Child and Adolescent Development

Child and Adolescent Development

A SOCIAL JUSTICE APPROACH

Kristine Anthis

cognella®

SAN DIEGO

Bassim Hamadeh, CEO and Publisher

Amy Smith, Senior Project Editor

Elisa Adams, Developmental Editor

Alia Bales, Production Editor

Jess Estrella, Senior Graphic Designer

Stephanie Kohl, Licensing Coordinator

Natalie Piccotti, Director of Marketing

Kassie Graves, Vice President of Editorial

Jamie Giganti, Director of Academic Publishing

3970 Sorrento Valley Blvd., Ste. 500, San Diego, CA 92121

Brief Contents

Detailed Contents

9 Emotional Development in Early Childhood 231

10 Physical and Cognitive Development in Middle Childhood 267

Preface

AFTER SEARCHING FOR a textbook that appreciates how inequitable resources and opportunities shape development—for better or worse—I decided to write my own. For those of you who know me, my author's journey has been a long one. Yet this prolonged path has given me the opportunity to reach my publication destination with a book that provides a timely and much-needed perspective on development—one that is tailored specifically to the needs of the next generation of college students. That book is *Child and Adolescent Development: A Social Justice Approach.*

Although there are many excellent developmental textbooks that now treat topics such as context and culture as standard, the majority of them shy away from systematically acknowledging the body of developmental science research that has demonstrated again and again how structural forces (such as social, economic, and political) alter the lives of children, teens, and their families.

Child and Adolescent Development: A Social Justice Approach does not shy away from such data. And it presents findings on how these data can be used to reduce inequities for children, teens, and their families, thereby optimizing development and allowing individuals to reach their full potential, no matter who they are.

The teaching tools within *Child and Adolescent Development: A Social Justice Approach,* designed to meet the needs of the next generation of college students, include

- a warm, conversational, and reader-friendly writing style;
- "their" as the pronoun used throughout the book;
- cutting-edge developmental science research data;
- *Snapshot* chapter openings that provide examples of diverse children and teens, including those who are of diverse races, ethnicities, languages, and genders, as well as those from working poor families, single-parent families, immigrant families, and refugee families;
- the inclusion of Risk–Resilience as a pattern of development;
- the *Cycle of Science* feature, which helps students become literate in developmental science by asking them to go through the process by identifying theory, research methods, and application of findings;

- a *Mentor Minute* feature, which provides students with career insights from interviews with diverse professionals in fields related to developmental science;
- the *Pan & Zoom* feature, which gives students the opportunity to practice thinking analytically in terms of the panoramic big picture versus a zoomed-in detailed view of a developmental science topic; and
- the *Tech & Media* feature, which validates students' interest in, and concerns about, technology and media use in their lives and the lives of others.

Child and Adolescent Development is therefore an ideal resource for courses in psychology, education, counseling, human services, and social work.

Acknowledgments

A village helped make this book available to students and instructors. They include the following reviewers: Tess Nicole Chevalier, Wake Forest University; Andrew Cummings, University of Nevada, Las Vegas; Crystal Hill-Chapman, Francis Marion University, University of South Carolina; Hilmar von Strunck, Northern Essex Community College; Melissa Atkins, Marshall University; Lawrence Eisenberg, William Peace University; Janelle McDaniel, University of Louisiana, Monroe; Cassendra Bergstrom, University of Northern Colorado; Jill Rinzel, University of Wisconsin Milwaukee at Waukesha; and Claire N. Rubman, Suffolk County Community College.

Others include Elisa Adams, my savvy and faithful developmental editor. Jess Estrella created the delightful cover art to remind us that we are always in the process of growing, developing, and becoming—and therefore need to care for one another in order to flourish. I am very grateful to Alia Bales, for her tremendous guidance in helping me navigate the production process; Faye Delosreyes and Alaina Munoz for their many efforts on the book's companion website; Tiffany Mok, Nicole Picotti, and Ivey Preston for helping us reach readers; Amy Smith to Tiffany Mok, Senior Content Marketing Specialist, and Nicole Piccotti, Director of Marketing at Cognella, both of whom helped us reach readers; Amy Smith, Senior Project Editor at Cognella, whose organization helped me keep my head above water; and Kassie Graves, Vice President of Editorial at Cognella, to whom I am grateful given her belief in my work.

I thank my honor's student, Jamiy Burey, for his creation of the book's flashcards. I am also thankful that, for almost two decades, my students and colleagues have stirred my thinking about all things developmental. I also very much appreciate the wisdom of the super staff Academy, and the many wise Mentors featured in the book who were so generous in sharing their expertise with students.

I am immensely grateful to my wife and son for their support, despite my time away from them while I wrote this book. I honor my parents and ancestors, the memory of my Νουνά, and I dedicate the book to current and future generations of children and teens, whom today live amidst staggering inequity and injustice.

I will be donating a portion of the book's proceeds to non-profit organizations that are working toward social justice.

And please consider what efforts you can make, no matter how limited your time, to ensure that all of us experience optimal development and have a chance to fulfill our potential.

Let's work now so that each us may be able to fulfill our potential and contribute to better development for everyone.

Introduction

CHAPTER 1

Snapshot

Every child has a right to high-quality education and high-quality healthcare. Both provide us with a solid foundation upon which we can build our lives. For example, children who experience high-quality daycare in early childhood, as well as more organized afterschool programs during middle childhood, show greater academic achievement at 15 years of age (Vandell, Lee, Whitaker and Pierce, 2018).

This is good news for children who attend high-quality preschools, but what about those children in the United States for whom high-quality preschool is unaffordable? Unlike many other economically developed countries that offer at least one year of government-funded preschool universally to all children, not all states in the United States provide such program (OECD, 2018). Those states in the United States that do fund universal preschool also vary considerably by the amount they spend per child, and data indicate that spending is related directly to preschool program quality—with quality being a predictor of children having better literacy and math skills that will help them achieve once they enter primary school (Bassok, Gibbs, & Latham, 2018; Friedman-Krauss et al., 2018).

The benefits of high-quality preschool even continue into adolescence if children's elementary classroom environments are of high quality as well (Ansari & Pianta, 2018). Perhaps because public schools in the United States are funded by local property taxes, research data show that the neighborhoods in which children grow up predict their college attendance and earnings (Chetty & Hendren, 2018).

FIG. 1.1   Kids Reading Books

Therefore, it is frustrating, but unfortunately not terribly surprising, that although the United States has been known as the land of opportunity, our citizens show less upward **social mobility**, or fewer opportunities to achieve greater economic changes from one generation to the next, than citizens in other countries (Bratberg et al., 2018).

These aforementioned examples represent a lack of equality in opportunity, an injustice that is one of many concerns this book considers in light of the well-being of children and their families, because this text takes a social justice approach to studying child and adolescent development **social justice** refers to the ability of people to reach their full potential within the societies in which they reside (Russell, 2015; Turiel, Chung, & Carr, 2016).

Keep in mind, though, that working toward *equality*, in which everyone is provided with the same thing to ensure they do their best, doesn't guarantee *equity*, in which everyone is provided with what they need to ensure they do their best.

These concepts of equality versus equity are illustrated in Figure 1.2, in which three individuals who are attending a soccer game may or may not see the game as a result of *if they receive support, the quality of the support they receive*, or *if the cause of inequity was addressed*.

That is, in the Equality panel, the view of the person on the left is the most comprehensive, unobstructed by the fence. The view of the game for the person in the middle of the Equality panel may be slightly obstructed by the fence given their height, but they can still likely see the game. The view of the individual on the right of the Equality panel is obstructed completely, so that they cannot see any of the soccer game. Notice that despite each individual being treated equally, via standing on equal size boxes, in the Equality panel, they cannot equally view the game.

In the Equity panel, all three individuals have a comparable view of the game as a result of the person in the middle being given a box to stand on so they have a view similar to the taller person on the left, and the person on the right being given two boxes to stand on so they have a view similar to the other two people. So these adjustments in the Equity panel are better than those in the Equality panel—but the inequitable environmental barrier that requires these adjustments still isn't addressed.

Therefore, if we imagine other people joining these three individuals to watch the soccer game with them, these additional attendees may also very well need supports and adjustments to correct the inequity caused by the systemic barrier (the wood fence in this example) so that they can see the game equally well.

Learning Goals

- ▶ Describe the stages of child and adolescent development
- ▶ Explain the domains of child and adolescent development
- ▶ Apply the patterns of child and adolescent development
- ▶ Compare traditional theories of child and adolescent development
- ▶ Evaluate contemporary theories of child and adolescent development

Equality

The assumption is that everyone benefits from the same supports. This is equal treatment.

Equity

Everyone gets the supports they need (this is the concept of "affirmative action"), thus producing equity.

Justice

All 3 can see the game without supports or accommodations because the cause(s) of the inequity was addressed. The systemic barrier has been removed.

FIG. 1.2 Equality, Equity, and Justice

Source: https://twitter.com/chdadvocate/status/1020488331338055681.

On the other hand, once the cause of the inequitable environment is addressed (that is, the chain link fence replacing the wood fence), such supports and adjustments are no longer needed for everyone to see the game. Only then is there justice for all.

So, in order to form a more perfect union to promote the general welfare and social justice of *all* its citizens, the United States might want to consider signing the Convention on the Rights of the Child (CRC). What's the CRC, you ask? The CRC is an international document that specifies the rights of children, rights that include the right to nondiscrimination, the right to have decisions made about them be based on what is in their best interests, the right to high-quality healthcare, and the right to a high-quality education that develops their individual talents, abilities, and personality to the fullest (UNICEF, 2018).

Countries that sign the CRC agree to protect these rights, and agree to do so by assessing their own educational systems, health systems, legal systems, and social services—as well as the funding of these services. All countries that are part of the United Nations have agreed to and ratified the CRC except one—that is, the United States.

By failing to sign the CRC, the United States government fails to ensure that it provides sufficient funding to protect children's rights. And by failing to sign the CRC, the United States government also fails to ensure that it provides our children with a high-quality education that develops each child's talents, abilities, cognitive functioning, and emotional well-being to the fullest.

Additionally, by failing to sign the CRC, the United States government fails to ensure that it provides children, teens, and their families the universal healthcare that many other countries provide, a vital right and one especially obvious during crises such as the corona virus (COVID-19) pandemic. How so?

As of the time of this book's publication when it has been relatively early in the history of this crisis, COVID-19 has caused devastation across the globe, and within the United States, it too has led to untold deaths. Yet within the United States, COVID-19 has also exacerbated inequalities and magnified our need for a true government safety net—and in turn has abandoned the physical health and well-being of countless American children, adolescents, and their families (Ahmed, Ahmed, Pissarides, & Stiglitz, 2020; Coven & Gupta, 2020; van Dorn, Cooney, & Sabin, 2020).

For instance, adults in millions of families have been experiencing sudden unemployment (which, along with a lack of access to their children's meals at school, can lead to food insecurity in the home) and the termination of their already limited safety net of non-universal but work-based health insurance (Ahmed, Ahmed, Pissarides, & Stiglitz, 2020; Coven & Gupta, 2020; van Dorn, Cooney, & Sabin, 2020).

Indeed, food insecurity in the U.S. during the time of COVID-19 has indeed unfortunately been soaring as well. In late April 2020, 35% of households with children under 18 years of age have reported food insecurity, an alarming increase since the 14.7% in 2018, especially because insufficient nutrition in childhood and adolescence can lead to long-term developmental delays (Bauer, 2020). This shameful state of the United States could have been prevented with a better government safety net, such as one that provides a universal basic income to all and/or an allowance to families with children, such as the child benefit we will learn more about in Chapter 8.

And members of low-income, Black, and/or Latinx families (who are already more likely to have chronic health conditions) have been placed at even greater risk of mortality during the COVID-19 crisis, given the adults in these homes who are still employed are more likely to work in essential frontline occupations that tend to offer lower wages and require workers to physically interact with others, such as in public transit, healthcare, custodial, and retail grocery—occupations which also tend to not provide workers with adequate health insurance in the face of illness, much less sufficient protective gear at work (Coven & Gupta, 2020; van Dorn, Cooney, & Sabin, 2020).

Clearly, things need to change. Throughout the book, we will investigate the empirical evidence on the how other social injustices affect development—as well as how such injustices can be rectified to ensure that the development of all children, adolescents, their families is optimized.

What Are the Stages of Child and Adolescent Development?

The term **development** implies *qualitative* change, as in the change from being a child who can think only *concretely* (such as counting how many books on homework help are in the local library) to being an adolescent who can also think *abstractly* (such as considering whether the distribution of books on homework help in different neighborhoods is fair and just), whereas the term **growth** implies *quantitative* change, as in the change from being a few inches taller since one's height was last measured; both development and growth in children and adolescents benefit when societies prevent an accumulation of adversities, such as limited opportunities to earn a living wage, unaffordable housing, and food insecurity (Black et al., 2017; Gottlieb, 1992).

TABLE 1.1 The Stages of Child and Adolescent Development

Stage of the Lifespan	Approximate Ages	Synopsis
Prenatal (see Chapter 4)	Conception to Birth	The transition from a fertilized egg to a newborn, in just nine months, includes numerous developments.
Infancy and Toddlerhood (Chapters 5, 6, and 7)	Birth to 2 years	Many dramatic physical changes, accompanied by cognitive and emotional changes, occur during the time a newborn becomes a 2-year-old.
Early Childhood (Chapters 8 and 9)	2 years to 6 years	The preschool or play years include a variety of changes, such as mastery of motor skills, rapid language development, and development of relationships with peers outside the home.
Middle Childhood (Chapters 10 and 11)	6 years to 12 years	The changes that occur during the school years include exposure to organized sports, the growth of logical thought, and the development of various facets of self-esteem.
Adolescence (Chapters 12 and 13)	12 years to 20–25 years	Puberty sets off a whirlwind of changes in this stage, changes that have implications for how teens think about the world around them and for how they come to define their identity.

Scientific research on child and adolescent development concerns how we change from the prenatal stage through middle childhood and adolescence. The five generally accepted stages of child and adolescent development, according to psychologists, are the following:

- *Prenatal*, from conception to birth
- *Infancy and Toddlerhood*, from birth to 2 years of age
- *Early Childhood*, from 2 to 6
- *Middle Childhood*, from 6 to 12
- *Adolescence*, from 12 to about 20–25

For a brief overview of the stages, see the synopsis in Table 1.1.

What Are the Domains of Child and Adolescent Development?

In the study of child development, the *physical development domain* includes all the biological changes that occur from birth through adolescence. These biological changes include increases in neuron connections within the brain during infancy and toddlerhood, physical growth of the bones, as well as the appearance of secondary sex characteristics during puberty.

The *cognitive development domain* includes all aspects of thinking and language development, such as babbling in infancy and learning the alphabet in preschool, as well as developing a greater attention span and acquiring a new language in school.

The *emotional domain* of development includes all aspects of social and emotional changes, such as attachment in infancy, developing relationships with peers upon initial entry into school, regulating our emotions in the face of bullying in middle childhood, and developing our identity in adolescence.

What Are the Patterns of Child and Adolescent Development?

FIG. 1.3 Standing in a Crop

Empirical research data on child and adolescent development are being collected, analyzed, and summarized all the time; the science of development is an ongoing process. With so much information available, though, how can we make sense of it all?

Well, just as views from an airplane help us notice patterns in a landscape (like the crop circles we would not see while standing in the thick of them), a big-picture view of the patterns within the research data on child development helps us better see and remember all that we know about what is happening in these stages. Here we consider lifelong patterns, multidimensional patterns, polydirectional patterns, and risk–resilience patterns.

Lifelong Patterns

Just as planting seeds today can yield a crop tomorrow, giving attention to aspects of our development now can influence our development at a later date. Each period of life is full of *within-stage* relationships, such as how brain development is related to language development in infancy and toddlerhood. The lifelong pattern of child development reminds us that there are also *between-stage* relationships, or relationships between various ages or stages.

For example, infants who were breastfed for more than six months show greater cognitive outcomes later on (such as having a lower risk of attention-deficit/hyperactivity disorder once in school) (Bar, Milanaik, & Adesman, 2016).

Another example of the lifelong pattern of development concerns how children living in poverty *who also possess greater self-regulation, or the ability to manage both their attention and their emotions, are at less risk* for the later aggression, substance abuse, and mood disorders such as depression that are generally associated with childhood poverty (Hanson et al., 2018).

Please note that these three aforementioned physical, cognitive, and emotional domains of child and adolescent development do not occur independently of one another. Development at any given point is a product of these domains interacting with one another, so a *multidimensional* approach to child and adolescent development best helps us understand the relationships between the domains that occur within a particular age. For example, in our discussion of within-stage relationships, we've mentioned how brain development is related to language development in infancy and toddlerhood; another example concerns how toddlers with more sleep difficulties—a concern of physical

FIG. 1.4   View of a Crop Circle from an Airplane

development—show worse performance on measures of cognitive development, such verbal skills (Hoyniak et al., 2018).

An additional example pertains to the popular concept of "grit," or perseverance, as a personality trait that helps us have stamina to meet long-term goals (Duckworth, 2016). So it is thought that an aspect of emotional development can help cognitive achievement. Most of the research associating grit with academic achievement has been conducted with college students, yet a recent study with school-age children indicates that grit alone cannot improve academic success in children, only grit in combination with improving students' *self-efficacy*, or their beliefs about their own capabilities (Usher, Li, Butz, & Rohas, 2018).

Polydirectional Patterns

An aerial view of a landscape also reveals peaks and valleys, much as the study of the *polydirectional* patterns can draw attention to the many directions that development can take. Child and adolescent development certainly includes losses, such as synaptic pruning of infrequent connections among neurons; but gains occur as well, such as in height, weight, vocabulary, and attention span (Guyer, Pérez-Edgar, & Crone, 2018) Some losses or decreases can be beneficial, too, as the loss of infrequently used connections among neurons may maximize brain efficiency (Stirrups, 2018).

Another example of polydirectional patterns concerns how neuroscience has improved our understanding of **sensitive periods**: times during development in which we are either particularly ripe for learning because an experience at that time will have its peak effect on our development, or time when we are especially harmed by adversity (Azañón, Camacho, Morales, & Longo, 2017; Dunn et al., 2017).

We now know that sensitive periods are often a function of nonlinear patterns of brain activity (Guyer, Pérez-Edgar, & Crone, 2018). Specifically, one study found that infants' performance on a measure of cognitive development is poor at 6 months, surges rapidly from 7 to 11 months of age, and then flattens at 12 months of age (MacNeill et al., 2018).

Risk-Resilience Patterns

The patterns of *risk-resilience* show the ways in which our development proceeds, for better or worse, due to the interactions among our genes and the environments in which we are developing —so that resilience is not simply a product of individual differences within a child or a teen, but a product of that individual child's or teen's genetic tendencies interacting with environmental conditions, including how equitable or inequitable one's society may be (Susman, 2019). Just as the surrounding environment helps shape the physical landscape of low coastal areas, grain-filled plains, and mountainous elevations, the contexts or environments in which we develop greatly influence our lives. Even within our own country and neighborhood, we meet people of different races/ethnicities, cultures, languages, economic backgrounds, countries of origin, and educational levels, so that the context in which each of us develops may be very different from the context in which others develop.

For example, **executive function** includes the ability to engage in sustained attention, filter out distractions, and have self-control over our impulses. This executive functioning appears to be a product of context. How so? Children growing up in families characterized by high socioeconomic status (SES) or high education, income, and/or occupational status, tend to have better executive functioning than children growing up in low-SES homes (Hartanto, Toh, & Yang, 2018).

These differences in children's cognitive abilities are likely a result of the extent to which their context includes material resources, social connections, and parents who are educated about child and adolescent development and/or who encourage executive function skills in their children. *Interestingly, though, the effects of SES on executive function are weak to nonexistent for bilingual children, so that growing up bilingual has cognitive advantages for all children, but especially for children growing up in a low-SES home* (Hartanto, Toh, & Yang, 2018).

Our *Mentor Minute* box features Allyson Criner Brown, MA, who has taught low-SES children and now works to promote social justice with early childhood educators.

A Mentor Minute

Allyson Criner Brown, MA

1) Describe your work, please.

I am the associate director of Teaching for Change, a nonprofit organization that provides teachers and parents with the tools to create schools where students learn to read, write, and change the world. By drawing direct connections to real-world issues, Teaching for Change encourages teachers and students to question and rethink the world inside and outside their classrooms; build a more equitable, multicultural society; and become active global citizens.

I am also an educator, facilitator, public speaker, advocate, and seasoned practitioner nationally known for my work at the intersection of racial equity and family engagement. I edited the second edition of *Between Families and Schools: Creating Meaningful Relationships* (2016) and have been featured in interviews, articles, symposiums, conferences, and workshops for Education Week, NPR, The Atlantic, the U.S. Department of Education, the Smithsonian National Museum of Black History and Culture, and more.

FIG. 1.5   Allyson Criner Brown, MA

I am a former middle school teacher and track and field coach, and my professional experiences are centered around schools and community-based organizations that focus on education, social justice, and youth development. I believe that deep and systemic inequalities that harm the rights, dignity, and potential of people of color and low-income families can be undone, and I pursue this ambition through my work in education.

2) How does social justice inform your work?

My approach begins with acknowledging that we do not live in a society where people are treated equally, particularly people of color and lower-income families. So, if we want to support children, we can't pretend they and their families haven't experienced oppression, nor can we be color-blind. To do so is to do a disservice to everyone, because ignoring our country's history of injustices allows those injustices to perpetuate. We all deserve equal opportunities no matter where we were born, what languages we speak, our gender, our religion, our ethnicity, and/or the color of our skin—but to realize this "American dream" we have to pursue social justice and equitable practices.

3) How did you become involved in social justice and/or advocacy?

My family belonged to the black middle class in Oakland, California, but I grew up seeing inequality in the lives of my friends and family members who were lower-income. At the time, I didn't have a vocabulary for it, but I now understand that the inequities in their opportunities were systemic. A lack of language for social inequalities (such as unequal funding of public schools) is akin to a silence or lack of consciousness, which perpetuates the systems that oppress them.

Words have power. To name an experience beyond and outside of one's self is a form of empowerment. If we want to help all children, we need to have language to identify the problems they encounter, as our good intentions are not enough.

(4) What are your thoughts on how social justice can improve child and adolescent development?

Integrating social justice and developmental science brings an asset-based approach to understanding children and their families, in which we see their full humanity and potential, rather than blaming them for being oppressed and/or seeing them as limited in their potential. Knowing that social justice starts by recognizing deeply rooted historical inequities provides us with a healthier perspective on what we can do individually—and what society can do to eliminate systematic inequalities and nurture the potential of our children and their families.

(5) What suggestions do you have for undergraduate students who are interested in making a change in child and adolescent development?

I recommend strongly that students spend time in the communities they want to serve, as it is important to get out of the college classroom and have real-world experiences that allow you to connect with children, their families, and their needs so you can respect and appreciate their full humanity.

• • • •

What Are the Theories of Development?

Now we consider theories of development, including both traditional theories and more contemporary theories. Let's consider an example. Maria is the youngest child in her family and the first to attend college. After five years of struggles and accomplishments, during which she learned a great deal about herself and explored professional careers unfamiliar to her working-class family, she graduated with honors. Maria now works with her local government implementing a "health in all" policy that aims to eliminate disparities in the social determinants of health, such as educational attainment, housing, transportation options, and neighborhood safety (American Public Health Association, 2018).

When Maria was a child, her family needed to move multiple times due to the lack of affordable housing near her parents' jobs, and the family ended up living far from work and school, which caused them major transportation and financial difficulties.

How would developmental science best explain Maria's path? Does one particular theory offer the "correct" explanation of Maria's behavior so others might learn how to emulate her success? No single theory has been able to account for the diversity of human lives from prenatal development through death, though each theory provides a unique perspective on our development. The multiple perspectives provided by the various theories we are about to discuss are like different-colored eyeglass lenses: All see the same person, but each theory's conclusion is influenced by assumptions that filter its view.

Here we consider those multiple perspectives, categorized as either traditional theories of development or contemporary theories of development. All the theories, whether they were first proposed in the twentieth century or the twenty-first, contain a set of assumptions that researchers can then attempt to empirically verify. Some theories may have historical precedent but are not used much by current researchers as a basis for hypothesis-testing; such theories can still be informative in hypothesis generation, though, and keep us informed about what has and has not been addressed in prior approaches to studying development. We will consider theories here according to the themes they emphasize, whether they be *physical*, *cognitive*, *emotional*, or a combination of such.

Traditional Theories: Psychoanalytic

Psychoanalytic theories propose that behavior is driven by unconscious *emotional* needs and early life experiences. For example, infants' need to know they can trust others to care for them, and their experiences of if and how others have met their needs, will create a unconscious mental template or set of beliefs (about which we are unlikely to be consciously aware) regarding what to expect in relationships, such as if others are there for us and are emotionally available to us.

The psychoanalytic theories advanced by Freud and Erikson are stage models in which they believe children resolve qualitatively different conflicts (e.g., the need for trust versus the need for autonomy) around their unconscious needs at different points in time during their development.

Freud's Theory

Some of the very first theories of development were the psychoanalytic theories focused on emotions and developed by Sigmund Freud and his followers. Although trained as a physician, Freud (1856–1939) found that medical explanations for some of his patients' ailments were insufficient, so he began to consider how patients' mental states could be contributing to their problems. He came to think that a large part of his patients' troubles was related to conflicts regarding the expression of pleasure inherent in the body, such as sexuality.

As a result, Freud advanced a theory of *psychosexual* development (the prefix "psycho" has its origins in the Greek word for "mind"). Freud proposed that an adult's anxieties can be explained by examining how the child fared during what Freud believed were five stages of development. These stages begin at birth and end at adolescence—revealing that Freud assumed that much of development occurs before adulthood, the point at which, he proposed, a person can love and work (Terr, 2000).

Later theorists criticized this idea, suggesting that while loving and working are necessary parts of adulthood, they are probably not a sufficient index of successful adulthood.

Freud's first three stages of psychosexual development cover birth to 6 years of age. The *oral stage* is a period of development during infancy (or the first year of life) in which oral issues are the child's primary focus, including feeding and putting things in the mouth (like their own fingers). From one to three years of age, roughly corresponding to the toddler stage and a bit beyond, the child enters the *anal stage*, in which elimination of waste becomes a central issue. It is during this stage that most Western toddlers are toilet trained.

Freud believed the anal stage was ripe for conflict with parents or other authority figures, since the expression of pleasure a child receives from various parts of the body in each stage must be approved by society. For example, children are taught to be proud of not soiling their pants and are not congratulated for impulsively eliminating at any time or in any place.

Another natural yet often impulsive act for young children is masturbation, which typically becomes prominent between the ages of 3 and 6. Parents teach their children that these body parts are private and should not be touched or revealed in public. Because Freud presumed that girls wonder why they do not have the penis that boys seem to be so proud of, he called this the phallic stage.

Most children have resolved major conflicts arising from weaning, toilet training, and sexual curiosity before age 6, which is when most begin formal schooling and are initiated into the world of schoolwork and peer relations. Sexual issues become latent or recede in importance during the school years until puberty, so Freud called this next stage the *latency stage*. According to Freud, what is most important during this time is achievement, whether it takes place in the classroom; on the playing field; or, for example, in the after-school music club. Next, with hormones flooding the bloodstream during puberty, adolescents become interested in sexual expression again, but then in genital contact with another person with whom they are emotionally intimate. Once reached, this mature sexuality, which Freud called the *genital stage* of development, continues into and lasts through adulthood.

Freud believed the conflicts inherent in any of these stages may not be resolved in childhood, perhaps due to harsh parenting. In that case, the adult would remain fixated in this stage. For example, a child who was excessively scolded for putting things in their mouth may now be an adult with an oral fixation and likely to be overly talkative, addicted to vaping, and/or constantly eating. The child who was humiliated for wetting their pants may now be an adult with an anal fixation and either extremely tidy and emotionally repressed or rather messy and lacking in emotional self-control. The child shamed for touching their genitals may experience romantic and/or sexual difficulties in adulthood. If Freud were alive today, he would likely remark that Maria and her determination, as described above, are a sign of her having completed the latency and even the genital period (with its emphasis on work).

Erikson's Theory

One of Freud's followers was Erik Erikson (1902–1994). Erikson's theory is similar to Freud's in that it proposes development to occur in stages, and that each of these stages includes some type of conflict that must be resolved. Only if the conflict is favorably resolved will the individual be able to fully master the subsequent stages. Difficulties in resolving these normative developmental crises may appear to be mental health issues, too, a topic to which we return in Chapter 13's discussion of anxiety and depression in college students (Côté, 2018).

In contrast to Freud's five stages, Erikson's theory offers eight stages, corresponding to the entire lifespan instead of childhood and adolescence. The first five of Erikson's stages correspond roughly to Freud's stages. Erikson's *Industry–Inferiority* stage, for instance, in which we acquire competence in one or more areas in school, is very similar to Freud's latency stage, in which achievement is the focus. The practical implications of Freud's and Erikson's two parallel stages are that all children and teens need to know they are good at something, and it is to the general public's benefit to help them discover what that is so that they can become happy and productive members of society; greater financial support for schools is a concrete example of how we can reduce injustices in this regard. It is noteworthy that children and teens who attend schools that are not facing budget cuts or being asked to boost test scores at the expense of art, music, and sports are more likely to successfully resolve this emotional stage of development and better contribute to society.

Another difference between Freud's and Erikson's ideas is the emphasis each placed on sexual versus social relationships. Erikson believed Freud concentrated on sexuality and did not give sufficient consideration to the role of social relationships throughout life, and not just those we have with our families. In contrast, Erikson's theory is a *psychosocial* theory of development.

For example, Erikson believed the conflict of identity versus role confusion characterized adolescence, because it is a period of exploring our uniquely personal and individual self within the realm of other people; we now know that this exploration process continues in adulthood and is related to the attachments or quality of emotional bonds we have with others (Kerpelman & Pittman, 2018). For instance, we saw above that although she had few professional role models before she attended college, Maria actively investigated possible careers before making her decision.

Erikson's later stages, from young adulthood to old age, are longer than the earlier stages, but this does not necessarily mean they are stable and without change. We will examine the details of these stages in later chapters, but note for now that Erikson's theory is one of the few to specifically address development beyond childhood and adolescence.

Traditional Theories: Learning

Learning theories also focus on observing aspects of *physical*, *cognitive*, and/or *emotional* development, as well as helping people change problems within such.

Pavlov's Theory

Ivan Pavlov (1849–1936) was a Nobel Prize–winning researcher who studied the digestive process, but he is best known for his discovery of **classical conditioning**, or the process by which two events are paired repeatedly so that eventually, presenting only one event can bring about the same result as presenting the other event. For example, classical conditioning can help explain why some students associate school with anxiety.

School is a seemingly neutral stimulus, but after a student experiences repeated anxiety-provoking incidents at school (such as being bullied or receiving poor grades on exams), the school itself rather than the bully or an exam becomes a conditioned stimulus that elicits anxiety from the student. Only by the school being repeatedly associated with events that are rewarding (such as the student learning how to cope with bullies or receiving better grades on exams) can the school become a conditioned stimulus that elicits confidence from the student rather than anxiety.

Skinner's Theory

Whereas in classical conditioning two stimuli (the neutral stimulus and the unconditioned stimulus) *that are precursors to behavior* eventually produce the same response, in **operant conditioning** the *consequences* of a behavior, either reinforcement or punishment, can increase or decrease the frequency of that behavior. B. F. Skinner's (1904–1990) research studies on operant conditioning were empirical verifications of the ideas put forth by John Watson (1878–1958). Watson proposed that development is a function of the environment to which we are exposed. He is famous for saying this:

> Give me a dozen healthy infants, well-formed, and my own specified world to bring them up in and I'll guarantee to take any one at random and train him to become any type of specialist I might select—doctor, lawyer, artist, merchant-chief and, yes, even beggar-man and thief, regardless of his talents, penchants, tendencies, abilities, vocations, and race of his ancestors. (1924)

To some extent, Skinner found empirical evidence for this assertion with his experiments on operant conditioning. Skinner found that when a behavior was reinforced, it increased in frequency, and when a behavior was punished, it decreased in frequency. For example, in a specified world that provides teens with no other viable alternatives than delinquent behavior, such behavior will likely be reinforcing; such behavior will likely not be reinforcing if schools, after-school programs, and employment are available and fully-funded. As another example, if studying for an exam is reinforced later by the consequence of a good grade, studying behavior will increase in the future. On the other hand, if slacking off and partying behavior is later punished by the consequence of a poor grade, slacking off and partying behavior will decrease in the future. Here we see how Maria's behavior can also be explained not only by classical conditioning, but also by operant conditioning. Her success in school was reinforced by teachers and family over time, leading to an increased likelihood that her performance in her courses would continue to remain strong.

Bandura's Theory

A third type of learning theory is **social learning theory**, which emphasizes learning through observing and imitating other people in social environments, such as at home, school, or work. Social learning theory proposed the concept of **modeling**, in which our own behavior is a reflection of what we have observed in others. Albert Bandura (1925–present) is a major proponent of social learning theory, and his latest revision of his theory is referred to as **social cognitive theory**. Bandura believes individuals actively attempt to understand others and model their own behavior on the behavior of others, rather than just behaving passively in response to the pairing of two stimuli (as in classical conditioning) and/or consequences that are reinforcing or punishing (as in operant conditioning).

Observing other people face-to-face—with all their gestures, minute changes in facial expressions, changes in spatial distance, and fluctuating body language—can add greatly to our understanding of them, which is one of the reasons why excessive screen time (which replaces face-to-face interactions) may interfere with learning social skills, a research result we discuss further in *Tech & Media: Reduced Screen Time Improves the Interpretation of Emotional Cues*.

Reduced Screen Time Improves the Interpretation of Emotional Cues

Researchers wanted to know whether screen time, such as use of mobile phones, promotes an understanding of the emotional cues that other people send us, as compared to in-person interactions (Uhls et al., 2014). They conducted a 5-day experiment with 12-year-olds, half of whom who atttended an overnight educational camp that emphasized hiking and outdoor skills while prohibiting the use of devices and access to screens; the other children attended school with no restrictions on their access to screens.

All of the children were avid users of technology, as they reported spending almost one hour a day texting, more than two hours per day watching television, and one hour a day playing video games. Streaming services for watching television and films, in combination with the proliferation of mobile devices, have likely blurred the categories, so technology use on average may be even higher than the amount reported in this particular sample (Uhls et al., 2014).

At the beginning of the study, both groups were tested on their ability to accurately identify the emotions (such as happy, sad, angry, and fearful) of children and adults in photographs and videos they were shown. At the end of the study, both groups were tested again using the same photographs and videos. The subjects who were away from devices and screens improved significantly more in their ability to accurately identify emotions of others in photographs and videos from the beginning to the end of the 5-day period than did those with unlimited access to devices and screens; other research has shown that the greater children's screen time at age 4, the worse their emotion understanding at age 6 and the greater their television viewing at age 6, the worse their emotion understanding at age 8 (Skalická et al., 2019; Uhls et al., 2014).

Let's think critically for a moment about these results. Is it the lack of device use that produced such results, or some other experience gained by eliminating media? Consider that media use impairs most when it *replaces* offline relationships rather than *supplements* them (Waytz & Gray, 2018)? Indeed, it is not unreasonable to think that the more children use media, the more they are missing out on offline opportunities—such as those they had time for at the camp—to learn emotional and social skills that can help them later in life as they navigate the job market and romantic relationships. Nor is it unreasonable to think that reducing one's use of technology is most beneficial for those who use it the most (Giedd, 2012; Skalická et al., 2019; Waytz & Gray, 2018).

Consider This: How can accurately interpreting emotional cues of other people help us during a job interview? In a relationship? Are the results of this study about screen time consistent with Bandura's concept of modeling? Why or why not?

• • • •

Traditional Theories: Cognitive Theories

Cognitive theories focus on how *cognitive* thinking functions and/or changes over time. Some cognitive theories—such as social learning theory, which also addresses *emotional* development—were revised to include thinking not just about ourselves, but the world around us as well. We will examine some of these theories now. We will examine these theories now.

Piaget's Theory

In Jean Piaget's (1896–1980) theory of cognitive development from infancy through adolescence, the focus is on **adaptation**, or the process by which our mental structures evolve to better fit our experiences. The mental structures that organize these experiences are called **schemes**. According to Piaget, adaptation includes two components: assimilation and accommodation.

In the **assimilation** process, we incorporate new information into our existing knowledge, or what we already know. In the **accommodation** process, in contrast, we change what we know in the face of new and different information. Let's say, for example, that you decide to bring your best friend's baby a rattle when you visit. The baby shakes the rattle with delight and you are pleased that you chose an appropriate gift. The next time you visit your friend and her baby, you bring a toy hammer.

But instead of instinctively knowing what to do with it, the baby shakes the hammer just as he shook the rattle. The baby has assimilated the hammer into his toy scheme, or he's done with it what he already knows, which is to shake it. Once you demonstrate to the baby that a hammer is something to pound with, he stops shaking the hammer like a rattle and begins using it to pound things. Now accommodation has taken place, because the baby has changed his toy scheme to incorporate this new information about how different toys are played with.

Assimilation and accommodation are processes, and schemes—which can be physical behaviors such as playing with toys, or emotional constructs such as romantic relationships—are what change in Piaget's theory. Piaget believed **equilibrium** occurs when more assimilation than accommodation takes place, and **disequilibrium** occurs when more accommodation than assimilation takes place (Figure 1.6).

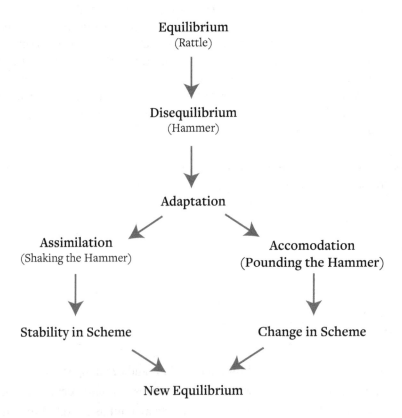

FIG. 1.6   The Adaptation Process According to Piaget

As Figure 1.6 shows, assimilation and accommodation must be balanced in order for a new equilibrium to occur, because each is part of the adaptation that allows schemes to change during Piaget's four stages of cognitive development: sensorimotor, preoperational, concrete operational, and formal operational. We will study the details and practical applications of each stage in subsequent chapters on cognitive development. But for now, note that although Piaget's ideas about the processes of adaptation no longer form the basis of much empirical research on cognitive development, his theory is still relevant to us because he studied universal aspects of children's rational thinking, whether it be with regard to children's understanding of morality and justice or with regard to their understanding of scientific concepts such as physics or object permanence—*and because he was one of the first to understand that development includes both gains and losses* (Barrouillet, 2015; Bjorklund, 2018a; Piaget, 1932).

Information-Processing Theory

Information-Processing theories are a second type of *cognitive* theory that describes the way thinking takes place, but typically without proposing age-related stages like Piaget's theory. Most Information-Processing theorists view the human mind as analogous to a computer: receiving input, then processing it, and then producing some type of output. For instance, listening to your favorite song provides your mind with lyrics that serve as input to process and think about. As you mull over these lyrics, you admire the ideas and attitudes suggested—which may also change your mind about how to deal with a situation that has been troubling you, such as a conflict with a friend or why you have not received a raise at work. As a result, one of the outputs or outcome behaviors that results from this processing of information is that you listen to your friend's perspective on the issue or request a raise from your boss.

Viewing the mind as a series of linear components, in which input leads to outcomes, allows us to illustrate thought processes with flowcharts, which can be helpful for conducting research on how we think. Research conducted under this framework can be useful for better understanding how children may incorrectly process social cues, such as misinterpreting an ambiguous act (such as when another child bumps into them) as intended to be hostile; research indicates that when they are in middle childhood, children who had poor-quality emotional bonds or attachments to their parents while they were infants make more hostile attributions of other children's ambiguous behavior (Zajac et al., 2018).

Vygotsky's Theory

According to our third example of a cognitive development theory, or the **sociocultural theory** of Lev Vygotsky (1896—1934), social interactions with more knowledgeable individuals—be they parents, teachers, or more experienced children—are what promote cognitive development in an individual.

For Vygotsky, interactions with others are a form of **guided participation**, in which both the student and the tutor are actively engaged in the learning process. In order for learning to be effective, though, the tutoring must be individually tailored to the student's current level of understanding. How does the more knowledgeable tutor provide such unique guidance? By catering to the learner's current level of competency and understanding.

For example, as students progress from high school to college and perhaps graduate school, they progress from being lectured at to actively participating in seminars and then perhaps to taking on an internship. Maria could not have participated in discussions in her senior seminar classes in college if she had not completed her foundation courses, and without the valuable internship experience she gained, she would not have been able to draw upon the advanced knowledge she acquired in those seminars. Therefore, the type and degree of instructional support changes as the learner's cognitive foundation grows and they become more competent—a process Vygotsky referred to as **scaffolding**, guidance that works in the same way that scaffolding at a construction site is rearranged as the building evolves.

Scaffolding by the more knowledgeable tutor allows the learner to progress from what they are unable to do independently, but can achieve with help. The range or zone of development between what we cannot do independently and what we can do with assistance is what Vygotsky referred to as the **zone of proximal development** (Esteban-Guitart, 2018) So, Maria's achievements may have seemed out of reach to her before she began taking college courses, but with the assistance of instructors and other students, she progressed along the zone of proximal development as she acquired the skills she needed to develop into a college graduate with internship experience, and a valued employee.

Contemporary Theories: Ecological Systems

In order to understand *physical*, *cognitive*, and/or *emotional* development, Ecological Systems theory considers how an individual interacts with and is influenced by various systems of the environment, such as how learning to read is a cognitive process that develops within different social practices, for example, how reading is or is not supported in the home and school (Jaeger, 2016).

Bronfenbrenner's Theory

Urie Bronfenbrenner (1917–2005)—a cofounder of the federally funded Head Start program for children in low-income families, and whose work is used by the United Nations International Children's Fund, or UNICEF—proposed a theory of development known as **Ecological Systems theory** (Bronfenbrenner & Morris, 2006).

According to Bronfenbrenner (1977), five systems influence our development, ranging from the immediate environment to seemingly distant but still influential forces: the microsystem, the mesosystem, the exosystem, the macrosystem, and the chronosystem. The *microsystem* consists of the setting in which the person lives and interacts directly with others. Maria's microsystem in college included her professors, classmates, coworkers, and/or roommates. When Maria was a child, her microsystem included her parents, siblings, teachers, and peers at school. The next level of the environment is the *mesosystem*, which consists of the connections between various microsystems, such as Maria's internship supervisor who communicated with her professor and classmates on a monthly basis, just like the monthly parent–teacher conferences that occurred during her childhood.

The *exosystem* refers to those environments that influence a person, even though the person typically does not participate in these environments. For example, Maria never met the president of her university, but she was certainly influenced by that person, who one year decided to increase the world language requirements for graduation in order for the school's graduates to thrive in a global economy. Maria also never met her father's boss while she was growing up, but the boss's policies affected the amount of time she was able to spend with her father.

Another system in which we typically do not take part but whose decisions influence us is the *macrosystem*, which consists of the general values, customs, and laws that are part of a culture. Although Bronfenbrenner originally proposed that culture is reflected in the macrosystem, reconceptualizations of his model posit that what we think of as culture is in fact the *microsystems* of daily activities in families, schools, and neighborhoods (Bronfenbrenner, 1977; Vélez-Agosto, et al., 2017).

On the other hand, the government is part of everyone's macrosystem, for instance. The values and financial decisions of the government in Maria's state influenced not only how much she had to pay for tuition, but also how many hours she had to work to earn this money, and therefore how many hours she had left for studying and, hopefully, some socializing and rest.

The current sociohistorical context, or the *chronosystem* in which an individual develops, influences whether and how each of the other systems changes over time. Not too long ago, females were not expected to graduate from college or consider pursuing a graduate degree. To some extent, Maria's accomplishments are a function of the social and historical period of the early twenty-first century in which she entered adolescence and early adulthood, when it was increasingly expected that all genders could succeed in higher education and in the professions.

In conclusion, Bronfenbrenner's (1977) theory provides us with a lens to understand complex interactions between *persons*, *contexts of development*, *processes of development*, and the *time period* during which such development takes place. This understanding of the multiple systems of development can therefore help contemporary researchers ensure that their research has ecological validity, so that studies occur in, or at least approximate, the real-world settings in which the behaviors in question actually occur, such as investigating bullying by observing children on a playground rather than by interacting with children in a lab setting (Adolph, Hoch, & Cole, 2018).

Pan & Zoom

Screen Time in Children AND Parents

In this box, we zoom in on a topic that has become especially applicable to the well-being of today's children. **Screen time** is the amount of time we spend looking at television, computers, and electronic devices. Over the last 10 years, the average amount of time that children 0 to 8 years of age spend using or simply looking at an electronic device each day has increased from 5 minutes in 2011 to 48 minutes in 2017 (Common Sense Media, 2018).

Although easier access to mobile electronic devices is convenient, such instant availability of distractions—which are often designed to be addictive—has negative consequences, especially for children. Screen time in childhood is so clearly associated with weight gains, sleep losses, and delays in cognitive and emotional development that the American Academy of Pediatrics recommends that children between the ages of 2 and 5 have *no more than one hour total per day* of screen time—and that when parents are with their children they reduce their own media use as much as possible, given that parent's own media use is associated with less parent attentiveness, as well as more parent-child interruption, along with greater (American Academy of Pediatrics Council on Communications and Media, 2016).

For example, one research study found that when parents were attempting to teach their 2-year-olds new words, children learned the word when their interactions were not interrupted by the parent taking a call on their phone, and the children did not learn the word when their interactions were interrupted by the parent taking a call on their phone (Reed, Hirsh-Pasek, & Golinkoff, 2017). More worrisome is research showing that when parents use technology to withdraw from the stress they feel over their child being easily frustrated or restless and/or having a hot temper, their children are more likely to become even more frustrated or restless and/or to have a hot temper—which is then followed by more parental withdrawal, and so on (McDaniel & Radesky, 2018).

Yet how would the results of this study differ if the United States had a law similar to the law in France in which people are not obligated to be part of an "always on" work culture—that is, if we had a **right to disconnect law**, which is a law based on the human right to protect people from being obligated to engage in work-related communication outside of business hours so that they can stay healthy, rest, and spend quality time with loved ones?

• • • •

Contemporary Theories: Ethological and Evolutionary Theories

Other theories, such as ethology, focus on aspects of *physical*, *cognitive*, and/or *emotional* development, aspects of which they propose are species-specific adaptations. While ethological perspectives of human behavior tend to focus on critical periods of development, evolutionary theories concentrate on explaining those behaviors that increase our reproductive success or appear to have a survival advantage, such as our physiological reaction to fear (increased heart rate, quickened pulse, sweating, and a sudden burst of energy), which mobilizes us to escape a dangerous situation. It may not surprise you to learn that evolutionary theories of human development include Charles Darwin's (1802–1889) theory of evolution via natural selection.

Lorenz's Theory

Konrad Lorenz (1903–1989), who won the Nobel Prize in Physiology or Medicine in 1973, is best known for his work studying **imprinting**, a process in which innate behaviors become manifest after exposure to certain stimuli. Lorenz observed that newborn geese followed the mother goose everywhere soon after they hatched. Yet once Lorenz made himself, rather than their mother, the first moving object to which the goslings were exposed, they followed *him* everywhere instead.

Thus Lorenz demonstrated that although some behaviors are innate, such as goslings following a moving object, their particular manifestation, such as following him instead of the mother goose, is dependent upon the specific events that occur within a critical or sensitive period of time, after which the behavior is less likely and/or more difficult to develop. In humans, for instance, there is a sensitive period for language development, after which the ability to learn a language in addition to our native tongue becomes much more difficult.

Lorenz's theory also has relevance for *emotional* development in infancy and toddlerhood, particularly in terms of the attachment or emotional bonds between children and their parents. Researchers measure attachment by noting a child's physical behavior when the child is in proximity to the parent, yet these physical behaviors are based on mental representations—that is, cognitive images in the researcher's mind of what we expect from emotional relationships (Laurita, Hazan, & Spreng, 2018).

The quality or type of attachment or emotional bond that develops during these early years tends to remain the same for other relationships throughout an individual's life—again suggestive of a critical or sensitive period in development. In Maria's case, it may be that during her early years, her parents were consistently emotionally available to her, which increased her trust in others and allowed her to develop both confidence in herself and the ability to focus on the task at hand (whether it be playing with building blocks in toddlerhood or completing assignments in college) rather than to be anxious about whether the people in her life are really there for her.

Bjorklund's Theory

Developmental scientists who adopt an evolutionary perspective may ask why evolution may have favored a tendency to behave in a specific way. For example, cognitive cognitive development may be a natural outcome of behavior typical for our species in order to solve problems associated with surviving, such as communicating with others (Bjorklund, 2018a).

Contemporary evolutionary approaches to understanding development, such as that proposed by David Bjorklund (2018b), do not propose that growth follows (genetically) predetermined paths.

Instead, many evolutionary approaches investigate **epigenesis**, or how genetic material is turned on and off in different contexts; two commonly studied epigenetic processes are **DNA methylation**, in which DNA is deactivated or turned off by different contexts, and **DNA acetylation**, in which DNA is activated or turned on by different contexts (Bjorklund, 2018b).

For example, epigenetic research is able to explain *how* stress (as a result of conditions such as poverty, which is associated with a range of public health concerns, from diabetes and depression) in early life turns off genes that help us engage in later self-regulation, such as impulse control. Thus, the binary *nature (e.g., genes) versus nurture (e.g., environment)* debate is overshadowed by a more complex and empirical understanding. With information such as this, public policy makers can make more data-driven government decisions in the interest of children—to eliminate social injustices by reducing, if not preventing, such stress (Conradt, 2017; Witherington & Lickliter, 2017).

How would evolutionary theory explain Maria? Her study behavior has ensured her survival, given that her parents' factory jobs are becoming increasingly scarce in the information age, which requires individuals to manipulate ideas rather than levers. It may also be that in childhood, Maria experienced low levels of stress and interacted with other children who were academically disciplined, helping to ensure that she developed self-regulation. Research has found that play in children is related to their being better able to be successful in relationships and to and to acquire socially acceptable behaviors that ensure their adaptation—so that the cognitive mechanisms of attention, memory, and reasoning that allow for solving problems in social play (and academic work) also foster survival, as do the emotional skills of communication, empathy, and cooperation (Bjorklund, 2018a; Greve & Thomsen, 2016).

Contemporary Theories: Developmental Neuroscience

Less a theory and more an approach, developmental neuroscience involves the study of the nervous system's development in order to inform our understanding of *physical*, *cognitive*, and/or *emotional* development (Lyle, 2011). For instance, one study found that when children and parents think about one another, those with better attachments or emotional bonds show less involvement of brain regions that are associated with relieving distress; this indicates that developing a secure emotional bond with someone and knowing that they are always there for you has a physical imprint—an imprint that does not require as much of the brain's resources for stress reduction, compared to those of people with less secure attachments (Laurita, Hazan, & Spreng, 2018).

Developmental neuroscience studies the relationships among the brain and various behaviors, while also addressing the roles of context and epigenetic processes of genes, as in how stressful life events may interfere with the functioning of receptors that bind to *cortisol*, a hormone that is released in response to stress (Guyer, Pérez-Edgar, & Crone, 2018). The combination of developmental neuroscience together with the traditional approaches to understanding developmental psychology are referred to **developmental science**, an interdisciplinary perspective adopted by this book (Bialystock & Werker, 2017).

The interdisciplinary approach of developmental science can be seen in a study in which researchers measured children's nervous system activity after exposing them to unpleasant images (such as sad or angry people). They found that those children who experienced low levels of exposure to Hurricane Sandy stress showed a reduction in their nervous system activity and corresponding attention to the unpleasant images, as compared to those children who experienced high levels of exposure to Hurricane Sandy stress, who did *not* show a reduction in their nervous system activity and corresponding attention to the unpleasant images (Kessel et al., 2018). Such findings suggest that stressful life events (such as poverty) do not just render nurture or the environment less than to be desired. The interaction of nurture and nature has exponential outcomes, such as poverty's potential to disrupt neurodevelopment and lead to continual high levels of vigilance in the face of threats, resulting in ongoing high levels of arousal that could lead to sleep disruption and its multiple negative consequences (Kelly & El-Sheikh, 2018).

Therefore, it is very likely that physical changes occur in the brain in response to social injustices, changes that then increase the risk for later adversities (such as difficulties in self-regulation). These physical changes in the brain, and their long-term outcomes, could be prevented with improved social policies that foster greater equity and social justice, which in turn improve everyone's well-being—that which is sorely needed now more than ever (Palacios-Barrios & Hanson, 2019; Tian & Liu, 2020).

Theory Summary

As you can see, all the theories we've looked at are correct about some aspect of human development, as each provides a valid interpretation of some aspect of behavior. This is especially clear when we look for explanations of what Maria achieved despite the hurdles she experienced. Yet no one theory is able to provide a comprehensive view of human behavior. Relying on one theory to try to explain Maria's life would limit our understanding of who she has become. In fact, each theory is like a puzzle piece that reveals only a little of the overall image on its own, but is necessary to include along with other pieces/theories in order for the total picture of an individual to emerge.

Many people working in developmental science and related fields typically adopt an eclectic approach, in which they consider elements of various theories rather than every aspect of just one theory. For example, understanding Maria's age-related developmental conflicts according to Erikson's stage theory (such as moving multiple times when she was young, which impacted her identity and her career interests) also informs our understanding of her—as does knowing the details of how each of Bronfenbrenner's Ecological Systems shaped where Maria came from and where she is going—and how her teachers and parents reinforced her academic success.

It may also very well be that Maria's attachment to her parents when she was young was of such high quality that not only did she develop strong emotional bonds with others throughout the rest of her life, but also her brain and nervous system were therefore wired to experience low levels of threats and stress so the genes that correspond to her ability to self-regulate and succeed in life stayed turn on by the DNA acetylation process. Further advances in developmental science will tell us more about Maria and others, based on the outcomes of empirical research studies. Research is the topic of our next chapter.

Key Terms

Accommodation	Classical Conditioning	Disequilibrium
Adaptation	Development	DNA Acetylation
Assimilation	Developmental Science	DNA Methylation

Ecological Systems Theory
Epigenesis
Equilibrium
Executive Function
Growth
Guided Participation
Imprinting

Modeling
Operant Conditioning
Right to Disconnect Law
Scaffolding
Scheme
Screen Time
Sensitive Period

Social Cognitive Theory
Social Justice
Social Learning Theory
Social Mobility
Sociocultural Theory
Socioeconomic Status
Zone of Proximal Development

Summary

1. **Describe the Stages of Child and Adolescent Development.** The stages of lifespan development are prenatal (from conception to birth), infancy and toddlerhood (from birth to age 2), early childhood (from 2 to 6), middle childhood (from 6 to 12), and adolescence (from 12 to about 20 or 25).

2. **Explain the Domains of Child and Adolescent Development.** The three domains of child development are physical, cognitive, and emotional. The *physical development domain* includes all the biological changes that occur from birth through adolescence. These biological changes include increases in neuron connections within the brain during infancy and toddlerhood, physical growth of the bones, as well as the appearance of secondary sex characteristics during puberty.

    The *cognitive development domain* includes all aspects of thinking and language development, such as babbling in infancy and learning the alphabet in preschool, as well as developing a greater attention span and acquiring a new language in school.

    The *emotional domain* of development includes all aspects of social and emotional changes, such as attachment in infancy, developing relationships with peers upon initial entry into school, regulating our emotions in the face of bullying in middle childhood, and developing our identity in adolescence.

3. **Apply the Lifelong, Multidimensional, Polydirectional, and Risk–Resilience Patterns of development.** *Lifelong* patterns reveal the relationships between the stages of development, or the way what we do today may affect the way we, or our offspring, develop in the future. *Multidimensional* patterns concern how physical development may affect cognitive and/or emotional development and vice versa in many aspects of lifespan development. *Polydirectional* patterns reveal that change over time is not always a decline; it can show growth and stability as well. *Risk–resilience* patterns show the ways in which our development proceeds, for better or worse, due to the interactions among our genes and the environments in which we are developing.

4. **Compare Traditional Theories of Child and Adolescent Development.** Psychoanalytic theories, such as those of Freud and Erikson, proposed that we develop in stages and must resolve a specific crisis at each stage. Ethological and evolutionary theories focus on behaviors that allow us to adapt and have survival advantage or increase our reproductive success.

    Learning theories include those of classical conditioning as well as operant conditioning, and both assume that our behavior changes as a function of association or what is paired with our behavior, either while we are behaving or after we behave. Cognitive theories include those of Piaget and Vygotsky; Piaget proposed that our thinking changes qualitatively across childhood in a series of stages, whereas Vygotsky proposed that we learn from a more knowledgable person, with that person teaching us in a way that changes as we advance, so that the instruction is tailored to whatever our level of understanding is at the moment.

5. **Evaluate Contemporary Theories of Child and Adolescent Development.** Bronfenbrenner's theory is one of ecological systems or various contexts in which we develop, each having a unique influence on us, and each interacting with one another. An example is how Maria's parents needing to move for their jobs impacted their interactions with her as a result of transportation and financial difficulties. Contemporary evolutionary approaches to understanding development do not propose that growth follows (genetically) predetermined paths (Bjorklund, 2018b).

Instead, some evolutionary approaches investigate epigenetic processes, or how genetic material is turned on and off in different contexts. Developmental neuroscience is more of an approach than a theory, and researchers who adopt these methods study the relationships among the brain and behaviors, while also addressing the roles of context and epigenetic processes.

Helpful Websites

According to their website, the National Association for the Education of Young Children (NAEYC) promotes high-quality learning by connecting practice, policy, and research. A description of their Anti-Bias Education program—which this chapter's Mentor, Allyson Criner Brown, works with—can be found here, including the four goals of an Anti-Bias Education: https://www.naeyc.org/resources/pubs/yc/nov2019/understanding-anti-bias

Diego Goldberg of Buenos Aires, Argentina, has photographed his family on June 17 over the years, providing a visual representation of how each family member has aged: http://zonezero.com/open/158-the-arrow-of-time

To learn about the increasing number of preschool programs being offered in the United States, check out the National Institute for Early Education Research's website: http://nieer.org/

UNICEF works internationally with the United Nations (UN) to ensure children's right to survive, thrive, and fulfill their potential—to the benefit of a better world. To learn more about UNICEF, the work they do, and how you can help, visit their website: https://www.unicef.org

Zero to Three is a nonprofit organization that informs, trains, and supports parents, professionals, and policymakers to improve the lives of infants and toddlers: https://www.zerotothree.org

Recommended Reading

Burman, E. (2017). *Deconstructing developmental psychology.* Oxford, UK: Routledge.

Payne, K. (2017). *The broken ladder: How inequality affects the way we think, live, and die.* New York, NY: Viking.

Barr, D. A. (2019). *Health disparities in the United States: Social class, race, ethnicity, and the social determinants of health.* Baltimore, MD: Johns Hopkins University Press.

Kendi, I. X. (2019). *How to be antiracist.* New York, NY: One World.

Putnam, R. D. (2015). *Our kids: The American Dream in Crisis.* New York, NY: Simon & Schuster.

Research

CHAPTER 2

Snapshot

Developmental science, the interdisciplinary perspective we learned about in Chapter 1, can promote social justice by informing policy makers, institutions, and others to rely on data-driven decisions that will provide people with the ability to reach their full potential within the societies in which they reside (Bialystok & Werker, 2017; Russell, 2015). How so? Well, for instance, research can demonstrate how environmental factors, including a lack of access to resources (inadequate school funding or inadequate healthcare) can turn on genes that contribute to developmental problems, such as a lack of self-control and/or increased risk of disease that interferes with a child's ability to succeed.

Additionally, the authors of these studies can identify the ways in which their findings can be used to reduce inequalities in society for children, teens, and their families, beginning by communicating the research and its implications with audiences who interact with children. They might also invite these audiences to participate in the research, such as by identifying issues for future studies (Golinkoff et al., 2017; Tebes & Thai, 2018).

FIG. 2.1

For example, a national initiative known as Mind in the Making provides training to parents and the professionals who work with children, and this training is based on such research (Galinsky et al., 2017).

For more information on Mind in the Making, including a discussion of what its organizers believe to be the seven essential life skills children need to acquire (focus and self-control; perspective taking; communicating; making connections; critical thinking; taking on challenges; being self-directed and engaged in learning), see their website in the *Helpful Websites* section of this chapter and the Mind in the Making book in the *Recommended Reading* section.

How Is Developmental Science Similar to Map-Making?

Suppose one day you take a wrong turn and get lost. What do you do? Some people look at a map. Maps provide us with an aerial or bird's-eye view of the landscape that reveals where we are in relation to others, much as the research of developmental science does. We realized in Chapter 1 that there are patterns within the research on child and adolescent development (such as lifelong, multidimensional, polydirectional, and risk–resilience) that rise out of the human landscape, just as crop circles become visible when we are flying above them in an airplane. So developmental science is akin to cartography, or map-making. Let's explore this idea further.

Map-making began as a way for explorers to visually symbolize the landscape they had just explored (Hellemans & Bunch, 1988). Early maps served two purposes. First of all, drawing a map allowed explorers to rely upon it if they later became lost. Secondly, it allowed explorers to describe the characteristics of their newly discovered land to other explorers. Map-making is a dynamic field, because maps become more accurate as more individuals explore and record details of the landscape.

For example, although they can bring up privacy issues, Google maps are a vast improvement over what early explorers might have created. And just as maps become more comprehensive and precise over time, so does the field of developmental science. As researchers continue to conduct studies, accumulate more data, and publish their findings in scholarly academic journals such as *Child Developmental*, our view or map of the human landscape becomes more accurate.

Learning Goals

▸ Describe how developmental science is similar to map-making

▸ Synthesize the cycle of science

▸ Distinguish the types of data and data collection methods

▸ Interpret the information obtained from correlational research designs

▸ Identify the necessary components of an experimental study

▸ Explain strengths and weaknesses of the three developmental research designs

▸ Critique the standards for ethical treatment of research participants

In developmental science, a **theory** is a description and explanation of human behavior that has been tested and retested by research studies in order to verify its claims. For a theory to be scientifically useful, it is tested with a **hypothesis**, or a precisely stated prediction. For example, Erikson's theory, introduced in Chapter 1, proposes that we must resolve a crisis at each stage in development. The crisis of middle childhood is one of Industry–Inferiority, when we must discover where our talents and strengths lie in order to develop competence that will serve us in all stages of our lives.

A hypothesis to test this theory might predict that adults who had resolved Erikson's Industry–Inferiority conflict during middle childhood will be more satisfied and more productive in their careers than those who did not resolve the conflict. If research shows that this is indeed the case, it gives support to the theory, and the results can be applied to schools in that budget cuts are prevented so that children have ample opportunities to discover if their talents lie not just in reading and math, but in art, music, sports, and other after-school programs as well.

How exactly we would go about testing our hypothesis, and then using the results, brings us to our next topic, The Cycle of Science.

FIG. 2.2   An Early Map

Copyright © 2012 Depositphotos/Andrey_Kuzmin.

FIG. 2.3   A Google Street View Car

Source: https://pixabay.com/en/google-view-camera-car-vehicle-2361156/.

The Cycle of Science

The three activities of theory, research, and application we've just described form what we call *The Cycle of Science*, a feature in every chapter of this book beginning with Chapter 3. In The Cycle of Science, the three processes of theory, research, and application are ongoing. As Figure 2.4 shows, it may start with a theory—say, of the factors that contribute to autism. Research is then conducted with this specific purpose in mind, using a particular type of design and yielding distinct findings. Application then involves using the research findings in various fields like public health, nursing, and

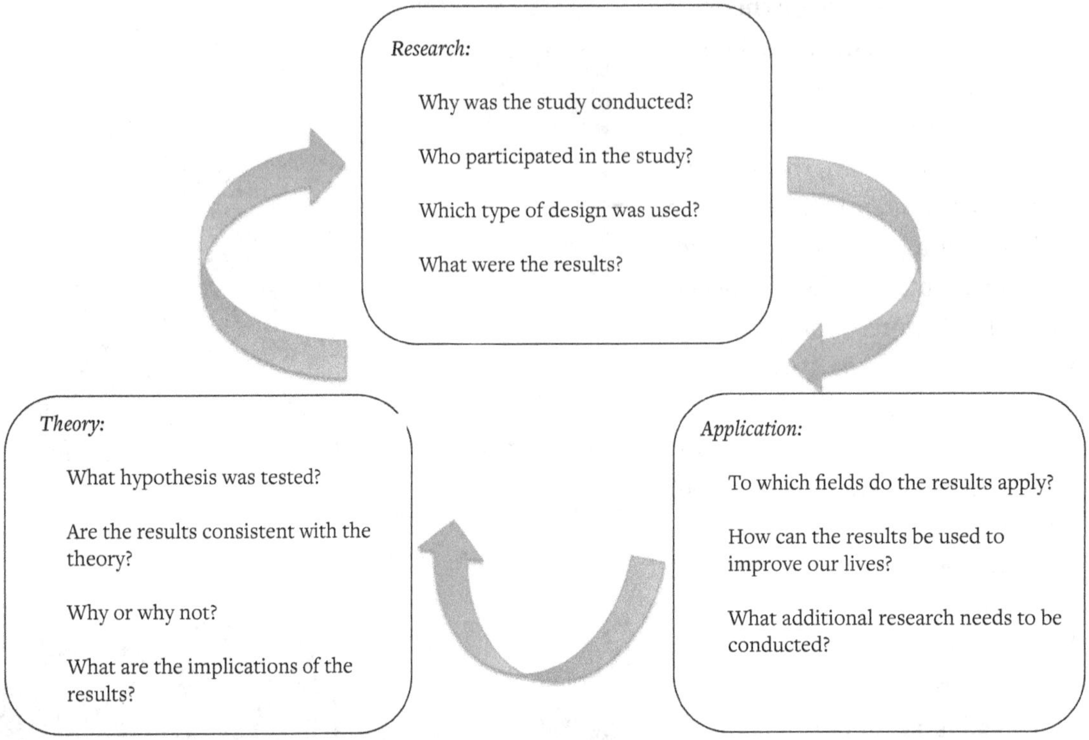

Research:

Why was the study conducted?

Who participated in the study?

Which type of design was used?

What were the results?

Theory:

What hypothesis was tested?

Are the results consistent with the theory?

Why or why not?

What are the implications of the results?

Application:

To which fields do the results apply?

How can the results be used to improve our lives?

What additional research needs to be conducted?

FIG. 2.4   The Cycle of Science

social work to help children and teens on the autism spectrum. This theory should then be revised, tested again with additional research, applied again, revised again, and so on.

What Role Do Data Have in Developmental Science?

How does research unfold? Where do researchers begin? Let's start with data.

What Are Data?

Most researchers start with a question they would like to answer (for instance, "When does conflict between teens and their parents peak?"). To answer their questions, researchers gather and then analyze data. **Data** are facts that researchers gather. When we gather data, we do so by measuring **variables**, which are values that can differ from person to person at one point in time (such as race/ethnicity), or that can change within a person over time (such as age or gender).

Researchers gather data in order to reach objective conclusions about a topic, rather than relying upon subjective and perhaps biased beliefs. For example, a researcher could ask his friends who have young adult children when they experienced the most conflict during their child's adolescent years. However, these friends of the researcher likely do not reflect the **population**—that is, the entire group of people of interest in regard to the research topic, such as all parents of young adults.

Instead, the researcher interviewed a limited **sample** or subset of the population that may or may not be representative of the entire population. Samples not being representative of the population of interest to a research study can be a major problem, limiting what the data can tell us, so research studies ideally include large representative samples of diverse individuals to approximate the general population as much as possible.

What Is the Role of Social Justice in Developmental Science as Map-Making?

Although it may not be possible for all researchers working in developmental science to address how to further social justice for children, teens, and their families (as in the Mind in the Making program we learned about in this chapter's *Snapshot*), the research that is being conducted needs to study children and teens from all backgrounds before making broad claims about development (Galinsky et al., 2017). Unfortunately, this is often not the case (Nielsen et al, 2017).

Why? Perhaps because issues such as equity and justice are only now starting to become focus areas in developmental science and/or because of the difficulty of obtaining an equivalent number of participants from all backgrounds (in terms of languages spoken, race/ethnicity, gender identity, SES, level of education, geography, culture, nationality, and so on), the people who participate in research have historically be involved based on their accessibility to researchers (Jager, Putnick, & Bornstein, 2017; Killen, Rutland, & Yip, 2016).

So the bulk of research in many areas is conducted on groups of people from Western, Educated, Industrialized, Rich, and Democratic (WEIRD) societies who are different substantially from people in non-WEIRD societies on a variety of measures, including moral reasoning, self-concept, and whether intelligence in children is judged according to their conformity or their creativity; cultures *within* WEIRD cultures can vary quite a bit on values as well, such as how parenting within the United States can be a function of culture—a topic we will discuss in greater detail in Chapter 9 (Clegg, Wen, & Legare, 2017; Henrich, Heine, & Norenzayan, 2010; Roubinov & Boyce, 2017). As a result, this lack of diversity in research participants may skew research findings, and it isn't always clear how (Nielsen et al., 2017).

For example, a recent study that investigated our aforementioned "When does conflict between teens and their parents peak?" question found that although prior research (conducted mostly on European Americans) has found conflict to peak in early adolescence, conflict between teens and their parents peaks in mid-adolescence for Chinese American families (Juang et al., 2018). And it is worth noting that Asian Americans show the fastest growth rate in the U.S. population of any racial or ethnic group (Lopéz, Ruiz, & Patten).

So if this study on the timing of parent–teen conflict in Chinese American families had not been conducted, Asian Americans, a major portion of our population (not to mention all the other non–European American parents and teens, who also deserve to be understood), would have been considered developmentally nonnormative. Most of the past research that has set the norm for when parents and teens experience the most conflict has been with European Americans (Juang et al., 2018).

Therefore, future research that tests theories must be specific about the groups to which the theory does and does not apply—perhaps by still using convenience samples but using those with homogeneous groups, such as with just one racial/ethnic group—so that similarities and differences between and among groups, and the reasons for them, can be compared and addressed in *The Cycle of*

Science—and so that developmental science can become **multicultural** in that it addresses cultural differences such as racial/ethnic differences in school achievement, along with the mechanisms of these cultural influences, such as unequal funding in public schools (Jager, Putnick, & Bornstein, 2017; Juang et al., 2018; Nagayama Hall, Yip, & Zárate, 2016; Syed et al., 2018).

Otherwise, to be **color blind**, and assume all racial/ethnic groups are similar to one another, is not only ethically irresponsible when trying to understand development in all populations and establish normative milestones for everyone, it is also bad science.

For example, out of a desire to reduce bias, researchers may minimize or simply choose not to address if and how their results apply to different racial/ethnic groups of children and teens—yet their doing so instead can unknowingly actually increase racism (Nagayama Hall, Yip, & Zárate, 2016; Syed et al., 2018).

Indeed, color-blind approaches to research, which are the opposite of multicultural approaches to research, are a more contemporary and subtle form of racism in which *raceless explanations* (such as individual choice) are given for *structural and environmental factors* (such as the housing discrimination that began after the end of slavery and that is now illegal but still exists in subtler forms, as with regard to rental apartments). Perhaps this is because American ideology tends to promote a belief in equal opportunity and encourages individualistic explanations for behavior that focus on motivation, will-power, and effort—rather than acknowledging difficult truths of structural inequities (Syed et al., 2018).

So if a research study found that there were racial/ethnic differences in children's school quality, a color-blind explanation would ostensibly be that such differences are found because these families choose to live in neighborhoods that have lower quality schools—rather than their schools being of lower quality because the structure of public school funding in the United States is based on local residential taxes (Bonilla-Silva, 2015; Syed et al., 2018).

The need to be multicultural and ethically responsible in The Cycle of Science holds for other groups, such as for researchers to no longer assume that children and their families belong to just one racial/ethnic group, and/or to a gender binary of either female or male. Consider this example in regards to class. If a working-class male wants to know how to help his children after his divorce and the postdivorce caregiving best practices he reads about are based on research done on upper-middle-class participants, the support being offered to him is misguided and potentially detrimental to his well-being and the well-being of his children (Dunham & Olson, 2016; Nielsen et al., 2017).

What Are the Types of Data?

Data can be qualitative or quantitative. **Qualitative data** describe characteristics we can categorize but not count or measure, such as gender and hair color. **Quantitative data** are numerical and describe features or qualities we can measure or count, such as height and weight. The ability to assign a meaningful number to a behavior or a trait makes quantitative data easier to use in conducting statistical analyses. As a result, quantitative data are more commonly used in research studies than are qualitative data.

This is not to say that the descriptive nature of qualitative data is not useful or valuable, however (Creswell, 2014). As we will see in later chapters, for instance, caregiving styles are qualitatively different ways in which parents relate to their children, with some parents being strict and unsupportive, others being warm and nurturing, and yet others being a combination. We cannot easily distinguish these differences by saying some parents have "more" or "less" of something than other parents.

The difference is one of style, not necessarily of amount. Therefore, qualitative data are best used to reflect differences such as these. Many researchers conduct studies in which qualitative data are a supplement to quantitative data.

Regardless of whether quantitative and/or qualitative data are used, researchers must use an **operational definition**, which is a description of the item or characteristic they are measuring; this definition needs be clear and precise so that other researchers will easily be able to measure the same variable, in the same way, in order to arrive at the same results.

For example, an operational definition of the degree to which parents are emotional coaches for their children might include how often they validate their children's feelings while also setting limits on their behavior. In fact, research has shown that compared to the parents of children with anxiety disorders, those children *without* anxiety disorders have parents who use more emotion coaching, at least in middle-class European Americans samples (Hurrell, Houwing, & Hudson, 2017). This type of operational definition is a good start. But how might you go about collecting data? You have a number of options, and your choice can influence your results. Let's see how.

What Are Observational, Self-Report, and Physiological Data Collection Methods?

In **observational methods** of data collection, a researcher watches participants behave, and then records the observations in order to use them as data. Observational methods include both naturalistic observation and structured observation. **Naturalistic observation** means watching individuals behave in their natural environment, such as observing children play in a playground or a park. A researcher might sit where children will be least likely to notice someone taking notes on how they play. Because the children are unaware of the researcher, they behave naturally. This is the advantage of naturalistic observation. A limitation is that the behavior in which a researcher is interested, such as how children resolve conflict, may not naturally appear while the researcher is conducting the observation. The researcher could sit at the local playground for a week and still not have the opportunity to observe how children resolve conflict, because no conflicts (or resolutions of such) occur during that week.

In **structured observation** methods of data collection, the researcher observes participants in a laboratory setting that has been set up for the sole purpose of observing how participants respond to it. For example, a researcher wishing to study how children resolve conflict might read them stories in a laboratory room about a bully on a playground and then ask them how they would respond to the bully's behavior. Structured observation is best suited for observing a specific behavior that may or may not occur during a naturalistic observation.

Yet structured observations have drawbacks as well. Listening to children talk about how they would respond to a bully's behavior is not necessarily equivalent to watching them respond. Or imagine a scenario where a researcher encourages children to "act naturally" and play with the toys in the lab room. But the children may not be able to act naturally, because they find the unfamiliar room strange and perhaps intimidating. As a result, when they do begin to play, they behave much less enthusiastically and/or aggressively than they would in a natural setting. Therefore, any conclusions the researcher makes based on observations of the children playing in a lab room may be limited. In this case, if there is no specific behavior the researcher wishes to observe, naturalistic observation is best.

Self-report methods of data collection are those in which participants provide their own data, such as their responses to survey questions. Self-report methods, no matter the research topic, include both clinical interviews and structured interviews. **Clinical interviews** ask participants a limited number of questions, with the intent of allowing them to guide the direction the interview takes.

This type of interview is best in the initial stages of designing a study, when researchers are choosing what variables they will include. For example, researchers conducting a study of parents' concerns regarding the way their children resolve conflict may decide to keep their questions open-ended so parents can voice their true concerns, rather than discussing only the topics the researchers are interested in, such as bullying. As a result, once the researchers conduct clinical interviews with parents, they find that many of the parents mention their children's conflict with siblings and say nothing about bullying at school.

Once researchers have designed their study to be inclusive and relevant to all participants, they may continue to do clinical interviews only to stumble upon another dilemma: That is, although most participants are discussing similar concerns, the free-form nature of the interviews prevents the researchers from comparing responses from participant to participant. At this point, the researchers should switch to **structured interviews.**

Structured interviews are conducted with a standard set of questions that all participants are asked, and in the same order. We can think of a survey as an example of a structured interview, because the standardization of questions across all participants ensures that everyone is asked the same questions, in the same way, with the same wording, and in the same order. Structured interviews are best for comparing responses across multiple participants, whereas clinical interviews are best for generating a report based on only a limited number of participants, usually in the beginning stages of designing a research study and deciding which variables to include.

Physiological methods of data collection are based upon subjects' biological indicators, such as blood pressure, heart rate, pulse, and sleep patterns. Physiological methods might be seen as objective and requiring little interpretation, but they can be misleading, as in the case of a researcher who measures heart rate as an index of anxiety. A person with a rapid heart rate may very well be anxious, or they may have just guzzled an energy drink that has produced the jitters. Therefore, physiological methods of data collection are often used in conjunction with systematic observation and/or self-report methods of data collection. If a researcher is interested in measuring anxiety and has the time and opportunity, they should measure heart rate, observe the subject's behavior, and ask the person to complete a survey that measures anxiety.

Assuming the measures are valid, a person who is truly anxious will most likely score similarly on two, if not all three, of these measures. A measure is valid or demonstrates **validity** if it assesses what it claims to measure, such as an anxiety scale that assesses a person's anxiety and not the levels of caffeine in the person's blood. On the other hand, a measure demonstrates **reliability** if it provides about the same score each time a person is assessed with it, such as a consistent score of "high anxiety" for a child traumatized by a natural disaster, after the child's anxiety level is measured a number of times over the course of a few days. Most measures of psychological traits establish reliability over a few weeks, because traits like extroversion do not typically change that much over a short period of time, whereas anxiety can fluctuate over the course of a few days or even hours.

Even with adequate validity and reliability, though, not all individuals are (understandably) comfortable sharing their personal data, especially with recent technologies, including sensory data obtained from people's smartphones, watches, and/or movement trackers. To learn more, see the *Tech & Media: Comfort Levels in Sharing Health and Personal Data* box.

Comfort Levels in Sharing Health and Personal Data

The data that people's smartphones, watches, and/or fitness trackers record could be used to improve their well-being, yet before the details of such improvements are even conceived, we need to consider individuals' privacy, and their comfort levels with the sharing of such data. One study of female-identified adults asked them about their comfort in sharing *health data*, such as patterns of their sleep, mood, and physical activity, as well as their *personal data*, such as their communication log, social activity, and location.

The participants reported that they were more comfortable sharing health data than personal data. They reported that it also matters whom they would be sharing such data with; their comfort in sharing data with physicians was much higher than their comfort in sharing such data with family members or with an electronic health record (Nichols et al., 2019). This study was limited in terms of the background characteristics, but it is a good start in identifying preliminary issues associated with smartphone, watch, and/or fitness tracker data— and the role that technology might play in allowing research access to improve our lives. Future research may want to ask similar questions to more diverse groups of individuals.

• • • •

What Are Case Study, Archive, and Ethnography Data Collection Methods?

Case study, archival, and ethnographic methods are used less often for research than are observational, self-report, and physiological methods of data collection. Yet the information they provide, because this information tends to be qualitative, is just as valuable, if not richer in detail. For example, the **case study method** generates a narrative report of a very small group of subjects, or even one individual, as a way to explore a topic in depth with rich detail.

Yet like the data from clinical interviews, the data obtained from a case study cannot be easily tied to quantitative measures. As a result, it is difficult for us to compare case study responses across individuals. And because case study methods typically rely on a very limited number of participants, they are often used to *generate* hypotheses as a study is being designed, rather than to *test* hypotheses after a study has been designed.

Once a case study has generated a hypothesis, that hypothesis can be tested with multiple participants, such as a self-report survey of many people. For example, a researcher who values the arts and/or whose son is taking a painting class may suspect that taking painting or guitar lessons can help a child develop attention, decision-making, planning, and problem-solving skills as much as a science class would. The researcher may notice that her son likes to paint rainbows, and that when he does, he needs to focus on gathering, opening, and stirring the different-colored paints; deciding which colors to paint and in which order; and then solving the problem of not having purple paint on hand by mixing red and blue paint.

The researcher might then hypothesize that children will have better attention, decision-making, planning, and problem-solving skills after they take a series of painting classes than they had before—and that these gains in their skills will be comparable to those of children who take science classes. Such a hypothesis is ripe for investigation; historically, developmental science has studied the development of scientific thinking and moral reasoning in children, whereas researchers have yet to find out about the developmental implications from the production of the arts and/or the reception of the arts, whether the production of or the reception of the arts, whether it be painting, practicing the guitar, or pretend play via theater arts (Goldstein, Lerner, & Winner, 2017).

Other forms of data collection include **archival methods** of data collection, which rely on data from archives or historical records, including newspapers, diaries, and public records such as birth and death certificates. The advantage of this type of data collection is that it allows a researcher to study people who lived in earlier periods of history, using data that have already been gathered. The disadvantage is that the researcher is limited to whatever data are available, especially if the people under investigation are deceased or otherwise unavailable for follow-up questioning.

Ethnographic methods of data collection draw from anthropological research that examines the similarities and differences between different cultures. Ethnographic research is frequently conducted within the culture(s) of interest, so researchers can be assured that whatever they are measuring is relevant to that culture.

For example, after attending a *quinceañera* (the 15th-birthday ceremony and celebration that marks the transition from childhood to adulthood for Latinx teens who identify as female), a researcher may be interested in investigating how various other groups celebrate the transition from childhood to adulthood. But in order to fully understand the meaning of a group's ceremony, especially before comparing and contrasting it to such ceremonies in other cultures, the researcher would need to appreciate a group's worldview and cultural values.

Once we have collected all this data, though, what do we do with it? How can we analyze it to find out whether it tells us something meaningful? How do we make sense of it? The answer depends whether on the research design we are using is correlational or experimental.

What Are Correlational Research Designs?

Correlational research studies examine the way two variables are or are not related to one another. In developmental science, correlational variables often reflect characteristics of children and their experiences, such as their *preschool experience* and their *readiness for kindergarten* (which could be defined as self-regulation). In correlational research studies, the variables are naturally occurring, meaning that researchers do *not* attempt to alter the participants' experiences.

For instance, in our example of children's preschool experiences and their readiness for kindergarten, the researchers in a correlational study would not attempt to improve or change children's preschool experiences or readiness; they would simply measure both variables to see if they change together, such as if one variable increases while the other variable increases. That is, does kindergarten readiness increase as preschool experiences (in terms of the *number of hours* experienced in preschool and/or the *quality* of the experiences) increase?

Also, in the same way that case studies can be used to generate hypotheses that are then tested with data from multiple participants, correlational research can provide researchers with a preliminary understanding of whether and how two variables may be related, a relationship that can then be tested experimentally. For instance, if researchers find a correlation between the quality of children's preschool experiences and their kindergarten readiness, the researchers could then conduct an experimental research study to determine what other variables—other than preschool quality—may boost kindergarten readiness, such as children's home literacy experiences and/or how engaged the children are with their teachers, their peers, and the tasks within their preschool classroom.

In fact, one preliminary study has found that beyond preschool quality, the more preschoolers are engaged, the greater their language skills and self-regulation (Sabol, Bohlmann, & Downer, 2018). So a subsequent experimental study could attempt to improve some preschoolers' engagement and see if children who show greater engagement also show greater school readiness compared to children with low or average engagement. To learn about being involved in research and policy on topics such as early education, visit the *Mentor Minute* box to learn about the work of Titus DosRemedios, MA.

Mentor Minute

Titus DosRemedios, MA

1) Describe your work, please.

I am the Director of Research and Policy at *Strategies for Children*, a small Massachusetts-based nonprofit organization, which works to ensure all young children have access to high-quality early education and are ready for success in kindergarten.

There is a wide equity gap in Massachusetts, and most states, in which there are populations of people with high levels of resources (i.e., education, multigenerational wealth) who are living near, in some cases down the street from, people with much fewer resources— families who have struggled with poverty, families experiencing trauma, recent immigrants just starting to build assets, etc. Social mobility in the U.S. is getting worse, with it being incredibly difficult for people at the bottom to make it out to the next level. High-quality early education

FIG. 2.5   Titus DosRemedios, MA

can play a small part in helping reverse this trend by providing all young children with a strong start in life, plus reliable, quality childcare so their parents can go to work.

I was initially hired at Strategies for Children (SFC) to help with research, data, and policy analysis, and have since grown to wear many hats. I organize state and local early education data, track state budget and legislative proposals, write policy briefs, and apply for grants. At SFC we assist our many partners (i.e., other nonprofits, elected officials, local early childhood teams) with their early childhood policy projects, which helps us all avoid reinventing the wheel. I manage the data on our website, which serves as a resource for parents, schools, local governments, state legislators, and journalists needing to know how individual communities in the state are doing and what they need. We have briefs, infographics, publications, and fast facts available to anyone at the "Research" tab on our website, http://www.strategiesforchildren.org, and a fantastic blog called Eye on Early Education.

2) How does social justice inform your work?

If society were just, many nonprofits such as Strategies for Children wouldn't need to do what they do now. We nonprofits are born when enough people want to see a societal need addressed, and try to fill the gaps that just aren't being addressed by government or business.

At Strategies, we feel it would be socially just for all children to have access to high-quality early education; that is basically our mission statement. Although we don't always use the phrase "social justice," it is our goal.

Preschool and childcare are very expensive for families, and costly for providers and schools to operate. Strategies for Children believes government should invest in helping make these programs available to more children, since research has long proven the benefits of high-quality early education—it is a societal good that gives kids a strong foundation for their future learning, and can even save governments money in the long term as those children progress through school and the workforce.

3) How did you become involved in social justice and/or advocacy?

After college, I worked in a few different teaching roles in Rhode Island, often as a community partner or guest presenter in schools. I was a Violence Prevention Educator, promoting nonviolence and conflict resolution strategies in middle schools throughout the eastern part of the state. I was also a Life Skills instructor in middle schools in Providence, and a teaching assistant at a very high-quality elementary school in Providence. Because I had seen so many different schools and communities within such a small state, it crystallized for me how wide the variation is of how kids experience school. That variation confused me—I thought that the poorest neighborhoods should have the best schools, but they unfortunately often had the worst.

I wanted to learn why the education system was set up the way it was, and learn new strategies for helping all children have equal opportunity and positive experiences in education. So, I enrolled in an Urban Education Policy masters program at Brown University, which gave me a great foundation for answering some of these questions, plus new skills to help me in my career going forward.

4) What are your thoughts on how social justice can improve child and adolescent development?

For people who are interested in achieving social justice, I want them to think about the first 18 years of a person's life, and all of the different opportunities that a child should have in order to have equal/equitable opportunities, a fair chance at a successful life. Think back on your own childhood as well, and the opportunities you may have had. It isn't just one or two things, such as graduating college or attending a quality preschool, but numerous things—playing a team sport, having mentors, living in a safe neighborhood—that all add up to a person's level of preparedness or advantage for the rest of their life.

Choose one of these topics and do some research, go meet people in your community who are working on the issue and offer to help them. This could be at the local or state level. It can be difficult to know where to start, but taking the initiative to attend community events and meet people who work on a given issue can help you better understand what you do, and do not, want to do. Local and state organizations are more approachable too, and not always on everyone's radar so they likely need any help you can offer.

5) What suggestions do you have for undergraduate students who are interested in making a change in child and adolescent development?

We have undergraduate and graduate-level interns who help us expand our capacity. For example, a recent graduate-level intern researched local governance structures in early education and wrote a policy brief for us. This will help inform our state policy strategy, and our work in local communities. Undergraduate students can come and work on almost anything—helping us update our contact lists and partner databases, reviewing and summarizing research reports, writing and delivering letters at the State House, and supporting our social media presence. Most of our interns are interested in developmental psychology, public policy, communications, and/or research.

We tell our interns, who may have preconceived ideas about how change happens, to be humble, have open minds, and learn as much as possible. We remind them that relationships are everything, so when people call us for information or ideas, it is important that we are helpful, respectful, and collaborative. Think of yourself as a collaborator, especially when you are starting out in your career.

And remember, "government" means federal, state, and local—if you find that one layer is stuck, you can always work at other layers. And these layers are interconnected. Local organizations can generate innovative ideas that can be used to inform state or federal policy. So do what you can, wherever you are, to help bring about the change you seek.

• • • •

Correlation Coefficients

The mathematical number that represents the correlation is called a **correlation coefficient**, and it is symbolized with a lowercase italic "r." The values a correlation coefficient can range from are –1.00 to +1.00, so the closer a correlation coefficient is to 1

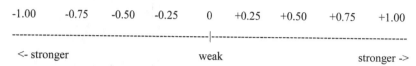

FIG. 2.6   The Closer Correlation Coefficients Are to –1.00 or +1.00, the Stronger They Are

(either –1 or +1), the stronger the relationship between the variables, and the closer a correlation coefficient is to 0, the weaker the relationship.

For example, a correlation of r = .80 is stronger than a correlation of r = .30. The size of the correlation is not the only piece of information a correlation coefficient provides, though. The direction is also important, and it can be positive or negative.

As can be seen in Figure 2.7, **positive correlations**, such as r = +.90, mean that as one variable *increases*, the other also *increases*. For example, our earlier example of how "the more engaged preschoolers are with their teachers, peers, and classroom tasks, the greater their language skills are" is a positive correlation, as is how "the more engaged preschoolers are with their teachers, their peers, and their classroom tasks, the greater their self-regulation is" (Sabol, Bohlmann, & Downer, 2018).

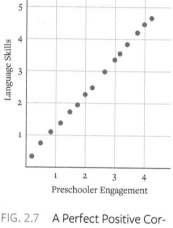

FIG. 2.7   A Perfect Positive Correlation of +1.0

Negative correlations, such as r = –.90, mean that as one variable *increases*, the other variable *decreases*. For example, there is a negative correlation between television viewing and school readiness, and this negative relationship is even stronger in low-income families (Ribner, Fitzpatrick, & Blair, 2017). From a social justice perspective, a finding such as this indicates that those who rely on television the most, perhaps to occupy their children if they are not able to pay for childcare, educational toys, and/or lessons, are most adversely impacted by it and therefore very much need universal preschool programs to level the playing field.

As you look at Figure 2.8, notice it is the absolute value of the number that matters when we are interested in how strong the correlation is; the positive or negative sign tells us only whether the direction of the correlation is positive or negative. Yet very few correlations are a perfect +1.0 or –1.0, as indicated in Figure 2.7 and Figure 2.8.

Instead, substantial correlations are usually +.80 or higher, yet even those around +.50 or +.60 can be meaningful. For instance, instance, although it is not a perfect correlation, there is a strong positive correlation between the number of library books a child reads per week and their literacy skills. And although it is not a perfect correlation, there is a strong negative correlation between the number of more library books a child reads per week, the greater their literacy skills. Another example of a negative correlation is the number of vaccines a child receives and their number of illnesses, as shown in Figure 2.10.

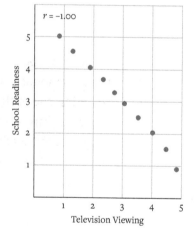

FIG. 2.8   A Perfect Negative Correlation of –1.0

Zero correlations are correlations that are zero (r = 00) or close to zero (such as r = .07), which means there is no or little relationship between two variables. An example of a zero correlation is

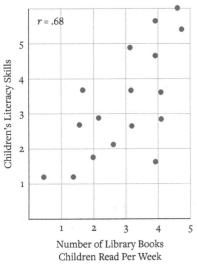

FIG. 2.9 A Positive Correlation Between the Number of Library Books a Child Reads per Week and Their Literacy Skills

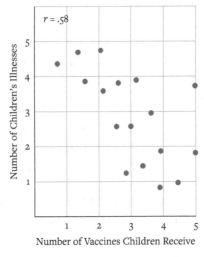

FIG. 2.10 A Negative Correlation Between the Number of Vaccines a Child Receives and Their Number of Illnesses

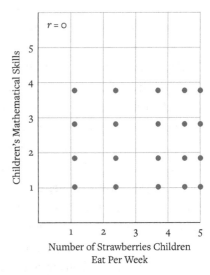

FIG. 2.11 A Zero Correlation

how many strawberries a child eats per week and their mathematical abilities. That is, there is no relationship between the two variables (see Figure 2.11).

Remember, all the correlations we have reviewed here compare two variables that provide *quantitative* data, because they consider whether one variable increases or decreases as the other variable increases or decreases.

Correlation Is Not Causation

It has been reported that a positive correlation exists between the amount of violent crime in an area and the amount of ice cream consumed. If this conclusion seems strange, the reason is that we are assuming one of the variables *causes* the other, when all we really know is that they are *correlated*. In fact, a third variable causes both these phenomena to increase at the same time: namely, the temperature outside. More violent crimes are committed during warmer months than during cooler months, and more ice cream is consumed then as well. As you can see, although two variables may be highly correlated, one does not necessarily cause the other.

Based on what we learned about correlational research, we know better than to conclude, for example, that confident and successful adults have always resolved the Industry–Inferiority conflict in middle childhood, even if we find a strong correlation between these two variables. The reason is that the feelings of competence may be either the cause *or* the effect of resolving the Industry–Inferiority conflict.

We cannot ethically require families to provide their children with opportunities for developing competence, which prevents us from determining what exactly causes confidence and success in adulthood.

So if correlational research is limited to identifying co-relations between variables, how can we best determine whether variables are causally related? By using experimental research designs, a topic to which we will now turn.

What Are Experimental Research Designs?

Experimental research examines the effect of one variable on another variable. Participants are assigned to different groups, each of which is treated differently so researchers can compare the results of the two experimental trials. Let's look at what this actually means.

Independent Variables and Dependent Variables

In an experimental study, an **independent variable** (IV) is a treatment the researcher manipulates or administers to the participants. The outcome the researcher is interested in measuring is the **dependent variable** (DV), so called because the participants' scores on this variable *depend on* the treatment. The result of experimental research studies is usually described as *the effect of* _____ (the independent variable) *on* _____ (the dependent variable).

For instance, researchers have identified a cause–effect relationship between packaging of STEM (science, technology, engineering, and math) toys and children's play. That is, they have examined if and how gendered toy packaging affects children's play with toys. They have found that toy packaging indeed makes a difference in how children play with toys.

Specifically, when using a building toy marketed for boys, children who identify as girls are more likely to build a design from the pages of a book that accompanies the toy, whereas children who identify as boys are more likely to build a design unrelated to the book that accompanies the toy (Coyle & Liben, 2018).

Experimental Groups and Comparison Groups

If the children who participated in one group, called the **experimental group**, played with a toy marketed to boys for the next four weeks, and researchers measured how much mechanical understanding (the dependent variable) the children had before and after playing with the toy, the first measure of their learning *before* playing with the toy is called "Time 1" or the pretest, and the second measure of their learning *after* playing with the toy is called "Time 2" or the posttest.

For example, if the children had an average mechanical understanding score of 5 (out of 10) at the pretest/Time 1, and an average mechanical understanding of 7 (out of 10) at the posttest/Time 2, we would compare the 5 and the 7 to see if the participants had significantly greater understanding of mechanics after playing with the toy. If the posttest levels of mechanical understanding are higher than the pretest levels of mechanical understanding, can we conclude that the independent variable (a toy marketed to boys) caused an increase in the dependent variable (mechanical understanding) and be done with the study? No.

We should conduct an additional study that now includes a **comparison group**, or a group that receives an alternative treatment—otherwise we cannot determine whether the difference between pretest and posttest is caused by the treatment or by some other variable, such as their taking a science class outside of the experiment and/or due to the child's gender. It could be that girls learn more from STEM toys marketed specifically to girls, and boys learn more from STEM toys marketed specifically to boys, yet preliminary evidence in this study indicates just the opposite, so further research is needed (Coyle & Liben, 2018).

What Are Developmental Research Designs?

So far, we have discussed the basics of research. But suppose we wanted our research to promote social justice, whether it be conducting studies to determine how to best help children in homeless families or how to reduce gender stereotypes of scientists. The latter topic of gender stereotypes of scientists can indeed seem frivolous compared to the former topic of how to best help children in homeless families.

Yet social justice includes the ability of people to reach their full potential, and if a significant percentage of children are discouraged from being mechanical because of their gender, then gender stereotypes of scientists merits our attention as well as homelessness, food insecurity, and all the other developmental science and social justice topics we will be discussing in future chapters.

So, gender stereotypes of scientists. Do children have them? That is, are children more likely to assume a scientist is male rather than female or nonbinary? If so, do these stereotypes vary according to different age groups of children and/or as children grow older? How can we know? Can we study groups of children at different ages or groups of children as they grow older over time?

Yes, and we do so by conducting **developmental research designs**, which measure *age differences*, *age changes*, or both *age differences and age changes*, using cross-sectional research designs, longitudinal research designs, or sequential research designs.

Cross-Sectional Research Designs

One common way researchers study age differences is by conducting research studies that use **cross-sectional** designs. Such studies compare multiple age groups on a dependent variable of interest, such as their height, their ability to count, or their level of emotional maturity. Age is the independent variable in any cross-sectional study.

In terms of our aforementioned example regarding gender stereotypes of scientists, cross-sectional research designs would allow us to answer the question of whether or not children's gender stereotypes of scientists varying according to their age. Okay, so how can we measure such stereotypes? Well, the Draw-A-Scientist test is a measure of children's attitudes and beliefs, and although it may be limited by children's drawing abilities and other factors, it does have the merit of not requiring children to be verbally articulate—or even to be conscious of whether they have stereotypes or what their stereotypes may be (Chambers, 1983; Finson, 2002; Reinisch et al., 2017).

It could be that because preschoolers have yet to have much exposure to scientists, they are less likely to have developed gender stereotypes of scientists, so older children are *more likely* to make gender stereotypes of scientists. *In other words, if this were the case, then children's gender stereotypes of scientists would seem to increase with age.* And research indicates this may indeed by the case (Miller et al., 2018). Therefore, we would see middle school children, compared to preschoolers, draw more men on the Draw-A-Scientist test, as can be seen in Figure 2.12.

But remember: cross-sectional studies can tell us only about *age differences* and not *age changes*, given that the children are studied at only one point in time rather than again and again as they grow older. Additionally, any age differences we might see in a cross-sectional study could actually be a cohort difference instead. **A cohort difference** is a generational difference, as in the case of differences among Baby Boomers, Generation X, Millennials, Gen Z, and so on. Cohort differences masquerading as age differences are one of the major shortcomings of cross-sectional research, as

FIG. 2.12   A Child's Drawing of a Scientist

they are a **confounding variable**. Confounding variables are variables that influence the actual variable(s) being measured, but are not measured themselves.

A cohort difference, rather than an age difference, in our question of gender stereotypes of scientists could be that, indeed, preschoolers have fewer gender stereotypes of scientists—but not because they have yet to encounter many scientists. Instead, it may be that in recent years there are more female (and hopefully nonbinary) role models of scientists, and that therefore preschoolers are exposed to portrayals of scientists (such as in picture books, including but not limited to *Ada Twist, Scientist,* by Andrea Beaty and a book that I, and my son, recommend highly) with more diverse characteristics compared to previous generations.

So it may be that compared to school-age children, preschoolers are less likely to assume that only males can be scientists—but this is because of the generation they grew up in, rather than because of their age per se. *In other words, if this were the case, then children's gender stereotypes of scientists would seem to be decreasing in more recent generations.* Therefore, we would see middle school children draw more men on the Draw A Scientist test compared to preschoolers, but it would be because the middle school children grew up in a period of history in which most of the role models for scientists were male. See Figure 2.13 for how these

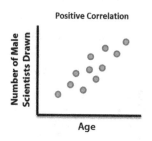

FIG. 2.13   Results of a Cross-Sectional Study on Children's Drawings of Scientists

results might look on a graph, with "Age" on the X axis and "Number of Male Scientists Drawn" on the Y axis.

Longitudinal Research Designs

While cross-sectional designs are often the most efficient way of conducting research on age-related research questions, they are not developmental in nature. To truly conduct developmental research, a study must examine not *age differences*, but *age changes,* that is, changes that occur as we age over time.

The best way to do this is by conducting research studies with **longitudinal research designs**, following the *same group of people* over a period of time. Longitudinal studies provide a more comprehensive view of participants, like photographing people repeatedly to see how they change with age. For example, a longitudinal study of children's gender stereotypes of scientists would first give the Draw-A-Scientist test to a group of 5-year-olds in 2020, and then measure the same children's opinions again in 2025, 2030, and 2035.

You might be thinking that longitudinal studies are time-consuming. Indeed, they are. Most longitudinal studies follow participants not just over a few months, but for years or even decades.

Because they are time-consuming to conduct, longitudinal studies are also less commonly used than cross-sectional studies—despite longitudinal studies providing more information than cross-sectional studies.

Longitudinal studies are also often more expensive (and therefore require researchers to obtain more financial support, say, via applying for and hopefully receiving grants) to conduct because they must provide participants with repeated incentives (such as a gift card to compensate them for their time) to help encourage these participants to remain in the study year after year. Even with incentives, some participants may become weary of the study and drop out. Others move without providing new contact information. Some may become ill, and some may die.

Again, although longitudinal studies provide richer information than cross-sectional studies, that is, they provide information on *age changes* rather than *age differences*, they are plagued by another issue besides the difficulty in conducting them. That is, The confounding variable of cohort differences also afflicts the results of longitudinal research studies.

Because there are more female and nonbinary role models of scientists in recent years compared to previous generations, it could be that if we were to conduct a longitudinal study that began in 2020, we would find that children are less likely to assume scientists are males as children grow older. *In other words, it would appear that gender stereotypes of scientists decrease with age.*

See Figure 2.14 for how these results might look in a graph, with "Age" on the X axis and "Number of Male Scientists Drawn" on the Y axis.

Notice something: The pattern of results from the Cross-Sectional study in Figure 2.13 is the exact opposite of the pattern of results from the Longitudinal study in Figure 2.14. Which study is accurate? Both are. The cross-sectional study provides information about *age differences* and children's gender stereotypes of scientists, and the longitudinal study

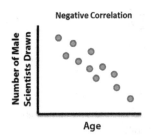

FIG. 2.14 Results of a Longitudinal Study on Children's Drawings of Scientists m

Source: https://www.spcforexcel.com/knowledge/root-cause-analysis/correlation-analysis.

provides information about *age changes* and children's gender stereotypes of scientists. Each study asks a different question, and therefore each has a different answer. Yet both include the confounding variable of cohort, making the results very murky to interpret. Is there a solution to this dilemma? Yes, and we find it in sequential designs.

Sequential Research Designs

Sequential research designs compare multiple age groups on a dependent variable of interest as in cross-sectional designs, but they also follow these same groups over a period of time as in longitudinal designs. As you can see, sequential designs are a combination of cross-sectional and longitudinal designs, and therefore provide the best of both worlds.

Because they follow multiple age groups over time, sequential studies are the most time-consuming of the three developmental designs. But their benefits outweigh the drawbacks, because the results can tell us two very meaningful pieces of information. One benefit is whether cohort differences are influencing the results. How do we know? We compare people at the same age who were born in different years.

For example, if we compare people born in 2020, 2030, 2040, and 2050 on the dependent variable when they are 3 years old and find that the results are all the same—meaning that all 3-year-olds, regardless of the generation into which they were born, are relatively the same—we can be much more confident that we are seeing true *age effects* (that is, age differences or age changes over time), rather than cohort effects.

This would be the case if we found that the majority of 3-year-olds of all future generations draw equal numbers of female, nonbinary, and male scientists when asked to Draw-A-Scientist. The second benefit of a sequential study is that it allows us to compare the cross-sectional results (where we compare people at the same age) and longitudinal results (where we compare people as they change as they age). The validity of the results is even stronger if the patterns are similar in each case.

Regardless of the design of our research study, we also need to be mindful when conducting research of the way participants are treated. This brings us to the topic of ethics.

What Are Research Ethics?

How can we be assured that participants in research studies are protected from harm as much as possible? It may not be completely possible to prevent research participants from being psychologically and/or physically harmed in a study, but researchers are ethically obligated to do all they can to protect participants.

For example, in a research study on the effectiveness of a new drug to treat ADHD in children, researchers are obligated to administer the lowest effective dosage in order to reduce harmful side effects. In the event of potential psychological harm, as in a research study that asks children to recall a traumatic event like witnessing a natural disaster, opportunities to speak with a therapist at the conclusion of the research study must be provided.

Yet how can we be assured that participants are informed about the aspects of a study that may affect their willingness to participate? That the research data containing the participants' responses will be kept confidential? That bias will be eliminated? That participants will be effectively debriefed after a study has concluded so that any concerns they have are addressed? That participants will be provided with beneficial alternative treatments whenever possible?

Institutional Review Boards

The answer to all these questions is the Institutional Review Board (IRB), or the committee within an institution (such as a university) that reviews researchers' proposals for studies before the studies can even begin. Proposals must meet strict guidelines to ensure they meet all the criteria we have discussed.

This is comforting to know. But who sets these guidelines? The American Psychological Association (APA) established the Ethical Principles of Psychologists and Code of Conduct, and the Society of Research in Child Development (SRCD) set the Ethical Standards for Research with Children. A description of the Code and the Standards can be found on these two organizations' websites. Links to the websites are provided in the *Helpful Websites* section at the end of this chapter.

Informed Consent and Confidentiality

Participants in research studies are required to give their **informed consent** before the study begins. Informed consent is an indication that the subject is willingly participating in the study and not being coerced. To obtain informed consent, researchers must first inform participants, with clear and age-appropriate language, about aspects of the study that might influence their decision to participate. For example, some participants may not be comfortable providing certain information in a survey, such as their SAT scores.

How do children under age 7 and people who have cognitive disabilities or dementia give their consent? In these cases, the individual's legal guardian or representative consents. If children are between 7 and 18, both the child and the parent must give informed consent.

Once informed consent has been obtained from participants and research data have been collected, researchers are required to practice **confidentiality**, or the ethical obligation not to share information they collect about people in order to ensure the participants' privacy.

Researchers do publish findings of their studies, but the names and other identifying characteristics of the participants are always omitted. In addition, confidentiality prohibits researchers from revealing participants' responses by other, less-formal means. For example, a researcher would never tell an adolescent's parent that during a clinical interview, the teen discussed their concerns about something they didn't want to get back to their parents.

Naturally Occurring Variables and Assigned Variables

In order to identify a causal relationship between variables, we know we must use experimental research designs. These designs use **assigned variables**, or variables assigned to the participants by the researcher. Yet some variables are what we refer to as **naturally occurring variables**, or those over which the researcher has no control. They include characteristics of participants such as their height or their gender.

We can still use naturally occurring variables in research, yet the conclusions we can draw from the quasi-experimental studies we use them in are limited because we cannot randomly assign subjects

Reducing Bias in Research

Unless they are specifically interested in one population (such as adolescents from low-income homes), most contemporary researchers have work to do in terms of eliminating bias, or the tendency to use only one group of people to represent all others. This means that most studies of child and adolescent development include equivalent numbers of participants who are different ages and genders, as well as different races/ethnicities.

Researchers must also be alert for differences *within* as well as between groups, whether these are differences of age, gender, race, or ethnicity. Just because a researcher includes both preschoolers and school-age children in a research study does not mean we can now predict that all the preschoolers will behave in one way and all the middle school children will behave in a different way. For example, some preschool-age children are aggressive while others are not, and the same holds true for middle school children.

The same cautions apply to race and ethnicity. Take the diverse group of people in the United States referred to as *Latinx*, the gender-neutral term now used to refer to people who are Latino/Latina. Some are of Mexican origin; others are Cuban, Dominican, or Puerto Rican; some identify their race as Black, others as European, and others as Hispanic. Yet they are all frequently grouped together and assumed to be similar, though they are not. European Americans too are often assumed to be similar, and they are not.

Ethnic gloss, or the assumption that no differences exist within ethnic groups when they certainly do, is not just a bias and a form of stereotyped thinking; glossing over differences among any groups is also a serious problem in research studies (Brittian et al., 2015; Phinney, 1996). People in any given group likely differ across a wide range of characteristics: norms, values, education level, profession, leisure activities, income, degree of acculturation, strength of ethnic identity, number of generations that have lived in the United States, languages spoken, and the experiences and attitudes associated with minority or majority status.

For example, we cannot assume that children who identify as Latinx are fluent in Spanish. While some may have parents or grandparents who are recent immigrants and spoke to them in Spanish, some may have parents or grandparents who are recent immigrants and spoke to them in limited Spanish because they themselves had limited opportunities for education, while still others may have parents or grandparents who are recent immigrants who also are highly educated and know English and speak to their children in English, whereas others may have parents or grandparents who immigrated many generations ago and may or may not speak Spanish, as is often the case for many ethnic European Americans in the United States.

To reduce bias in research, therefore, researchers often include additional variables associated with those they are studying (such as education level, gender and/or race/ethnicity) because of the vast within-group differences on each variable.

· · · ·

to groups. That is, we can't tell people to be tall or short, or male, female, or nonbinary. No matter the variables, though, researchers must work to reduce bias as much as possible, as we see in the *Pan & Zoom: Reducing Bias in Research* box.

The Debriefing Process

The debriefing process in research studies is the process by which researchers reveal the purpose of the study to participants once the study is over and address any concerns that participants may have. You might be wondering why this even occurs if the participants gave informed consent at the beginning of the study. Aren't the researchers obligated to explain the study before it begins? Yes, they are, but in some cases, saying too much would spoil the results.

For instance, imagine you are conducting research on whether teens who snack between meals are responding to internal cues such as hunger, or to external cues such as seeing or being offered a tasty treat. You decide to conduct a study in which one group of participants is told to arrive at your research lab immediately after eating lunch, with the other group is told to arrive before lunch when they are presumably hungry.

You offer fresh-baked cookies to both groups and tell them you are studying their ability to tolerate boredom. Then you show them a boring film. Afterwards, you count and compare the number of cookies eaten by each group. If you had told them beforehand that you were studying the internal and external cues that encourage snacking, however, they might not have taken any cookies at all.

So that your participants are not upset to find out the real purpose of the study, another aspect of your debriefing them is to reassure them that your intent was not to deceive but to encourage them to act naturally, rather than the way they thought you expected them to. Researchers then need to answer any questions the participants may have and address any concerns they may have. A final step is to provide your subjects with contact information in case they think of a question after they leave.

The Peer Review Process

Before we conclude this chapter, there is one more subject worth discussing about research ethics, and about research in general. The peer review process is the method by which experts scrutinize research and decide whether a study is worthy of publication. If the experts agree, the report will be published as an article in a peer-reviewed academic journal. These articles are the gold standard for researchers, because such publications have stringent requirements about the quality of the studies they publish.

Key Terms

Archival Methods

Assigned Variables

Case Study Methods

Clinical Interviews

Cohort Difference

Color Blind

Comparison Group

Confidentiality

Confounding Variable

Correlation Coefficient

Correlational Research Studies

Cross-Sectional Research Designs

Data

Dependent Variable

Developmental Research Designs

Ethnographic Methods

Experimental Group

Experimental Research Studies

Hypothesis

Independent Variable

Informed Consent

Longitudinal Research Designs

Multicultural

Naturalistic Observation

Naturally Occurring Variables

Negative Correlation

Observational Methods

Operational Definition

Physiological Methods

Population

Summary

1. **Describe how developmental science is similar to map-making.** Developmental science relies upon objective data obtained from the scientific method, rather than opinion. Researchers collect more information about development over time in order to make a more accurate map of human development. Thus, we can think of this process as similar to continually gathering information to make more accurate maps of the physical world.

2. **Synthesize The Cycle of Science.** In developmental science, the process we call The Cycle of Science continues beyond research into an application of the findings to everyday life, and then a return to the theory that generated the research study's original hypothesis.

3. **Distinguish the types of data and data collection methods.** Facts that researchers gather in order to reach objective conclusions about a topic are what are referred to as data. Qualitative data describe characteristics we can categorize but not count or measure, whereas quantitative data are numerical and describe features or qualities we can measure or count. Ways to collect data include naturalistic observation, structured observation, self-report, clinical interviews, structured interviews, physiological methods, case studies, archival method, and ethnographic methods. Each method must provide both valid and reliable measures of human behavior in order to be considered useful.

4. **Interpret the information obtained from correlational research designs.** Correlational research can tell us only whether two variables are related; it cannot tell us how variables affect one another. Yet correlational research studies still provide us with valuable information, such as the size (or strength) of the relationship between the two variables, and its direction. Just because two variables are related does not mean their relationship is a cause–effect one.

5. **Identify the necessary components of an experimental study.** The components of experimental research are independent variables, dependent variables, experimental groups, and comparison groups. Experimental research compares an experimental group that receives a treatment (the independent variable) to a similar control group that does not. If the outcome for the experimental group is different from the outcome of the control group, we can reasonably conclude that the treatment caused the difference.

6. **Explain the strengths and weaknesses of the three developmental research designs.** Although cross-sectional research studies can be completed much sooner than longitudinal research studies, they can tell us only about age differences, or how people are different depending on their age. Longitudinal studies tell us how people change over time, but the changes may be due not to the participants' getting older, but to a characteristic of the generation to which they belong.

The best and most informative developmental research design is the sequential research design, which combines the methods of cross-sectional and longitudinal studies to provide us with information about age differences and age changes for multiple generations of participants. If all the participants change in similar ways, we can then attribute these changes to aging per se and not to something specific to their generation.

7. **Critique the standards for ethical treatment of research participants.** Ethical treatment of research participants includes protection from harm, working with Institutional Review Boards, obtaining informed consent and ensuring confidentiality, incorporating both naturally occurring and assigned variables, working to eliminate bias, involving participants in the debriefing process, and proceeding through the peer-review process in order to publish one's results and share them with stakeholders.

Helpful Websites

The website of the national initiative Mind in the Making has many resources for parents and professionals: https://www.mindinthemaking.org/

To learn more about the research on *Sesame Street*, visit the Sesame Workshop website: http://www.sesameworkshop.org/what-we-do/our-results/

A description of the American Psychology Association's Ethical Principles of Psychologists and Code of Conduct is available here: http://www.apa.org/ethics/code2002.html

A description of the Society for Research in Child Development's Ethical Standards for Research with Children is available here: https://www.srcd.org/about-us/ethical-standards-research-children

Recommended Reading

Galinsky, E. (2010). *Mind in the making: The seven essential life skills every child needs.* New York, NY: HarperCollins.

Our Genes and Our Environment

CHAPTER 3

Snapshot

Does prenatal adversity (such as unemployment, financial insecurity, and/or an unstable support network) play a role in how aggressive a child is when a toddler? Yes. For example, one review of the research reveals that children born to women who had high levels of stress during pregnancy are more likely to show decreased self-regulation, compared to children born to women who had average levels of stress during pregnancy (Gartstein & Skinner, 2018).

And when we consider prenatal adversity as interacting with other factors, such as the child's physiological functioning, we see further evidence for the ways in which prenatal adversity plays a role in how aggressive a woman's child is as a toddler. That is, research has found that children who are exposed to high levels of prenatal adversity *and* who have low levels of parasympathetic activity when they themselves are distressed are most likely to be aggressive as toddlers (Suurland et al., 2018).

Remember, the sympathetic nervous system is responsible for a "fight or flight" response or heightened heart rate and respiration when we are distressed, and the parasympathetic nervous system is responsible for decreasing our heart rate and respiration in response to sympathetic nervous system activity. So, low levels of parasympathetic activity suggest that high levels of sympathetic nervous system activity continue or exacerbate when children are stressed.

Also, keep in mind that physical aggression is developmentally appropriate for toddlers (they have yet to acquire sophisticated language abilities to express their needs), so aggression peaks from age 2 until about age 3, then declines during preschool—yet frequent aggression in toddlerhood is associated with a risk of later negative outcomes, such as antisocial behavior (Tully & Hunt, 2017). Therefore, physical aggression is an example of the multidimensional pattern of development, because understanding and ideally preventing what contributes to unusually high levels of such in toddlerhood can prevent emotional and academic problems for children—and help them instead best fulfill their potential.

What Are the Basics of Genetics?

Most people would correctly say that both nature and nurture influence human behavior. This is indeed the case, but better yet, we can address *how* nature and nurture do so. Before we consider the specific ways in which nature interacts with nurture, though, let us examine what nature and nurture entail. Obviously, not all environmental forces (such as radiation) are favorable, and not all natural genetic predispositions (such as aggression) are beneficial to society.

Yet without realizing it, we often assume that what is innate or traditional is superior. Some people protest, "That's not natural," when something is unfamiliar and makes them uncomfortable. But it is worth emphasizing here that natural and innate influences on development are not necessarily any better or any worse than learned or environmental influences on development. Let's take a look at the ingredients that make up what we call "nature."

The nucleus of every cell in the human body contains 46 **chromosomes**, which are the structures in our cells that contain genetic information and that are capped at the ends with structures called **telomeres**. Every time a cell divides, these telomeres shorten; if telomeres shrink beyond a certain point, the cell will die. So telomeres can be thought of as similar to the protective tips at the ends of shoelaces that prevent the laces from unraveling.

Chromosomes are arranged in pairs. One member of each of these 23 pairs comes from a person's genetic mother, and the second comes from the genetic father. As you can see in Figure 3.1, the 23 pairs of chromosomes contain strands of deoxyribonucleic acid (DNA). **DNA** is a double helix or twisted ladder-shaped molecule containing the genetic code that contributes to each individual's development. Units of DNA, which direct the development of one or more traits, are referred to as **genes**.

The genetic code produces a person's **genotype**, or heredity. Does this genotype guarantee that our appearance and traits will develop in a certain way? No. Just as a brownie recipe does not guarantee

Learning Goals

- ▶ Define telomeres, chromosomes, DNA, genes, genotype, and phenotype
- ▶ Describe the four different patterns of genetic inheritance
- ▶ Identify some chromosomal and gene-linked abnormalities
- ▶ Contrast environmental and nonenvironmental influences
- ▶ Explain the "Which one?" question in regard to the relationships among nature and nurture
- ▶ Discuss how measures of hereditary influence answer the "How much?" question
- ▶ Evaluate ways to answer the "How?" question in regard to how nature and nurture interact

that the brownies will turn out the same every time, our **phenotype**, or observable characteristics, may not always match our genetic code or human recipe. Consider a teenage boy who may have a genotype and phenotype for black hair; if he decides to dye his hair blue, he still has a genotype for black hair, but now he has a phenotype for blue hair.

Because our phenotype includes our physique, our physiological state, and our behavior, no two individuals will ever have the same phenotype—including how our traits, as well as any disease we may develop, become manifest; such variability has prompted medical professionals and families to contribute to a Human Phenotype Ontology (HPO), which provides in-depth information on clinical cases of various diseases and how they may appear different in different people, or differently within the same person over time (Köhler et al., 2019; Vasilevsky et al., 2018). Such complexity may be appreciated when we consider how even identical twins can have different phenotypic appearances as a result of environmental factors such as lifestyle and diet.

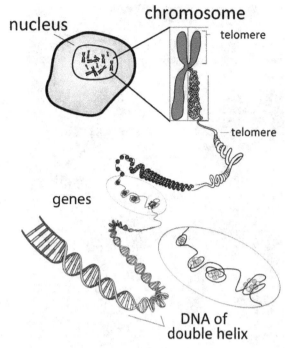

FIG. 3.1   Chromosomes, DNA, and Genes

What Are the Patterns of Genetic Inheritance?

If chromosomes, DNA, and genes are the *"what"* of genetic inheritance—that is, the raw materials—then the specific patterns by which nature and nurture influence behavior are the *"how,"* or the processes by which these materials operate in order to produce genetic inheritance. There are a number of these *"how"* patterns or processes, so we'll consider them separately here.

Sex Chromosomes and Autosomes

Of each cell's 23 pairs of chromosomes, only one pair—the **sex chromosomes**, the 23rd pair—differs between females and males. Females have two copies of the X chromosome, whereas males have one copy of the X chromosome and one copy of the Y chromosome. In the sex chromosomes, each member of the pair may contain different information. For example, the X chromosome is larger than the Y chromosome, so it typically contains more genes than the Y chromosome does.

Sex-linked traits are those that are determined by the X chromosome only. An example of a sex-linked trait is *hemophilia*, in which the affected person bleeds excessively after injury or surgery (and can bleed to death if left untreated) because they lack a substance that ensures blood clotting.

FIG. 3.2   Actor Javier Bardem

Copyright © 2012 Depositphotos/s_buckley.

	D	D
D	DD	DD
d	Dd	Dd

FIG. 3.3   Inheritance of Dimples.

The genes associated with hemophilia are found only on the X-chromosome; hence hemophilia is a sex-linked trait.

The **autosomes**, or the other 22 pairs of chromosomes, are similar in males and females, and each member of the pair, called an **allele**, carries the same genetic information as the other member. Alleles that are expressed phenotypically with only one copy of the allele are *dominant alleles*. Those alleles that are expressed phenotypically but need two copies of the allele (one from each genetic parent) to do so are *recessive alleles*. When both alleles in the pair of chromosomes are the same, dominant or recessive, they are called a **homozygous pair**. When they are different, they are called a **heterozygous pair**.

Where can we see the result of dominant and recessive alleles? Dimples are indentations in the cheeks that are especially apparent when a person smiles, as you can see in the photo of actor and activist Javier Bardem. Dimples are a dominant trait, so having them is a result of inheriting either one or two dominant alleles, and not having them is a result of having two recessive alleles. For a person's phenotype to show a recessive trait, the person must inherit a recessive allele from both parents. But someone inheriting a dominant allele for dimples from one parent and a recessive allele for dimples will always have dimples because dimples are a dominant trait.

Figure 3.3 illustrates both dominant and recessive inheritance of dimples. The allele for having dimples is dominant (represented by a capital letter "D"), and the allele for not having dimples is recessive (represented by a lowercase letter "d"). If a woman who is homozygous (DD) for dimples and a man who is heterozygous (Dd) for dimples have the four children shown in Figure 3.3, represented by the symbols DD, DD, Dd, and Dd, note that all of their children will have dimples. If one of the children had been dd, then that child would not have had dimples.

Incomplete Dominance

People who inherit two recessive alleles for sickle cell anemia develop the full-blown disease, Sickle Cell Disease (SCD), which causes blood cells to be sickle- or half-moon-shaped. Because the blood cells are not the usual full round shape, they fail to carry sufficient oxygen, and people with sickle cell anemia experience anemia, pain, swelling, and tissue damage. They have a shortened life span as well, living two to three decades fewer than those without the disease. SCD not only causes much emotional and physical suffering, as well as pain, fatigue, and impaired functioning, but also costs hundreds of thousands of dollars over a person's lifetime. There is an "urgent need to develop disease-modifying therapies that can improve the underlying morbidity and mortality of individuals living with SCD" (Agodoa et al, 2018).

Rates of SCD are higher in populations of people of African, Latinx, and/or Mediterranean descent, likely because these areas of the world have had high rates of malaria, and sickle cells are resistant to the parasite that carries malaria. So although SCD can be deadly, it appears to be passed from generation to generation as an evolutionary advantage to people with ancestry from areas in which it proved adaptive in avoiding malaria.

The patterns of dominant alleles and recessive alleles do not always hold, though, and sometimes an individual with heterozygous alleles is influenced by the dominant allele and recessive allele, rather than just the dominant allele. Based on what we learned about the dominant–recessive patterns of genetic inheritance, you would imagine that people who inherit just one recessive allele for sickle cells do not develop the disease, but this is not necessarily the case.

When people have Sickle Cell Trait (SCT)—that is, they inherit one recessive allele for SCD and one nonaffected dominant allele—they experience mild and temporary symptoms when their oxygen levels decrease, such as during exercise (which may be implicated in the sudden death of high school athletes), suggesting that everyone at risk for SCT or SCD needs to know their status (Crowder et al., 2018; Mayo-Gamble et al., 2018). In this case, **incomplete dominance** is occurring, because the symptoms of the recessive-linked disease manifest themselves only under certain conditions.

Polygenetic Inheritance

The sex-linked and dominant–recessive allele patterns of inheritance we have covered so far are each based on one particular chromosome. Yet many human characteristics, such as eye color, weight, height, and intelligence, are a product of multiple genes and thus represent **polygenetic inheritance**. Genes also interact with one another to produce a range of different phenotypes depending upon how they interact with environmental factors. For example, cancer risk can be a function of genetics, but it may also be curtailed by efforts to increase exercise and reduce sedentary behavior such as sitting (Ekelund et al., 2018; Yang & Colditz, 2014).

Recent research indicates that Parkinson's disease is likely a polygenetic disorder. Parkinson's is a neurodegenerative disease in which the neurons that dictate movement become impaired or die, and as a result the body produces less dopamine (a chemical messenger that allows the different parts of the brain to communicate) (Paul, Schulz, & Bronstein, 2018). As a result of the lack of communication among the various brain regions in Parkinson's disease, a person suffering from it, such as the actor Michael J. Fox, experiences tremors, rigidity, and decreased mobility. Some evidence suggests that embryonic stem cells, which we discuss in the *Tech & Media* box, can differentiate into cells that function like the neurons that degenerate in Parkinson's, but more research is needed (Sontag et al., 2018).

Tech & Media in Our Lives: Stem Cell Research

Cells differentiate, or change from generic embryonic cells to specialized cells such as nerve cells, muscle cells, and skin cells. So, stem cells are undifferentiated cells, which means that they haven't yet specialized into a particular structure or function. There are two forms of stem cells: *Embryonic stem cells* are those that may be obtained from a blastocyst. A blastocyst is a 5-day-old zygote or fertilized egg that may have been created for **in vitro fertilization (IVF)**, a form of assisted reproduction in which multiple eggs are fertilized by sperm outside of a woman's body and then only the *most* healthiest are transferred back to her uterus for a potential pregnancy (Rossant & Tam, 2018).

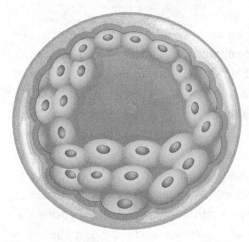

As you can see in Figure 3.4, blastocysts resemble hollow balls, so they have neither a nervous system nor organs. Therefore, embryonic stem cells are able to develop into a wide range of specialized cell types. Research indicates that our ability to genetically program embryonic stem cells into specific types of cells may help develop treatments for Parkinson's disease (Gao et al., 2018; Sontag et al., 2018).

The second type of stem cell is an *adult stem cell*, which is derived from developed tissue, such as bone marrow, muscle, heart, lung, and skin. Adult stem cells are usually only able to develop into only a limited range of cell types. Thus, they may or may not be as useful as embryonic stem cells for developing treatments for conditions such as heart disease, diabetes, autism, and Parkinson's disease.

FIG. 3.4   A Blastocyst

Copyright © 2012 Depositphotos/blueringmedia.

The International Society for Stem Cell Research (ISSCR) has developed guidelines for embryonic stem cell use, and many ethical issues about these techniques are now being discussed. One of these issues is that in order to avoid conflicts of interest, the individuals conducting the research on stem cells need to be different people than the physicians performing assistive reproductive techniques such as IVF (International Society for Stem Cell Research, 2016). You can read about these guidelines at the ISSCR's website, listed in the *Helpful Websites* section of this chapter.

• • • •

What Are Chromosomal and Gene-Linked Abnormalities?

Genetic disorders can be classified according to whether they result from chromosomal abnormalities or gene-linked abnormalities. *Chromosomal abnormalities* occur as either numerical abnormalities of chromosomes or structural abnormalities of chromosomes. *Gene-linked abnormalities* pertain are the result of defects to specific genes. Let's look more closely at a few examples of each.

Chromosomal Abnormalities

A *numerical chromosomal abnormality* occurs when a person is missing one of the chromosomes of a pair, or has more than two chromosomes in a pair. One of the best-known examples of the latter is Trisomy 21 or Down Syndrome, which occurs because an individual possesses a third chromosome in pair number 21. Characteristics of individuals with Down Syndrome include a prominent crease in the palm of the hand, an upward slant to the eyes, and flattened facial features. Individuals with Down Syndrome are at risk for congenital heart disease and cognitive dysfunction as well, including early-onset dementia, although promising new research indicates that aerobic exercise may stave off such (Capone et al., 2018; Ptomey et al., 2018;).

Down Syndrome occurs equally across racial/ethnic groups and socioeconomic statuses at a rate of about 1 in 700 live births, and the risk increases with parental age—both of the mother and the father—as well as *consanguineous relationships* (as a result either of incest or of relationships among people who are second cousins or closer) between the biological parents (Jennings, Owen, Keefe, & Kim, 2017; Ray et al., 2018). A *structural chromosomal abnormality* occurs when a chromosome's structure is somehow altered, as in the case of Cri du Chat syndrome (also called Cat Cry syndrome), in which babies have a high-pitched cry, poor muscle tone, and small head size, which is caused by a deletion of chromosome 5.

Gene-Linked Abnormalities

Two noteworthy gene-linked abnormalities are phenylketonuria (PKU), which is preventable, and Huntington's disease, which is not. Individuals with PKU cannot metabolize the amino acid phenylalanine, so it builds up in their system and causes damage to the nervous system so severe that cognitive disabilities are often the result. Yet PKU can be prevented. Newborns who test positive for the disorder can be put on a special phenylalanine-restricted diet, which research indicates may prevent PKU from interfering with the intellectual abilities of children and teens with severe PKU (Feldmann et al., 2018).

Huntington's disease, which is uniquely caused by a dominant gene, is associated with progressive inability to plan ahead, remember things, control movements, and swallow; eventually, dementia occurs. These characteristics develop because the neurons in the brain are genetically programmed to degenerate in a person who inherits the defective gene. Treatment for tremors is available. But because there is no available remedy for preventing neuron degeneration or replacing afflicted neurons, there is no known cure for Huntington's disease at this time (Ghosh & Tabrizi, 2018).

The most common form of Huntington's disease is adult-onset, meaning it typically develops in middle age. Thus, through genetic testing, individuals can find out before developing any symptoms whether they have the mutated gene. Yet unlike other diseases for which genetic tests are available, Huntington's disease cannot be prevented or slowed. So, while testing for the disease may allow some people to prepare for the onset of symptoms, other people may find such knowledge unbearably distressing. This is particularly true when people unexpectedly learn about their defective gene via genetic testing done for some other purpose.

What Are Environmental and Nonenvironmental Influences?

In discussing Bronfenbrenner's Ecological Systems theory in Chapter 1, we saw that we can take a more precise view of environmental influences on behavior than just the general concept of "nurture." Likewise, we can be more specific about hereditary influences on behavior, rather than relying on the general concept of "nature."

In this section, we take a look at the four types of nonenvironmental influences on development, as well as the possible relationship(s) among them. We will follow with a discussion of genetic counseling, a field that helps people understand the practical implications of hereditary influences. We'll complete the section with a look at the two main types of environmental influences.

Nonenvironmental Influences

As you can see in Figure 3.5, the most basic of the four types of nonenvironmental influences is *hereditary*. Hereditary influences on development are acquired from our genetic parents or our more remote ancestors; they are considered to be the most basic of nonenvironmental influences on development because they are the least prone to interact with the environment. These influences include the likelihood of having a certain eye color or a trait like sickle cell anemia.

The second type of nonenvironmental influence *is innate*, which encompasses not only characteristics we inherit but also those that come to us via a gene **mutation** or a change in a DNA segment, such as childhood leukemia—the risk of which is associated with pesticide use (Van Maele-Fabry, Garnet-Payrastre, & Lison, 2019). *This example reminds us not to equate nature and "internal," or nurture and "external," because external influences can cause internal changes.* Additionally, the cost of testing for genetic mutations is prohibitively expensive and not always covered by insurance policies, which renders these tests and their corresponding necessary treatments out of reach for many families, so that unequal access to healthcare as a social justice issue is relevant here.

The third type of nonenvironmental influence is *congenital*, or those influences that are present at birth. Congenital influences include fetal alcohol syndrome (physical and cognitive differences that may be acquired if a woman drinks during her pregnancy), intellectual deficits due to maternal smoking, and HIV when transmitted during vaginal birth. Congenital influences can be positive too. For example, although the evidence is mixed on why the prevalence of peanut allergies has tripled within the past 20 years, medical guidelines to expectant mothers also changed during this time; nonetheless, children may be less likely to have peanut and tree nut allergies if their mothers eat peanuts and tree nuts during pregnancy and/or if they are given infant-safe forms of peanuts (such as peanut butter thinned with warm water) within the first year of life starting around six months of age (Anvari et al., 2017; Sicherer et al., 2017).

The fourth and final type of nonenvironmental influence on development consists of the *constitutional* influences that occur as a result of life experiences, such as impaired neurological

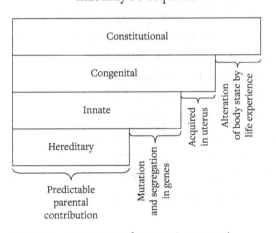

FIG. 3.5   Four Types of Nonenvironmental Influences:

development in children exposed to lead or the negative relationship researchers have found between consumption of sugar-sweetened beverages (such as soda) and telomere length. This latter example indicates that lifestyle factors clearly influence the aging process: telomere length illustrates the life-long pattern of development; that is, telomere length is correlated negatively with risk of later diseases (Freitas-Simoes, Ros, & Sala-Vila, 2018).

So there we have it. Instead of just relying on the general concept of "nature," we can offer more specific explanations of nonenvironmental influences on development. But how do we make practical sense of some of these nonenvironmental influences? They can loom large when we need to make healthcare decisions, as we know all too well. For example, based on her genetic testing results, which showed she had a high risk of breast cancer and ovarian cancer, the film star Angelina Jolie opted to have a preventive double mastectomy as well as removal of her ovaries and fallopian tubes. No matter who we are, we all can benefit from making better-informed decisions about our healthcare, and we have a right to access the information that is necessary to guide such decisions. Making wise decisions is where genetic counseling can play an invaluable role in our lives.

Genetic Counseling

According to the website of the National Society of Genetic Counselors (Senter et al., 2018), "Genetic counselors are professionals who have specialized education in genetics and counseling to provide personalized help patients may need as they make decisions about their genetic health." That is, genetic counselors help us make decisions about a variety of diagnoses, whether it be Down Syndrome in a fetus, cystic fibrosis in a newborn, or cancer in an adult. Genetic counselors use pedigrees to illustrate disease risk, and they help people make decisions to err on the resilience side of the risk–resilience

FIG. 3.6   Pedigree Symbols

Martin Alexander Kennedy, Pedigree Symbols, from "Mendelian Genetic Disorders," Encyclopedia of Life Sciences. Copyright © 2001 by John Wiley & Sons, Inc.

FIG. 3.7 Proposed Pedigree Symbols for Transgender People

Source: https://twitter.com/NicolaCadenas/status/1063111550926499840.

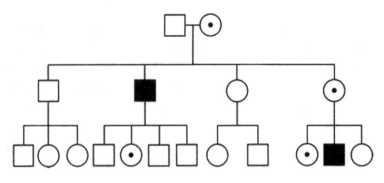

FIG. 3.8   A Sample Pedigree for an X-Linked Recessive Trait

Martin Alexander Kennedy, A Sample Pedigree for an X-Linked Recessive Trait, from "Mendelian Genetic Disorders," Encyclopedia of Life Sciences. Copyright © 2001 by John Wiley & Sons, Inc.

pattern of development. *Pedigrees* are created with a standardized set of symbols, as you can see in Figure 3.6.

A sample pedigree is shown in Figure 3.8 for an X-linked recessive trait or disorder, such as red-green color blindness. Although genetic counseling is typically conducted postconception, it can also estimate risks before pregnancy and explore issues unrelated to pregnancy, such as confirming a genetic disorder in the parent and suggesting treatment.

The National Society of Genetic Counselors has a Code of Ethics and standards for reporting genetic counseling interventions to better help research results be translated into the practice of genetic counseling. The practice of genetic counseling is expected to grow, given that there is a predicted future shortage of genetic counselors who work directly with patients (Hooker et al., 2017; Hoskovec et al., 2018; Senter et al., 2018).

Mentor Minute

FIG. 3.9   Barbara Harrison, MA

Barbara Harrison, MA

Barbara Harrison is the director of the Genetic Counseling Training program at Howard University College of Medicine, where she teaches and mentors students and coordinates students' clinical rotations.

Barbara also provides direct clinical services, including genetic counseling. Most of her patients come to her with prenatal or pediatric concerns. The opportunity to help people make decisions about serious medical concerns was the primary reason she chose to go into genetic counseling.

1) Describe your work, please.

As a genetic counselor, I assist individuals and families who have a known or suspected genetic disorder, working with them through the diagnostic evaluation, understanding the implications of a diagnosis for the person's medical management and their personal life, and reproductive implications. Genetic counselors work in all areas of medicine, including pediatrics. The process of finding a diagnosis can often be a long, tedious, and frustrating journey for parents. When a child is affected by a genetic condition, it often causes some level of disability, physical and/or mental. These families may have challenges with securing adequate healthcare, daycare, and education for their children.

2) How does social justice inform your work?

Although many do not want to acknowledge it, the study of genetics rose out of the practice of eugenics, which has negative connotations. However, we know that understanding the genetics of our health can have significantly positive effects on treatment and management of disease. It is imperative, then, that we ensure that those who have a genetic condition (Sickle Cell Disease, cystic fibrosis, Down Syndrome, etc.) or are at risk for a health issue based on an increased susceptibility in the family (cancer, diabetes, Alzheimer's disease, etc.) have equal access to healthcare, employment, and opportunities to live a fulfilling life and provide for their families.

3) How did you become involved in social justice and/or advocacy?

I have spent time advocating for those with genetic conditions and those at risk. For example, throughout the 2000s, I assisted in the efforts that led to the eventual passing of the Genetic Information Nondiscrimination Act in 2008, which provides protections for individuals, who know they are at risk for a condition based on genetic testing, from discrimination in health insurance (no increased premiums or coverage decisions) and employment (information cannot be used in hiring, firing, or promotion decisions). Also, I have advocated on behalf of the Sickle Cell Disease community, as they strive to ensure that adequate federal funds are committed to research and eventual cure for this disease, and that patients are treated with dignity and respect.

4) What are your thoughts on how social justice can improve child and adolescent development?

Access is the key to optimal child development. Even if a child has a genetic makeup that will limit their overall learning potential, reaching that ultimate potential is primarily based on that child being in a supportive learning environment, at school and at home. Having an individualized education plan that is followed and updated regularly, having access to skilled teachers who are dedicated to that child's learning, and having a home environment that provides basic needs is critical to any child being all that they are destined to be.

5) What suggestions do you have for undergraduate students who are interested in making a change in child and adolescent development?

Stay passionate! It is important to get a solid educational foundation and use this time to build your skill set, both inside and outside of the classroom. Be involved on your campus and begin to build your network through alumni and others in your field of interest. Take advantage of internships on Capitol Hill or in your local government, so you can build your skills and network further. Seek out local nonprofits in an area you care about (Special Olympics, National Down Syndrome Congress local affiliations, etc.) so you can learn how grassroots organizations make a difference in their communities. These experiences will get you started on the way to making a difference in the lives of children.

· · · ·

To help you find genetic counselors in your area, see the *Helpful Websites* section at the end of this chapter for the directory on the website of National Society of Genetic Counselors. The site can searched by ZIP code. You can also learn about career options in genetic counseling in the *Mentor Minute: Barbara Harrison, MA* box.

Environmental Influences

Throughout this book, we will consider environmental influences on development, from our personal health habits to the quality of the air we breathe. In this section, however, we consider only the two specific types of environmental influences that genetic researchers most frequently investigate: shared and nonshared influences. Both are usually studied through research on siblings, so we can better understand whether and how siblings are similar to and different from one another.

A common question, for instance, is why siblings are often different even when they are raised in the same home. One reason is that parental influence is not the same across siblings. We tend to assume that children with the same parents are treated in the same way or share the same emotional environment. But our **shared environment**, or the environment we do have in common with our siblings, is only one small part of our experience. For example, parents may respond to a difficult child with impatience and their shy sibling with tenderness. It is this **nonshared environment**, or the environment siblings do *not* have in common, that seems to be most influential as we grow older.

In studying twins, researchers identify how much of a behavior in question, such as deviant behavior like stealing and breaking rules, is due to each of three things: genetic effects or the genes the twins have in common, shared environmental events that happen to both twins, and nonshared environmental effects that happen to one twin but not the other. The influence of shared and nonshared environments illustrates the polydirectional pattern of development. That is, the polydirectional pattern of development in this regard means that environmental influences tend to decrease with age, while nonshared environmental influences tend to increase with age, because as they grow older, children interact more with others at school and eventually the outside world.

So the influences of school and neighborhood grow in importance with age—with disparities in the quality of schools and neighborhoods having a particularly strong influence with increasing age. Indeed, one study of ethnically and socioeconomically diverse twins in 3rd to 12th grade found that inequalities in the quality and composition of their schools and neighborhood SES predicted their academic achievement above and beyond the influence of their family (Engelhardt, Church, Harden, & Tucker-Drob, 2018).

What Do We Know When We Ask About Which One?

So far, we have learned a lot about nonenvironmental and environmental influences on human development. But how did researchers arrive at this point? That is, did people working in the fields related to developmental science always have such a clear understanding of what influences us? And if not, what exactly did past thinkers propose? Let's look into this question to better understand how developmental science evolves.

What in the world do sea monkeys—toy sets for children that consist of dehydrated brine shrimp eggs that grow after you add water—have to do with nature–nurture, you ask? We will see in a minute. For now, though, consider this.

We may chuckle at the absurdity of the ancient Greek myth that the goddess Athena burst out of her father Zeus's head fully grown, completely armed for battle, and ready for the Parthenon to be her sacred temple. Athena's springing forth as a mature adult has inspired a great deal of art over the years. Fine, you say. Art need not accurately represent reality, and often it is fantastically metaphorical. Yet even in the 17th century, the field of biology was dominated by a similar perspective, called *preformationism*, which proposed that preformed humans were contained in sperm cells in miniature size, so that development entailed only quantitative increases in organ size, a process thought to be fueled by nutrition from the mother's egg (Lewontin, 2000).

Consider Figure 3.10, which is an illustration of human sperm by the 17th-century microscopist Nicolaas Hartsoeker. The "just add water" view of development might be appropriate for explaining the metamorphosis of sea monkeys, but it is obviously *not* development. Although we might assume that preformationistic explanations of human development are extinct in modern science, remnants of this type of thinking are found in those who believe in *genetic determinism*: the idea that human traits are determined completely by our genes so that the human genome must be a complete blueprint or map for a human.

Such a belief fails to remember that not all the genes are used by all cells, nor does this view include the "nurture" component of the nature–nurture set of influences. Surely there is no environment without organisms (people included), and there are no organisms without environments, given that both are interacting constantly with one another (Bjorklund, 2018b; Sweatt, 2019).

Any emphasis of genes over the study of the environment also offers a very limited—and incorrect—understanding of nature–nurture. This type of genetic determinism thinking is frequently found in popular discussions that describe DNA as "the stuff of life," offering a "complete" understanding of human life, with our fate determined by our genes. Also worrisome are the research findings

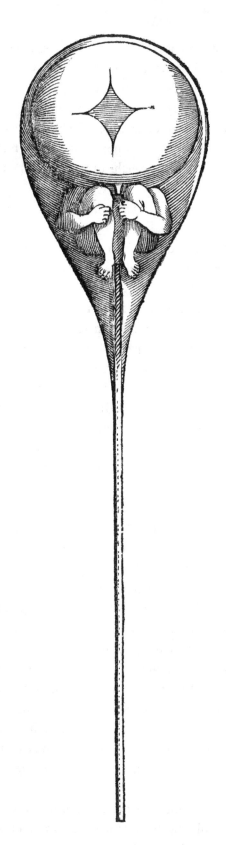

FIG. 3.10   A 17th-Century View of Sperm

that indicate that when college students are taught genetics without an emphasis on the developmental contexts in which we may or may not possess such traits, students are more likely to endorse a genetic determinism view of the role of genes in development—so that in science education and science journalism, the importance of appreciating environmental influences on development cannot be overstated (Carver et al., 2017; Jamieson & Radick, 2017).

Asking "Which one?"—that is, "Which one, nature or nurture?"—fails to address how much of each influence weighs in on development. We turn to that question of how much now.

What Do We Know When We Ask About How Much?

Our brief detour into past beliefs about the nature and nurture of human development has shed some light on how the questions we ask determine the answers we find. Other questions—such as "How much of nature and how much of nurture contribute to development?" and "How do nature and nurture interact to produce development?"—which we will discuss in this section and the next, offer more promising insights. The "How much of nature and how much of nurture contribute to development?" question refers to *how much* of the difference between people is due to heredity and *how much* is due to environment.

Let's turn now to how researchers go about answering such a question. As we learned in Chapter 1, multiple disciplines can contribute to our knowledge of development. One of these disciplines is Behavioral Genetics, the scientific study of the relative roles of nature and nurture in accounting for individual differences in behavior. By computing estimates of **heritability**, behavioral geneticists can identify what portion of the differences among people, such as personality differences, is due to genes. They then assume that the remaining variation is due to environmental factors.

The symbol used to represent heritability is h^2, and estimates can range from 0 to 1.0; the higher the score, the greater the genetic influence. One study found that the heritability of a personality trait was 0.57 (Melchers et al., 2018). This means that 57% of the personality differences in a group of people is due to genes, suggesting that the other 43% is due to environmental influences.

Heritability estimates can vary depending upon environmental conditions, such as a family's SES or their education, income, and/or occupational status. The *Scarr–Rowe hypothesis* predicts that heritability is higher in more privileged economic conditions, which are able to provide optimal environmental conditions for development (Anastasi, 1958; Gottschling et al., 2019).

And indeed, research has found support for the Scarr–Rowe hypothesis, in that IQ score differences in more advantaged environments are more likely due to genetic differences than compared to less advantages environments; the research support for the Scarr–Rowe hypothesis is particularly strong in the United States compared to European countries, where we have unequal access to educational environments and greater social injustice (Turkheimer, Beam, & Davis, 2015; Zavala et al., 2018).

What does this mean? Children and teens with affluent backgrounds tend to develop in similarly stimulating and nurturing environments, so genetic differences among them are accentuated. The fact that heritability of intelligence is lower for children and teens in impoverished families also means that *environmental influences appear to be most powerful when the environment is least ideal.*

Remember, though, that heritability estimates identify only genetic contributions to development, and those working in the field have suggested that attention would be better spent on identifying environmental contributors to development as well, and the interactive relationships among them (Esposito, Azhari, & Borelli, 2018; Lerner, Batanova, Ettekal, & Hunter, 2015; Tenesa & Haley, 2013; Timpson et al., 2018).

Asking the "How much of nature and how much of nurture contribute to development?" question is not much of an improvement over asking the "Which one?" question. Instead, we need to ask the "How?" question—"How do nature and nurture interact to produce development?"—because it recognizes that 100% of nature and 100% of nurture always *interact* with one another in influencing development, rather than simply adding up with one another.

What Do We Know When We Ask About How?

By now you can see that instead of asking how much of development is due to nature and how much is due to nurture, we should ask *how* the two interact (Anastasi, 1958; Bjorklund, 2018b). In our opening *Snapshot*, we learned that children who are exposed to high levels of prenatal adversity and who have low levels of parasympathetic activity when they themselves are distressed are most likely to be aggressive as toddlers (Suurland et al., 2018). This is an example of a gene-environment interaction.

Once we answer the question "How?"—that is, "How do nature and nurture interact to produce development?"—we will see that related concepts, such as cultural change, genetic-environmental correlations, genetic–environmental interactions, range of reaction, norm of reaction, and epigenetic theory, help us take our understanding even further. Let's look at how they do so.

Evolution Confronts Cultural Change

Over the course of human history, evolution has selected for genes whose expression fits an environment demanding high levels of physical activity. For the hundreds of thousands of years humans have been on Earth, the activities of hunting and gathering food, creating shelter, and escaping danger were essential for survival and maintaining health—so that inactivity may very well lead to early onset of chronic diseases, which is particularly worrisome in light of research data showing physical activity in children has decline dramatically in recent years (Booth et al., 2017; Pontzer, Wood, & Raichlen, 2018).

Today, the genotype for high levels of physical activity interacts with an environment of sedentary lifestyles to produce maladaptive phenotypes, such as chronic diseases like type 2 diabetes, which has risen greatly in recent years (Zheng, Ley, & Hu, 2018).

The overproduction of corn and subsequent creation of high-fructose corn syrup in the 1970s made sugary soda and corn-fed meat cheaply available. These products being sold in high quantity for low prices aggravated the problem, as does the limited time that working families have to regularly prepare healthful meals (Alston & Okrent, 2017). As a result of maladaptive phenotypes, normal gene expression is sometimes altered; for example, an individual who had regular insulin sensitivity becomes insensitive to insulin after a period of being obese and/or inactive and develops diabetes.

Genotype–Environment Correlations

Why do some people stay healthy while others fall ill? Could one reason be that some of us avoid fast food and spend active time with friends and family, and limit how much time we are passively entertained by media? Yes. **Genotype–environment correlations** occur when different genotypes are exposed to different environments (Dobewall et al., 2018; Plomin, DeFries, & Loehlin, 1977).

There are three types of genotype–environment correlations. The first type is **passive genotype–environment correlation**, so called because children play a passive role in choosing the type of environment in which they find themselves. For example, parents choose what to feed an infant, how to dress a child, and what books to read aloud to them, and choose whether they themselves read parenting books such as *Raising an Emotionally Intelligent Child* (Gottman & DeClaire, 1998), so children's ability to self-soothe and regulate their emotions may be a direct result of their parents' behavior (Bridgett et al., 2015).

The second type of correlation is **evocative genotype–environment correlation**, in which the child's genetic predisposition evokes a response from the environment. For example, a music teacher may notice a child has an especially good sense of pitch and encourages the child's parent to have the child pursue singing, as is rumored to be the case for pop star Beyoncé (Kopala-Sibley et al., 2018)

The third type of correlation is **active genotype–environment correlation**, in which the child actively plays a role in choosing their environment; this is also referred to as **niche-picking**, because we seek positions for ourselves in the world that are best suited to our talents and interests (Klahr et al., 2017). For example, an extraverted teen will likely seek out very different after-school activities than an introverted teen.

Genotype–Environment Interactions

Genotype–environment correlations are often confused with **genotype–environment interactions**, which acknowledge that different people may respond differently to the same environment (Molenaar et al., 2013; Plomin, DeFries, & Loehlin, 1977; Saltz et al., 2018). For example, among a group of children who all attend a high-quality school, some will still perform better than others. If those who performed less well were to then enroll in a remedial program and those who performed very well were to then enroll in a gifted program, a genotype–environment *correlation* would also be occurring in that children with different genotypes are being exposed to different environments.

But what exactly is happening in genotype–environment interactions that cause children to respond so differently to the same environment? Consider these three different ways of thinking about *how* genes interact with the environment: range of reaction, norm of reaction, and epigenetic theory.

Range of Reaction

The **range of reaction** describes the way the possible phenotypic behavioral outcomes for a genotype interact with different types of environments—and in what way the range of behavior outcomes for one genotype differs from the range for another (Gottesman, 1963). For example, it helps us understand why a remedial program can be more beneficial to some children than to other children. Imagine a working poor family with four children. Their environment is very restricted, and the parents have few opportunities to spend time with their children or provide stimulating toys and books. When

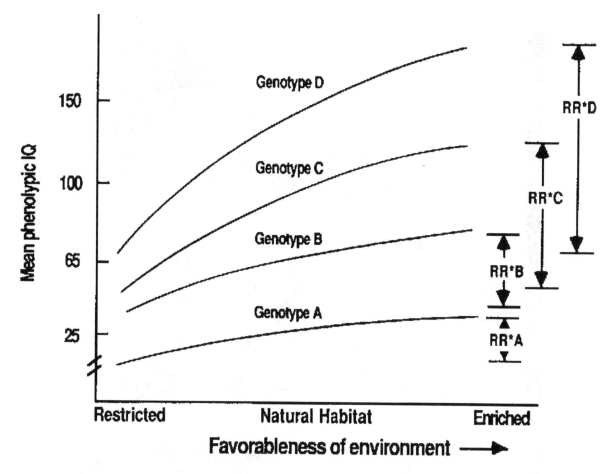

FIG. 3.11   Range of Reaction for Four Phenotypes

Steve Anderson Platt and Charles A. Sanislow, Range of Reaction for Four Phenotypes, from "Norm-of-reaction: Definition and Misinterpretation of Animal Research," Journal of Comparative Psychology, vol. 102, no. 3. Copyright © 1988 by American Psychological Association.

the children are tested at school, their IQ scores are all below the average or mean score of 100, but they are somewhat different from each other as well (Fig. 3.11).

When the parents find better work to make ends meet, they need to work long hours, so the grandmother offers to raise the children for a while and she is able to spend more time with them. A year later, the children's IQ scores are all higher—and still quite different from each other. Then, a few months later the parents receive promotions and their work options improve markedly. The children are now able to live with and spend a lot of time with their parents, enjoying enriching books and toys. Each child's IQ score is higher than ever—but each is still very different from the others.

This reveals that the range of each child's possible outcomes or phenotypic reactions to various environments differs, depending on the child's genotype. As is noted in the double-arrow lines on the right side of the figure, compared to the range of reaction for child 'D', the range of reaction for child 'C' is smaller, but child C's range of reaction is greater than child B's, which is in turn greater than child A. All four children benefit when the environment becomes better, but they do not benefit equally.

Concepts such as this range of reaction remind us that while it is true that all children need to demonstrate competence in basic skills that will allow them to be productive in the modern information age, it is not realistic to expect that all will be high-functioning on all outcomes when assessed, such as on standardized tests.

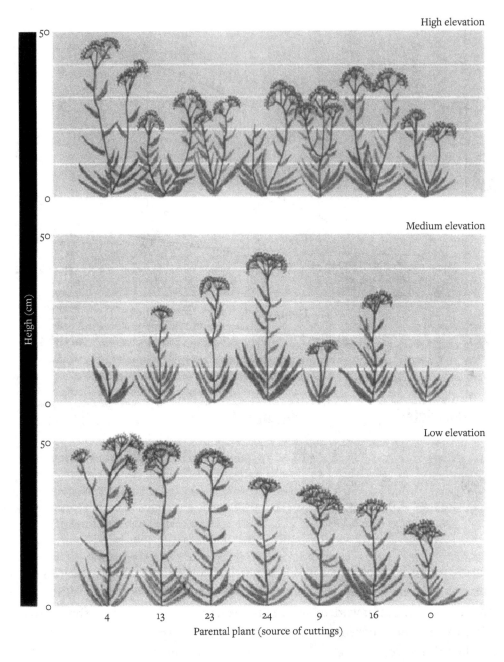

FIG. 3.12   The Norm of Reaction for Plants at Different Elevations

Richard Lewontin, "The Norm of Reaction for Plants at Different Elevations," Human Diversity. Copyright © 1982 by W. H. Freeman & Company.

Norm of Reaction

Does range of reaction mean we should not enrich some people's environments because those people are never going to measure up? Absolutely not. Consider this example. Three cuttings were taken from each of seven different plants (Gupta & Lewontin, 1982). As you can see in Figure 3.12, one

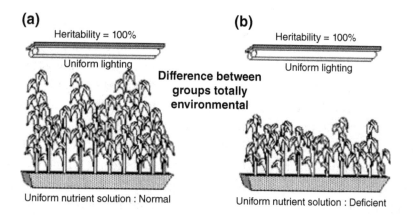

FIG. 3.13 Environment Still Plays a Role When Heritability Is High

David S. Moore and David Shenk, Environment Still Plays a Role When Heritability is High, from "The Heritability Fallacy," WIREs Cognitive Science, vol. 8, no. 1-2. Copyright © 2016 by John Wiley & Sons, Inc.

set of cuttings was grown at a low elevation where plant #1 grew the most, which suggests that its genotype is superior.

Plants #6 and #7 grew the least, which suggests that their genotypes are inferior. The differences among these seven genotypes at one elevation are similar to the "range of reaction" concept we just studied. But when the second set of the cuttings was grown at medium elevation, the growth patterns were remarkably different, with plants #5, #7, *and* #1 growing the least. Plant #1 is genotypically identical at all three elevations, but phenotypically it is quite varied depending on how it interacts with a certain environment. This **norm of reaction**, or the way an individual's normative or average reaction varies with the specific environment, tells us that plant #1 may not necessarily possess a superior genotype after all, but that it simply develops best in a particular environment.

The norm of reaction also helps us see why heritability estimates can be misleading. A common error is to assume that if a trait is high in heritability, the trait is permanent and not malleable or open to experience. The differences among our seven plants at each elevation are 100% due to genetic factors, but this 100% heritability does not mean different elevations do not make a difference. And as you can see in our final plant metaphor, illustrated in Figure 3.13, the differences *between* the window boxes are totally environmental, yet the differences *within* a window box, such as box "A" on the left, are 100% due to genetics.

When the deficient soil has been replaced with soil high in nutrients, as in window box "B" (analogous to improving the quality of children's access to high-quality healthcare, food, and education), *all* the plants benefit from the improved quality of the environment, but the differences within the group are still 100% due to genetics. A heritability estimate of 100% for IQ might lead people to think IQ score differences among children are completely due to genetic factors, so that there is no point in providing high-quality education to all. Yet this is simply not the case.

Epigenetic Theory

Neither genes nor environment cause (?) development; instead, they interact with one another to produce development. And it is with this understanding in mind that epigenetic theory was developed. **Epigenetic theory** (*epigenetic* means "near or around genes") proposes that over the course of an individual's development, interactions among genetic activity, neural activity, behavior, and environmental influences occur to produce development; because the field of epigenetics goes beyond the binary of what is due to innate factors and what is due to experience, it renders the nature–nurture debate obsolete (Gottlieb, 2007; Lickliter & Witherington, 2017; Witherington & Lickliter, 2017).

The process of **epigenesis** involves how genes are activated and/or deactivated depending on the environment, so changes in the expression of and activity of genes do not involve changes in the gene sequence (Moore, 2015; Sage & Burgio, 2018).

For example, a review of research found evidence for changes not in DNA, but in expression of neurological development (such as problems in memory, learning, attention, as well as symptoms similar to ADHD and autism), for children who are exposed to electromagnetic fields via persistent exposure to wireless technologies—suggesting that should we have the privilege of access to them, we may want to limit our use of Wi-Fi and wireless devices as best we can, despite them being increasingly necessary for school and work (Sage & Burgio, 2018).

Pan & Zoom

School Inequity as a Source of Epigenetic Influences on Development

In this box, we are going to pan—or take a panoramic, wide-angle look at—research that has investigated how stress in the educational system may be a source of epigenetic influences on child development.

It is fairly well established that epigenetic processes affect development as a function of severe environmental events, such as war, famine, and child abuse. But less is known about subtler but ongoing sources of stress, such as the socioeconomically unequal school system that occurs in the United States and also in other countries with high inequity such as Chile (Frias-Lasserre, Villagra, & Guerrero-Bosagna, 2018).

Research has found that students' physiological stress, which impacts their ability to focus and learn, is a function of teachers' occupational stress, and it is well known that classrooms and schools in general are among the many contexts that can either support or undermine development (Oberle & Schonert-Reichl, 2016; Osher et al., 2018).

One mechanism of school inequity stress may be bullying. Researchers in Canada and England have found that high levels of economic disparity between schools and among students within a school are risk factors for bullying. Exposure to bullying in childhood is associated with depression and increased levels of anxiety up to two years after the bullying has occurred. The chronic social stress of bullying can have long-term health consequences as well, such as an increased risk for heart disease in adulthood as a function of epigenetic alterations to the body's stress response (Fink et al., 2018; Napoletano et al., 2015; Singham et al., 2017; Zarate-Garza et al., 2017). Clearly, much work needs to be done to eliminate these inequities.

• • • •

As we have previously discussed, a gene–environment interaction was illustrated in our opening *Snapshot*. The study covered there found that children who are exposed to high levels of prenatal adversity and who have low levels of parasympathetic activity when they themselves are distressed are most likely to be aggressive as toddlers (Suurland et al., 2018).

Why is this an example of a gene–environment interaction? Well, as we will learn in Chapter 7, there is a biological basis to temperament, a collection of traits such as emotionality, irritability, and reactivity (Dalimonte-Merckling & Brophy-Herb, 2018; Zvara et al., 2018).

One possible mechanism of epigenesis by which DNA activity is changed without the actual DNA sequence being changed, is the methylation to which we were first introduced in Chapter 1. **Methylation** is a biochemical process that involves the transfer of one carbon atom and three hydrogen atoms in order to turn on and off the biological switches that produce biochemical reactions in the body that regulate various systems, including neurological systems; one study found that children who were prenatally exposed to alcohol had numerous methylated genes that were associated with lower IQ scores and greater ADHD problems (Bjorklund, 2018a; Frey et al., 2018).

Continued research on methylation is needed, but it does seem to be a promising avenue for understand the "How?" question—that is, *"How do nature and nurture interact to produce development?"* For example, as we will see in the *Pan & Zoom: School Inequity as a Source of Epigenetic Influences on Development* box, inequities in the school system may very well indeed be a source of epigenetic influences on development.

Key Terms

Active Genotype–Environment Correlation

Allele

Autosomes

Chromosome

DNA

Epigenesis

Epigenetic Theory

Evocative Genotype–Environment Correlation

Genes

Genotype

Genotype–Environment Correlation

Genotype–Environment Interaction

Heritability

Heterozygous Pairs of Alleles

Homozygous Pairs of Alleles

Incomplete Dominance

In Vitro Fertilization

Methylation

Mutation

Niche-Picking

Nonshared Environment

Norm of Reaction

Passive Genotype–Environment Correlation

Phenotype

Polygenetic Inheritance

Range of Reaction

Sex Chromosomes

Sex-Linked Traits

Shared Environment

Telomeres

Summary

1. **Define telomeres, chromosomes, DNA, genes, genotype, and phenotype.** *Telomeres* are the caps at the end of our chromosomes, which are the structures in our cells that contain genetic information. DNA is a double-helix or twisted ladder–shaped molecule that contains the genetic code that contributes to each individual's development, and segments of DNA are

referred to as genes. The *genotype* is our genetic code, and the *phenotype* refers to observable characteristics, which may or may not always match our genetic code.

2. **Describe the four different patterns of genetic inheritance.** Some genes are inherited via *recessive* inheritance, in which at least one of the offspring of a pair of biological parents will inherit a recessive trait, such as not having dimples. Other genes are inherited via *dominant* inheritance, in which at least one of the offspring of a pair of biological parents will inherit a dominant trait, such as dimples. A third pattern of genetic inheritance is *incomplete* dominance, in which the symptoms of a recessive-linked disease, such as Sickle Cell Trait, manifest themselves only under certain conditions. A fourth pattern of genetic inheritance is *polygenetic* inheritance, which occurs when a trait, such as eye color, is the product of multiple genes.

3. **Identify some chromosomal and gene-linked abnormalities.** The chromosomal abnormality in Down Syndrome occurs when an individual has a third chromosome on pair number 21. Huntington's disease is caused by a dominant gene, and symptoms include a progressive worsening in the ability to plan ahead, remember things, control movements, and swallow; dementia eventually occurs as well.

4. **Contrast nonenvironmental and environmental influences.** Hereditary nonenvironmental influences are those that we acquire from our biological parents or remote ancestors. Innate nonenvironmental influences on development include what we inherit, but they also change in inherited cellular characteristics as a result of gene mutations. Congenital nonenvironmental influences on development are those that are present at birth. Constitutional nonenvironmental influences on development occur as a result of life experiences. Environmental influences include both shared influences and nonshared influences.

5. **Explain the "Which one?" question in regard to the relationships among nature and nurture.** During the 17th century, the dominant perspective in biology was preformationism, which assumed that preformed humans were contained in sperm cells and just needed to grow in size. Some of the more modern views of development emphasize nurture, yet a "Which one?" type of perspective tends to emphasize nature *or* nurture, not both.

6. **Discuss how measures of hereditary influence answer the "How much?" question.** Heritability measures how much the differences among people in a group, such as their height, are due to genes and how much to environmental influences.

7. **Evaluate ways to answer the "How?" question.** Genotype–environment correlations occur when different genotypes are exposed to different environments. Genotype–environment interactions examine how different people may respond differently to the same environment. Range of reaction looks at all the possible outcomes when a genotype interacts with the environment. The norm of reaction reminds us that even if heritability for a trait such as IQ is 100%, this does not mean the environment does not play a major role in development. Epigenetic theory explains how influences occur among genetic activity, neural activity, behavior, and the environment, leading to long-term changes in gene expression and activity.

The Cycle of Science

The Cycle of Science feature asks us to consider the theoretical implications of the results of research studies—and to reflect upon how these empirical findings can be applied to fields. The feature will be included here and at the end of all subsequent chapters.

Research

Why was the study conducted?

The researchers wanted to know what might determine the length of telomeres in newborns; we learned earlier in this chapter that telomere length is correlated negatively with risk of later diseases (Bosquet Enlow et al., 2018; Freitas-Simoes, Ros, & Sala-Vila, 2018).

Who participated in the study?

The participants were 151 mothers and their infants.

Which type of design was used?

A correlation design was used. No independent variables or experimental methods used; the researchers simply wanted to identify any patterns among newborns' telomere length and risk–resilience variables, such as maternal SES and stress exposures (Bosquet Enlow et al., 2018).

What were the results?

The researchers did not find any relationships among newborns' telomere length and risk–resilience variables in female infants. Yet they did find telomere length in male infants was correlated negatively with the risk variables of maternal smoking during pregnancy, maternal body mass index during pregnancy, and maternal depressive symptoms during pregnancy, as well as maternal sexual abuse during childhood; they also found that telomere length in male infants was correlated positively with the resilience variables of level of maternal education during pregnancy and household income during pregnancy, as well as level of mothers' emotional support from their families while they were children (Bosquet Enlow et al., 2018).

Are the results consistent with theory?

The results are consistent with the theory of gene–environment interactions in that development is a product of nature and nurture interacting.

How can the results be used to improve our lives?

The results can help government officials be more informed about the importance of creating, and funding, policies that promote optimal health for pregnant women, such as universal access to high-quality prenatal care and paid time off during pregnancy.

Exercises

1. What pattern of results would you expect to find if the study had been longitudinal in design and looked at physical and mental health outcomes in children when they were adults?

2. Explain why the results are consistent with epigenetic theory.

3. If this study had included participants from other countries with both high levels of inequity and low levels of inequity, the results may have been more powerful. How so?

Helpful Websites

The website of the International Society for Stem Cell Research has guidelines for the use of stem cells. You can read about the research here: https://www.isscr.org/policy/guidelines-for-stem-cell-research-and-clinical-translation

The website of the National Society of Genetic Counselors has information for healthcare providers and patients, as well as people who are looking for a genetic counselor: https://www.nsgc.org/page/find-a-genetic-counselor

The Minnesota Center for Twin & Family Research has research findings on its website, as well as information about how to participate in research, if you are a twin or a sibling: https://mctfr.psych.umn.edu/index.html

The University of Utah's Health Sciences program has a website dedicated to all things epigenetic, as well as information about how what you eat can change your gene expression: http://learn.genetics.utah.edu/content/epigenetics/

Recommended Reading

Carey, N. (2013). *The epigenetics revolution: How modern biology is rewriting our understanding of genetics, disease, and inheritance.* New York, NY: Columbia University Press.

Gottman, J., & DeClaire, D. (1998). *Raising an emotionally intelligent child: The heart of parenting.* New York, NY: Simon & Schuster.

CHAPTER 4

Prenatal Development, Birth, and Neonates

Snapshot

A pulmonary embolism, a blood clot in the lungs, is a medical condition that tennis champion Serena Williams was prone to before her pregnancy. That is, prior to her pregnancy, Ms. Williams had suffered multiple pulmonary embolisms that left her short of breath and almost ended her life.

The day after she had her daughter, Ms. Williams suspected she was again having a pulmonary embolism when she started having trouble breathing; but when she asked for a blood thinner and a scan, her request was initially dismissed and she was told the pain medications had left her confused. She persisted, and she was eventually given a scan that found several blood clots in her lungs (Salam, 2018). So, even a highly successful, famous, and informed new mother needed to be her own healthcare advocate.

Unfortunately, not all cases of complications associated with pregnancy end as well. According to the Centers for Disease Control (CDC), a *pregnancy-related death* is the death of a woman while pregnant or within one year of the end of pregnancy—and despite major medical advances in the last 25 years, pregnancy-related deaths began to rise during this time, resulting in a public health crisis (Gingrey, 2020). A pregnancy-related death, in addition to being a tragic event, is often preventable. One report summarizing the data found 63% of pregnancy-related deaths were preventable, with most of them being due to hemorrhaging,

FIG. 4.1   Serena Williams on the Tennis Court

Copyright © 2014 Depositphotos/zhukovsky.

FIG. 4.2   Serena Williams in the American issue of *Fader* Magazine.

cardiovascular conditions, infections, and embolism (Brantley et al., 2018).

The report also found that these preventable deaths were most often a result of factors associated with the *patient,* such as lack of knowledge on warning signs; factors associated with the *provider,* such as misdiagnosis and/or ineffective treatments; and/or factors associated with *systems of care,* such as lack of coordination among providers (Brantley et al., 2018). If these data weren't bad enough, enormous racial disparities exist with pregnancy-related deaths, as well as newborn deaths (Janevic et al., 2018). That is, 13 deaths occur for every 100,000 live births for European American women, 30 deaths occur for every 100,000 live births for American Indian/Alaska Native Women, and 41 deaths occur for every 100,000 live births for Black women (Petersen et al., 2019).

What may be the cause of this state of disgrace? Well, the data from one study found that although Black women are at an increased risk for high blood pressure and diabetes before conception, and although their newborns are significantly more likely to have complications, these risk factors do not account for racial disparities in birth outcomes. The data do indicate that non–European American infants have worse outcomes than European American infants within the same intensive care unit in the same hospital (Harville et al., 2018; Howell, Hebert, & Zeitlan, 2019; Vance, McGrath, & Brandon, 2018). So racial/ethnic disparities in preexisting health differences prior to conception do not explain racial/ethnic disparities in pregnancy-related deaths.

Learning Goals

- ▸ Describe the stages of prenatal development
- ▸ Identify the factors affecting the prenatal environment
- ▸ Explain fertility, infertility, and miscarriage
- ▸ Analyze the stages of birth, the fetus's experience, and birth options
- ▸ Summarize the newborn's characteristics, potential complications, and kangaroo care
- ▸ Discuss events in the postpartum period

Yet other research suggests an epigenetic mechanism of a societal and political context rife with racism (M'hamdi et al., 2018; Penkler, Hanson, Biesma, & Müller, 2019).

Not only do the empirical data indicate that women of color report significant disrespect, unmet information needs, and inconsistent support during their pregnancy-related healthcare experiences, but also researchers have found that a given geographical area's proportion of Internet searches using the 'n-word' is correlated positively with mortality rates of Blacks in the same area, as well as the rates of preterm and low-birth-weight babies born to Black women in that same area (Chae et al., 2015; 2018; McLemore et al., 2018).

Fortunately, attention is now starting to be paid to the need for high-quality healthcare for all individuals before, during, and after pregnancy, and some of the research being conducted even involves women of color, so that their concerns are better addressed (Howell, 2018). Let's hope that, therefore, the lives of these families improve immediately.

What Occurs During Prenatal Development?

As we consider the events that occur during prenatal development, we will organize them into the three periods commonly used to understand these nine months. These three periods of prenatal development are as follows: the **germinal period**, which lasts from conception to the end of week 2, the **embryonic period**, from the beginning of week 3 to the end of week 8, and the **fetal period**, which begins at week 9 and ends at birth.

Note, however, that these three periods are not equivalent to the three **trimesters** of pregnancy, each of which corresponds to approximately three months. The *first trimester* is from the beginning of week 1 to the end of week 12, the *second trimester* is from the 3˜ beginning of week 13 to the end of week 26, and the *third trimester* is from the beginning of week 27 to the end of pregnancy, an end that occurs on average between 38 and 42 weeks.

Many of the most dramatic changes in prenatal development occur within the first trimester, which corresponds to all three periods of prenatal development. Before we begin discussing the germinal period and the two others, though, we need to consider conception.

Conception

Approximately every 28 days, a healthy woman who is of childbearing age usually *ovulates*, meaning she releases an egg or ovum from her ovaries. If sperm penetrate this ovum as it travels through one of the fallopian tubes, **fertilization** or **conception** takes place, as shown in Figure 4.3. The fertilized egg is now referred to as a **zygote**, which is a single cell and contains 46 chromosomes, 23 from the mother's egg

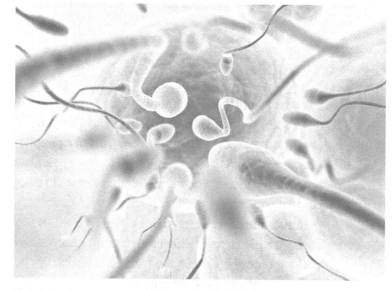

FIG. 4.3   Sperm Approaching an Egg

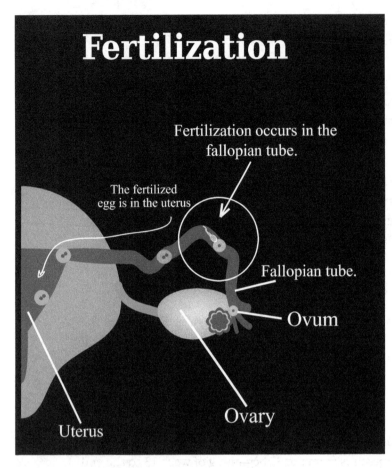

Fertilization

Fertilization occurs in the fallopian tube.

The fertilized egg is in the uterus

Fallopian tube.

Ovum

Ovary

Uterus

FIG. 4.4   Fertilization Occurs in the Fallopian Tube

and 23 from the father's sperm. As you can see in Figure 4.4, when fertilization occurs, it usually takes place in the outer third of the fallopian tube, or the area closest to the ovary.

Keep in mind that conception is no guarantee of pregnancy, since about one-third to one-half of all zygotes never implant in the uterine wall, which is necessary for continued growth. And as we know, not all eggs are even fertilized. If no sperm are present within 24 hours after the egg has been released and travels down one of the fallopian tubes, the egg disintegrates and is shed during menstruation, along with the protective lining of the uterine wall that has developed in the event that fertilization takes place.

The Germinal Period

The first of the three periods of prenatal development is the germinal period, which corresponds to the first two weeks after conception. Within 24 hours of conception, the zygote divides for the first time. On day 5, or within about 120 hours after conception, the zygote consists of multiple cells and is now called a *blastocyst*.

The Embryonic Period

The embryonic period begins at the start of the third week of gestation. Cell differentiation and *organogenesis*, or the development of major organs such as the brain, lungs, and heart, are primary characteristics of the embryonic period. For example, a hollow groove or *neural tube* in the developing body cavity begins to close by folding over, usually around the fourth week. This neural tube will eventually differentiate into the components of the central nervous system, the brain and the spinal cord, as you can see in Figure 4.5.

In the fourth week, the neural tube closes so that it can thicken to form the brain and spinal cord. At this time the heart also begins to beat and the buds of the legs form. The buds that will become the arms have formed a bit earlier, usually around 24 days. At seven weeks, the embryo is about 18 to 20 mm or 3/4 of an inch in size, and the digits (fingers and toes) become increasingly prominent.

Human Embryonic and Foetal Development

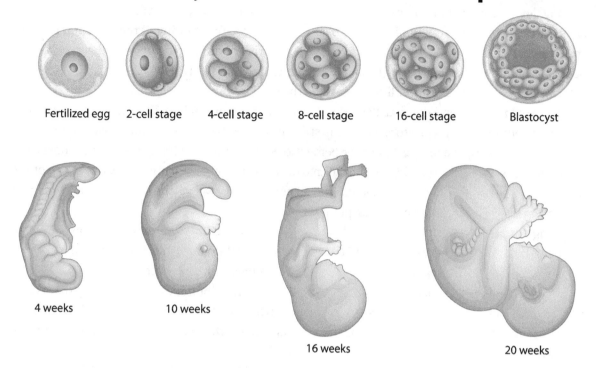

Fertilized egg   2-cell stage   4-cell stage   8-cell stage   16-cell stage   Blastocyst

4 weeks   10 weeks   16 weeks   20 weeks

FIG. 4.5   Key Stages in Embryonic Development

Limb movements occur at 8 weeks. While most organs are present by now, only the heart and blood vessels are functional at this point. Many of the other organs become fully mature only after birth.

The 8-week-old embryo is about 27–31 mm or 1.20 inches in size and has a more human appearance. This is the last week of the embryonic stage.

The Fetal Period

In the final period of prenatal development, the **fetal period**, the fetus continues to grow. At nine weeks, the eyelids close, the fetus is around 50 mm or 2 inches and about 8 grams or 0.02 pounds, and the head is about half the length of the body. The first trimester is complete at the end of the 12th week. By this time, rapid body growth has occurred, so the fetus is 8.5 cm or about 3 inches and weighs 45 grams or 0.09 pounds. Twelve weeks is also the point at which sexual differentiation in the fetus is apparent, so distinguishing features such as a vulva or a penis can be identified.

The **placenta** is the organ in the mother's body that delivers oxygen and nutrients to the fetus while also removing fetal waste. It is fully functional by 12 to 14 weeks of pregnancy and delivers the hormones necessary for sexual differentiation and genital development. While the placenta allows maternal blood and fetal blood to remain separate, it does not protect the fetus from drugs taken by the pregnant person.

The placenta does, however, allow maternal antibodies to enter fetal circulation, a process that will protect against infections, such as measles, from which the newborn is not able to defend itself until the immune system matures. The placenta's efficient functioning plays a major role in the baby's lifelong development: poor nutrition during pregnancy can lead to deficits of micronutrients—deficits that can impair the functioning of the placenta. Impaired functioning of the placental proteins that support the function of neurons may increase the risk of developing obesity, diabetes, and/or neurological problems later in life (Briana & Malamitsi-Puchner, 2017; Hofstee et al., 2018).

From 12 to 16 weeks, the lower limbs lengthen; the head is now relatively smaller. The growth that has occurred rapidly slows down at 17 weeks. A fetus born prematurely at 17 weeks would be unable to survive because the respiratory system is still immature. Between 17 and 20 weeks, pregnant persons begin to experience *quickening*, or perceptions of faint fetal movements. This is considered the midpoint of pregnancy, giving us another means of verifying **gestational age**, or the age of the pregnancy in weeks from a woman's last menstrual period. By 20 weeks, the fetus is 190 mm or about 7.5 inches and weighs 460 grams or 1.01 pounds.

The **age of viability**, or the age at which a fetus could survive if born prematurely, has traditionally been thought to be between 24 and 26 weeks. Recent technological advances have pushed this average age of survival back to 22 weeks, but such an average is no guarantee of survival or of freedom from complications such as intracranial bleeding, potential blindness, chronic lung disease, or death of part of the intestine; one study in Norway, which has an excellent and equitable healthcare system, found that the chance of survival at 22 weeks is 18%, whereas at 26 weeks it is 90% or more (Stensvold et al., 2017; Welty, 2019).

At 26 weeks the eyes are open, and body fat has increased to about 3.5% of the fetus's body weight. At 28 weeks, the fetus is 270 mm or about 10 inches, with a weight of 1,300 grams or 2.87 pounds. Ten weeks later, near the end of pregnancy, the fetus has typically grown to 500 mm or about 20 inches and weighs 3,400 grams or 7 pounds, 5 ounces.

What Factors Influence the Quality of the Prenatal Environment?

We tend to think of environmental influences on development as those existing in our local communities, but the womb is just as much an environment as any other, and it too can influence the development of the zygote, embryo, and fetus.

The concept of *developmental origins of health and disease* (DOHaD) proposes that much of our health during adulthood, such as our risk of depression, high blood pressure, obesity, or heart disease, is a function of our environments (maternal stress, low family income, poor nutrition, smoking, etc.) when we were in our mother's womb—or even earlier when our father's sperm was produced, given that research shows paternal age is correlated positively with the child's risk of autism spectrum disorder (Bhat et al., 2018; Longo, 2018; Kimura, Yoshizaki, & Osumi, 2018; Sata, 2019).

These findings remind us not to blame parents, nor to be fatalistic and assume that biology is destiny, given how many factors can affect any one developmental outcome. Focusing attention on and/or blaming parents by assuming that the primary cause of pregnancy effects is the pregnant person can lead to a self-fulfilling prophecy in which research questions on DOHaD fail to address other factors so that the research literature on DOHaD is imbalanced and flawed, as represented in Figure 4.6 (Sharp, Lawlor, & Richardson, 2018).

It is in the best interests of all of us to do whatever we can as individuals, as communities, and as a society, with better public health initiatives and greater social justice, to ensure that prenatal development occurs under circumstances as nearly ideal as possible. Also, now that there are data to show the context does indeed affect health, likely via epigenetics (M'hamdi et al., 2018), society has a great responsibility to reverse health inequities. Before we consider some ways to achieve that, though, consider the *Pan & Zoom: Developmental Origins of Health and Disease* box to learn more about the fascinating topic of DOHaD.

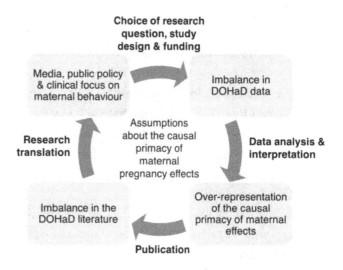

FIG. 4.6 How Assumptions About Maternal Effects Perpetuate Flawed Understanding

Gemma C. Sharp, Deborah A. Lawlor, and Sarah S. Richardson, How Assumptions About Maternal Effects Perpetuate Flawed Understanding, from "It's the Mother!: How Assumptions about the Causal Primacy of Maternal Effects Influence Research on the Developmental Origins of Health and Disease," Social Science & Medicine, vol. 213, pp. 21. Copyright © 2018 by Elsevier B.V.

Pan & Zoom

Developmental Origins of Health and Disease

In this box, we zoom in on and take a detailed look at the developmental origins or health and disease (DOHaD) by investigating the specific role of the *microbiome*, or the microorganisms in the body. Factors that affect the early-life microbiome include the microbes in the intrauterine environment, how a child is born (vaginally or via Cesarean section), how a child is fed (primarily with breast milk or primarily with formula), antibiotic usage, and other factors that influence a child's bacterial composition (Stiemsma & Michels, 2018).

How does the microbiome affect health? Well, preliminary work is establishing relationships among early-life *dysbiosis,* or the disruption of gut microorganisms, and long-term health consequences such as asthma, obesity, inflammatory bowel disease (IBD) and neurode-

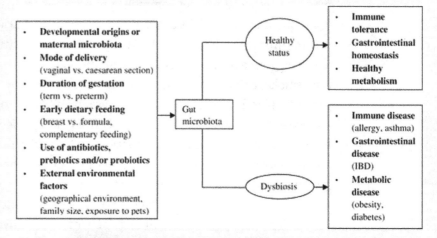

FIG. 4.7 Factors Contributing to Dysbiosis or Healthy Gut Status

Yeong Yeh Lee, et al., Factors Contributing to Dysbiosis or Healthy Gut Status, from "Gut Microbiota in Early Life and Its Influence on Health and Disease: A Position Paper by the Malaysian Working Group on Gastrointestinal Health," Journal of Paediatrics and Child Health, vol. 53, no. 12. Copyright © 2017 by John Wiley & Sons, Inc.

velopmental disorders; Figure 4.7 provides a diagram of these relationships (Lee et al., 2018; Stiemsma & Michels, 2018). Additionally, the later-life microbiome may also be the source of the connection between social context and physical health, such as the link between racism and mortality rates in Blacks that we learned about earlier in this chapter (Chae et al., 2018; Dowd & Renson, 2018)

• • • •

Prospective biological parents today may want to take stock of their health and lifestyle prior to conception, especially now that we know more about the role of preconception factors that influence development, whether it be the the pregnant person's microbiome or the quality of the sperm. Research indicates that those who receive *preconception care* are more likely to receive timely prenatal care, which is important because untimely prenatal care is associated with negative birth outcomes (Wally et al., 2018).

Preconception care can be immensely helpful for well-being. For example, these care providers can answer prospective parents' questions; remind the pregnant person to start taking prenatal vitamins with folic acid (important for preventing birth defects of the brain and spinal cord); discuss with them the benefits of breastfeeding and of avoiding antibiotic use; help them quit smoking; improve them diet to include micronutrients and fatty acids; manage prospective parents' health conditions, such as hypertension and diabetes; discuss the various sources of birth defects; and perhaps, depending on family history, suggest genetic counseling. Genetic counseling is a screening process for genetic risk during preconception care or prenatal care; note that it needs to be especially thorough, given the recent research showing that some screenings aren't comprehensive and result in healthcare providers missing important indicators of genetic risk (McClatchey et al., 2018).

Prenatal care should certainly begin immediately after a person suspects they are pregnant. A healthcare provider will assess the pregnant person's general health; calculate their estimated due date; discuss nutrition, exercise, and medications during pregnancy; and answer any questions they may have, especially about common symptoms of pregnancy such as fatigue and morning sickness. Subsequent prenatal visits are recommended every four weeks until 28 weeks gestation, then every two to three weeks between 29 and 36 weeks, and every week from 37 weeks to delivery.

During prenatal care visits, healthcare providers will ask the pregnant person whether they exercise, smoke, drink alcohol, and have any health conditions. These providers will check their blood pressure, blood sugar (for signs of gestational diabetes, or the onset of diabetes during pregnancy), and weight (to determine whether they are gaining adequate but not excessive weight); check the fetus's heartbeat; discuss birthing options, such as birthing pools; and recommend childbirth classes and pediatricians. Healthcare providers may also recommend prenatal testing, which we discuss further in the *Tech & Media: Prenatal Testing* box.

Prenatal care can also be a good opportunity for future parents to discuss male circumcision and its risks (pain, infection) as well as its benefits (easier hygiene and lower risk of urinary tract infections, HPV, HIV, and other sexually transmitted diseases). Male circumcision is a personal and/or religious decision that many parents report wishing they had more information about before making a decision, but it is also a medical decision that should consider the best interests of the child. The World Health Organization suggests considering circumcision as an effective intervention for HIV prevention, and the American Academy of Pediatrics indicates that the benefits of circumcision outweigh the risks for families who choose it (American Academy of Pediatrics, 2012a; Sardi & Livingston, 2015; Rasheed, 2018).

Prenatal Testing

Prior to birth, multiple tests can check the status of a pregnant person's health, as well as the health of the fetus. Some are lab tests, also known as the *prenatal panel*, which can test for blood count, blood type, rubella, hepatitis, syphilis, and HIV on the basis of blood drawn in a medical office. *Ultrasounds* use sound waves to produce images that help estimate the size of the fetus and thus the probable due date, identify sex, and check heart function. Ultrasounds can also measure the back of the fetus's neck, which helps assess the risk of Down Syndrome.

Prenatal genetic testing can screen for chromosomal abnormalities and genetic defects, as well as defects in the brain and spinal column, such as spina bifida. These genetic tests include amniocentesis and chorionic villus sampling (CVS). Amniocentesis requires extracting some of the amniotic fluid that surrounds the fetus, using a needle inserted into a pregnant person's uterus via her belly, usually during the 15th week of pregnancy or later. The amniotic fluid is then tested for chromosomal abnormalities such as Down Syndrome.

With CVS, some of the placenta is removed via a needle into the abdomen or the cervix, usually between the 10th and 13th week of pregnancy. The amniotic fluid is then tested for chromosomal abnormalities or genetic disorders such as cystic fibrosis. Both amniocentesis and CVS are considered to be safe, but they do increase the risk of miscarriage. At approximately the 25th week of pregnancy, glucose screenings of the blood are conducted to discover whether a pregnant person has gestational diabetes, a condition that goes away a few weeks after delivery but must be addressed during pregnancy through nutrition, exercise, and/or insulin.

Genetic counselors (see Chapter 3) can help a pregnant person or a couple make decisions about which prenatal tests are best for them. This guidance can be especially useful regarding invasive tests such as amniocentesis and CVS. Genetic counselors can also discuss whether any fetal surgery options are available to treat a birth defect, such as spina bifida.

• • • •

Teratogens

Teratogens, or agents that can cause birth defects, are usually most damaging in the embryonic period while the organs are developing, but they can cause harm during the fetal stage as well. Teratogens can also lead to miscarriage and perinatal mortality, that is, death during the **perinatal period**, which is between the 22nd week of prenatal development and the 28th day after birth.

Teratogens can be both recreational drugs (alcohol, tobacco, cannabis) and therapeutic drugs (vitamin A, the acne drug Accutane, anticonvulsants, and so on). However, they also include the lead in drinking water, mercury in fish, and parasites in cat feces as well as other sources. We discuss substance abuse first.

Substance abuse during pregnancy has two major effects: damage to the fetus, and withdrawal symptoms in the newborn, including hyperirritability, gastrointestinal dysfunction, and respiratory distress. No amount of alcohol is safe during pregnancy.

Even small amounts of alcohol consumed by the pregnant person during pregnancy and/or the father within three months prior to conception can result in fetal alcohol spectrum disorders or full-fledged **fetal alcohol syndrome**, both of which include the following symptoms: abnormal facial features, small head size, poor coordination, hyperactivity, poor attention, poor memory, learning disabilities, low IQ, and/or vision problems. Yet both of these conditions can also be diagnosed with neurodevelopmental assessments throughout development in order to attempt to improve some outcomes for those affected (Cook et al., 2016; Hollander et al., 2018; Xia et al., 2018).

Symptoms of fetal alcohol syndrome, the more severe disorder of the two, can include severely deformed skulls and/or the absence of a nose or an eye, as well as stunted growth, behavior problems, central nervous damage, cognitive disabilities, and the typically distorted facial features.

Antidepressant use during pregnancy is associated with a greater risk of autism spectrum disorders. However, although the research evidence is extensive, the majority of these studies are correlational, so definitive cause–effect relationships are not possible at this time (Morales et al., 2018).

Cannabis consumed by either parent prior to conception and cannabis consumed by the pregnant parent during pregnancy are also associated with their offspring's heightened acting out (aggression, disobeying rules, stealing, cheating, etc.) during middle childhood (El Marroun et al., 2018). Even a drug that some think is least offensive, nicotine, can have devastating consequences. Nicotine constricts blood flow to the fetus, increasing the risk of miscarriage, fetal death, and even *sudden infant death syndrome* or SIDS (we will discuss SIDS in greater detail in the next chapter). Nicotine has intrauterine effects not only when the pregnant parent smokes but also if they are vaping, using nicotine gum, or has nicotine patches.

Although the evidence is mixed regarding whether amphetamines (such as diet pills) are associated with an increased risk of congenital malformations such as heart defects, <u>absence of evidence of a risk is not the same thing as evidence of an absence of risk</u>, so all amphetamines should be avoided during pregnancy (Andrade, 2018). Use of opioid prescriptions, such as Oxycontin and Vicodin, from preconception through pregnancy increases the risk of autism spectrum disorder as well (Rubenstein et al., 2018).

Regardless of what substance(s) a pregnant person may be abusing, healthcare providers and mental health professionals should provide emotional and practical support to help prevent as many complications as possible for parent and baby. The research evidence suggests that although pregnant persons discontinue using some substances during pregnancy, they find it much more difficult to discontinue others and need treatment help in doing so (Latuskie et al., 2018).

Sexually transmitted diseases (STDs) can act as teratogens too. **Syphilis** is a sexually transmitted disease that can cross the placenta and infect the fetus, resulting in perinatal death, preterm labor, or delayed growth. Treatment is available, though, and it is highly recommended that all pregnant people have a syphilis test. The human immunodeficiency virus (HIV) can be transmitted via the placenta, through fluid and blood exchange during birth, and while breastfeeding.

Most infants who acquire HIV congenitally (between conception and birth) do not survive beyond 2 years of age. The likelihood that HIV will be transmitted during pregnancy can be reduced with antiretroviral medication, Caesarean delivery, and avoidance of breastfeeding. Last but not least, chlamydia is the most commonly diagnosed sexually transmitted disease, but when it goes untreated, it (and untreated gonorrhea) can cause pelvic inflammatory disease. Chlamydia can also lead to preterm labor, as well as conjunctivitis, blindness, and pneumonia in newborns.

Less-well-known teratogens are just as dangerous. Although some do not realize it, a pregnant person's contact with parasites in the feces of an infected domestic cat (often when changing a litter box), on root vegetables such as carrots, in sandboxes, and in gardening soil and undercooked meat can be dangerous to the fetus. All these locations serve as potential hosts for the *Toxoplasma gondii* protozoa, which causes the *toxoplasmosis* infection to enter the central nervous system and cause inflammation in the brain. Symptoms are minor, so infected pregnant people do not always become aware they are infected or seek medical attention.

Yet miscarriage, seizures, blindness, and hydrocephalus (water on the developing brain, which can lead to learning disabilities) can result if the infection spreads to the fetus; some treatments are available, and in addition, it has been suggested that the United States should begin screening pregnant people for toxoplasmosis; the screening is done routinely in countries such as Argentina, Germany, Lithuania, France, and Uruguay (Montoya, 2018).

Lead, which can be found in tap water and in old paint that chips off walls, is associated with miscarriage, and even very low levels of exposure to lead during pregnancy can interfere with the development of a newborn's nervous system. This exposure can lead to problems in brain development, including lower test scores, but also higher impulsivity, anxiety, and depression (Green, 2019; Muller, Sampson, & Winter, 2018; Sampson & Winter, 2016; Winter & Sampson, 2017).

People of color who also live in poor communities have the highest blood lead levels; this is likely a result of living in housing and/or using water supplies that have been neglected by public officials. These supplies sometimes even show lead levels above Environmental Protection Agency (EPA) limits. One example of this is the devastating case of Flint, Michigan, where schools are overwhelmed with students whose behavioral and neurological problems are likely a result of such lead exposure. This is an example of *environmental inequality*, but one that can be remediated. In Chicago, for example, greater regulation has resulted in significantly lower lead levels in children over the past 20 years (Green, 2019; Muller, Sampson, & Winter, 2018; Sampson & Winter, 2016; Winter & Sampson, 2017).

Other Sources of Birth Defects

Rubella or German measles in the pregnant person is associated with miscarriage, **stillbirth** (death of the fetus), fetal blindness, heart disease, and other health problems—and rubella rates have increased in recent years, perhaps as a result of misconceptions about the science of vaccines (Schwarz, 2017). Miscarriage rates also increase substantially with contraction of the varicella zoster virus, the virus that causes chicken pox. Gonorrhea, the sexually transmitted disease that infects the cervix but can be asymptomatic, increases the risk of miscarriage and preterm labor. Stillbirth rates are increased when pregnant people contract Lyme disease, which is transmitted by the bite of infected ticks.

Iodine deficiency disorders (IDDs) result from insufficient iodine in the salt supply. Once they occur, these disorders are irreversible and can lead to miscarriage, stillbirth, delayed physical growth, and impaired neurocognitive functioning in childhood (such as reduced IQ) (Eastman & Zimmermann, 2018).

Insufficient leafy greens and/or synthetic forms of folic acid increase the risk of neural tube defects, which occur when the neural tube fails to fold completely and/or close. Given that the risks to the fetus of folic acid deficiency are greatest when this deficiency occurs before or early in pregnancy, it is recommended that all potential pregnant people of childbearing age take a daily dose of folic acid, even if they have no known risk of neural tube defects.

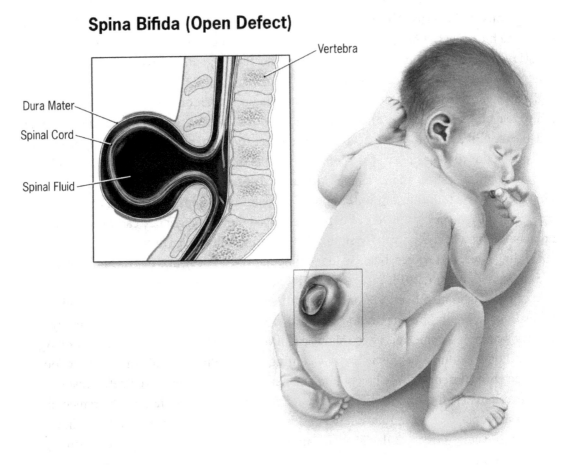

Spina Bifida (Open Defect)

Vertebra

Dura Mater

Spinal Cord

Spinal Fluid

FIG. 4.8   Spina Bifida

Source: https://commons.wikimedia.org/wiki/File:Spina-bifida.jpg.

Scoliosis is a curvature of the spine that can be corrected with a brace, or in more severe cases, with surgery. *Spina bifida* occurs when the vertebra in the spine fail to fuse, usually within the lower lumbar region. As a result, the spinal cord extends outside the bones. Surgery can close the vertebra, but it does not necessarily eliminate the side effects of spina bifida, such as paralysis.

Anencephaly occurs when the upper end of the neural tube does not close. As a result, the brain and skull fail to form fully. Embryos with this devastating condition often survive until the late fetal stage or even birth (yet without any experience of consciousness or ability to feel pain), but they usually die within a few hours or days of birth.

Caffeine consumption during pregnancy has adverse outcomes: it increases the risk of smaller head circumference, earlier gestational age, and low birth weight. Remember that caffeine is found not just in coffee but also in soda, tea, energy drinks, food bars, and chocolate, so all of these should be eliminated or consumed sparingly during pregnancy (Chen et al., 2018).

The case of chocolate is intriguing, however. Research has shown that it reduces blood pressure and anemia, and it prevents preeclampsia (a dangerous condition discussed later in this chapter). In addition, pregnant people who eat chocolate with a high cocoa content daily during their pregnancy report their infants' emotional state to be more positive at 6 months of age, suggesting a multidimensional relationship between prenatal food consumption and infant mood (Babar et al., 2018; Brillo & Di Renzo, 2015; Latif, 2018).

Parental Influences During Pregnancy

Poor nutrition in the second half of pregnancy affects fetal growth and is often responsible for newborns being small for their gestational age. Pregnant people should speak with their healthcare provider to establish what levels of protein, healthy fats, calcium, iron, and folic acid are ideal. They may also wish to discuss herbs, which have the potential to be either dangerous or beneficial during pregnancy.

Massage, when practiced safely to accommodate the needs of pregnant people, can be therapeutic during pregnancy. Massage increases circulation, enhances muscle function by releasing the buildup of lactic acid, relieves stress on weight-bearing joints, reduces the stress hormone cortisol, encourages physical and emotional relaxation, and can reduce depression and anxiety, relieve neck and back tension, and reduce muscle cramps.

Also, massage—as well as bright light therapy and/or acupuncture—can reduce symptoms for pregnant people diagnosed with depression during pregnancy. This is an important decrease, because prenatal depression and anxiety have lifelong and multidimensional consequences for both parent and baby; that is, depression affects a child's later socioemotional well-being (Madigan et al., 2018; Smith et al., 2018).

In addition to its usual benefits, exercise during pregnancy can help tone muscles (including the heart), increase physical stamina, and reduce stress and tension. Stress reduction is important and has lifelong and multidimensional consequences for both parent and baby. Research reveals that pregnant people who engage in relaxation techniques (such as guided imagery and diaphragm breathing) report less perceived stress, fewer symptoms of depression and anxiety, and a greater feeling of control (Katziari et al., 2017; Nasiri et al., 2018). Engaging in physical activity and practicing yoga during pregnancy have also been found to reduce back pain and depression during pregnancy, as well as reducing labor pain and the duration of labor (Jahdi et al., 2017; Kinser, 2017).

Stress reduction is also vital because hypertension (high blood pressure) poses dangers to the fetus. Such hypertension can be *pregnancy-induced hypertension* (PIH), which reverses after delivery, or *chronic preexisting hypertension*, which occurs before pregnancy and does not end with delivery. Regardless of the origin, hypertension in the parent reduces oxygen supply to the fetus's major organs such as the brain and liver, so it is vital to monitor, if not prevent.

When hypertension is joined by abnormal proteins in the urine and blood plasma that leaks into tissues, *preeclampsia* occurs, which research shows is the leading cause death of the pregnant person and perhaps is also linked to autism spectrum disorders in the child, likely because of inflammation or chronic activation of the body's immune system (Cornelius, 2018; Maher et al., 2018).

If the symptoms of preeclampsia are accompanied by seizures, the condition is referred to as *eclampsia*. Both preeclampsia and eclampsia are extremely serious and can lead to death of the pregnant person (due to cerebral hemorrhage), as well as fetal death (due to placental insufficiency). Any pregnant individual experiencing headaches, altered consciousness, and/or blurred vision should seek medical care immediately, since these symptoms usually precede eclamptic seizures.

So far in this section we have discussed factors that affect the fetus as a result of the pregnant person, but partners certainly matter too. Research indicates that although many cisgender and heterosexual families are still characterized by parenting inequality or an unequal division of labor regarding child and household responsibilities (whereas same-sex couples are more egalitarian), father involvement in child-rearing has increased over time and is associated with greater breastfeeding rates and the likelihood of the mother receiving appropriate prenatal care, as well as a lowered risk of lower birth weight and infant mortality (Garfield, 2018; Rossi, 2018).

Partners' mental health bears notice as well. Research indicates that partners who have symptoms of anxiety and depression during pregnancy (and who have had adverse childhood experiences of their own) are more likely report stress and negative perceptions of their children's behavior at 6 months of age. So their mental health needs should be addressed just as much as those of the pregnant person—which reminds us how vital it is that therapy for parents be supported both via insurance coverage and by cultural acceptance without stigma (Misri, 2018; Skjothaug, Smith, Wentzel-Larsen, & Moe, 2018).

How Can We Explain Fertility, Infertility, and Miscarriage?

Female fertility, or a person's ability to conceive and carry a pregnancy to term, is correlated negatively with age (de Kat & Broekmans, 2018; Wallace & Kelsey, 2010). For instance, those who are born with *follicles*, or cells that produce eggs, are likely born with all they will ever have. *Ovarian reserve*, or the ability of a person's ovaries to produce eggs capable of being fertilized for pregnancy, is a function of their age, as well as interactions among their genes and environments (Hardy et al., 2018; Wallace & Kelsey, 2010).

Measures of ovarian reserve in potential pregnant people of older reproductive age (between 30 and 44 years of age) that show a diminished reserve are not necessarily predictive of infertility, though, so such measures should be used and interpreted cautiously. But diminished ovarian reserve is indeed associated with age-related infertility, as well as an increased risk of chromosomal abnormalities in the offspring if a pregnancy occurs (Cimadomo et al., 2018; Tal & Seifer, 2017; Steiner et al., 2017).

Regardless of age, though, ovarian reserve is correlated negatively with body mass index, so it is in a potential pregnant person's best interests to take care of their health if they are interested in becoming pregnant, particularly if their own birth parent reached menopause before age 50. Research shows that the daughters of such mothers have a diminished ovarian reserve (Moreau et al., 2018; Nazanin et al., 2018).

Sperm fertility, or the ability of a person to fertilize an egg, is maintained for most of a person's life span for those people who have sperm, unless they become obese or seriously ill. But the quality of sperm declines with time even in healthy people, and this decreased quality with increasing age has been associated with a number of outcomes in their children, such as stillbirth, cleft palate, autism spectrum disorders, and schizophrenia (Bazzi et al., 2018; Eisenberg, & Meldrum, 2017; Janecka et al., 2017).

According to the American Society for Reproductive Medicine (2018), approximately 10% of the reproductive-age population suffers from infertility. What is **infertility**, though? For individuals 35 years of age and younger, infertility is the inability to conceive or carry a pregnancy to term after 12 months of trying; for individuals over 35 years of age, it is the inability to conceive or carry a pregnancy to term after 6 months of trying.

Approximately one-third of all cases of infertility are a result of the sperm; another one-third the egg; and the remaining one-third both, or both but for unexplained reasons. Causes of sperm infertility include overexposure to chemicals and toxins (steroids, pesticides, radiation, drugs); the use of saunas and hot tubs; genetic diseases; undescended testicles; surgery; and prior infections, including untreated STDs. Causes of egg infertility include uterine abnormalities; fallopian tube damage; early menopause; disorders of ovulation; cancer; thyroid disorders; genetic diseases; and prior infections, including untreated STDs.

Even when conception occurs, though, a **miscarriage**, or spontaneous abortion (as opposed to a medical abortion), which is the loss of a fetus before the 20th week of pregnancy, can occur. The risk of such is correlated positively with parental age (Brandt et al., 2018; Carolan & Wright, 2017; Frederiksen et al. 2018).

Miscarriages can occur as a result of defective chromosomes in the fetus, as well as a range of factors in the pregnant person, including uncontrolled diabetes, obesity, infection, hormonal problems, and drug use. Most miscarriages occur in the first trimester. For pregnant people who aren't yet aware they are pregnant, the miscarriage rate is approximately 50%; for pregnant people who know they are pregnant, it is approximately 15%–20%.

Fertility Treatment Options

A range of fertility treatments are available to people who seek to have a child but are unable to do so on their own. Some of the most common treatments make use of *fertility drugs*, *intrauterine insemination* (IUI), *in vitro fertilization* (IVF), *donor eggs*, *donor sperm*, and *surrogacy*. Fertility drugs help potential pregnant people who don't ovulate regularly or who do ovulate regularly but don't produce many eggs. Fertility drugs, which are often hormones taken p˜ in pill form or via injection, have physical and emotional side effects that can be mild or substantial.

IUI involves injecting sperm directly into the uterus via a catheter tube. IUI can help if sperm are insufficient, low-quality, and/or slow-moving. It can also help potential pregnant people who are using a donor sperm, whether they have a same-sex partner or are single.

IVF extracts eggs directly from a potential pregnant person's ovaries via surgery, and then fertilizes them with sperm in the lab. If any embryos result, the individual or couple chooses how many embryos to implant in the uterus, and any remaining embryos can be stored. Fertility drugs are required to enable a potential pregnant person to produce as many viable eggs as possible. Although it is commonly assumed that IVF pregnancy success is near impossible after potential pregnant people are older than 42 years of age, research indicates that outcomes are better than commonly believed, especially if multiple attempts are made (Gleicher et al., 2018; Raz et al., 2018).

IVF can help if sperm are few in number, low-quality, or slow-moving; it can also help if a potential pregnant person is older and not producing many eggs or has scarring on their fallopian tubes. Potential pregnant people who wish to delay childbearing, potential pregnant people who don't have a partner and would prefer to have one before they begin childrearing, and/or potential pregnant people who receive a medical diagnosis and would prefer to reserve their eggs before initiating a medical treatment also use IVF for fertility preservation, mainly via freezing their eggs or embryos to implant later (Inhorn et al., 2018).

Donor eggs can help if a potential pregnant person is not producing viable eggs because of genetic disorders, chemotherapy/radiation, ovarian damage, or advanced age, and/or if they are a lesbian and desire shared-motherhood IVF, in which one partner becomes pregnant with the other partner's egg (Bodri et al., 2018).The use of donor eggs requires retrieving eggs from a donor with healthy ovaries via surgery, then fertilizing them in the lab with sperm, as in IVF.

Donor sperm can help an opposite-sex couple if a male partner has insufficient, low-quality, and/ or slow-moving sperm; a donor sperm can help a same-sex female couple by providing one or both of the partners with sperm, and can do the same for single women and same-sex male couples who conceive with a surrogate may or may not cover the costs of fertility treatment options, so policies that could improve affordability would ensure greater economic equity in options for becoming biological parents (Stanford, 2018).

How Does Birth Occur?

A **full-term pregnancy** can last anywhere from 38 to 42 weeks. A **preterm pregnancy** is one in which birth occurs at or prior to 37 weeks, and a **postterm pregnancy** is one in which birth occurs at or after 42 weeks. *Birth*, the process of bearing offspring, can take many long hours in humans and occurs over the course of three stages. In this section, we will learn about those stages, as well as the various birthing options that are available and the potential complications that can occur.

The Stages of Birth

Labor is the sequence of involuntary uterine contractions that results in the dilation of the cervix, the delivery of the baby, and the delivery of the placenta. These three events also define the stages of labor, each of which we will discuss below.

FIG. 4.9   A Newborn

Pregnant people often know labor is about to begin when a variety of symptoms appear. These include *lightening*, or "the baby dropping," which can result in increased ease of breathing for them as a result of the fetus moving down into the pelvis; a bloody show from the expelled mucous plug of the cervix; gastrointestinal changes; and "nesting," or an exciting emotional time in which the pregnant person experiences an unexpected burst of energy 24–48 hours before labor.

There are three stages of labor. In the first stage, *dilation* occurs. This begins with regular uterine contractions and ends when the cervix has been completely dilated. The second stage of labor is the *expulsion stage*. It begins with the cervix fully dilated and ends with the birth of the baby. Once the fetus has been delivered, we use the term **neonate** or newborn; specifically, *neonate* refers to infants from birth until they are 28 days or 4 weeks old.

You may not think anything else needs our attention after such a monumental event as birth. Yet the third stage of labor is important in its own right; it includes the delivery of the placenta and the clamping and cutting of the umbilical cord. Once the cord has been cut, the neonate wears a clip around the area where the cord entered the body, until the stump dries and falls off. The remainder forms the navel. Clamping the umbilical cord can be delayed a few minutes after birth in order to prevent anemia in the newborn; it allows more blood to flow to the newborn from the placenta, and research shows that the delay of clamping is especially beneficial for preterm infants (Fogarty et al., 2018).

The American Academy of Pediatrics discourages banking the blood in the umbilical cord for the newborn, because although stem cells are plentiful in umbilical cord blood, most of the conditions that can be treated with these cells (such as leukemia) already exist in them, rendering them useless to the particular newborn (say, with leukemia). However, since the cells could be immensely helpful to individuals with other conditions (such as amyotrophic lateral sclerosis, or ALS—Lou Gehrig's disease), new parents are encouraged instead to donate cord blood to a bank for public use (Shearer et al., 2017). Such donations may reduce the use of embryonic stem cells; some individuals have ethical concerns about this.

It has been suggested that there is a fourth and final stage of labor, known as the recovery stage. This stage begins as soon as the placenta has been delivered and contractions continue as a means of preventing excessive bleeding in the uterus, and it ends about two hours later.

The Fetus's Experience

Amid all our concern that the birth process proceeds smoothly, it can be easy to forget about the fetus's experience of birth, a transition from intrauterine life to extrauterine life that is both physical and emotional (Lorente-Pozo et al., 2018; Morton & Brodsky, 2016). While undergoing the birth process, the fetus experiences the onset of breathing, as well as changes in body temperature, hormones, and blood flow—not to mention sudden and overwhelming visual and auditory input from the extrauterine environment that activates the sympathetic nervous system we learned about in Chapter 3 and leads to states of arousal. These overwhelming states of arousal require emotional support from the outside world in order for the neonate to self-regulate. Such support is especially necessary for male neonates, because although males fetuses are more likely to survive in utero than female fetuses, male neonates tend to be less physiologically mature than female neonates (Lorente-Pozo et al., 2018).

Neonates are not completely passive beings: They can move their eyes, arms, and legs to express themselves and to seek attention from and interaction with a sensitive adult. Such behavior may not be indicative of self-awareness, but it does suggest that neonates possess motive and are capable of communication in which they sense the purpose of another's behavior—a type of will that even Darwin recognized in his own child. In this we have an example of the risk–resilience pattern of development: A responsive and sensitive context of care in the first year of a child's life is associated with greater emotional self-regulation in the child (Darwin, 1877; Steele, 2017; Trevarthen & Delafield-Butt, 2017).

Birthing Options

The number of birth options available has never been greater. Pregnant people can choose to give birth at a hospital, at a birthing center, or at home; birthing options also include choices of procedures (birthing tubs, pain relief, Cesarean sections) and types of care.

And choice matters; birth parent's subjective birth experiences are determined by their personality traits and by how well they felt they were true to their values in making choices about how to give birth. Also, such experiences predict how they later perceive their babies, as well as their caregiving attitudes and self-esteem as parents (A. F. Bell et al., 2018; Conrad & Stricker, 2017; Reisz, Jacobvitz, & George, 2015; Wolf, 2017).

During pregnancy, a birth parent or couple can choose an obstetrician or a midwife. *Obstetricians* are physicians whose have earned a medical degree and specialize in pregnancy, labor, and birth. Obstetricians usually delivery babies in hospitals and may be best for pregnant people who have or have had medical conditions that may interfere with labor and delivery. Obstetricians tend to follow a *medical model*, which focuses on diagnosing and treating complications, so pregnant people experiencing complications may prefer to choose an obstetrician for care, especially if they need a Cesarean section.

Cesarean sections, in which a fetus is delivered via a surgical procedure than requires incisions into the uterus, are recommended when a birth parent is pregnant with multiple fetuses, is infected with HIV, or has high blood pressure, or when the fetus has an abnormal heart rate or is in the breech position (with the feet near the birth canal rather than the head), which complicates vaginal birth. The number of Cesarean sections has plateaued in recent years, but the rates are still higher than recommended by the World Health Organization (DeClercq, Cabral, & Ecker, 2017).

Although Cesarean sections may be more convenient for the purpose of scheduling, they are also more expensive and pose more harm to both parent and fetus, including chronic pain and complications from anesthesia and infections, as well as later childhood asthma and respiratory illness (Ranjit et al., 2018). There is no shame in having a Cesarean section, but they are probably best avoided for pregnant people with uncomplicated pregnancies.

Certified nurse midwives have earned a nursing degree and advanced training in pregnancy, labor, and birth—as well as in postpartum care and primary care to parents needing family planning resources, gynecological exams, and/or menopausal care. Midwives deliver babies in hospitals, birth centers, and homes.

Midwives tend to follow a model different from the medical model, as the *midwifery model* (which has been misunderstood by some) assumes that pregnancy, labor, and birth are normal biological processes, and that unnecessary diagnostic tests and interventions should be avoided for pregnant people who are healthy and not experiencing complications. The midwifery model is relationship-based and tends to offer longer appointments in order for midwives to offer parents informed choices and provide them with emotional support (Guilliland & Dixon, 2017; McRae et al., 2018).

To learn more about midwives, and the career of one midwife in particular, see the *Mentor Minute: Mariah Valenzuela Farrell* box. Marinah is a practicing midwife and the president of Midwives Alliance of North America.

Marinah Valenzuela Farrell

1) Describe your work, please.

My work is better described as my life; it is very hard for me to separate out my career in concrete ways. I see this often with medical professionals—our work is a bit all-consuming. I think, especially in this country. To be a midwife is another level of consciousness because we continue to be seen as outside of the system, whereas research worldwide has shown that midwives are an essential part of the maternal health solution to end maternal mortality.

I have my own practice in Phoenix, Arizona, as a homebirth midwife, but I have also worked quite often in birth centers. I am also politically active in formal ways, as past president of a national midwifery association, and representative to various national efforts to increase access to midwifery. I've also had the blessings to work internationally, both as a provider and politically. Finally, I do a lot of grassroots work in Phoenix around healthcare justice—including helping found a free clinic in Phoenix for the community and working as a street medic during political protests, among just a handful of things that are currently happening politically.

FIG. 4.10 Marinah Valenzuela Farrell

2) How does social justice inform your work?

It is my everything ☺. As a medical professional, my work in the United States is based in a system of inequalities. U.S citizens have been told this is the best country, and yet our country does not offer healthcare to everyone, and the majority of people in the U.S worry every day about the cost of healthcare or the lack of access to healing. And yet our population in general is unhealthy, and the most vulnerable communities are—and this is literal—dying because of the inequalities in our healthcare system injustices. I tell people who ask how I became a midwife that it was because of politics that I understood my role is to model the community healer that I believe would change the system, and also to help make a "good birth" accessible to everyone.

3) How did you become involved in social justice and/or advocacy?

I started my first organized group in the third grade, and have always loved bringing people together and recognized from an early age the power behind an organized group. Being a child of the US and Mexican border, with parents who walked that world, and growing up in Arizona—well, I knew well about racism and also the loss of my cultural identity and, somewhat, my language. It was clear that I was different, and that led me to go to college and find ways to get involved in organizations where I was able to be outspoken about systems where there were injustices.

From there I started my path in midwifery and immediately recognized all the areas where there needed to be more organizing. At that time, I was determined to become a professor of political theory, and did not have midwifery as a career on my horizon. I worked a lot in midwifery legislation as an advocate. Once I moved toward specific midwifery study, I went to El Paso, Texas, where I have family on both sides of the border. At that time, the women were disappearing in Juarez, Mexico. So, I was able to study midwifery and still maintain the social justice work by going into Juarez and finding the activists who were working on the matter of women disappearing and police/government complicity. I have followed that same path my whole career—in every facet of midwifery I am doing something political as well. And, as I write that, I can just say that midwifery IS political just in the act of birth and rights of women/families birthing.

4) What are your thoughts on how social justice can improve child and adolescent development?
A good birth, one ☺. Social justice is all about equity and access to better opportunities to live a fuller, healthier life. By healing the elders, or by hearing the elders, the future generations can have a larger understanding of how they were impacted genetically by a system that has created huge power imbalances. Current children being born are impacted by generations of colonization, slavery, and the effects of poor health options, and by changing that (starting with including the elders in the conversation as well as children) there will be generational healing. This heals communities.

5) What suggestions do you have for undergraduate students who are interested in making a change in child and adolescent development?
To start in their own living room. It starts there with your close friends and family. And yourself. If you don't have a social justice heart at home, you won't have it in your professional life where the risks and hard work of social justice are intense. If you change even one life, you are a hero. To do social justice in child development means that you do your work and ensure everyone has access to the healing you offer. It is simple.

• • • •

What Are the Characteristics of Newborns?

The average newborn is 20 inches in length and weighs 7.5 pounds. *Small-for-date* or *small for gestational age* (SGA) babies are those who are in the 10th percentile compared to babies born at the same gestational age; *large for gestational age* babies (LGA) are those in the 90th percentile. Besides length and weight, though, a number of characteristics in the newborn are of interest and have developmental implications, so we discuss them next.

Newborn Characteristics

The bones of a newborn's skull are not fused together, which allows them to overlap, compressing the head as it passes through the birth canal. As a result, a newborn's head may be temporarily misshapen, though it usually returns to a rounded shape within a few days or weeks after birth. The seams created when the bones fuse are called *sutures*. Before the sutures form, the tender spaces between the skull bones are referred to as *fontanels*. These soft spots remind us of how fragile baby's brains are and that we must always handle infants with care.

One of the most common ways that healthcare professionals assess newborn health is with the APGAR score, which was developed by Virginia Apgar, an obstetrical anesthesiologist. APGAR also stands for the five criteria assessed in the test: appearance, pulse, grimace, activity, and respiration. APGAR scores are taken at 1 minute after birth and again at 5 minutes after birth.

Appearance or color can range from pink all over and healthy to blue (indicating a lack of oxygen), but healthcare providers must take into account the race/ethnicity of a baby when assigning an appearance score in the APGAR test and focus on the mouth, palms of the hands, and soles of the feet for babies of color (Adams & Grunebaum, 2014). A healthy *pulse* or heart rate is over 100 beats per minute. The third APGAR criterion, *grimace*, checks reflexes, which can range from facial grimaces in response to pain to sneezing, crying, and coughing. The newborn should be *active* with good muscle tone to meet the fourth criterion. The fifth criterion measures *respiration*; a newborn who is breathing well can manage a good, lusty cry.

Depending on the newborn's state, healthcare providers rate each of the five scales of the APGAR as 0, 1 or 2; total scores of 7 and up are signs of good health, whereas scores under 7 indicate that the newborn needs medical attention and may be at later risk of autism spectrum disorder. The APGAR test can also therefore be considered one of the first postnatal indicators that one's child may not necessarily have tremendous problems, but may perhaps be *neurotypical* or might show some atypical development (Modabbernia et al., 2018).

Potential Complications

Newborns may experience complications after birth, and complications tend to occur more frequently in babies who were preterm and/or of low birth weight. Preterm labor occurs before 37 weeks gestation and is the most powerful predictor of negative and potentially lifelong outcomes in the baby, yet outcomes tend to be worse for males, likely due to a combination of genetic, hormonal, and immune system functioning (O'Driscoll, McGovern, Greene, & Molloy, 2018).

One common symptom of a baby having been born preterm is *low birth weight* (LBW), defined as less than 2,500 grams or 5.5 pounds. Babies with LBW are not all preterm, though.

Very low birth weight (VLBW) babies weigh less than 1,500 grams or about 3.3 pounds. Modern prenatal care has drastically improved the prognosis for preterm infants compared to just a few decades ago, but schoolchildren who were preterm and/or VLBW are still quite impaired relative to others in terms of general cognitive development, academic achievement, social relationships, and mental health. Sensitive parenting can help mitigate some of the long-term negative outcomes, though (Wolke, 2018).

In the case of respiratory disorders, such as *respiratory distress syndrome*, in which the lungs are not fully developed and don't fill with air, treatment may require a mechanical breathing machine and extra oxygen. Other potential birth complications include breech position; anoxia, or a lack of oxygen; and birth injuries such as bruising of the head if the baby is large, the birth parent's pelvis is small, the birth parent is extremely overweight, a Cesarean section is performed, forceps are used in delivery, and/or a baby is born prematurely.

In general, the care of and outlook for babies born prematurely may depend on environmental factors, such as an individual hospital's practice; some hospitals offer no active treatment to 22-week-olds, whereas other hospitals treat such cases quite aggressively (Rysavy et al., 2015). Parental education plays a role in long-term outcomes as well. Research has found positive correlations among birth parents' educational level and the neurocognitive and academic performance of their children at 10 years of age (Joseph et al., 2018).

The birth parent's emotional well-being matters, too. Children who were VLBW have better physical skills and cognitive skills if their birth parent engages in sensitive emotional interactions with them. Interventions to help birth parents relax and get help taking care of themselves and their baby, so that they can focus on reading and responding to their preterm babies' cues, are vital. This is particularly true because preterm babies' cues are more difficult to read and because birth parents of preterm babies are at a higher risk of distress, depression, and PTSD than birth parents of full-term babies (Anderson & Cacola, 2017; Vanderbilt, Mirzainan, & Schifsky, 2018; White-Traut et al., 2018).

Kangaroo Care

Newborns, and especially those who are preterm, can benefit greatly from **kangaroo care**—the direct skin-to-skin contact achieved by holding a baby on the parent's chest for extended periods of time. Kangaroo care facilitates physical warmth, which helps the newborn regulate their body temperature, as well as psychological warmth via the emotional bond developing with the parent. A review of the research indicates that newborns who receive kangaroo care have greater self-regulation skills in infancy (Akbari et al., 2018).

Kangaroo care facilitates breastfeeding as well, and research indicates that it is just as effective as conventional care (that is, an incubator) in promoting newborn weight gain (Cunningham et al., 2018).

The benefits of kangaroo care are consistent with the multidimensional and lifelong patterns of development. Longitudinal research has found that infants who receive kangaroo care have higher IQ scores in young adulthood (Ropars et al., 2018).

What Does the Postpartum Period Involve?

The period after birth, and what occurs during this time, has developmental consequences for both the newborn and the parents. In this section, we discuss these outcomes and how best to support development during a special time in development.

Breastfeeding

Lactation, or production of milk, usually begins within 24 to 48 hours of birth, starting with the production of colostrum. **Colostrum**, a fluid secreted before the first production of milk, contains high levels of protein and antibodies to help protect the newborn from infection. Healthy newborns have a strong sucking reflex, and they will turn their head toward a nipple in response to having their cheek stroked.

Breast milk has many benefits that reflect the polydirectional pattern of development: It is easy for infants to digest, it promotes development of brain tissue, it boosts the maturation of the immune system, and it results in less diarrhea, as well as fewer respiratory and urinary tract infections. Some research indicates that breastfeeding may protect against infections, obesity, and diabetes as well. Breastfeeding has outcomes associated with the multidimensional and lifelong patterns of development, too; research shows that breastfeeding is associated with greater gains in intelligence, school achievement, and income in adulthood (Horta, de Sousa, & de Mola, 2018).

Breastmilk, as well as fish, contains docosahexaenoic acid, or DHA, an omega-3 fatty acid that promotes the development of brain tissue, so people who wish to conceive or who are pregnant may wish to speak to their healthcare provider about how much and what type of fish is safest to eat and/or how much and what type of DHA supplementation is best. Research indicates that the higher a birth parent's DHA levels, the higher their child's problem-solving skills at 1 year of age (Braarud et al., 2018).

Breastfeeding benefits the child in protecting their birth parent's life too; those who follow the American Academy of Pediatrics' (2012b) recommended guidelines and breastfeed exclusively for the first 6 months, then continue to do so for the first year of life while introducing solids to their baby, are at a reduced risk of breast cancer, ovarian cancer, endometrial cancer, metabolic syndrome, hypertension, type 2 diabetes, and heart attack (Louis-Jacques & Stuebe, 2018).

Birth parents who are malnourished, infected with HIV, and/or on medication that can interfere with quality of milk are not usually advised to breastfeed and should consult their healthcare provider. Those who are healthy yet are concerned that they don't produce enough milk can be reassured that the longer the baby suckles, the more milk they will produce, so it is important not to give up breastfeeding prematurely. Birth parents should seek help if they are struggling with depression; research has found that those who struggle with perinatal depression are more likely to give up breastfeeding prematurely (Stark, Shim, Ross, & Miller, 2018).

Lactation consultants are available at hospitals and birthing centers to help a new parent get started with breastfeeding, and most hospitals have breastfeeding groups where parents can meet others, share concerns, learn techniques to help them breastfeed for as long as they wish to do so, and form bonds with others who can support them.

The Emotional Transition to Parenthood

Consistent with Bronfenbrenner's (1977) Ecological Systems theory, researchers have found five aspects of the context of family life that influence the transition to parenthood—along with strategies that can be used to improve relationship processes at any stage in this transition (Cowan & Cowan, 2000, 2018). The first aspect is *the inner life of each parent*, which includes the parent's identity, view of the world, and level of emotional well-being or distress (Is the individual more anxious and ambivalent than confident about the decision to become a parent?). The second aspect is *the quality of the relationship between the parents*, particularly in terms of their family roles (Do they follow traditional sex roles, or are they more egalitarian in sharing responsibilities?) and quality of communication (Do they share their feelings, and without blaming or verbal aggression?).

The third aspect is *the quality of the relationships among the parents and grandparents* (Do the parents receive support from their own parents in the first few months of the baby's life?). The fourth aspect of family life that influences the transition to parenthood is *the relationship the parents have with others outside the family*, including coworkers, friends, and childcare workers. The fifth and final aspect is *the quality of the relationship between each parent and the child*.

Prenatal coparenting behavior predicts a couple's postnatal coparenting as well, with implications for children that are consistent with the lifelong pattern of development. Research with an *inconsolable doll* (a doll that the parents were shown how to soothe and stop crying before they were left alone with the doll, then whose crying in fact did not stop when the parents were left alone with the doll) shows that when expectant couples are asked to play with the doll in order for researchers to observe their interaction under stress, children whose parents displayed destructive communication and negative emotions with the inconsolable doll performed worse on measures of cognitive development at 18 months of age (Shai, 2019).

Same-sex couples' and transgender couples' to parenthood has additional unique concerns (Gash & Raiskin, 2018). They must first consider and then choose a parenting option, which can be emotionally and financially draining, such as fostering, adoption, and/or reproduction. If they end up going with the last option, family and friends may pose intrusive questions, such as about any donors involved and/or the means of conception, that they likely would not ask opposite-sex and/or cisgender couples. Same-sex parents may then struggle with an unsupportive or even a hostile context, including a lack of legal protections that opposite-sex couples do not experience, such as a lengthy and expensive process of second-parent adoption even in states that recognize same-sex marriage.

No matter their orientation or gender though, those new parents, living in the United States face a multiplicity of additional stressors as a result of unique government policies that fail to provide paid time off to new parents, fail to provide universal healthcare independent of a parent's employment status, and fail to provide universal childcare.

Postpartum Depression

Maternal postpartum blues occur in 50%–80% of new birth parents. This is a limited and transitory state, lasting for a few days after the birth, in which a new birth parent experiences crying, anxiety, fatigue, irritability—feelings fueled at least partially by sudden hormonal changes and drastic sleep deprivation (Bass & Bauer, 2018). The best treatment is to prepare pregnant birth parents by explaining that postpartum blues are expected, and to encourage families to provide emotional support and practical help with food preparation, laundry, pet care, errands, etc.

Postpartum blues are different from **maternal postpartum depression** (PPD), which occurs in 13% to 20% of new birth parents, lasts for several weeks, and is more severe. The symptoms of postpartum depression are similar to those of postpartum blues, but they are more severe in intensity and longer in duration. They are also associated with caregiving practices inconsistent with professional recommendations; that is, depressed birth parents are less likely to follow advice from their pediatricians, less likely to use a car seat appropriately, less likely to cover electrical outlets, etc. (Bass & Bauer, 2018).

Paternal depression occurs in 14% of new partners is most likely to occur between 3 and 6 months postpartum. Partners who are most at risk are those who are of low SES, have a prior history of depression, and have other children—and/or whose partner is also depressed. Yet unlike new birth parents, new non-birth parents usually are not screened for depression, although they deserve to be (Bass & Bauer, 2018).

Whereas children of depressed birth parents are less likely to engage in social interactions, are more likely to be delayed in their development, and may experience difficulties in emotional bonding, children of depressed parents are at risk for experiencing negative parenting, hyperactivity, and developmental delays as well, so screening and treating all parents is in their best interests and that of the child (Bass & Bauer, 2018; Field, 2018). To learn more about how all expectant couples can benefit from a mindfulness-based relationship education program in their transition to parenthood, consider the *Cycle of Science* box at the end of this chapter, which features a research study on mind-fulness-based childbirth and parenting courses for birth parents and non-birth parents (Warriner et al., 2018).

Key Terms

Age of Viability	Infertility	Placenta
Colostrum	Iodine Deficiency Disorders	Post-Term Pregnancy
Conception	Kangaroo Care	Preterm Pregnancy
Embryonic Period	Labor	Stillbirth
Fertilization	Maternal Postpartum Blues	Syphilis
Fetal Alcohol Syndrome	Maternal Postpartum Depression	Teratogens
Fetal Period	Miscarriage	Trimester
Full-Term Pregnancy	Neonate	Zygote
Germinal Period	Paternal Depression	
Gestational Age	Perinatal Period	

Summary

1. **Describe the stages of prenatal development.** Prenatal development is divided into three trimesters, each approximately three months long, and three periods of pregnancy—germinal, embryonic, and fetal. The germinal period begins at conception and ends at the end of week 2; the embryonic period lasts from week 3 to week 8; and the fetal period lasts from week 9 to birth, which typically occurs 38 to 42 weeks from conception.

2. **Identify the factors affecting the prenatal environment.** Factors that affect the prenatal environment include the womb itself and preconception care and prenatal care. The prenatal environment can be profoundly influenced by teratogens, which are any agents that can cause birth defects. Parental influences during pregnancy also affect the prenatal environment and include a multitude of behaviors, such as smoking and the use of alcohol and drugs.

3. **Explain fertility, infertility, and miscarriage.** Fertility treatment options include fertility drugs, intrauterine insemination (IUI), in vitro fertilization (IVF), donor eggs, donor sperm, and surrogacy. A miscarriage, or spontaneous abortion (as opposed to a medical abortion), is the loss of a fetus before the 20th week of pregnancy. Miscarriages can occur as a result of defective fetal chromosomes, as well as uncontrolled diabetes, obesity, infection, hormonal problems, and drug use in the pregnant person.

4. **Analyze the stages of birth, the fetus' experience, and birth options.** The stages of birth include dilation; expulsion; and the delivery of the placenta, along with the clamping and then cutting of the umbilical cord. The fetus experiences the onset of breathing, as well as changes in body temperature, hormones, blood flow, as it undergoes the birth process. The neonate also experiences sudden, overwhelming visual and auditory input that activates their

sympathetic nervous system. Birth options include giving birth at a hospital, at a birthing center, or at home.

5. **Summarize the newborn's characteristics, potential complications, and kangaroo care.** Newborn characteristics are assessed typically with the APGAR score, which measures appearance, pulse, grimace, activity, and respiration. Potential complications include preterm birth, low birth weight, respiratory disorders, and birth injuries such as bruising of the head. Kangaroo care, the skin-to-skin contact that is achieved by holding a baby on the parent's chest for extended periods of time, facilitates physical warmth, which helps the newborn regulate their body temperature, and psychological warmth via the emotional bond developing with the parent.

6. **Discuss the postpartum period, including breastfeeding, emotional transitions, and depression.** Breast milk has many physical benefits for babies, including immunity protection gained from the birth parent. The emotional transition to parenthood is influenced by the inner life of each parent, the quality of the parents' relationship, the relationships among the parents and grandparents, the parents' relationship with others outside the family, and the relationship between each parent and the child.

   Depression during and/or after pregnancy can result in difficulty providing appropriate infant care and can bring about thoughts of hurting oneself or the child. Children of parents with postpartum depression show symptoms of being withdrawn, irritable, or inconsolable; show insecurity and behavior problems; and are at risk for anxiety and depression themselves. They may experience cognitive and emotional difficulties later.

The Cycle of Science

Research

Why was the study conducted?
The researchers wanted to know if a mindfulness-based childbirth and parenting course for pregnant people and their partners could improve their prenatal mental health, such as decrease their prenatal depression that is a risk factor for postnatal depression (Warriner et al., 2018). The study was conducted in the United Kingdom as part of that nation's National Health Service—a publicly funded health service that is 98% paid for with taxes and was founded after World War II with the intent of its services being free, universal to all UK residents, and comprehensive in its coverage.

Who participated in the study?
The participants 88 individuals who identified as female and 69 individuals who identified as male.

Which type of design was used?
A correlational and longitudinal design was used; that is, the participants' level of depression was measured before they participated in a mindfulness-based childbirth and parenting course, then again after the course.

What were the results?

The researchers found that depression in both the pregnant people and their partners decreased after the course, as did their anxiety and stress.

Are the results consistent with theory?

The results are consistent with Bronfenbrenner's (1977) theory, which posits that many contexts influence our development, such as the macrosystem of the general values and laws that are part of a culture. The results are also consistent with the risk–resilience pattern of development, which studies how interactions among our genes and our environments can alter our development, for better or worse.

How can the results be used to improve our lives?

The results can be used to improve our lives in that other countries, such as the United States, may want to consider diverting tax dollars away from wars and border walls to ensuring all its citizens' health.

Exercises

1. What pattern of results would you expect to find if the study had been experimental in design and looked at depression outcomes in a second group of expectant parents who did not participate in a mindfulness-based childbirth and parenting course? Would such a study be ethical? Why or why not?

2. Explain why the results are consistent with social justice, which we defined in Chapter 1.

3. If this study were conducted in the United States right now, the results might be different. How so? Remember that the United States is the only industrialized nation across the globe that does not provide universal healthcare coverage.

Helpful Websites

A sequel to *The Miracle of Life*, the Emmy Award–winning program that tracks development from conception to birth, is available on the PBS website: http://www.pbs.org/wgbh/nova/body/life-greatest-miracle.html

RESOLVE, the National Infertility Association, is a nonprofit organization that promotes reproductive health and works to ensure equal access to family-building options. Their website has many resources, including a directory of professional services, fact sheets, support group listings, and an online support community: http://www.resolve.org/

If you or someone you know is interested in having the support of a birth and/or postpartum doula, the website of the Doulas of North America (DONA) has a location search, as well as publications and resources: http://www.dona.org/

La Leche League International, the international group that encourages and supports breastfeeding, has helpful information on their website for mothers who wish to breastfeed but experience difficulty doing so and/or have legal questions about nursing when returning to work: http://www.llli.org/

The American Association of Pediatrics' website has a special section for parents, which includes information on how to obtain free or low-cost health insurance for children, a guide to using car seats safely, facts about immunizations, and a brochure for tracking a child's physical development: https://www.healthychildren.org/English/Pages/default.aspx

Recommended Reading

Gaskin, I. M. (2008). *Ina Mary's guide to childbirth*. New York, NY: Bantam.

Jana, L. A., & Shu, J. (2015). *Heading home with your newborn: From birth to reality*. Elk Grove Village, IL: American Academy of Pediatrics.

Karp, H. (2015). *The happiest baby on the block*. New York, NY: Bantam.

Medina, J. (2014). *Brain rules for baby: How to raise a smart and happy child from zero to five*. Seattle, WA: Pear Press.

Morbacher, N., & Kendall-Tackett, K. (2010). *Breastfeeding made simple: Seven natural laws for nursing mothers*. Oakland, CA: New Harbinger Publications.

Pregnancy Experts at the Mayo Clinic (2011). *Mayo Clinic guide to a health pregnancy: From doctors who are parents too!* Boston, MA: Da Capo Lifelong Books.

Silverberg, C. (2012). *What makes a baby*. New York, NY: Seven Stories Press.

Tsiaras, A. (2002). *From conception to birth: A life unfolds*. New York, NY: Doubleday Vermillion.

Weschler, T. (2006). *Taking charge fertility, 10th anniversary edition: The definitive guide to natural birth control, pregnancy achievement, and reproductive health*. New York, NY: Harper-Collins.

CHAPTER 5

Physical Development in Infancy and Toddlerhood

Snapshot

Mateo entered the world weighing 8 pounds, 2 ounces, and measuring 20 inches long. His mother reports that her pregnancy was uneventful, that Mateo's birth at 40 weeks was without complications, and that Mateo is doing well.

How do we know Mateo's birth weight and height were within the normal healthy range though? And what does it mean for an infant or toddler be doing well? In this chapter, we will learn how to understand physical development in infancy and toddlerhood, the stages that occupy the first two years of life.

"Infant" and "toddler" may appear to be synonyms for "baby." But "infant" describes a baby who cannot yet walk or talk, while a "toddler" is one who does walk and talk. When exactly do children begin walking? Is it typical for a child to do so within the first year of life? And what if a child is not yet walking by 1 year of age? In this chapter, we will answer these questions, and more.

What Body Growth Changes Occur During the First Two Years of Life?

You have probably noticed that infants crawl while toddlers toddle or walk. That may not seem like a very meaningful difference. But once we regard these events in light of the multidimensional pattern of development, you will see how, for example, a child's

FIG. 5.1   Mateo

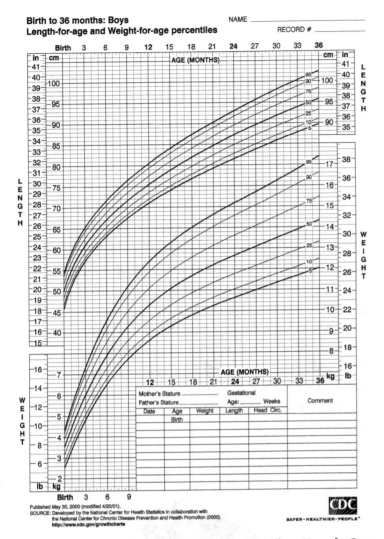

FIG. 5.2 Average Length and Weight Over the First Three Years for Boys

Source: https://www.cdc.gov/growthcharts/clinical_charts.htm.

transition from crawling to walking changes the way they think about the world, and how they relate to the people within it.

Measuring Growth of the Body

As you can see in Figure 5.2, average length or height of a male newborn falls between 18 and 21.5 inches, with a mean or average of 19.75 inches (the bold line in the 'Length' section of Figure), and the average weight falls between 5.5 and 9.5 pounds, with a mean of 7.7 pounds.

Figure 5.3 provides similar information for females (no data are available for infants who are *intersex* or those with reproductive anatomy that doesn't fit the traditional female-male binary). This chart is remarkably similar to Figure 5.2, and it reveals a pattern that we will see repeatedly throughout development.

Learning Goals

▸ Summarize the growth of the body, including size and proportion, in the first two years of life

▸ Paraphrase what we know about the growth of the brain in the first two years of life

▸ Recall what we know about sleep in the first two years of life

▸ Discuss the growth of teeth and the importance of high-quality nutrition

▸ Describe what occurs during well-baby exams

▸ Explain why vaccines are safe and necessary

▸ Identify the milestones of motor development in the first two years of life

▸ Illustrate sensory and perceptual development in the first two years of life

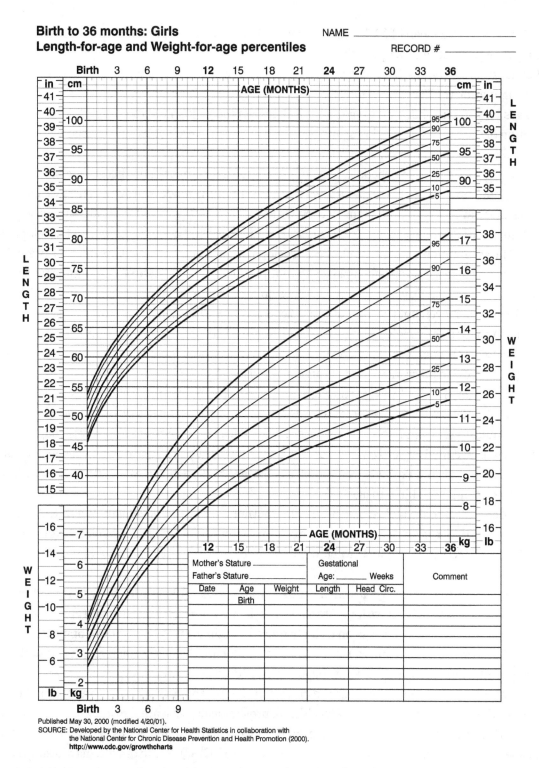

Birth to 36 months: Girls
Length-for-age and Weight-for-age percentiles

NAME _____

RECORD # _____

Published May 30, 2000 (modified 4/20/01).
SOURCE: Developed by the National Center for Health Statistics in collaboration with
the National Center for Chronic Disease Prevention and Health Promotion (2000).
http://www.cdc.gov/growthcharts

FIG. 5.3 Average Length and Weight Over the First Three Years for Girls

Source: https://www.cdc.gov/growthcharts/clinical_charts.htm.

That is, the differences *among* boys and differences *among* girls are far greater than the differences *between* boys and girls. Specifically, with numbers much like those in Figure 5.2, Figure 5.3 shows that the average height for newborn girls falls within a range (the two outer bold lines) of 18 to

21.25 inches, with a mean of 19.5 inches (the inner bold line). Average weight falls between 5.75 and 9 pounds, with a mean of 7.5 pounds.

Let us go back to our earlier question, "How do we know Mateo—or any child—is of normal height and weight at birth?" This question is a crucial one, because it reminds us of the significance that averages play in our understanding of physical development. Inspired by Darwin's ideas about the evolution of the species, psychologist and pediatrician Arnold Gesell (1880–1961) studied the average ages at which various physical developments occur.

His Gesell Development Schedule, a list of such ages, is no longer in use because it was not based on sufficient numbers of children, but it was a precursor of the modern growth charts we use today, such as those in Figure 5.2 and Figure 5.3. As Gesell et al. (1940) wrote, "There are laws of sequence and of maturation which account for the general similarities and basic trends of child development" (p. 7). The assumption here is that physical development is mainly, if not completely, nature-driven.

The process of maturation encompasses the entire timetable of **milestones**, or significant achievements in physical, cognitive, and emotional development. **Norms** are the average ages at which these milestones or achievements occur. For example, the ability to sit up without support is a milestone, and the norm for this event is 6 months. In addition to Gesell, other scientists who were also working from the 1920s through the 1940s focused on how infants' bodies change over time, whereas later researchers became more interested in infants' minds.

Not long after Gesell's work, further examination of the norms for infant milestones was conducted by Nancy Bayley (1899–1994). Bayley created the Bayley Scales of Infant Development to measure milestones from birth to age 4, which we will learn more about later in this chapter. Some pediatricians use the Denver Developmental Screening Test (DDST) for birth until age 6. Another available measure is the Peabody Developmental Motor Scales, which measure fine motor skills and gross motor skills from birth to age 7.

Regardless of which scale we use, it tells us whether a child's achievement of a milestone is on time, or typical. Is a child who reaches a milestone after the average age atypical? Not necessarily. We usually consider "typical" to be within a range that includes *but is not limited to* the norm or average.

For example, the average age at which children walk alone is 12 months, but the typical range is 8.2 to 17.6 months, which allows for quite a bit of variability in what is considered typical or healthy. Throughout this chapter's discussion of body growth, brain growth, motor development, and sensory and perceptual development, we will come to understand what normative or typical physical development is. Armed with this knowledge, we can consider how to best prevent, identify, and/or treat atypical development—and enhance optimal development during infancy and toddlerhood.

Besides these screening tools used by healthcare professionals, what are the other sources of data on infant and toddler growth? In the past, many practitioners in the United States have relied upon those published by the government's Centers for Disease Control (CDC). But in order to have a single international standard of physical growth—one that is updated for the 21st century and establishes children who are predominantly breastfed for the first 4 months and then continue to be breastfed throughout the first 12 months while other foods are introduced as the normative model for development—the World Health Organization (WHO) collected data from 8,500 high-socioeconomic-status but ethnically diverse and culturally diverse children from Brazil, Ghana, India, Norway, Oman, and the United States between 1997 and 2003.

The results of this Multicentre Growth Reference Study (MGRS) study were published in 2006 and serve as international standards of growth. These results assume that no matter where in the world a child is born, that child has the potential to develop within the same range of height and weight as any other—as long as they have access to high-quality care in the first few years. Using growth charts such as these, we are better able to detect and/or intervene in the event of malnutrition and other less-than-ideal conditions at an early age.

Changes in Body Proportions

Growth during infancy and toddlerhood is not always smooth and gradual; it can occur in spurts over periods as short as 24 hours. And growth does not proceed equally in all parts of the body, so we can characterize changes in body proportions by means of two unique growth patterns, as well as one set of growth curves.

The first growth pattern is the **proximodistal** (prox-eh-mo-DIS-tal) growth pattern, or the *near-to-far and inside-out* trend. In this pattern of growth, the chest (because it contains the internal organs vital to survival) grows more rapidly than the arms and legs, which in turn grow faster than the hands and feet. And because toddlers' chest circumference begins to exceed their abdominal circumference, they start to look leaner as they grow than they did as infants.

In addition to the proximodistal growth pattern, changes in body proportions also follow a **cephalocaudal** (sef-fa-lo-CAW-dal) growth pattern or trend, which is also known as the *head-to-toe or top-down* trend. Because the brain develops more rapidly than the lower part of the body, it also takes up a greater proportion of overall body size during early life, both prenatally and postnatally.

The brain's relatively advanced development early on, compared to other parts of the body, is likely a result of the brain being responsible for so many vital functions, such as heart pumping and breathing, as well as receiving necessary signals from other organs such as the eyes and ears.

Examination of growth curves, as in those within Figure 5.4, also reveals that physical growth is **asynchronous**, meaning it does not occur at the same rate in every bodily system; in fact, it varies in both timing and rate. Each curve in Figure 5.4 illustrates the rate and timing of

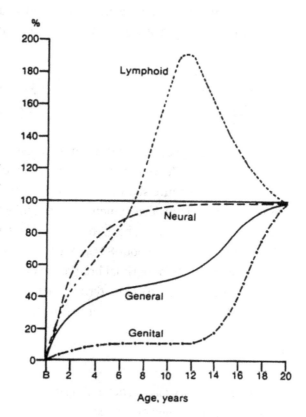

FIG. 5.4   Growth Curves Over the First 20 Years of Life

K. Fujii, Growth Curves Over the First 20 Years of Life, from "Re-vericia-tion with Regard to Scammon's Growth Curve Proposal of Fujimmon's Growth Curve as a Tentative Idea," *American Journal of Sport Science*, vol. 5, no. 3. Copyright © 2017 by Science Publications.

growth in a different body system, such as Neural, Lymphoid, Genital, and General. Together the curves reveal that the growth of the body exemplifies the polydirectional pattern of development, because the various bodily systems change in different directions, at different rates, during different periods (Fujii, 2017)

For example, the Neural Growth Curve represents growth of the brain, nervous system, eyes, and upper face (the jaw does not mature until the adolescent growth spurt). Notice that this system grows quickly compared to the other three body systems. Why? The reason is that the brain is responsible for controlling many bodily functions, such as heart rate and breathing, so it is vital that this body system develop at a rate that seems not unlike the speed of light.

The Lymphoid Growth Curve shows the development of the lymph glands (which are part of the immune system and contain the white blood cells that protects us from infection), along with the thymus gland, the tonsils, and the appendix. The relatively rapid growth of this system during infancy and childhood indicates the need for protection against disease while our bodies are still immature. The growth of the Lymphoid system peaks at approximately age 12 and then declines as the thymus and tonsils being to shrink, revealing a polydirectional pattern of development.

The General Growth Curve refers to height, weight, bone growth, and muscle growth. The shape of this curve is sigmoid or an S-curve, which suggests that growth occurs rapidly in infancy and early childhood, becomes slow but steady during middle childhood, reverts back to rapid growth in adolescence, increases slightly after adolescence, and then stops—reminding us that most people reach their adult height by age 20, and that growth is indeed polydirectional.

What Brain Growth Changes Occur During the First Two Years of Life?

Let's go back to the Neural Growth Curve for a moment. We saw, in Figure 5.4, rapid development in the Neural Growth Curve that slows down around age 4 (note that growth does not stop, it merely slows down). The figure shows the curve beginning at birth, but the "brain growth spurt" really begins during prenatal development, at about mid-pregnancy when nerve cells in the fetal brain and nervous system, or *neurons*, begin to differentiate and migrate to different parts of the brain.

The rest of this spurt, about 83%, takes place postnatally, revealing that adequate stimulation is necessary after birth for optimal brain development. This suggests that parenting is so vital that it actually "chisels" children's brain development, from infancy and continuing through early adulthood (Belsky & deHann, 2011; Guyer, Pérez-Edgar, & Crone, 2018).

Plasticity

Our brain is relatively plastic, depending upon our age. **Plasticity** refers to the capacity of an object or a substance to be formed or shaped. Describing the human brain as "plastic" is appropriate, because the brain is certainly shaped or molded by experience.

Brain plasticity is consistent with the lifelong pattern of development (though stronger in infancy and childhood than in later life), and it results from two different types of processes. The first type is **experience-expectant** processes, or experiences that are generally expected to occur in most individuals' lives because they have occurred over the course of evolutionary history, such as acquisition of language. The second process that contributes to brain plasticity is called **experience-dependent**. It occurs when we are exposed to information unique to us in both timing and character, such as the learning of multiple languages.

The concepts of experience-expectant and experience-dependent processes emphasize *which* experiences occur in our individual context. How do we describe *when* they occur? There are two types of windows of time during development in which we must experience, or ideally should experience, certain events.

The difference between them is that **critical periods** are time intervals in which an event *must* occur in order for normal development to take place, while **sensitive periods** are time intervals in which an event *ideally* occurs for optimal development to take place. For example, there is a critical period in early life during which exposure to speech is necessary in order for us to learn a language; exposure to multiple languages ideally occurs during a sensitive period in childhood when we can acquire additional languages quite easily. After adolescence, it is much more difficult to train the brain's wiring to comprehend, and produce, new sounds and structures.

The existence of critical and sensitive periods means that our brain's degree of plasticity may be a function of our age. Thus we know that a gene–environment interaction takes place in which the brain changes in response to different experiences (starting in utero and continuing through childhood, adolescence, and even beyond), and behavior occurs as a result—rather than the brain merely commanding behavior, as is often assumed (Mariotti, Palumbo , Pellegrini, 2019; van Dyck & Morrow, 2017).

Myelination, Synaptogenesis, and Synaptic Pruning

Human brain development undergoes rapid and drastic changes in the first two years after birth, as a result of a number of processes, including myelination and synaptogenesis (Zhang et al., 2019). **Myelination** is the process by which myelin, the fatty sheath that insulates a neuron's axon, thickens; this thickening allows signals to travel throughout the nervous system more efficiently (Lebel & Deoni, 2018).

Because myelin is fat-based, children need a fatty diet in the first two years of life, ideally from breast milk. Myelination does not occur evenly across the different lobes of the brain but begins in the regions most necessary to infants' and toddlers' functioning, namely, the motor and sensory areas of the cerebral cortex.

The more myelination has occurred, the more quickly we think when we see or hear something. A diet poor in both quantity and quality of food during the first two years can lead to a smaller brain, lower IQ, and poor performance in school, illustrating the multidimensional as well as lifelong patterns of development. Myelination continues to about age 30, but at a slower rate than during the brain's growth spurt.

The brain growth spurt we have been discussing takes place in both the brain stem and the outer layer of gray matter, called the *cerebral cortex* or *cerebrum*. The exception to the spurt is the *cerebellum*, the structure at the base of the brain that looks like a miniature brain. The cerebellum controls voluntary movement and balance—just those abilities that are necessary, say, when a toddler learns to ride a balance bicycle—and the coordination of hand and eye movements, such as when using a

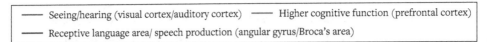

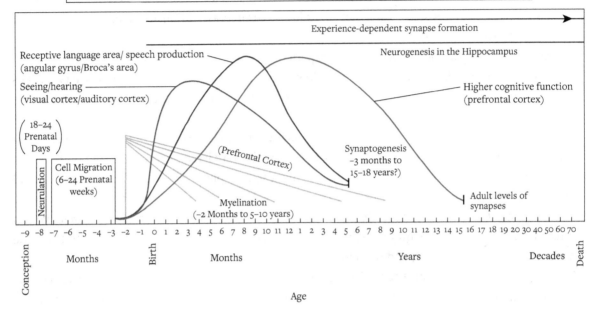

Note. This graph illustrates the importance of prenatal events, such as the formation of the neural tube (neurulation) and cell migration; critical aspects of synapse formation and myelination beyond age three; and the formation of synapses based on experience, as well as neurogenesis in a key region of the hippocampus (the dentate gyrus), throughout much of life.

FIG. 5.5   Milestones of Brain Development

Thompson & Nelson, 2011.

spoon to eat. The cerebellum has its own growth spurt, beginning about 1 month before birth and continuing to about 18 months of age. Overall, however, the brain reaches 80% of adult size by age 3 and 90% of adult size by age 5 (Malina, Bouchard, & Bar-Or, 2004). That this interval is so short indicates that the cerebellum's growth spurt occurs at a faster rate and over a shorter period of time than that of the brain in general, perhaps because the need to crawl, step, and walk is such a vital part of early life.

As you can see in Figure 5.5, the majority of the neurons are initially formed between the first and second trimesters of pregnancy. During this time, the neurons also begin to migrate to different regions of the brain and then begin differentiating by producing axons, dendrites, and synapses (Hadders-Algra, 2018; Thompson & Nelson, 2001).

Synapses are the gaps between neurons where they come close together, but do not touch, in order to communicate with one another via chemical substances or **neurotransmitters** such as serotonin, which cross the gap. The number of synapses in the average child exceeds that of the average of adult; as we will learn in the next section, this is because synapses are pruned over time (van Dyck & Morrow, 2017). The process by which synapses are created is referred to as **synaptogenesis**. Synaptogenesis occurs primarily in childhood as a result of gene–environment interactions.

The role of the environment in synaptogenesis is that it is an experience-dependent process in which children's brains thrive with a broad range of stimulating experiences in which they are interacting with other people (such as hearing someone speak to them slowly while making eye contact, being massaged, interacting with soft dolls, looking at board books) versus watching a screen.

In fact, research documents a relationship between exposure to fast-paced television in the first three years of life and later attention deficits (Christakis et al., 2018; Gao et al., 2019).

So not all forms of brain stimulation are equal, nor are all forms of stimulation developmentally appropriate. Understimulation (such as sitting in a crib for the majority of the day, or moving around with an adult but not being engaged in eye contact and/or interaction) of a child's brain can also put them at a disadvantage.

Neurons may die because of a lack of developmentally appropriate stimulation. And when they die, the synapses created between these neurons will also die, a process referred to as **synaptic pruning**.

Although the loss of neurons may be the result of the person receiving too little brain stimulation from their environment, pruning or "sculpting" of the structure of the brain, via the loss of connections between neurons, is not always a problem. In fact, a lack of pruning, and the resulting overabundance of neuronal connections, is associated with autism spectrum disorder (Gilmore, Knickmeyer, & Gao, 2018; Muhle, Reed, & Stratigos, 2018).

In addition to infants needing developmentally appropriate stimulation for healthy brain development, they also need a complete lack of stimulation—sleep—for healthy brain development, a topic to which we now turn (Dutil et al., 2018).

What Is Necessary for High-Quality Sleep in the First Two Years?

According to the National Sleep Foundation (2019), infants need between 14 and 17 total hours of sleep every 24 hours during the first 2 months of life, as you can see recommended in Figure 5.6.

Most infants divide these hours into small blocks of about 1 to 3 hours each and wake up in between to be fed, given that an infant's stomach is approximately the size of a cherry and empties quickly.

Such short intervals of infant sleep mean that new birth parents, especially those who are breastfeeding (and perhaps pumping milk to store for future use), very much need support from others to tend to every-day chores of food shopping, meal preparation, laundry, and so on. Such support would give them some time to rest adequately, given their own fractured sleep, and therefore be as present, engaged, and attached as possible with their babies.

Around 3 months of age, infants become sensitive to patterns of day and night; this is when they begin to shift to a schedule of 13 to 15 total hours of sleep every 24 hours. In fact, Mateo had his first extended period of sleep (lasting 6 hours) at exactly 12 weeks of age.

National Sleep Foundation's Sleep Duration Recommendations:

Age	Recommended	May be appropriate	Not recommended
Newborns			
0-3 months	14 to 17 hours	11 to 13 hours	Less than 11 hours
		18 to 19 hours	More than 19 hours
Infants			
4-11 months	12 to 15 hours	10 to 11 hours	Less than 10 hours
		16 to 18 hours	More than 18 hours
Toddlers			
1-2 years	11 to 14 hours	9 to 10 hours	Less than 9 hours
		15 to 16 hours	More than 16 hours
Preschoolers			
3-5 years	10 to 13 hours	8 to 9 hours	Less than 8 hours
		14 hours	More than 14 hours
School-aged Children			
6-13 years	9 to 11 hours	7 to 8 hours	Less than 7 hours
		12 hours	More than 12 hours
Teenagers			
14-17 years	8 to 10 hours	7 hours	Less than 7 hours
		11 hours	More than 11 hours

FIG. 5.6   Sleep Recommendations by Age

Hirshkowitz, et al., Sleep Recommendations by Age, from "National Sleep Foundation's Sleep Time Duration Recommendations:Methodology and Results Summary," Sleep Health, vol. 1, no. 1, pp. 41. Copyright © 2014 by Elsevier B.V.

By 6 months of age, most infants sleep through the night, but night waking increases again around 12 months of age, typically because of a toddler's increasing imagination. This emotional development often leads to fears and nightmares, but a transitional object like a security blanket or a stuffed animal "lovey" can help then.

By about 12 months of age, most children establish a consistent nighttime sleep cycle with just one daytime nap (Dias et al, 2018). The 13–15 hour schedule lasts until approximately 18 months of age, and then it shortens to 12–14 hours with about one daytime nap, until about 3 years of age (National Sleep Foundation, 2019).

Despite the impact that infant sleep (or lack thereof) can have on parents, waking at night for feedings is thus normal and is not considered problematic. It should be noted that the lack of paid leave time for new parents in the United States can magnify the enormous stress with which birth parents must cope while trying to express milk every two to three hours at work at (and consider how such stress and lack of support for wanting to do what is in the best interest of one's child could multiply, say, for individuals who are a trans man, that is, their identity is male yet they are certainly able to give birth and breastfeed); this may lead them to stop breastfeeding prematurely, given that employers' compliance with the law about milk expression in the workplace varies quite a bit, as does employers' implementation of available spaces for such (Demirci et al., 2018; Furman, 2018). Colic, on the other hand, unlike waking at night for feedings, may be problematic. Let's consider it now.

Colic

Colic is a condition that professionals have not always understood very well, but they diagnose it based on an infant's continual crying that cannot be relieved by the usual comforting techniques, such as gentle rocking. Most cases of colic end between 2 and 3 months of age and are not associated with any negative long-term outcomes for the child (Bell et al., 2018).

Yet because there is no known cause (although it may be due to abdominal pain) and no known treatment for colic, it can be especially frustrating to parents. During those first few months, parents want nothing more than to relieve the crying and then sleep themselves. (Remember, no matter how understandably frustrated one is with an infant's chronic crying and one's own sleep deprivation, to never ever shake a baby. Such shaking can cause brain damage or death. As long as a baby is safe in a crib, for the adult to do some deep breathing and/or meditation in a different room can help quite a bit if no other adults are available to help.)

How can a parent know an infant does indeed have colic after having checked whether a sleepless child is hungry, is hot or cold, has a soiled diaper, or is allergic to their sleepwear (some children will not tolerate polyester and need cotton sleepwear)? One classic way is to use Wessel's *rule of three*: If an otherwise healthy and well-fed infant cries for more than 3 hours a day for more than 3 days in 1 week over the course of 3 weeks, colic is the likely cause (Wessel et al., 1954).

If parents use this rule and find their babies are indeed colicky, one suggestion for helping the baby is the *colic carry*. In the colic carry, the parent rocks the baby gently while holding the baby's belly close to their own body. Colic is likely physical in origin, but this does not mean emotional soothing cannot help. Massaging the infant's back at the same time can be particularly helpful, and experimental research shows that lavender oil inhaled via aromatherapy reduces infant crying and may also improve parental mood (Vaziri et al., 2018).

Intriguing new research also suggests that colic represents stomach inflammation and dysbiosis, which we learned in Chapter 4 is the disruption of gut microorganisms, so that certain strains of probiotics may be helpful to infants with colic. Ask your MD or ND physician before using any child probiotics. The correct strain, dosage, and duration of use need to be determined on a case-by-case basis (Lee et al., 2018; Pärtty, Rautava, & Kalliomäki, 2018; Rhoads et al., 2018).

Sleep Hygiene in Infants and Toddlers

So far, we have discussed how much sleep children need in the first 2 years of life, as well as what may or may not be problems with sleep during this time. But how can parents ensure sleep hygiene for their babies, as well as for themselves? This is very important, because low levels of **health literacy**, or the ability to obtain, understand, and use health information, in parents are associated with suboptimal parenting practices.

Low levels of health literacy in parents are also associated with suboptimal parenting practices specifically with regard to sleep, such as allowing a television or other such device in a child's bedroom or not ensuring that a child sleeps for a sufficient duration. High levels of health literacy are associated with parents perceiving that there are benefits to shared reading (Bathory et al., 2016; Hutton et al., 2017; Ogi et al., 2018).

Tech & Media

Online Training to Teach Parents Safe Sleep Space Creation

Online instruction is an effective way to help parents of infants and toddlers learn better sleep hygiene, particularly with regard to creating safe sleep environments. After researchers developed an online training program that taught parents how to create a safe sleep environment, which incorporated instructions, modeling, rehearsal, and feedback, the researchers measured parents' understanding of how to create a safe sleep environment—before and after they had the parents complete the online training program (Austin, Doering, & Davies, 2018).

Parents' understanding of how to create a safe sleep environment increased significantly from the pretest to the posttest, as did parents' ability to identify sleep risks on photos provided to them. The research showed that more prenatal care providers, as well as pediatricians, may wish to provide parents with similar online training programs to improve parents' understanding of good sleep hygiene, specifically in terms of safe sleep space creation (Austin, Doering, & Davies, 2018).

• • • •

Health literacy specific to infant sleep can be taught effectively, which is great news for our ability to err on the resilience side of the risk–resilience pattern of development, as we see in the *Tech & Media: Online Training to Teach Parents Safe Sleep Space Creation* box.

Let's consider some best practices regarding sleep, especially for the early months that set the stage for later sleep patterns, for better or worse in the child and the rest of the family (Bathory & Tomopoulos, 2017; Voltaire & Teti, 2018).

Sleep hygiene for infants and toddlers includes shared reading as soon as possible after birth. The American Association of Pediatrics also recommends swaddling; pacifiers; placing babies on their backs with no blankets, toys, or stuffed animals, nor any loose bedding that could cause suffocation; using a firm sleep surface; and never placing a baby to sleep on a sofa or an armchair (American Academy of Pediatrics, 2020.

Also recommended are regular bedtime routines (bath and books), earlier bedtimes and sufficient hours of sleep (to ensure physical growth, memory consolidation, and language learning, as well as to prevent separation anxiety). These are greatly enhanced by a *sleep-promoting environment* of quiet and calm behavior before bedtime, darkness or lights off along with the use of a night light (a star projector night light has been a favorite of my son), no devices in the room other than a sound

Pan & Zoom

Bed Sharing

In this box, we pan across or take a panoramic wide-angle view of what the research data tell us about co-sleeping or bed sharing. Bed sharing between infants and parents is biologically appropriate, as it is an evolutionary adaptation of ensuring survival and it facilitates a plethora of benefits, including breastfeeding, sleep for infant and birth parent, monitoring of the infant, and bonding. In fact, a review of the research indicates that infants who bed-share experience longer breastfeeding time per night and are significantly older when they stop breastfeeding (Baddock et al., 2019; Bartick, Tomori, & Ball, 2018).

Yet this same research review found bed sharing to be associated with an increased risk of sudden infant death syndrome at least in cultures where bed sharing isn't the norm (SIDS is rare in cultures where bed sharing is the norm), when bed sharing occurs on a sofa, when infants heads aren't clear of bedding, and/or when parents smoke or use alcohol/drugs before bedtime, as well as when parents carry excess weight and/or are overtired (Baddock et al., 2019). So there are both risks and benefits to bed sharing.

Although the dominant culture in the United States can be critical of bed sharing, parents have a right to make an informed decision and not be stigmatized by healthcare professionals about their choices—especially if it has a chilling effect on communication with providers (Baddock et al., 2019; Tully & Sullivan, 2018).

Further, when emphasis and energy are spent on warning of the dangers of bed sharing, it diverts attention away from providing families with greater structural support to address other risk factors—risk factors that, when taken care of, help us err on the resilience side of the risk–resilience pattern, such as extended sleep deprivation (due to a lack of universal paid parental leave), a lack of universal healthcare and mental healthcare to address problems that could interfere with sleep, and our lack of paid universal home visitations from nurses in the newborn period (Bartick, Tomori, & Ball, 2018).

• • • •

machine, a cool room after a warming bath, and the use of lavender or rose aromatherapy (Field, 2017; Hutton et al., 2017; Mindell et al., 2017; Mindell & Moore, 2018). Quiet can be hard to come by for families in low-income neighborhoods, so again, resources that some take for granted reflect inequities in children's development.

We haven't yet discussed bed sharing; please see the *Pan & Zoom: Bed Sharing* box.

What Do We Know About the Growth of Teeth and Nutrition Quality?

Infants begin drooling at around 4 months of age, which is an initial sign that teeth will soon arrive. Then, between the ages of 6 months and 12 months, the front teeth (both upper and lower) rupture through the gums.

This process is referred to as tooth eruption or **teething**
and is the final stage of the process in which teeth form; increases in a child's weight and/or height are associated with an earlier emergence of primary teeth (Shaweesh & Al-Batayneh, 2018). Teething can cause more than drooling, including night waking and sleep problems. To determine whether a child is teething, you may want to run your finger along the gum line to feel whether it is swollen.

The 20 primary teeth are formed inside the gums at birth, and typically all of them will have erupted by 3 years of age. As you can see in Figure 5.7, the timing of tooth eruption depends on the location of the tooth.

The American Dental Association recommends that a child's first dental appointment occur within 6 months of the appearance of the first tooth and no later than the first birthday (American Academy of Pediatric Dentistry, 2018). Early attention is especially valuable because tooth decay in the primary teeth can damage the underlying permanent adult teeth or cause them to be poorly aligned.

Age Tooth Comes In (months)	Age Tooth Is Lost (years)
Central incisor (8 - 12)	Central incisor (6 - 7)
Lateral incisor (9 - 13)	Lateral incisor (7 - 8)
Canine/cuspid (16 - 22)	Canine/cuspid (10 - 12)
First molar (13 - 19)	First molar (9 - 11)
Second molar (25 - 33)	Second molar (10 - 12)
Second molar (23 - 31)	Second molar (10 - 12)
First molar (14- 18)	First molar (9- 11)
Canine/cuspid (17 - 23)	Canine/cuspid (9 - 12)
Lateral incisor (10 - 16)	Lateral incisor (7 - 8)
Central incisor (6 - 10)	Central incisor (6 - 7)

FIG. 5.7   The Timing of Tooth Eruption

Breastfeeding as a Social Justice Issue

In Chapter 4, we talked about the superior nutrition that breast milk provides to children. Research also shows that breastfeeding is associated with the lifelong pattern of development. That is, babies who are breastfed for at least 6 months are less likely to be overweight or obese when they enter preschool as well as adolescence (Pattison et al., 2019).

But breastfeeding is a social justice issue, and not just because women who are incarcerated are often separated from their babies and receive little to no informational support or practical physical space support to breastfeed and/or pump. This puts their babies at a disadvantage in terms of the polydirectional pattern outcomes of breastfeeding, which include *physical development*, such as a decreased chance of obesity; *cognitive development*, such as increased risk of lower intelligence; and *emotional development*, such as an increased risk of disrupted bonding and attachment (Shlafer et al.,

2018). The criminal "justice" system often seems to be, intentionally or not, focused less on reform and more on punishment—in this case, women and their children.

Breastfeeding is also a social justice issue given that workplace support for breastfeeding varies by employment type, with professional and management industries providing more support than service and transportation industries. If a birth parent works in a service position, they and their baby are more likely to be prevented from receiving the advantages that breastfeeding provides to both of them (Boutwell, Young, & Meldrum, 2018).

That is, they loses the health benefit (breastfeeding protects against a birth parent later developing breast cancer) and their baby loses the health and cognitive benefits (lower risk of obesity, greater chance of higher intelligence). The latter therefore advantages other children in school who were breastfed and puts their baby at a disadvantage, decreasing their baby's chance of academic success relative to others and perhaps also perpetuating class differences and the cycle of the working poor; *social inequalities are therefore both an effect and a cause of unequal access to power and resources* (Boutwell, Young, & Meldrum, 2018; Dodgson, 2018; P. H. Smith, 2018).

Just as disturbing is how one study found that even birth parents who are physicians, a career often considered the epitome of professions and with the greatest knowledge about health, struggle to find sufficient time and dedicated private space to pump when they return to work (Melnitchouk, Scully, & Davids, 2018).

The Affordable Care Act requires employers with 50 or more employees to provide sufficient break time and private space (that is not a bathroom) for an employee to express or pump milk. But without specific insurance benefits to cover the breast pump and supplies, as well as lactation consultants who can provide support and a work schedule that allows for breaks of sufficient length to express milk, even many of the birth parents whose workplaces provide lactation rooms end up being unable to provide their babies with breast milk throughout the first year of life (Salganicoff, 2018).

Consumption of Solid Food

Solid food should be introduced at around 5 to 6 months, because by that time the intestines are mature enough to digest baby food, and because this is the age at which stronger neck muscles allow infants to turn their head away to indicate *satiety* or satisfaction of hunger. Cow's or goat's milk can be introduced at 12 months of age, but not before (goat's milk has the same calories and nutrients as cow's milk but more essential fatty acids, and children are less likely to develop allergies to it).

Breastfeeding and consumption of solid foods should be negatively related to one another; that is, solid foods should be postponed until at least 6 months of age, while breastfeeding should continue until at least 6 months of age. Once children reach somewhere between 18 and 24 months of age, toddlers can become picky eaters and prefer to simply "graze," eating small amounts rather than entire meals. Much of this change is due to the slowing down of growth in toddlerhood (children triple their birth weight in the first year, but gain an average of only 5 pounds in the second year). Toddlers' newfound ability to feed themselves and therefore choose what they eat also plays a role in this change. Another factor is the rapid changes in other areas of their lives; children tend to prefer the safety of just a few familiar foods as they begin to explore walking, running, and climbing (as we will learn later in the section on motor development).

Since toddlers tend to eat small amounts, it is extremely important that these small amounts be of high quality—including finger foods like carrots, yogurt, cheese, broccoli, peanut butter, and fresh and dried fruit. Infants and toddlers are less fussy eaters and eat more nutrient-dense food if they eat during family meals—these may not be practical all the time, but the more often regular family meals occur, the better (Verhage et al., 2018).

Parents may also want to resist any temptation to pressure children to eat vegetables, as the research data indicate that parent pressure to eat vegetables and/or parent use of other foods (sweets) to reward vegetable consumption is associated with children being fussier and more resistant to wanting to eat vegetables (Holley, Haycraft, & Farrow, 2018).

Repeated exposure to new foods, including not just the actual food but picture-book portrayals of fruits and vegetables, may increase children's willingness to accept such foods (Owen, Kennedy, Hill, & Houston-Price, 2018). A new food should be presented up to 15 times before a child is willing to try it, so parents should not give up preparing and serving the vegetables and other food they prefer their children eat; exposure to a certain flavor also predicts acceptance of such flavor later on, revealing a lifelong pattern of development in food preference (Ahern et al., 2019).

Infants are more accepting of new flavors (and require fewer exposures) than toddlers and older children, suggesting that infancy may be an ideal, and sensitive, period for introducing a wide array of new foods into a child's diet. The number of foods to which an infant is exposed also matters greatly, especially vegetables cooked so that they are tasty: Children are more likely to eat vegetables if they are offered a variety of vegetables at a single meal rather than one vegetable, which they may or may not like (Carstairs et al., 2018).

What Do Well-Baby Exams Involve?

During the first year of life, babies need routine checkups to make sure they are growing adequately, to identify any problems as soon as possible, and to provide any necessary interventions. These well-baby exams include measuring a child's length, weight, and head circumference (percentile changes in head circumference may be a marker for autism spectrum disorders); conducting a physical exam; providing vaccines; and assessing the child in terms of motor development.

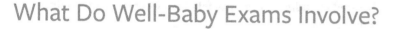

Mentor Minute

Dr. Sandra Braganza

1) Describe your work, please.
I am a general pediatrician and director of the Social Pediatrics Residency program at The Children's Hospital at Montefiore. The program's focus is on training residents to care for children in underserved communities. We prepare residents with the knowledge, skills, and attitudes required to practice social medicine to improve the health status of vulnerable and underserved populations, and we teach residents to partner in and promote efforts to create social change that will promote equity and health for all. Residents receive a comprehensive educational curriculum on advocacy for children, families, and communities.

FIG. 5.8   Dr. Sandra Braganza

2) How does social justice inform your work?

We are a social medicine program, so we focus on the major role that equity, wealth, and opportunities—or lack thereof—play in a given community's health. We teach residents to create social change to promote equity. How? We involve them in activities that focus on individual advocacy, such as how to help individual family members acquire resources (such as free breastfeeding support groups). We also have residents engage in a great deal of self-exploration: We ask them about all the things that helped you become a doctor and how much more difficult it may have been for students with many obstacles, and then to understand the obstacles in their patients' lives, such as housing insecurity, food insecurity, and/or a lack of social capital.

We work in interdisciplinary teams, including clinical psychologists, to help residents appreciate all the biopsychosocial factors when working with families. For instance, before they suggest better nutrition, they need to understand if the family lives in a food desert and/or if the family has the budget to buy fruits and vegetables. Residents visit local bodegas and local schools and make home visits to see what their patients' worlds are like. Once they understand their patients' communities, we teach them how they can link their patients to better resources. The socioeconomic backgrounds of the residents are mixed, but no matter where they come from, they have all made a commitment to working with the underserved.

3) How did you become involved in social justice and/or advocacy?

When I was an undergraduate, I had done a lot of volunteering, including in a daycare, a childcare, and mentoring younger students. The seed for reaching out to others was planted very early in my career. Social justice is part of my day-to-day practice, and advocacy is one tool to implement some social change.

4) What are your thoughts on how social justice can improve child and adolescent development?

Providing children early on with appropriate resources and stimulating their brain development provides them with a foundation to grow. Early-childhood education is fundamental, and opportunities for children to play and interact with others therefore improves everyone's well-being.

5) What suggestions do you have for undergraduate students who are interested in making a change in child and adolescent development?

Learn the research methods and the findings. Appreciate what developmental science can tell us about brain stimulation. Become involved in any community organization that concerns development in any way. Most importantly, find out what matters to you and then learn all you can about it to make it a difference.

· · · ·

We will discuss vaccines and motor development in subsequent sections. For now, also note that well-baby exams give parents a chance to ask their pediatrician any questions they may have about their child or themselves (such as treatment options for postpartum depression). Most pediatricians recommend that children have well baby exams at 2 weeks of age, once a month from 1 to 6 months, then at the ages of 9 months, 12 months, 18 months, 24 months, 30 months, 36 months, and finally once a year.

In the meantime, to learn more about the role of social justice in the practice of pediatrics, read the *Mentor Minute: Dr. Sandra Braganza* box.

Why Are Vaccines Necessary for Everyone's Health?

Research indicates that autism rates appear to be rising over time, and in numerous countries across the globe (Fombonne, 2018). Yet the scientific data do not support the view that rising autism rates are associated with vaccines.

It is worth discussing how the misunderstanding about vaccines and autism came about in the first place. In the late 1990s, one case study (with a sample of a mere 12 children) reported that thiomersal, the mercury preservative used in some of the MMR vaccines (to prevent measles, mumps, and rubella) was associated with the onset of autistic symptoms (Wakefield et al., 1998).

This study was later retracted, given its questionable sample size and some ethical concerns—and because it failed to address the possibility that the relationship between the MMR vaccine and autism may not be causal but rather temporal. That is, the study did not consider the weakness of correlational conclusions—that is, that the onset of autism might co-occur with the MMR vaccine simply because of timing (such as how the onset of autism symptoms can co-occur with the timing of some vaccinations), rather than cause and effect.

Yet vaccination rates began to drop as a result of the attention given to this study and the lack of critical questioning of it, and an antivaccine movement began to burgeon. Unfortunately, some have begun to err on the risk side of the risk–resilience pattern of development, and the number of vaccine-preventable diseases has since risen sharply—for example, the highly preventable outbreak of measles at Disneyland in 2015 and in Minnesota in 2017 (Dubé, Vivion, & MacDonald, 2015; Kubin, 2019).

Let's stop for a minute and consider something else. The increase over time in autism is confounded by cohort effects we learned about in Chapter 2, as is the case with a good deal of longitudinal data. For instance, during the period when autism rates began to rise, changes were made to broaden the diagnostic criteria for autism; in addition, public awareness and recognition of autism rose, and diagnoses began to be made earlier.

All these changes certainly may have increased the rate of diagnosis of autism without implicating the use of vaccines, at least for European American children. But the data show troubling racial and ethnic disparities: Black and Latinx children on the autism spectrum are less likely to receive their first evaluation by the recommended age of 36 months of age—and early diagnosis is key to effective treatment (Bennett, Webster, Goodall, & Rowland, 2019; Christensen et al., 2018; Presmanes, Zuckerman, & Fombonne, 2014; Szatmari, 2017).

Yet keep in mind that a sole focus on treatment can ignore the resiliency of people on the autism spectrum, as well as devalue them and their contributions to society (Bennett, Webster, Goodall, & Rowland, 2019; Christensen et al., 2018; Presmanes, Zuckerman, & Fombonne, 2014; Szatmari, 2017).

So the concept of **neurodiversity**, in which neurological differences among people are respected as much as any other human variation, is one we need embrace. It provides a nonpathological understanding and acceptance of people who have different needs than others—needs that society can better meet once we appreciate them

What Changes Occur in Motor Development During the First Two Years of Life?

At what age do most infants first sit up unaided? Is it normal for children to pull themselves up and stand but not walk?

After reading the first part of this chapter, you should be able to correctly answer that the basis for answering these questions is knowledge of norms for the milestones of motor development. Let's talk about these now, starting with an overview of the normative reflexes seen in neonates or newborns.

Reflexes

Reflexes are involuntary responses to a stimulus, such as blinking when a puff of air is blown at our eyes. Some reflexes are necessary for survival, such as the **rooting reflex**, which occurs when we touch the area around a neonate's mouth and the baby moves in the direction of this stimulation, ensuring that the infant will be able to eat.

Another reflex with survival advantages is the **sucking reflex**, which allows the baby to adjust the sucking pressure according to the flow of milk. This reflex begins almost immediately after birth. The rooting reflex disappears at approximately 5 months of age, and the sucking reflex disappears around 6 months of age.

The **Moro reflex**, which is also called the *parachute reflex*, results in the baby's arms and legs spreading open if the head is dropping abruptly. It seems to be a defensive clinging reaction to being dropped. The Moro reflex is apparent at birth and disappears at approximately 6 months of age.

Other reflexes without a clear survival value but which are (?) certainly valuable to everyday functioning include the **Babinski reflex**, in which a baby's toes will curl out like a fan when the bottom of the foot is stroked. The Babinski reflex disappears at approximately 12 months of age. The **Palmar grasp** reflex occurs when a baby's fingers grip an object placed in the palm. This reflex disappears typically around 4 months of age.

The **standing reflex** and the **stepping reflex** occur when a neonate is held under the arms with feet touching a flat surface like a tabletop or the floor, and it appears as if the baby is making rudimentary movements to stand or step. Both these reflexes disappear around 3 months of age, perhaps because babies' legs become too heavy at this point relative to their weak leg muscles. If so, this indicates that infants are capable of learning, because they adapt their location to their changing body dimensions.

Learning may explain why babies are willing to persist in their attempts to walk when crawling has served them well. That is, they learn that although walking is difficult, it allows them a richer visual experience, offers opportunities to interact with parents in qualitatively new ways, and allows them to cover more ground quickly (Adolph & Hoch, 2019).

Milestones of Fine Motor Skills and Gross Motor Skills

While reflexes occur automatically, motor skills and corresponding advances in cognitive and emotional development benefit when the child is in an optimal environment. For example, when a toy on the floor piques interest so that the infant crawls to it, cognitive development is being stimulated.

Emotional development is occurring as well, because children experience feelings of mastery and accomplishment when they engage in crawling, rolling, sitting up, and reaching—especially in an atmosphere where parents encourage and support their exploration. Therefore, providing infants with ample opportunities to crawl, instead of leaving them for a long time in a stroller or a playpen, stimulates their intrinsic pleasure in movement, an interest that is consistent with the Lifelong pattern of development, that is, an interest in movement pays lifelong. What different types of skills can such nurturing influence?

To answer, we first categorize motor skills into fine and gross. **Fine motor skills** rely on small muscle groups, such as those of the hand. Acts that demonstrate precision and dexterity, like drawing, cutting, and painting, require fine motor skills. Fine motor skills are also needed for the **manipulative skills** with which we move objects, such as throwing and catching.

Percentile	Sitting without Support	Standing with Assistance	Hands and Knees Crawling	Walking with Assistance	Standing Alone	Walking Alone
99th	9.2	11.4	13.5	13.7	16.9	17.6
90th	7.5	9.4	10.5	11.0	13.4	14.4
75th	6.7	8.4	9.3	10.0	12.0	13.1
Average	6.0	7.6	8.5	9.2	11.0	12.1
50th	5.9	7.4	8.3	9.0	10.8	12.0
25th	5.2	6.6	7.4	8.2	9.7	11.0
10th	4.6	5.9	6.6	7.4	8.8	10.0
1st	3.8	4.8	5.2	5.9	6.9	8.2

FIG. 5.9 The Mean Age (in Months) at Which Children Reach Each of the Six Milestones

World Health Organization, "The Mean Age (in Months) at Which Children Reach Each of the Six Milestones," WHO Multicentre Growth Reference Study Group. Copyright © 2006 by World Health Organization.

When we speak of **gross motor skills**, the term *gross* refers to "large," that is, large muscle groups such as those of the legs. Because they activate major segments of the body, or even the entire body, gross motor skills are useful for the **locomotor skills** that move our bodies in space, such as crawling, swimming, running, and walking.

The WHO's Multicentre Growth Reference Study released a Windows of Achievement standard that provides averages for six gross motor milestones. These norms were based on observations by investigators and parents of 816 children in Ghana, India, Norway, Oman, and the United States (WHO Multicentre Growth Reference Study Group, 2006).

Such norms or milestones are important to know because motor development delays have been found in children who had extremely low birth weights, as well as in children who show symptoms of autism spectrum disorder at 1 year of age (Kovaniemi et al., 2018). Longitudinal research has also found that children who achieve motor milestones later tend to have lower IQs when followed up in early adulthood (Flensborg-Madsen & Mortensen, 2018;).

In approximately 90% of the children in the WHO study, five of the six milestones occurred in a fixed sequence (sitting without support occurred first, then standing with assistance, then crawling on the belly, then walking with assistance, and finally walking alone). Crawling on hands and knees sometimes occurred between sitting without support and standing with assistance.

As you can see in Figure 5.9, the mean or average age (in months) at which children reach each of the six milestones is close to the 50th percentile, which is where we expect it to be. For example, the 50th percentile of sitting without support is 5.9 months, and the mean is 6.0.

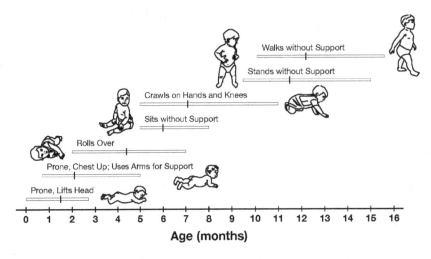

FIG.5.10   Average Ages at Which Infants and Toddlers Reach Gross Motor Milestones

Karen E. Adolph and Scott R. Robinson, Average Ages at Which Infants and Toddlers Reach Gross Motor Milestones, from "Motor Development," Cognitive Processes. Copyright © 2015 by John Wiley & Sons, Inc.

The Motor Skill Trajectory

Figure 5.10 shows the average ages at which infants and toddlers reach major gross motor milestones, with the horizontal bars representing average ranges for age of onset and vertical lines representing median age of onset or the age in the middle of the range (Adolph & Robinson, 2013; Adolph, Hoch, & Cole, 2018). Keep in mind that any one child may or may not follow the milestones in sequence and may even skip some milestones, so viewing the milestone trajectory as obligatory is unfounded and doing so likely causes parents unnecessary stress (Adolph & Robinson, 2013; Adolph, Hoch, & Cole, 2018).

Notice how the horizontal bars or average ranges overlap with one another, if not also show a reversed pattern.

For example, the median age of Crawls on Hands and Knees is 7 months, and the median age of Stands without Support is 11.5 months, so we might expect a child to crawl before standing.

Yet any individual child might meet one milestone later than average (such as Crawling on Hands and Knees at 11 months) yet meet another milestone earlier than average (such as Standing without Support at 10 months).

In this particular example, notice the average ranges for these two milestones not only overlap, but the median ages at which this individual child met these milestones were reversed from average. Yet because each falls within the median range, neither is considered problematic.

Most infants can lift their chins around one month of age. Starting around this time, infants need **tummy time,** or time on their tummies while awake and supervised by an adult, to strengthen their shoulders and neck muscles in order to prevent delays in such motor development as turning over and sitting up. Tummy time should occur for about 20 minutes per day until babies are approximately 6 months of age, or whenever they can roll over on their own. Tummy time can also prevent **plagiocephaly,** or a flattened head (as you can see in Figure 5.11), which occurs as a result of infants being left too long with one side of their head against a flat surface, whether it be a crib mattress, a playpen, or a stroller.

To avoid plagiocephaly (and to increase cognitive development and emotional bonding), infants should not be left in car seats, strollers, swings, or playpens for extended periods; instead, they need be picked up, propped up with a "boppy," held, spoken to, sung to, etc. In addition, infants should be placed to sleep with the head to one side for a week, then the head to the other side for the next week, with the rotation to either side continuing thereafter.

The supine position is much preferred for preventing Sudden Infant Death Syndrome (SIDS), a devastating occurrence that, although it has been on the decline in recent decades, still occurs—with approximately 3,500 sleep-related death still occurring in the United States each year (Bombard et al., 2018). We can reduce SIDS, if not eliminate it, by educating people about proper infant sleep recommendations, as listed in Figure 5.12, as well as by changing public policy.

Regarding public policy, the United States has the highest SIDS rate among developed countries, and it is the only country that does not provide its citizens with universal healthcare, home visitations from nurses in the newborn period, nor universal paid maternity—all of which research indicates protect against SIDS (Carlin & Moon, 2018).

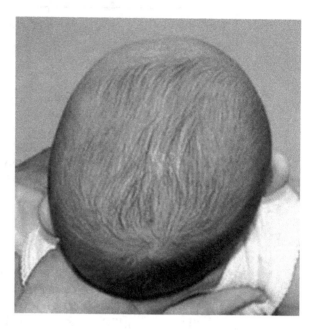

FIG. 5.11   Plagiocephaly

Two-month-olds can demonstrate a "chest up" as they begin to be able to elevate themselves with their arms. Voluntary reaching starts at 3 to 4 months of age with the **ulnar grasp**, in which the fingers clamp an object down against the palm without the thumb, allowing infants to yank on parents' hair, ties, glasses, clothing, and anything else in their path. The ulnar grasp replaces the finger-curling **palmar grasp** of neonates, which was just a grasp, rather than a harbinger of reaching. Newborns will often move their arms toward objects and people, but this is not considered reaching because they don't obtain their desired object.

Voluntary reaching occurs at 3 or 4 months, when infants achieve the ability to voluntarily switch their gaze from one object or person to another, which in turn fosters further cognitive development. It is also at 3 months that infants begin to change their type of cry depending on their need, so it becomes easier for parents to determine whether a child is wet, hungry, or in need of attention. At 3 months babies become relatively less fussy, because they begin to trust that someone takes care of them on a consistent basis.

By 4 months of age, most infants can roll themselves over, and at 5 months they can momentarily sit up alone. Some roll from their tummy to their side and then eventually to their back as early as 3 to 4 months if they are active babies, but calmer babies tend to roll for the first time around at 5 or 6 months. At 5 months of age, after they have spent weeks practicing reaching, infants want to put everything in their mouth. Baby-proofing the residence is vital at this time.

By 6 months of age, most infants weigh approximately 15 pounds, or double their birth weight. Their neck muscles have strengthened so that now they can be lifted up by an adult without their

FIG. 5.12   Recommendations for Preventing SIDS

Recommendations for Preventing SIDS, from "SIDS and Other Sleep-Related Infant Deaths: Updated 2016 Recommendations for a Safe Infant Sleeping Environment," Pediatrics. Copyright © 2016 by American Academy of Pediatrics.

head lagging or falling back (which can damage the neck or spinal cord). Once they can hold up their own heads at this age, infants can turn and look at different objects and consider the differences and similarities between them, taking another step in their cognitive development. They can now also sit up alone for an extended period.

Another milestone that can occur as early as 6 months is achievement of the **pincer grasp** (from the French word for "pinch"), which allows us to pick up a small object with the thumb and forefinger. The pincer grasp replaces the ulnar grasp, and we can usually observe babies using it consistently starting anywhere between 9 and 12 months. When a baby reaches 6 to 9 months of age, most parents begin to notice hand dominance, a preference for using the right hand or the left hand.

Most infants begin to engage in locomotion, or traveling, by crawling, usually by 6 or 7 months of age. As we will see in more detail in Chapter 7, the ability to move actively away from a parent marks the first form of psychological independence.

Parents need to encourage locomotion (in safe areas), rather than showing excessive fear or fretting over it. Parents should note any concerns they have over their child's motor skills at this time, though, since research shows that infants with poorer motor skills at 6 months of age are more likely to develop autism spectrum disorder and/or delays in expressive language and therefore may benefit from a screening for such (LeBarton & Landa, 2019).

Because the ability to release a held object appears at around 7 to 8 months, many infants enjoy repeatedly dropping objects, requiring patience on the part of parents. If dropping becomes excessive and/or includes food, parents may wish to alter the environment by trying to feed a child relatively quickly, then placing the child on the floor to play with toys (especially if a toy bucket or toy trash can is handy to drop objects into).

Admonishing children not to drop things at this age can be a form of reinforcement that increases the behavior, given the pleasure children may receive from defying the adult's wishes.

Most infants begin to *cruise*, or walk from place to place while holding onto a piece of furniture, at around 9 or 10 months. Cruising helps infants explore their environment more actively than ever

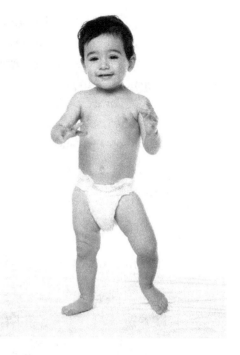

FIG. 5.13   Mateo's First Step

Copyright © 2012 Depositphotos/phakimata.

before, but it also means they are now able to grab things sitting on tabletops. Should a child pick up something potentially dangerous, it is best to squeeze their wrist to release their grip on the object rather than attempt to pull the object out of their hand.

Children begin walking between 9 and 18 months, and parents can help by holding a child by both hands while they move along. One study of infants from the Bloomington, Indiana, Pittsburgh, and New York City areas found that children who lived in homes with stairs went up stairs earlier than infants in single-level homes (at 10.46 and 11.42 months, respectively). Yet the two groups of children did not differ in the age at which they first navigated their way *down* a flight of stairs they encountered (Adolph, Hoch, & Cole, 2018; Berger, Theuring, & Adolph, 2007).

This tells us that we cannot think of motor development as determined by a gradual unfolding of predetermined milestones that are the result only of nature. Rather, they are also a product of the context in which they develop.

By 11 months, infants can stand alone without support. Not long after, at approximately 12 months of age, most can walk three steps alone. *Notice in Figure 5.13 that at 12 months Mateo is not holding his parent's hand.*

The term "toddler" is an apt description, too, because most children do indeed toddle back and forth or stagger as they begin to walk. The average 12-month-old has tripled their birth weight and is about 29 inches tall. These increases in height, along with increasing locomotion and decreasing appetite, make toddlers leaner than infants.

Remember that optimal development of the motor skills we have reviewed can be fostered by nurture, that is, by the child's context. Parents can place blocks, stuffed animals, and rattles just out of reach so infants will move and stretch to reach them. An ideal collection of infant toys has blocks, bubbles, balls, dolls, and trucks (for both girls and boys), pots, pans, and any other household items that can be used in imaginative play and that together offer a variety of colors, shapes, sounds, and textures.

The acquisition of motor skills allows the child to move away from parents and represents the first step not just in physical independence, but also in psychological independence (Mahler, 1974; Walle, 2016). For example, what some people refer to as the "terrible twos" may just be the sprouting of the child's self, less compliant with the parents' wishes and demands and more verbally assertive as vocabulary (including the word "no") grows.

What Occurs in Sensory and Perceptual Development During the First Two Years?

The first **social smile**, a smile that occurs in response to other people rather than, say, to feeling full after a good meal, tends to appear at approximately 6 weeks. If you're wondering what social interactions have to do with this chapter on physical development, consider that the ability to respond to another person—and the ability to develop attention, memory, and language—requires sensation and perception, such as the ability to see, touch, or hear that person. So while we learn next about the multiple changes in our sensory skills during the first two years, keep in mind that it will be easier to remember and apply them when you consider them in relation to the cognitive and emotional domains of development—in other words, the Multidimensional pattern of development.

Newborn   4 weeks   8 weeks   3 months   6 months

FIG. 5.14   A Face as It May Appear to a Newborn and to Us

A. Fogel, " A face as it may appear to a newborn and to us," Infancy: Infant, Family, & Society, ed. 4. Copyright © 2001 by Wadsworth Publishing Co.

Sensation is a physical event, whereas **perception** is a psychological one. Sunlight allows us to see our significant other with the sense of sight, but our brain makes the perception that this person as lovely to us. Reaching for and manipulating objects provides a child with knowledge about an object's properties, such as whether it is malleable or rigid, smooth or rough, and hot or cold to the touch. The coordination of actions, such as a child moving their hands together to grab a cookie, requires depth perception as well. We see again that actions are goal-directed or intentional, which distinguishes them from reflexes.

Vision

Visual acuity, or the lens's ability to focus, is 20/600 (legal blindness is defined as 20/200 vision) in a newborn. This measure indicates that their vision is really quite poor and resembles a blurry photograph as is evident in Figure 5.14.

Yet by the time infants are 6 months of age, their acuity has improved to 20/80, and it reaches 20/20 levels by 4 years of age (Slater et al., 2010). *Binocular vision*, or the ability to use both eyes to focus on the same image, is typically established around 2 to 4 months of age, just when infants begin to voluntarily reach for objects (Wang & Candy, 2010).

Newborn acuity is best when they are looking at something about 8 to 10 inches away from them, such as their parent's face. Newborns show a preference for looking at facelike stimuli as well. Also, they better discriminate among female faces if their primary parent identifies as female, suggesting that experience certainly plays a role in infant facial preference (Reynolds et al., 2017; Reynolds & Roth, 2018).

Infants also show a preference for faces of their own race over those of other races, a preference that is likely based on experience—given that a preference can be reversed and that subsequent racial prejudice can hopefully also be prevented with exposure to others (such as friends, as well as childcare providers) who are racially diverse (Anzures et al., 2013; Quinn, Lee, & Pascalis, 2018).

Hearing

Most neonates have excellent hearing, a physical capability whose implications are consistent with the multidimensional pattern of development, because hearing prepares them for cognitive development,

Tech & Media

Tech & Media in Our Lives: A Sensitive Period for Cochlear Implants?

A cochlear implant is a device surgically implanted behind the ear under the skin, and it contains a microphone and speech processor (to pick up sounds from the environment, especially speech), as well as a receiver that converts the speech signals into electrical impulses that are sent to the auditory nerve system.

By stimulating the auditory nerve, cochlear implants can help foster the development of language in children who experience the onset of deafness. They can also provide us with opportunities to enjoy music and become more aware of surroundings, improving the quality of life.

Is there a critical or sensitive time for hearing development, indicating when children with hearing impairments can or should receive a cochlear implant in order to derive these benefits?

Longitudinal research has shown that both the auditory skills and language skills are greater for children who received cochlear implants before 12 months of age compared to children who received the implants after 12 months of age, and other work indicates that speech and language outcomes are even better when children receive cochlear implants prior to 6 months of age—a practice consistent with guidelines that early hearing detection and intervention include screening by 1 month of age, confirmation of impaired hearing at 3 months of age, and any interventions by 6 months of age (Ruben, 2018; Yoshinaga-Itano et al., 2018).

Thus, there does appear to be an optimal time for cochlear implantation, but missing out on such does not doom a child with hearing impairment to an impoverished life. In fact, some proponents of deaf culture feel deafness is not necessarily a medical condition to be cured, but rather a life to be lived, so parents should be fully informed before making a decision for their child that has lifelong implications.

Hearing-impaired individuals certainly develop optimally and lead successful and satisfying lives. Many in the deaf community advocate raising children bilingually, that is, giving them cochlear implants but also teaching them American Sign Language; nonbinary thinking about cochlear implants is recommended: assuming that one way is the only "right" way fails to consider the many complex variables that families need to consider in order to make decisions in the best interests of their child (Komesaroff, Komesaroff, & Hyde, 2015).

• • • •

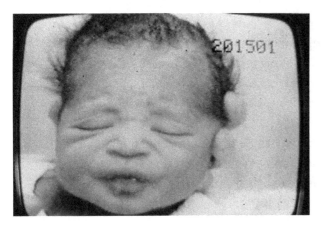

FIG. 5.15 A Neonate after Being Given a Sucrose Solution

Diana Rosenstein and Harriet Oster, "A Neonate after Been given a Sucrose Solution," What the Face Reveals: Basic and Applied Studies of Spontaneous Expression Using the Facial Action Coding System (FACS), ed. Paul Ekman and Erika L. Rosenberg, pp. 310. Copyright © 1997 by Oxford University Press.

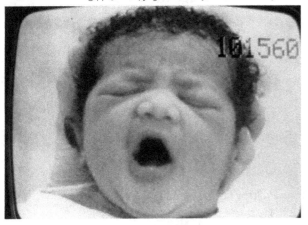

FIG. 5.16 A Neonate after Being Given a Bitter Solution

Diana Rosenstein and Harriet Oster, "A Neonate after Been given a Bitter Solution," What the Face Reveals: Basic and Applied Studies of Spontaneous Expression Using the Facial Action Coding System (FACS), ed. Paul Ekman and Erika L. Rosenbergpp. 311. Copyright © 1997 by Oxford University Press.

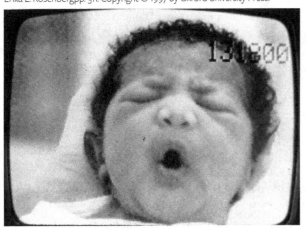

FIG. 5.17 A Neonate after Being Given a Sour Solution

Diana Rosenstein and Harriet Oster, "Neonate after Been given a Sour Solution," What the Face Reveals: Basic and Applied Studies of Spontaneous Expression Using the Facial Action Coding System (FACS), ed. Paul Ekman and Erika L. Rosenberg, pp. 312. Copyright © 1997 by Oxford University Press.

—namely, language acquisition—and for emotional bonding because it allows infants to differentiate between their parents and strangers. What makes this hearing response possible is that auditory development starts in the prenatal stage, and response to external sounds begins sometime in the third trimester. How do we know this?

One classic study had birth parents read Dr. Seuss's *The Cat in the Hat* out loud during the last six weeks of their pregnancy—a study that later research confirmed is evidence that in the womb is where we first hear speech and first learn about intonation, tone, and rhythm (DeCasper & Spence, 1986; Gervain, 2018).

A few days after birth, the newborns were given the opportunity to suck on a pacifier that could turn on a recording of their birth parent's voice reading *The Cat in the Hat* or a different story, depending upon how the babies sucked. The researchers found that after a few trials, the newborns began to suck on the pacifier for *The Cat in the Hat* significantly more than an equivalent group of newborns whose birth parents did not read *The Cat in the Hat* aloud during pregnancy.

But what if the brain is not allowed the opportunity to develop hearing, as in the case of a child who is born hearing-impaired? Will the preference for human speech be possible if we intervene with hearing aids or cochlear implants? To learn more about congenital deafness and whether there is a critical or sensitive period for cochlear implants, see the *Tech & Media in Our Lives: A Sensitive Period for Cochlear Implants?* box.

Taste and Smell

A classic study of newborn reactions to the basic tastes found that 2-hour-old neonates respond consistently to the different sensations of sweet, sour, and bitter, but not salt. *As you can see in Figure 5.15, an initial negative reaction is followed by relaxation and sucking after the neonate is given a sucrose solution. Figure 5.16 and Figure 5.17 show, respectively, neonates' reactions to a bitter solution and a sour solution.*

The lack of consistent response to a salt solution suggests that newborns do not detect the salt taste very well, and preference for salt does not begin until approximately 4 months of age. This indicates that taste seems to mature after birth, so that infants' parents who eat a variety of vegetables easily learn to like vegetables during breastfeeding (Mennella, Daniels, & Reiter, 2017).

Yet flavor preferences develop prenatally as well. Amniotic fluid is altered by context, that is, the foods a birth parent eats, so newborns prefer those flavors at birth. Flavor learning continues after birth, as infants are exposed to breast milk or formula.

It may be that infants who are breastfed for shorter duration or are exclusively formula-fed are more picky eaters of solid foods later on because formula provides a more restricted range of flavor experiences than breastmilk (breastfeeding allows babies to be exposed to the flavors of the food their mothers eat). So they are less accepting of flavors not found in formula and therefore show more **food neophobia**, or fear of novel foods (Bell et al., 2018; Specht et al, 2018).

Newborns have the ability to both detect odors and discriminate among them. The capacity to recognize odors that belong to the parent may facilitate the process of emotional bonding or attachment, too. And both full-term and preterm newborns exposed to the odor of breastmilk show reduced heart rates in response to a medical procedure (Alemdar, 2018; Zhang, Su, Li, & Chen, 2018).

Touch

Infants certainly respond to touch. A review of the research on infant massage shows that it is not only safe but also has many positive benefits: It can reduce crying, improve sleep, lower stress reactions, improve interactions with the mother, and lead to greater physical growth. Massage can help increase necessary weight gain, as well as reduce jaundice and shorten the stay in neonate intensive care units (NICUs), and these benefits are especially pronounced for infants who were born prematurely (Garg, Kabra, & Balasubramanian, 2018; Taheri et al., 2018).

Bedtime routines that include massaging one's infant can help parents achieve better sleep as well (Mindell et al., 2018). To learn about how to care for new parents, who very much need mothering themselves at this point in their lives, see *The First Forty Days: The Essential Art of Nourishing the New Mother* in the *Recommended Reading* section at the end of this chapter.

You might not think that healthy and cared-for babies suffer much pain. Yet even when a birth is free of complications, newborns must undergo a number of procedures that can be painful, such as *venipuncture* or the drawing of blood from the back of the hand for purposes of screening for phenylketonuria and Sickle Cell Disease and for blood typing

Unsurprisingly but delightfully, research shows that those babies exposed to the odor of their their birth parent cry less after venipuncture compared to babies exposed to an odorless diffuser (de Chanville et al., 2017). To learn about a research study that examined the effects of music on newborn pain perception, read the *Cycle of Science* feature at the end of this chapter.

Key Terms

Asynchronous

Babinski Reflex

Cephalocaudal Trend

Critical Periods

Experience-Dependent

Experience-Expectant

Summary

1. **Summarize the growth of the body, including size and proportion, in the first two years of life.** The proximodistal growth pattern means that the chest (because it contains the internal organs vital to survival) grows more rapidly than the arms and legs, which in turn grow faster than the hands and feet. The cephalocaudal (sef-fa-lo-CAW-dal) growth pattern or trend is also known as the *head-to-toe* or *top-down* trend. Physical growth is asynchronous, meaning it does not occur at the same rate in every system.

2. **Paraphrase what we know about the growth of the brain in the first two years of life.** Experience-expectant processes are generally occur in most individuals' lives. Experience-dependent processes occur when we are exposed to information unique to us in both timing and character. Myelination is the process by which myelin, the fatty sheath that insulates a neuron's axon, thickens, allowing signals to travel throughout the nervous system more efficiently. When neurons in the brain die because of a lack of stimulation, the synapses created between these neurons will also die, a process referred to as synaptic pruning. Synaptogenesis is a result of neuron activity that is both spontaneous and a result of experience.

3. **Recall what we know about sleep in the first two years of life.** Infants need between 14 and 17 total hours of sleep every 24 hours during the first 2 months of life. Around 3 months of age, infants shift to a schedule of 13 to 15 total hours of sleep every 24 hours. And by about 12 months of age, most children establish a consistent nighttime sleep cycle with just one daytime nap.

   Sleep hygiene includes shared reading as soon as possible after birth; placing babies on their backs with no blankets, toys, or stuffed animals; no electronic devices; quiet and calm behavior before bedtime; regular bedtime routines (bath and books); and earlier bedtimes and sufficient hours of sleep. Other important elements of good sleep hygiene are a *sleep-promoting environment* of darkness or lights off, along with the use of a night light, a sound machine, a cool room after a warming bath, and the use of lavender or rose aromatherapy.

4. **Discuss the growth of the teeth and the importance of high-quality nutrition.** Between the ages of 6 and 12 months, the front teeth (both upper and lower) rupture through the gums. Between 18 and 24 months, toddlers can become picky eaters; their food preferences are likely related to those of their parents. Repeated exposure to new foods may increase children's willingness to accept them.

5. **Describe what occurs during well-baby exams.** A typical well-baby exam includes measuring a child's length, weight, and head circumference; conducting a physical exam; providing vaccines; and assessing the child in terms of motor development. Well-baby exams also give parents a chance to ask the pediatrician any questions they may have.

6. **Explain why vaccines are safe and necessary.** Not only have vaccines been a major public health success and contributed to the rise in average life expectancy, but also research involving over 90,000 children shows no relationship between the MMR vaccine and an increased risk of autism. Broader diagnostic criteria for autism, earlier diagnosis, and greater public awareness may have increased the rate of diagnosis of autism.

7. **Identify the milestones of motor development in the first two years of life.** Reflexes are involuntary responses to a stimulus, such as blinking when a puff of air is blown at our eyes. Fine motor skills rely on small muscle groups, such as those of the hand. Gross motor skills require large muscle groups such as those of the legs. Because they activate major segments of the body or even the entire body, gross motor skills are useful for the locomotor skills that move our bodies in space, such as crawling, swimming, running, and walking.

8. **Illustrate sensory development and perceptual development in the first two years of life.** The average visual acuity of newborns is really quite poor. Most neonates have excellent hearing. Taste develops before and after birth. Newborns have the ability to both detect odors and discriminate between them. Infant massage is not only safe but also can reduce crying, improve sleep, lower stress reactions, improve interactions with the baby's mother, and lead to greater physical growth and weight gain, especially for infants who were born prematurely.

The Cycle of Science

Research

Why was the study conducted?
The researchers wanted to know if newborns' pain perception while undergoing painful medical procedures could be reduced with exposure to music and/or heartbeat sound recordings (A. Rossi et al., 2018).

Who participated in the study?
The participants were 80 full-term newborns who were between 1 day old and 3 days old.

Which type of design was used?

An experimental design was used, and the independent variable was the music or the sound to which the babies were exposed: Mozart's Sonata for Two Pianos K.448, Beethoven's Moonlight Sonata, a heartbeat recording, or no music. The dependent variables were babies' scores on a neonate pain scale (which measured facial expressions, crying, breathing patterns, and arousal levels), their heart rate, and the oxygen levels in their blood; the oxygen levels are presumably lower with shortness of breath, a sign of stress (A. Rossi et al., 2018).

What were the results?

The researchers found that compared to newborns not exposed to any music, newborns exposed to either of the two musical pieces or the heartbeat recordings showed lowered heart rate and pain perception, as well as increases in oxygen levels in the blood (A. Rossi et al., 2018).

Are the results consistent with theory?

The results are consistent with our understanding that newborns experience pain—and that there are simple, inexpensive, and pleasurable interventions that can reduce such pain.

How can the results be used to improve our lives?

The results can help midwives, birthing centers, and hospital maternity wards engage in better practices to reduce newborn pain.

Exercises

1. What pattern of results would you expect to find if a similar study were conducted with babies born prematurely?

2. Describe an experimental research study that examines the effect of exposure to different bedtime music on 6-month-olds' ability to sleep through the night.

3. If this study had included babies with parents with low levels and high levels of health literacy, the results may have been more powerful. How so?

Helpful Websites

Dr. John Medina is a developmental molecular biologist, and his book *Brain Rules for Baby,* with corresponding website, provides a wealth of information for parents on how to promote their child's brain development: http://brainrules.net/brain-rules-for-baby

The University of Utah's PediNeuroLogic Exams are online videos of pediatric exams with newborns, 3-month-olds, 6-month-olds, 12-month-olds, 18-month-olds, and 2.5-year-olds that demonstrate how normal and abnormal development are assessed via developmental milestones: http://library.med.utah.edu/pedineurologicexam/html/introduction.html

Zero to Three is a national and multidisciplinary nonprofit organization that educates professionals, the public, and parents about the importance of the quality of the first three years of life: https://www.zerotothree.org/

Recommended Reading

Heath, A., Bainbridge, B., & Moore, D. (2004). *Baby massage: The calming power of touch.* London, UK: DK Publishing.

Karp, H. (2015). *The happiest baby on the block.* New York, NY: Bantam Books.

Lim, R. (2001). *After the baby's birth: A complete guide for postpartum women.* Berkeley, CA: Celestial Arts Press.

Ou, H., Greeven, A., & Belger, M. (2016). *The first forty days: The essential art of nourishing the new mothers.* New York, NY: Stewart, Tabori, & Chang.

Cognitive Development in Infancy and Toddlerhood

CHAPTER 6

Snapshot

Suppose you work for a toy company and one of your many duties is to correctly identify the recommended age range for the company's various new toys. These include an activity quilt that makes noise when different areas are pressed, a grab and teethe toy, a soft book with a toy bone that can be hidden in multiple places, a mobile, a pretend car, and a highchair and table toy that bounces when pressed. Baby toys may seem all the same, but your boss tells you that in order to make accurate decisions regarding each toy's recommended age range, you need to use research, rather than your personal beliefs or opinion. You decide to investigate the work of Jean Piaget.

Piaget's theory regarding cognitive development in children was not concerned with toys per se, but rather with the way our schemes (mental structures) develop over time as we interact with the objects and people in our environment. By understanding how these schemes change during the first two years of life, we can identify the types of interactions with the environment—including playing with toys—that best promote the development of infants and toddlers at different ages. Let us now learn how schemes develop in infancy and toddlerhood.

FIG. 6.1   Mateo and a Friend

As we learned in Chapter 1, Piaget's ideas of regarding the processes of adaptation no longer form the basis of much empirical research on cognitive development, yet his theory is still relevant because he studied universal aspects of children's thinking, including scientific concepts such as the physics of object permanence, which have implications for how Mateo and other children play with toys; some have also suggested that his theory can help us better organize and therefore apply what we are learning in developmental neuroscience research about age differences and/or age changes in neural processing (Arsalidou & Pascual-Leone, 2016; Barrouillet, 2015; Bjorklund, 2018a; Piaget, 1952).

What Is Piaget's Theory of Cognitive Development in Infancy and Toddlerhood?

Piaget's theory of cognitive development is a **constructivist** theory. This means that Piaget believed we *construct* our understanding of the world from the basic perceptual and cognitive achievements we acquired in earlier stages—and that we develop cognitive skills by immersing ourselves in age-appropriate activities within the environment (Burchinal, 2018; Newcombe, 2013).

So, in his view, development follows not only an inevitable sequence but also a hierarchy, with more complex behaviors and cognitions evolving over time (Arsalidou & Pascual-Leone, 2016; Flavell, 1963; Pascual-Leone, 2012). For example, the ability to understand that a parent will return after leaving for work requires that a child understand that people and objects continue to exist when they are out of sight.

Constructivist Theories

Unlike **nativist** theories, which propose that we come into this world with a set of abilities allowing us to understand the world around us, constructivist theories like Piaget's assume we arrive with nothing but reflexes and motivation to satisfy our curiosity to learn about the world (notice the

Learning Goals

- ▸ Paraphrase Piaget's theory of cognitive development in infancy and toddlerhood
- ▸ Illustrate the six substages of Piaget's Sensorimotor stage with examples
- ▸ Interpret the available empirical evidence on object permanence
- ▸ Summarize the core knowledge approach to infant and toddler cognitive development
- ▸ Explain cognitive processes in infancy and toddlerhood
- ▸ Evaluate the effects of childcare on cognitive development in infancy and toddlerhood
- ▸ Trace the development of language over the first two years of life
- ▸ Describe the symptoms, potential causes, and treatments of autism spectrum disorders

assumption here that people are active agents in their own development). This is the reason why theorists such as Piaget (1932) believe experience is vital for constructing knowledge.

Chapter 2 explained how, according to Piaget, schemes develop via the adaptation and organization processes. Recall that schemes are initially physical and then evolve into cognitive schemes, and that *organization* is an internal process by which children connect their previously developed schemes, such as grabbing a toy and then pulling it toward themselves, while *adaptation* requires interacting directly with the environment.

Although it seems like a relatively short period of time, the period between birth and 2 years of age is vast in terms of the many dramatic changes that occur, especially with regard to schemes; we begin this stage with nothing but reflexes and leave it capable of using language.

Piaget referred to the first two years of life as the *Sensorimotor* stage because, for the first 18 months or so, children know or understand the world only by interacting with it using their senses and their motor skills. By 24 months of age, most children are capable of **representational thought**, which means that children can think symbolically (such as leaning back-and-forth in a cardboard box and pretending it is a vehicle) and which signals the end of the Sensorimotor stage.

What Occurs in the Six Substages of the Sensorimotor Stage?

Referring back to the example of the employee of a toy company in our opening *Snapshot*, how do we know at what age a toy such as shape sorter, in which children must insert the correct circle, square, or star shape into a hole, is appropriate for an infant or a toddler?

We know by being well versed in Piaget's six substages of the Sensorimotor stage, which are increasingly complex and occur in a set sequence (Piaget, 1952). These stages, the topic to which we now turn, provide a precise account of the many milestones that take place within the first two years of life, as you can see in Figure 6.2.

Stage 1: Reflexes (Birth to 1 Month)

For Piaget, reflexes such as the palmar grasp (which we discussed in Chapter 5) serve as our first schemes. Reflexes and sensory stimulation such as seeing, hearing, and tasting dominate a child's first month of life. Chapter 5 described how a newborn's visual acuity is best at seeing objects 8–10 inches away.

Sensorimotor Substage	Approximate Age in Months	Overview of Substage
1) Reflexive Schemes	0-1	The use of reflexes
2) Primary Circular Reactions	1-4	Repetitive motor behaviors that are focused on the infant's body and the first acquired adaptations
3) Secondary Circular Reactions	4-8	Repetitive motor behaviors that are focused on external objects
4) Coordination of Secondary Circular Reactions	8-12	Goal-directed behaviors and object permanence
5) Tertiary Circular Reactions	12-18	Variation in behaviors and accurate A-not-B searches

FIG. 6.2   The Six Substages of Piaget's Sensorimotor Stage

So a crib mobile is an ideal toy for Stage 1, because the sensation of seeing moving shapes and patterns above the crib stimulates an infant's visual development—and because in terms of motor skills newborns are quite passive.

Stage 2: Primary Circular Reactions (1–4 Months)

From 1 month to 4 months, an infant's first adaptations occur; that is, new behaviors first appear. Here in stage 2, these new behaviors are based on innate reflexes—and they are the first form of intentional behavior. As a result, the behaviors in stage 2 take the form of *primary circular reactions*.

Circular reactions are acquired behaviors that are repeated over and over (Baldwin, 1958/1998). They are called primary because although they are an aspect of cognitive development, they are also physical given that they are focused <u>primarily</u> on the infant's own body, and therefore can be considered consistent with the multidimensional pattern of development.

A stimulating toy will encourage the primary circular reactions the infant has already begun—such as repeatedly placing something in their mouth (behavior based on the sucking reflex). So although teething isn't full-blown until about 6 months of age, a grab and teethe toy is appropriate for this age.

Stage 3: Secondary Circular Reactions (4–8 Months)

If the primary circular reactions of stage 2 are focused on the body, the *secondary circular reactions* of stage 3, from 4 to 8 months of age, are repetitive behaviors focused on interesting external objects and events, such as when an infant drops their spoon from their high chair, time after time. As in stage 2, the intention in stage 3 is to repeat the behavior for its own sake. As you can probably guess, a toy that bounces when pressed is a good bet for stage 3.

Stage 4: Coordination of Secondary Circular Reactions (8–12 Months)

In stage 4, from 8 to 12 months of age, infants become capable of combining more than one secondary circular reaction in order to reach a goal. For the first time in an infant's development, they can use one circular reaction in the service of another. They show intention, and their behaviors serve as a means to an end rather than merely being repeated. For example, an infant who coordinates grabbing and throwing would certainly benefit from toys he can grab in order to throw them to see how they land.

Such coordination means that goal-directed behavior, as well as an understanding of cause and effect, begin to appear in children's behavior. Imagine an infant playing with an activity ball, only to have it roll under a footstool where it is partially hidden. To reach their goal of obtaining the ball again, the child can crawl over to the footstool, and then reach under it to grab the toy. Observe the aspects of this situation that are consistent with the multidimensional pattern of development, in the way milestones of physical development, such as reaching and crawling, support cognitive development.

Another notable characteristic of infants in stage 4 is that they are now capable of **object permanence**, or the understanding that toys in baskets, parents who are at work, and biscuits in jars continue to exist even though they are not visible.

Stage 5: Tertiary Circular Reactions (12–18 Months)

The *tertiary circular reactions* of stage 5 appear at 12 to 18 months of age. This third variation of circular reactions consists of repeated behaviors on external objects, combinations of repeated behaviors on external objects, and combinations of repeated behaviors with variations on external objects.

So if variation is the theme of this stage, along with true mastery of object permanence, a soft book with a toy bone that can be hidden in multiple places within the book would be suitable for a toddler in this stage, given they can actively vary the places in which they hide the toy bone in the book.

Stage 6: Mental Representation (18–24 Months)

Piaget's sixth stage occurs from 18 to 24 months of age when toddlers become capable of using internal symbols, such as words, to mentally represent objects and ideas. Because toddlers now understand that one object, such as a word, can function as another object—they understand that the word *cat* refers to the family pet in the next room—this is also the time when they are able to engage in pretend or make-believe play, such a imagining they are making a building with toy blocks. They might even appreciate that small empty boxes can serve as symbols for bricks. And at this point, children now appreciate that the toy car represents a real car.

Toddlers also master mental combinations in stage 6, which means they can consider multiple ideas at once, such as planning the dialogue between two characters for a puppet show. They are also capable of **deferred imitation**, or the ability to replicate the actions of others at a later point in time, such as by using a puppet to imitate actions a parent engaged in the day before (Ótuari, Kolling, & Knopf, 2018). The ability in stage 6 to mentally represent or think about what is not currently visible also means that the use of schemes based solely on sensations and motor skills has come to an end.

Evaluation of Piaget's Theory

Piaget's theory has historic value because of the role it has played in bringing us to an understanding of the processes of cognitive development in infants and toddlers, and in generating numerous hypotheses as a result. Yet aspects of the theory, such as the concept of object permanence, continue to be debated because they are not always supported by empirical research. We examine that research here.

But one last thing before we do: *Consider that it may still be worthwhile to study Piaget's theory because it parallels the practice of scientific thinking.* That is, science is indeed a process of balancing assimilation (holding on to current beliefs) and accommodation (updating one's information), via hypothesis generation, hypothesis testing, hypothesis revision, further hypothesis testing, and so on.

And just because empirical research does not verify all aspects of a major theory, whether it be Piaget's, Classical versus Operant Conditioning, or Evolutionary Theory, we do not discard the theory altogether—especially given how developmental neuroscience and evolutionary theory can inform Piaget's theory (Arsalidou & Pascual-Leone, 2016; Bjorklund, 2018a).

What Does the Empirical Research Conclude About Object Permanence?

On the first day of her Child and Adolescent Development course, Sam located her classroom, which was in the university's former visual arts building. To her delight, Sam found the classroom's walls were painted with murals. During the first few weeks of the semester, she always took pleasure in gazing at the murals as class began. As the semester progressed, though, she no longer even noticed the murals.

Then, during final examinations, Sam told her best friend Jackie to come by her class when Jackie had finished her own exam so they could go out afterwards. When Sam finished her exam, Jackie greeted her with "Wow! Cool classroom." Sam replied "Oh, yeah, I forgot about that."

Has this happened to you? Have you ever found yourself overlooking familiar things in your surroundings? If so, you are not alone. In fact, psychologists have capitalized on this normal human tendency in order to study Piaget's concept of object permanence in infants.

The tendency of our attention to wane after continuous or repeated to exposure to a stimulus is referred to as **habituation**. Habituation is an adaptive form of learning. How so? We would not get through our day if we paid attention to everything in our environment all the time. The less we notice the things in the environment that stay the same, the better we can focus on the stimuli that need our attention.

Dishabituation refers to the tendency of our attention to *increase* after a change to the stimulus, as happens when a parent adds a new object to dangle from the baby's crib. Because infants are preverbal and cannot talk about what they know, researchers have relied on habituation and dishabituation for quite some time to measure whether and when babies notice changes in their environment (Fantz, 1964).

Piaget proposed that object permanence began to develop between 8 and 12 months of age. But his reasoning was based on his assumption that this cognitive milestone depends on the physical milestone of reaching, which begins around 5 months of age. Later researchers developed an experiment, using habituation, that did not require reaching, to see whether it would uncover evidence of object permanence occurring before 8 months of age. These studies have demonstrated evidence of what appears to be object permanence in infants between 4 and 8 months of age (Baillargeon, 1987; 2008; Jin et al., 2018). How so? The next section explains.

The Violation-of-Expectation Method

Babies demonstrate habituation when they stop looking at something we show them, so researchers used a **violation-of-expectation method**, which violates the expectations infants have about physical events by measuring their habituation to physically possible events and physically impossible events.

If infants look longer at impossible events than they look at possible events—that is, they habituate to possible but not impossible events—it tells us they likely possess object permanence because they know there is something unusual about the impossible event.

Let's look at an example. In Figure 6.3, the Habituation Events infants are shown include the short carrot moving behind the screen and then reappearing on the other side of the screen, and the tall carrot doing the same. Then infants are then shown the two Test Events: a possible event and an impossible event.

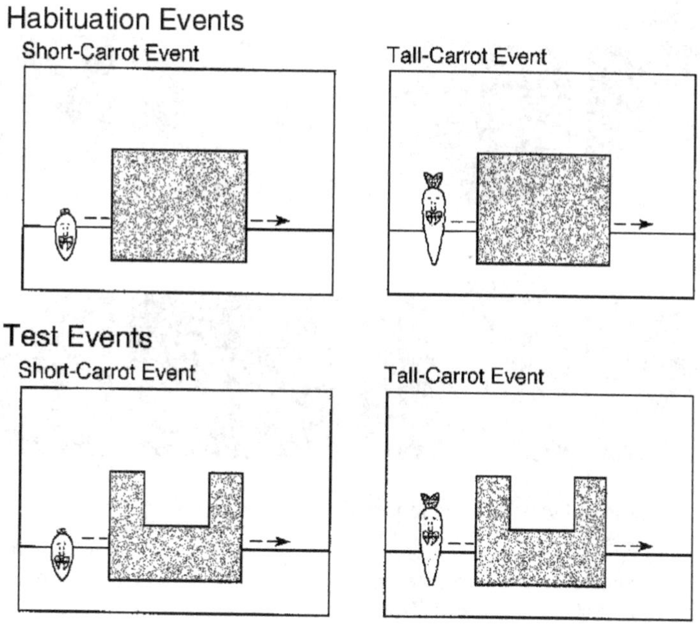

Habituation Events

Short-Carrot Event

Tall-Carrot Event

Test Events

Short-Carrot Event

Tall-Carrot Event

FIG. 6.3   Habituation Events and Test Events in the Violation-of-Expectation Method

Adriana F. S. Aguiar and Renée Baillargeon, Habituation Events and Test Events in the Violation of Expectation Method, from "2.5-Month-Old Infants' Reasoning about When Objects Should and Should Not Be Occluded," Cognitive Psychology, vol. 39, no. 2. Copyright © 1999 by Elsevier B.V.

In the possible Short-Carrot Event, the short carrot moves behind the screen and reappears on the other side. In the impossible Tall-Carrot Event, the tall carrot moves behind the screen without its stalk appearing at the top of the screen's window, and then reappears on the other side. Infants who possess object permanence will expect the stalk of the tall carrot to appear at the top of the window as it moves behind the screen.

If infants possess object permanence, they should look at the impossible Tall-Carrot Event longer than they look at the possible Short-Carrot Event. Do 8- to 12-month-olds do so?

Indeed they do, as do infants as young as 2.5 months of age. From this research, it seems that infants possess object permanence much earlier than Piaget believed, based on the assumption that they have an innate understanding that objects persist in time and space (Baillargeon, 2008; Jin et al., 2018).

More recent research confirms these findings using a paradigm, as shown in Figure 6.4, in which the infant sees a woman performing household chores when a nearby baby begins to cry—and the woman either comforts the baby (the Comfort Event) or ignores the baby (the Ignore Event). How do babies who watch the Comfort Event video know the woman is indeed comforting for the baby? Notice two things; that is, after the baby cries she both stops folding clothes and she goes over to the bassinet to attend to the baby.

On the other hand, how do babies who watch the Ignore Event know the woman is indeed ignoring the baby? Notice now two different things; that is, after the baby cries she both continues to fold laundry and she does not even approach the baby's bassinet.

As is illustrated in Figure 6.5, babies were provided with either event on different touch screen monitors, and they were taught that by touching either monitor, they could watch the respective event (adult comforts or adult ignores) again. At 4, 8, and 12 months of age, babies were significantly more likely to

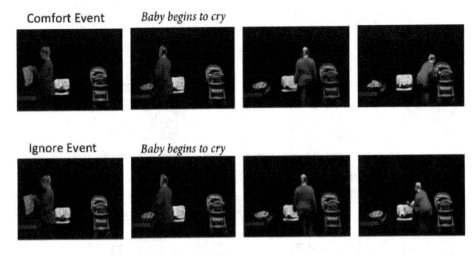

Comfort Event   *Baby begins to cry*

Ignore Event   *Baby begins to cry*

FIG. 6.4   The Comfort Event and the Ignore Event

K-S. Jin et al., The Comfort Event and the Ignore Event, from "Young Infants Expect an Unfamiliar Adult to Comfort a Crying Baby: Evidence from a Standard Violation-of-expectation Task and a Novel Infant-Triggered Task," Cognitive Psychology, vol. 102. Copyright © 2018 by Elsevier B.V.

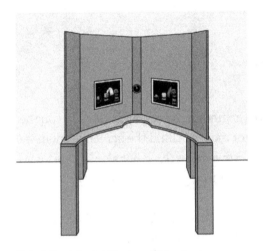

FIG. 6.5   Infants' Choice of Monitors

K-S. Jin et al., Infants' Choice of Monitors, from "Young Infants Expect an Unfamiliar Adult to Comfort a Crying Baby: Evidence from a Standard Violation-of-expectation Task and a Novel Infant-Triggered Task," Cognitive Psychology, vol. 102. Copyright © 2018 by Elsevier B.V.

choose watching the adult Ignore Event again, which may suggest that it violates their expectations, given that adults usually respond to another baby in distress (Jin et al., 2018).

Critics of the violation-of-expectation method have suggested that infants may be looking longer at impossible events not because these events violate their expectations, but simply because the events are novel. Or it may be that what appears to be innate knowledge really is information that babies are learning in the first few months of life, an argument worth merit in light of the difficulty of conducting research with newborns (Bremner, Slater, & Johnson, 2015).

While more research is being conducted to shed light on this as well as the neural processes underlying Piaget's concepts, some researchers who study cognitive development in infancy have turned to the theory of Core Knowledge, which we will now explore.

What Is Core Knowledge Theory?

Opposed to Piaget's view that knowledge is constructed and requires experience, the Core Knowledge theory assumes that we have innate core knowledge of the world.

This view is consistent with Baillargeon's (2008) assumption that infants have an innate understanding that objects persist in time and space. But the Core Knowledge theory specifies further that humans innately understand *objects* (that they move on a continuous path), *actions* (that they serve a purpose in helping us reach a goal, such as physical reaching helping us obtain an object), *numbers* (in which infants understand basic addition and subtraction), and *space* (in which infants understand spatial relationships, such as one object blocking another). Thus, Core Knowledge theory details exactly what knowledge is innate (Skerry & Spelke, 2014).

Yet Core Knowledge theory, like many other theories, does not always hold up completely under empirical scrutiny.

For example, some research with infants as young as one day old has found that these babies respond to changes in number. Yet other research has found that infants' understanding of actions as motivated by goals actually improves as their own physical actions develop, indicating that knowledge not just reflects the multidimensional pattern of development in that thinking is cognitive but often relies upon physical actions, but also that knowledge may require us to gain experience interacting with and observing the world after all (de Hevia et al., 2014; Saffran & Kirkham, 2018).

What Cognitive Processes Develop in Infancy and Toddlerhood?

Recall that Information-Processing theory (Chapter 1) assumes the human mind functions like a computer, as it processes visual, auditory, and olfactory input and generates thoughts, feelings, and speech as output. In exploring cognitive development in infants and toddlers, Information-Processing theorists may emphasize a specific aspect of cognitive processes, such as affordances, attention, joint attention, memory, and infantile amnesia. Let's take a look at these processes now.

Affordances

The first cognitive process in infancy and toddlerhood that we consider is affordances. Reaching for and grabbing objects illustrate the concept of **affordance** or the opportunity to act, which depends on the characteristics of a child's body and of their environment and context (Gibson, J. J., 1979; Gibson, E. J., 2000). For example, objects on a coffee table afford the opportunity to pick them up for investigation if the child has the motor skills to reach the table. Researcher Eleanor Gibson (1997) has said that "Perception and action are interdependent: Perception obtains information for action, and action has consequences that inform perception" (p. 25).

Gibson's claim was a result of her having designed a classic study of depth perception. Gibson and Walk (1960) had infants crawl along a *visual cliff*, or a contraption made of Plexiglas with a checkered tablecloth underneath. The checkered tablecloth was directly under the Plexiglas on one side, and about three feet lower on the other side, creating an illusion of depth as you can see in Figure 6.6.

Only infants who have had experience crawling or walking appear to avoid the deep side of the cliff—not because they are afraid of heights, but because although they perceive an affordance for moving to the deep side, they fail to see a good fit between the drop-off and their current abilities (Adolph & Hoch, 2019; Adolph, Kretch, & LoBue, 2014).

So experienced crawlers are *less* likely to cross over the drop-off than inexperienced crawlers, yet experienced crawlers will cross a cliff whose drop-off is ambiguous, if parents stand nearby exhibiting positive facial and vocal expressions (Adolph & Hoch, 2019).

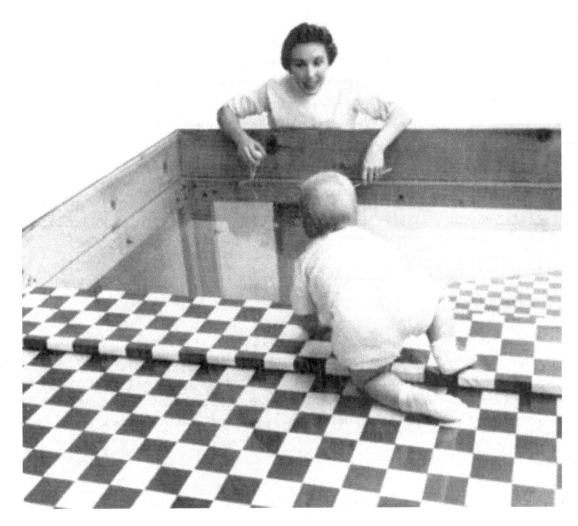

FIG. 6.6   The Visual Cliff

This tells us that affordances are consistent with the multidimensional pattern of development in that the opportunity to act physically depends on cognitive perceiving the opportunity to do so and, depending on the situation, if they are emotionally supported (Adolph & Hoch, 2019).

So, locomotion experience and the perception of one's own movements play a role in wariness of heights. Also, depth perception, rather than being an unfolding of a preformed maturation, follows the principle of epigenesis that we learned about in Chapter 3: Behavior is a function of genetic activity, neural activity, behavior, and environmental influences, such as the motivation to cross over unknown flooring to reach one's parent (Adolph, Hoch, & Cole, 2018; Bjorklund, 2018b).

Attention

The second cognitive process in infancy and toddlerhood that we consider is attention. **Attention,** or the focus on selective information, is an example of the multidimensional pattern of development. That is, our ability to focus is certainly affected by our emotional state. In infants, the physical connections among neurons in various brain structures are in place; these connections are required for the cognitive process of focusing, yet they require maturation over time to be fully developed (Xie, Mallin, & Richards, 2019).

Interestingly, research that tracks infants' eye movements has found that 1-year-old babies pay equal amounts of attention to the eyes and mouth of a person speaking to them in their native language, but they pay more attention to the mouth of a person speaking to them in a nonnative language (Niedźwiecka, Ramotowska, & Tomalski, 2018; Pons, Bosch, & Lewkowicz, 2019).

This same study also found that the more babies paid attention to a speaker's eyes, the greater the babies' degree of social interaction and jointly paying attention to the same object such as a toy, both of which are related to greater learning—perhaps because interaction and mutual gaze between infants and parents has been found to be related to infants' being better able to focus their attention (Niedźwiecka, Ramotowska, & Tomalski, 2018; Pons, Bosch, & Lewkowicz, 2019).

Children who were born prematurely and/or with low birth weight show difficulty fixing their attention during infancy, and are at an increased risk of later being diagnosed with ADHD (Downes et al., 2018; Franz et al., 2018; Zuccarini et al., 2018).

Yet research shows that the more that preterm 6-month-olds actively explore objects (using both mouth and hands with toys, such as a teething toy, a rattle, or a musical toy), the greater their word comprehension and word production at one year of age. Perhaps this is because physical exploration of objects elicits greater joint attention—that is, joint attention that may subsequently facilitate interaction and language input from parents (Downes et all, 2018; Franz et al., 2018; Zuccarini et al., 2018).

Again, this reminds us that in order to err on the resilience side of the risk–resilience pattern of development, parents can facilitate development quite a bit, and just with a few simple things— playing with and speaking to their infants as much as possible. And although redirecting an infant's or toddler's attention is useful and even necessary at times (such as when they may be about to do something dangerous), it is not recommended as a usual means of interacting with an infant.

Research has found that infants of parents who are highly redirective and regularly attempt to shift their babies' focus are highly distractible and have difficulty focusing their attention; instead, parents should *focus on focusing*, that is, engage in joint attention on one object at a time, and for greater periods of time (Mason et al., 2018). What's joint attention? Redirect your attention to the next section and you will find out.

Joint Attention

Infants become capable of shifting their attention at approximately 9 months of age. **Joint attention** occurs when two or more individuals pay attention to the same person, object, or event at the same time. Infants' engagement in joint attention at approximately 1 year of age is usually the result of a parent initiating such and/or the infant initiating such by pointing to an object. Yet at approximately one and a half years of age, infants begin to initiate joint attention by focusing on the object and their parent (Loy, Masur, & Olson, 2018).

Joint attention predicts a child's later vocabulary size, likely because attending to an object to which a parent is also attending, while also naming it, scaffolds babies' attention to words for objects (Yu, Suanda, & Smith, 2019).

In the context of joint attention, pointing serves an interrogative function for infants. That is, when they are looking at something with others, infants are able to obtain information about the object by pointing at it. Research shows that infants' pointing gestures also correlated positively with later vocabulary size—perhaps because adults often respond by naming the object or the person to which their baby pointed, so infants who gesture and point are likely exposed to more vocabulary words (Lucca & Wilbourne, 2018, 2019; Suarez-Rivera, Smith, & Yu, 2019).

Even if/when infants aren't pointing, parents can err on the resilience side of the risk–resilience pattern of development and facilitate infants' joint attention by manipulating objects while looking at their baby, then shifting their own gaze to the object, then talking about the object.

The research data show that similar to infants' use of gestures, the more that infants respond to parents' attempts to elicit their joint attention, the greater the infants' later language ability (Deák, Krasno, Jasso, & Triesch, 2018; Salo, Rowe, & Reeb-Sutherland, 2018).

Infants' responding to, and not just initiating, joint attention is also predictive of language skills. Consequently, parents of children who are developing typically and children who may be on the autism spectrum might want to consider eliciting infants' joint attention as much as possible. Also, as we will learn in the section on autism spectrum disorders later in this chapter, interventions on increasing joint attention in children on the autism spectrum are available (Kourassanis-Velasquez & Jones, 2018).

Memory

Another process in infancy and toddlerhood that we consider is memory. **Implicit memory** is unconscious and unintentional; it is the type of memory that helps us remember, for example, how to ride a bike. **Explicit memory** is conscious and intentional; it is the type of memory that helps us talk

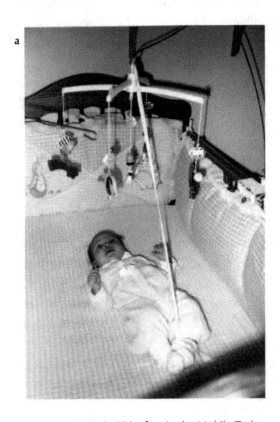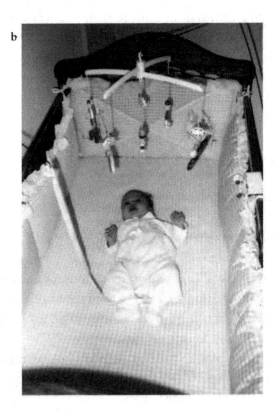

FIG. 6.7   A 3-Month-Old Infant in the Mobile Task

Carolyn Rovee-Collier, A Three Month-old Infant in the Mobile Task, from "The Development of Infant Memory," Current Directions in Psychological Science, vol. 8, no. 3. Copyright © 1999 by SAGE Publications.

about how we remember the particular day we learned to ride a bicycle. Implicit memory develops within the first few months of life (Vöhringer et al., 2018).

Our initial understanding of infants' implicit memories is a result of the wonderful work of Rovee-Collier (1999), whose research had infants learn to kick a mobile hanging over their crib by using a ribbon tied to their foot, as you can see in Figure 6.7.

These studies first measured how frequently an infant kicked without the ribbon, to get a baseline measure of kicking. Rovee-Collier and her colleagues then tied one end of the ribbon to the infant's ankle and the other end to the mobile, and then measured kicking frequency again.

The independent variable in this research is the length of time that passes between infants' first learning to kick a mobile with a ribbon tied to their foot, and their being presented with the ribbon and mobile again weeks later. If infants kick immediately and intentionally (rather than only sporadically and randomly) when the ribbon and mobile are reintroduced after a delay, this indicates they remember they can move the mobile by kicking.

Rovee-Collier's (1999) research shows that infants are indeed capable of forming such implicit memories. And a further study found that 3-month-olds can show memory for 1 week after their initial exposure to the ribbon and mobile, and six-month-olds show memory for kicking 2 weeks after (Rovee-Collier & Cuevas, 2009).

Other studies on implicit memory examine if and how infants imitate an adult, a research paradigm that has been a fruitful test of recall. The studies indicate that infants can imitate adults and that doing so serves an evolutionary purpose, given that bonding with parents ensures the infants' own survival and that cultural information is conveyed to them (Piaget, 1952; Meltzoff & Marshall, 2018).

Such findings regarding infant imitation also indicate that infants do indeed form memories and that the length of such memories increases over time, likely as a function of a reciprocal relation between maturation of the brain's hippocampus and sleep; the latter is known to consolidate memory in all ages (Friedrich et al., 2018; Wange et al., 2018). We will talk more about the relations among learning, memory, and sleep in Chapter 12 when we discuss adolescents' sleep hygiene in relation to their study habits.

As for the development of explicit memory, it too develops as the brain's hippocampus grows, reminding us that infants' and toddlers' ability to remember is a function of their brain development (Jabès & Nelson, 2015).

Yet because explicit memory requires language, unlike implicit memory, it begins developing later than explicit memory. A certain type of explicit memory, called **autobiographical memory,** involves

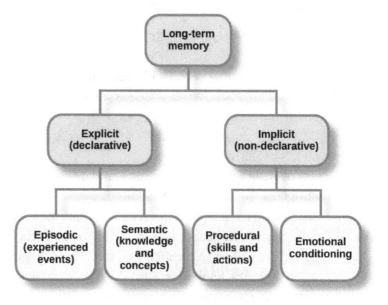

FIG. 6.8   The Different Types of Long-Term Memory

remembering events that have occurred in our lives alongside facts, such as where we were when the first Black president was elected.

As you can see in Figure 6.8's illustration of the different types of long-term memory, explicit memory is a combination of **episodic memory**, which is memory for events that have occurred in our lives, and **semantic memory**, which is memory for knowledge of the world, such as facts we learn in school (Tulving, 1972).

Infantile Amnesia

The study of autobiographical memories is a fascinating one. Many people cannot remember events that occurred early in life, before they were 3 or 4, a phenomenon that psychologists refer to as **infantile amnesia**. How do we explain this apparent memory failure? We know from Rovee-Collier's research that infants do indeed form memories, so infantile amnesia likely isn't a result of memories never being formed.

One explanation is that lack of autobiographical memories could be an access issue, an inability to reexperience the context in which an original event occurred, such as the apartment in which we were raised but no longer inhabit.

On the other hand, infantile amnesia could be a function of not having words with which to express our experiences in infancy, so it may be that early memories are inherently fragile or that forgetting processes simply reflect the polydirectional pattern of development; for example, it may be that early life is a period of rapid forgetting, and one that decelerates with age, perhaps as our brain matures (Bauer, 2015; Howe, 2019). Others researchers have proposed that neurogenesis in the hippocampus drops precipitously in the first year of life (Sorrells et al., 2018).

What Are the Effects of Childcare During Infancy and Toddlerhood?

Research on the effects of childcare fills volumes, so we will come to back to different aspects of this topic in other chapters, such as when we discuss whether and how childcare influences a child's emotional attachment to their parent(s).

Let us limit our discussion here to how the quality of childcare during infancy and toddlerhood affects cognitive development.

The quality of childcare matters immensely, especially with regard to erring on the resilience side of the risk–resilience pattern of development. Research has also found evidence for outcomes associated with the lifelong pattern of development.

In general, language, general cognitive, and school readiness skills at the end of the preschool period are highest in children who received high-quality childcare during infancy/toddlerhood *and* during the preschool years. Such skills are next-highest in children who received high-quality childcare during infancy and toddlerhood *or* during preschool years. Such skills are lowest in children who did not receive high-quality childcare during infancy and toddlerhood *nor* during the preschool years (Li et al., 2013; Son & Chang, 2018).

Yet what constitutes a context of high-quality childcare that ensures optimal development of infants and toddlers? And what constitutes a context of high-quality childcare that ensures optimal development of their lives later on, given that studies have shown high-quality early childcare is associated with higher grades at the end of high school, a greater likelihood of being accepted into more selective colleges, and fewer externalizing problems such as physical aggression and bullying (Vandell, Burchinal, & Pierce, 2016; Vandell et al., 2018)?

Characteristics of high-quality care for infants and toddlers include *positive affect* (smiling and talking calmly), *sensitive physical contact* (offering a hand to a child rather than grabbing theirs), *responsiveness to the infant's vocalizations and behavior, reading to the infant,* and *a continuity of caregivers*; the last of these is associated with greater attachment, self-control, and initiative for children in infant–toddler rooms (Horm et al., 2018).

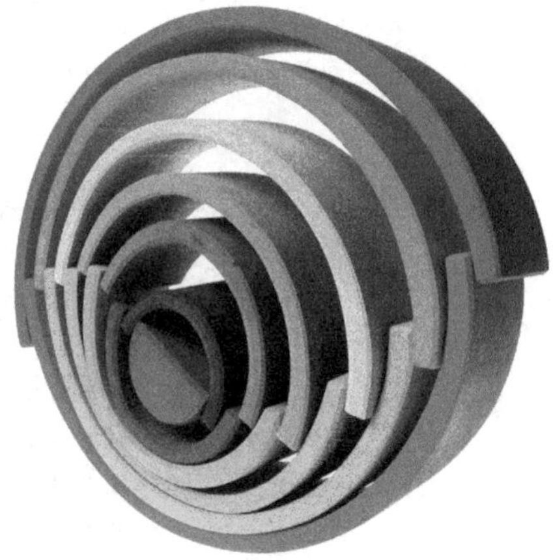

Other characteristics are a caregiver–child ratio of no more than 1:3 for infants and 1:6 for toddlers; caregivers who are trained in child development and first aid; a low turnover, so that children are able to form bonds with staff; regularly scheduled activities for play, naps, and healthy snacks; licensing, which is required by the state; and play materials that are developmentally appropriate—and if at all possible, simple, natural and beautiful, as in Figure 6.9.

For instance, this rainbow stacker is consistent with Waldorf approaches that emphasize stimulating a child's sensory and aesthetic experiences, as well as inspiring their imaginations with toys that lack specific details and that are open-ended and flexible. *This way, the child can visualize the toy as more than one thing—which trains the child's mind to consider not just what is, but also what is possible.*

To learn more about Waldorf toys such as these and about Allison Klein, the founder of the company, see the website for *rose & rex* in the *Helpful Websites* section at the end of this chapter.

Voluntary accreditation is available to childcare centers as well, so those centers that choose to become accredited are likely to be of high quality. National funding of childcare centers, which occurs in many other countries, could ease the burden on families; provide caregivers with the

FIG. 6.9   A Waldorf-Inspired Stacking Toy

Copyright © by Agactanya Toys (cc by-sa 4.0) at https://commons.wikimedia.org/wiki/File:A%C4%-9Fa%C3%A7tanya_Waldorf_Oyuncak.jpg.

Mentor Minute

Deborah Seok, BA

1) Describe your work, please.

Child Trends is a nonprofit, nonpartisan organization that seeks to improve the lives of children, youth, and families by conducting and sharing high-quality research. As a senior research assistant in the Early Childhood department, I support research and policy projects addressing the various programs and systems that serve children from birth through early elementary school across the nation. Examples of topics include home visiting, center- and home-based childcare, state-wide quality rating systems, and opportunities for the early childhood workforce. We conduct data collection and analysis efforts around the implementation and evaluation of these services, in partnership with

FIG. 6.10   Deborah Seok, BA

clients ranging from the federal government and state agencies to local foundations and communities. We also play an essential role in translating scientific research into resources and reports for a broad audience of policy makers, practitioners, and the general public.

2) How does social justice inform your work?

In thinking about how to improve the lives of children, youth, and families, researchers need to consider people from all kinds of backgrounds. For example, at Child Trends we are devoted to examining programs and policies geared toward families in poverty due to the particular risks poverty poses on young children's development. Likewise, developing best practices for certain racial or ethnic groups requires targeted research around that population, often best conducted by people who look like them and have had similar life experiences. The Hispanic Institute at Child Trends is dedicated to serving the needs of Hispanic children and families. We believe that conducting research around issues like poverty and inequality can help identify the areas of need and develop tailored systems and practices to fill in the gaps.

3) How did you become involved in social justice and/or advocacy?

I first began to understand the impacts of race and socioeconomic status on child development while conducting research at Head Start centers. There, I witnessed families and children who were restricted by poverty, adverse or traumatic experiences, lower parent education levels, and even cultural and linguistic barriers. It was evident to me that these families did not have equal access to or capacity for high-quality care for their children. Besides being unable to financially afford resources, such as enriching toys or books, some parents could not even afford the time or energy due to long, nonstandard work hours or single parenthood. While these realizations were unsettling at first, I was encouraged by the care and resources offered by Head Start centers to meet these families' needs. Additionally, I was motivated by the very mission that I and many others were working toward—research that seeks to develop and contribute to interventions for families from disadvantaged backgrounds.

4) What are your thoughts on how social justice can improve child and adolescent development?

At the systems level, social justice can play a role in providing families with access to different services that promote child development, such as home visiting and high-quality childcare. By targeting specific populations, like low-income parents, we can reach children who are at particularly high risk of poor developmental outcomes, such as social-emotional and behavior problems. One example of policies geared toward low-income families is the childcare subsidy programs that provide financial assistance to eligible families for childcare needs. Within these services, a focus on social justice can also ensure that we are meeting the precise needs of all families and children by hiring a racially and ethnically diverse workforce and using culturally relevant practices in early care and education classrooms. Overall, we want to provide every child with the opportunity for positive growth and development.

5) What suggestions do you have for undergraduate students who are interested in making a change in child and adolescent development?

Based on what I have learned from my own coursework and professional experience, my advice to undergraduate students interested in making a change is to be aware of and keep an open mind about the various levels of influence on a child's development. If you are interested in working directly with children, as a childcare provider or school counselor, make sure to be informed by the latest research and current events around the field that may impact how you interact with children. Ask questions like "What type of pedagogy will best support my students' learning? How can I practice trauma-informed care in school settings?" And if you are interested in working for children in research and policy contexts, try to understand decisions from the perspective of those who are on the ground. Ask questions like "What amount of training is appropriate for counselors and teachers to take on? How can physicians play a role in coordinating early childhood services for families?" No one individual or even group of people works in isolation, and the old proverb goes "It takes a village to raise a child." Collaborating and working with others, especially with those outside of your own niche, will strengthen our nation's support for children and maximize the potential for their positive development.

• • • •

professional-level salaries and benefits they deserve, given their education and experience; improve and standardize the quality of childcare centers; and possibly reduce the achievement gap, since children from low-income families are more likely to be in poorer-quality childcare or not be in childcare at all. Research shows that childcare subsidies increase parents' employment (Child Care Aware America, 2017; Davis et al., 2018; Zigler, Marsland, & Lord, 2009).

For suggestions on how to choose a childcare facility, see the Child Care Aware America link in the *Helpful Websites* section at the end of this chapter. To learn more about research on childcare, see the interview in *A Mentor Minute: Deborah Seok, BA.*

How Does Language Develop During Infancy and Toddlerhood?

Language learning begins in utero, during the third trimester. Newborns just 2 days old can clearly distinguish between the language to which they were exposed as fetuses and an unfamiliar language—which suggests that we retain postnatally what we learned prenatally (Moon, 2017; Moon, Zernzach, & Kuhl, 2015).

This prenatal processing of speech is an example of the lifelong pattern of development, given that it produces postnatal neural memory traces, particularly when it comes to the language of music. For example, research has found that when mothers play "Twinkle, twinkle, little star" five times a week in their last trimester, their babies show greater brain activity immediately after birth—and later on at 4 months of age—than do babies whose mothers did not play this melody (Partanen et al., 2013).

It may be that the fetus's learning of songs in particular is focused more on the melody than the sounds of the words (which makes sense, given their unfamiliarity with words), particularly because other research has found that when English-speaking adults hear toddlers singing in other languages, they are able to identify the name of the song, which refutes prior belief that children first learn the *words* of songs rather than the *tunes* (Gudmundsdottir & Trehub, 2018). Regardless, infants' musical experiences, particularly those that involve interactions with their parents, provide a foundation for lifelong engagement with music for social bonding, mood regulation, and well-being (Trehub & Cirelli, 2018).

One fascinating experiment with premature newborns (born between week 25 and week 32) found that those who received standard care had smaller auditory brain regions than premature newborns whose care was enriched with audio recordings of their birth parent voice and heartbeat.

This indicates that the auditory region of the brain's cortex is more responsive to parental sounds than to general environmental noise—which provides evidence for experience-dependent plasticity in the brain (Webb et al., 2015).

Postnatally, language acquisition can be divided into the vocal period and the verbal period. The *vocal period*, also referred to as *prelinguistic speech*, includes the crying, cooing, and babbling noises that infants make. The *verbal period*, also referred to as *linguistic speech*, begins after the vocal period when infants start making one-word utterances (Shormani, 2014).

Within the vocal period, infants and toddlers achieve remarkable accomplishments in communication. The first of several milestones is the production of vowel sounds like "oo" and "aa" that imply contentment. This is **cooing**, and it begins typically at 6 to 8 weeks of age (Hoff, 2013; Stephens & Matthews, 2014). By 3 weeks of age, infants are more attentive to adults and show more joy, via cooing and smiles, in the presence of adults (Labouvie-Vief, 2015).

By 6 to 9 months, **babbling** begins (Shormani, 2014). Infants babble when they use vowel and consonant combinations, such as "goo" and "gaa," as well as "mamamama," "dadadada," "babababababa," and "nananana." Babbling is practicing sounds, but also communicating. It is a clear example of experience-expectant development, because all babies babble, even those with hearing impairments (although they may babble a little later and don't necessarily increase the range of the sounds they make over time, likely because they don't receive such input).

Babbling is communication because infants vocalize when their parents cease interacting with them, and even more so when their parents reengage with them. This shows that as early as 6 months of age, infants know they are able communicators who can engage their parents' attention, and that they know vocalizing has emotional value (Cohen & Billard, 2018; Elmlinger, Schwade, & Goldstein, 2019).

As infants babble, they often attempt to imitate sounds that their parents make, especially sounds called **infant-directed speech** (IDS). IDS elicits infant attention and bonding, via a higher pitch, slower rate, and shorter sentences with longer pauses between them (Spinelli, Fasolo, & Mesman, 2017). IDS is used across the globe, yet cultures vary in how much they use IDS.

One study found that Lebanese mothers use more IDS than American mothers, and the researchers speculated that this might be because non-Western cultures such as Lebanon may value being interconnected more than independence, whereas the dominant US culture seems to have the opposite set of values (Farran et al., 2016).

Children prefer to listen to **child-directed speech** not only during infancy, but also into toddlerhood. It is noteworthy that the amount of child-directed speech to which a child is exposed is positively correlated with the size of the child's later vocabulary (Golinkoff et al., 2015; Ramírez-Esparza, García-Sierra & Kuhl, 2014).

Parents should be mindful, however, that environmental factors, such as a television running in the background, reduce the amount of child-directed speech they offer their children—a serious issue because children's ability to acquire language depends on adult input (Masapollo, Polka, & Ménard, 2015; Masur, Flynn, & Olson, 2016).

Sometime between 4 and 8 months, infants appear to understand their first word, and by 8 months they usually comprehend a select number of phrases, such as "Give me a hug." It is also around this time that infants beginning looking at the mouth, as well as the eyes, of the communicator.

At 9 months of age, infants begin to make the external world the topic of conversation. This is a major achievement in communication, because it allows infants to create a joint frame of reference with another person (Stephens & Matthews, 2014).

Children typically speak their first word around the time of their first birthday. Common first words are "mama," "daddy," "hi," "bye," and "uh-oh" (Shormani, 2014). **Holophrases** are single words children used to convey an intention, such as when a toddler says "More!" during mealtime

Pan & Zoom

Education as a Cause and as an Effect of the Social Injustice of Low Literacy

In this box, we zoom in on how research has revealed a risk–resilience pattern of development in the way the socioeconomic status (SES) of a family affects a child's language abilities.

As early as 1995, researchers were discovering that the achievement gap starts early, with children in professional families hearing more words than children in working-class families, who in turn hear more words than children in families needing welfare. As a result, children in professional families know almost twice as many words as children in working-class families, who in turn know a few hundred more words than children in families needing welfare (Hart & Risley, 2003).

More contemporary research confirms these patterns, and although some have argued that children in lower-SES homes hear more words that this classic study indicated, only speech spoken to children (versus overheard speech) predicts their language learning (Golinkoff et al., 2018; Levine et al., 2019; Sperry, Sperry, & Miller, 2018).

And low levels of language development in infants and toddlers unfortunately illustrate the lifelong pattern of development. Low levels of language development are associated with a lack of school readiness in kindergarten, an increased risk of academic difficulties later on, reduced career success, and lower levels of health literacy, which can lead to greater chronic illness and mortality rates.

What are often SES differences may be a function of parents' education level (Levine et al., 2019; Rindermann & Ceci, 2018). Yet even if parents have yet to pursue a degree, they can be educated about language development in order to err on the resilience side of the risk–resilience pattern of development.

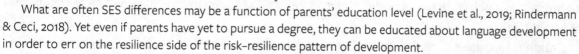

There are research data to show that interventions with parents work. Researchers educated parents on how intelligence is malleable, and how they themselves can improve their children's intelligence by pointing to objects more often and talking about such objects more often with their children. The more these parents began pointing, the more their children's vocabularies grew (Rowe & Leech, 2018).

Teaching parents about the role they play in developing their children's skills for optimal development is not a devaluing of lower-SES cultural and/or language differences, but a public health issue in which low literacy environments suppress our future workforce, and each child's inherent potential. We know that the absence of expected environmental inputs affects the brain's neuronal proliferation and pruning, which in turn affects children's academic success and their ability to contribute meaningfully to society (American Academy of Pediatrics, 2014; Hoff, 2013; Rosen et al., 2018).

Some of these environmental inputs can be remediated by teaching parents, but the inputs could also be remediated by government policies that choose to fully fund public libraries in order to provide comprehensive programming and services to communities during days, evenings, and weekends (Pateman & Vincent, 2010). For instance, the public library system in my current hometown of New Haven, Connecticut (which has a 1-in-4, or 25%, poverty rate, whereas the national poverty rate average is 12%), has only some of its branches open on certain days, and none open on Sundays, when working families have the time to take advantage of library resources.

• • • •

(Hantman, 2011). At around the same time, a child will start to notice the gaze of another person, which provides an understanding of other people's minds. In fact, the extent to which 12-month-olds follow the gaze of others and look at their mouths predicts these same children's later vocabularies and social skills (Brooks & Meltzoff, 2013, 2015; Pons, Bosch, & Lewkowicz, 2019).

By 18 months of age, toddlers are using two-utterances ("more give"), and these noun–verb combinations are an example of **telegraphic speech**, which conveys the minimal words necessary to communicate. Research indicates that toddlers who are spoken to with telegraphic speech are no more likely to respond than when they are spoken to in full grammatical sentences, so that the latter is equally or perhaps even more beneficial for language learning, since complete sentences teach them more words and more realistic usage (Bredin-Oja & Fey, 2014; Shormani, 2014).

Literacy is a product of many factors, though, including education. We turn to this topic in the *Pan & Zoom: Education as a Cause and as an Effect of the Social Injustice of Low Literacy* box.

At 18 months of age, most toddlers have a vocabulary of approximately 50 words. Let's back up for a minute. If children speak their first word at around 12 months of age and have a vocabulary of 50 words by 18 months, their initial rate of word learning is relatively slow.

Yet by 6 years of age, most children have a vocabulary of approximately 14,000 words. And by the end of high school, most adolescents have a vocabulary of approximately 60,000 to 80,000 words, and perhaps double that number if they read a lot. Such an increase would require that we learn approximately 10 new words per day on average (Bloom, 2000b).

Researchers had believed a **naming explosion** began around 18 months of age. This spurt was thought to be an abrupt, drastic, and discontinuous change in the rate of word learning, especially because 30-month-old children have, on average, a 200-word vocabulary (Hoff, 2006). Instead, the rate of word learning seems to increase at 18 months of age, but it is a gradual increase rather than the abrupt change that was once hypothesized. Three-year-olds are more likely to learn about 10 words per week, after learning about 5 per week at 17–18 months of age; any spurts are therefore unique to individual children in terms of their intensity as well as their timing (Bloom, 2000b; Dandurand & Shultz, 2011).

Children who are exposed to two languages simultaneously master both languages at the same rate as children who learn only one language. Some studies show that being bilingual helps improve executive function, which we learned in Chapter 1 includes the ability to engage in sustained attention, filter out distractions, and have self-control over our impulses—and which is a function of our context, such as how our parents interact with us (Sorge, Toplak, & Bialystock, 2017). And true fluency in a language is not required for children to reap the benefits of learning another language. How fluent they become likely depends on their age of exposure, forms of exposure (e.g., home, school, friends), frequency of their use of the language, and so on. The environments in which children become bilingual or multilingual vary substantially (Birdsong, 2018; Hoff, 2018).

In fact, even the children of monolingual parents can learn a language in addition to the one their parents speak. One childcare center in Madrid taught babies (between the ages of 7 months and 33 months) English 1 hour a day for 18 weeks, and parents were told not to expose the babies to English outside the class. Amazingly, the results indicated that compared to a control group of babies in a monolingual childcare facility, these babies produced significantly more English words at the end of the 18 weeks of classes—and retained what they had learned for another 18 weeks (Ramirez &

FIG. 6.11   Mateo and His Sister with Their Mother

Kuhl, 2017). Clearly, any combination of babysitters, community groups, and library media, as well as other books, music, and videos, can make a difference.

Reading and Talking

What is the most significant predictor of career success? It is achieving reading proficiency by third grade. Yet 66% of third graders (and 80% of those living below the poverty line) in the United States lack competency in reading skills (American Academy of Pediatrics, 2014; O'Keefe, 2014).

The American Academy of Pediatrics (2014) names parent–child reading as an epigenetic factor that promotes school readiness, so another means of scaffolding language and general cognitive development in infancy, toddlerhood, and beyond is regular reading aloud (Price & Kalil, 2018).

You may wonder why this is so when infants and toddlers are preverbal, but reading to young children can boost language development because it fosters paying attention, comprehending words, listening to what is spoken, enjoying books, and appreciating what makes for a good narrative or story—as is the case for Mateo and his sister with their mother each night.

Because both the child(ren) and the person reading to the child are focused on the same task, reading for even as little as 3 minutes a day also provides another opportunity for joint attention. Putting a book in their mouth is developmentally appropriate behavior for infants, as is a short attention span for toddlers, so parents should read shorter books while pointing to and naming objects within them (O'Keefe, 2014).

Regular reading will allow parents to err on the resilience side of the risk–resilience pattern of development by helping to develop the child's attention span in the process and establishing a lifestyle in which reading is an important part of everyday life. Therefore, in addition to a child's parents, childcare and healthcare providers should also be doing all they can to promote children's literacy skills via providing a wide range of beautiful and developmentally appropriate books.

Notice that these parent–child interactions are consistent with Vygotsky's theory that we learned about Chapter 2, in that more-knowledgeable adults are necessary to promote cognitive development in children. Books can even foster emotional bonding, since parents can teach their children to pair the pleasure of their mutual interactions with the pleasure of a book, so children learn to associate books with delight and an eagerness to read.

Research shows that daily reading at 6 months of age is associated with children's greater socio-emotional skills at 12 months of age—a finding parallel to that of research showing that difficulties in language development are associated with later problem behaviors, perhaps because communicating one's needs with verbal language is an emotional regulation strategy (Chow & Wehby, 2018; Curtis et al., 2019; O'Farrelly et al., 2018).

To learn more about a parent-led language intervention that sought to reduce children's problem behaviors, see *the Cycle of Science* box at the end of this chapter.

Early Literacy Promotion

The American Academy of Pediatrics and the National Association of Pediatric Nurse Practitioners have endorsed officially the Reach Out and Read model of early literacy promotion. In this program, pediatricians give children a specific developmentally appropriate book during the well-child visit (as opposed to just telling the parents to take a book on their way out). These healthcare practitioners discuss with parents the literacy gains in children who are read to regularly, and they provide parents with guidance on how best to enjoy the book with the child.

Reach Out and Read can dramatically alter the mood of a well-child visit for the child, changing it from one of fear to one of excitement and anticipation. A review of the research confirms other benefits for those who participate in Reach Out and Read, with parents reading more to their children, and their children showing greater vocabularies (American Academy of Pediatrics, 2014; Saravillo & Agapinan-Alfonso, 2018; Zuckerman & Khandekar, 2010).

Other programs to support literacy in the home include the Providence Talks program, in which families in Providence, Rhode Island, receive a biweekly coaching visit to help them speak more frequently with their kids. This program also uses a novel "word pedometer" technology to assess the words to which a child is exposed each day. Providence Talks interventions last for 2 years, and then the data are analyzed and published.

Preliminary findings indicate that parents who start out at the lowest levels of word use are increasing their word use by 50% after starting the Providence Talks program, that ongoing coaching is helping parents sustain these changes, that parents are subsequently engaged in more interactions with their children, and that families enjoy participating in the program (Providence Talks, 2019).

Because parents serve as children's first teachers, they must do all they can to promote early learning. Books with illustrations that can help children infer a word's meaning are helpful, although parents

Tech & Media in Our Lives: Consequences and Alternatives to Infant and Toddler Screen Time

Despite the American Academy of Pediatrics' (2016) recommendation that children's screen use be limited to video chatting until 2 years of age, and then limited to no more than 1 hour a day of high-quality programming until age 5, researchers have found children under 2 years of age spend 45 minutes a day using screen media (Rideout, 2017). Some children watch much less, and some watch much more.

There are physical, cognitive, and emotional consequences of not following the American Academy of Pediatrics' recommendation. Toddler screen time is an example of the polydirectional pattern of development. That is, screen time is correlated negatively with their attention, language, and social skills in preschool, as well as their engagement at school in adolescence, and it is correlated positively with their weight when they are adolescents (Carson et al., 2019; Kostyrka-Allchorne, Cooper, & Simpson, 2017; Simonato et al., 2018).

It is certainly understandable that parents are sorely tempted to set a child in front of a screen whenever they need to accomplish some tasks. Yet no matter how savvy marketers may seem in promoting their media as "educational," screen viewing is detrimental during the first two years of life, a research finding that many in the field of mobile app development technologies (who clearly value innovation and thinking about what could be, rather than just what is) are aware of—given their decisions to not let their own children use such and their restricting their children's technology use in general (Weller, 2018).

Once children reach the preschool years, though, a limited amount and frequency of high-quality educational content can improve academic performance (Kostyrka-Allchorne, Cooper, & Simpson, 2017).

• • • •

can use gestures and facial expressions to help children make sense of the words in any book. When the library is closed, parents can use new vocabulary words in everyday conversations by speaking to babies and naming objects during everyday routines.

As Fletcher and Reese (2005) note in their review of research on adults' picture book reading with children under the age of 3, those parents who provide support while reading with their child, by asking age-appropriate questions, are more likely to have children who feel a sense of competence with books.

Both Vygotsky's and Erikson's theories should come to mind here. Old-fashioned sitting on the floor to interact and engage with a child appears to be more beneficial than showing an "educational" app for a child to watch passively. In fact, research indicates that some educational videos are correlated *negatively* with a child's vocabulary. For more information, see the *Tech & Media in Our Lives: Consequences and Alternatives to Infant and Toddler Screen Time* box.

In the meantime, on snow days or at times when parents need to accomplish something, such as meeting deadlines while working from home, they can plan ahead by taking their babies out early in the day so they will be tired for a nap at midday, pull out toys reserved for special days that are novel enough to sustain infants' and toddlers' attention a bit more, plan ahead with other parents to take turns leading while the children play together, and build a list of trusted care providers.

Even Dr. Rovee-Collier needed to invent ways to keep her son entertained while she studied at home during graduate school. Her method of researching infant memory came to her serendipitously after she tied her son's foot to the musical mobile he liked so much, which hung over his crib, so that she could study uninterrupted. Her own innovation spurred our understanding of infant memory (Vitello, 2014).

What Is Known About Autism Spectrum Disorders in Infancy and Toddlerhood?

We discussed the relationship between vaccines and autism in Chapter 5, but autism is just one of a number of **autism spectrum disorders** (ASD) or what are also known as *pervasive developmental disorders* (PDDs).

PDDs often have have symptoms associated with the Multidimensional pattern of development, which, include deficits in communication and social interactions; rigid behaviors with a strong dependence on routine and a consistent environment; and under- or over-stimulation in response to sensations, such as indifference to pain but repeated smelling of objects. PDDs also include intense focus and preoccupation with unusual objects (American Psychiatric Association, 2013; Chawarska et al., 2014).

Assessments are available to diagnose ASD by age 2 (and are often based on children's decreased social responsiveness, such as lack of receptivity to joint attention), yet symptoms are broad and may be complicated by attentional disabilities, language impairments, and/or anxiety, making ASD difficult to diagnose, especially during the early years. Thus, most ASD diagnoses are made when the child is around 4 years of age (Hedges, Shea, & Mesibov, 2018; Powell et al., 2018). No one gene seems to cause autism spectrum disorders. In fact, not only do multiple genes probably contribute to the development of ASD, but PDDs are likely epigenetic in that genes and environment interact with one another to produce the symptoms typically associated with them (Eshraghi et al., 2018).

For instance, it could be that the proteins regulating the genes involved in the architecture of synapses are altered for some children via neuronal activity, yet are not altered in others. There is also promising new research that ties early disruption of infants' microbiome (which we first learned about in Chapter 3) to the differences found between the guts of individuals on the autism spectrum and those who are developing typically (Bourgeron, 2015; Eshraghi et al., 2018; Quesnel-Vallières et al., 2018).

Connectivity issues within the brain do seem to be relevant to understanding children on the autism spectrum. Research suggests that the symptoms of ASD may be due partially to a *pruning problem*, in which the peak of synaptic pruning that occurs in infancy and toddlerhood is disrupted so that the brain has excessive synapses, rather than an *overgrowth problem* that results from an excess amount of synapses being produced in the brain from the start (LeBarton & Landa, 2019; Lewis et al., 2017).

As a result of their difficulty communicating and interacting with others, children on the autism spectrum may have difficulty learning language—because, as we saw above, we typically map new words onto objects by following a speaker's gaze. Individuals on the autism spectrum pay less attention than do others to a speaker's gaze, or to faces in general, yet interventions specifically designed to improve the joint attention of children on the autism spectrum are effective. Before choosing an early intervention program, though, parents are encouraged to investigate evidence-based practices (Kucharczyk et al., 2018; Reichle, 2018).

To learn more, see the link to the ASD Toddler Initiative in the *Helpful Websites* section.

Key Terms

Affordance

Attention

Autism Spectrum Disorders

Autobiographical Memory

Babbling

Child-Directed Speech

Constructivist

Cooing

Deferred Imitation

Dishabituation

Episodic Memory

Explicit Memory

Habituation

Holophrases

Implicit Memory

Infant-Directed Speech

Infantile Amnesia

Joint Attention

Naming Explosion

Nativist

Object Permanence

Representational Thought

Semantic Memory

Telegraphic Speech

Violation-Of-Expectation Method

Summary

1. **Paraphrase Piaget's theory of development in infancy and toddlerhood.** Piaget believed we *construct* our understanding of the world from the basic perceptual and cognitive achievements we acquired in earlier stages, and that we develop cognitive skills by immersing ourselves in age-appropriate activities within the environment. As a result, development follows a sequence but also a hierarchy, with more complex behaviors and cognitions evolving over time.

2. **Illustrate the six stages of Piaget's Sensorimotor stage.** Reflexes corresponds to birth until 1 month of age. Primary Circular Reactions corresponds to 1 to 4 months of age. During this stage, an infant's first adaptations occur; that is, new behaviors first appear. During Secondary Circular Reactions, at 4 to 8 months of age, infants engage in repetitive behaviors focused on interesting external objects and events. Coordination of Circular Reactions corresponds to 8 to 12 months of age. Children show intention, and their behaviors serve as a means to an end. Tertiary Circular Reactions corresponds to 12 to 18 months of age, and involves combinations of repeated behaviors on external objects. In Mental Representation, children 18 to 24 months of age become capable of using internal symbols, such as words, to mentally represent objects and ideas.

3. **Interpret the available empirical evidence on object permanence.** Object permanence refers to the understanding that partially hidden toys, parents who are at work, and cookies in cookie jars continue to exist even though they are not visible. There are ample data that children look longer at impossible events, or at least those which appear novel.

4. **Summarize the Core Knowledge approach to infant and toddler cognitive development.** Core Knowledge theory assumes that we innately understand objects, actions, numbers, and space.

5. **Explain cognitive processes in infancy and toddlerhood.** Implicit memory is unconscious and unintentional. Explicit memory is conscious and intentional. One type of explicit memory is episodic memory, which is memory for events that have occurred in our lives; another is semantic memory, which is memory for knowledge of the world, such as facts. Autobiographical

memory involves remembering events that have occurred in our lives alongside facts, such as where we were when the first Black U.S. president was elected.

6. **Evaluate effects of childcare on cognitive development in infancy and toddlerhood.** The language, general cognitive, and school readiness skills at the end of the preschool period for children who received high-quality childcare during infancy and toddlerhood are significantly better than those skills for children who received low-quality childcare. Children in high-quality care also show greater ability to regulate their attention, and their emotions, as they grow older.

7. **Trace the development of language over the first two years of life.** Cooing typically begins at 6 to 8 weeks of age. By 6 to 9 months, babbling begins, and it is characterized by vowel and consonant combinations. Sometime between 4 and 8 months, infants appear to understand their first word, and by 8 months they usually comprehend a select number of phrases. At 9 months of age, infants begin to make the external world the topic of conversation, and children typically speak their first word around the time of their first birthday. By 18 months of age, toddlers are using two-word utterances and typically have a vocabulary of approximately 50 words.

8. **Describe the symptoms, potential causes, and treatments of autism spectrum disorders.** Autism spectrum disorders are a category of developmental disorders whose symptoms include deficits in communication and social interactions, as well as rigid behavior with a strong dependence on routine and under- or over-stimulation in response to sensations. Connectivity issues within the brain seem to be an issue for children on the autism spectrum, as research indicates synapses are not being cleared away over the course of development. Intensive interventions designed to improve the joint attention skills of children on the autism spectrum are effective.

The Cycle of Science

Research

Why was the study conducted?
The researchers wanted to know if their parent-led language intervention to reduce problem behavior in children with language delays was effective (Curtis, Kaiser, Estabrook, & Roberts, 2019).

Who participated in the study?
The 97 children who participated in the study were, on average, 30 months of age at Time 1, or the baseline at the beginning of the study; 45 of these children participated in the intervention condition and 52 participated in the control condition. All participants met the criteria for a language delay and 815 of them were male, a percentage consistent with the greater prevalence of language delays in boys. Participants were Black, European American, and Unspecified.

Which type of design was used?
An experimental design was used, with intervention/no-intervention as the independent variable, and both problem behaviors (both internalizing and externalizing) and rate of communication (the number of their utterances when playing with their parent in a clinic) as dependent variables. The intervention, which lasted 3 months, taught parents how to facilitate their children's language, via responding to their children's nonverbal request by modeling effective language use to make verbal requests, noticing and responding to their child's utterances, expanding their utterances, etc.

What were the results?
The researchers found that compared to children in the no-intervention control group, the problem behaviors of the children in the intervention group decreased significantly when measured 12 months after the intervention. The decreases were seen in children's total number of problem behaviors, as well as their specific internalizing problem behaviors and specific externalizing problem behaviors.

Are the results consistent with theory?
Yes. Improvements in these children's communication indicate that verbal language is indeed an emotional regulation strategy. Additionally, the changes in the parents' behaviors may have led to greater quality in their relationships with their children, as a result of parents being more observant of their children and their needs and being more responsive to such needs by expanding on their utterances, which could have fostered more secure attachment within the dyads.

How can the results be used to improve our lives?
Interventions such as this suggest that improving children's language development has outcomes associated with the multidimensional pattern of development. Being able to better communicate improves the quality of their lives. It allows them to be more likely to express their needs clearly and have them met, which helps them better fulfill their potential in the long term.

Exercises

1. What pattern of results would you expect if the participants were Asian American or Latinx and bilingual?

2. What pattern of results would you expect if the intervention was conducted for a longer period of time?

3. How might such an intervention be adapted to refugee children who have not yet learned the language of their host country and who may also have special emotional needs after the trauma of experiencing violence, organized conflict, war, death of loved ones, frequently dangerous journeys of crossing national borders, being detained in settlements or refugee camps that often have harsh living conditions and treatment, forced displacement, etc.?

Helpful Websites

Zero to Three, the non-profit organization devoted to educating and supporting adults who have the opportunity to influence the lives of children, has a fantastic collection of resources for parents (and recommended by parents, including your author) on their website: https://www.zerotothree.org/resources/series/parent-favorites

To see a *Ted Talk* with Professor Anne Fernald, director of the Language Learning Lab at Stanford University, on why talking to little kids matters, click this link: https://www.youtube.com/watch?v=IpHwJyjm7rM

The Providence Talks program, in which families received a biweekly coaching visit to help them speak more frequently with their kids, uses a novel word pedometer technology to assess the words to which a child was exposed each day. To learn more about Providence Talks, visit their website: http://www.providencetalks.org/

Child Care Aware is a program of the National Association of Child Care Resources and Referral Agencies, and they help parents choose care, including their "5 Steps to Choosing Care": https://www.childcareaware.org/

To learn more about toys such as the Waldorf rainbow stacker and to learn more about Allison Klein, the founder of the company (Allison has a master's degree in early childhood education from the Bank Street College of Education), see the website *rose & rex* here: https://www.roseandrex.com/pages/about-us

The ASD Toddler Initiative provides learning modules on assessment, intervention, and treatment for toddlers on the autism spectrum: https://asdtoddler.fpg.unc.edu

Recommended Reading

Allyn, P. (2009). *What to read when: The books and stories to read with your child—and all the best times to read them.* New York, NY: Penguin.

Golinkoff, R. M., & Hirsh-Pasek, K. (2016). *Becoming brilliant: What science tells us about raising successful children.* Washington, DC: APA.

Golinkoff, R. M., Hirsh-Pasek, K., & Eyer, D. (2004). *Einstein never used flashcards: How our children REALLY learn—and why they need to play more and memorize less.* Emmaus, PA: Rodale Books.

Gopnik, A., Meltzoff, A. N., & Kuhl, P. K. (2000). *The scientist in the crib: What early learning tells us about the mind.* New York, NY: Harper Collins Publishers.

Smolen, P. (2015). *Can doesn't mean should.* Durham, NC: Torchflame Books.

Trelease, J. (2013). *The read-aloud handbook.* New York, NY: Penguin Books.

Emotional Development in Infancy and Toddlerhood

CHAPTER 7

Snapshot

One of Mateo's favorite stories is *The Color Monster: A Pop-Up Book of Feelings* by Anna Llenas. It's about a monster who begins to articulate his many emotions with the help of a friend. The five different feelings are represented with visually arresting artwork and pop-up displays that engage Mateo's attention for long periods of time and help him better understand himself, particularly when he is sad then angry.

In this chapter, we will learn about the emotions that infants and toddlers experience and how these emotions develop over time; we'll also examine the theories and research on temperament and attachment. Before we do, though, it is worth taking a moment to discuss some characteristics of picture books that best facilitate development.

All picture books help young children learn about the world in addition to themselves; the books also promote language development. However, although pop-up or manipulative (in which, say, the child lifts a flap) books are designed to engage infants and toddlers, the data indicate that children are less likely to learn from such books compared to traditional books, perhaps because in traditional books parents are more likely to point to and label letters (Horst & Houston-Price, 2015; Strouse, Nyhout, & Ganea, 2018).

Some pop-up and manipulative books are great, especially if they are beautiful and they focus on emotions, but ideally the majority of books to which babies and toddlers are exposed via joint reading should be traditional books. Electronic books on a device support preschoolers' comprehension of stories, but more research is

FIG. 7.1   Mateo

needed to determine the risks and benefits of adults' use of ebooks in shared reading with infants and toddlers (Strouse & Ganae, 2017).

How Can Emotions That Develop in the First Two Years Be Best Supported?

An **emotion** is a person's state of mind. Emotions typically have corresponding physiological states, including arousal or pleasantness. This means that we can be aroused in a positive sense, such as elated or alert, or in a negative sense, such as tense or stressed.

Ancient Hindu philosophers believed there are eight basic emotions, Descartes proposed six, and modern researchers' estimates range from three to eleven depending on their theoretical orientation; for example, evolutionary psychologists consider an emotion basic if it serves to help reproduction of the species or solves an adaptive problem (Al-Shawaf, Conroy-Beam, Asao, & Buss, 2016; Plutchik, 2003). Regardless of their number, emotions are evident at different ages—even within the first year of life.

Emotions in the First Year of Life

Some people have suggested that mad, sad, glad, and afraid are the most basic of emotions. We will certainly cover those here, along with others. For instance, newborns display facial expressions that appear to correspond to emotions, such as disgust, distress, joy, and interest. We know newborns are attentive to the environment, because immediately after birth they are alert and orient their eyes to sights and sounds.

Disgust and distress probably occur as a way for newborns to communicate that their needs are not being met, whereas joy and interest are likely present to help them begin creating mental representations of themselves and the world outside. Interestingly, research has also found that 2-day-old babies are able to distinguish between faces that express happiness and faces that express disgust—and that they prefer the former (Addabbo et al., 2018).

Learning Goals

▸ Identify how emotions in the first two years of life can be best supported

▸ Describe what Erikson's theory can tell us about early emotional needs

▸ Explain how the self develops, including the role of self-recognition

▸ Summarize what is known about how temperament develops in infants and toddlers

▸ Analyze how the quality of a child's attachment is a cause and an effect of development

Infants seek eye contact at approximately 6 weeks of age, around the time that they first coo and smile in response to parents' expressions. Infants smile reflexively when satiated or relaxed, but their first smile that is intentional and reflects happiness, the *social smile*, occurs typically by 3 months of age.

Anger occurs when infants are frustrated, such as when an object they are exploring is taken away from them or their mobility is restricted. Although these frustration flare-ups are evident as early as 2 to 3 months of age, anger is most clearly and immediately expressed beginning at 4 months of age (Sullivan & Lewis, 2003).

Anger is a developmentally appropriate way for infants and toddlers to get their needs met when they aren't able to express them otherwise. Yet children vary greatly in how much anger they experience, and those infants who show the most hitting, negative moods, biting, and temper tantrums at 6 months of age are more likely to make aggressive choices in a computer game at 7 years of age (Hay et al., 2018). A parent's sensitivity to an infant's emotional cues may play an indirect role in sparking anger because a lack of sensitivity increases the baby's stress responses.

Indeed, research has found evidence for the risk–resilience pattern of development in the fact that greater parental insensitivity is associated with stronger reactivity in the infant's sympathetic nervous system, which increases their levels of the stress hormone cortisol. Therefore, the importance of parents learning to regulate their own distress (and having sufficient paid time off to focus on their new baby), especially such as in response to their infants' distress, cannot be understated given the potential for negative interactions to escalate (Enlow et al., 2014; Firk et al., 2018).

Being sensitive to but nonreactive to shrieking infants and angry toddlers can be difficult at times, though, despite those behaviors being developmentally appropriate. So parents who find themselves being more reactive and less patient than they want to be can benefit from a mindfulness practice. To learn more about research on a mindfulness training that helps parents, see the *Cycle of Science* box at the end of this chapter.

In terms of other emotions, infants do not typically express surprise until about 5 to 7 months of age, not long after the time when they also develop the cognitive capacity for expectation (Sullivan & Lewis, 2003). Researchers who use the violation-of-expectation model that we learned about in Chapter 6 find that surprise appears to motivate infants to learn. For example, infants who saw a ball go through a wall that was in its path were later more interested in learning about the ball's ability to make sounds, whereas infants who saw the same ball stop at the wall were later less interested in the ball's sounds—indicating that surprise may serve the purpose of propelling inquiry and curiosity (Stahl & Feigenson, 2015; 2018).

Children are indeed capable of empathy in the first year of life; infants are sensitive to the distress of others (such as their peers in childcare), and this concern for others forms the basis of social competence and moral behavior (Crespo-Llado, Vanderwert, Roberti, & Geangu, 2018; Spinrad & Eisenberg, 2017). Interestingly, researchers have found that infants who show more sadness and distress in response to others' distress behave with more empathy in toddlerhood if they have both acquired sufficient self-regulation and if prosocial behavior is modeled to them (Abramson, Paz, & Knafo-Noam, 2018; Schuhmacher, Köster, & Kärtner, 2018).

Infants begin to detect fear in others at approximately 7 months of age and begin to engage in helping behaviors at approximately 14 months of age (Grossmann & Jessen, 2017). Not surprisingly, those babies who show heightened attention to, and then disengagement from, fearful faces at 7 months of age show greater prosocial behavior, such as helping an experimenter obtain an out-of-reach object at 14 months of age (Grosmann, Missana, & Krol, 2018).

Such findings reflect the polydirectional pattern of development; that is, *less* engagement after attending to fear is a sign of self-regulation and *greater* development of the brain's prefrontal cortex, which tempers our emotions and social behaviors (Grosmann, Missana, & Krol, 2018).

Infants start to respond differently to strangers around 7 or 8 months of age, a noteworthy change given that babies' social circles can be very limited in the first few months of life (Brooker, 2013). Infants begin to experience **stranger anxiety** at approximately 7 months of age, as their world expands and they begin to encounter more unfamiliar people (Brand, Escobar, & Patrick, 2020).

Near the end of the first year of life, children can start to feel separation anxiety. **Separation anxiety** includes crying, clinging, and the other forms of distress that children show when their parents are about to leave them, such as at childcare when the parent leaves for work. Separation anxiety is normal at this time of development, and if anything, it becomes intensified during the second year before beginning to taper off in most children.

Also near the end of the first year of life, children begin to engage in **social referencing**, or looking to familiar adults in order to interpret a novel situation, such as when a new person is at the door (Moore, 2014). If the trusted adult appears frightened by the new person at the door, the child will act accordingly. If, on the other hand, the trusted adult appears happy to see the new person at the door, so will the child.

Emotions in the Second Year of Life

Consciousness or self-awareness begins to emerge in the second year of life. This awareness, along with brain maturation, provides a foundation for the emergence of **self-conscious emotions**, such as embarrassment, envy, and empathy (Kagan, 2007; Muris & Meesters, 2014).

Around the same time, a toddler begins to be able to maintain an overt expression of an emotion that may or may not reveal their internal feelings, which is an example of emotion regulation. **Emotional regulation** is the process of modifying our emotional experiences and the physical reactions that underlie them—not to suppress or eliminate them, but to identify them and transform them into an adaptive state of mind.

The mindfulness we learned about in Chapter 4's *The Cycle of Science*, in which we cultivate awareness and acceptance of the present moment, is associated with healthy emotional regulation when practiced as a form of meditation (Kral et al., 2018). This is because it reduces activation of the brain's **amygdala**, a structure in the brain that plays a role in emotional responses such as anxiety, fear, and aggression (Kral et al., 2018). In fact, research shows that infants have fewer negative emotional behaviors if their birth parent's mindfulness was greater prior to their birth (Braeken et al., 2017).

The process of modifying our emotions can focus on their *quality* (seeing the humorous side of having done something embarrassing), *duration* (extending our pleasure over good news by sharing it with others), or *intensity* (becoming excited about an upcoming event or toning down our anxiety before meeting with our boss). Thus, emotional regulation can have multiple goals (Eldesouky & English, 2018; Gross, 2015).

Emotional regulation is not static either. This skill changes over time and can certainly mature throughout our lives (Zimmermann & Iwanski, 2018). A toddler's growing ability to modify how they feel will pay later dividends; research has found that self-regulation sets the foundation for outcomes that illustrate the lifelong pattern of development, particularly those regarding school success. Specifically, greater self-regulation is associated with greater academic achievement from preschool through at least second grade, perhaps because it allows us to focus our attention on learning—rather than on being preoccupied with how we feel or being flooded by stress hormones (Skibbe et al., 2019).

Emotional regulation illustrates the multidimensional pattern of development, too, because modifying our emotions requires modifying our physical reactions, as well using language to modify our thoughts and feelings. Indeed, a lack of physical well-being, especially a lack of sleep, can interfere with emotional well-being for all of us.

One study with toddlers compared those who did and did not have a nap as they attempted to complete an unsolvable puzzle, and those who did not have a nap were less able to modify their emotions. They focused on pieces that did not fit and insisted on trying to complete the puzzle (Miller et al., 2015). Sleep really is necessary for emotional regulation. This has been found to be particularly true for toddlers whose families may not be able to afford childcare or other help that assists the parents in getting their babies to stick to a regular sleep schedule (Bocknek et al., 2018).

Facilitating Emotional Development in Infants and Toddlers

Given what we have learned about emotional development so far, is the "terrible twos" a fair nickname for the toddler years? Probably not. Toddlers' increasing use of the word "no" is a signal of increasing autonomy; it also reflects the child's growing understanding of the difference between self and other. And because of their newfound physical mobility, toddlers preoccupy themselves with exploring the environment, an activity motivated by curiosity rather than by a desire to be naughty.

Toddlers are, in a sense, little scientists—wanting to know about everything; the desire to learn is a human instinct. Yet because self-regulation and patience have yet to develop much by toddlerhood, flares of anger and temper tantrums are common in the second year of life. Inhibition of these emotions increases during the preschool years, as does control over behavior.

Resistance to parents is normal during toddlerhood, and it shows a pattern consistent with the polydirectional pattern of development. It peaks at around 24 months of age and begins to decline, so that aggressive acts usually decline after about 3.5 years of age (Teymoori, Côté, & Jones, 2018). If aggression continues significantly beyond this age, it may indicate a poor child–parent relationship, as in attachment security, a topic we discuss later in this chapter (Roskam, 2018).

The normative decline in aggression reminds us, though, that the polydirectional pattern of development can be healthy, that is, not all decreases in development are negative; sometimes they co-occur with increases in maturity. Children's aggression declines partially due to their becoming increasing capable of using words to express their needs, but they require practice and reminders from adults, such as "Use your words."

Better yet, a means of interaction that respects a toddler's autonomy is that of Resources for Infant Educarers (RIE). This philosophy emphasizes sensitively <u>observing</u> children to understand their needs (nighttime distress could be a need for more daytime bonding), <u>involving</u> them in all care activities (such as clothes changing) to encourage them to be an active participant, and <u>validating</u> their emotions (such as frustration) while also <u>setting</u> clear and consistent limits (Gerber & Johnson, 2012; Lansbury, 2014). Certification in RIE training is available, and RIE® associates work in various settings helping parents and childcare professionals provide excellent care to infants and toddlers. For a list of associates, see the link to the RIE website in the *Helpful Websites* section at the end of this chapter.

Also consider Lansbury's excellent book *No Bad Kids: Toddler Discipline Without Shame*, listed in the *Recommended Reading* section. (Don't miss the fantastic corresponding podcast, "Janet Lansbury Unruffled," #1 Kids & Family.)

To learn more about someone who practices RIE, read about Angela Fisher-Solomon, PhD, in the *Mentor Minute* box.

Mentor Minute

FIG. 7.2   Angela Fisher-Solomon, PhD

Angela Fisher-Solomon, PhD

1) Describe your work, please.

My work as an Infant Developmental Psychologist and Parent–Infant Specialist allows me to work in multiple capacities to serve parents, children, and staff in various areas of early childhood development. My work serves to provide training and technical assistance to federally funded programs across the country to promote the implementation of evidence-based practices across early childhood systems. I develop resource materials and provide training to Head Start/Early Head Start grantees on topics such as the implementation of home-based curriculum and the promotion of secure parent–child relationships to support the parent's implantation of learning experiences in the home. In this capacity, I provide professional development training to managerial leaders and staff in the early care and education field.

The families served typically range in a low socioeconomic level and are often challenged with multiple ACES (Adverse Childhood Experiences) (e.g., poverty, mental illness, trauma, depression, abuse). Also, I work in private practice and teach Certified RIE (Resources for Infant Educators) Parent–Infant Guidance classes, and Certified RIE Before Baby Care (e.g., observation, infant massage, and support healthy parent–infant relationships across cultural backgrounds).

As a Certified RIE Associate, I teach and educate parents and adults on respectful, responsive caregiving practices. I support parents in their learning process of how to view their infants as competent and authentic humans, to build confidence in the parent on their journey of parenthood, and support the adult–child relationships.

2) How does social justice inform your work?

The magnitude and role of social justice informs my work in the early childhood field on a consistent basis. I provide training and technical assistance for early childhood program managers and staff all over the country who represent and serve diverse families from different socioeconomic and cultural backgrounds, as well as families with children who have special needs.

3) How did you become involved in social justice and/or advocacy?

I became involved in social justice from an early age. I grew up in a low-income environment that provided me with firsthand experience of the importance of equal quality or inequality with resources, family supports, and limited materials that can affect a child's school choices and quality of education. Not to mention, how inequality of resources and materials can affect a child's confidence, self-esteem and feeling of self-worth. The power of social justice affects children and parents on both a micro and macro level of development and system formation within the environment.

4) What are your thoughts on how social justice can improve child and adolescent development?

Social justice can improve child development at its core foundation. Social justice, equality, and social awareness can influence the quality of how an infant comes into the world or the quality of prenatal care and access a mother has before her child is born, the quality of food she has access to in her particular neighborhood, the quality of childcare the parents may have access to in their environment, and the types of jobs, resources, social services that are available to the family; as well as schools, libraries, parenting classes, and overall support systems within a neighborhood in a specific state.

5) What suggestions do you have for undergraduate students who are interested in making a change in child and adolescent development?

I recommend to undergraduate students to be aware and focused on what's happening in the world, and not just their "immediate' environment." To understand that the babies are our future—and for those who are studying child development, that their voices matter. I suggest to students to be open to looking at what makes children thrive and grow to their full potential. Ask students to take an authentic and intentional interest in their peers from a different cultural group that they have limited knowledge about. Review the most up-to-date literature to remain current on social issues, changes, and new opportunities for inclusion against prejudices across multiple groups and situations that affect infants, toddlers, and families.

Lastly, I would suggest that undergraduate students recognize they have so much to offer the world in understanding child development and parenting. I would emphasize to undergraduate students to be willing to mentor someone younger, mentor parents, offer your services and skills to make a difference in the lives of a child and family. Keep the faith that the world can and will be a better place because they [the student] can make a difference in the life of a child not yet seen or heard!

· · · ·

What Can Erikson's Theory Tell Us About Early Emotional Needs?

Recall from Chapter 1 that Erikson's psychosocial theory of development proposes eight life stages, each presenting us with an emotional crisis (with two opposite potential outcomes) that we must resolve. Ideally, in each stage we become acquainted with both the positive and negative aspects of the crisis but have more positive experiences than negative ones.

Erikson's theory is similar to Freud's in that both theories proposed stages of development, but Erikson extended Freud's ideas *up and out* into a theory of healthy development over the life cycle

(Adams-Price et al., 2018; Kivnick & Wells, 2013; Hoare, 2005). That is, Erikson's theory is more concerned with the following:

- a dynamic balance of opposites, in terms of positive and negative experiences
- motivation occurring in conscious awareness rather than in the unconsciousness
- environmental factors that influence development within each stage
- the entire life span

Trust–Mistrust

For Erikson (1964), the crisis of infancy is between **trust and mistrust**. Trust begins in infancy as we start to recognize that other people are separate from ourselves and that we can rely on them to attend to our needs. Infants learn to pin their hopes on others feeding them, bathing them, and cuddling them, because they cannot do these things for themselves. Yet if the only experiences a child ever has are those in which they can trust people, the child might become a gullible adult.

So not having people available *all* the time to care for our needs may result in our being less reliant upon others and more independent, because it is unhealthy for parents to respond to a child's every single need, when the child must learn eventually to self-soothe. Thus, our having a parent who is relatively, if imperfectly, consistent in caring for us—what psychoanalyst Donald Winnicott (1953) called a "good enough parent"—will result in our being able to tolerate others leaving us temporarily because we know they will come back.

Outer predictability leads to inner certainty. That is, consistent caregiving leads to an understanding that we can trust other people to be there for us (Erikson, 1963). Erikson believed that infants who experience more trust than mistrust possess the virtue of hope, or the "enduring belief in the attainability of fervent wishes" (Erikson, 1964).

Hope is rendered beautifully in Eric Carle's classic children's book *The Very Hungry Caterpillar.* In the words of Carle, "It is a book about hope. If you're an insignificant caterpillar, you can grow up to be a big butterfly in the world" (Setoodeh, 2009). Such hope is not to be undervalued. According to Erikson, positive resolution of this first crisis, as well as every other, serves as a prerequisite for successfully resolving crises in subsequent stage of development.

Without being able to depend on others, we may find the crisis in each subsequent stage of development insurmountable. Infants who experience large amounts of mistrust growing up may become suspicious and lack self-confidence because they have learned *not* to depend on others to be there for them. These children are therefore likely to experience difficulty in resolving the next qualitatively different stage.

Autonomy–Shame and Doubt

Erikson proposed that the second crisis, to be resolved in toddlerhood, is **Autonomy–Shame and Doubt**. Autonomy, or the ability to begin controlling or directing our behavior, develops because of the physical changes that occur in toddlerhood and that enable us to crawl and walk away from our parents to explore the environment. Such physical changes have psychological repercussions, with frustration mounting as toddlers go from experienced skillful crawlers to inexperienced unskilled walkers (Adolph & Hoch, 2019; Adolph & Tamis-LeMonda, 2014).

At the other end of the crisis continuum in this stage is the following: If parents are overly controlling and do not allow a child much liberty in deciding what to do or what to play with, they cause the toddler to feel ashamed, helpless, and doubtful of their decisions and determination. Thus, the way parents respond to toddlers' growing autonomy and budding self-control has a significant influence on whether and how children resolve Erikson's crisis of the second year of life.

The way that parents respond to a toddler's growing autonomy also plays a role in how toddlers feel about their parents.

Research has found that during middle childhood, children show more positive emotions toward their mothers if their mothers showed greater regard for their autonomy during toddlerhood. Researchers also found that children's academic outcomes as well as their emotional well-being in middle childhood are greater, likely as a result of their mothers' respect helping to instill self-regulation in them, as compared to the disrespect and insensitivity that can cause stress hormones to surge and flood a child with stress and negative emotional states (Ispa et al., 2015; Liew et al., 2018).

Parents may inadvertently encourage shame and doubt in their children when they engage in behavior that is disrespectful of the child, even though they may think they are just being funny or teasing. If the parents are especially harsh and criticize or ridicule the child's choices, the child will be engulfed in a sense of shame, which is extremely unhealthy when it arises out of behaviors that are hardly shameful, such as a clothing ensemble that is merely unusual.

To err on the resilience side of the risk–resilience pattern of development, parents need to allow toddlers to explore the environment safely, via encouraging the careful touching of most objects as well as the banging of pots and pans. It is also helpful to allow toddlers to choose and follow their interests, to support their desire to do things for themselves, to encourage them to keep trying, to ask questions in order to encourage thinking, to reinforce what they do well, and to engage in conversations about their feelings. All of these will help children learn to identify and eventually manage different emotional states.

Allowing children to have a choice—and a voice—in matters that concern them raises an interesting issue in the era of social networking. Infants and toddlers do not have a say in whether photos and videos of them are posted online or whether parents speak for their thoughts and feelings there. See the *Tech & Media in Our Lives: Social Networking and Babies?* box for a consideration of whose needs might be being served online.

Tech & Media

Tech & Media in Our Lives: Social Networking and Babies?

Although the opportunity to post photos, videos, and journal entries about a child's milestones on a standard social networking site sounds inviting, it does bring up ethical concerns. First, of course, the child has had no say in the matter.

Second, there is no guarantee that such sites will safeguard members' privacy or that the sites can avoid being hacked at some future date. Of course, it might seem like it's the parent's prerogative to engage in seemingly harmless media sharing.

But parents must be mindful of their children's desires from a very early age, particularly if the parents enjoy posting images that are less than flattering or respectful and may haunt a child at a later age, even if such images are not digitally "kidnapped" so that the child experiences identity theft, bullying, and/or having their photos exploited on a pornography site. As for the last concern, a survey in Australia found that a significant portion of photos on a child pornography website had initially been posted to social networking sites by parents, but were now edited with inappropriate comments (Battersby, 2015).

Nor should parents speak for their children or deny children their own voice, even if that voice is preverbal. Having a voice and a choice are vital to a child's developing a healthy sense of autonomy and self-control, prerequisites for successful resolution of later stages of development.

Also, research indicates that twice as many children as parents want rules on what parents can digitally share, indicative of their need, and their right, for respect and privacy, as well as control over their digital footprint (Hiniker, Schoenebeck, & Kientz, 2016).

• • • •

Cultural Influences on the Development of Autonomy

A family's cultural values influence their child-rearing techniques. Some families interpret autonomy as desirable evidence of the separateness required for self-esteem. For others, autonomy is not nearly as important as relatedness to others.

Families that value independence and self-reliance tend to live in or at least value individualistic cultures, whereas families that value the needs and feelings of the group tend to live in or value collectivistic cultures (Triandis, 2001).

Individualistic cultures like that of the United States place the individual's needs and feelings first, whereas *collectivistic* cultures like that of Japan tend to place the individual's obligations to others first. Regardless of where parents live, however, their own cultural values influence their responses to their children's emotions, which in turn can result in cultural differences in children's subsequent emotions and thinking.

One study with non-WEIRD (see Chapter 1 for a discussion of the importance of involving research participants from countries other than Western, Educated, Industrial, Rich, and Democratic) preschool-age and school-age children asked them to distribute candy to hypothetical recipients. When the recipients varied in whether they had a broken leg or not, children from collectivistic cultures were more likely to distribute candy *equitably* rather than *equally* (see Chapter 1 for a review of equality versus equity) than were children from individualistic cultures (Huppert et al., 2018).

Of course, differences exist within cultural groups as well. Research on Mexican American preschoolers' vocabulary is predicted positively by mothers' reading beliefs, reading frequency, and creation of a home literacy environment, which are in turn predicted by mothers' educational level and socioeconomic status (Gonzalez et al., 2017).

How Does the Development of the Self Occur in Infancy and Toddlerhood?

A number of the emotions that we have discussed so far rely on a child's understanding of their self as unique and separate from others. We know that newborns do not possess this knowledge but that toddlers do, because self-conscious emotions do not become apparent until the end of the second year of life.

Is it possible to measure a child's recognition of their self? And if it is, how does the ability to recognize ourselves as unique and separate from others influence other aspects of development?

Self-Recognition in Other Animals

The **mirror test** is the traditional criterion by which researchers determine whether we possess self-recognition (Gallup, 1970). This test was first implemented by biologists, who found that chimpanzees recognized themselves in a mirror. The chimps didn't just smile at the image in the mirror and think it was another friendly chimp; they realized it was themselves because they moved their fingers to their faces (not their images) in order to touch red marks the researcher had placed there.

Subsequent research has found that not all animals recognize themselves in the mirror. Monkeys, magpies, and pigeons do, as evidenced by their passing the mirror test, but pandas do not (Ma et al., 2015; Toda & Platt, 2015; Uchino & Watanabe, 2014).

Self-Recognition in Humans

When the mirror test is used with humans, some infants will touch a mark on their face around 18 months of age, and most do so by 24 months, a trajectory that is consistent with the onset of self-conscious emotions (Amsterdam, 1972). When videos are used instead of mirrors, most infants do not recognize themselves until 36 months of age unless they are specifically trained to do so, likely due to perceptual differences in responses to different media (Suddendorf & Butler, 2013; Reiß, Krüger, & Krist, 2017).

Research results such as these suggest that contrary to beliefs about the educational value of 'baby' apps and videos, children in the second year of life do not learn from screens—what is known as a **video deficit effect**—but instead do from real life (Suddendorf & Butler, 2013; Reiß, Krüger, & Krist, 2017).

A longitudinal study that followed toddlers from 15 to 23 months of age revealed that the ability to consistently pass the mirror test takes time to develop. Just because a child recognizes their self once does not mean that they will do so the next time. And there are cultural differences in this ability as well.

One study that compared children in Scotland, Turkey, and Zambia found that toddlers in Scotland performed

FIG. 7.3   A Girl Touching Her Face

FIG. 7.4   The Body-as-Obstacle Test

Chris Moore, Jennifer Mealiea, and Nancy Garon, The Body-as-Obstacle Test, from "The Development of Body Self-Awareness," Infancy, vol. 11, no. 2, pp. 161. Copyright © 2007 by Lawrence Erlbaum Associates.

best on a test of self-recognition when a mirror test was used, whereas Turkish and Zambian toddlers performed best on a test of self-recognition when a *body-as-obstacle* test was used. The body-as-obstacle test involves a toy shopping cart with a mat attached to the axle; the toddler stands on the mat, as can be seen in Figure 7.4 (Ross et al., 2017).

When you look at the Body-as-Obstacle Test, imagine a child standing on the mat that is attached to cart, and becoming frustrated and upset as they unsuccessfully try to push the cart. They are unable to push the cart because they are standing on the attached mat, but younger children don't always realize their standing on the mat is the reason why.

Previous research found that 21-month-olds are much more likely to appreciate they need to step off the mat to make the cart go than are 15-month-olds, and that the cultural differences found on this task may reflect caregiving practices (Moore et al., 2007; Ross et al., 2017). Why? Because Western cultures such as the culture of Scotland tend to emphasize independence and communicate more verbally, whereas more Eastern cultures such as those in Turkey and Zambia emphasize interrelatedness and communicate more, both verbally and via physical contact (Moore et al., 2007; Ross et al., 2017).

How Does Temperament Develop in Infants and Toddlers?

Mateo is calm and pleasant, but his older sister Ana was cranky when she was an infant. What explains these differences? One explanation with a great deal of empirical support is temperament.

Temperament accounts for the stable and seemingly innate individual differences in the way we each respond to the world, specifically our emotional reactivity, or the intensity of our emotional arousal levels, and our self-regulation. Aspects of temperament in infants also include soothability, impulsivity, and tolerance for new stimuli, characteristics that are likely are product of gene–environment interactions; for example, a parent training intervention can be helpful in improving both caregiving and child impulsivity, but only for children showing one version of a dopamine receptor gene, reminding us that not all interventions are helpful for all people (Posner & Rothbart, 2018; Rothbart, 2015).

Researchers measure temperament with observer ratings and/or parent reports. The New York Longitudinal Study (NYLS), which began in 1956, was conducted by Stella Chess and Alexander Thomas and observed individual differences among 141 subjects from infancy all the way to adulthood. The NYLS is notable not only because of the unprecedented interval of time during which Chess and Thomas observed human development, but also because their work began during a period in which Behaviorism was a dominant perspective in psychology. In the 1950s, most scholars were investigating the role of reinforcement, and general environmental influences, on development and were not especially welcoming of theories proposing that the characteristics (such as temperament) distinguishing us from one another may be present from birth (Thomas & Chess, 1977).

The NYLS was concerned more with the *how* of behavior rather than the *what*. For example, all infants show interest in a new toy, but they differ in the way they approach it. Through intensive observations, the researchers came to understand that infants vary in terms of how much interest they show in the toy versus something else, how long they look at it, how intense their reaction is, and so on. After establishing that these responses vary from individual to individual and over time, Thomas and Chess (1977) developed a theory of temperament that proposes nine dimensions upon which individuals vary. Let's take a look.

Temperament Classifications

Thomas and Chess (1977) gathered data from various sources. While the children were still infants, parental reports of their behavior were the primary data sources. As the children grew, teacher reports were included, along with the researchers' interviews with children and their direct observations of the children at school.

As the researchers gathered all these sources of data for the entire sample of 141 children, consistent pattern or themes became apparent. In particular, the following nine categories of temperament across which individuals differed were clear:

1. *Activity Level*: Degree of physical energy, from low to high levels
2. *Rhythmicity or Regularity*: Predictability in terms of waking, hunger, and becoming tired
3. *Approach or Withdrawal*: Positive or negative responses to new people and environments
4. *Adaptability*: How long it takes to adjust to changes in routines
5. *Threshold of Responsiveness*: Sensitivity to noises and other changes in the environment
6. *Intensity of Reaction*: The energy level when responding, can be positive or negative
7. *Quality of Mood*: A joyful and cheerful demeanor or unpleasant and stormy demeanor
8. *Distractibility*: Degree of concentration and focus in the face of distractions
9. *Attention Span and Persistence*: Ability to pursue an activity over a length of time in the face of obstacles

The advantage of having any of these characteristics is age-dependent. For example, *distractibility* is advantageous in an infant attempting to poke an electrical socket because parents can easily redirect them, but it can be problematic in a school-age child who needs to pay attention in class.

As if nine categories of temperament weren't provocative enough, the researchers' longitudinal findings revealed that scores on these categorical dimensions were stable over time and tended to cluster into patterns we can think of as *temperament styles*. For example, approximately 40% of the children whom Thomas and Chess studied were classified as **Easy**, meaning they were

> characterized by regularity, positive approach responses to new stimuli, high adaptability to change and mild or moderately intense mood which is predominantly positive. These children quickly develop regular sleep and feeding schedules, take to most new foods easily,

smile at strangers, adapt easily to a new school, accept most frustration with little fuss, and accept the rules of new games with no trouble. (1977, pp. 22–23)

About 10% of the NYLS sample were classified as **Difficult**, a temperament style characterized by

irregularity in biological functionings, negative withdrawal responses to new stimuli, non-adaptability or slow adaptability to change, and intense mood expression which are frequently negative. These children show irregular sleep and feeding schedules, slow acceptance of new foods, prolonged adjustment periods to new routine, people, or situation, and relatively frequent and loud periods of crying. Laughter, also, is characteristically loud. Frustration typically produced a violent tantrum. (1977, p. 23)

Approximately 15% were **Slow-to-Warm-Up**, with

a combination of negative responses of mild intensity to new stimuli with slow adaptability after repeated contact. In contrast to the difficult children, these youngsters are characterized by mild intensity of reactions, whether positive or negative, and by less tendency to show irregularity of biological functions. (1977, p. 23)

What are we to make of the 35% of children who do not match one of these three temperament classifications? They usually exhibit a combination of more than one style.

Other Theories of Temperament

Jerome Kagan has conducted longitudinal studies on temperament using observations of children's physical behavior in response to novelty, such as how they respond to a new mobile swung above their car seat while in a research lab, and the way their reactions predict their personalities when older.

Temperament is fairly stable over time (Bornstein et al., 2015). It therefore casts a long shadow on development, according to Kagan and Snidman (2004), because "a 45-minute laboratory observation of 16-week-old infants revealed dispositions that were preserved in some children for over 10 years" (pp. 244–245).

However, consistent with Figure 3.13 in Chapter 3's discussion of how genetically similar seeds may grow differently depending on the soil, temperament is more an inclination than a guarantee (Kagan, 2012; 2018). For example,

No temperamental bias determines a particular cluster of adult traits. Life experiences, acting in potent and unpredictable ways, select one profile from the envelope of possibilities. A young boy born with a temperament that favors bold, sociable behavior may become the head of a corporation, a politician, a trial lawyer, or a test pilot if raised by nurturing parents who socialize perseverance, control of aggression, and academic achievement. A child born with exactly the same temperament is at some risk for a criminal career if his socialization fails to create appropriate restraints on behaviors that violate community norms. (Kagan & Snidman, 2004, p. 5)

For an in-depth look at how infants' distress in reaction to novelty may predict their later well-being, see the *Cycle of Science* section at the end of this chapter. For now, though, note that some of Kagan's work in conjunction with colleagues has focused on two extreme types of infant **reactivity**, or the ease with which they are emotionally and physically aroused (Fox et al., 2015; Kagan, 2018).

High-reactive infants tend to become shy, inhibited, and introverted children; *low-reactive* infants tend to become bold, sociable, and extraverted children. The differences among infants are apparent in their reactions to strangers, and these differences usually manifest between 6 and 9 months of age. The differences also have consequences that illustrate the lifelong pattern of development.

For instance, infants who are high-reactive and physically active at 4 months of age are significantly more likely show symptoms of ADHD during middle childhood, but only if they are male and their parents' caregiving behaviors was of poor quality. Such poor caregiving behaviors may involve being *less* likely to be sensitive in interacting with one's infant, less likely to be accepting, encouraging, and/or available, as well as *more* likely to be interfering with rather than cooperating with their infants' activity (N. V. Miller et al., 2018). In the second year of life infants who are high-reactive (perhaps as a result of an excitable amygdala, part of the brain involved in emotional reactions) are more likely to exhibit **behavioral inhibition**, that is, crying in reaction to and/or avoidance of unfamiliar events, people, or objects (Kagan, 2012; 2018).

Behavioral inhibition is stable over time, with high-reactive infants more likely to be shy and avoidant as kindergartners than low-reactive infants. Also, while high-reactive children are not necessarily timid and anxious adolescents, they are less likely to be completely uninhibited and consistently fearless and sociable as they grow older (Kagan, 2018). According to Kagan, temperament may not be a perfect predictor of who we will become as we age, but it is able to predict with some confidence who we will *not* become.

Mary Rothbart views temperament as a result of two factors, reactivity and self-regulation (Posner & Rothbart, 2018; Rothbart, 2011). **Self-regulation** is the processes infants use to regulate reactivity, such as shifting their attention or self-soothing (clinging to a favorite blanket or thumb-sucking, which can reduce a child's negative emotions). Self-regulation develops considerably from infancy to the early preschool years as a function of the multidimensional pattern of development, such as increasing connectivity among the brain's structures over time, as well as a function of a strong emotional bond or attachment to a parent (Pallini et al., 2018; Posner & Rothbart, 2018).

Effortful control, a specific form of self-regulation, is the ability to suppress an impulse, such as eating a snack or opening a gift placed in front of you. Effortful control begins to appear between 6 and 12 months of age. Infants, toddlers, and preschoolers who are relatively low in effortful control are more likely to exhibit externalizing problems such as physical aggression and bullying in middle childhood and early adolescence (Jonas & Kochanska, 2018). Other work indicates that an adolescent's degree of effortful control predicts their level of educational attainment in early adulthood (Véronneau, Hiatt Racer, Fosco, & Dishion, 2014).

Why do some children have better effortful control than others? Again, as with self-regulation, one contributing factor to better effortful control is the emotional bond that parents have with their children (Birmingham, Bub, & Vaughn, 2017). For example, when parents err on the resilience side of the risk–resilience pattern of development, they do so by offering a respectful, warm, and supportive context in which they validate children's negative emotions and then offer ways to cope with these feelings.

As a result, children are able to decrease their arousal in response to the negative event. This decreased arousal, in turn, increases the child's effortful control, to which sensitive parents often respond with even more validation and support—so that there is likely a bidirectional relationship between child temperament and parent responses to children's emotional experiences (Finch, Johnson, & Phillips, 2015; Klein et al., 2018).

On the other hand, parents who—intentionally or unintentionally—increase their children's risk of poor effortful control do not validate the children's feelings, but instead control, dismiss, ridicule, and/or punish them. By these actions they also do not teach the children strategies for coping with their feelings.

 Such lack of empathy also has consequences consistent with the polydirectional pattern of development. That is, lack of empathy increases children's negative emotions, causing the children to feel overaroused; they are therefore less likely to regulate themselves over the long term, and they are also less likely to show empathy for others (Arnett et al., 2018; Spinrad & Eisenberg, 2017; Stern & Cassidy, 2018).

Goodness of Fit

Such differences in the way parents respond to children brings up to a concept proposed by Chess and Thomas (1999). They considered development to be optimal when there is a **goodness of fit** between the individual and the context.

For example, the adoption of regular sleep cycles, feeding schedules, toilet training, and other milestones of infancy and toddlerhood may proceed smoothly for children with an Easy temperament, yet be a struggle for children with a Difficult temperament. Difficult children need calm, quiet environments, and Slow-to-Warm-Up children must be given time to acclimate to new situations.

Parents therefore need to learn to respect a child's individuality, particularly if there is more than one child in the home and/or if the home environment has changed considerably from one child to the next; what was an effective strategy with one child may not be with another child. Goodness of fit occurs when the demands of the environment match the individual's style of behavior. It can play a considerable role in development, given that research shows it to be related to children's later well-being (Newland & Crnic, 2017; A. S. White et al., 2018).

How Is the Quality of a Child's Attachment a Cause and an Effect of Development?

"Mateo loves me, but he loves you, his mama, more than me because you're the one who feeds him," Mateo's father Edgar remarked to Mateo's mother Luz.

Could Edgar be right? Actually, it is unlikely. Let's consider the evidence.

Freud, Erikson, Harlow, and Bowlby on Attachment

Attachment is the emotional bond infants form with their parents. It is not evident in the first few weeks of life but rather emerges over time.

Why do children develop this emotional bond with their parents? Freud believed the reason was that infants' parents feed them (Holmes, 1993). This *cupboard theory* of attachment may seem a bit silly, but consider Erikson's belief that infants learn to trust their parents because their parents attend to their emotional and physical needs.

In a now-classic (as well as ethically questionable) experiment, Harry Harlow set about testing the cupboard theory empirically with newborn rhesus monkeys that were separated from their mothers soon after birth. Harlow placed cubicles alongside the monkeys' cages, one cage containing a wire "mother" and the other containing a cloth "mother." The wire mother provided milk, and the cloth mother did not.

Harlow and his colleagues found that the monkeys spent only as much time with the wire mother as needed when they wanted milk; otherwise they spent up to 18 hours a day with the cloth mother because of *contact comfort*, or the solace provided by physical contact with a parent (Harlow, 1958). This work showed that the cupboard theory is not valid.

Just as importantly, when the monkeys were placed in an unfamiliar room with novel toys, it was clear that the cloth mothers provided them with the security to explore the environment, as you can see in the right panel of Figure 7.5. When the cloth mother was absent from the room, the infant monkeys froze in a crouched position.

Recall that in ethological theory, introduced in Chapter 1, attachment is likely based on our evolutionary history. It serves to keep infants in close physical proximity to their parents, which helps ensure that they are protected from harm and are capable of surviving—and thus caring for future generations (Szepsenwol & Simpson, 2019; White, 2014).

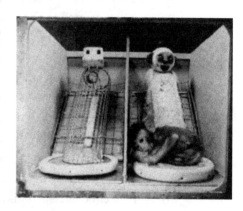

FIG. 7.5   A Monkey with a Cloth Mother

Source: https://commons.wikimedia.org/wiki/File:Natural_of_Love_Wire_and_cloth_mother_surrogates.jpg.

John Bowlby proposed that attachment develops through a series of stages, roughly corresponding to different ages. Based on Lorenz's theory of critical or sensitive periods in development (Chapter 1), Bowlby's *discontinuous model of socioemotional development* proposes that changes in attachment proceed universally, but that individual differences occur in the *rate* of development.

For example, in *Stage 1: Indiscriminate Orientation*, infants orient or respond to others, but their ability to discriminate between people is quite limited—and this limitation lasts for the first two or three months of life (Bowlby, 1969). It is at least partially a function of physical development, since infants' vision does not reach 20/20 until 6 months of age. It should therefore not surprise you that for first few months of life, infants do not display a preference for one person over another.

In *Stage 2: Discriminate Orientation*, infants show more positive reactions to familiar people. This stage begins at about two to three months—*right around the time that many parents' unpaid leave ends and they must return to work*. In light of attachment research, policy makers need to rethink our government's social injustice in their lack of support for families and their erring on the risk side of the risk–resilience pattern of development. This stage lasts until approximately 6 months of age.

The name *Stage 3: Discriminate Proximity Maintenance* means that children show evidence of a strong attachment to one or more parents, and attempt to maintain proximity or physical closeness to them. They can do this now by crawling and later by walking. A rise in cautiousness around strangers appears in this stage.

Stage 3 begins around 6 months of age, when Stage 2 ends, but for children who spend a great deal of their day without a main parent (in crowded orphanages or in childcare centers with high staff turnover), this stage may begin as late as 1 year of age. Stage 3 concludes around 2 or 3 years of age, depending on the child (Bowlby, 1969).

Speaking of childcare, children who experience more continuity of care in infant–toddler classrooms show a number of positive emotional outcomes, such as fewer behavioral concerns (poor self-regulation) as well as greater self-control, initiative, and attachment (Horm et al., 2018).

Yet the shorter a parent's parental leave, the less likely it is that their child's attachment to them is secure. This is the case perhaps because a parent who is not given much, or even any, paid time off is prevented from being able to spend the quality time with their child that is necessary for the parent to become attuned to the child's needs and cues (Plotka & Busch-Rossnagel, 2018).

The public policy implications of these findings are clear, especially when we learn that paid leave is good for employers as well as families: States such as Rhode Island have reported public savings after implementing a paid leave policy: Employee medical costs went down (Mejeur & Poppe, 2014).

In *Stage 4: Goal-Corrected Partnership Formation*, the child forms a partnership with the individual to whom they have become attached, and begins taking the other person's behavior into consideration. For example, the child may no longer chase after their father in the grocery store if the father tells the child he is going to the other end of the aisle for an item.

Partially because of gains in cognitive development that occur from Stage 3 to Stage 4, such as a decline in egocentrism, children now appreciate the motives and intentions of their parents and do not need to maintain constant proximity with these emotional partners. As a result, we develop what Bowlby (1976) referred to as **internal working models** of attachment, or mental representations of relationships that consist of our expectations regarding relationships (that people will treat us well or that people will reject us), as well as any needs, emotions, and behaviors that correspond to these expectations.

Negative expectations can lead us to misinterpret others' actions and words, and then to engage in defensive strategies that initially prevent us from paying attention to our emotions and that then perhaps cause us to ruminate over the emotions that later bubble up for us, as well as those of others. Such a process can create a cycle of insecure attachment (Koback & Bosmans, 2019; Mikulincer & Shaver, 2019).

Attachment Styles Measured by the Strange Situation

Just as important as the *process* by which attachment to a parent forms is the *quality* of this attachment. A protégé of Bowlby, Mary Ainsworth, observed mother and child interaction in the African country of Uganda (Ainsworth, 1967). She then moved back to the United States and developed a laboratory procedure to measure attachment quality within the first two years of a child's life. This procedure is called the **Strange Situation**.

The Strange Situation consists of a series of eight different separations and reunions between a child and their parent in a strange or at least unfamiliar playroom. It begins with the child and the parent alone in the room for approximately 30 seconds. Then, every 3 minutes a new episode begins in which the parent or a stranger (a confederate of the researchers) leaves or enters the room. The procedure was designed so that the predictable ways in which a child relates to their parent can be identified.

As a result, researchers using the Strange Situation are able to observe how the child behaves in four different situations, that is, with the parent, with the parent and the stranger, with the stranger, and alone. Within these different situations, observers focus on three behaviors, that is, the child's exploration of the toys in the playroom, the child's reaction to the separation (when the parent leaves the room), and the child's reaction to the reunion (when the parent returns to the room). Using Ainsworth's procedure, researchers have discerned that there are four attachment types (Ainsworth et al., 1978; Thompson, 2013). Let's examine them.

Children classified as having an **Insecure-Avoidant** (Type A) attachment avoid proximity and interaction with the parent while in the playroom, continue playing when the parent leaves, then ignore the parent or greet them very casually when the parents returns; the child also may squirm to be released when picked up by the parent. Approximately 20% of toddlers studied in the United States demonstrate this attachment type; interestingly, longitudinal research measuring avoidance on a continuum has shown that it declines from adolescence to early adulthood, perhaps because such decreased avoidance—and therefore less stability of attachment in adolescence relative to other life stages—allows young people to begin initiating romantic relationships (Chopik, Moore, & Edelstein, 2014; J. D. Jones et al., 2018).

Children having a **Secure** (Type B) attachment seek proximity to and interaction with the parent while in the playroom, stop playing temporarily when the parent leaves, smile at and approach the parent upon the reunion, and enjoy being picked up by the parent. Approximately 70% of U.S. toddlers studied demonstrate this attachment type, a good thing considering that the Secure attachment style is associated with optimal well-being later in childhood—and also that Secure attachments reflect the lifelong pattern of development in that they can alter developmental cascades for infants with difficult temperaments who otherwise would be at greater risk of relationship difficulties (Kochanska, Boldt, & Goffin, 2018).

Some have asked if Secure attachments are possible for children who are adopted. The answer is yes. Although preadoption adversity can have implications for children's thoughts and feelings about close relationships, their attachments improve significantly after the children are adopted; and regardless of the lack of genetic relatedness between parents and adopted children, the adopting parents' own attachments tend to be transmitted to their adopted children, reminding us that the intergenerational transmission of attachment is not bound by biology (Raby & Dozier, 2019).

Children with an **Insecure-Resistant** (Type C) attachment show such strong proximity-seeking behavior with the parent that they may fail to explore the toys in the playroom, become highly distressed when the parent leaves, express anger during the reunion (may even hit or push the parent when they return), resist being comforted easily upon being picked up, and then protest after being put down. Approximately 10% of toddlers studied in the United States demonstrate this attachment type, and the data indicate that Insecure-Resistant (as well as Insecure-Avoidant) children are also lower in effortful control than Secure children, and that these children tend to have parents who are less sensitive to their distress (Leerkes & Zhou, 2018; Pallini et al., 2018).

The **Insecure-Disorganized** (Type D) attachment style is clear in children who show flat or depressed emotions when with their parents, seem confused, or behave inconsistently or oddly, quiet one moment and aggressive the next. These children often have parents who are less likely to initiate joint attention, are ambiguous in whether or not they serve as safe havens, and are intrusive and/or psychologically controlling. For example, these parents regularly induce guilt; instill anxiety; and excessively criticize, shame, and/or ridicule their child in an ineffective and damaging attempt to manipulate the child's behavior (Reisz, Duschinsky, & Siegel, 2017).

 Consistent with the Lifelong pattern of development, all of the attachment styles have long-term consequences for the quality of teens' and adults' relationships, a quality that often parallels their attachment styles in early life unless they engage in extensive self-exploration and/or participate in effective therapy, so that

> the missing experience of having feelings recognized and acknowledged by another person, particularly of having strong feelings tolerated by another person, is provided by the therapist. Most important of all, when therapist and client fail to understand each other, or disagree

Pan & Zoom

Disorganized Attachment

In this box, we zoom in on Disorganized attachment. Attachment disorganization is a risk factor not only for emotional outcomes, but also for cognitive and physical outcomes. Children who experience Insecure-Disorganized attachment with two parents are more at risk in middle childhood for cognitive distortions, such as misinterpreting social cues as hostile and disrespectful, and therefore express more anger (Zajac et al., 2018).

 Children who experience Insecure-Disorganized attachment are also more at risk in adolescence for struggling with Borderline Personality Disorder (BPD), a diagnosis characterized by instability in relationships, with drastic swings from idealizing others to devaluing them within short periods of time. Parents who are ambiguous in whether or not they serve as a safe haven contribute to the development of BDP, given that they may alter between being a **secure** base to which children can return for validation and solace, and being a source of threat (Miljkovitch et al., 2018).

Research shows that among children who were involved in Child Protective Services in infancy, those with Disorganized (or Insecure) attachments were more likely to show negative outcomes consistent with the multidimensional pattern of development, such as having high levels of inflammation in their bodies or chronic activation of their immune system in early childhood (which can interfere with brain function and increase the risk of later depression). They also may have a higher body mass index, which increases the risk of later obesity and metabolic disease—*so that maltreatment becomes physically embedded in our bodies* (Bernard, Hostinar, & Dozier, 2019; Li & Danese, 2018).

 All is not lost for the emotional, cognitive, and physical well-being of children with Insecure-Disorganized attachment styles, though. Research shows that adults who complete treatment shift in their attachment patterns and experience fewer interpersonal problems. Interventions that prevent Disorganized attachment in children are also effective and help families function more out of the resilience side of the risk–resilience pattern of development (Facompré, Bernard, & Waters, 2018; Keating, Muller, & Classen, 2017).

• • • •

about something important and there is a "rupture" in the relationship, the therapist demonstrates that relationships can be "repaired." This cycle of rupture and repair is the key to secure relationships. (Gerhardt, 2004, p. 205)

To appreciate the multidimensional pattern of development in the consequences of one of the most worrisome attachment styles—that is, Disorganized attachment—see the *Pan and Zoom: Disorganized Attachment* box.

Keep in mind, though, that the Strange Situation that measures all attachment types reflects only a small fraction of the attachment interactions between parent and child. A true understanding of the quality of the bond a child has with a parent is perhaps best delineated with repeated observations as well as more naturalistic observations, including those reunions that occur when a parent picks up a child from childcare (Burman, 2017; Ziv & Hotam, 2015).

Attachment to Fathers

Most studies on attachment tend to examine the relationship between one parent (usually the birth parent) and the child. In the case of lesbian families in which children have two mothers, the mothers' own attachment experiences and current functioning—not whether each mother is biologically related to the child—are good predictors of their emotional involvement with their children (Barone, Carta, & Ozturk, 2018).

Yet partners substantially influence a child's developmental outcomes. A child with a mother and a father but with whom the child has two Insecure attachments is even more at risk for later difficulties than a child with only one Insecure attachment to a parent. Alternatively, a Secure attachment to one parent can buffer the child from the negative consequences of their Insecure attachment to the other parent (Dagan & Sagi-Schwartz, 2017).

In recent generations, fathers are increasingly (although not yet equally in many cases) involved in their children's lives. Fathers with the most paternal self-efficacy, or greatest perceived ability to deal with the demands of parenting, as well as the most expectations that fathers should be involved in their children's lives, are indeed the most involved (Trahan, 2017).

Just as a Secure mother–child attachment is correlated positively with children's emotion understanding, so is a Secure father–child attachment (Psychogiou et al., 2018). On the other hand, children of fathers who experience depression during the postnatal period are more likely to display conduct problems in the preschool years. These children are also likely to struggle with depression themselves while in adolescence, indicating that disruptions in fathers' ability to meet the needs of their babies is just as problematic as disruption in mothers' ability to meet their needs (Gutierrez-Galve, Stein, & Hanington, 2018).

Therefore, it behooves future research to involve more fathers in studies, particularly in terms of coparenting and fathers' interactions with mothers (or with their male spouses in the case of same-sex male couples—with gay fathers receiving even less research attention than straight fathers, and transgender parents even less so) to better understand how the parents together influence the child (Burke & Bribiescas, 2018; Fabiano & Caserta, 2018).

Key Terms

Amygdala

Attachment

Autonomy–Shame and Doubt

Behavioral Inhibition

Difficult

Easy

Effortful Control

Emotion

Emotional Regulation

Goodness of Fit

Insecure-Avoidant

Insecure-Disorganized

Insecure-Resistant

Internal Working Models

Mirror Test

Reactivity

Secure

Secure Base

Self-Conscious Emotions

Self-Regulation

Separation Anxiety

Slow-to-Warm-Up

Social Referencing

Strange Situation

Stranger Anxiety

Temperament

Trust and Mistrust (Trust–Mistrust)

Video Deficit Effect

Summary

1. **Identify how emotions in the first two years of life can be best supported.** Newborns display facial expressions that appear to correspond to emotions such as joy and disgust. Infants are capable of empathy in the first year of life and they smile reflexively when satiated or relaxed, but the first smile that is intentional and reflects happiness, the *social smile*, occurs typically by 3 months of age. Anger is most clearly and immediately expressed beginning at 4 months of age. Infants do not typically express surprise until about 5 to 7 months of age, around the time when they also develop the cognitive capacity for expectation.

    Infants begin to experience fear in the second half of the first year of life, and they start to respond differently to strangers around 7 or 8 months of age. Near the end of the first year of life, children begin to experience separation anxiety and to engage in social referencing, looking to familiar adults in order to interpret a novel situation. The emergence of consciousness or self-awareness in the second year of life provides a foundation for the emergence of self-conscious emotions, such as embarrassment, envy, and empathy. Around the same time, a toddler begins to be able to maintain an overt expression of an emotion that may or may not reveal their internal feelings, an example of emotion regulation.

2. **Describe what Erikson's theory can tell us about early emotional needs.** The crisis of infancy is Trust–Mistrust. Infants who experience mistrust may become suspicious and lack self-confidence because they have learned not to depend on others.

    The crisis to be resolved in toddlerhood is Autonomy–Shame and Doubt. When toddlers experience more autonomy than shame and doubt, they acquire the virtue of will. A parent who is overly controlling, on the other hand, causes the toddler to feel ashamed and helpless and to doubt their decisions and determination.

3. **Explain how the self develops, including the role of self-recognition.** Emotions rely upon a child's understanding of their self as unique and separate from others. Newborns do not possess this knowledge, but toddlers do. Some infants can pass the mirror test at around 18 months

of age, and most do so by 24 months, consistent with the onset of self-conscious emotions. Cultural differences in self-regulation suggest that the understanding of the self develops as a function of risk–resilience factors, such as how parents interact with their toddlers.

4. **Summarize what is known about how temperament develops in infants and toddlers.** According to Thomas and Chess, some children are Easy, meaning they show positive responses to new stimuli and high adaptability to change. Others are Difficult, meaning they are irregular in their sleep and eating patterns, have intense moods, and adapt slowly to change. Yet others are Slow-to-Warm-Up, meaning they are slow to adapt but have less intense reactions and less irregularity. Kagan focused on two extreme types of infant behavior, measured in terms of reactivity or how easily someone is emotionally and physically aroused.

   Rothbart views temperament as a result of two factors, reactivity and self-regulation, in which children shift their attention or self-soothe. Chess and Thomas considered development to be optimal when there is a goodness of fit between the individual and the context.

5. **Analyze how the quality of a child's attachment is a cause and an effect of development.** Attachment is the emotional bond that infants form with their parents. Harlow found that infant monkeys were more likely to cling to cloth "mothers" than to wire "mothers" even though the cloth "mothers" did not provide food, casting doubt on Freud's cupboard theory. Bowlby proposed that attachment develops through a series of stages roughly corresponding to different ages. Ainsworth developed the Strange Situation technique to measure different types of attachment, using eight different separations and reunions between a child and their parent in an unfamiliar playroom.

The Cycle of Science

Research

Why was the study conducted?

The researchers wanted to know how effective a "Mindful with Your Toddler" training program was for mothers and toddlers who have difficulties with co-regulation, or difficulties in self-regulation of attention, thoughts, and emotions that exacerbate the other person's difficulties in self-regulation (Potharst, Zeegers, & Bögels, 2018).

Problems in co-regulation are important to address in toddlerhood, because it is during this stage that children transition from being other-regulated to being self-regulated. Toddlers whose parents struggle to regulate themselves are at risk for later cognitive and emotional struggles, given that their parents weren't able to respond to them appropriately.

Who participated in the study?

The participants were 18 mothers of toddlers between the ages of 18 and 49 months; 68% of them were boys. The majority of the mothers were Dutch or otherwise European, lived with the fathers of their toddlers, and had earned a master's or bachelor's degree.

The majority of the mothers struggled in their relationship with the child's father; struggled with depression, anxiety, and/or post-traumatic stress disorder. Consequently, they were overreactive with their child; they were excessively demanding of their child; and/or their child had sleeping problems, eating problems, or problems with excessive crying.

Which type of design was used?

A quasi-experimental design was used, and the control group was a waitlisted group who received the training as well, but approximately 8 weeks after the experimental group. The 2-hour training sessions occurred weekly over the course of 9 weeks. Pretest assessments occurred 1 week before the training started, then again directly after the training, then 2 months after the training, and finally 8 months after the training. The assessments included measures of each mother's sensitivity to her child, acceptance of her child, overreactivity to her child (harshness); and sensitivity to her child's dysregulation (anxiety, depression, aggression); as well as parenting stress, internalizing and externalizing, mindful parenting, and so on.

The first four weeks of the training, mothers learned mindfulness skills, such as patience, acceptance, and trust in themselves. At week 5, mothers were joined by their toddlers in order to start practicing being mindful in the presence of their child—as well as being aware of their child's experience and their relationship with the child. They then practiced being mindful during stressful interactions with their child.

What were the results?

The researchers found that mothers' sensitivity to and awareness of their children increased in the experimental group, but not the control group. They also found that children's dysregulation improved in the experimental group, but not the control group. At the 2-month follow-up, maternal stress and incompetence decreased; but stress and incompetence had not decreased further by eight months, suggesting that the training could be even more effective if continued over longer periods of time.

Are the results consistent with theory?

The results are consistent with our understanding of self-regulation, or the process infants and toddlers use to regulate reactivity, which is a function of their brain structures' increasing connectivity and their having a strong emotional bond or attachment to a parent.

How can the results be used to improve our lives?

The results can be used to improve our lives by knowing that "Mindful with Your Toddler" group training programs are effective for mothers and toddlers who experience co-regulation difficulties—so that hopefully these programs can be effective with other groups of participants as well.

Exercises

1. What pattern of results would you expect to find if the study had been longitudinal in design and looked at outcomes in children when they were in preschool?

2. What pattern of results would you expect to find if the study had been conducted with toddlers and their fathers?

3. If this study had included participants from the United States and/or with mothers who were not as highly educated, the results might have been different. How so?

Helpful Websites

RIE® Associates has a list of providers who train parents and child care professionals: https://www.rie.org/about/alliance-of-rie-associates/

The State University of New York at Stony Brook has video clips of the Strange Situation, radio interviews with Mary Ainsworth, information on attachment for attorneys on placement decisions, and a wide range of other materials on attachment: http://www.psychology.sunysb.edu/attachment/

Zero to Three has a number of resources on Infant–Toddler Specialists, including this list of states with networks: https://www.zerotothree.org/resources/466-infant-and-toddler-specialist-network-factsheet

Recommended Reading

Bowlby, J. (1990). *A secure base: Parent-child attachment and healthy human development*. New York, NY: Basic Books.

Hoffman, K., Cooper, G., & Powell, B. (2017). *Raising a secure child*. New York, NY: The Guilford Press.

Kagan, J., & Snidman, N. (2004). *The long shadow of temperament*. Cambridge, MA: Belknap Press.

Katz, C., & Katz, J. (2007). *Dirty wow wow and other love stories: A tribute to the threadbare companions of childhood*. Berkeley, CA: Ten Speed Press. http://dirtywowwow.com/

Lansbury, M. (2014). *No bad kids: Toddler discipline without shame*. Los Angeles, CA: JLML Press.

CHAPTER 8

Physical and Cognitive Development in Early Childhood

Snapshot

Like many working-class parents (and, increasingly, middle-class parents as well), Dawn and Kevin struggle to make ends meet each month, and they are frustrated that things aren't getting any easier for them, no matter how hard they work.

They want the best for their 5-year-old twins, Crystal and Jimmy, and they're now starting to read about whatever they can do make sure their children's lives are better than their own. In this chapter, we will discuss what Crystal and Jimmy are learning, in terms of the twins' physical development during the preschool years, as well as the twins' cognitive development through the preschool years.

We will also see how Crystal's early fondness for building blocks has taken flight into a fascination with all things STEAM (science, technology, engineering, art, and math) after her exposure to the book *Rosie Revere, Engineer* (by Andrea Beaty and David Roberts) in their Pre-K class—and how this educational influence is affecting her development in a myriad of ways.

FIG. 8.1   Crystal and Jimmy

In the next chapter, we will learn how Jimmy's consuming passion for a different book, Maurice Sendak's *Where the Wild Things Are*, is helping him better understand and regulate his emotions.

What Are the Normative Changes in Physical Development During Early Childhood?

In this section, we consider normative or typical changes in physical development during early childhood, also called the preschool years. This is the stage of the life that corresponds to approximately 2 to 6 years of age.

General Growth

During early childhood, children like Crystal and Jimmy learn to eat, bathe, and dress themselves—primarily because of improvements in the fine and gross motor skills that are the result of brain development. Thus, it may not be surprising to learn that the brain reaches approximately 80% of its adult weight by 4 years of age (Haywood & Getchell, 2020).

In terms of preschoolers' total weight, we learned in Chapter 3 that the average newborn weighs 7.5 pounds. By 6 months of age, the infant weighs three times what they weighed at birth. Does this mean that weight triples every 6 months during early childhood?

No. During early childhood, growth is steady, as you can see in Figures 8.2 and 8.3. Most preschoolers gain approximately 5 pounds per year, and this pattern continues through middle childhood (Haywood & Getchell, 2020).

Gains in height during early childhood are also steady, as you can see in Figures 8.4 and 8.5. Each year, the average preschooler grows approximately 2 to 3 inches taller. So although the average newborn is 21 inches long, and by 12 months of age height has

Learning Goals

▸ Summarize the normative changes in physical development during early childhood

▸ Identify what nonnormative changes in physical development within the first two years entail

▸ Describe what Piaget's theory can tell us about cognitive development in early childhood

▸ Explain the cognitive processes that are most relevant to development in early childhood

▸ Demonstrate how preschoolers' language development, literacy, and numeracy can be supported

▸ Evaluate what family and government investments can do for development in early childhood

Weight-for-age GIRLS
2 to 5 years (percentiles)

World Health Organization

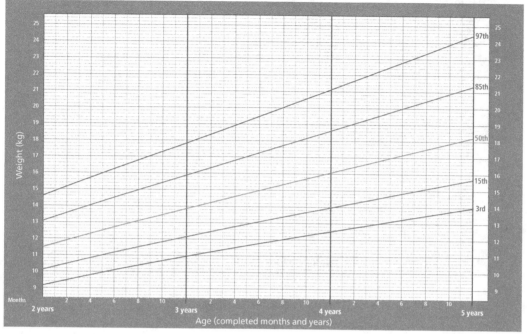

WHO Child Growth Standards

FIG. 8.2   Weight-for-Age for Girls from 2 to 5 Years of Age

Source: https://www.who.int/childgrowth/standards/cht_wfa_girls_p_2_5.pdf?ua=1.

Weight-for-age BOYS
2 to 5 years (percentiles)

World Health Organization

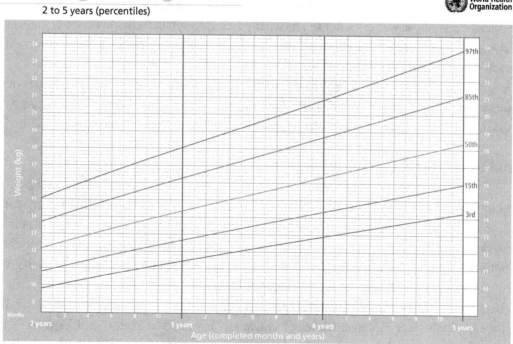

WHO Child Growth Standards

FIG. 8.3   Weight-for-Age for Boys from 2 to 5 Years of Age

Source: https://www.who.int/childgrowth/standards/cht_wfa_boys_p_2_5.pdf.

Height-for-age GIRLS
2 to 5 years (percentiles)

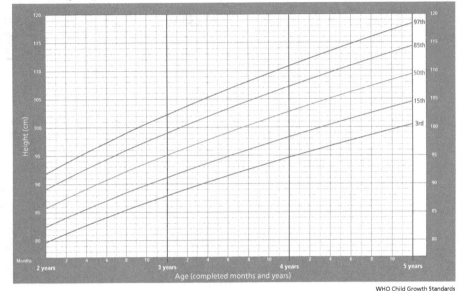

WHO Child Growth Standards

FIG. 8.4   Height-for-Age for Girls from 2 to 5 Years of Age

Source: https://www.who.int/childgrowth/standards/cht_hfa_girls_p_2_5.pdf.

increased by only 50%, height has doubled by the time children are 4 or 5 years of age. For instance, the average 5-year-old girl is 110 centimeters or 43 inches, which is double the average length of a newborn, or 21 inches.

Weight-for-stature is a measure of body weight that takes height into account. It is often computed as body mass index (BMI), and calculators for it can be found online. BMI is used to screen individuals for overweight and obesity. It does not tell us what percentage of an individual's body mass is made up of fat rather than muscle, though, so its use is limited. Yet it does provide a better understanding of physical growth than does weight alone.

Notice, in Figure 8.6 and Figure 8.7, that BMI for females and males actually *decreases* over the preschool years. This is a result of "baby fat" declining as children enter early childhood. As a result, preschoolers are leaner than toddlers, although weight issues can begin in early childhood.

Skeletal Growth and Tooth Eruption

Experts agree that the best measure of physical maturity is in our bones. Why? Because we can determine the beginning and end points of skeletal growth—unlike the case with height, for which we know only the beginning. That is, we know that most newborns are approximately 21 inches, but we do not know what each child's final, adult height will be. Yet we know when bones finish growing, which is when their growth centers are no longer visible.

Let's back up for a minute, though, to before the growth centers are even visible. Bones come into existence during the embryonic stage of prenatal development, as an early skeleton made of cartilage. This skeleton hardens into bones during this same stage, and then continues to grow into early adulthood. Like brain growth, bone growth is consistent with the polydirectional pattern of development, in that much of it occurs rapidly and early, and then slows down later in development.

Height-for-age BOYS
2 to 5 years (percentiles)

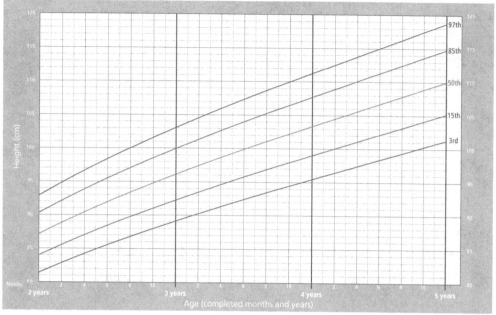

WHO Child Growth Standards

FIG. 8.5 Height-for-Age for Boys from 2 to 5 Years of Age

Source: https://www.who.int/childgrowth/standards/cht_hfa_boys_p_2_5.pdf.:

BMI-for-age GIRLS
2 to 5 years (percentiles)

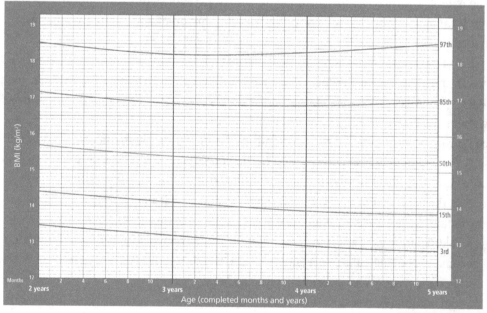

WHO Child Growth Standards

FIG. 8.6 BMI-for-Age for Girls from 2 to 5 Years of Age

Source: https://www.who.int/childgrowth/standards/cht_bfa_girls_p_2_5.pdf.

World Health
Organization

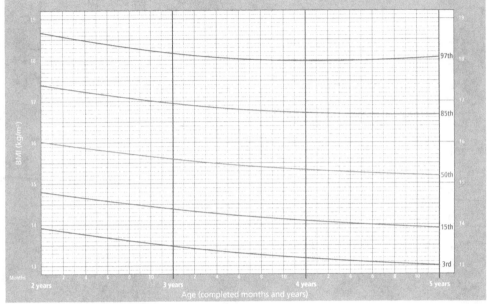

WHO Child Growth Standards

FIG. 8.7   BMI-for-Age for Boys from 2 to 5 Years of Age

Source: https://www.who.int/childgrowth/standards/cht_bfa_boys_p_2_5.pdf?ua=1.

As growth occurs, it tends to take place at the end of the bones. There, the *growth plates*, as Figure 8.8 shows, contain cartilage cells that eventually harden and thus lengthen the bone. An X-ray can reveal the extent to which the growth plate areas are present, which is considered a measure of a child's **skeletal age**. What differs from individual to individual, and therefore what we measure in assessments of skeletal age, is the *rate* of bone development.

Because skeletal age is an index of physical maturity, we can use it to compare one child at different points in time, or many different children at the same point in time. For example, each x-ray in Figure 8.9 is of a 14-year-old boy's hand, but the boy on the left is considered to have a skeletal age of 12, whereas the boy on the right has a skeletal age of 16.

Notice how **epiphysis** areas, or rounded ends of the bones, on the hand of the skeletally younger boy have yet to completely fuse with the rest of the bone, resulting in clearer lines at the end of each hand bone, indicating that the growth areas are still active. So imagine if you saw the x-ray on the left and were told the hand was of a 14-year-old. That would be typical, given skeletal age doesn't always match chronological age. Yet now imagine if you saw the x-ray on the left and were told the hand was of a 16-year-old. That would be atypical, because although a one-year or two-year mismatch between skeletal age and chronological age certainly occurs, the difference of four years—with skeletal age behind chronological age—can indicate delayed growth.

The epiphysis of long bones, such as the femur, or thigh bone, typically fuse by 18 or 19 years of age (Haywood & Getchell, 2020).

We know from Chapter 5 that most, if not all, of the 20 primary teeth erupt by about the time a child turns 3 years of age, with the first tooth showing at approximately 6 *months* of age, although the range is anywhere from 4 to 17 months. By 2 to 3 years, most of the primary teeth have erupted. But

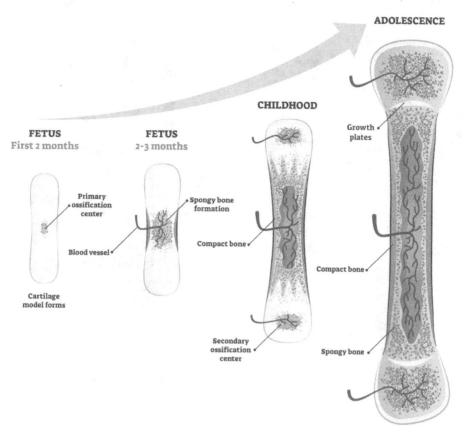

FIG. 8.8   The Growth of Bones

Copyright © 2019 Depositphotos/VectorMine.

when do the permanent teeth, illustrated in Figure 8.10, first arrive or begin to erupt? Have Crystal's? Jimmy's? Likely not, given the average is approximately 6 years of age.

Preschoolers usually don't yet have the motor skills to brush their teeth effectively, so parents need to be sure they do so, especially in light of the fact that 28% of preschoolers have tooth decay or cavities. Those children who live in lower-income families tend to have more tooth decay or cavities—likely because many pediatric dentists don't take Medicare and because the bacteria that cause cavities thrive off carbohydrates, which are bountiful in foods that are less costly (National Institute of Dental and Craniofacial Research, 2020; Rosenbaum, 2017).

By 12 to 13 years of age, most of the permanent teeth have finished erupting. Although some individuals never develop their third molars or wisdom teeth, those who do usually experience this eruption between 17 and 21 years of age.

Brain Development

As we saw in Chapter 4, synaptogenesis occurs as connections between neurons are created. The brain quadruples in weight before 6 years of age, when it also reaches approximately 90% of its adult volume (Brown & Jernigan, 2012). This helps explain the increasing head circumference of both girls and boys during the preschool years.

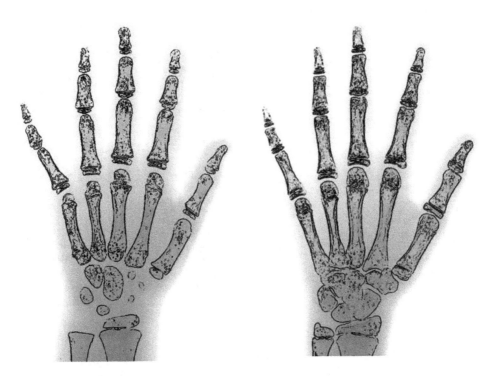

FIG. 8.9   X-Rays of 14-Year-Old Boys' Hands, with Skeletal Age of 12 (Left) and with Skeletal Age of 16 (Right)

Vicente Gilsanz and Osman Ratib, "Bone age," Hand Bone Age: A Digital Atlas of Skeletal Maturity, pp. 13-14. Copyright © 2005 by Springer Nature.

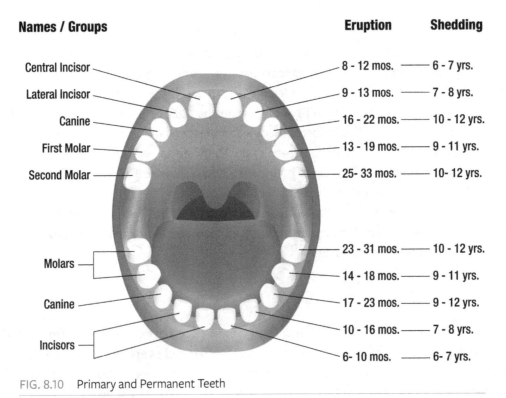

FIG. 8.10   Primary and Permanent Teeth

Copyright © 2015 Depositphotos/Furian.

As we learned in Chapter 4, neurons are produced and migrate to various areas of the brain primarily during prenatal development. But this process of neurogenesis continues during the preschool years, so that the brain's cortex is thickest by the end of this stage (Vértes & Bullmore, 2015).

Synaptogenesis is mostly complete at the start of early childhood, but these preschool years are a time of heightened myelination and **synaptic pruning**, or the elimination of excessive synaptic connections that we first read about in Chapter 5. Synaptic pruning is the way the volume of *gray matter* in the brain (synapses, neurons, and glial cells) decreases, whereas *white matter* (myelin) increases during this stage (Dean et al., 2015; Vértes & Bullmore, 2015).

These physical changes lead to children showing increasing levels of self-regulation during the preschool years. Yet the extent to which children self-regulate is also determined by parents' own self-regulation, which in turn contributes to how self-possessed (versus reactive) they are when their child is having difficulty self-regulating (Bridgett et al., 2015; Morawska, Dittman, & Rusby, 2019).

Children who exposed to the stressors of poverty often show impaired self-regulation, likely because chronic threats to children's well-being interferes with the functioning of their parasympathetic nervous system, their levels of the stress hormone cortisol, and the activity of their amygdala—setting them up for a greater likelihood of being reactive (Palacios-Barrios & Hanson, 2019).

Parenting interventions for parents living in poverty are especially necessary then, given the magnitude of their children's risks while growing up in poverty during a sensitive time of brain development. Also, parents who can't get their basic needs met are most at risk themselves for being able to provide for their children's needs (Morawska, Dittman, & Rusby, 2019; Palacios-Barrios & Hanson, 2019).

Nutrition

Food allergies are real—and their consequences can range from mild skin reactions to *anaphylaxis*, in which the throat swells and, in extreme cases, death can result. So it is important to be supportive of children with food allergies, as well as their parents, whose quality of life can be seriously diminished by the stress of constantly monitoring their child's food intake, and perhaps even dealing with other adults who dismiss their concerns (Warren et al., 2015; Williams & Hankey, 2014).

The causes of food allergies are not just genetic. They are a function of multiple lifestyle factors, including the timing of exposure to foods, insufficient vitamin D, the consumption of unhealthy fats, obesity, and even the season of a child's birth. Researchers have found that children born in the summer tend to have the lowest level of immune cells (Matsui et al., 2019; Sicherer & Sampson, 2014).

Some food allergies are more common, and more severe. Children can be allergic to cow's milk, shellfish, soy, and tree nuts. Yet peanut allergies account for approximately 25% of food allergies in children; are the most severe of all allergies; and are the type that children are least likely to outgrow, although novel treatments for peanut allergies are in development (Turnbull, Adams, & Gorard, 2015; Vickery et al., 2019).

Optimal nutrition is therefore important in any stage of development, but of particular importance in early childhood, not least because children's habits and preferences take form during the preschool years. Research shows that families who are most involved with food preparation have preschoolers who have a healthier food intake (Baranowski, Diep, & Baranowski, 2013; Metcalfe et al., 2018).

Malnutrition is obviously a problem, and when malnutrition comes not from the *quantity*, but from the *quality* of food, it is often referred to as **undernutrition**, meaning that independent of the child's weight, the child's diet is deficient in nutrients. Preschoolers who suffer chronic undernutrition have reduced amounts of muscle mass, their motor skill development is delayed or even impaired, and they may suffer stunted growth of the brain (Haywood & Getchell, 2020).

Undernutrition can be a consequence of eating more prepackaged food than fresh fruits and vegetables and/or a consequence of *food insecurity*, in which a family does not have reliable access to sufficient quantity and quality food (Moradi et al., 2018). For example, research has found that children's consumption of fried foods is correlated positively with their fat mass, whereas their consumption of vegetables is correlated positively with their bone mass and negatively with their fat mass.

Children's vegetable and fruit intake is also a function of role modeling, that is, how often their parents eat these foods and prepare them for their children. Yet children's vegetable and fruit intake is also clearly a function of how available these foods are—and when they aren't available, the lack of such a basic need negatively impacts parents too, understandably making the parents unnecessarily stressed and more likely to frequently discipline their children, as was the case of Dawn and Kevin in the past when one of them had lost a job (Gill, Koleilat, & Whaley, 2018; Harris & Ramsey, 2015).

Sleep

We know nutrition is key to growth and development, but sleep is important as well, particularly because it enables the release of growth hormone. Although more research on sleep recommendations for different age groups is needed, most available recommendations suggest that preschoolers need to sleep 11 to 13 hours in every 24 hours.

It isn't always easy to adhere to such recommendations, but doing so as consistently as possible is vital. Insufficient or irregular sleep (which research shows is more frequent in low-SES families) has outcomes consistent with the multidimensional pattern of development. These outcomes include a higher risk of obesity; poorer verbal abilities and self-regulation (understandably, even adults tend to be less patient, more irritable, and more likely to overeat when sleep deprived); and greater anxiety, depression, and aggressiveness (Cremone et al., 2017; Hoyniak et al., 2018; M. M. Miller et al., 2018).

In general, the quality of sleep changes in early childhood. Talking and laughing in one's sleep, as Jimmy does, are not uncommon for preschoolers. And because of their burgeoning imaginations, young children commonly experience sleep terrors and nightmares as well.

Sleep terrors, when children do not wake fully but scream in fear, usually occur during the early part of a sleep cycle or period of sleep, whereas **nightmares** occur later in the sleep cycle. Children often don't remember sleep terrors in the morning, although they may remember nightmares, which are usually more involved and can include a frightening story with an extended plot. Nightmares in children are thought to be a result of an irregular sleep schedule and/or stress.

Physical Activity

There are many valuable forms of physical activity in early childhood. Yoga has been found to improve preschoolers' attention, and their teachers' report that preschoolers show greater self-regulation and emotional skills when they practice yoga—all benefits that enhance their academic readiness as well (Cohen et al., 2018; Wolff & Stapp, 2019).

In general, though, preschoolers need at least 60 minutes and up to several hours of child-initiated **unstructured play** (make-believe play, such as playing house or playing doctor) per day. They also need at least 60 minutes per day of intentionally planned and adult-facilitated **structured play** (such as tricycle riding, running, climbing, dancing, hopscotch, and anything that involves hopping, skipping, jumping, and tumbling—all of which improve bone health and reduce excess fat). Therefore, children should be engaged in around 3 hours a day total of both kinds of play, particularly the more active types, and at all intensity levels—from light, to moderate, to vigorous (Centers for Disease Control and Prevention, 2019b).

Older preschoolers are ready for lessons in swimming, skiing, and skating. Not until middle childhood are children ready for organized or competitive sports, though. Preschoolers' level of physical development and cognitive development is not yet on par with the demands of sports (American Academy of Pediatrics, 2019).

A child with developmental delays need not miss the opportunity to play, either, thanks to new specially designed tricycles. Children with mobility-limiting disabilities such as cerebral palsy are able to take part in dance lessons at some facilities as well.

Most importantly, all preschoolers should spend time outdoors, to prevent what Richard Louv refers to as **Nature-Deficit Disorder** (Suttie, 2016). Nature Deficit Disorder is not a clinical diagnosis, but it certainly has a clear set of symptoms that appear in response to alienation from nature and insufficient *green time*, or time spent with nature. Perhaps this occurs because children are now more likely to be overscheduled or a *backseat generation*, being driven to multiple activities rather than spending unstructured time outside, compared to prior generations of children (Driessnack, 2009).

The aforementioned symptoms include obesity, depression, attention deficit disorder, lack of awe and wonder in response to nature, and lack of respect for the environment. Louv is the chair of the Children & Nature Network, a national nonprofit organization that provides opportunities for children to reconnect with nature and unplug from the allure of constant media. To learn more, visit their web page via the link in the *Helpful Websites* section at the end of this chapter.

Sufficient physical activity, ideally outside, is especially important during early childhood. Longitudinal research shows that physical activity declines substantially between 3 and 4 years of age and stays at lower levels throughout the rest of early childhood (Li, Kwan, King-Dowling, & Cairney, 2015; Taylor, Williams, Farmer, & Taylor, 2013).

Sufficient physical activity is a social justice issue too, as can be seen in the socioeconomic disparities in the contributors and consequences of asthma. That is, urban areas with traffic-related pollution make it difficult for children to obtain sufficient physical activity—urban areas with traffic-related pollution that contributes to children developing asthma in the first place (Kravitz-Wirtz et al., 2018).

Global and cultural differences are apparent too. For example, a comparison of cities across the globe with similar weather conditions found that children in northern Europe and southeast Australia are significantly more active than children in western Europe and the United States. It may be that, regarding preschool play, the cultures of western Europe and the United States have yet to appreciate the wisdom in the mantra "There's no such thing as bad weather, only inappropriate clothing." Also, northern European and Australian preschools may budget to provide for such clothing in order to better support children's needs and development (Harrison et al., 2017).

In the United States, unless a childcare center is exempt from state licensing, they are legally required to meet minimum health standards set by the state in which they operate. Yet as of this writing, only four states and one city have regulations for a specific amount of physical activity (Neelon et al., 2017).

Unfortunately, while physical activity varies among childcare centers, it is in general quite low—with less than 5% of preschoolers' time being spent in moderate-to-vigorous activity. Such inactivity is exacerbated by some childcare centers allowing children to have access to computer screens, which is very much against best practices for reducing sedentary behavior. Not surprisingly, the data show that the more screen use is restricted in childcare centers, the higher preschoolers' levels of total physical activity (Staiano et al., 2018).

Gross Motor Skills

Thanks to rapid growth in the cerebellum, which is involved in motor control just prior to and during early childhood, the quality of physical activity in early childhood is typically spontaneous, unorganized, and of short duration.

Running usually begins about 6 months after a child first walks; by about 24 months of age, most children are proficient runners. Preschoolers can usually jump from a height of about a foot off the floor by the time they are 3 years of age, hop on one foot a few times at 3.5 years of age, and jump over a rope approximately 8 inches high around the same time. Skipping usually develops later, between 4 and 7 years (Haywood & Getchell, 2020). A game that helps preschool children practice muscle and cognitive control, and that both Crystal and Jimmy enjoy regularly, is to line up pieces of paper on the floor and jump from "island" to "island."

Gross motor skills rely upon energy, which most preschoolers have in abundant supply; fine motor skills require patience, which isn't always at hand in early childhood. So fine motor skills may seem to lag behind gross motor skills for a few years. Yet they certainly improve with age.

Fine Motor Skills

Most 2- to 3-year-olds can stack blocks, hold an eating utensil, take off their shoes and socks, and draw simple lines. Around 3 years of age, children show a clear preference for using their left or right hand, yet approximately 25% of children have a mixed preference, which indicates that their hand preference may still be developing. This finding is consistent with how most children don't show true dominance of one hand until around 6 years of age (E. L. Nelson et al., 2018).

By 4 years of age, children can hold a crayon or a pencil in an adult manner with three fingers (that is, primarily using their thumb and index finger, and resting the tool on their middle finger). Also, 4-year-olds can usually brush their teeth and perhaps bathe on their own, print some letters, and draw an image of a person with a head, a torso, and legs. At approximately 4 to 5 years of age, children are able to cut paper fairly accurately with scissors and color mostly within the lines.

A child's drawings are a provocative example of the use of fine motor skills. The drawings might seem like mere child's play, but preschoolers who had lower birth weights or did not attend kindergarten tend to produce less sophisticated drawings.

Culture plays a role in children's drawings too: All children's drawing skills grow more proficient over time, and especially in recent years with the world becoming more visual. But Chinese American children's drawings are more proficient at all ages compared to those of other children, perhaps because Chinese American parents value the acquisition of drawing skills (such as via lessons) and artistic competence more than other groups of parents do (Genovese, 2018; Huntsinger et al., 2010).

No matter their culture, art provides a window into children's development because it gives us information about an individual child's fine motor skills—as well as their sensory abilities, cognitive functioning, and emotional experiences. It can also reveal symptoms of post-traumatic stress disorder.

For example, Palestinian children in Gaza and the West Bank live under chronic military occupation and are exposed to regular violence; the high level of violent content in their artwork is indicative of their distress levels. Research shows that children who have been traumatized and/or are at risk (such as those with unstable housing situations) benefit greatly from access to expressing themselves with art (Kamens, Constandinides, & Flefel, 2016; Saulle et al., 2018).

In fact, in 2020, the Sesame Workshop is releasing three new characters for *Ahlan Simsim*, the Arabic-language version of *Sesame Street*, one of whom likes to engage in painting to deal with trauma. The characters were created in order to change the course of a generation of a group of children for the better.

That is, *Ahlan Simsim* is set to help child refugees from Syria who are understandably struggling with the overwhelming fear, loneliness, and/or hopeless they have experienced since 2011, when over 5.6 million Syrian people—50% of them children—began to flee their country (and when another 6.6 million became trapped in their homes), when the violent government crackdowns began (UNHCR, 2019).

To create the new episodes, Sesame Workshop joined with the International Rescue Committee, received grants from the MacArthur Foundation and the Lego Foundation, then consulted with early-childhood professionals, psychologists, language specialists, writers, and artists. The first season will deal with how children can manage their emotions and cope with difficulties, through child-friendly actions such as belly breathing and art (Dahir, 2019).

In *Ahlan Simsim*, the new characters are yellow-furred Jad (who, tellingly, likes to paint with the brush he brought from where he used to live), who is welcomed to his new neighborhood by purple-furred Basma. The two are followed around by a baby goat named Ma'zooza, who eats circle-shaped objects.

To learn more about *Ahlan Simsim*, as well as how art therapy can help with post-traumatic stress disorder, see the links in the *Helpful Websites* section at the end of this chapter.

Regardless of any traumas to which they may be exposed, almost all children become better at representing reality in a drawing as they age, as you can see in Figure 8.12 on the next page (Basgul et al., 2011). In **Random Scribbling**, toddlers use a writing instrument not in order to draw something, but as a motor expression. The movements are usually broad back-and-forth strokes. Therefore, their random lines don't intend to be a representation of someone and therefore would occur prior to (a) in Figure 8.11.

With **Controlled Scribbling**, which occurs at the onset of early childhood, they attempt to reproduce at least part of an object, such as sweeping horizontal lines

FIG. 8.11 Children's Drawings of People by Age

John Willats, "Children's Drawings of People by Age," *Making Sense of Children's Drawings*, pp. 146. Copyright © 2005 by Taylor & Francis.

Age	Drawing Milestone
18 to 24 months	Random Scribbling
2 to 3 years	Controlled Scribbling
3 to 4 years	Lines and Patterns
4 to 5 years	Descriptive Symbolism
5 to 6 years	Letters and Word Practice

FIG. 8.12   The Progression of Children's Drawing Skills

that they declare are the family pett, as is now the case in (a) of Figure 8.11.

In the **Lines and Patterns** stage, 3-year-old and 4-year-old children begin using single movements of a writing instrument rather than broad back-and-forth movements, and first use lines to represent the boundaries of objects, such as a circle for a person's head. Yet representations in the Lines and Patterns stage are not entirely accurate at this point, something that is especially clear when 3- and 4-year-old children draw a person.

As can be seen in (b) in Figure 8.11, the **tadpole person**, typical of this age, consists of a single circle representing a person's head and body, with protruding lines for legs and arms.

And as can be seen in (c) in Figure 8.11, In the **Descriptive Symbolism** stage, drawings by 4- and 5-year-olds become more realistic descriptions and symbols of reality. For instance, at this age children's drawings of people begin to incorporate a separate head and body.

And as can be seen in (d) in Figure 8.11, gains in physical development and cognitive development are likely contributors to children's ability to then enter the **Letters and Word Practice** stage from 5 to 6 years of age. There is also increasing realism in all children's drawing at this stage. For example, although this particular drawing does not include writing, it does show increasing realism compared to (c)—notice how the torso is more proportional to the head in (d) than in (c), as well as the realistic details of the face and hat in (d). Such increased realism by the end of early childhood is universal including children with special needs, such as blind children who can also produce representational drawings (Jolley, 2010; Toomela, 2002).

The changes we see in children's drawings reflect the multidimensional pattern of development too, because they reflect corresponding changes in cognitive as well as physical development. Notice in Figure 8.12 that the maturation of children's drawing skills reflects the proximodistal trend, with increasingly control of the arms, then the hands, then the fingers, over time.

The sketchy appearance of "a" in Figure 8.11 is due partially to a child's limited fine motor skills, which prohibit them from making controlled and exact marks. Detail is more advanced in older children. Approximately 50% of 4-year-olds can draw a three-part person, or a person with a torso as in "c," so this is one assessment that nurses and physicians may give during a well-child exam. When asked to draw a three-part person, most 6-year-olds should be able to do so.

By the time children are between 3 and 5 years of age, they have a better attention span and can work on their own for approximately 10 minutes. Many have better control over their fingers and wrists, allowing them to produce drawings with finer lines and details (as in "d," "e," and "f")—making crayons, markers, paint, and modeling clay ideal tools to facilitate creativity and self-expression. Children 5 and 6 years old can work independently for up to 30 minutes, can work in small groups, and may even be able to share supplies.

By the time they are in primary school, children should be able to work independently on any creative task, including STEAM (Science, Technology, Engineering, Art, and Mathematics) projects, for approximately 1 hour, as Crystal and Jimmy have begun to do after one of their teachers taught

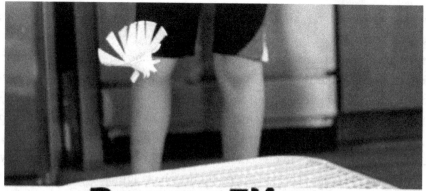

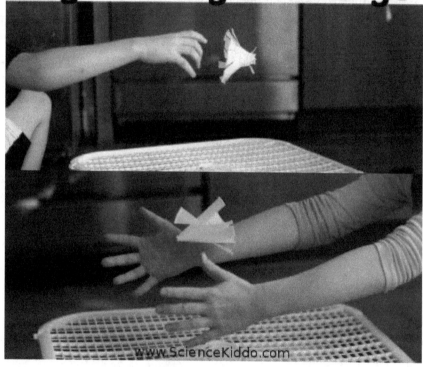

FIG. 8.13   Paper Fliers Engineering Challenge

Source: https://www.sciencekiddo.com/paper-fliers-rainy-day-boredom-busters/.

Crystal how to engineer using a box fan to fly papers fliers made out paper with different patterns of cuts, as can be seen in Figure 8.13 (Koster, 2009; Mohammed, 2018).

Notice in the top panel how they are experimenting with one particular flier as they drop it down over a box fan, whereas the second panel teaches them how the very same flier responds when they attempt to sail it over the fan instead. The last panel reveals another flier possibility, this one with a more aerodynamic nose, which teaches them about the role of cuts as well as shape.

To learn about stages of artistic development in both childhood and adolescence, and to learn which stages correspond to Piaget's stages of cognitive development in both childhood and adolescence, see the book *Understanding Children's Drawings* (Malchiodi, 1998) listed in the *Recommended Reading* section at the end of this chapter; this book also provides a fascinating overview of important of art therapists.

To best support children's creativity, teachers and parents should be flexible so that children can explore materials and ideas that the children themselves select from a range of choices provided to them (such as investigating the seeds within a real sunflower, via painting, counting, or sprouting the seeds—rather than being handed a closed and teacher-driven task such as coloring a paper plate to make it look like a sunflower). Teachers and parents should be playful and surprising (wear something unusual or decorate an entire room in one color) so that children understand it is okay to take risks and try something new. They should be patient, so children have sufficient time to immerse themselves in a project without becoming frustrated or sensing that their work isn't worthwhile. Especially, they should be careful with their praise so children do not feel they are not really worthy of consideration.

That is, the physical act of creating is influenced by and influences how we think about what to make, which, in turn, influences and is influenced by our emotions. For example, instead of saying "Great job!" an adult may wish to respond with "I noticed you made line and circle shapes to glue to the board. The lines and circles really helped you make a tree shape" (Koster, 2009; Mohammed, 2018).

The former comment suggests to the child that some of their work may not always be great, so that they may give up if and when their parent provides realistic feedback on not-so-great work; the latter comment provides positive reinforcement for the child's *effort*, not the *outcome*, and it is this effort that children will continue to engage in with such reinforcement (Costa & Faria, 2018; Dweck, 1999). We will talk more about the consequences of these very different types of praise in Chapter 12.

For a lively, informative, and practical guide with concrete ideas on what really makes for best practices with preschoolers, check out Christakis's (2016) *The Importance of Being Little: What Preschoolers Really Need from Grownups*, listed in the *Recommended Reading* section at the end of this chapter.

How Can We Identify Nonnormative Physical Development?

Sometimes development during the preschool years does not proceed typically, or as expected. In this section, we review the various ways in which growth and development during early childhood veers from the normative path.

Overweight and Obese Preschoolers

A **secular trend** is a historical trend in which generations vary, usually because of risk–resilience factors. Secular trends in physical development are evident. For instance, the average height and weight of children and adolescents have increased in recent generations, while the age of menarche, or a female's first menstrual cycle, and other indices of biological maturation have declined (Wagner, Sabin, & Kiess, 2015).

Researchers have speculated that the reasons for these trends include improvements in public health and nutrition, which is a good thing and reflects the risk–resilience pattern of development, but another reason may be the increased average BMI of girls in recent generations (Le-Ha et al., 2018). Body fat contains estrogen, and estrogen/body fat levels are correlated negatively with menarche;

earlier onset of puberty is worrisome, given, that it is associated with a greater risk of type II diabetes, heart disease, and cancer in adulthood (Binder et al., 2018).

To counteract this trend, the use of consumer products with parabens, phthalates, and phenols (chemicals that are quickly metabolized) should be reduced. Research reveals negative correlations between puberty onset and exposure to these chemicals, exposure both in utero and during childhood in both boys and girls—and as we learned a moment ago, earlier onset of puberty is associated with a greater risk of a number of life-threatening diseases in adulthood (Harley et al., 2019).

Current data indicate that approximately 14% of preschoolers are obese, a percentage that has declined in recent years but is still worrisome. Research shows that obesity-related cancers (such as colorectal and uterine) are now occurring much more often in young adulthood, compared to middle adulthood and late adulthood, for unknown reasons, but quite possibility due to obesity being higher in recent generations of young children (Centers for Disease Control and Prevention, 2019a; Sung, Siegel, Rosenberg, & Jemal, 2019).

BMI is correlated negatively with preschoolers' degree of self-regulation, and it is also correlated negatively with the education level of preschooler's main parent, reminding us of the role that parent education can play in erring on the resilience side of the risk–resilience pattern of development (Schmitt et al., 2019).

Overweightness is defined as having a BMI of 25 to 29.9, and **obesity** is defined as having a BMI of 30 or greater. Researchers have examined the many characteristics of a preschooler's context that increase the risk of them being overweight or obese; they include child characteristics, family characteristics, community characteristics, and government policies (Congdon, 2019; A. S. Williams et al., 2018). Let's consider each now.

Child characteristics include having been breastfed very little or not at all, spending relatively little time in tummy time to promote motor development, being primarily formula-fed (which alters the intestinal microbiome), consuming high-energy but low-nutrient foods as well as juices and other sweetened beverages, maternal obesity or diabetes, obtaining insufficient sleep, having a lack of bedtime rules, and engaging in little physical activity but regular screen time (Koren, Kahn-D'Angelo, Reece, & Gore, 2019; Mueller & Blaser, 2018; Porter et al., 2018).

A sedentary lifestyle during the early years is particularly problematic. It sets the stage for a cascade of consequences consistent with the lifelong pattern of development, including a sedentary lifestyle later on, which is a risk factor for many chronic and life-threatening diseases, such as heart disease and diabetes.

Community factors that increase the risk of a preschooler's being overweight or obese include characteristics associated with the risk–resilience pattern of development. Among these are urban sprawl without adequate sidewalks; low proximity to playgrounds and/or healthful food, leading some children to become overweight or obese but simultaneously malnourished, given their insufficient intake of nutrients; unsafe neighborhoods; a lack of opportunity to exercise in childcare and preschool; preschool settings without jumping or balancing equipment, hilly terrains, or sand but with seesaws and gravel; an emphasis on academics over play in preschool settings; and childcare providers' limited ability to change practices despite their knowledge of children's need for regular intervals of movement (Congdon, 2019; Connelly, Champagne, & Manningham, 2018; Määttä et al., 2019).

On the other hand, positive factors associated with the risk–resilience pattern of development—such as excellent maternal mental health, neighborhood safety, school safety, and child resilience—all contribute to erring on the resilience side of the risk–resilience pattern of development when it comes to children being overweight or obese (Lynch et al., 2018).

Government policy characteristics that contribute to the increasing number of overweight and obese preschoolers include limited dietary guidelines in childcare centers and schools. Related risks include nonparticipation in the USDA's Child and Adult Care Food Program rules for nutrition standards, variable policies on recommended serving sizes for children, and unequal legal protections for birth parents to breastfeed at work (Andreyeva & Henderson, 2018; Smith, 2018).

The Affordable Care Act's "Break Time for Nursing Mothers" requires employers to provide a reasonable amount of time and nonbathroom private space for parents to breastfeed or pump breast milk until their children turn 1 year of age. But it does not require employers to pay employees for these breaks, nor does it specify what is a reasonable amount of time or where the private space may be located. Further, it applies only to employers with at least 50 employees and to hourly, not salaried, employees (Raju, 2014). As a result, employers who don't provide sufficient time or space for parents risk having more disgruntled employees; and employees risk having to take more days off to care for sick infants, and having to pay higher insurance premiums to care for these infants' medical bills (Raju, 2014).

Increasing portion sizes also seem to play a role in the rising numbers of overweight and obese children. The resulting increased food intake in both children and adults is referred to as the *portion size effect* (Keller et al., 2018). Healthcare professionals recommend that parents take the time to cook—and have their children help by washing vegetables, reading recipes, preparing equipment, and learning how to plan ahead. The professionals also recommend that parents consider visual examples of what a recommended portion of food is, in order to avoid "portion-distortion."

An example of portion-distortion is how, 20 years ago, an average bagel was 3 inches in diameter and 140 calories. Most bagels are now 6 inches in diameter and 350 calories. Another contributor is the lack of policies governing commercials pitched to children, alongside the huge investments some

Tech & Media

Tech & Media in Our Lives: The Marketing of Food to Children

Children learn what to eat and how often to eat after observing the eating habits of the adults in their lives. But what we eat is not only a result of personal preferences, but also a function of government policies and the food industry—which has a history of opposing such guidelines over the last four (Nestle, 2018).

Thus, patterns set in early childhood are a major contributor to whether an adult is of a healthy weight, and children and adolescents may not live as long as their parents as a result of the current obesity crisis (Preston, Vierboom, & Stokes, 2018). Therefore, children should never be forced to clean their plates, fruit should be served regularly, high-calorie snacks should not be kept in the household, and screen time should be reduced. Obesity often begins during the preschool years, is difficult to reverse, and has serious health consequences consistent with the lifelong pattern of development (Langian, Tee, & Brandreth, 2019).

Why screen time, though? Because the snacks marketed to children—via "advergames" (games on food-company and other websites), on television, or within video games and various forms of media—tend to be foods or *food-like* products that are energy-dense but nutrient-poor. Research data on advergames indicate that they promote unhealthful food and also induce unhealthful eating in children, who consequently have greater BMIs (Folkvord, & van't Riet, 2018; Norman et al., 2018; Russell, Croker & Viner, 2018).

Food industry groups claim that government regulation of food marketing to children would violate the First Amendment, yet the First Amendment does not protect speech that is "inherently misleading." Research shows that children are not able to recognize the persuasive intent in advertising. Inherently misleading advertising, aimed at those who cannot recognize it as such and have little or no advertising literacy, is considered beyond the scope of constitutional protection—so marketing restrictions and packaging redesign to reduce the appeal of low-nutrition food-like products sold to children must be implemented as a preventative public health measure (Kelly et al., 2015; Kersh & Elbel, 2019).

• • • •

corporations make in tailoring their advertising and marketing of food to children. More information on this is available in the *Technology & Media in Our Lives: The Marketing of Food to Children* box.

Nocturnal Enuresis

Imagine babysitting a 4-year-old who wets the bed long after you put them to sleep. You change the sheets, assure the child it was just an accident, and encourage them to go back to sleep. When the parents come home, they ask you what you recommend, given that this has become a regular problem. What do you say?

The American Psychiatric Association's Diagnostic and Statistical Manual (DSM-5) defines **nocturnal enuresis** as urinating in the bed or clothes at least twice a week for at least three consecutive weeks in children over 5 years of age (American Psychiatric Association, 2013).

Nocturnal enuresis is thought to have many causes, the most common being weak bladder control. Other contributing factors include excessive nocturnal urine production; low bladder capacity; inability to wake up when the bladder is full; a poor diet, which leads to constipation and corresponding pressure on the bladder; urinary tract infections; diabetes; sleep apnea; and/or being overweight or obese (Tobias, 2018).

Most cases of nocturnal enuresis are a product of weak bladder control because the nervous system is still developing. For this reason, most children outgrow the condition as they advance in age and physical maturation. Children who wet themselves and/or the bed should therefore not be punished, since they are not intentionally misbehaving.

Parents' sensitivity is vital; children who do not receive treatment and support are more at risk for behavior problems and low self-esteem than children of the same age who have bladder control. Many older children have found enuresis alarms helpful, perhaps more so than hormonal medication to reduce urine. However, alarms may require several weeks to be effective, so both the child and the parents must be sufficiently motivated to adhere to treatment guidelines—and the underlying problem contributing to nocturnal enuresis should be determined before any treatment begins (Kuwertz-Bröking & von Gontard, 2018).

Enuresis alarms, which go off if a sensor detects wetness, are not a form of punishment—nor should they be used as such. These alarms work via negative reinforcement, in which children's learning to wake up and go to the bathroom is reinforced by the absence of a wet bed. Parents can also make a *sandwich bed*, in which they alternate a clean sheet with a plastic sheet. That way, if a child has an accident, parents can pull the wet sheet and underlying plastic sheet off the bed quickly and easily without major effort or distress.

Injuries

The leading cause of death in early childhood is not disease or homicide but *unintentional injuries*, such as a motor vehicle accident, drowning, being burned in a fire, or suffocating (Centers for Disease Control, 2017).

Figure 8.14 shows that adult supervision is influenced by and influences adults' recognition of the factors that contribute to preschool-age children's injuries. In this model, *child factors* that put children at risk for injury include their larger heads, over which they have less control than the rest of their bodies, so they are top-heavy and can drown in as little as one inch of water.

Another factor, and an example of the multidimensional pattern of development, is preschoolers' limited logical thinking, which leads them to engage in risky behavior such as standing on unstable objects to obtain toys or cookies. *Environmental factors* include drawstrings from window treatments, access to harmful plants and medications, poorly lit stairways, and toys with magnets that can be swallowed and then stick together and stay in the body.

Agent factors refer to the means by which an injury occurs, such as a toy's sharp edge and/or toxic paint, a window screen's inability to hold the weight of a child leaning against it, and a motor vehicle's

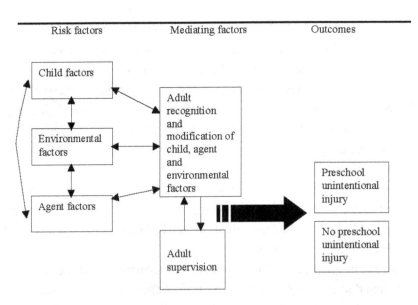

FIG. 8.14 Risk Factors, Mediating Factors, and Outcomes for Unintentional Injuries to Preschoolers

Dawn Lee Garzon, Risk Factors, Mediating Factors and Outcomes for Unintentional Injuries to Preschoolers, from "Contributing Factors to Preschool Unintentional Injury," Journal of Pediatric Nursing, vol. 20, no. 6, pp. 442. Copyright © 2005 by Elsevier B.V.

speed. These hazards can occur in any home, so even though it can be difficult to make time for preventive actions, it is vital for parents to modify the home environments and teach children safety rules—as well as first being aware of risk factors, such as a lack of safety bars on windows, which can prevent falls (Ablewhite et al., 2015; Hogan et al., 2018).

Child Maltreatment

Child maltreatment is an umbrella term for any context that can include physical abuse or the inflicting of physical injuries, but also physical neglect, sexual abuse, emotional abuse, and/or emotional neglect. **Physical neglect** is a failure to meet children's basic health and safety needs, a failure that places them in harm's way. Parents who neglect children fail to provide the physical, cognitive, or emotional conditions essential to a child's development. **Physical abuse** is the deliberate inflicting of injuries, bruises, burns, and wounds from firearms.

Sexual abuse includes making contact with a child's genitals and/or exposing children to sexual photography. **Neglect** refers to the failure to provide basic physical needs (food, healthcare, a safe and clean home), emotional needs (nurturance, warmth, and support), and/or educational needs.

Emotional abuse includes ridiculing, mocking, belittling, threatening, imposing developmentally inappropriate expectations on the child, rejecting, limiting the child's learning and exploration, engaging in hostility, and using the child to fulfill the adult's needs (Berzenski, Madden, & Yates, 2019). Although its symptoms may not always be as visible as other forms of child maltreatment, emotional abuse should not be disregarded, given that it is associated with later outcomes, such as a heightened risk of anxiety, depression, and/or aggression. Unfortunately, emotional abuse is the most pervasive but least studied form of maltreatment (Lavi et al., 2019; Warmingham et al., 2019).

The evidence on whether or not parents who were mistreated as children are more likely to mistreat their own children is mixed, and depends on many factors (Capaldi et al., 2019). Indeed, though, parents who experienced emotional abuse in their own childhoods may struggle more to create secure attachments with their preschoolers—and they are most likely to display verbal aggression, anger, poor emotional regulation, and poor coping strategies.

Although parents may be ashamed of such, they need to remember that if they didn't have the opportunity to acquire effective coping skills in the past, they can learn them now. This includes regulating one's emotions and tolerating distress via Dialectical Behavior Therapy, or DBT (Lavi et al., 2019). See the *Recommended Reading* section at the end of this chapter for a suggested DBT workbook.

The consequences of child maltreatment in general illustrate the multidimensional and lifelong patterns of development. They include obesity, chronic inflammation, high blood pressure, heart disease, memory impairments, depression, anxiety disorders, substance abuse, difficulty achieving developmental milestones, heightened reactivity to later stress, impaired relationships, diminished emotional regulation, and parenting difficulties. The last of these may increase the likelihood of intergenerational transmission of child maltreatment (Albott, Forbes, & Anker, 2018; Goodman, Freeman, & Chalmers, 2018; Rasmussen et al., 2019; Suglia et al., 2017).

Again, however, these outcomes are not inevitable. Whether maltreated children suffer them depends on the children's general resilience or ability to adapt to adversity, their stress reactivity, the quality of support they receive in childhood, the form of intervention or psychotherapy treatment as teens or adults, and their willingness to experience and process painful private thoughts and memories rather than suppress them (Mongan et al., 2018; Toth & Manly, 2019). Prevention, which research has shown to be effective with parenting programs, is vital; all children are entitled to grow up without denigration (Tiwari et al., 2018).

If a child discloses maltreatment to a professional (such as a social worker, teacher, principal, physician, nurse, counselor, therapist, childcare provider, and/or law enforcement officer), this adult should listen but not inquire about the details—nor promise confidentiality—but instead explain to the child that the adult is required to pass the information on to others, such as Child Protective Services. Failure to report abuse or suspected abuse to Child Protective Services is a violation of the law in 44 states and can result in fines and/or imprisonment (Kenny et al., 2018).

What Can Piaget's Theory Teach Us About Cognitive Development in Early Childhood?

Today, Jimmy is upset because he thinks his little sister (by a few minutes) Crystal got more pieces of cinnamon toast for breakfast than he did. Jimmy's father Kevin cut Crystal's toast into eight small pieces, but was rushing to turn off the noisy tea kettle so he cut Jimmy's toast in halves for a total of four larger pieces.

As soon as Jimmy became upset, however, Kevin cut Jimmy's toast again, so he now had eight pieces of cinnamon toast. Jimmy smiled and began eating his breakfast, content with what he thought was finally an amount of cinnamon toast equal to Crystal's. But why did Jimmy become upset in the first place? What was it about Jimmy's thinking that Kevin understood?

Let's take a look, and keep in mind that, according to Piaget, three of the four major characteristics of children's thinking during the preschool years are *weaknesses* rather than *strengths*, but weaknesses that are normative and that children will overcome in later stages of development.

The major strength of children's thinking during the preschool years is their capacity for representational or symbolic thought. This means they come to understand that one thing is capable of representing or symbolizing something else, such as a banana that a child can place at their ear and speak into as if it were a mobile phone. As we will see in Chapter 9, representational or symbolic thought has major implications for children's capacity for play, especially make-believe play, an activity that can further boost cognitive development and emotional development. For now, though, let us better understand some of the aforementioned weaknesses in children's thinking during this stage.

Egocentrism

Operations are mental schemes that describe the ways children interact with the world, and operations rely on logical thought because they follow a system of rules; preschoolers tend to be Preoperational because their thinking is not yet logical (Bjorklund & Causey, 2018). An example of operational thinking occurs when we understand just by looking that two rows of equal numbers of grapes are still equal even though the grapes in one row are farther apart, making that row appear longer than the other.

Because preschoolers do not yet use operations accurately, their thinking is more intuitive than logical. According to Piaget, for instance, preschoolers are **egocentric** in the sense that they are incapable of distinguishing their perspective from the perspectives of other people.

Piaget and his colleague Inhelder (1948) developed the *three-mountain task* to measure egocentrism in children. After sitting at a table with a display of three mountains of different sizes, children were shown photographs of the display. When they were asked to choose the photograph that corresponded to the experimenter's view of the mountains, only school-age children were able to do so correctly. Preschool-age children chose the photograph that corresponded to their own perspective of the mountain display, indicating that in early childhood, we tend to assume everyone has the same perspective as our own.

Another quirk of preschoolers' egocentrism is that they assume that, just like themselves, all people and objects are conscious and engage in mental activity—an idea referred to as **animism**. For example, preschoolers might assume that thunder happens because the clouds are angry or the sun moves across the sky during the day because it wants to follow people home.

Such magical thinking or to be encouraged in order for children to fulfill the potential of their imaginative capacities, yet they can also influence emotional development by resulting in a great deal of fear, especially around bedtime. Preschoolers often aren't sure what is real and what is pretend. It is important that adults do not discount, ignore, or ridicule these fears, because they are very real and very disturbing to children. If a child continues to be extremely fearful of the dark, pain, masks, crowds, animals, and so on after 5 years of age, counseling may be helpful to the child and the family.

Research has shown that preschoolers have a tendency to assume fantastical creatures (such as monsters) are real. Children with greater nighttime fears show more confusion about the distinction between fantasy and reality, but this distinction grows clearer with increasing age.

Since the distinction between fantasy and reality is much less clear for preschoolers than it is for school-age children, it may just be a matter of time before older preschoolers appreciate that monsters are not real. In the meantime, parents can encourage children to express these fears via the arts; research shows that children with imaginative fears tend to have strong creative imaginations (Gündoğan, 2018; Martarelli et al., 2015).

Lack of Hierarchical Classification

Piaget proposed that because preschoolers are not yet capable of logical thinking, they show another weakness in their thinking. That is, they show a *lack of hierarchical classification*, in which they struggle to organize or classify objects into categories and subcategories in the process we call hierarchical classification.

For example, when asked whether there are more dogs or more animals in the drawing shown in Figure 8.15, most preschoolers say there are more dogs, because they see that there are more dogs than cats. Yet they are unable to

FIG. 8.15   An Example of a Class-Inclusion Task

Robert S. Siegler and Matija Svetina, An Example of a Class-Inclusion Task, from "What Leads Children to Adopt New Strategies? A Microgenetic/Cross Sectional Study of Class Inclusion," Child Development, vol. 77, no. 4. Copyright © 2006 by John Wiley & Sons, Inc.

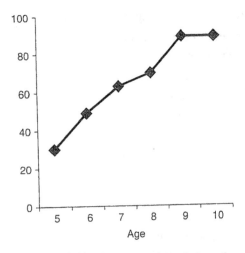

FIG. 8.16   Children's Correct Completion of a Class-Inclusion Task by Age

: Robert S. Siegler and Matija Svetina, Children's Correct Completion of a Class-Inclusion Task by Age, from "What Leads Children to Adopt New Strategies? A Microgenetic/Cross Sectional Study of Class Inclusion," Child Development, vol. 77, no. 4. Copyright © 2006 by John Wiley & Sons, Inc.

simultaneously see that there are more animals than dogs, because they typically don't have the ability to combine these multiple mental counting strategies until they are in the next stage in Piaget's theory, that is, Concrete Operational thinking (Börnert-Ringleb & Wilbert, 2018; Siegler & Svetina, 2006).

The percentage of children who complete a **class-inclusion** task like this correctly increases with age, a finding shown in Figure 8.16 and consistent with Piaget's theory. Notice that this is an example of the polydirectional pattern of development; magical thinking decreases and logical thinking increases as children enter middle childhood.

Consider a 6-year-old who is inquiring about the Tooth Fairy and wants to know how it is possible that she flies into the house while he is sleeping. As children transition into middle childhood, they begin asking questions such as these because their thinking is becoming more logical.

With age, children become more rational and more scientific, so they increasingly question things that are not explained by reason. Research indicates that children who are more advanced in their ability to distinguish between physically possible events and impossible events are more likely to question the feasibility of magical beings such as the Tooth Fairy—and more so to the extent that parents have conversations with them about fantasy and reality (Carrick, Sawaya, & Palisoc, 2018; Shtulman & Yoo, 2015).

Lack of Conservation

Jimmy's dismay over being given what he thought was less cinnamon toast than his sister Crystal was due to another normative weakness in thinking during this stage: a lack of understanding of conservation. In Piaget's Cognitive Development theory, **conservation** means we are able to understand that the characteristics of an object stay the same, or are conserved, despite changes in its appearance. Piaget is probably best known for his work on conservation, particularly the tasks or measures he used to assess whether a child was capable of it.

One such measure was the conservation of liquid task (Piaget, 1941). In this task, children are shown two glasses of the same shape and size and holding the same amount of liquid. When asked whether the two glasses contain the same amount, preschoolers typically respond correctly.

Next during this task, the experimenter pours the liquid from one glass into a third glass that is a different shape and size. For example, as seen in Figure 8.17, the third glass may be tall and narrow. Once the liquid from one of the original glasses has been poured into the third glass, children are asked once again whether the two filled glasses hold the same amount.

Preschoolers invariably say the taller glass has more. When asked why, they say the glass is taller. This answer indicates one of the reasons why preschoolers struggle with conservation tasks: They

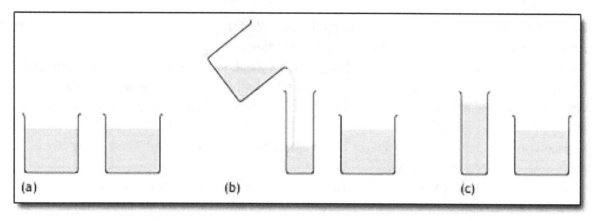

FIG. 8.17   A Conservation of Liquid Task

engage in **centration**, focusing on one characteristic of something, such as the height of the glass, while ignoring others, like its narrow width. Centration is another example of preschool children's inability to think about multiple things at one time.

Another reason why preschoolers typically fail conservation tasks is that they engage in **irreversibility**. This means they are incapable of mentally reversing previous events. That is, a preschooler, when asked what would happen if the liquid from the third glass were poured back into its original glass, is unable to consider that the amount of liquid would still be the same.

Generally speaking, conservation tasks can also ask children to determine *mass* (in which researchers smash one of two equal-size balls of dough and ask children whether the balls are still the same size) and *number* (researchers stretch out one of two equal-length rows of equal numbers of grapes and ask whether the rows still contain the same number of grapes).

Regardless of the type of conservation task, remember that the *rate* or speed with which children progress through each of Piaget's four stages is variable, but the *sequence* or order of these four stages is fixed and always remains the same. The rate seems to be determined by the quality of a child's environment. Piaget proposed that the lack of logical abilities in children under age 7 was due to deficiencies of the nervous system, but that maturation of the nervous system—and the support of the environment of ideal conditions for children to explore—only creates the condition for logical thinking to develop (Inhelder & Piaget, 1964).

So progression through the Preoperational stage is characterized by multidimensional and risk-resilience patterns of development, because the stage is characterized by a number of cognitive weaknesses that may be a function of physical development or increasing connections between the brain's neurons, and because it requires children to interact with a stimulating environment in order to develop their thinking.

Symbolic Thought

Jimmy holds a banana to his ear and says, "Hello." Obviously he is pretending the banana is a phone, but does he understand that pretending is not just a physical behavior, but a mental activity as well?

During the preschool years, children develop the capacity for *symbolic thought*, that is, the understanding that an object or a word can represent something else.

The physical object of a banana can represent a mobile phone, and the word *banana* can represent a real banana, a toy banana, or a banana that is a figment of the imagination—such as one that a child draws on paper. Understanding that preschool children use symbolic thought can help us appreciate why thinking in early childhood is often fanciful rather than logical; this is why explaining that there are no sharks in the closet because sharks need water to survive does not always assuage a child's fears.

Their use of symbolic thought also explains why preschoolers often think that inanimate objects like clouds are animate or have a life force and intention behind them (it is raining because the clouds are sad). However, symbolic thought is a strength too, because it means preschool children are deeply creative in their thinking and are not tied to the physical limitations of the real world—for instance, a child who is encouraged regularly to consider that the child's "loveys" are consider, that inanimate objects might propose that the child's "loveys" are jealous of their ability to go out and play in the snow, or that the toothbrush is really wants to brush the child's teeth tonight, or that their homemade puppet is wondering if it can give the child's younger sibling a hug when they are sad.

Symbolic thought seems to shift at around 3 years of age. In a classic study, researchers had 2.5-year-olds and 3-year-olds watch as the researchers hid a toy in a miniature room (built to scale so that it resembled a real room next door and was different only in size). The researchers first asked the children to go fetch the toy in the miniature room. Then they asked them to go fetch a larger version of the toy in the real room next door that the miniature room represented.

The 3-year-olds were able to find the larger version of the toy in the real room next door, but the 2.5-year-olds were not, which suggests that before age 3, children are unable to understand that the miniature scale model was a symbol of the actual room—perhaps because the miniature scale model was akin to a map, which preschoolers are limited in reading (Callaghan & Corbit, 2015; DeLoache, 1987; Dillon & Spelke, 2018).

Piaget's theory of cognitive development, including his emphasis on symbolic thought, is just one way of looking at the changes in children's thinking throughout the preschool years. To have the most comprehensive understanding, we need to consider other approaches, such as cognitive processes.

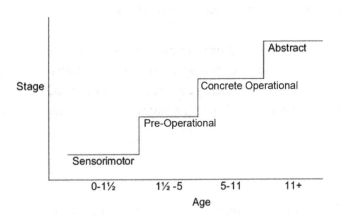

FIG. 8.18   A Staircase Model of Development

Robert Siegler, A Staircase Model of Development, from "Continuity and Change in the Field of Cognitive Development and in the Perspectives of One Cognitive Developmentalist," Child Development Perspectives, vol. 10, no. 2. Copyright © 2016 by Society for Research in Child Development.

What Cognitive Processes Are Most Relevant to Development in Early Childhood?

As we learned in Chapter 1, Information-Processing theories, which concern themselves with specific thinking processes such as strategy use, view the human mind as analogous to a computer, receiving input (like this chapter) and producing output (like your notes to study from).

Unlike Piaget's theory, Information-Processing theories do not see development as a kind of staircase with relatively stable age-related stages and qualitative and dramatic differences between them (Fig. 8.18). In this section, we learn about the processes that these theories emphasize as most relevant to development in early childhood, including strategy use, theory capabilities, intelligence, and eyewitness testimony.

Overlapping Waves of Strategy Use

Instead of a stage model, the *overlapping waves* model of strategy use proposes that children use many different types of thinking, or different strategies, at the same time (Siegler, 2002; van der Ven, Boom, Kroesbergen, & Leseman, 2012).

As children become older and wiser (as a result

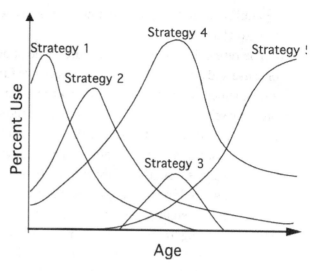

FIG. 8.19   The Overlapping Waves Model of Strategy Use

Robert Siegler, The Overlapping Waves Model of Strategy Use, from "Continuity and Change in the Field of Cognitive Development and in the Perspectives of One Cognitive Developmentalist," Child Development Perspectives, vol. 10, no. 2. Copyright © 2016 by Society for Research in Child Development.

of experience), they use some strategies more and others less, and they add new ones, as you can see in Figure 8.19. For instance, when first-graders are asked to solve simple addition (3 + 2) and advanced addition (9 + 11) problems, they tend to use <u>more</u> *retrieval strategies* (calling the answer to mind after having memorized it) and *counting strategies,* especially with simple addition problems. They are <u>less</u> likely to use more advanced *decomposition strategies* (decomposing 11 into 10 + 1, adding the 1 to 9, then adding 10 + 10) (Lindberg et al., 2013).

Other studies have provided additional empirical verification of the overlapping waves model of strategy use, a model of continuous forms of development that is consistent with the polydirectional pattern of development. This model is now being increasingly conceptualized as relevant to education, particularly in terms of how children learn reading, writing, mathematics, and scientific reasoning (Siegler, 2016; van Dijk & van Geert, 2015).

Theory Capabilities

Earlier in this chapter, we mentioned STEAM (Science, Technology, Engineering, Art, and Mathematics) projects, which are the focus of much recent attention. Careers in these fields tend to be well-paying, yet people who identify as female, Black, Latinx, Native American, and/or from other racial/ethnic backgrounds tend to be significantly underrepresented in them (Funk & Parker, 2018). Something happens between early childhood and later career development, because all preschoolers are capable of scientific literacy, including knowledge of scientific facts as well as scientific processes—such as using theories to test hypotheses of cause and effect.

One study showed three-year-old children a timeline of photographs in which something underwent a change, such as from a flowerpot to a broken flowerpot or from a tomato to a sliced tomato, and then measured the children's ability to make causal inferences. That is, they asked them to choose one among four photos of objects that could have caused the change—such as a hammer, a light bulb, a paintbrush, and glue for the flowerpot, and a whisk, a spatula, measuring cups, and a knife for the tomato (Bauer & Booth, 2019).

The researchers found that children who showed the greatest overall scientific literacy in terms of cause and effect had the greatest executive function and were most accurate in their causal inferences, which suggests that practicing the ability to make accurate causal inferences may not only promote self-regulation, but also promote children's scientific literacy, including hypothesis-testing of theories (Bauer & Booth, 2019). Such practice need not be difficult, either. Parents can sketch these items, and a corresponding timeline, however roughly, and children are often fully intrigued by such puzzles from their parent's own hand.

In terms of self-regulation, remember from Chapter 1 that *executive function* includes the ability to engage in sustained attention, filter out distractions, and have self-control over our impulses. Although having limited impulse control is a symptom of adult personality disorders (such as Borderline Personality Disorder, which we read about in Chapter 7), having limited impulse control is developmentally appropriate for preschoolers; yet the more that parents and teachers can do to support it, the better for children.

One such way is via playing Head, Toes, Knees, and Shoulders (HTKS), first by having children touch their head, touch their toes, touch their knees, and touch their shoulders after each corresponding body part is called out. Then the game is played the opposite way, so that children are to touch their toes when "head" is called out and so on. Research on HTKS shows that children's performance on such games is correlated not only with their ability to control their impulses, but also with their memory, their mathematical ability, and their literacy skills. One study showed improvements in children native to and living in rural Hawai'i and at risk for poorer self-regulation given that they tend to live in poverty (Hee, Yu, & Krieg, 2017; McClelland et al., 2014). These results are promising and suggest the HTKS task may help children err on the resilience aspect of the risk–resilience pattern of development, particularly those who also live in poverty or are otherwise at risk.

To learn more about what parents and others can easily do to greatly help their children's self-regulation skills, read the excellent *Executive Function & Child Development*, listed in the *Recommended Reading* section of this chapter. The book is chock full of practical ideas (for example, the "We're going on a trip" car game, in which the person to begin identifies something they have in the car, with the child repeating the item and adding another item that's in the car, the parent repeating and extending, etc.). The book contains illuminating case studies of children helped by such, as well as reminders of what children really are and are not capable of, so that we don't inappropriately and unfairly pathologically label them as "not paying attention" or as "lazy" (Yeager & Yeager, 2013).

In addition to scientific theories, preschoolers are capable of theorizing about other people's minds. The way we come to understand the desires, emotions, knowledge, beliefs, and intentions of ourselves and others is referred to as our **theory of mind** (Saracho, 2013). By age 3, most children use the words *think* and *know*, yet most fail a major milestone of theory of mind, that is, **false-belief** tasks. A false-belief task is one in which children are asked whether another person has a false belief about an object or a situation.

For example, consider a research study in which the researcher empties a crayon box and places birthday candles inside the box while a child watches. The child is then asked about what someone else, who hasn't seen this change of the box's content, believes about what is in the box when they later pick it up. If the child believes that someone else will think the box has birthday candles in it, the child has failed the false-belief task. If the child believes that someone else will think the box has crayons in it, the child has passed the false-belief task, because this child understands the other person has a false belief (in this case, that the box contains crayons, which is false because it no longer contains crayons but now candles).

False-belief tasks help us understand children's theory of mind: specifically, whether they can distinguish between their (true) beliefs and those (false) beliefs of another person (Bauminger-Zviely, 2013). Although 2-year-olds appreciate that others may have different emotions than they have, and 3- and 4-year-olds can sometimes pass false-belief tasks, children don't usually pass false-belief tasks consistently until they are 5 years old or around the transition to kindergarten. However, the performance of 3- and 4-year-olds can be improved by the researchers engaging in joint attention with

Pan & Zoom

Theory of Mind and Patterns of Development

In this box, we pan across or take a panoramic wide-angle view of what is known about theory of mind in terms of the patterns of development. Empathy is an aspect of emotional development and refers to our ability to share another person's emotional state and feel similarly, whereas theory of mind is an aspect of cognitive development (and one informed by other cognitive skills, such as verbal ability and executive function) and refers to our reasoning about another person's mental state (Brock et al., 2019; Dvash & Shamay-Tsoory, 2014).

Yet theory of mind certainly exemplifies the multidimensional pattern of development. It has its own neurological bases in the brain, and it has major emotional implications: Theory of mind and empathy are both needed in order for a person to be socially competent (Preckel, Kanske, & Singer, 2018; Westby & Robinson, 2014; Y. Xiao et al., 2019).

Not surprisingly, research has found a polydirectional pattern of development in children with less advanced theory of mind skills. These children are not only *less likely* to pass a false-belief task but also *more likely* to be friendless than children with more advanced theory of mind skills, who are more likely to be rated as popular by their peers—perhaps because they tend to be more cooperative as a result of thinking about what others need (Etel & Slaughter, 2019; Fink et al., 2015; Slaughter et al., 2015). Theory of mind illustrates the lifelong pattern of development too, because false belief understanding predicts children's academic adjustment, behavioral adjustment, social skills, and emotional skills in kindergarten and beyond (Brock et al., 2019; Carr et al., 2018).

The risk–resilience pattern of development is clearly evident in theory of mind as well, because social experiences shape children's understanding of their own mind, as well as the minds of others (Hughes & Devine, 2015).

Children's exposure to both storybooks and conversations with *mental state talk* or verbs about cognitive mental states (*think, believe, know, remember, imagine, pretend*, and so on) promotes the development of their theory of mind, as does parents' emotional availability—which serves as a cradle for children's understanding of others (Farkas et al., 2018; Slaughter, 2015; Tompkins et al., 2018).

• • • •

them about what happening in the task, rather than merely narrating (Psouni et al., 2019; Rhoades & Brandone, 2014).

Theory of mind very much reflects all the patterns of development, which you can learn more about in the *Pan & Zoom: Theory of Mind and Patterns of Development* box.

Intelligence

Most adults who interact with Crystal and Jimmy would agree that they are intelligent. But what is intelligence? **Intelligence** has been defined as the ability to learn from past experience, as well as to adapt to, select, and shape our environment so that we may be successful in life (Sternberg, 2012; 2018).

Preschoolers' intelligence level has serious implications for life associated with the lifelong pattern of development: Longitudinal research reveals that regardless of a child's health and their family's SES, lower intelligence in early childhood is associated with worse health in midlife, including increased risk of stroke and heart disease, and premature death (Bratsberg & Rogeberg, 2017; Wrulich et al., 2015).

Intelligence in preschool children is correlated negatively with both maternal and paternal BMI. This suggests that parents' physical lifestyles and/or genes influence children's cognitive development, perhaps because our brains' abilities to navigate spatially and engage in decision-making evolved in order to help us obtain scarce food, with physical activity benefiting cognitive activity (Mattson, 2019). But intelligence in preschool children is a product of many factors. Among these are parents' IQ, parents' education, the birth parent's consumption of long-chain polyunsaturated fatty acids (as in fish) while pregnant, regular interaction with parents, the experience of being read to, participation in music lessons, and preschool quality and quantity (Linnavalli et al., 2018; Protzko, Aronson, & Blair, 2013).

Eyewitness Testimony

The accounts that people give of events they have witnessed is referred to as *eyewitness testimony*. Young children may be asked to provide eyewitness testimony in court. But are they credible witnesses? Not especially, even for children who have not experienced trauma nor who are being asked to appear in court alone to defend themselves against deportation, such as Crystal and Jimmy.

Migrant children such as those who were separated from their parents at the southern border of the United States are even less capable, given how the unconscionable actions by the government may have disrupted their emotional attachments (Jewett & Luthra, 2018).

In police lineups of suspects, children under 5 years of age are less likely than older children to correctly identify a suspect (Brubacher et al., 2019; Fitzgerald & Price, 2015). This is not to say that preschoolers should not be able to participate in legal decisions affecting their lives, whether as witnesses, victims, or even suspects (Lamb et al., 2015).

During early childhood, children can accurately remember events, particularly those that occurred within the last year or two. Yet they are susceptible to contextual factors, including suggestive interview technique; "loaded" questions ("Her dad did that, right?"); close-ended yes/no questions; and repeated questions, especially those to which they have previously answered no (Bruck & Ceci, 2015; Stolzenberg, McWilliams, & Lyon, 2017).

So it is imperative that those questioning children use nonleading and open-ended questions ("What happened?") when interviewing or questioning them in court. Judges and juries should certainly consider a child's developmental level, but they should also consider the factors associated with the multidimensional pattern of development. Such factors include children's language skills, which make them better able to respond to open-ended questions correctly, and their personalities, given that shy children appear less likely to recall as many details of an event or to respond correctly to nonleading questions (Hritz et al., 2015; Wyman et al., 2019).

How Can Preschoolers' Language Development, Literacy, and Numeracy Be Best Supported?

The preschool years are a sensitive time for language development. Although we can learn languages throughout our lives, mastering vocabulary, pronunciation, and grammar is easiest in early childhood, whether it be one's first language or an additional one.

Early language development requires sufficient audiovisual speech perception, so children with suspected symptoms of hearing problems, developmental language disorder, and/or autism spectrum need intervention as soon as possible, and as tailored to their specific processing needs as possible (Irwin & Turcios, 2017). Language development in the preschool years shows multidimensional and lifelong patterns of development too. Preschoolers who have better vocabularies have better self-regulation—indicating that language helps us understand and master not only the world around us, but also ourselves (Cadima et al., 2019).

As we learned in Chapter 6, toddlers experience a naming explosion at approximately 18 months of age; by 30 months, most speak 200 words or more. After 30 months, language development continues vigorously—by 6 years of age, preschoolers' vocabularies have typically acquired 10,000 words (Law et al., 2017).

Language Development

The development of vocabulary in early childhood is characterized by **fast-mapping**, a process in which children connect new words to the concepts of those words, often after a single exposure ("dog" refers to the furry creature in the house that woofs and pants). Yet it can take preschoolers a number of years to appreciate the specifics of some types of words they use accurately. It usually isn't until 5 years of age that children can reason about the past and the future, including the ability to locate past and future events on a timeline. This indicates that fast-mapping is likely not critical for word learning (O'Connor, Lindsay, Mather, & Riggs, 2019; Zhang & Hudson, 2018). For example, in addition to fast-mapping, preschoolers learn vocabulary words via **syntactic bootstrapping**, a process by which they infer the meaning of words based on their syntax or the way they are used grammatically in sentences. For example, when shown different apples, a child who is learning colors will come to understand that the *red* and *green* in "This is a red apple" and "This is a green apple" refer to different colors and not to different types of fruit.

Now there is another one. There are two of them. There are two _____.

FIG. 8.20   The Wug Test

Source:: https://en.wikipedia.org/wiki/File:WugTest_NowThereIsAnotherOne_FairUseOnly.jpg; https://commons.wikimedia.org/wiki/File:Wug.svg

In terms of learning grammar, Jean Berko Gleason's (1958) classic research established that children internalize the structure of language and apply it even to words they have never heard before. When Gleason asked children to respond to her "Wug Test,"—that is, when she showed children a drawing of a `wug' as in Figure 8.20 with the sentences, "Now there is another one. There are two of them. There are two _____.", children were able to respond that there were two wugs.

As children continue to apply grammatical rules, they inevitably make mistakes and incorrectly apply the rules to verbs that are exceptions, a type of error that is normative and called **overregularization**. In English, this often occurs with tricky irregular verbs, as in the case of *go*: "I goed to the store with Mommy today."

Parents and other adults can help children learn the correct grammar by using **recasts**, or restructures of inaccurate language use into the correct form, such as "Oh, you went to the store," which is more helpful than telling them that what they said was wrong. A review of more than 30 scientific studies indicates that recasts are an effective means of informally teaching and improving grammar (Cleave et al., 2015; Justice, Jiang, & Strasser, 2018). One can imagine that they also foster a strong emotional bond and trust with the caregiver.

Literacy

"Children who are dependent on school for their literacy experience begin their reading careers with a deficit" (Desmond, 2001, p. 31). This truth cannot be overstated when we consider that reading skills correlate strongly with academic achievement, and that academic achievement correlates strongly not only with personal development, but also with career success.

By 3 years of age, children should be accustomed to playing with alphabet blocks, should understand that print corresponds to speech, and should be attempting to write and identify some, if not all, the letters of the alphabet—a task they need to accomplish by the end of the preschool years if they are to not fall behind in kindergarten. *Alphabet knowledge* consists of letter recognition, letter naming, and knowledge of letter sounds and lowercase and uppercase forms. Mastery of alphabet knowledge is a significant predictor of children's later literacy and general achievement (Heilmann, Moyle, & Rueden, 2018).

As we learned in Chapter 6, the context of socioeconomic status matters: Children from lower-SES families tend to be less prepared for formal literacy instruction when they start school. Research indicates that these class differences may be due to parents from lower-SES families talking less to their children than do parents from higher-SES families, emphasizing the order of the alphabet rather than asking questions about letters ("Can you find all the examples of letter 'M' in the room?"), and emphasizing the letters of a child's name instead of all the letters of the alphabet (Robins et al., 2014; Treiman et al., 2018).

Understanding the correspondence between letters and sounds, as well as having the capacity to notice changes in the spelling and pronunciation of words (such as knowing that when the "s" is dropped from "small," the remaining word is "mall," not "wall" or "ball"), constitutes **phonological awareness**—a skill vital to reading comprehension (Knoop-van Campen, Segers, & Verhoeven, 2018). So formal and informal literacy instruction during the preschool years must include efforts to increase phonological sensitivity. Instruction must not be limited to just vocabulary; it should include rhyming as well (Read & Quirke, 2018).

In addition, **interactive book reading**—in which the parent or teacher stops and asks children questions—about the objects on the page, what else is happening in the story, and what will happen next—seems especially helpful to children's emerging literacy. Having children touch and trace the shape of letters while reading is helpful as well (Cabell et al., 2019; Han & Neuharth-Pritchett, 2014; Labat et al., 2015). A home literacy environment that includes a wide variety of children's books and parents who read to children regularly, even prior to early childhood, is also associated with children having better literacy skills (Demir-Lira, Applebaum, Goldin-Meadow, & Levine, 2018).

To learn about how best to read aloud to children (and what to expect in their behavior and questions in response), as well as which books are best at what age, visit the website of Pam Allyn, author of *What to Read and When*, and the website of Jim Trelease, author of *The Read-Aloud Handbook*. Both are listed in the *Helpful Websites* section at the end of this chapter.

This advantage has implications associated with the lifelong pattern of development, because research shows that children who are frequent readers are more successful students from preschool through college—likely because of momentum. That is, children with better reading abilities read more; and because they read more, their literacy skills continue to improve far beyond those of children who read less (Kalb & van Ours, 2014; Mol & Bus, 2011; van Bergen et al., 2018).

Creating a home literacy environment with a wide variety of children's books is a social justice issue too. It can be a struggle for low-SES families who have neither the income nor the access to bookstores, not to mention high-end boutique book and toy stores for children; unfortunately, these families often tend to live in *book deserts*.

To clarify, one study had researchers walk and bike every street in neighborhoods, with either 18% to 40% of families living in poverty, or neighborhoods with more than 40% of families living in poverty. They found that the latter, higher-poverty, neighborhoods had significantly fewer places to buy print books for preschoolers—and fewer appropriate books within the available print resources

Mentor Minute

Darren Glenn, MS

1) Describe your work, please.

My name is Darren J. Glenn. I have a master's degree in Library and Information Science and my job title is Outreach Librarian. An outreach librarian could mean many different things, even within the same library system. I work as an outreach librarian for Brooklyn Public Library, and I'm assigned exclusively to the two library branches situated in the Brownsville neighborhood. In addition to some of the standard librarian duties—such as processing holds on books and other materials, staffing the information desk and assisting with locating materials, and providing assistance to patrons using our computers—it's my unique responsibility to bring library services outside of the four walls of the library building and to bring as many people [as possible] from the community into the four walls of the library building. So I table and put on programs at various schools and shelters and community spaces and local events—wherever the community is. Essentially, I can be thought of an evangelist or an ambassador for the library within Brownsville community limits.

FIG. 8.21   Darren Glenn, M.S.

2) How does social justice inform your work?

To quote my library system's own self-description, "Brooklyn Public Library is among the borough's most democratic civic institutions, serving patrons in every neighborhood and from every walk of life." This declaration of a commitment to supporting the democratic spirit at the local level really excites me because it speaks to the fundamental ethical aspects of librarianship that made this career so attractive to me in the first place. We often underestimate the role that public libraries can play and have always played in the body politic; we forget that the great library of Alexandria was just as much a center of discourse and civic engagement within and between societies as it was an impressively large collection of written texts.

That being said, I believe that, in a 21st-century America that is seeing the rise of moderate and extreme right-wing sentiments, the kinds of discourses that really promote equitable civic participation are ones that actively and consistently engage with structural forces that conserve inequities. When I go to work in Brownsville, I push programs that foster dialogue about racist and overtly classist public policies at every level of government. I promote library services that could have the most currency with people who have experienced generational poverty and people facing chronic joblessness or homelessness or trauma from neighborhood violence. I create resource collections and classes or discussion groups that seek to help equip members of this neighborhood with some of the tools they will need to know lasting social, economic and environmental justice.

3) How did you become involved in social justice and/or advocacy?

My parents brought me here from Trinidad blindly convinced that the American Dream narrative applied fully and unconditionally to anyone. But growing up, we really were blindsided by the harsh reality that discriminatory practices in employment, housing, bank finance, every aspect of life, promised us that nothing we hoped for would be easy to attain. And myself growing up a black, queer, immigrant boy really felt a lot of pressure to be less ambitious and less visible and to settle. Going to college and discovering that I could actually resist and advocate for myself and that I wasn't alone and that other people were depending on more people like me to speak up and take up more space and demand an equal chance at happiness and success and justice, really changed my relationship to the structural forces that made me feel like an unwelcome member of society. Toward the end of my undergraduate studies I'd say I received a "call" to champion social justice causes. I came to believe what Audre Lorde famously declared: Silence would not protect me.

4) What are your thoughts on how social justice can improve child and adolescent development?

When doing programs for children, no matter what those programs may be, we are fostering their understanding of the world and themselves. If we have an equity lens—an awareness that some children are coming from disadvantaged backgrounds and will require extra support and resources—we can start shaping a world in which an entire generation is starting out on less uneven footing. We want to foster an understanding that impoverished or working-class children aren't less deserving of success than children with wealthier backgrounds. This is one of the things I love about the library: its potential to fill in those gaps in support for child development if only this equity lens is properly and consistently applied.

5) What suggestions do you have for undergraduate students who are interested in making a change in child and adolescent development?

Always ask questions. My advice is to resist the fear that comes with questioning yourself and questioning what you know and the way things are done. It's only through this sort of thorough, Socratic interrogation that the changes in need of being made will reveal themselves.

• • • •

(for example, excluding coloring books, which they usually have minimal print). Some cities did not have *any* preschool age books available, even in local drugstores (Neuman & Moland, 2016).

So as a consequence of income segregation in neighborhoods, children who live in neighborhoods with few resources suffer greatly, both in the short term and in the long term. Yet libraries, assuming they are fully funded so that they have abundant resources for any and every community with ample hours during the week and weekend, can mitigate some of the restrictions that are experienced in neighborhoods segregated by income.

To learn more about the role of libraries in social justice, see the *Mentor Minute* box with Darren Glenn, MS, TEFL Certification, who serves as the Outreach Librarian for the Brownsville neighborhood in the Brooklyn Public Library system.

Numeracy

Math matters. Although most children can count by the time they are 5 years old, the strength of their number skills, such as general counting ability—as well as their *spontaneously focusing on numerosity* (SFON) or spur-of-the-moment focusing of attention on numbers in a set of items (such as "There are three bananas left on the counter") in preschool—predicts their math skills in fifth grade (McMullen, Chan Mazzocco, & Hannula-Sormunen, 2019; Nanu et al., 2018). These examples of the lifelong pattern of development have been verified by quasi-experimental research as well, which has found math learning during the preschool years to be associated with math achievement in late elementary school (T. W. Watts et al., 2018).

What determines preschoolers' mathematical learning, though? One factor is the quality of the preschool they attend. Research has shown that the growth of preschoolers' mathematical knowledge over a school year is predicted by how much math-related talk their teachers engage in and the extent to which the teachers guide complex play, such as with building blocks (Geary & van Marle, 2018; Trawick-Smith et al., 2017).

The more frequently preschool teachers mention concepts like counting; **cardinality**, or the total number of people or things ("Sure, all three of you can help me"); **equivalence**, or a match between two or more things ("Each child gets one arch block"); and **ordering**, or a sequence of things ("What comes after nine?"), the earlier children acquire these concepts and the more their math knowledge grows over the course of the school year (Geary & van Marle, 2018; Trawick-Smith et al., 2017).

The home environment has a major influence on children's numeracy as well. As we have learned before, it's best to avoid screen time as much as possible. Screen time is correlated negatively with preschoolers achieving general developmental milestones, some of which reflect the memory skills that enable mathematical abilities (Madigan, Browne, & Racine, 2019).

And there are a number of environment factors that should be embraced. Although not all parents speak more than one language, the more they can expose their children to additional languages, the better—including for a child's math skills. Preschoolers who are exposed to more than one language show greater skill in identifying numbers as well as greater skill in addition, no matter their families' SES. This is likely because speaking more than one language helps a child develop greater executive function (Daubert & Ramani, 2019). Regardless of the number of languages to which they are exposed, though, the greater a child's executive function, the greater their math skills (Nesbitt, Fuhs, & Farran, 2019).

And the more their parents engage in home numeracy practices such as SFON (How many cars in the train set are red?) during play, the greater children's own spontaneous attention to numbers. The more parents ask number questions during storybook reading, the greater children's number ability too (Braham, Libertus, & McCrink, 2018; del Río et al., 2017; Uscianowski, Almeda & Ginsburg, 2018).

Parents can also encourage the practice of *spatial skills*, or the ability to mentally transform spatial information, such as children realizing they can recreate the photo on a box of blocks by adjusting the way their blocks are stacked currently), along with *patterning skills*, or the ability to identify what comes next in a pattern, such as photo of an umbrella after a photo of a sun in a sequence of sun-umbrella-sun-umbrella photos. Both spatial skills and patterning skills predict math knowledge at the end of prekindergarten (Rittle-Johnson, Zippert, & Boice, 2019).

What Can Family and Government Investments Do for Development in Early Childhood?

So far, we have learned about physical and cognitive development during the preschool years. Now we will address what parents, as well as childcare providers and preschool teachers, can do to optimize such development during early childhood.

Parents

The types of investments parents make in their children's lives are often at least partially a function of the family's income. Parents may not have the financial capital to pay for ideal schooling for their children, but they can make sure they have access to books (and toys, if possible) that stimulate learning. They can attend cultural events and visit museums. Depending on their resources, they can provide informal or formal music, dance, sports, and/or language lessons to develop not just a skill, but discipline in general. Even short-term training in early childhood of a second language and/or music lessons improves children's attention skills, which is of obvious importance for later learning, especially in an age of heightened digital distractions (Groussard et al., 2014; Moreno et al., 2015).

Parental investment refers to the regular activities, experiences, material goods, and lessons that parents provide or obtain in order to enrich their children's human capital and foster their development and well-being. Social-class differences can be seen in the level of parental investment. Many working-class parents tend to adopt a child-rearing perspective called **accomplishment of natural growth**, which assumes that if they provide love, food, and shelter, their children will thrive own their own. Many middle-class parents take a **concerted cultivation** approach to child-rearing, which leads them to feel personally responsible for actively fostering the skills and talents of their children and perhaps to having their children enroll in extracurricular activities—both for enjoyment and as a means of securing skills for future educational and occupational payoffs (Lareau, 2011; Vincent & Maxwell, 2015; Weininger, Lareau, & Conley, 2015).

Parents who believe in the accomplishment of natural growth are not uncaring, nor will their children fail to do well in life. Rather, these children may not have the educational and cultural advantages that others do when trying to get ahead. Research shows that children from working-class families adopting the accomplishment of natural growth approach progress academically at a level typical for their background, while their peers whose families adopt the concerted cultivation approach progress academically above what is typical (Mayo & Siraj, 2015). So although motivation, intellect, and general gumption are necessary for everyone, these characteristics likely play a large role in the success of children from the former group.

Government Policies

It is often said that children are the future. Given such, the United States may wish to better invest in its future. For example, for each child that they have, coupled parents in Sweden receive 480 days leave that they can split between them, with 80% of their salary covered by taxes for 390 of those days, and with the time that can be taken lasting until each child is 8 years of age (Crisp, 2017).

The U.S. government does not guarantee any of the safety net benefits provided by other countries regarding paid maternal leave or paid paternal leave. The U.S. Family and Medical Leave Act (FMLA) requires that employers offer 12 weeks total per year of *unpaid* leave for the care of a new child in the family, or for care of an ill family member, or for when the employee is ill.

But not everyone is eligible for FMLA benefits (an individual must have worked for the employer for at least 1,250 hours during 12 months prior to the start of leave, the worksite must have at least 50 employees, and so on). And bringing a new child into one's family is one of the events in a family's life cycle in which the family likely simply cannot afford to not be paid.

Citizens in many other countries pay higher federal tax rates than U.S. citizens, but when we realize that U.S. citizens pay both state and local in additional to federal taxes, and much higher real estate taxes, the rates become comparable—and Americans receive a lot less for our money. For example, citizens in countries such as Sweden receive low-cost and high-quality childcare, free college tuition, extensive paid vacation time, etc., whereas Americans must pay out-of-pocket for tuition, fees, surcharges, insurance premiums, copayments, and various additional hidden charges—in addition to our taxes—in order to receive benefits that are often not even be comparable in cost or quality (Hill, 2013).

So educating and illuminating voters about how our tax revenues could be used to better support everyday citizens, as opposed to taking from the poor (as in the slashing of food stamps) and giving to the wealthy (as in tax cuts when they don't need them), may help change the tide for future generations.

In addition to the aforementioned services covered by taxes, in many countries families receive a child benefit. The *Kindergeld* or child benefit in Germany is provided to help cover the costs of child-rearing, and every month until their child turns 18, it transfers into parents' bank accounts an allocation of $220 for each of a family's first two children, $227 for the third child, and $255 for each subsequent child. In addition to the Kindergeld, Germany provides $100 per year to pay for school materials, funding for children's school travel, and additional support for low-income families (Federal Office for Migration and Refugees, 2019).

Consider that, and the no-cost or low-cost but high-quality childcare in other countries, alongside how childcare in the United States costs, on average, $8,933 per year, and is not always of high quality (U.S. Department of Education, 2016; Whitehurst, 2018). Even more discouraging (and fundamentally disrespectful of those who care for children) is that these startling childcare fees often don't even cover the cost of a living wage for most preschool teachers—who are paid less that pest control workers—yet who contribute extensively to children's physical, cognitive, and emotional development (U.S. Department of Education, 2016; Whitehurst, 2018).

The policies that many other countries have designed to support parents during a child's first few years of life, by providing paid time off then low-cost and high-quality childcare paid by the government, seem to create a national context that is not only preschool-teacher friendly, but also truly in the best interests of children—who are indeed our future.

$16.14 in Returns for Every $1 Invested

Indeed, the benefits of investing in children's physical and cognitive development accrue not only to the individual children and their families, but also to society. Like physical diseases, delinquency is much more effectively prevented than treated.

For example, when concerns over social justice were raised in the 1960s, programs like Head Start were created to provide early-childhood educational programs, including nutritional, physical health, and mental health services, to children in low-income families. The beneficial effects of Head Start fade over time, but children who participate in Head Start preschool programs do show significantly greater school readiness across the year. In addition, the benefits of Head Start are greater over time, when children have then had access to well-funded elementary schools (Bassock, Gibbs, & Latham, 2018; Bustamante & Hindman, 2019; Johnson & Jackson, 2017).

Another successful early-childhood education program was the High/Scope Perry Preschool Project, which provided high-quality preschool to 58 children for 2 years. Longitudinal follow-up with these children, now adults, found lifelong dividends. Specifically, by age 27, more than 29% of people who had been in the control group (who were similar to those who participated but weren't allowed access to the preschool program due to limited funding) as children had been arrested more than

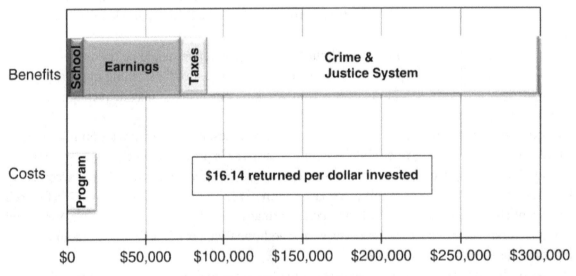

FIG. 8.22   High/Scope Perry Preschool Project Public Costs and Benefits

: Adapted from L. J. Schweinhart, et al., Lifetime Effects: The HighScope Perry Preschool Study Through Age 40. Copyright 2005 by Highscope Educational Research Foundation.

five times, compared to only 7% of the people in the experimental group who did have access to the preschool program (Schweinhart, 2019; Zigler & Styfco, 2001).

Some taxpayers make pejorative statements about government-funded programs, indicating that they are unwilling to contribute to the commons if they are unable to take directly from such. Yet consider that in addition to satisfying a moral obligation for members of society to take care of our own, these programs—especially high-quality childcare in early childhood—yield financial, personal, and societal dividends to us all, including but not limited to providing young, healthy, and educated future workers for an aging population.

Specifically, as you can see in Figure 8.22, the economic benefits to society are worth $16.14 for every $1 invested in childcare, a return unheard of even in some of the most lucrative financial investments. Further, it has benefits associated with the polydirectional pattern of development: It *reduces* special education expenses, criminal justice costs, and victim costs; and it *increases* achievement and taxes, given that individuals make higher earnings with high-quality childcare in early childhood (Schweinhart, 2019).

Even more impressively, increases in the quality of childcare beyond acceptable levels do not have diminishing returns; rather, they have *increasing* returns. Early mastery of skills eases mastery of more advanced skills later on (and therefore increases worker productivity). The result is that early interventions actually lower the cost of later interventions—and increase labor productivity in adulthood, which leads to greater economic growth for all citizens (Balart, Oosterveen, & Webbink, 2018; Delalibera & Ferreira, 2019; Heckman, 2011).

The greater one's school success, the greater one's health and longevity. These are clear indicators of a better quality of life as well as reduced government spending on chronic health issues in adulthood—so that investments in early education would clearly help all preschools become *drivers of opportunity* rather than *reproducers of inequality* (Ramon, Chattopadhyay, Barnett, & Hahn, 2018; Zajacova & Lawrence, 2018).

The United Nations Convention on the Rights of the Child

High-quality education for children is viewed as a right, not a privilege, in many other countries. In 1990, the United Nations created the **Convention on the Rights of the Child** (CRC), a set of standards and obligations that promote the rights of children, including their right to survival, the right to be free of harmful influences, and the right to develop their full potential. Not surprisingly, children who are provided the resources to develop such potential experience more life satisfaction (Brusdal & Frønes, 2014; Reyes, 2019). Article 18 of the CRC specifies that member nations agree to support the child-rearing responsibilities of parents, which includes providing childcare and education services to working parents.

As an example, the microcontext of children's development in France is often similar to that of children in the United States; research found that mothers in both countries had similar child-rearing beliefs and long-term goals for their infants, toddlers, and preschool-age children (Claes, et al., 2018; Suizzo, 2004). Yet the macrocontexts of children's lives in these two countries are very different.

France, for example, which spends approximately 4% of their gross domestic product on family services (whereas the United States spends less than 1.5%) has relatively high levels of fertility. This may be a function of their government providing parents financial support for paid parental leave, plus a child benefit allowance, as well as free preschool for children between 3 and 6 years of age (United Nations Expert Group Meeting on Policy Responses to Low Fertility, 2015).

France's belief that "children are the future" is not just rhetoric but an actual practice in which families and government share the responsibility for children's development. Those who work in France's *crèches*, or infant and toddler daycare centers that serve children from birth to 3 years of age, also have a year of schooling in nursing. Additionally, and perhaps unsurprisingly, France's preschools, or *écoles maternelles*, are staffed by teachers who have master's degrees in education and are well compensated. Compared to the United States, where parents pay 100% of their childcare costs unless they are living in poverty, parents in France pay only about 20% of daycare costs and 25% of preschool costs.

As of 2019, only one of the UN's member nations has not ratified the CRC. It is the United States.

Key Terms

Accomplishment of Natural Growth

Animism

Cardinality

Centration

Child Maltreatment

Class-Inclusion

Concerted Cultivation

Conservation

Controlled Scribbling

Convention on the Rights of the Child (CRC)

Descriptive Symbolism

Egocentric

Emotional Abuse

Epiphysis

Equivalence

False Belief Task

Fast-Mapping

Gift Wrap Task

Intelligence

Interactive Book Reading

Irreversibility

Letters and Word Practice

Lines and Patterns

Nature-Deficit Disorder (NDD)

Neglect

Nightmares

Nocturnal Enuresis

Obesity

Operations

Ordering

Overregularization

Overweightness

Parental Investment

Phonological Awareness

Physical Abuse

Physical Neglect

Random Scribbling

Recast

Secular Trend

Sexual Abuse

Skeletal Age

Sleep Terrors

Structured Play

Synaptic Pruning

Syntactic Bootstrapping

Tadpole Person

Theory of Mind

Undernutrition

Unstructured Play

Summary

1. **Summarize the normative changes in physical development.** General growth in height and weight is steady during early childhood, and synaptogenesis within the brain continues. Food allergies can be a product of genetics as well as environmental factors. Preschoolers need 11 to 13 hours of sleep every 24 hours. Sleep duration during the preschool years is correlated negatively with a host of multidimensional factors, revealing how necessary sufficient sleep is. Preschoolers need at least 60 minutes and up to several hours of unstructured play and at

least 60 minutes and up to several hours of structured play each day in order to stay healthy and develop their motor skills.

2. **Identify what nonnormative changes in physical development within the first two years entail.** The average BMI of preschoolers has increased significantly in recent years, and it reflects child characteristics, community factors, and government policies. The causes of nocturnal enuresis are many, although some treatments are available. Unintentional injuries during early childhood can range from mild to fatal; prevention is essential. Child maltreatment during early childhood can include physical abuse, physical neglect, sexual abuse, emotional abuse, and neglect—all of which have serious correlates associated with the multidimensional and lifelong patterns of development.

3. **Describe what Piaget's theory can tell us about cognitive development in early childhood.** Three of the four major characteristics of children's thinking during early childhood, according to Piaget, reflect weaknesses. They are egocentrism, or the inability to differentiate between one's own perspective and the perspective of another person; a lack of hierarchical classification, or an inability to organize or classify objects into categories and subcategories; and a lack of conservation, or an inability to understand that the characteristics of an object stay the same despite changes in the object's appearance.

   On the other hand, children's capacity for symbolic thought is a major strength of preschoolers' thinking, because it allows them to be creative.

4. **Explain what cognitive processes are most relevant to development in early childhood.** Many cognitive processes characterize preschoolers' thinking—including the overlapping waves model, in which children use many different types of thinking, often at the same time. Differences in intelligence levels during early childhood predict later outcomes, including physical health, so supporting children's cognitive development during the preschool years is vital. Although preschoolers can accurately remember events within the last year or two, they are highly susceptible to suggestive interview techniques.

5. **Demonstrate how preschoolers' language development, literacy, and numeracy can be supported.** Fast-mapping, in which children connect new words to concepts with very few exposures, and syntactic bootstrapping, in which children infer the meaning of words based on their syntax or how they are used grammatically in sentences, characterize children's vocabulary development during early childhood.

   Alphabet knowledge and phonological awareness are predictors of children's later literacy achievement, as is interactive book reading. Children's verbal skills are correlated positively with their numeracy or number skills, and number skills are a predictor of later school achievement. Children's degree of numeracy shows benefits when parents spontaneously discuss numbers.

6. **Evaluate what family and government investments can do for development in early childhood.** Parental perspectives can assume the accomplishment of natural growth, or they can undertake concerted cultivation. The latter is associated with greater achievement in children from working-class families. U.S. government policies that reflect investments (or lack thereof) in early childhood include a lack of guaranteed paid parental leave, a lack of social security child benefits, and a lack of guaranteed and free access to high-quality childcare. All of these are associated with a range of positive lifelong outcomes.

In the United Nations' Convention on the Rights of the Child (CRC), high-quality education is considered a right. As of 2019, the United States is the only UN member nation that has not ratified the CRC.

The Cycle of Science

Research

Why was the study conducted?

The researchers wanted to know why children from low-income families who receive a prekindergarten math intervention (because children's mathematical knowledge tends to vary by their family's SES) still enter kindergarten behind children from middle-income families in math readiness (DeFlorio et al., 2019).

Who participated in the study?

The participants were 526 children from 44 different schools that were either Head Start or pre-K state schools. The children were, on average, 3.38 years of age. Also, 52% were female, and in terms of race/ethnicity, 58% were Latinx, 18% were Black, 6% were Asian American, 5% were European American, and 14% were multiethnic.

Which type of design was used?

An experimental design was used. Children in the first experimental group received 2 years of a math intervention program, children in the second experimental group received 1 year of a math intervention program, and children in the control group received no math intervention at all. The math intervention consisted of training teachers to implement math activities (involving number, space, geometry, arithmetic, and patterns) within small groups of children and providing similar home activities for parents. Teachers were observed twice per month to support their implementation of the intervention.

Over the course of 2 years (preschool and prekindergarten), children's math skills and self-regulation skills were measured three different times. Time 1 was the fall of preschool, Time 2 was the fall of pre-K, and Time 3 was the spring of pre-K. Math skills were assessed with a measure of counting, number sense, arithmetic, geometry, measurement, and patterns. Self-regulation skills were assessed with a variety of inhibitory control measures, including the **gift wrap task**, in which children were told they would be receiving a present, but that it needed to be wrapped so they should face forward and try not to peek while the experimenter pretended to noisily wrap a gift; children who did not peek received a 4 score, children who peeked over their shoulder received a 3 score, children who turned in their chair received a 2 score, and children who left their chair to peek received a 1 score (Kochanska, Murray, & Harlan, 2000).

What were the results?

The researchers found that children enrolled in either a 1-year or 2-year math intervention had significantly higher math scores at Time 3, compared to children enrolled in the control group. The researchers also found that children's math scores at Time 1 predicted their scores on the gift wrap task at Time 2. Children's math skills at Time 2 predicted their scores on the gift wrap task at Time 3. In addition, children's performance on the gift wrap task at Time 1 predicted their math scores at Time 2, and their performance on the gift wrap task at Time 2 predicted their math scores at Time 3.

Are the results consistent with theory?

The current study found that the relationship between math skills and self-regulation skills was bidirectional, so it may very well be that math interventions that don't seek to also improve self-regulation explain why children from low-income families who receive a pre-kindergarten math intervention still enter kindergarten behind children from middle-income families in math readiness.

How can the results be used to improve our lives?

The researchers found that children's level of self-regulation did not play a role in how beneficial the math intervention was for them, so even children with poor self-regulation can benefit from a math intervention.

Exercises

1. What pattern of results would you expect to find if the math intervention in this study had been designed to also improve self-regulation?

2. What pattern of results would you expect to find if the study had not included math activities for parents?

3. If this study had not been conducted with children who were regularly exposed to more than one language, the results may have been different. How so?

Helpful Websites

The Children & Nature Network is a national organization that helps children reconnect with nature. Local events are listed on their website: http://www.childrenandnature.org/

The new characters on *Ahlam Simsim* have the chance to change the course of a generation of refugee children for the better. You can make their acquaintance here: https://www.sesameworkshop.org/what-we-do/shows/ahlan-simsim

The American Art Therapy Association website provides information about the many benefits of art therapy. In particular, on this page you'll find information about how art therapy can help those who are struggling with the traumatic impact and aftereffects of gun violence: https://arttherapy.org/news-traumatic-impact-gun-related-violence/

What to Read and When is a fantastic chronological overview of which books parents can choose to best connect with their children over the lifecycle of childhood. Author Pam Allyn has been the recipient of awards for bringing literacy to under-resourced communities, and she is now vice president of innovation and development at Scholastic Education: https://www.pamallyn.com/books

The *Read-Aloud Handbook* is an excellent and classic guide for parents on which books are best to read aloud to children and what to expect in response from children in terms of questions and request. The website of author Jim Trelease has free excerpts from his book: http://www.trelease-on-reading.com

For information on policies and programs that promote the well-being of children, visit the website of the Children's Defense Fund: http://www.childrensdefense.org/

Recommended Reading

Christakis, E. (2016). *The importance of being little: What preschoolers really need from grownups.* New York, NY: Viking.

Golinkoff, R. M., & Hirsh-Pasek, K. (2016). *Becoming brilliant: What science tells us about raising successful children.* Washington DC: APA LifeTools.

Louv, R. (2008). *Last child in the woods: Saving our children from nature-deficit disorder.* Chapel Hill, NC: Algonquin Books.

Malchiodi, C. A. (1998). *Understanding children's drawings.* New York, NY: The Guilford Press.

McKay, M., Wood, J. C., & Brantley, J. (2007). *The dialectical behavior therapy skills workbook: Practical DBT exercises for learning mindfulness, interpersonal effectiveness, emotion regulation and distress tolerance.* Oakland, CA: New Harbinger Publications.

Metropolitan Museum of Art (2001). *What can you do with a paper bag?* San Francisco, CA: Basic Books.

Singer, D. G., & Singer, J. L. (2000). *Make-believe: Games and activities for imaginative play.* Washington, DC: American Psychological Association.

Yeager, M., & Yeager, D. (2013). *Executive function and child development.* New York, NY: W.W. Norton.

CHAPTER 9

Emotional Development in Early Childhood

Snapshot

We first encountered 5-year-old twins Crystal and Jimmy in Chapter 8, where we learned more about Crystal. In this chapter, we learn more about Jimmy.

Like many preschoolers, Jimmy loves to be read Maurice Sendak's (1963) classic children's book, *Where the Wild Things Are*. It's a story about a little boy named Max who, while wearing a wolf costume, makes mischief around his house, including chasing his dog with a fork!

In response to his impulsive behavior, Max's mother calls him a "wild thing," to which he replies, "I'll eat you up"—so she sends him to his room without dinner. As Max pouts, his bedroom morphs into a forest! So he sails off in a boat to a land of "wild things," creatures that gnash their teeth and roar.

Max tames the wild things and eventually becomes their king. But soon he becomes lonely. Because he is now ready for human interaction, having mastered

FIG. 9.1   Crystal and Jimmy

the wild things (who represent his wild emotions and impulsive behaviors), Max sails back home. Before he leaves, the wild things threaten him by saying "We'll eat you up," but Max, who is now unafraid of wild things, says, "No." He drifts home to his room, to find a hot meal waiting for him.

This beloved story entertains millions of children but also provides a glimpse into the world of preschoolers. So throughout this chapter, we will reflect upon the meaning of *Where the Wild Things Are* in terms of the emotional milestones of early childhood.

What Can Erikson's Theory Tell Us About Preschoolers' Emotional Needs?

We first encountered Erikson's (1993) theory of development in Chapter 1, and we considered the first two stages of his theory (Trust–Mistrust; Autonomy–Shame and Doubt) in detail in Chapter 7.

In this chapter, we will explore his third stage, Initiative–Guilt, which corresponds to the preschool years or early childhood, the stage of development that corresponds to approximately 2 to 6 years of age.

Initiative–Guilt

For Erikson (1950), the crisis of early childhood is between initiative and guilt. In Erikson's context, taking initiative means being motivated and confident to choose tasks and activities for ourselves, carrying out goals, and generally making things.

"Making" can mean constructing arts and crafts; building structures from toy blocks; singing songs and telling stories; and role-playing, whether it be about Max in his wolf costume, superheroes, pirates, astronauts, or more everyday roles like teacher, physician, firefighter, and chef.

Because of the rise of initiative during this stage of development, preschoolers often become frustrated if adults attempt to help or even simply hurry them while they are feeding or dressing themselves. They will make clear that "I want to do it myself!"

Learning Goals

- ▶ Interpret what Erikson's theory tells us about preschoolers' emotional needs
- ▶ Discuss how preschoolers' emotional understanding can be best scaffolded
- ▶ Illustrate how self-concept, self-esteem, and self-regulation can be best supported
- ▶ Explain what gender can teach us about children developing their full potential
- ▶ Identify how play can be better facilitated and how play can be therapeutic
- ▶ Analyze how the quality of preschoolers' relationships affects their lives
- ▶ Describe what we know about moral development in early childhood

This self-assertion is developmentally appropriate, and certainly not a sign that the child is difficult or outrageously strong-willed. And because children are busy taking initiative to explore their environment, their constant question "Why?" is also developmentally appropriate and will fade over time (Hurrell & Stack, 2017).

Note that children's attempts to create should be reinforced, but as Erikson (1993) stated,

> Children cannot be fooled by empty praise ... they may have to accept artificial bolstering of their self-esteem in lieu of something better, but their ego identity gains real strength only from wholehearted and consistent recognition of real accomplishment—i.e., of achievement that has meaning in the culture (pp. 235–236).

For Erikson, the virtue of this stage is **purpose**, or the ability to visualize and pursue goals (Erikson, 1997). Children who resolve this stage successfully tend to be proactive and use their imagination freely, such as how Jimmy told his mother one morning that he was going to go into the preschool classroom and take two toy cars and build a parking lot for them—and how he subsequently used his shoe as a pretend car when he could only find one car. Jimmy then proceeded to pursue his goal by using crayons on the ample supply of cardboard in the classroom to delineate a parking lot lines.

Children who resolve successfully this stage also have been allowed to be responsible, such as by having the opportunity and duty to clean up their toys on a regular basis, as opposed to having it done for them.

On the other hand, in Erikson's view, children who do not resolve this stage successfully tend to be passive, inhibited, and/or paralyzed with guilt over the emotional needs that are typical of this stage—wanting to be independent, to do things on their own, and to choose the activities in which they are involved.

Such excessive guilt can result from a context of criticism or excessive control from parents. Let's talk more about guilt, as well as shame, with which it is often incorrectly confused.

Shame versus Guilt

Shame and guilt are both examples of *self-conscious emotions*. That is, they are a result of evaluating ourselves through the eyes of another person, and they become apparent at the end of the second year of life.

Although the terms *shame* and *guilt* are often used interchangeably, they are not the same emotion—and they correspond to overlapping but quite distinct areas of the brain (Michl et al., 2014; Muris & Meesters, 2014; Zhu et al., 2019).

Shame is a negative evaluation of our self ("*I* did that horrible thing") whereas **guilt** comes from negatively evaluating a specific behavior of ours ("I *did* that horrible thing"), so that guilt during the preschool years serves a purpose in moral development—and a lack of guilt indicates a risk factor for later psychopathology (Glenn, 2019; Lewis, 1971).

Preschoolers who experience guilt, and display such, are more likely to engage in behaviors that repair a ruptured relationship with—and elicit the cooperation of—someone against whom they misbehaved (Vaish, 2018).

Guilt is perhaps a more mature emotion, because it is voluntary and evoked solely from within, whereas shame is involuntary and is evoked in relationship to another person. Therefore, shame is the more comprehensive, and the more painful, of the two emotions.

The maturational difference between shame and guilt is also apparent in children's relationship to empathy. "Shame is typically an acutely painful experience that involves a marked self-focus. This preoccupation with the self is likely to draw one's focus away from a distressed other, thus precluding or interrupting other-oriented feelings of empathy" (Tangney, 1995, p. 1137).

In Erikson's (1997) theory, guilt indeed develops later than shame; research indicates that shame is more disruptive; is more likely to lead us to believe we are a failure; and interferes more with our functioning, such as leading to anger and other aspects of our functioning consistent with the multi-dimensional pattern of development, such as impairing our memory (Cavalera et al., 2018; Zhu et al., 2018). Shame is appropriate when children are misbehaving, but like guilt, it can become excessive.

So if both excessive shame and guilt impair children's well-being, what works?

Not punishment. Punishment (including threats, as well as spanking and physical force) is ineffective, and it backfires, given that it causes children to become resentful, aggressive, and unable to learn what behaviors they should engage in instead.

On the other hand, caregiving that provides much freedom as well as clear limits, along with warmth and **inductive discipline** (discussing a conflict as a problem that a parent and child can solve together, offering explanations for limits, and reasoning about how one's actions affect others), is most effective for its outcomes associated with the polydirectional pattern of development. That is, it helps preschoolers *decrease* their problem behavior over time and *increase* their **prosocial behavior** over time (Gershoff et al., 2018; Olson, Choe, & Sameroff, 2018).

How Can Preschoolers' Emotional Understanding Be Best Scaffolded?

Children need help identifying their emotions, even the negative ones. Parents should avoid saying, for instance, "We don't get angry."

Instead, it is best to first mirror the child's feelings and say, "You seem angry. Is that right?" Then, display empathy for the child's anger and say, "I'd be angry too if I wasn't allowed to do what I want—*and* you can't hit your brother/throw things at people/run in the street/etc."

Parents need to then make it clear to the child that anger is certainly appropriate, but that it must be expressed in healthy ways, by doing a mad dance, ripping paper, punching a pillow, jumping on a bean bag, drawing a picture about how angry one is, making up a puppet story about the anger-inducing situation, reading a story about taming your anger like *Where the Wild Things Are*, and so on. For more suggestions on helping children manage difficult emotions (with plenty of empathy from the authors for parents who are flummoxed by their child's behavior), see *How to Talk So Little Kids Will Listen: A Survival Guide to Life with Children Ages 2–7* (Faber & King, 2017) listed in the *Recommended Reading* section at the end of this chapter.

Preschoolers' emotional understanding improves when parents try to help them imagine the emotions of others as well, such as by asking a child, "Why is Keisha crying? How do you think she feels? How can we help her feel better?"

Research indicates that the more preschool teachers help children recognize, identify, and understand emotions, the greater the children's emotional regulation over time (Housman, Denham, & Cabral, 2018). Providers of family childcare (which is set in a provider's home) are more likely to be responsive to children's negative emotions when their own perceived stress is low. In the same way, preschool teachers who feel greater control over their job, and who perceive greater job resources, have more positive attitudes regarding teaching children about emotions (Denham, Bassett, & Miller, 2017; Jeon, Kwon, & Choi, 2018).

Greater support for childcare providers' and teachers' well-being (including but not limited to their pay and benefits) is vital if we want future generations of all children—not just those whose parents can afford high-end preschools—to be able to regulate their emotions and therefore contribute to everyone's well-being (Denham, Bassett, & Miller, 2017; Jeon, Kwon, & Choi, 2018).

To learn about a public television show that aims to foster emotional well-being in preschoolers, see *Tech & Media: Daniel Tiger's Neighborhood*.

Tech & Media

Daniel Tiger's Neighborhood

As we learned in Chapters 6, 7, and 8, children's exposure to screen time during the first 2 years should be nonexistent. After that, it should be limited to no more than 1 hour per day from ages 2 to 5.

These guidelines are determined as such largely because the *more* that children are sitting with screens, the *less* time they are moving their bodies so they can later rest, the *less* opportunity they have to interact with parents to develop a secure attachment and learn about emotions, and the *less* time they are acquiring social skills with peers (Hinkley et al., 2018).

In addition to these serious negative consequences of screen time, much of what is available for preschool age children on television, over streaming services, and via apps is of poor quality. Sometimes it is even violent, despite proclaiming that it is age-appropriate.

FIG. 9.2   Daniel Tiger's Neighborhood

Source: https://en.wikipedia.org/wiki/File:Daniel_Tiger%27s_Neighborhood_logo.png.

There are some exceptions, though. One is especially notable, because it is prosocial with a focus on empathy and because it teaches emotion regulation strategies. This is *Daniel Tiger's Neighborhood*, a show for preschoolers based on the *Mister Rogers' Neighborhood* show watched by many in prior generations.

Both the television show and the app for *Daniel Tiger's Neighborhood* value emotional intelligence, along with respect for others, and they teach preschoolers emotion regulation strategies via modeling: In one scenario, Daniel Tiger and his friend are so frustrated that they can't go to the beach as planned, since it's a rainy day, that they become mad. But then they begin singing "When you get so mad that you want to roar, take a deep breath [big inhale sound] and count to four—1, 2, 3, 4!"

Research indicates that that the show and the app work. Preschoolers who watched *Daniel Tiger's Neighborhood* showed more empathy and emotion recognition one month later, those who used the app showed more knowledge about emotions one month later, and those who both watched the television show and used the app showed more emotion regulation strategies a month later (Rasmussen et al., 2016; 2018).

. . . .

How Can Self Concept, Self-Esteem, and Self-Regulation Be Best Supported?

According to William James, one of the earliest presidents of the American Psychological Association, the self consists of the Me-Self and the I-Self.

The **Me-Self** is the *object* of other people's knowledge, or the way we are perceived by others; the **I-Self** is the *subject* of our knowledge, the knower, or "the sense of our own personal identity" (James, 1890/1998, p. 334).

Max's thinking of himself as the king of the wild things, as we learned about in the opening *Snapshot* with Jimmy, is a clear manifestation of his I-Self. The I-Self develops as children's autobiographical memories grow, an advancement that later gives way to the Me-Self, which the I-Self constructs (Harter, 2016).

Self-Concept

When asked to describe themselves, preschoolers typically use concrete and tangible traits, such as being male and having brown hair. In middle childhood, children begin typically to use group memberships and some psychological traits to describe themselves, such as what grade they are in and their being smart or nice. Adolescents often compare themselves to other people, but they typically use more abstract and internal personality traits ("I'm an introvert") when asked to describe themselves.

The development of **self-concept**, or the collection of traits, skills, attitudes, and values we believe in order to define our self, occurs during childhood and adolescence (Harter, 2012).

More specifically, from age 2 to age 4, the **taxonomic self** is one in which children understand themselves in terms of taxonomy or classifications, such as what color their hair is, what gender they are, and what their favorite color is.

Notice that children's emotional understanding of themselves during this time is related to their cognitive development in that it focuses most on concrete and tangible characteristics rather than on abstract traits. As Chapter 7 discussed, preschoolers' limited ability to mentally juggle multiple pieces of information at the same time, the reason they usually fail Class Inclusion problems, also is consistent with the multidimensional pattern of development in that makes it difficult for them to make social comparisons.

Social comparisons are a way to evaluate ourselves in relationship to others who are similar to us. Because children in the preschool stage struggle to make these social comparisons, they also tend to overestimate their competencies and as a result often experience frustration. For example, Jimmy might think he is strong and therefore capable of walking the dog, but he overestimates his ability to hold on to the leash when the dog pulls, and as a result, Jimmy falls down and cries.

From 5 to 7 years of age, children understand themselves in terms of the **interrelated taxonomic self**, in which they begin to appreciate the relationships among their various traits. For example, Jimmy mentions that he is good at riding his bike but not his skates.

Educational television programs that focus on opposites also help facilitate this kind of thinking; therefore, cognitive development can certainly boost emotional development (Harter, 2012). Social comparisons are limited at this stage, but preschool children are beginning to make temporal comparisons.

Temporal comparisons are those we make between our current selves and ourselves in the past. Jimmy's statement that "I can run faster now that I could last summer" reflects such a temporal comparison, as well as a belief about his competency.

Competency beliefs change over time as children take in both the comments about their performance that they receive from parents, teachers, and other adults, as well as the support they receive in order to achieve tasks (Muenks, Wigfield, & Eccles, 2018). Comments should focus on *effort* rather than *outcome*, as we learned in Chapter 8; support, of course, should be developmentally appropriate and fall within a child's zone of proximal development.

Self-Esteem

Self-esteem is a judgment we make about our worth. Children with high self-esteem are *more* likely to take initiative, whereas children with low self-esteem are *less* likely to persevere and more likely to give up on a task even when they do take the initiative to begin it. This indicates that the emphasis in Erikson's (1993) theory not only is consistent with the polydirectional pattern of development, but also has real practical consequences.

Most preschoolers have high self-esteem for reasons associated with the multidimensional pattern of development we discussed earlier. That is, because they cognitively struggle to keep two things in mind (recall their lack of hierarchical classification ability, discussed in Chapter 8), they are unable to mentally consider and compare their behavior to that of another child, so they tend to assume that their own behavior is excellent. Another example: Jimmy's ability to color within the lines is developmentally appropriate in that it leaves a bit to be desired, yet he describes his coloring as "the best."

We also discussed above how the crisis of Erikson's theory means preschoolers must develop the confidence to choose activities proactively, with the support of parents who provide opportunities for the child to show responsibility so that they balance what could happen in fantasy with the societal demands of reality. Otherwise, children may become passive and paralyzed, perhaps as a result of excessive control from parents who don't appreciate the developmental need that children have for open messy places to play, and/or criticism from parents who don't appreciate that children thrive when their feelings are mirrored and validated, rather than reacted to, and sternly so (Berzoff, 2016).

Jimmy's parents suggest regularly that they use objects in pretend play, which is likely why he so readily used his shoe as a car when he found only one car in his preschool classroom as we discussed earlier in this chapter. Jimmy's parents also provide him, and Crystal, a wide range of choices for books each night after their bath, so Jimmy and Crystal have developed the confidence to choose and know they will be able to continue to choose what they read with their parents as long as they take care of their bodies first.

So the risk–resilience pattern of development is apparent when we consider how important the home environment is to the development of self-esteem during early childhood, particularly emotional interactions between parents and preschoolers. Indeed, parents can promote children's (healthy, rather than excessive) self-esteem by providing them with opportunities to make choices, take initiative, and be responsible. Parents can also provide specific scaffolding support to help a child master a task depending on where the child is, adjust their expectations to just above the child's current level of performance—as in Vygotsky's concept of a zone of proximal development that changes over time, which we learned about in Chapter 1—and ensure that their interactions are characterized regularly by positive affect (Eun, 2019; Wang, Morgan, & Birigen, 2014).

Self-Regulation

The self-regulation we first learned about in Chapter 7 is a precursor to the adult personality trait of *conscientiousness*—or the extent to which we regulate our impulses so that we can be responsible, accurate, motivated to achieve, compliant with norms, and disciplined in our work, health, and social relationships (Kim & Kochanska, 2019). Self-regulation develops most dramatically during the preschool years and includes *effortful control* and *executive functions*, including children's abilities to calm their physical bodies, perhaps via mindful breathing and yoga (Cole et al., 2017). In Chapter 7, we learned that effortful control is a specific form of emotional regulation that allows us to resist our impulses.

Executive functions are our abilities to control our behaviors and our thoughts, often via cognitive function, such as by planning and achieving goals, as well as by delaying gratification (Ma et al., 2018). Delaying gratification is an emotional function too, and it likely depends on whether children perceive the world to be safe and fair, especially in light of research showing that children are more likely to wait to receive two stickers later (instead of receiving one now) if they perceive others to be trustworthy (Ma et al., 2018).

Additional cognitive processes that contribute to children developing these executive function abilities include attention shifting, working memory (which we will learn about in Chapter 10), and the behavioral inhibition needed for planning ahead, solving problems, and engaging in goal-directed activities. All of these processes bolster preschoolers' school performance, health, and social skills. They require not only parents' scaffolding, but also parents' encouragement, praise, warmth, support for children's autonomy, acceptance of children's needs, and acceptance of children's emotions (whether the emotions are positive or negative) (Merz et al., 2017; Valcan, Davis, & Pino-Pasternak, 2018).

We will have more to say about parents' role in children's self-regulation in a moment. For now, though, note that executive functions are an example of the multidimensional pattern of development because they occur in the physical brain, require cognitive processes, and depend on emotional bonds.

Self-regulation overall is characterized by the lifelong and risk–resilience patterns of child development too, as indicated in the classic "Marshmallow" studies on the ability to delay gratification, and the contemporary replications of such (Mischel, Ebbesen, & Zeiss, 1972; Mischel, Shoda, & Rodriquez, 1989). In these studies, preschoolers were brought one by one into a research room with nothing but a desk, and on it a bell and a marshmallow. The experimenter then said they had to leave the room, and the rule of the game was that if the child could wait until the experimenter returned (15 minutes later) without eating the marshmallow, the child would receive two marshmallows. A child who could not wait could ring the bell, and the experimenter would return and give the child one marshmallow. Some of the children were able to wait; others were not.

Once these same preschoolers reached adolescence, those who were able to delay gratification and wait for the experimenter to return had higher SAT scores that those teens who had not been able to wait for the experimenter as children—and as adults, those who were able to wait were more successfully educationally and economically and were less likely to be overweight, abuse drugs, have low self-esteem, and suffer from mental disorders (Mischel, 2011; 2012).

Yet when contemporary researchers attempted to replicate these studies, they found that the link between preschoolers' ability to delay gratification and their later achievement (along with the general well-being) as teenagers was be much weaker when researchers ruled out the role of executive functioning (Watts, Duncan, & Quan, 2018).

Results such as these suggest that any intervention designed to improve children's ability to delay gratification without first addressing their executive function, along with their abilities to calm their bodies (such as after having been taught mindful breathing and yoga, as in the *Cycle of Science* study at the end of this chapter), may be limited.

To learn about how self-regulation reflects the four patterns of child development, see the *Pan & Zoom: Self-Regulation* box.

Pan & Zoom

Self-Regulation

In this box, we pan across, or take a panoramic, wide-angle view of self-regulation and how it is related to the patterns of development.

In terms of the multidimensional pattern of development in which aspects of physical, cognitive, and/or emotional interact with one another, children's cognitive abilities, especially their vocabulary ("Use your words"), can help or hinder their ability to self-regulate in the present—and throughout their development.

Children's emotional well-being matters for self-regulation too. Parents' creation of a context in which they optimize secure attachment, as well as socialize self-regulation—by accepting emotions, discussing emotions and how to cope with them, and valuing self-regulation—likely provides a foundation for the relationship between self-regulation and language (Cooke et al., 2018; Hanno & Surrain, 2019; Meyer et al., 2014; Pallini et al., 2018).

How? Well, parents' fostering of a secure attachment promotes self-regulation in which children know psychologically that they have a secure base to which they can return when they need to fill their emotional cup (Saltzman, Fiese, Bost, & McBride, 2018). This security, in turn, also fosters another multidimensional pattern: children's regulation of their literal cup, that is, their appetite. Children with secure attachments are more likely to begin eating when physically hungry and stop eating when sated or full, instead of eating for emotional reasons (Saltzman, Fiese, Bost, & McBride, 2018).

In terms of the lifelong and polydirectional patterns of development, parents who suspect they may be highly controlling should pause and rethink their behavior, given that research has shown the negative effects of such. That is, children who have highly controlling parents at age 2 are *less* likely to possess emotion regulation at age 5, and as a result, are *more* likely to exhibit emotional and academic problems and *less* likely to possess social skills and be academically productive at age 10 (Perry et al., 2018).

Instead of harsh control, discipline and self-control can be taught with limit-setting that provides boundaries, but that allows and supports children in making a choice, both within the context of emotional support and affection. For instance, parents can tell children they must wear a sweater, but the children can certainly choose which sweater to wear.

When children are given choices, they feel more in control of their behavior. When supported with guidance from others, they are more likely to master a task, which prevents excessive shame and guilt, fosters healthy self-esteem, and perpetuates self-regulation over development. Yet parents' expectations about choices need be developmentally appropriate—expectations that are too high leave children chronically feeling like failures, and expectations that are too low diminish a child's value and signal to them that others do not believe in them, and/or send a message to the child that they are out of control.

The polydirectional pattern of development is also relevant in how social rejection or being rejected by peers *decreases* a child's development of self-regulation, and poor self-regulation *increases* the likelihood of subsequent self-regulation (Stenseng et al., 2015).

In terms of the risk–resilience pattern of development, interventions are available for helping children learn to better interact with their peers. General interventions, such as yoga in kindergarten classrooms, are also effective in improving children's self-regulation as well as improving specific problem behaviors such as inattention and hyperactivity (Jarraya et al., 2019; Pahigiannis & Glos, 2018).

To learn more about a particular research study that investigated the relationship between yoga and self-regulation in preschoolers, see *The Cycle of Science* at the end of this chapter.

⚬ ⚬ ⚬ ⚬

Child Self-Regulation via Parent Self-Regulation

Before we end this section, we need discuss one more critical aspect of children's ability to develop self-regulation during the preschool years, and that is parents' own self-regulation.

Parents' fostering of their own self-regulation is just as important as their fostering of children's self-regulation, especially because caregiving is emotionally demanding and requires consistent positive interactions with children. Many of these interactions are particularly challenging because of preschoolers' need for continual attention, redirection, and managing of strong emotions (Xiao, Spinrad, & Carter, 2018).

Yet when parents are reactive to these stressors and unable to regulate their emotions and/or they are unavailable emotionally, children lack secure attachments and support for managing their emotions. As a result, the children withdraw from the parent, and/or have difficulty regulating their own emotions (Tsotsi et al., 2019).

Ideally, all parents demonstrate **reflective capacity**, or the ability to interpret one's own behavior, as well as others' behavior as a function of people being separate and differentiated psychologically from one another, with different thoughts and feeling (Wade et al., 2018). When parents demonstrate reflective capacity, they regularly consider *the motivations behind their children's behavior* (so that a meltdown is correctly interpreted as a result of sleep deprivation, and not as the result of a "bad" or "irritating" child merely "acting out"), as well as *the motivations behind their own behavior* (so that rather than acting on their temptation to "blow a fuse" and disrupting the parent–child attachment, parents engage in the very same response inhibition they ask of their children). For example, they acknowledge their anger to themselves and hold it internally with self-compassion, as they reassure themselves of how difficult parenting truly is and the skills and emotional tools they can practice.

Reflective capacity in the face of preschoolers' need for continual attention, redirection, and managing of strong emotions is understandably even more difficult to practice when a parent is stressed. Research confirms that the more mothers' lives are characterized by risk factors (teen motherhood, single parenthood, high levels of marital conflict, low education, low income, and/or depression), the less likely they are to demonstrate reflective capacity (Wade et al., 2018).

Indeed, the more reactive parents' sympathetic nervous systems are to the stress in their lives (perhaps as a result of not having an adequate support system, not engaging regularly in stress-reduction techniques, and/or not resolving their own unresolved emotional issues), the greater their risk of expressing negative affect toward or even maltreating their child (Oosterman et al., 2019; Reijman et al., 2016).

Parents who are more effective in creating a context in which they model how to self-regulate end up helping their children learn to self-regulate, which ultimately lowers children's risk for maladjustment (Morris, Cui, Criss, & Simmons, 2018). Therefore, it is essential that parents who experience difficulties in emotional regulation learn to regulate their emotions. Research has found that parents with lower levels of emotional regulation (and lower levels of coping skills in general) show higher levels of verbal aggression, anger, and depression (Johnson et al., 2017; Lavi et al., 2019).

Other work indicates that the *less* likely parents are to "coach" their children through their difficult emotions and the *more* likely they are to dismiss or reject their child's emotions, the *more* their child is at risk for having conduct problems such as aggression, disruption, and/or antisocial behavior (Johnson et al., 2017; Lavi et al., 2019).

Remember, emotional regulation is a simply set of skills that need to be learned, and there is no shame in parents, or anyone, not (yet) knowing them. These tools certainly can be acquired. Options include yoga, meditation, exercise, massage, therapy, and/or reading relevant books.

To learn more about how parents can develop reflective capacity and become more emotionally available to their children, even when they are struggling with their own issues and/or regulating their own emotions, see *Raising a Secure Child* (Hoffman, Cooper, & Powell, 2017), listed in the *Recommended Reading* section at the end of this chapter.

Other reading suggestions include *Dialectical Behavior Therapy Skills Workbook*, listed in the *Recommended Reading* section at the end of Chapter 8 as well as this chapter, and *Self Compassion for Parents*, which reassuringly validates and normalizes parents' struggles with great warmth and support (Pollak, 2019).

It indeed takes a village to raise a child, so it is in the best interests of children for their parent(s) to find a preschool that has emotion-coaching as part of the curriculum. The preschool should also employ teachers who practice emotion co-regulation, given that such co-regulation is associated with children's greater self-regulation (Silkenbeumer, Schiller, & Kärtner, 2018).

What Can Gender Teach Us About Children Developing Their Full Potential?

Sex can refer to the physical act, of course, but it also refers to the biological category to which we were assigned at birth, such as female, male, or **intersex**—that is, people whose sex characteristics (in terms of chromosomes, hormones, and/or genitals) don't fit the typical definitions of *female* or *male* (United Nations Office of the High Commissioner for Human Rights, 2016).

Gender, on the other hand, refers to the psychological traits, roles, and expectations society has of people—and the gender with which people identify, such as female, male, or **nonbinary**. A nonbinary gender includes children and adults who are gender nonconforming, genderqueer, gender fluid, gender neutral, and so on.

These nonbinary terms may also be used by people who identify as **transgender**, in that their gender identity does not match the sex to which they were assigned at birth. But do note that some transgender people identify with a gender binary—such as a female-to-male (FTM) transgender person or a trans man, who may or may not opt for sex reassignment surgery (American Psychological Association, 2015).

In terms of the aforementioned psychological traits, societal attitudes deem feminine traits to be nurturing and sensitive as well as passive and dependent, and masculine traits to be analytical and confident, as well as assertive and independent.

So society tends to be "gendered" or to encourage a *gender binary*, that is, a split into two sets of gender roles, despite many children and adults showing both feminine and masculine traits such as being both nurturing and assertive—and despite research showing that having a wider range of emotional competence including "feminine" and "masculine" traits is associated with greater well-being (Gartzia, Pizarro, & Baniandres, 2018).

So this binary is unfortunate, yet not everyone (including adults, as well as preschool-age children) internalizes it, nor needs to do so. In this section, we will learn specifically about how preschoolers begin to understand gender typing and gender identity.

Gender Typing

Gender is one of the first social categories that children make, and research shows that children who are less flexible about gender stereotypes (e.g., answering "boys" rather than "both" when asked who likes to play with trucks and answering "girls" rather than "both" when asked who likes to play with dolls) have more negative attitudes about other genders (Halim et al., 2014; Skinner & Meltzoff, 2019). Such negative attitudes may not be innocuous, either, given that social exclusion and discrimination can have real consequences for children's health and well-being (Halim et al., 2018; Skinner & Meltzoff, 2019).

Gender typing (also known as gender stereotyping) is the process by which anything, including psychological traits but also clothing, activities, and toys, are *prescribed* as appropriate for one gender but *prohibited* for other genders (Liben and Bigler, 2002; Weisgram, 2018). Criticisms of same-sex marriage laws have suggested that gender typing is an ideal to uphold (which, as we will see below in light of research data on negative out-group attitudes, is questionable) and that children of same-sex parents will not learn such gender stereotypes; yet the data indicate otherwise—that is, that children's gender-typed behavior does not vary depending on the orientation of their parents (Farr et al., 2018a).

In fact, it may be that the long-term positive adjustment found in children of *queer* or **LGBTQIA +** (lesbian, gay, bisexual, transgender, questioning, intersex, asexual, and related communities—such as Two-Spirit, about which we will learn more in Chapter 13) parents is a result of their learning early on to cope with different, if not also sometimes difficult, life circumstances such as stigma and/ or bullying. So the quality of family interactions is more important than parents' sexual orientation (Lick, Patterson, & Schmidt, 2013; Sasnett, 2014). Indeed, research shows that children raised by same-sex parents have an overall equivalent quality of life and are just as psychologically healthy and socially and academically well-adjusted as children raised by opposite-sex parents (Fedewa, Black, & Ahn, 2015; Lamb, 2014; Titlestad & Pooley, 2014).

Also, although many parents, regardless of their *affectional orientation* (heterosexual or queer), may dress their children in gender-neutral clothing and state that they encourage their children to be *psychologically androgynous*—that is, both feminine and masculine in their psychological traits—they may still (perhaps unconsciously) perpetuate gender typing, via the contents of their children's bedrooms. How so? Well, a 2019 study of preschoolers' bedrooms found that they were very gender-typed, and unfortunately not unlike the gender-typed preschoolers' bedrooms when a similar study was conducted in 1975 (Macphee & Prendergast, 2019).

It is more than okay for boys to play with dolls. In fact, it is not just authors like Maurice Sendak and actors like Daniel Kaluuya (whose films include *Black Panther*) who possess sensitivity and insight into interpersonal relationships. All people who work with other people need to get along with them, so it is vital that children be allowed to pursue any and all of their interests so they can develop their full potential. Dolls in particular help children practice interpersonal relationships.

Additionally, studies show that parents judge neutral-gender toys and same-gender-typed toys as more desirable toys for their children than cross-gender-typed toys (Kollmayer et al., 2018). This is especially true for parents whose own attitudes toward gender are more traditional and less egalitarian, as indicated by their agreement with statements to the effect that "girls enjoy helping with the household more than boys" and that "male police officers provide a stronger sense of security than female police officers." The same study also found that parents who are male, are younger, and/or have less education tend to endorse such traditional gender role attitudes, whereas parents who are female, are older, and/or have more education tend to endorse more egalitarian gender role attitudes (Kollmayer et al., 2018).

It is not just parents who may be encouraging children to fortify some parts of themselves while cutting off other parts of themselves. For instance, studies show that preschool teachers are less likely to encourage feminine activities (e.g., art, pretend play, kitchen play) than masculine activities (e.g., blocks, vehicles, climbing) or neutral activities (e.g., books, music, math, clean up) during free play (Granger et al., 2017). This is especially true when teachers facilitate activities with mixed-gender groups of children or all-male groups of children. Such devaluing of the feminine is discouraging, yet it could simply reflect teachers' preference to have children obtaining exercise or focusing on academics, or it could be that they don't appreciate or value the creativity, nurturance, and complex thinking that feminine activities help children to develop (Granger et al., 2017).

Regardless, other research does indicate that preschool teachers often transmit very gendered expectations for children, with the data indicating, for example, that girls are more likely to be held back from a subsequent activity if they didn't clean up, whereas boys are more likely to be allowed to transition to the next activity regardless of whether they clean up—or how girls are more likely to be excused from an activity if they become physically aggressive, whereas boys are likely to be told they need to talk out their conflict in an activity (Gansen, 2019).

Peers also end up limiting the range of children's behaviors. Research has shown that both girls and boys who "gender-police," by encouraging adherence to gender norms and discouraging or even punishing cross-gender activities with teasing and rejection, are more likely to be aggressive overall. It has also been found that the more time a child spends with a gender-police peer, the more time that child spends with same-gender peers (Xiao, Cook, Martin, & Nielson, 2019).

Increasing children's flexibility about gender stereotypes is not difficult. One study found that, compared to children who were shown a magazine page that portrayed a similar-age child playing with a gender-stereotypic toy, those children who were shown a magazine page that portrayed a similar-age child playing with a gender counter-stereotypic toy were subsequently more likely to show gender flexibility themselves when playing with toys. Children from this second group were more likely to choose either a boy or a girl when asked with whom they would like to play (Spinner, Cameron, & Calogero, 2018).

On the other hand, this same study also found that children who were shown a magazine page that portrayed a similar-age child playing with a gender-stereotypic toy were more likely to choose a same-gender playmate. Results such as these tell us that media have the potential to disrupt the gender typing of toys, as well as gender-biased playgroups (Spinner, Cameron, & Calogero, 2018).

Greater encouragement of cross-gender toys could thus expand children's psychological and behavioral repertories, rendering them three-dimensional and better able to fulfill their potential in all arenas of life (Kollmayer et al., 2018). Girls might not then be deprived of more opportunities to learn about, say, engineering; nor would boys be deprived of more opportunities to learn about, say, expressing their emotional depths.

Gender Identity

So far, we have been discussing gender-related *behaviors*. These are different from gender identity, a topic we turn to now.

When did Jimmy know that he is a boy? When he was around 2.5 years of age, which is typically when children establish their **gender identity**, or their understanding of their own gender.

Yet when did Jimmy not only know that he is a boy, but also know that he will likely always be a boy? **Gender stability**, our understanding of the fact that our gender will remain stable over time,

is appreciated by most preschoolers by about 3 years of age.

Around the end of the preschool years, somewhere between 5 and 6 years of age, children also begin to develop **gender constancy**, or the understanding that gender doesn't change despite a change in someone's appearance, such as when a male wears a skirt (doing so is not unusual in Scotland, a remind to us that gender roles are specific to a culture).

Before the end of the preschool years, children may think that a physical change, such as a female suddenly sporting a short haircut, means a change in gender. Why? Because of their tendency to *centrate*, an aspect of cognitive development we learned about in Chapter 8. This reminds us that gender development is a clear example of the multidimensional pattern of development (Kohlberg, 1966, 1969; Leaper, 2015).

Because preschoolers tend to focus on one piece of information at the expense of other sources of information, it shouldn't surprise us that gender is an especially salient category in early childhood. In middle childhood, children become better able to make multiple and subtler distinctions between people, so gender becomes less important

FIG. 9.3   Jimmy Is a Boy

: Copyright © Depositphotos/iordani.

over time, especially for children who are encouraged to develop complex thinking skills and consider multiple sources of information when making judgments about others. For example, when a child says "Zoë is crying because she is a girl, and that's what girls do," adults need to encourage other explanations for Zoë's crying, such as her personality traits (Zoë is empathic), her environment (other children are bullying Zoë), her well-being (Zoë is sick), and/or her situation (Zoë's grandfather just died).

Preschoolers' tendency to concentrate of physical features, such as appearance, before gender constancy is established is also consistent with research that shows children's *appearance rigidity* (e.g., girls insisting on wearing pink, and/or dresses, day after day) from 2 to 4 years of age is followed by greater *appearance flexibility* (e.g., girls starting to be willing to wear blue or pants or ...) between 5 and 6 years of age (Halim et al., 2014, 2018).

Flexibility in our understanding of gender is a developmental process—and it is also a cultural characteristic. As we learned in Chapter 2, although differences *among* people in WEIRD (Western, Educated, Industrialized, Rich, and Democratic) societies differ substantially from one another, there are also substantial differences between people in WEIRD and non-WEIRD societies (Clegg, Wen, & Legare, 2017; Henrich, Heine, & Norenzayan, 2010).

Because most developmental science research involves participants from WEIRD societies, this lack of diversity may distort our understanding of the concepts that researchers study (Nielsen et al., 2017). An example: For decades, research on gender development in WEIRD cultures has assumed a gender binary of people being only female or male, but a gender binary is a cultural assumption that isn't universal. For instance, many non-WEIRD cultures acknowledge a *gender nonbinary*, such as the third gender *Hijra* in India or *Two-Spirit* individuals in Native American communities. We will get to know one of these individuals in Chapter 13 (Dunham & Olson, 2016; Hyde et al., 2019).

Increasingly, many children within the United States are also recognizing and accepting a gender nonbinary, in themselves or others, whether it be as *gender variant, gender nonconforming, transgender,* or *gender-expansive*. Let's learn more about them now.

Gender-Expansive Children

Until recently, developmental science research has endorsed the gender binary (perhaps without realizing so)—and as a consequence, failed to understand the development of children who are nonbinary; nonbinary children are often referred to as **gender-expansive**, meaning that their expression of their gender identity does not match their sex at birth. Children (and adults) who are gender-expansive may sometimes refer to themselves as gender variant, gender nonconforming, transgender, or nonbinary as well.

Please understand that children who are gender-expansive are not pretending to be another gender, nor are they confused about their gender identity. Instead, they are expressing their gender identity—interestingly, gender-expansive children are less likely to endorse gender stereotypes (Olson & Enright, 2018; Olson, Key, & Eaton, 2015).

Current researchers are working to reverse the perpetuation of the field's formerly limited understandings of gender and of children. For example, researchers have found that transgender preschoolers are no different from preschoolers who are **cisgender**, or whose gender identity expression corresponds to their sex at birth (*cis* is Latin for "on the side of," and *trans* is Latin for "on the other side") in terms of their behavior, but they are less likely than cisgender preschoolers to believe in gender constancy, or that gender is stable over time (Dunham & Olson, 2016; Fast & Olson, 2018).

Gender-expansive children are no different from cisgender children in terms of their depression levels, although they are slightly higher in anxiety—perhaps because they sense that others may be uncomfortable with and/or rejecting of them.

Indeed, research reveals that, unfortunately, adults rate children who violate stereotypes as less likeable, and gender-expansive children with more peer relation problems show more internalizing problems, such as anxiety, as well as externalizing problems, such as aggression (Durwood, McLaughlin, & Olson, 2017; Kuvalanka et al., 2017; Sullivan et al., 2018). Later in this chapter we will learn more about aggression, including what is developmentally normative for preschoolers and what is not.

For now, it is important to know that the (often cisgender) parents of gender-expansive children experience anxiety themselves (and corresponding health consequences such as sleep loss), not necessarily because they are uncomfortable with their children or reject them but as a result of *gender minority stress*. That is, they are also dealing with their own worry over rejection by family, friends, and other parents; concerns over discrimination at their child's school and in society in general; practical concerns such as the need of documentation while traveling; and unfortunately, quite legitimate concerns about their child's risk of exposure to victimization and violence (Hidalgo & Chen, 2019).

Parents, Families and Friends of Lesbians and Gays (PFLAG) supports the families of lesbian, gay, bisexual, transgender, and queer (LGBTQ+) children and teens—and they are available in person at a family's local PFLAG chapter, or online, via their website. See the *Helpful Websites* at the end of this chapter.

How Can Play Be Better Facilitated and How Can Play Be Therapeutic?

Play is any activity in which we engage without a clear purpose for doing so, at least, other than for pleasure. Play is both appropriate and necessary for children.

The types of play that children engage in change over time, and one particular type, make-believe play, greatly improves children's cognitive and emotional skills. Thus, play is not trivial. Developmentally appropriate play with parents and peers contributes substantially to school readiness too, given its cognitive, language, emotional, and self-regulation benefits (Pyle & Danniels, 2017; Yogman et al., 2018).

The shared interactions and emotional connections available within play can also help a child in regulating their body's stress response system, so the benefits of play are truly reflective of the multidimensional pattern of development. So while pediatricians have already begun to support reading initiatives, they are beginning to embrace the idea of writing 'prescriptions' for play (Yogman et al., 2018).

Physical play outside during the day, with other children in particular, provides children a physical outlet to release energy, an opportunity to learn problem-solving and conflict resolution with their peers, and the ability to focus during subsequent class time once they have increased oxygen levels to the brain through activity. Children who have access to outdoor classrooms are less likely to be off task and less likely to need to be redirected (Bohn-Gettler & Pellegrini, 2014; Largo-Wight et al., 2018).

Play can also be therapeutic and help preschoolers who are having difficulties, such as with ADHD or autism spectrum symptoms, because play provides them with an opportunity to express what is troubling them when words may not come readily.

In this section, we consider all aspects of this wonderful world of play.

The Stages of Social Play

One of the very first theories of social play, in which children play with others, was advanced by Mildred Parten (1932). Parten proposed that play develops in stages, and that these stages are tied to preschoolers' developing social skills.

The first of the six stages in this model occurs when young preschoolers begin interacting with others through **unoccupied behavior**, in which they are not playing but simply standing around or following the teacher. Soon after, children enter the second stage, **onlooker play**, in which they observe other children who are playing and may even talk to these other children, yet not play with them. Next comes the third stage, **solitary independent play**, or play during which one or many children are playing, but not together.

Parallel play develops next. Parallel play is similar to solitary independent play, but in it children share materials, though still without working on or playing with the same thing. Soon after, the fifth stage, **associative play**, develops as children share materials and still work independently, but now they begin to comment on each another's play. Last but not least, **cooperative play** brings children truly together with a common goal—typically pretend or make-believe play with rules about each character's behavior (Parten, 1932).

More complex forms of social play tend to increase as children progress through the preschool years, but not all children follow these stages in a clear sequence. Some of the stages overlap, so a 4-year-old, for example, might be engaging in solitary independent play at one point in the day and parallel play later that same day.

Variability in the rate and sequence of the stages of social play is particularly noticeable in children on the autism spectrum, who may be advanced in one type of play and delayed in another type of play, but whose further progress can be prompted via modeling (Charlop, Lang, & Rispoli, 2018; Humpal, 2015; Nelson et al., 2017).

Make-Believe Play

Jimmy, like Max in *Where the Wild Things Are*, dresses up and imagines he is a wolf, sailing off in a cardboard box boat to a land of "wild things," where he can tame them and become their king. Exploring a hypothetical world such as this prepares children's minds to explore alternate reactions to real-world situations, especially emotional ones. Children are more likely to engage in make-believe play if the adults in their lives, such as parents and preschool teachers, create a context in which they regularly guide and scaffold such play, such as creating a scenario and playing with the children "in role" (Ilgaz et al., 2018; Loizou, Michaelides, & Georgiou, 2019).

Chapter 1 introduced Vygotsky's concepts of scaffolding and the zone of proximal development, in which children master and progress more in the zone of development than they would on their own if they receive tailored guidance from a more experienced person (Esteban-Guitart, 2018).

FIG. 9.4   Jimmy and His Cardboard Boxes

: Copyright © Depositphotos/iordani.

Scaffolding is consistent with Erikson's (1950) concept of initiative too, because in this preschool stage children are interested in learning what they can do, including with help. The more experienced helper gradually increases the task difficulty to just beyond the child's current capabilities, so that the child can slowly master each level and feel a sense of accomplishment and self-control, rather than becoming frustrated.

For Vygotsky, preschoolers demonstrate the greatest self-control over their behavior when they engage in make-believe play. Why? Well, let's consider what happens when children pretend. Of their own *initiative*, they give up an immediate attraction, such as toys, to follow the social rules of the pretend situation, such as one that governs when they, as dragons, can approach castle, and with or without other creatures. So, make-believe or pretend play helps children make controlling their impulses fun, rather than regrettable or frustrating.

Preschoolers who engage in make-believe or pretend play, especially if it is characterized by fantasy and negative emotions, benefit in ways consistent with the polydirectional pattern of development. That is, they are *more* likely to have higher levels of emotional expressiveness, emotional knowledge, emotional regulation, language development, math skills, and spatial skills—as well as being *less* likely to exhibit internalizing symptoms such as anxiety (Hassinger-Das, Hirsh-Pasek, & Golinkoff, 2017; Lindsey & Colwell, 2013; Marcelo & Yates, 2014).

They are also likely to have the greater *theory of mind* or understanding of the desires, emotions, knowledge, beliefs, and intentions of themselves and others, which children acquire through social interactions (Jankowska & Omelańczuk, 2019; Miller & Aloise-Young, 2018). This is likely because pretend play—even when involving preexisting characters such as Batman but when also asked questions such as "What would Batman do?"—facilitates self-control via psychological distance from ourselves and our current situation, a distancing via pretending to be a character that is particularly effective for children with weaker executive function (Grenell et al., 2019; White & Carlson, 2016).

Better yet, pretend play with puppets singularly captures children's attention (even more than storytelling), which reduces behavioral problems. Also, when children (and adults) are allowed to manipulate the puppets themselves, they possess the ability to express internal mental and emotional states in a concrete and physical form (Aminimanesh, Ghazavi, & Merhrabi, 2019). This allows them both psychological distance and expression of specific thoughts and feelings that are not necessarily available with prefabricated characters. Puppets also support children's understanding of narratives, so mental health professionals often use them for healing purposes (Schaefer & Drewes, 2018).

Engaging in puppet play to entertain children, and to role-model to them, can be intimidating to some parents at first (including yours truly), but as with many things, it can be learned. One excellent resource for how to do so is the classic *Storytelling Made Easy with Puppets* (VanSchuyver, 1993), which is listed in the *Recommended Reading* section at the end of this chapter.

Last but not least in the development of pretend play is **sociodramatic play**, pretend play with others. It is important to know that most children can enjoy sociodramatic play by 4 years of age. This type of play is similar to general make-believe or pretend play in its multidimensional benefits, as long as the narrative of the imaginary story is sustained among the children, ideally with the help of parents and/or preschool teachers (Loizou, 2017; Robertson, Yim, & Paatsch, 2018). Puppets can also be used in sociodramatic play, with similar if not stronger benefits.

Speaking of imaginary, although not all preschoolers have an imaginary friend (and they are less common in cultures where parents are unfamiliar with them and/or anxious about them, as research shows is the case in Japan), they are without a doubt a good thing (Moriguchi & Todo, 2018). Children with imaginary companions show greater theory of mind and emotional understanding of others, and they are also more likely to be psychologically sophisticated in their thinking about others, so they are viewed more positively by peers. Also, when they describe their real-life friends, they use mental characteristics such as "He is kind," rather than behavioral or physical characteristics such as "He has straight hair" (Davis, Meins, & Fernyhough, 2014; Lin et al., 2018).

Play Therapy

Erikson was a proponent of play as a means for children to express their inner conflicts, whether regarding Initiative–Guilt or other issues, and to find potential solutions to such conflicts in an accepting environment. This is particularly helpful for children who are marginalized for any number of reasons, whether it be their gender identity, their ethnicity, class, etc. (Davis & Pereira, 2014; Erikson, 1997; Post, Phipps, Camp, & Grybush, 2019).

Mental health professionals who use play therapy with children do so one-on-one or in conjunction with family therapy; they also use play therapy in their offices or outdoors in nature settings.

Play therapy illustrates the multidimensional pattern of development. The relationship the child establishes with a therapist is an emotional one, but it allows the child to cognitively construe a conflict or an issue in a symbolic way (such as via a sandbox) that helps them express feelings in a safe environment.

The empirical research on play therapy indicates that it is effective for a variety of children, including those struggling with anxiety, those with intellectual disabilities, and those who have been exposed to adversity such as poverty or violence and/or trauma such as the death of a parent (Humble et al., 2018; Mora, van Sebille, & Neill, 2018; Patterson, Stutey, & Dorsey, 2018).

How Does the Quality of Preschoolers' Relationships Affect Their Lives?

Early childhood is a time in which we begin to experience greater exposure to people outside the home, especially other children and adult teachers at preschool. These early relationships provide children with a variety of relationships and interpersonal influences, although a child's primary parent(s) are still likely to be the child's most influential relationship during the preschool years.

In this section, we consider different caregiving styles, as well as the impact that other relationships typically have during early childhood.

Caregiving Styles

The ways in which parents interact with their children on a regular basis creates a context of caregiving styles; these styles vary from person to person. Parents' styles may also evolve over time, as the parents themselves change, and/or as they experience stressors in their lives. The four caregiving styles examined here are based on a classification system developed by Baumrind (1971) that categorizes how *accepting and warm* parents are, as well as how *demanding and controlling* they are.

Authoritarian parents are characterized by low levels of acceptance and warmth, but high levels of demandingness and control. That is, they value obedience to an authority figure, and they favor status distinctions between themselves and their children (Baumrind, 2012).

These parents do not typically engage in many verbal exchanges with their children, nor do they encourage their children to question what the parents deem is correct. Their frequent responses to their children are "Because I said so."

Unfortunately, authoritarian parents are often more interested in controlling their children (via threats, ridicule, and criticism) than in teaching them how to control themselves via self-regulation. Thus it shouldn't be too surprising to learn that children whose authoritarian parents emphasize a conformity to parental authority are later more likely to struggle with obesity and issues regarding eating, and more likely to score more poorly on measures of theory of mind (Kuntoro, Dwiputri, & Adams, 2018; Pace, D'Urso, & Zappulla, 2018; Yavuz & Selcuk, 2018).

Additionally, characteristics of the Authoritarian caregiving style also include psychological control *psychological control* (intrusiveness, guilt induction, love withdrawal) and *parental disrespect*, the latter which is associated with both internalizing and externalizing symptoms in children (Smetana, 2017).

In addition, parents' negative emotions and criticism are associated with children having lower levels of executive function or less ability to control their impulses, whereas parents' fostering a home learning environment via regular reading, counting, and scaffolding activities is correlated positively with children's executive function (Hughes & Devine, 2019).

Authoritative parents, like Jimmy's and Crystal's, are characterized by high levels of warmth and acceptance, as well as high levels of demandingness and control. Their control is different from that of Authoritarian parents, though, because Authoritative parents assert their power via high expectations, coupled with support for children in reaching those expectations. Their support helps their children meet expectations through self-regulation (Baumrind, 2012).

These parents also regularly engage in give-and-take discussions with their children and explain the reasons behind the rules they set. So Authoritative parents are responsive and accepting, yet they also establish firm rules and boundaries that they practice consistently.

As a result of such support for their autonomy, the children of Authoritative parents show outcomes that illustrate positive lifelong patterns of development.

FIG. 9.5   Jimmy and Crystal with their Mother

: Copyright © Depositphotos/iordani.

That is, they are able to engage in self-regulation and control their own behavior, rather than being controlled by outside factors like rewards and punishments.

After being the recipients of firm monitoring with high support, later on these children may be less likely to struggle with issues involving weight and food; they also are more likely to be successful in terms of time management, with lower levels of procrastination (Baumrind, 2012; Sokol, Qin, & Poti, 2017; Won & Yu, 2018).

Permissive-Indulgent parents are characterized by high levels of warmth and acceptance, but low levels of demandingness and control. These parents set few or no limits on their children, rarely provide consequences for their misbehavior, and regularly indulge their desires. As a result, the children of Permissive-Indulgent parents are at risk for externalizing problems and having high self-confidence to the point of entitlement and narcissism—showing high levels of stress, and tending to perform poorly in school—perhaps because they have had little experience with obeying limits and learning self-control (Barton & Hirsch, 2016; Pinquart, 2017).

Although being indulged probably sounds pretty good from a child's perspective, it could set a child up for failure. There can be negative consequences associated with the lifelong pattern of development in the sense of not learning the discipline needed to succeed in school and at work, for instance. It is almost as if Permissive parents are afraid or unable to say "no" to their children, perhaps as a result of their own lack of assertiveness.

Research has shown that the children of Permissive parents have a very difficult time delaying gratification, managing frustration, and following through with plans—all behaviors that are necessary for academic success and career success, not to mention emotion regulation for satisfying social relationships (Barton & Hirsch, 2016; Kenney et al., 2015; Steele & McKinney, 2018). Unfortunately, but perhaps not surprisingly, these children's later adjustment to college is quite poor compared to that of children whose parents demonstrate Authoritative styles. However, the internalizing and externalizing symptoms of children with Permissive parents tend to be lower if the quality of the relationship among the child and their parent(s) is high (Barton & Hirsch, 2016; Kenney et al., 2015; Steele & McKinney, 2018).

Rejecting–Neglecting parents are characterized by low levels of warmth and acceptance, as well as low levels of demandingness and control. During adolescence, the children of Rejecting–Neglecting parents are less able to delay gratification and are at a higher risk of not finishing their schooling, likely because their parents are so overwhelmed by their own stressors that they are unable to support their children. In fact, the Rejecting–Neglecting caregiving style is most likely to occur when parents are undergoing stressful life transitions (Kimmes & Heckman, 2017; Majumder, 2016; Schroeder & Mowen, 2014).

Keep in mind that parents not only vary from one another in their caregiving styles; they may change from one style to another as they themselves or the situations change, or they may use a combination of styles. Although flexibility in response to children's needs is vital, one particularly problematic combination may be Authoritative and Permissive. Parents who seesaw between being harsh and lax (likely due to their own emotional needs, rather than their children's needs) have children who are much more likely to manifest internalizing symptoms such as anxiety and depression (Brassell et al., 2016; Parent, McKee, & Forehand, 2015).

Cultural Differences in Caregiving Styles

The context of culture certainly plays a role in caregiving styles. Chinese parents tend to show higher levels of control, and research indicates that the parent's own self-worth may be contingent on their children's academic success—their warmth toward their children declines when their children fail at a task (Ng, Pomerantz, Lang, & Deng, 2019).

Chinese parents who value greater emotional skills tend to adopt a more Authoritative caregiving style, and as a result they have preschoolers with better emotional skills as well as better pre-academic school readiness skills (Ng, Pomerantz, & Deng, 2014; Pomerantz, Ng, Cheung, & Qu, 2014; Ren & Edwards, 2017).

The positive correlation between Authoritative caregiving and academic success is by no means restricted to Chinese or European American children. The same pattern is found in Latinx children, who show greater academic engagement, perspective-taking (including greater prosocial behavior, such as a tendency to help people in need), and self-regulation when their parents adopt an Authoritative caregiving style. This is especially true when their parents are highly involved in their education, via engaging in learning at home, communicating regularly with teachers, and/or volunteering at school (Carlo et al., 2018; Jabagchourian et al., 2014; Jeynes, 2017).

Research with Black families is complex. Some studies indicate that Authoritative caregiving styles are best for children, whereas others suggest that Authoritarian may best serve Black children, at least in families who are *underresourced* low-SES families and/or struggle against community violence (Pearl et al., 2014; Pezzella, Thornberry, & Smith, 2016; Varner et al., 2018). Yet no matter a family's resources, parent involvement (as is the case with Latinx parents) and racial pride also play a strong role in the academic achievement of Black youth (Pearl et al., 2014; Pezzella, Thornberry, & Smith, 2016; Varner et al., 2018).

To learn more about underresourced families of all backgrounds and those who help them one-on-one, and also to examine some of the broader societal changes that need to be made, visit *A Mentor Minute Jonathan Foiles, LCSW*. Foiles is the author of *This City Is Killing Me: Community Trauma and Toxic Stress in Urban America*.

Mentor Minute

Jonathan Foiles, LCSW

1) Describe your work, please.

I am a psychotherapist at an outpatient mental health clinic that primarily serves the south and west sides of Chicago. I work with an adult population that is primarily Black and Latinx. Decades of structural racism and disinvestment in the surrounding neighborhoods have combined to create a high level of community and individual-level trauma that impacts almost all of the people I see.

2) How does social justice inform your work?

For starters, it's one of the reasons I chose to work at my current position. I also operate from a framework that acknowledges that many of the things that impact my patients and contribute to their suffering are the result of deliberate policy choices made at the federal, state, and local levels. It's not enough to merely assign a diagnosis of depression to someone without identifying the circumstances that help create and sustain such symptoms. Further, many of my patients are parents, which means that their struggles impact not just their own lives but those of their children.

FIG. 9.6   Jonathan Foiles, LCSW

3) How did you become involved in social justice and/or advocacy?

Social justice has always been an important value to me (and to my field, social work) but I became much more invested after the 2016 election. While I had strong personal feelings about it, I also realized that it was not me but rather my patients who would bear the brunt of what was to come (and that has proven to be true time and again). That's when I began using my voice to advocate against structural oppression in its many guises.

4) What are your thoughts on how social justice can improve child and adolescent development?

Children are deeply vulnerable, a fact that has only become more apparent to me now that I have children of my own. All children deserve an opportunity to grow up in a safe, affirming environment, and far too often they are not provided with that. The majority of child protective services cases come about not because of abuse but neglect which is often caused by a lack of resources. Children truly are our future, and ensuring that all of them have access to such love and support is not just a parenting issue but a policy issue as well.

5) What suggestions do you have for undergraduate students who are interested in making a change in child and adolescent development?

I think we often do a good job of accounting for the ways that parents influence the development of their children, but I would encourage them to take a broader view. The economic opportunities (or lack thereof), unjust policing practices, and availability of needed resources in the surrounding community all have a huge impact upon the life of the developing child. Never be afraid to ask the big structural questions of why things ended up this way and whether or not such a development was inevitable. History is not set in stone—it's being written right now.

• • • •

More research involving Native American, Caribbean, Pacific Islander, mixed, and other families is needed, but until then, we do know this: A review of over 400 studies across the globe found that the Authoritative caregiving style was associated with at least one positive outcome for children, whereas the Authoritarian caregiving style was associated with at least one negative outcome for children (Pinquart & Kauser, 2018; Segrin & Flora, 2019).

Other work shows that inductive discipline (such as providing explanations for appropriate behavior), rather than parents asserting their power, cultivates greater emotional and social intelligence in children (Pinquart & Kauser, 2018; Segrin & Flora, 2019).

Speaking of power assertion, researchers are beginning to turn their attention to characteristics of caregiving, and not just the four styles. Relationships among parents and children are often more complex than one variable (caregiving styles) causing another variable (child outcomes). Many children have more than one parent at home (both of whom may show different styles over situations and time), children influence their parents as much as their parents influence them, and parents' styles likely serves as more of a context for their specific caregiving practices (Darling & Steinberg, 2017).

Siblings

Siblings provide children with another socialization context beyond that of parents.

If the relationship quality among siblings is high, as it is for Jimmy and Crystal, children have the opportunity to teach one another about comforting, sharing, helping, and emotional regulation—perhaps via a function of modeling by the older child. Research has found that a younger child's empathy grows over time if their older sibling shows empathic concern for them (Dirks et al, 2015; Howe & Recchia, 2014; Hughes, McHarg, & White, 2018; Jambon et al., 2018).

Aggression among siblings is typical, and often viewed as benign. It is recognized that in children, the preschool period is a time during which aggression is a normative misbehavior. Of course, children need to learn to replace that aggression with words such as "I don't like it when you push me" instead of hitting a child who pushed them. Yet aggression among siblings becomes atypical when it occurs on most days and/or involves bullying (Dirks et al., 2018).

There are consequences for children whose siblings bully them. The victims of such treatment report lower levels of competence and self-esteem, as well as higher levels of internalizing problems later on—which indicates that parents must take seriously any bullying that occurs among siblings (CAPTA Reauthorization Act, 2010; Child Welfare Information Gateway, 2016; Perkins & Barry, 2019; Plamondon, Bouchard, & Lachance-Grzela, 2018).

FIG. 9.7   Jimmy and Crystal

Copyright © Depositphotos/iordani.

This is particularly true in light of how some have argued that ongoing sibling violence is an example of the *failure to protect* in the Child Abuse Prevention and Treatment Act (CAPTA), which defines *child abuse and neglect* as "Any recent act or failure to act on the part of a parent or caretaker, which results in death, serious physical or emotional harm, sexual abuse, or exploitation, or an act or failure to act which presents an imminent risk of serious harm" (CAPTA Reauthorization Act, 2010; Child Welfare Information Gateway, 2016; Perkins & Barry, 2019; Plamondon, Bouchard, & Lachance-Grzela, 2018).

Parents who are concerned about the bullying between or among their children may want to seek out social skills training for them. Research shows that sibling victimization is associated with later mental health problems as well as delinquency (Tippett & Wolke, 2015; Tucker & Finkelhor, 2015; van Berkel, Tucker, & Finkelhor, 2018).

Additionally, a review of the research studies on interventions for bullying among siblings shows that children's relationship quality with one another improves after they are taught perspective-taking, conflict management, and problem-solving. Also, positive parent behaviors such as praise, hugging, talking with children about matters that are important to them, and spending quality time with children protect against the risk of sibling bullying (Tippett & Wolke, 2015; Tucker & Finkelhor, 2015; van Berkel, Tucker, & Finkelhor, 2018).

So while it is often assumed children with siblings are better off, they may or may not be. The *quality* of their relationship determines whether these relationships are a source of of either the risk or of the resilience aspects of the risk-resilience pattern of development (Dirks et al., 2015).

Only-children are not necessarily always at a disadvantage either. Although they are less physically active and therefore at greater risk for being overweight or obese compared to children with siblings, only-children are no different from children with siblings in terms of psychological well-being once they're in adolescence. In fact, they are better off academically: They spend more time on homework and have better grades than children who have siblings (Chen & Liu, 2014; Kracht et al., 2018).

Peers

As we learned in Chapter 8, most children don't consistently pass false-belief tasks until they are approximately 5 years of age, which tells us that although theory of mind may begin at around age 3, it takes time to develop. Most preschoolers have a fairly poorly developed theory of mind, so they don't typically appreciate that others may have thoughts and feelings that are different from their own. As a result, it doesn't usually occur to them to choose friends on the basis of personal characteristics. Instead, preschoolers consider a friend to be someone with whom they can play.

Therefore, friendships in early childhood are focused primarily on the sharing of toys and/or activities rather than on exchanges of information and feelings; if someone is a playmate, that person is a friend. In fact, Jimmy's best friend is Diego, another boy with whom he engages in pretend or make-believe play, imagining that the two of them are firefighters speeding to an emergency, or sometimes, at the suggestion of their parents, superheroes helping other children resolve conflicts (for example, "Batman is here to tell you that if someone pushes you, instead of pushing back, you can use your words and say that you don't like it when others push me").

Then, as children mature through the preschool years to become less egocentric and develop a greater theory of mind, their friendship preferences tend to change. When researchers examine the differences between a child's mutual friends and that child's acquaintances, preschoolers whose teachers rate them as more *prosocial*, in that they contribute positively to social interactions, are found to express both more positive and more negative emotions with mutual friends than with acquaintances. Also, of the negative emotions that they do express with mutual friends, anger is most common (Lindsey, 2019).

These findings indicate that preschoolers are more likely to express anger with those peers whom they feel close to, whereas preschoolers whose teachers rate them as less prosocial are more likely to express anger with acquaintances, with such anger as both a *cause* and an *effect* of being less deemed less prosocial.

This same study also found that preschoolers without a mutual friend were also more aggressive, more withdrawn, more shy, and less skilled at interacting with other children and had more difficult entering play groups than children with a mutual friend (Lindsey, 2019).

Keep in mind that not all anger is problematic. Children who are more likely to express anger when treated unfairly (such as when a researcher shares candy equally with children but then eventually takes all of this particular child's candy) are also more likely to behave prosocially toward a stranger (such as offering a researcher a toy or asking if they are okay after the researcher bumped their elbow) one year later. *Children's sensitively to justice predicts their later care for others* (Xiao, Spinrad, & Risenberg, 2018).

We will learn more about preschoolers' moral reasoning later in this chapter. For now, let's return to a child's status as having mutual friends, or not, and how this changes over time. One longitudinal study of more than 2,000 kindergartners from the beginning to the end of the school year found that some children were friendless, some had stable friendships, others had fluid friendships in which they lost friends, and yet others had fluid friendships in which they gained friends (Proulx & Poulin, 2013). To what were the researchers able to attribute these polydirectional patterns?

They found that friendless children were more aggressive but also more withdrawn, as well as less accepted by their peers than all the other children. Children who had stable friendships, at least relative to children who had fluid friendships, were less shy, and more prosocial in their willingness to help others, and were more likely to be accepted by their peers (Proulx & Poulin, 2013).

Children who lost friends over the course of the school year became less accepted by their peers and less prosocial over time, whereas children who gained friends showed the opposite pattern in that they became more accepted by their peers and more prosocial over time. Other research with 5- and 6-year-olds reveals that friendships tend to be especially stable over the course of a year when they exist within same-gender pairs as well (Proulx & Poulin, 2013; Wang et al., 2019).

Prosocial behavior—in which we are helpful, we share, and we cooperate—is an important aspect of everyday life that contributes to our well-being. It is a variable that is often considered in the study of moral development, a topic to which we now turn.

What Do We Know About Moral Development in Early Childhood?

What does it mean for a preschooler like Jimmy to be moral? **Morality** concerns the norms regarding other people's welfare, rights, fairness, and justice (Dahl & Killen, 2018).

Research on morality began with a framework proposed by none other than Piaget (1932). Later, Kohlberg (1984) revised Piaget's model of moral development. Both theories propose that moral development proceeds through a series of universal stages with an invariant sequence. That is, there are discontinuous stages in which children's reasoning about social-emotional issues regarding ethical behavior matures, and it is the responsibility of parents and other adults to ensure that children progress through these stages while they interact with others (Dahl & Killen, 2018; Snarey & Samuelson, 2014; Wren, 2013).

So both Piaget's and Kohlberg's theories consistent with the multidimensional pattern of development. Let's look at each.

Piaget's Theory of Moral Development

Piaget (1977) developed a theory of moral development after noticing the rules to which children of different ages adhered while they played with marbles—and after listening to their responses to stories he told them about other children's moral dilemmas. His subsequent theory of moral development proposed two distinct stages of moral development: Moral Realism and Autonomous Morality.

Moral Realism, which begins at age 5 and ends at approximately age 9, is a stage of thinking in which the morality of a behavior is based on clear objective standards that adults set regarding right and wrong. As a result, children in this stage believe behavior is moral when it conforms to the rules parents or teachers establish. As Piaget (1977, p. 195) noted, "Right is to obey the will of the adult. Wrong is to have a will of one's own."

Because morality is objective in this stage, children in the Moral Realism stage believe misbehavior should always be punished, regardless of the wrongdoer's intentions. For example, Piaget (1977, p. 122) presented the following scenarios to children:

> A little boy who is called John is in his room. He is called to dinner. He goes into the dining room. But behind the door there was a chair, and on the chair there was a tray with fifteen cups on it. John couldn't have known that there was all this behind the door. He goes in, the door knocks against the tray, bang go the fifteen cups and they all get broken!

> Once there was a little boy whose name was Henry. One day when his mother was out he tried to get some jam out of the cupboard. He climbed up on to a chair and stretched out his arm. But the jam was too high up and he couldn't reach it and have any. But while he was trying to get it he knocked over a cup. The cup fell down and broke.

When Piaget asked children who was naughtier and should therefore receive more punishment, 6-year-olds were more likely to say John should receive more punishment because he broke 15 cups, rather than Henry who broke just 1.

In other words, children in the Moral Realism stage believe punishment is proportional to the damage caused by misbehavior, and they don't excuse accidental behavior. On the other hand, 9- and 10-year-olds were more likely to think Henry deserved more punishment, because the cup he broke was a direct result of his intentional misbehavior (trying to access out-of-reach jam), whereas John's breaking 15 cups was accidental.

This suggested to Piaget that at approximately 9 years of age, most children enter the **Autonomous Morality** stage of moral development, a stage of thinking in which we decide the morality of a behavior based on the wrongdoer's intentions. Children in this stage believe behavior is moral depending on the circumstances, because they believe rules are social agreements that can be changed if need be. Such thinking is a result of children's greater perspective-taking and ability to appreciate the intentions, desires, and needs of others. Therefore, in Autonomous Morality, punishment should be worse for individuals who misbehave intentionally.

Central to Piaget's thinking about moral development is that children's action precedes their reasoning about moral situations, so they learn as a result of interacting with others in their context.

This assumption illustrates the multidimensional pattern of development, given that moral development encompasses behaviors and thoughts. This distinction becomes increasingly clear during the preschool years; research shows that 3.5-year-olds are more likely to consider when someone is in need—and therefore are more likely to help someone in need—than are 1.5-year-olds (Hammond, 2014; Paulus, 2019).

Kohlberg's Theory of Moral Development

Inspired by Piaget's (1977) theory of moral development, Lawrence Kohlberg expanded his ideas to provide a more detailed view of how moral development changes, and throughout development.

According to Kohlberg, there are three levels of moral development (Kohlberg, 1981). He arrived at this set of levels based on children's responses to any of a set of moral dilemmas he provided. One such dilemma is the case of Heinz, which was as follows:

> In Europe, a woman was near death from a special kind of cancer. There was one drug that the doctors thought might save her. It was a form of radium that a druggist in the same town had recently discovered. The drug was expensive to make, but the druggist was charging 10 times what the drug cost him to make. He paid $200 for the radium and charged $2,000 for a small dose of the drug. The sick woman's husband, Heinz, went to everyone he knew to borrow the money, but he could only get together about $1,000, which is half of what it cost. He told the druggist that his wife was dying and asked him to sell it cheaper or let him pay later. But the druggist said, "No, I discovered the drug and I'm going to make money from it." So Heinz got desperate and broke into the man's store to steal the drug for his wife. Should the husband have done that?

Children's responses to this question typically fall into one of these three levels: Preconventional Reasoning, Conventional Reasoning, and Postconventional Reasoning. Keep in mind that Kohlberg emphasized a child's reasoning or *process* of thinking, rather than the child's answer or the *end result* of thinking.

Preconventional Reasoning is the most immature form of moral reasoning, in which children determine the morality of a behavior based on rewards and/or punishments from an individual person, such as a parent, rather than from the larger societal context. This Preconventional level is most common during childhood.

For example, a child at this level might respond to Heinz's dilemma by saying he should not steal the drug because he will go to jail. Using Preconventional Reasoning, children conform to societal rules, not for conventional reasons of *societal interest*, but instead for reasons of *self-interest* (to avoid punishment).

Conventional Reasoning, which is concerned with social approval, comes to dominate children's thinking at the end of middle childhood and the beginning of adolescence. For example, a child at this level might respond to Heinz's dilemma by saying he should not steal the drug because it will dishonor and shame his family.

Notice that this level of reasoning considers the way others will view a situation. Conventional Reasoning represents a change from a relationship between an individual and another, to a relationship between an individual and society (Kohlberg, 1981). At this level, children conform to societal rules, and for reasons of societal interest.

Postconventional Reasoning, which is concerned with universal ethical principles such as justice, may develop later in adolescence and adulthood. For example, an adolescent or adult at this level might respond to Heinz's dilemma by saying he should not steal the drug if he thinks stealing is a greater injustice than letting his wife die. At this level, adolescents and adults conform to societal rules, but for reasons of interest to all humans, regardless of their specific society.

Diversity issues such as tolerance, rights, and inequity therefore become increasingly important in this stage, as does symbolic thinking. So teens and adults in this stage might be inclined to notice that the secure base that attachment researchers speak about is relevant to the study of moral development in that a government's failure to invest adequately in education and a social safety net is both lacking and perhaps even intentionally undermined, as some have suggested (Burman, 2016).

Recent research using brain imaging has found that individuals in the Postconventional Reasoning stage have increased gray matter in the ventromedial prefrontal cortex of their brains, an area that corresponds to both decision-making and emotional regulation (Fang et al., 2017; Prehn et al., 2015).

Future longitudinal research may wish to pursue the chicken-or-egg question regarding this relationship that exemplifies the multidimensional pattern of development. That is, does brain maturity lead to more advanced moral development, or does advanced moral development help the brain mature?

Moral Reasoning About Aggression

Moral reasoning about aggressive interactions with friends, as compared to disliked peers and bullies, varies for preschoolers. Aggression takes a number of different forms during early childhood. Before we consider the research findings, let's consider those various types of aggression.

Physical aggression is behavior that intends to hurt another person via physical acts, such as hitting, kicking, biting, and shoving. Although seemingly alike, verbal aggression and relational aggression are separate constructs.

Verbal aggression is behavior that intends to hurt another person and includes typically overt or conspicuous behaviors such as verbal threats, name-calling, and teasing. Max's "I'll eat you up" in response to his mother's calling him a "wild thing" in *Where the Wild Things Are* is a form of verbal aggression.

Relational aggression or **social aggression** is also behavior that intends to hurt another person, but it typically includes covert or hidden behavior such as rumor-spreading, social exclusion, and sudden rejection of a close friend.

Instrumental aggression is any behavior that hurts another person but with the intent of obtaining something, such as a toy.

Hostile aggression is behavior in which the intent is simply to hurt someone. It includes physical aggression, verbal aggression, and relational aggression (such as social exclusion and spreading rumors).

Instrumental aggression and physical forms of hostile aggression occur fairly frequently as opportunities to interact with others increase after infancy and toddlerhood. Yet both these forms of aggression decline by the end of the preschool years as children's language skills improve and their executive function develops.

Bullying is an additional type of aggression that involves repeated physical and/or psychological intimidation against individuals whom an instigator perceives to have less power (Smetana & Ball, 2017).

Researchers have found that when they present children with stories in which a hypothetical child *morally transgresses* against another child via physical harm, psychological harm, or an unfair distribution of resources (such as giving a child one cookie and giving all the other children two cookies), children view transgressions against bullies as more acceptable, whereas transgressions against friends are seen as causing the transgressor to experience more negative emotions (Smetana & Ball, 2017). Findings such as these suggest that children understand remorse to be a result of not a moral transgression in general, but a result of a moral transgression against someone they like.

When studying preschoolers' moral reasoning, researchers may tell them a story about a hypothetical child who *conventionally transgresses* (such as standing during story time or putting their backpack on the ground instead of placing it in the cubby) or *morally transgresses* (such as acting negatively toward another child in order to obtain a toy). Researchers then ask the children how bad they would feel if they did something similar to the hypothetical child—even if there was no longer a rule about the transgression and the teacher would not disapprove of the transgression.

What researchers have found is that children who report feeling the most negative in response to a moral transgression are those with the lowest aggression levels 9 months later (Jambon & Smetana, 2018). Because the children were asked how badly they would feel even if there was no longer a rule about the transgression, this tells us that the degree of their negative emotions does not reflect anxiety or fear of punishment, but instead true concern for other people's welfare.

Key Terms

Associative Play

Authoritarian

Authoritative

Autonomous Morality

Bullying

Cisgender

Conventional Reasoning

Cooperative Play

Executive Functions

Gender

Gender Constancy

Gender Expansive

Gender Identity

Gender Role

Gender Stability

Gender Typing

Guilt

Hostile Aggression

I-Self

Inductive Discipline

Initiative–Guilt

Instrumental Aggression

Interrelated Taxonomic Self

Intersex

GBTQIA+

Me-Self

Moral Realism

Morality

Nonbinary

Onlooker Play

Parallel Play

Permissive–Indulgent

Physical Aggression

Play

Postconventional Reasoning

Preconventional Reasoning

Prosocial Behavior

Purpose

Reflective Capacity

Rejecting–Neglecting

Relational Aggression

Self-Concept

Self-Esteem

Sex

Shame

Social Aggression

Social Comparisons

Sociodramatic Play

Solitary Independent Play

Taxonomic Self

Temporal Comparisons

Transgender

Unoccupied Behavior

Verbal Aggression

Summary

1. **Interpret what Erikson's theory tells us about preschoolers' emotional needs.** For Erikson, early childhood is a time when children take initiative; the conflict that must be resolved in the preschool years is Initiative–Guilt in order to obtain the virtue of Purpose. In his theory, children who do not resolve this stage successfully tend to be passive, inhibited, and paralyzed with guilt. Guilt focuses on negative evaluations of our behavior, as opposed to the more immature Shame, which is focused on negative evaluations of ourselves.

2. **Discuss how preschoolers' emotional understanding can best be scaffolded.** Children need help understanding and identifying their emotions, particularly so that they can then regulate their emotions. So rather than dismissing children's emotions, especially the negative ones, it is much more helpful to children to have parents mirror children's emotions, then show empathy for such.

3. **Illustrate how self-concept, self-esteem, and self-regulation can be best supported.** Starting at approximately 5 years of age, children begin to understand themselves in terms of the interrelated taxonomic self, in which they can understand the relationships among their various traits, such as being good at drawing and not so good at singing. During early childhood children acquire effortful control, a type of emotional regulation, and their executive functions improve, which allows them to control their behavior and thoughts by planning and by delaying gratification. Self-regulation in general is a function of children's cognitive abilities, as well as the quality of their attachment to parents.

4. **Explain what gender can teach us about children developing their full potential.** Gender is one of the first social categories that children make, and their flexibility in gender typing benefits their becoming a more complete person and not discriminating against others. Increasing children's flexibility about gender stereotypes is not difficult; plus, it is necessary, given that gender typing is not innocuous. Over time, children's gender identity progresses on to gender stability and gender constancy. Gender-expansive children are children for whom their expression of their gender identity doesn't identify their sex at birth, and they are similar in many but not all ways to cisgender children.

5. **Identify how play can be better facilitated and how play can be therapeutic.** In **unoccupied behavior**, children are not playing but simply standing around or following the teacher. In **onlooker play**, they observe other children who are playing and may even talk to these other children, yet not play with them. **Solitary independent play**, during which one or many children are playing but not together, is the third type of play.

   Parallel play is similar to solitary independent play, but in it children share materials, though still without working on or playing with the same thing. Soon after, the fifth stage, **associative play**, develops as children share materials and still work independently, but now they begin to comment on each another's play. Finally, **cooperative play** brings children truly together with a common goal, typically pretend or make-believe play with rules about each character's behavior.

6. **Analyze how the quality of preschoolers' relationships affect their lives.** Authoritarian parents show low levels of acceptance and warmth, but high levels demandingness and control. Authoritative care consists of high levels of warmth and acceptance, as well as high levels of demandingness and control. Parents who show high levels of acceptance and warmth but low levels of demandingness and control are Permissive–Indulgent. Those with low levels of acceptance and warmth and low levels of demandingness and control are Rejecting–Neglecting.

Children whose parents are Authoritative are best able to engage in self-regulation and be successful both emotionally and academically. The characteristics of children raised by these different types of parents can vary as a function of context though. Siblings can learn many aspects of emotional as well as cognitive development from one another, yet they can also suffer from sibling bullying.

In terms of peers, preschoolers tend to choose friends on the basis of shared activities rather than personal characteristics, especially if their theory of mind is not yet well developed. Preschoolers who are more prosocial tend to express different emotions, with different people, and for different reasons.

7. **Describe what we know about moral development in early childhood.** Piaget's theory of moral development has two stages. During Moral Realism (from 5 to 9 years of age), children view right and wrong according to objective standards set by others, such as parents and teachers. In the Autonomous Morality stage (at age 9 and up), children start to appreciate a wrongdoer's intentions as part of their decision about the morality of an action.

For Kohlberg, in the Preconventional Reasoning stage preschoolers conform to society's rules for reasons of self-interest (to avoid punishment). At the Conventional Reasoning level, older children and adolescents conform to societal rules, and for reasons of societal interest. Postconventional Reasoning, which is concerned with universal ethical principles such as justice, may develop later in adolescence and adulthood as teens and adults conform to societal rules, but for reasons of interest to all humans. Research also considers how children's prosocial behavior, their actions intended to help others, changes over time, as do the different types of aggression in which they engage—along with their moral reasoning regarding moral transgressions versus conventional transgressions.

The Cycle of Science

Research

Why was the study conducted?

The researchers wanted to know if a mindfulness-based yoga intervention improved self-regulation in preschool children (Razza, Bergen-Cico, & Raymond, 2015).

Who participated in the study?

The participants were 29 children who were between 3 and 5 years of age. Of the children, 16 were in the intervention group and 13 were in the control group.

Which type of design was used?

A quasi-experimental, pretest, posttest design was used. Children in the experimental group received 40 hours of mindful yoga over the course of 25 weeks, which started with 10 minutes a day and increased to 30 minutes a day. The classroom teacher had completed a yoga certification. The teacher had children engage in breathing exercises and poses during morning circle time, poses during literacy activities in the afternoon, and breathing exercises during transition periods. The teacher of the children in the control group did not have a background in yoga nor in mindfulness, and did not incorporate either in her classroom.

In late September (Time 1) and again in late May (Time 2), children's self-regulation (such as their performance on the Head, Toes, Knees, and Shoulders assessment and their ability to delay gratification via the gift wrap task we learned about in Chapter 8) was measured by the researchers as well as reported on by the children's parents.

What were the results?

The researchers found that from Time 1 to Time 2, compared to children in the control group, children in the intervention group improved in their Head, Toes, Knees, and Shoulders performance as well their ability to delay gratification via the gift wrap task. The researchers also found that children in the intervention group who struggled most with self-regulation at Time 1 benefitted the most by Time 2.

Are the results consistent with theory?

Yes, self-regulation has the potential to develop dramatically during the preschool years, and includes effortful control, executive function, and children's abilities to calm their bodies, such as via mindful breathing and yoga.

How can the results be used to improve our lives?

Children with poor self-regulation are not damaged; they simply need to be taught tools to engage in self-regulation. Providing preschoolers with the opportunity to regularly engage in mindfulness-based yoga, including breathing exercises and poses, can help them significantly.

Exercises

1. What pattern of results would you expect if children had learned only breathing exercises?

2. What pattern of results would you expect if children had learned only poses?

3. If this study had been conducted with gender-expansive children, who tend to be higher in anxiety than cisgender children, the results might be different. How so?

Helpful Websites

The National Association for the Education of Young Children (NAEYC) has numerous resources on their website, from supporting children's reading and writing skills to eliminating bias: https://www.naeyc.org/resources

Tools of the Mind, an early childhood program based on the work of Vygotsky, has suggestions on its website for how parents can support children's make-believe play at home, both alone and with other children: http://www.toolsofthemind.org/parents/make-believe-play/

PBS has information on its websites about which books and television shows can help preschoolers express their feelings and develop health relationships with others, including other children: http://www.pbs.org/parents/childdevelopmenttracker/three/socialandemotionalgrowth.html

Melissa & Doug create fantastic high-quality toys, including those for pretend play as well as puppetry. Cofounder Melissa Bernstein also hosts a *Living Playfully* podcast with developmental behavioral pediatrician Dr. Jenny Radesky. You can find more about it here: https://www.melissaanddoug.com/podcast-living-playfully.html

Parents, Families and Friends of Lesbians and Gays (PFLAG) supports the families of lesbian, gay, bisexual, transgender, and queer (LGBTQ+) children and teens. They are available in person at local PFLAG chapters, or they're online at https://pflag.org.

Recommended Reading

Faber, J., & King, J. (2017). *How to talk so little kids will listen: A survival guide to life with children ages 2–7.* New York, NY: Scribner.

Foiles, J. (2019). *This city is killing me: Community trauma and toxic stress in urban America.* Cleveland, OH: Belt Publishing.

Hoffman, K., Cooper, G., & Powell, B. (2017). *Raising a secure child.* New York, NY: The Guilford Press.

McKay, M., Wood, J. C., & Brantley, J. (2007) *Dialectical behavior therapy skills workbook: Practicing DBT exercises for learning mindfulness, interpersonal effectiveness, emotion regulation, and distress tolerance.* Oakland, CA: New Harbinger Publications.

Pollak, S. M. (2019) *Self compassion for parents: Nurture your child by caring for yourself.* New York, NY: The Guilford Press.

Sendak, M. (1963/1988). *Where the wild things are.* New York, NY: HarperCollins.

Siegel, D. J., & Bryson, T. P. (2011). *The whole-brain child: 12 revolutionary strategies to nurture your child's developing mind.* New York, NY: Random House.

VanSchuyver, J. (1993). *Storytelling made easy with puppets.* Phoenix, AZ: Oryx Press.

CHAPTER 10

Physical and Cognitive Development in Middle Childhood

Snapshot

Ten-year-old Francine, or Frankie, is preoccupied with *Heroes of Olympus* now that she has finished *Percy Jackson and the Olympians*, both series by author Rick Riordan. She has read each of the novels four times, has seen each film at least five times, and is learning archery to be like the Zoë Nightshade character.

Frankie's parents are thrilled with her wanting to get outside and exercise—and with her curiosity—so they provide her with as many activities and opportunities to foster her interests as they can. But they are a little concerned about her strong emotions regarding the novels.

Why? Well, Frankie not only spends hours playing with everything *Camp Half-Blood*, but also she becomes very upset when her parents try to clean up and organize her things. Frankie claims they don't understand how important it is that her *Heroes of Olympus* and *Percy Jackson* items not be rearranged.

FIG. 10.1   Frankie

Her mother and father are sensitive and engaged parents, and are educated professionals. Yet they have not had a course in child and adolescent development, so they don't always appreciate that her arranging and rearranging is part of her exercising the cognitive abilities typical of school-age children.

In fact, at Frankie's age many children are obsessed with their own collections, whether they are baseball cards, stuffed animals, or rocks. In this chapter, we learn why.

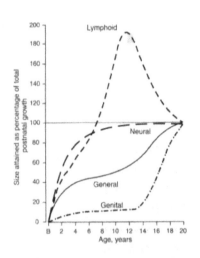

FIG. 10.2 Growth of the Four Bodily Systems

R. E. Scammon, Growth of the Four Bodily Systems, from "8 — Controlling for Maturation in Pediatric Exercise Science," Pediatric Exercise Science, vol. 12, no. 1. Copyright © 1930 by Human Kinetics Publishers.:

What Normative Changes in Physical Development Occur in Middle Childhood?

Physical development in middle childhood, from approximately age 7 to age 12, consists of general growth patterns, pubertal timing, brain development, motor skill development, and changes in physical activity.

As you might imagine, each of these aspects of normative physical development during the school years often influences other aspects of physical development; for example, gender differences in general growth patterns contribute to gender differences in pubertal timing.

Let's take a look.

Growth Patterns

In Chapter 5, we learned that physical growth is asynchronous, meaning that the body's different physical systems grow at different rates.

Learning Goals

▶ Outline normative physical development within middle childhood

▶ Describe the nonnormative changes in physical development within middle childhood

▶ Summarize what Piaget's theory can tell us about school-age cognitive development

▶ Identify what cognitive processes are most relevant to middle childhood

▶ Illustrate how children are smart

▶ Explain how language develops in middle childhood

▶ Analyze how literacy and numeracy develop in middle childhood

▶ Discuss what is known about parenting and schools in the United States

Figure 10.2 shows that during middle childhood, while the permanent molars erupt at the beginning of this stage, there are slow gains in general growth. Skeletal growth decelerates, while the lymphoid system continues to increase and the brain approaches a peak in its overall volume. The genital system remains relatively dormant until the end of this stage (DelGiudice, 2018). It is near the end of this stage that we begin to see gender differences in physical growth.

While there are few significant differences among the sexes in terms of cognitive development, we do see some meaningful differences in physical development.

Regarding the eruption of permanent teeth, the data are mixed, with only some studies showing gender difference, usually with girls obtaining their first permanent tooth before boys (Listl et al., 2018). Yet longitudinal research does show that the higher the SES of a child's family and the greater the number of books in the home, the more likely these children are to have their natural teeth later on at age 50. All of these factors are perhaps due to sufficient financial resources for the family to afford dental care and/or dental insurance premiums, less stress and therefore greater regularity in adhering to a tooth-brushing ritual, and/or higher quality nutrition (Listl et al., 2018).

The data are clearer regarding the timing of puberty when considering gender differences, at least between girls and boys (there aren't yet enough data on gender-expansive children). Because girls are growing faster than boys, they are also becoming heavier. Between the ages of 5 and 13, the percentage of an average female's body mass that is composed of muscle increases from 40% to 45%; between 5 and 13, the percentage of an average male's body mass composed of muscle increases from 42% to 54%. So are girls losing muscle mass over time?

Not typically; instead, they are usually accumulating fat (Malina, Bouchard, & Bar-Or, 2004). Yet the more body fat a girl has (relative to other girls), the earlier her **menarche**, or onset of menstruation; and the earlier a girl's age of menarche, the more likely she is to be at subsequent risk for being overweight or obese, as well as developing insulin insensitivity and eventual type II diabetes (O'Keefe et al., 2019; Wilson et al., 2015).

There are other consequences of early menarche that are consistent with the multidimensional and lifelong patterns of development. Let's delve a little deeper into these topics for a moment.

Pubertal Timing

Those who are advanced in skeletal age reach their adult height (and consequently stop growing) earlier than children with a less advanced skeletal age.

So children and adolescents are considered to be **early maturing** if their skeletal age is more than one year *ahead* of their chronological age, **late maturing** if it is more than one year *behind* their chronological age, and **on time** if their skeletal and chronological ages are less than one year apart (Malina, Bouchard, & Bar-Or, 2004). And skeletal age is a better predictor of menarche than is chronological age.

In fact, menarche, and **spermarche** or the time of a boy's first ejaculation, may start during middle childhood rather than adolescence. Boys usually reach spermarche between 11 and 15 years of age, with most falling within this normal range.

As we consider menarche, though, let's look at averages. The current average of 12.5 years of age reflects the polydirectional pattern of development. The average age of menarche was 15.5 during the Industrial Revolution. Why the decrease?

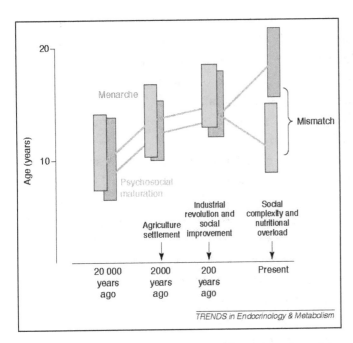

FIG. 10.3   The Mismatch Between Menarche and Psychosocial Maturation

Peter D. Gluckman and Mark A. Hanson, The Mismatch Between Menarche and Psychosocial Maturation, from "Evolution, Development and Timing of Puberty," Trends in Endrocrinology and Metabolism, Vol. 17, No. 1, pp. 10. Copyright © 2006 by Elsevier B.V.

A **secular trend** is a historical pattern in which generations vary, usually as a result of environmental factors. Changes in a number of such environmental factors are likely at play when it comes to the secular trend found in pubertal timing.

First, most children today have access to high-quality nutrition and medical advances. Also, general living conditions have improved greatly since the Industrial Revolution. Increased (but recently stable) numbers of overweight and obese children may contribute to this secular trend as well. In addition, there is exposure to humanmade chemicals, such as the phthalates that make plastic soft (such as those in plastic food wrap) and the types of bisphenol used in hard plastic (such as in hard plastic water bottles and food containers); these are very similar to naturally occurring estrogens, and they act as endocrine disruptors (Hashemipour et al., 2018; Malina, Bouchard, & Bar-Or, 2004; Papadimitriou, 2015; Rochester & Bolden, 2015).

Regardless of the reasons, though, the earlier menarche begins, the earlier there is a mismatch between a girl's physical maturity and emotional maturity. For example, a girl may be physically ready to have children at 12 years of age, but she is unlikely to be psychologically ready to be a parent at this point in her development.

As you can see in Figure 10.3, this discrepancy between the two forms of maturity is a relatively new phenomenon in human history.

Also, the earlier menarche occurs, the more potentially worrisome consequences there are that exemplify the lifelong and multidimensional patterns of development.

A woman's lifetime exposure to estrogen (which increases with earlier menarche) may heighten her risk of breast cancer. Likely this is because of the epigenesis we learned about in Chapter 3, in which DNA activity is changed without the actual DNA sequence being changed. Methylation turns on and off the switches that produce biochemical reactions in the body that regulate various systems (Johansson et al., 2019).

As we know, the mind and the body are not always in sync. For instance, a girl may look like an adult woman (and hence attract the attention of suitors) before her mind has fully matured and before she is ready to make adult decisions, whether it be in terms of sexual activity or otherwise. As a result, such changes in the body increase the risk of certain emotional outcomes such as later depression and/or antisocial behavior (Mendle, Ryan, & McKone, 2019).

Yet we can view these increased risks as a window of opportunity for erring on the side of resilience in the risk–resilience pattern of development.

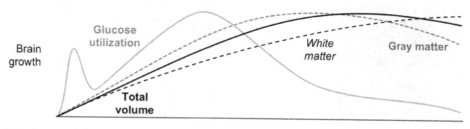

FIG. 10.4   Polydirectional Developmental Trajectories

Why? Because they're providing children and teens with prevention and/or interventions that tap into what neuroscience tells us are their brains' increasing sensitivity to rewards.

Doing so means that young people are given opportunities to engage in appealing activities (such as structured afterschool programs; mentoring programs; and fully funded afterschool classes in music, art, sports, coding, and so on) that may have a greater impact on their choices, as compared to, say, campaigns that attempt to convince them to abstain from things—without offering rewarding choices they can make instead (Dorn et al., 2019).

Brain Development

The brain reaches its maxiumum size by 6 years of age (DelGiudice, 2018). Yet within the brain itself, we see different patterns of development.

As we learned in Chapter 5, the brain's outer layer that is the cerebral cortex or cerebrum is also referred to as *gray matter*, and the brain's myelin is referred to as *white matter*. The volume of gray matter in the brain peaks near the end of childhood, whereas the volume of white matter continues to increase into adolescence, a difference consistent with the polydirectional pattern of development seen in Figure 10.4. The top panel of the figure specifically illustrates differences between white matter and gray matter (DelGiudice, 2018).

These polydirectional patterns of gray matter and white matter development are normative. So environmental influences may contribute to different outcomes. For example, as we learned in Chapter 1, children growing up in homes characterized by high socioeconomic status (SES), education, income, and/or occupational status tend to have better executive functioning than children growing up in low-SES homes. This occurs perhaps because low SES is associated with less gray matter, which itself is associated with lower performance on cognitive tasks that require executive functioning's ability to engage in sustained attention, filter out distractions, and have self-control over our impulses (Farah, 2017a; Hartanto, Toh, & Yang, 2018).

This tells us that neuroscience can inform SES-related policy decisions. It also tells us that neuroimaging could be used to "check on" the efficacy of interventions (such as the High/Scope Perry Preschool Project we learned about in Chapter 8) that were designed to benefit the brain functioning of children of low-SES homes and, ultimately, the development and well-being of these children (Farah, 2017b; Leonard et al., 2019).

FIG. 10.5   Frankie's Trampoline Jumping

Copyright © Depositphotos/belchonock.

Children who are not yet fluent readers show delayed white matter development. There are data indicating that interventions, such as those to improve reading skills, do result in widespread changes in the white matter of children's brains as their reading skills improve (Huber et al., 2018; Lebel, 2019).

Motor Skills

As the brain becomes more differentiated and provides children with greater control over their bodies, motor skills improve. By the end of early childhood, most children can run, hop, and skip, so the school years are ripe for playing hopscotch, red rover, kick the can, and jacks—games that are child-organized and are found throughout the world (Haywood & Getchell, 2020).

These activities come just in time, because the period between 5 years and 8 years is considered a transitional time for motor skills. Children become capable of more complex actions with age (such as the archery that Frankie from our opening *Snapshot* is learning), although there are still wide variations within abilities during the early part of middle childhood (Malina, Bouchard, & Bar-Or, 2004).

As Table 10.1 shows, *within-stage* development occurs for gross motor skills, so fewer children are proficient in catching a ball at age 7 than are proficient in jumping at that age. Any type of play that provides children an opportunity to practice motor skills enhances their physical activity too, including the trampoline-jumping that Frankie so loves (Lima et al., 2017).

Physical Activity

According to the U.S. Department of Health and Human Services (2019), children need to engage in at least 60 minutes of moderate-to-vigorous exercise each day, whether it be via physical activity during or after school, organized sports, and/or neighborhood games that incorporate aerobic activity, muscle-strengthening activity, and bone-strengthening activity. Getting less exercise is associated with being overweight or obese.

Because daily physical activity levels drop from middle childhood to adolescence, the more that children are exercising *before* they make the transition to the next stage of development, the better off their health and well-being will be.

So, what influences children's activity levels during the school years?

Well, research indicates that those children in fifth grade who perceive their parents to be encouraging of physical activity, providing support (such as transportation) for physical activity; who spend time outdoors; who have access to social spaces (such as parks) for physical activity in their communities; and who live near facilities for physical activities (such as baseball fields) are most likely to be physical active two years later in seventh grade as they transition from elementary to middle school (Pate et al., 2019).

Clearly, government investments in educational and community facilities, as well as government support for working families, could do more to foster the physical development (and cognitive development, as we will see in a moment), and therefore level the playing field, of and for children from underresourced families. Not surprisingly, therefore, a neighborhood's economic status tends to be correlated negatively with the prevalence of obesity in that community (Kim, Cubbin, & Oh, 2019).

One research study found that the brains of 7-, 8-, and 9-year-old children who participated in an after-school physical activity program showed gains in white matter over time (Chaddock-Heyman et al., 2018; Zarrett et al., 2018). This tells us that educational policies that reduce or eliminate children's opportunities for daily routine physical activity, often so that more academic content can be covered, are misguided and may be counterproductive, whereas afterschool programs that can meet the developmental needs and personal interests of children will foster their well-being (Chaddock-Heyman et al., 2018; Zarrett et al., 2018).

Further, the data indicate that physical activity does improve children's engagement with school and the time they spend attending to academic tasks, perhaps because physical fitness improves executive function (de Bruijn et al., 2018; Maykel, Bray, & Rogers, 2018; Owen et al., 2016).

What Are Nonnormative Changes in Physical Development in Middle Childhood?

Most school-age children are relatively healthy. Yet illnesses and other problems can arise during middle childhood. In this section, we examine a variety of *nonnormative*, or nontypical, changes that may occur, including obesity, sleep disturbances, illnesses, and injuries.

We start our discussion regarding children who are overweight or obese.

Obesity

Approximately 20% of school-age children are obese. Longitudinal research has shown that children are more likely to be obese if they enter kindergarten overweight, if they are from low-SES homes, if they are Black or Latinx, and when they are on summer break (Fleming-Milici, Harris, & Liu, 2018; Hardy et al., 2019; Spinosa et al., 2019).

This last finding reminds us that families who can *least* afford pay-to-play sports programs for their children are the ones likely *most* in need of school and neighborhood support for their children's health. These families also are very much in need of policies restricting food marketing to children, which we first learned about in Chapter 8 (Fleming-Milici, Harris, & Liu, 2018; Hardy et al., 2019; Spinosa et al., 2019).

Consistent with the *evocative genotype-environment correlation* we learned about in Chapter 3, in which the child's genetic predisposition evokes a response from the environment that research has found that parents are more likely to limit their children's food intake if the children's body mass index is high and are more likely to pressure their children to eat more food if the children's body mass index is low (Selzam et al., 2018).

Other factors contributing to the risk of children becoming obese include increased time spent indoors playing with media, and greater reliance on fast food by families who have demanding jobs and/or are on strict budgets. And an **obesogenic environment**, or one that gives rise to obesity by encouraging energy intakes that exceed energy expenditures, increases the likelihood of a child's physical development erring on the side of risk rather than resilience side of the risk-resilience pattern of development.

Characteristics of environments that are obesogenic include fresh fruits and vegetables being more costly than calorie-dense but nutrient-poor foods prepared by others, and also more costly than sweets and soft drinks. Public health researchers have found that taxes on junk food and sugar-sweetened beverages are both legally and practically feasible. This indicates that citizens could demand that legislators enact such taxes along with greater subsidies for high-quality fruits and vegetables so that this healthful food is more accessible to everyone (Pomeranz et al., 2018).

Food deserts, or regions with little to no access to healthful food, are another characteristic of obesogenic environments, especially when they occur in combination with limited public transportation (Widener, 2018). Alternatively, **food swamps** are those with a high density of fast food and junk food outlets; research shows that food swamps predict local obesity rates even more than food deserts do (Cooksey-Stowers, Schwartz, & Brownell, 2017).

Food insecurity, in which a family experiences a limited or an uncertain ability to acquire nutritionally adequate and safe food in socially acceptable ways, in childhood is associated with higher weight in adulthood. Perhaps this brings about a motivation to consume more calories than are expended whenever the opportunity to do so arises (Nettle et al., 2019).

Sleep Disturbances

The recommended number of hours of sleep for school-age children is approximately 10 to 11 hours in every 24, compared to preschoolers' 11 to 13 hours (Marceau et al., 2019; Miller et al., 2018).

The risk of children being overweight or obese is greater for children who obtain less sleep than this—perhaps because insufficient sleep disrupts the hormones that regulate hunger and satiety, such as ghrelin and leptin (Marceau et al., 2019; Miller et al., 2018). Short sleep also illustrate the multidimensional pattern of development, given externalizing symptoms such as aggression. Poor-quality sleep is associated with worse cognitive and academic functioning (El-Sheikh et al., 2019; Short et al., 2018).

So how can parents help children obtain more and better sleep, other than by adhering to daily sleep rituals of a regular bedtime and reading before bed?

Well, research shows that improving a child's nutritional intake improves their sleep. Reducing caffeine consumption can certainly help too, given that consumption of caffeine in children is related to restless sleep (Watson et al., 2017; Yackobovitch-Gavan et al., 2017). Additionally, reducing family stress, whether via counseling for parents and/or via greater opportunities for emotional attachments among parents and children, is associated with better sleep in children (El-Sheikh & Kelly, 2017).

Better sleep may in turn eliminate some of the differences in cognitive functioning between children of different races and/or SES backgrounds. For example, research reveals that Black and Latinx children and children from low-SES homes report greater daytime sleepiness, which in turn is associated with poorer cognitive functioning as well as poorer academic performance (Guglielmo et al., 2018; Philbrook et al., 2018).

Although it may not be a magic wand, obtaining proper sleep can make a big difference in children's lives, especially given that its physical, cognitive, and emotional benefits are consistent with the multidimensional pattern of development.

Illnesses and Injuries

Are allergies on the rise in children, or has awareness of allergies increased so that families and physicians are reporting them more often?

We do not have sufficient data yet to know, but one study did find that children's hospital visits for *anaphylaxis* (a severe and sudden allergic reaction that can be life-threatening) are on the rise. Approximately half of these visits are due to allergic reactions to foods such as peanuts, tree nuts, milk, eggs, fish, or shellfish (McBride, 2019).

One possible reason for the trend is the **hygiene hypothesis**, which refers to how our improved ability to stay clean has resulted in exposure to fewer microbes. This lessened exposure gives the immune system less work to do, so it overcompensates (McBride, 2019; Walter & O'Mahoney, 2019).

The hygiene hypothesis certainly does not mean that all germs are good for you, nor that we no longer need to practice good hygiene habits. It simply is one potential explanation for why allergies and/or the reporting of such seems to be on the rise (Alexandre-Silva et al., 2018).

The hygiene hypothesis cannot explain all allergies, though. Certain populations are at greater risk for specific allergic and inflammatory conditions, and those conditions are more likely to be a product of interactions between *environment exposure* (or lack thereof, such as to important gut bacteria) and *genetic predisposition* (Bach, 2018; Frew, 2019).

One other potential explanation for the allergy trend is parents not appreciating the importance of introducing allergen-producing foods early enough in the child's development. The data show that exposing children to peanuts (approximately four watered-down teaspoons of peanut butter, per week, between 4 and 11 months of age) reduces the likelihood of a child later having a peanut allergy. Another potential explanation for allergies is climate change, because higher temperatures and more carbon dioxide in the atmosphere encourages plants to grow more quickly and therefore create more pollen (Du Toit et al., 2018; Katelaris & Beggs, 2018; McBride, 2019).

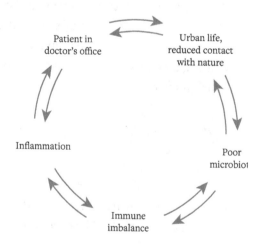

FIG. 10.6   An Illustration of the Biodiversity Hypothesis

Tari Haahtela, An Illustration of the Biodiversity Hypothesis, from "A Biodiversity Hypothesis," Allergy, vol. 74, no. 8. Copyright © 2019 by John Wiley & Sons, Inc.

Last but not least, let us consider the **biodiversity hypothesis**, as illustrated in Figure 10.6. This hypothesis proposes that reduced contact with nature and declining diversity *within* nature (which is evidenced by the collapse of honey bee colonies, likely from increased use of pesticides) leads to poor microbiota ingestion, which then contributes to an immune imbalance, which then gives rise to inflammation and subsequent medical conditions (Booton et al., 2017; Haahtela, 2019; Li, G. et al., 2018).

These allergic and inflammatory medical conditions include asthma, which sometimes occurs alongside allergies; the factors contributing to asthma are also environmental. But perhaps they are societal as well: Of Black children, 16% have asthma, whereas among European American children only 7% have asthma. There are not sufficient data on other racial/ethnic groups (Centers for Disease Control and Prevention, 2019c).

Just as importantly, Black children are more likely to have poorly controlled asthma and a worse quality of life and are more likely to experience more asthma-related emergency visits than European American children. Perhaps this is the case because they are more likely to live in poor-quality housing. Strategies to reduce inequalities are needed to reduce disparities in children's health (Cazzola et al., 2018; Guilbert et al., 2019; Hughes et al., 2017).

Also consistent with the biodiversity hypothesis, one study found that exposure to more green spaces with greater vegetation diversity, in addition to reducing systematic inequities in housing, education, and healthcare access, can also lower the risk of asthma in children (Donovan et al., 2018).

Unintentional injuries, or damage to the body that is not deliberate, result from falls, crashes, and drowning. The leading cause of death for children during the school years is unintentional injuries, and specifically, those involving motor vehicles (CDC, 2019d).

Most alarming is that although the death rate for children declined from 1999 to 2013, it increased from 2013 to 2016 and includes unintentional injuries as well as suicides. This alerts us that public health efforts need to address cause, intent, age, sex, race, and regional factors in preventing such deaths (Ballesteros et al., 2018; Curtin et al., 2018).

By the way, we use the term *unintentional injuries* rather than *accidents*, because *accident* suggests that the event cannot be prevented. This is often not the case if precautions are in place. For example, one study found that of the children who went to an emergency room for a bicycle, scooter, skateboard, or inline skate injury, only 58% of them were wearing a helmet. The 42% who were not wearing a helmet were more likely to be admitted to the hospital and have sustained a major head injury (Ong et al., 2018).

What Can Piaget's Theory Tell Us About School-Age Cognitive Development?

In Chapter 6, we learned about the Preoperational stage of Piaget's theory of Cognitive Development, which suggests that children from ages 2 to 6 are perception-bound, egocentric, and not very capable of logical thinking.

Beginning around age 6 or 7, children are no longer so perception-bound, are less egocentric, and are more capable of logical thinking. But how do we know? Primarily because of empirical research that has verified at least some of Piaget's original observations of school-age children. Let's learn about it here.

Concrete Operations

Piaget's observations of his own children, as well as of many others, led him to propose that school-age children enter a stage of Concrete Operations. We learned in Chapter 8 that *operations* are mental schemes or internal mental actions that are logical because they follow a system of rules; for instance, they help us understand that two rows of equal numbers of grapes are truly equal, despite one row's being more spread out than the other.

Therefore, Concrete Operational children are not as intuitive and are less influenced by their perceptions than are preoperational children. Concrete Operational children are more logical. They are also more likely to understand cause–effect relationships and to solve conservation problems.

Conservation problems require us to distinguish between what is real and what is apparent, and they depend on the operations of reversibility and decentration. Children who are less adept at conservation problems tend to show deficiencies in their use of the strategies (such as counting) that we first encountered in Chapter 8 (Bruner, 1974; Börner-Ringleb & Wilbert, 2018).

Keep in mind that children's conservation in tasks does not occur all at the same time. Instead, **horizontal décalage**, a time interval or a gap within a stage, occurs when children understand a concept on some conservation tasks earlier than on other conservation tasks, such as how a child might achieve conservation of liquid earlier than conservation of mass or volume (Flavell, 1963; Rogoff, Dahl, & Callanan, 2018).

School-age children are also more likely than preschoolers to solve other types of problems in addition to conservation, such as class inclusion, seriation, and transitive inference, as operational thought develops. This is because "classifications and seriations are essentially operational forms of behavior" (Inhelder & Piaget, 1964, p. 282) and because the greater maturation of school-age children's brains provides them with greater inhibitory control. This greater control helps them suppress incorrect solutions to problems, such as the temptation to organize books by color instead of alphabetically (Borst et al).

That is what happens in **seriation**, or the understanding of a continuum. Examples might be arranging sticks according to their length—or arranging the *Heroes of Olympus* and *Percy Jackson* novels according to their size, or alphabetizing them, or arranging them according to their publication date, or whatever Frankie might be thinking as she arranges and rearranges.

In addition to wanting to be sensitive to and supportive of school-age children's needs, why else might seriations be noteworthy? It's important because the ability to understand seriation allows children to solve **transitive inference** problems—that is, to understand that a combination of two quantitative relationships creates a third relationship. One classic example of transitive inference requires children to specify what the relationship is between A and C after learning that A > B > C, and that A is a large stick, B is a medium-size stick, and C is a small stick.

Piaget proposed that children must have memory of the relationships among A, B, and C in order to solve a problem of this type. Indeed, researchers have found that children with ADHD have problems maintaining in their memory a unified representation of the related items (Brunamonti et al.,

FIG. 10.7   Frankie Pondering What Could Be

Copyright © Depositphotos/belchonock.

2017). Even when children's memories are well-developed, though, success at Piagetian tasks is not just age- or nature-driven; context plays a role too.

For example, there are cross-cultural differences in children's performance on tasks such as class inclusion, seriation, and transitivity. Children from more nonindustrialized countries, such as the Aboriginal Australians, tend to perform just as well on Concrete Operational tasks, but tend to take longer to achieve these cognitive milestones. Perhaps this is a function of their lack of familiarity with the test materials, since Aboriginal culture involves symbols and beautiful rock paintings but doesn't rely on a system of numbers of measurement (de Lemos, 2019).

As a result, it appears that Piaget is still relevant today, but that he failed to appreciate the environmental influences on their development (Bjorklund 2018a; Piaget & Inhelder, 2000). So, most children between 6 and 12 years of age are eventually able to reason and do so systematically, noticing relationships between concepts (A is greater than both B and C). Also, although school-age children's thinking is more advanced than that of preschoolers, it still has some shortcomings.

For instance, school-age children's thinking is primarily reality-based, rather than being concerned with the hypothetical and what could be. It isn't usually until about age 12 (and with education in scientific reasoning, including the testing of hypotheses) that children begin to ponder on their own what is possible or what could be. Thus, Frankie might be pondering a new method of outsmarting the antagonistic Ares war god in *Percy Jackson*, creating affordable electric cars, or finding a new and different way to respond to someone who is being cruel.

Piaget's Theory and the Theory of Mind

We learned in Chapter 8 that children develop a theory of mind during the preschool years. Thus, most 4-year-olds can pass a false-belief task in which they understand that other people can have beliefs that are not true.

Yet at the beginning of middle childhood, most children still have a limited understanding of how the mind can actively interpret sensations in more one way, such as the classic vase–face image in Figure 10.8. Reasoning about ambiguity is not something most children can do until they are 10 years of age or older (Barquero, Robinson, & Thomas, 2003; Osterhaus, Koerber, & Sodian, 2016).

But how is theory of mind related to Piaget's theory of concrete operations? The answer is that school-age children can focus on multiple characteristics of a situation at a time, as in the case of irony. Unlike *sarcasm*, which is aggressive humor intended to hurt another and may include irony—as when someone may remark, "You're so graceful!" when another person trips—*irony* uses the literal meaning of a statement to suggest its opposite, as when the weather is crummy and we say, "What a gorgeous day!"

For children to understand irony, they must appreciate the difference between what is stated and what is intended. Most children notice the difference between a stated meaning and an implied meaning by 6 years of age; but even at 9 years of age, differences are apparent, with children who show greater empathy development showing greater appreciation of irony (Colston, 2019; Nicholson, Whalen, & Pexman, 2013).

One study showed 8- and 9-year-old children a series of short puppet shows, which ended with a statement by one of the puppets. The statements were either *literal compliments* ("That was so good"), *literal criticisms* ("That was so bad"), or *ironic criticisms* ("That was so good"). The children were asked to judge the puppet's final statement as "nice'" or "mean" by placing a "nice" duck or a "mean" shark in the answer box, as can be seen in Figure 10.9.

FIG. 10.8   The Face–Vase Illusion

FIG. 10.9   A Puppet Show to Measure Empathy and Irony Understanding

The researchers found that the greater a child's empathy development, the greater their ability to identify the statements correctly. Other work confirms that children's understanding of irony is related to their social skills and theory of mind (Colston, 2019; Nicholson, Whalen, & Pexman, 2013).

Theory of mind also predicts the appreciation of irony in children with autism spectrum disorder. These children usually perform poorer than typically developing children, but certainly adequately (Huang, Oi, & Taguchi, 2015; Saban-Bezalel et al., 2019).

Although puns such as "To write with a broken pencil is pointless" may elicit groans from adolescents and adults, school-age children tend to find them highly amusing. Why? Likely because of their gains in verbal intelligence, which predict understanding and appreciation of metaphors, and because of their recent understanding of concrete operations, as necessary to grasp the humor in the following joke:

Samuel goes into a restaurant and orders a whole pie. The waitress asks whether she should cut the pie into four slices or eight. "Four," says Samuel. "I'm on a diet." (Deckert et al., 2019; Goldstein & Ruch, 2018; McGhee, 1974).

By about 7 years of age, most children express cynicism or doubt when speakers make statements that are in the speaker's self-interest, so they are no longer as naïve as during the preschool years. At this later age they also are more likely to question and explore claims that are counterintuitive to them, such as when they are told that the smallest toy in a group of toys is also the heaviest (Mills & Kail, 2005; Ronfard, Chen, & Harris, 2018).

Notice, too, that these aforementioned milestones require considering more than one aspect of a situation at a time, the major achievement of concrete operations.

What Cognitive Processes are Most Relevant to Middle Childhood?

FIG. 10.10   Frankie Completing Her Homework

Copyright © Depositphotos/belchonock.

Frankie has an amazing memory, especially for *Percy Jackson and the Olympians* and *Heroes of Olympus* trivia. She has been enchanted by each series for a long time, and she has only recently found it easy to postpone tinkering with her collection of *Percy Jackson* and *Heroes of Olympus* odds and ends until she has finished her homework.

Such changes in behavior might mean Frankie is losing interest in all things *Percy Jackson* and *Heroes of Olympus* as she grows older. Yet it could also be that the ways in which she processes information have changed with age, because of both her brain's maturing frontal lobe and her improved study skills.

Here we consider how things have changed, via the information-processing approach to studying Cognitive Development in middle childhood.

Executive Function

We learned in Chapter 1 that executive function includes the ability to engage in sustained attention, to filter out distractions, and to have self-control over our impulses, and that it is a function of our context.

How so? Well, in terms of how our parents interact with us and the educational and economic resources they have. Research shows that children's executive function performance is correlated positively with their family's SES, but in fact it is likely the product of multiple interactions among environmental and genetic influences (Lawson, Hook, & Farah, 2018).

Most of the aspects of executive function that begin to develop in middle childhood include goal setting, cognitive flexibility, prioritizing and organizing, accessing working memory, and self-monitoring (Meltzer, 2018).

Goal setting includes identifying short-term and long-term objectives, as well as planning actions in advance and approaching tasks in an efficient and strategic way. Frankie figured out that she needs to study a little bit each day rather than cramming all her study time in the night before a test.

Cognitive flexibility refers to the ability to switch between approaches, and to learn from mistakes. Frankie really began to appreciate a few weeks ago that she really does need to study for tests.

Prioritizing and **Organizing** refer to ordering based on the relative importance of information and subsequent arranging of such information, such as Frankie tackling a science problem before she completes her math homework. She finds math easier than science, and has come to realize it is

Pan & Zoom

Patterns of Brain Rhythms in Children's Executive Functions

In this box, we zoom in on the specifics of executive functions which illustrate the multidimensional pattern of development.

Executive function is associated with physical development—specifically, the resting state of the brain's various rhythms. These rhythms are measured by the number of neurons firing within a given frequency range. The neurons that fire slowly are *theta* bands, the ones that fire faster are *alpha* bands, and those that fire even faster are *beta* bands.

These frequency bands illustrate the polydirectional pattern of development, because there are age-related differences in them over time. Specifically, researchers have found that theta waves *decrease* with age and alpha waves *increase* with age (Perone, Palanisamy, & Carlson, 2018).

The same researchers also looked at ratio of theta/beta bands in relation to executive function. High theta/beta ratios reflect a brain that is more stimuli-driven (and perhaps distracted), whereas low theta/beta ratios reflect a brain that is more goal-driven. Past research has found that high theta/beta ratios are associated with ADHD, a topic to which we turn in a moment (Zhang et al., 2017). For now, though, know that these researchers who found age-related changes in brain rhythms also found individual differences in children's theta/beta band ratios, which predicted their executive functions skills. That is, children with high theta/beta bands (a characteristic of brains that are more stimuli-driven, rather than goal-driven) show poorer executive function skills than children with low theta/beta bands (Perone, Palanisamy, & Carlson, 2018).

• • • •

best to devote more mental energy to more difficult tasks earlier on in studying, rather than later on when she feels mentally drained.

Working Memory refers to juggling information mentally, via a small amount of information that we hold temporarily in a heightened state of availability, such as Frankie writing her English class paper on Greek Mythology in modern life and working on a paragraph about Tiresias the blind seer, who communicated among both mortals and gods/goddesses—while simultaneously remembering to add a paragraph on him as having changed genders, as did the Asian goddess Quan Yin (both of whom may serve as role models for some transgender youth).

Self-monitoring refers to finding errors in our work and/or thinking, such as Frankie taking ample time to proofread her paper after letting it sit for a few days, as well as realizing that she forgot to clean up sufficiently in art class yesterday, and remembering to clean up, and help others clean up, in class today.

In the *Pan & Zoom: Patterns of Brain Rhythms in Children's Executive Functions* box, we zoom in on the patterns of brain rhythms associated with individual differences in children's executive function.

Why some children have poorer executive function than others could be a result of being born prematurely and/or being on the autism spectrum (both of which are associated with brain irregularities, such as reduced brain volume and/or reduced brain activity), but also with traumatic brain injuries (Burnett et al., 2018; Demetriou et al., 2018a; Nassar et al., 2019; Resch et al., 2019).

No matter. Substandard executive function skills predict poor reading comprehension and poor arithmetic, as well obesity, given that poor executive function involves difficulties in self-regulation, including the regulation of eating and exercising. Most promising, though, is the finding that when obese children participate in interventions to improve executive function skills, they lose weight too (Hayes et al., 2018; McDonald & Berg, 2018; Meixner et al., 2019).

We don't yet know if interventions to change brain rhythms are effective. But we have empirical evidence that interventions (such as aerobic activity, music, art, learning of strategies, and mindfulness) structured to improve the executive function skills, of both typically developing and neurodiverse children, are effective (de Greeff et al., 2018; Kassai, Futo, Demetrovics, & Takacs, 2019). And those interventions that train working memory, inhibitory control, and cognitive flexibility together rather than training each one in isolation, are best (de Greeff et al., 2018; Kassai, Futo, Demetrovics, & Takacs, 2019).

To learn more about a **meta-analysis,** or a review that combines results from multiple studies, on such interventions, visit the *Cycle of Science* feature at the end of this chapter.

Attention Deficit Hyperactivity Disorder

Approximately 5% to 7% of children have **Attention Deficit Hyperactivity Disorder (ADHD),** a neurodevelopmental disorder in which individuals show inappropriate levels of inattention, hyperactivity and impulsivity—symptoms that can impair functioning at school, home, or social situations. Another 5% struggle with these same symptoms at levels that are just under clinical diagnostic levels (American Psychiatric Association, 2013; Sayal et al., 2018).

The prevalence of ADHD in the United States is among the highest in the world—likely as a function of a number of things, including the diagnosis being broadened and the rise of medical treatments for such (as opposed to psychotherapy). Perhaps the prevalence is also due to the enormous increase in pharmaceutical companies' direct-to-consumer advertising over the last few decades (Bergey & Conrad, 2018; Raman et al., 2018).

The latter trend appears to be related to the increasing influence of American psychiatry practices across the globe, and to pharmaceutical industries' growing international reach. Increased medication use is now being seen in other countries as well (Bergey & Conrad, 2018; Raman et al., 2018).

We know that some characteristics in earlier developmental stages seem to predict later ADHD. For instance, children who were born preterm and/or at low birth weight are at a significantly higher risk for ADHD (Franz et al., 2018).

Also, as we learned in Chapter 7 on emotional development in infancy and toddlerhood, one aspect of temperament is **reactivity**, or the ease with which infants are emotionally and physically aroused (Fox et al., 2015; Kagan, 2018). *High-reactive* infants tend to become shy, inhibited, and introverted children; *low-reactive* infants tend to become bold, sociable, and extraverted children.

In that chapter, we learned that infants who are highly reactive and physically active at 4 months of age are significantly more likely show symptoms of ADHD during middle childhood. But this is true only if they are male and their mothers' caregiving behaviors are of poor quality. For example, the mothers are less likely to be accepting, less sensitive in interacting with their infant, less available, less encouraging, and less likely to cooperate (rather than interfere) with their infants' activity (Miller et al., 2018).

We also know that infants who respond positively to novelty are significantly more likely to show symptoms of ADHD during middle childhood, but only if they are female and their mothers' caregiving behaviors are of poor quality—so that early intervention that can promote greater sensitivity in caregiving may reduce children's risk of ADHD (N.V. Miller et al., 2018). Additionally, approximately 70% of children who are on the autism spectrum show clinically meaningful symptoms of ADHD (Gargaro et al., 2018).

International research (with participants from Brazil, India, Saudi Arabia, South Africa, and Sweden) indicates that children diagnosed with ADHD often show a strong drive to meet challenges, whether it be participating in physical exercises, studying for exams, and/or showing heightened creativity. Still, treatment may be necessary for children whose ADHD interferes with their ability to learn (Mahdi et al., 2017; 2018). Also, the earlier these symptoms are addressed, the better the children's later outcomes (Sayal et al., 2018).

Traditional treatments for ADHD include stimulant medications (which improve executive functioning in children, but can have side effects of increased anxiety, irritability, and/or apathy) or behavioral therapies—at least for whom such treatments are recommended. For instance, research indicates that children who regularly display problem behaviors at school (such as disobedience and/or bullying) are at risk of being suspended or expelled, regardless of their race and/or ethnicity, yet among children with less-severe behavior problems, Black and Latinx children are more likely to be punished for such behaviors than are European American children (Pozzi et al., 2018; Ramey, 2018).

Also, while European American children are more likely to be *overmedicated*, Black and Latinx children are more likely to be *undermedicated*—when in fact they may need such a potentially helpful treatment (Hooven et al, 2018; Ramey, 2018). This is particularly true when other data indicate that Latinx families are more likely to miss, cancel, or need to reschedule appointments for their children's

ADHD medication management even when they do receive it, and unfortunately are instead often treated as future criminals (Hooven et al., 2018; Ramey, 2018).

A review of the research reveals that stimulant medications are effective in the time period during which they are taken. However, it is unclear that they have long-term benefits (Caye et al., 2019; Rajeh et al., 2017). On the other hand, behavioral therapies with a trained teacher or therapist, coaching programs (that help to improve time management, prioritizing, and sustaining effort over time), and cognitive training strategies (that help to strengthen attention, inhibitory control, and working memory) are associated with *long-term* improvements in executive functioning (Caye et al., 2019; Rajeh et al., 2017).

Further, it is necessary for parents to adhere to treatments in which they teach and reinforce children's skills and behaviors. Parents' adherence is less important in treatments in which there is shared responsibility among parents, teachers, and clinicians (Rooney et al., 2018).

Children with ADHD are likely to have a deficiency of omega-3 **polyunsaturated fatty acids**, or **PUFAs**, and supplementation with such can help (Caye et al., 2019; Healey-Stoffel & Levant, 2018). PUFAs are found in foods such as flax, salmon, and fish oil. They influence various functions in brain

Tech & Media

Tech & Media in Our Lives: Neurofeedback as a Treatment for ADHD

Within our discussion of executive function in this chapter, we learned that the resting state of the brain's various rhythms is measured by the number of neurons firing within a given frequency range.

That is, those that fire slowly are *theta* bands, those that fire faster are *alpha* bands, and those that fire even faster are *beta* bands. Also, high theta/beta ratios reflect a brain that is more stimuli-driven (and perhaps distracted), whereas low theta/beta ratios reflect a brain that is more goal-driven. Past research has found that high theta/beta ratios are associated with attention deficit hyperactivity disorder (ADHD).

A nonpharmacological and noninvasive treatment technology called *neurofeedback* shows success at decreasing theta activity and/or increase beta activity. Neurofeedback can better regulate the brain's activity, via a series of training steps based on both operant conditioning and skill learning (Enriquez-Geppert et al., 2019). The training steps are as follows:

1. The person's brain activity is measured by a software system to which they are connected via electro-encephalogram (EEG) technology that attaches electrodes to their scalp.
2. The software calculates a specific brain frequency that is translated back to the person.
3. The person adjusts to this type of brain activity while working on a task over and over.
4. The person eventually learns to regulate their brain activity on their own.

Research indicates that neurofeedback is a viable treatment option for children with ADHD, with documented treatments effects lasting for at least 6 months. However, uniform standards are needed for training practitioners to use neurofeedback (Enriquez-Geppert et al., 2019; Strehl et al., 2017; Van Doren et al., 2019).

• • • •

development, including the modification of cell membranes in the central nervous system in order to alter the transmission of neurotransmitters involved in executive function (Artukoglu & Bloch, 2018; Del-Ponte et al., 2019; Lu et al, 2019).

Some research indicates that nutritional choices (fish and vegetables versus sugar and saturated fats) may help children err on the side of resilience in the risk–resilience pattern of development when it comes to ADHD. More experimental research on the role of nutrition (or lack thereof—given that food insecurity in children raises their risk of ADHD) is needed (Artukoglu & Bloch, 2018; Del-Ponte et al., 2019; Lu et al., 2019).

In addition to medication, behavioral interventions, and/or better nutritional choices, preliminary evidence suggests that neurofeedback may also help children with ADHD (Caye, et al., 2019). To learn more, see the *Tech & Media in Our Lives: Neurofeedback as a Treatment for ADHD* box.

Memory

Information-processing (IP) theories provide a model of memory by which researchers study how information flows through our minds, both before and after we pay attention.

The model compares the mind to a computer, receiving input and then generating output. In terms of the human mind, sensations (hearing, smelling, and so on) are the input, and the operations we execute or behaviors in which we engage (turning up the volume on our favorite song, reaching for a cinnamon roll) are the output, or the end of the flow of information.

This view of the mind as a computer, and of memory in particular, is often portrayed in a flowchart as in Figure 10.11. General memory performance is weaker in children than in adults, but it certainly improves over time, telling us that the processes in these models are not static; rather, they change over the course of a child's development (Fandakova et al., 2019; Shiffrin & Atkinson, 1969).

Information first enters the sensory register. The **sensory register** retains multiple sources of information, but for only a fraction of a second. Any information in the sensory register that we attend to moves on to short-term memory, such as what you heard in your instructor's lecture that you thought was important and wrote in your class notes.

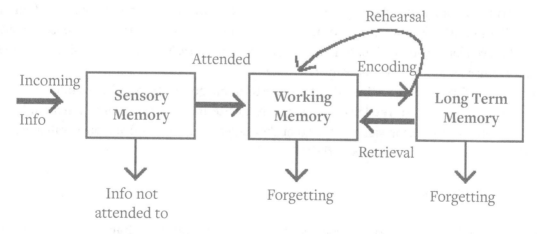

FIG. 10.11   The Information-Processing View of Memory

Source: https://rongtu.wordpress.com/2014/12/03/srl-solo-phase-3/.

On the other hand, if you weren't paying *attention*, as noted in Figure 10.11, the information won't be retained in your memory, and you therefore won't have a chance to move it to working memory. Is that a big deal? Yes, it is. Without working memory, we would have no long-term memory; without long-term memory, we wouldn't have ourselves, much less remember our name, address, or date of birth.

Recall that *working memory* refers to juggling information mentally, via a small amount of information that we hold temporarily in a heightened state of availability (Cowan, Li, Glass, & Saults, 2018). That is, working memory "works on" or transforms the information held in the short-term storage space. Some examples: when students do math problems in their head now that they can count; when they can complete a sentence in Chinese now that they have stored letters, words, and grammatical rules; and when they rehearse mentally before asking a question about what they just heard in class.

Working memory is vital for understanding, planning, reasoning, language acquisition and language use, as well as problem-solving. This is consistent with what we learned earlier about the role of working memory in executive functions. It is also during middle childhood that children should be learning the *encoding*, *rehearsal*, and *retrieval* strategies shown in Figure 10.11 for effective study skills (Cowan, 2014; Cowan, Li, Glass, & Saults, 2018).

Greater connections among neurons in the brain's parietal cortex and prefrontal cortex are likely responsible for the more-effective working memory seen across middle childhood and adolescence. This also tells us that the brain systems that support working memory change over time (Bathelt et al., 2018; Perone, Almy, & Zelazo, 2018).

Working memory improves through middle childhood due to an increase in memory capacity or the *amount* of material held within it, as well as increases in children's **metamemory**, or their knowledge about memory (Bathelt et al., 2018; Cottini, Basso, & Palladino, 2018; Flavell, 1979). Working memory is also influenced by parents' ability to scaffold their children's learning, an ability which is a product of a parent's own working memory, and an ability that can be affected negatively by increasing age, stress, anxiety, and/or sleep deprivation (Wilson & Gross, 2018). Interventions that are designed to improve children's working memory—such as via practicing inhibition; learning to better discriminate, remember and manipulate sounds; and engaging in fantasy play—can improve working memory as well (Rowe et al., 2019).

Once sensory information is held in working memory, we need to move it into long-term memory. **Long-term memory** is the relatively permanent store of information that we have learned throughout our lifetime. Although we hold information in working memory longer than in sensory register, we hold it even longer, in fact indefinitely, in long-term memory. The capacity or size of long-term memory is also larger; it is theoretically indefinite.

How does information move in and out of long-term memory? **Storage** moves information *into* long-term memory, whereas **retrieval** moves it *out of* long-term memory. When children (and adults) forget something, the reason can be either that they failed to retrieve it from long-term memory or that they initially never truly stored it there.

Eyewitness Testimony

For children to be able to testify in court and provide **eyewitness testimony** or give statements under oath in a court of law, they must have "sufficient intelligence, understanding, and ability to observe, recall, and communicate events; an ability to comprehend the seriousness of an oath; and an appreciation of the necessity to tell the truth" (Pantell, 2017).

Children as young as 3 years of age are able to accurately recall experiences, but as a memory weakens over time, children (and adults) may fill in the gaps with similar but unrelated events (Blizard & Shaw, 2019; Pantell, 2017). Although it used to be thought that false memories only decrease with age, they may very well increase with age too (Brainerd, Reyna, & Holliday, 2018; Paz-Alonso & Goodman, 2016).

In addition to the aforementioned qualifications for children to provide eyewitness testimony, other factors influencing the credibility of child witnesses include the length of time since the event in question, the child's experiences in being prepared for court, and the nature of the courtroom experience (Pantell, 2017). Children's participation in legal proceedings can be extremely upsetting to them, so their involvement in any legal case needs to be kept to the absolute minimum required (Milojevich, Quas, & Yano, 2016).

All states have laws that help reduce the distress of children appearing in court by requiring children to bring comfort objects with them, for allowing a support person to attend with them, providing a *court-appointed special advocate* (CASA) and/or *guardian ad litem* (GAL) or court-appointed guardian to protect the interests of the child and/or excluding the press. Yet these protections may apply to some cases, such as to children who are victims of abuse, and not to others, such as children who are witnesses to violence, even within their own family (Pantell, 2017).

Extending such laws to *all* cases could help greatly, particularly for children who witness violence in the home and fear speaking ill of a parent on whom they are dependent and from whom they might anticipate punishment.

To learn about becoming a volunteer CASA or GAL to advocate in court on behalf of children who have experienced abuse or neglect, see the of CASA/GAL website listed in the *Helpful Websites* section at the end of this chapter.

How Are Children Smart?

Think of someone you know who is smart. What is it about this person that makes you think they are smart? What *is* intelligence exactly?

Defining Intelligence

Early theorists in the field of intelligence often took a **psychometric**—literally, 'measuring the mind'—approach to intelligence. According to this approach, **intelligence** is a score on an IQ test, and it reflects the ability to learn, to reason, and to solve problems (Plomin & von Stumm, 2018).

Spearman (1927) proposed that intelligence is made up of "**g**," a general form of intelligence that includes working memory, control of our attention, mental flexibility, being aware of our mental processes, and making inferences (Demetriou et al., 2018a). So many measurements of intelligence are really attempting to assess g.

The heritability of g, or how much of the difference in IQ *within a group* is due to genes, varies from study to study but is approximately 50% (Plomin & von Stumm, 2018). This means that when we see IQ differences among people, 50% of those differences are due to genetic factors, and 50% are environmental.

Although people frequently assume that some folks just are or are not smart, this isn't true. Like height, intelligence has a genetic component but is influenced substantially by the environment (including the quality of home and school environments).

Longitudinal research shows that the higher a family's SES, the greater the child's brain gray matter volume, cortical thickness, and hippocampal volume. So SES may alter brain development and corresponding brain processes in the areas of language, working memory, and learning that predict IQ (Aeschlimann, Voelke, & Roebers, 2017; McDermott et al., 2019; Tourva, Spanoudis, & Demetriou, 2016).

Remember that correlations are not causal, but findings such as these make it clear—and physically concrete in the brain—that family resources play a role in children's development (Aeschlimann, Voelke, & Roebers, 2017; McDermott et al., 2019; Tourva, Spanoudis, & Demetriou, 2016). Schools certainly play a role as well and can help children from disadvantaged backgrounds. Children who perceive greater academic support and higher expectations also exhibit greater cortical thickness (Piccolo et al., 2017).

Gardner's Theory of Intelligence

Gardner proposes that rather than a general "g," multiple intelligences exist, and they help us process information in order to solve problems or create things of value within our culture, whether they be abstract engineering designs for a new electronic product, a television series, a sculpture, or a musical piece (Chen & Gardner, 2018; Gardner, 2011).

Therefore, all children (and adults) possess multiple forms of intelligence, yet they differ in their relative strengths (Chen & Gardner, 2018). According to Gardner (2017), the multiple intelligences (which are basic cognitive capacities) are as follows: **Musical** (the ability to sing, play an instrument like Frankie with her guitar after listening to a song on her headphones, identify a ring tone), **Bodily-Kinesthetic** (the ability to compete in dance and/or sports), **Logical-Mathematical** (the ability to solve Piagetian problems or play chess well), **Linguistic** (the ability to write, translate, tell a gripping story), **Spatial** (the ability to design a building and/or navigate a ship), **Intrapersonal** (the ability to identify and manage one's own emotions), **Interpersonal** (the ability to identify and respond sensitively to the emotions of others), and **Naturalist** (the ability to distinguish different elements of nature, such as types of dinosaurs, clay in which archeological treasures are buried, plants, and clouds).

Again, we all have these forms of intelligence as potential, with some currently developed better than others (Chen & Gardner, 2018).

For Gardner, then, the question is not "How smart are you?" but "How are you smart?"

The reason there is no "artistic" intelligence is that each intelligence can be applied artistically; sculptors use spatial intelligence aesthetically, and surgeons use it routinely. Notice too that the various types have been valued differently across historical contexts.

For example, Hunter-Gatherer and Industrial societies required kinesthetic and spatial skills for success in manual work that relied on physical brawn. Modern Information and Technological societies, on the other hand, require linguistic and mathematical-logical intelligence as well as both interpersonal and intrapersonal intelligence, because we must not only understand conceptual knowledge but also apply and make decisions with it—often while navigating relationships with others (Chen & Gardner, 2018). Thus, a child may have figured out what to do for an upcoming school science project but needs their irritable parent's support in obtaining materials. Or an adult may have figured out how to increase profits when competitors are outsourcing to other countries, but they need to be able to suggest to the boss that they be open about how to achieve such.

Additionally, intrapersonal intelligence and interpersonal intelligence together may be considered *emotional intelligence*, which is correlated positively with children's psychosocial adjustment (Peachey, Wenos, & Baller, 2017; Piqueras et al., 2019).

Not surprisingly, perhaps, emotional intelligence is lower in all children who engage in bullying, as well as in boys who are victims of bullying. This indicates that interventions that aim to reduce and prevent bullying best support children's ability to identify and manage their own emotions, and their ability to identify and respond sensitively to the emotions of others (Peachey, Wenos, & Baller, 2017; Piqueras et al., 2019).

How Does Language Develop in Middle Childhood?

During middle childhood, vocabulary growth continues, and at an even more rapid pace than in early childhood. Children have approximately 10,000 words in their vocabulary by first grade, approximately 20,000 by third grade, and 40,000 by fifth grade—so that they tend to gain more words from third grade to fifth grade than from first grade to third grade (Anglin, Miller, & Wakefield, 1993; Hoff, 2014).

In addition to age/grade-level differences over time, there are individual differences in children's vocabulary growth. Research data on fourth-graders' reading skills reveal that above-average readers show a higher rate of vocabulary growth than average readers, which is consistent with other studies finding a **Matthew Effect** (in which those who have more obtain more, and those who have less have more taken away from them). In other words, initial skills predict growth over time, in that children whose early skills are poor fall increasingly behind their peers, which leads to an ever-widening gap among children (Duff, Tomblin, & Catts, 2015; Petscher, Justice, & Hogan, 2018).

Neuroscience research finds that at the beginning of middle childhood, the amount of adult–child conversation in which a child participates is correlated positively with the degree of connections among neurons in left hemisphere of the child's brain (Neuman & Kaefer, 2018; Ozernov-Palchik et al., 2019; Romeo et al., 2018). This tells us that one means of erring on the resilience side of the risk–resilience pattern of development—and therefore reducing, if not closing, the language gap (and preventing a *Matthew Effect* at the start of middle childhood) between children from low-SES homes and high-SES homes—is campaigns and/or interventions directed at parents and care providers about the importance of conversation. Another valuable means is shared book reading—a regular ritual

FIG. 10.13   Frankie and Her Father's Regular Reading Ritual

that Frankie shares with her father (Neuman & Kaefer, 2018; Ozernov-Palchik et al., 2019; Romeo et al., 2018).

Children's grammar development corresponds to their vocabulary development, and it follows a trajectory consistent with the development. That is, the growth of grammar begins to plateau by third grade, while vocabulary continues to increase (Brinchmann, Braeken, & Halaas Lyster, 2019; Justice et al., 2018).

A common source of influence on both grammar development and vocabulary development is the *home literacy environment*, which includes how often a child is read to, how many books are at home, how much a child enjoys reading, as well as parents' education levels (Brinchmann, Braeken, & Halaas Lyster, 2019; Justice et al., 2018). Musical exposure can help as well: Children's understanding of rhythm is associated with better judgments of whether sentences are grammatically correct or incorrect, as well as literacy in general (Chern et al., 2018; Ozernov-Palchik, Wolf, & Patel, 2018).

Therefore, we now consider literacy, as well as numeracy, and school.

Literacy and Numeracy

Middle childhood is informally referred to as the school years, a stage during which children receive intentional instructional in literacy and numeracy.

Literacy, or the ability to read and write, is one of these skills. **Numeracy**, or the ability to understand and use numbers, is another skill that's vital to our success. Children must learn other skills too, including social skills, and a wide array of knowledge. Here we will focus on literacy and numeracy, along with how schools can best foster such learning.

Literacy

The development of literacy is similar to general cognitive development in Piaget's theory. Children develop through a series of three stages during middle childhood by interacting with the environment (Chall, 1979).

In *Stage 0: Prereading*, children are exposed to letters, words, and books, but as the name of this particular stage suggests, they can't yet read. Stage 0 is normally the longest of the stages of reading, lasting from birth until approximately 6 years of age.

Stage 1: Initial Reading or Decoding corresponds approximately to the time from first grade through second grade, or 6 to 7 years of age. During or even before this stage, children learn the parts of spoken words that correspond to the letters of the alphabet, so that *reading comprehension* is really a product of *decoding*, such as phonological awareness, and *language*, such as vocabulary and listening (Hjetland et al., 2018).

Remember from Chapter 8 that **phonological awareness** refers to understanding the correspondence between letters and sounds, as well as having the capacity to notice changes in the spelling and pronunciation of words (such as knowing that when the "s" is dropped from "small," the remaining word is "mall," not "wall" or "ball") (Knoop-van Campen, Segers, & Verhoeven, 2018).

The relationship between decoding and literacy is consistent with the polydirectional pattern of development in that at the beginning of middle childhood, decoding skills are a stronger predictor of children's reading comprehension, so that children with poor letter knowledge will be at risk of having poor reading comprehension (Hjetland et al., 2018).

Later in middle childhood, when decoding skills have ideally developed to a sophisticated level, language is a stronger predictor of children's reading comprehension; children with poor vocabularies and listening skills will be at risk of having poor reading comprehension (Hjetland et al., 2018). This tells us that in order to best support children's ability to understand fully what they read, they need to develop a variety of skills at different times within, if not also prior to, middle childhood.

Stage 2: Confirmation and Fluency, corresponds to grades two to three or approximately ages 7 to 8. Some children begin to fall behind in this stage if their home context does not foster reading in the home; they are losing the time needed to practice reading. As we learned in Chapter 8, children with better reading abilities read more, and because they read more, their literacy skills continue to improve far beyond those of children who read less (van Bergen et al., 2018).

The more children engage in leisure reading, ideally with books rather than magazines or online blogs, the greater their comprehension, so it is imperative that parents help children find novels with stories and characters children can relate to and are excited about—as did Frankie's parents (Torppa et al., 2019). Differences in reading are often a function of disparities in household wealth and education. Yet they are not necessarily static over time, which indicates that government policies that guide public school programming, library funding, and outreach to parents could eliminate this social injustice (Reynolds et al., 2017).

One technique that can help eliminate or at least reduce the ever-increasing vocabulary gap between children from low-SES homes and children from high-SES homes during the school years—in addition to ensuring high-quality schooling for all, fully funded libraries, and programs that teach parents about interactive book reading and the importance of child-directed conversations—is a school curriculum that teaches children strategies for learning new words, such as imagining a picture of the context as they are reading. The more knowledge children have of what is happening in a sentence or a paragraph, the more readily they can integrate an unknown word's meaning (Maguire et al., 2018).

Regardless of family income, language interventions are helpful to many children, including those with permanent childhood hearing loss. Such children are more at risk for later emotional and/or behavioral difficulties if their language and reading comprehension skills are poor during middle childhood (Stevenson et al., 2018).

Note that the transition from Stage 2 to Stage 3 marks the transition from *learning to read* to *reading to learn*. This is a "pivot point" that can catalyze school disengagement, especially for children who are struggling to read (Garrett-Peters et al., 2019; Hernandez, 2012).

In *Stage 3: Reading for Learning*, which corresponds to grade 4 to grade 8, or approximately ages 9 to 13, children begin to read to acquire knowledge. But usually this is only from one viewpoint or perspective; it's about reading for facts, concepts, and information about how to do things. In order to read a (print or online) newspaper and comprehend it—a basic skill necessary for a democracy—individuals must reach at least Stage 3.

Skills developed in this stage are consistent with the lifelong pattern of development. The degree of children's reading proficiency in third grade predicts later outcomes; one in six children who do not read proficiently by this time do not graduate from high school on time (Hernandez 2012).

However, reading comprehension interventions that occur across the fourth-grade school year as well as the summer before fifth grade are effective for children who struggle with reading difficulties. This tells us that as long as school resources are made available to them, we can certainly help children (and the rest of society) err on the resilience side of the risk–resilience pattern of development (Wanzek et al., 2019).

Reading is best taught when it combines **phonics** instruction, in which letter–sound correspondences are taught explicitly (phonological awareness is the best predictor of reading skills), with a **whole language approach** that emphasizes understanding what is read and provides motivation for children to read (American Psychiatric Association, 2013; Castles, Rastle, & Nation, 2018). Phonics instruction is especially beneficial for children struggling with what is now understood as **specific learning disorder** (formerly called *dyslexia*). This results in difficulties in word reading, word comprehension, spelling, and written expression (it can also include difficulties in number sense, calculations, mathematical reasoning), so that children's progress in such is substantially and quantifiably lower than would be expected given a child's chronological age (American Psychiatric Association, 2013; Castles, Rastle, & Nation, 2018; Schaars, Segers, & Verhoeven, 2017).

Therefore, reading instruction should combine phonics instruction with the whole language approach and should use what is otherwise known as a **balanced instruction**. But such balance does *not* mean devoting equal time to phonics and comprehension, as is often practiced (Castles, Rastle, & Nation, 2018; Hoff, 2014). Instead, instruction must be tailored to where children are developmentally *and* what they need—so that, for instance, children need to have mastered basic decoding skills before they are taught strategies for text comprehension (Castles, Rastle, & Nation, 2018; Hoff, 2014).

If a child's literacy level does not match their age, even with balanced instruction in school and reading in the home, parents may want to contact a speech pathologist. To learn about how speech pathologists work with school-age children, see the *Mentor Minute: Samah Saidi, MA* box.

Samah Saidi, MA

1) Describe your work, please.

I am an elementary school–based speech language pathologist. I work with children from preschool to eighth grade. I work in a public school but I am also employed in a few private schools as well.

2) How does social justice inform your work?

My current special education team and I always try to ensure that the families we work with know their rights and the rights of their child(ren). I speak Arabic and work with a large population of Arab American families. I advocate for my families by providing translation during meetings whenever necessary, directing them toward the correct person when they have specific questions that I cannot answer, and referring families to advocacy groups that are mentioned on the procedural safeguards.

3) How did you become involved in social justice and/or advocacy?

Being an American-born, Arab, Muslim woman who has worn a hijab since the age of 8, I feel as though I have been drawn to social justice work or awareness at the very least for most of my life. There have been many times where I have felt that I was treated negatively because of the way I look or because of some preconceived

FIG. 10.14   Samah Saidi, MA

notions about me or people who look like me. Although these experiences are not ideal, I believe that they do help to strengthen an individual's beliefs and character. My experiences have helped to shape my values, personality, and worldviews in many ways. Because of this, I try to ensure that those around me feel that their voices are being heard and that they are treated with respect.

4) What are your thoughts on how social justice can improve child and adolescent development?

Many students in college learn a great deal about Bloom's Taxonomy and the domains that help children develop cognitive skills. As important as this framework is, it is also critical to remember the importance of Maslow's hierarchy of needs. If a child's basic needs are not met (e.g., shelter, food, safety, and health), then it is unlikely that they will excel in any of the domains outlined in Bloom's Taxonomy.

5) What suggestions do you have for undergraduate students who are interested in making a change in child and adolescent development?

In order to make change, I believe that undergraduate students should realize that they can have a huge impact on the lives of the children they will encounter or work with in the field. We most often consider parents to be a child's first or biggest advocate. But not all children have this luxury, or parents may have the best of intentions but may not necessarily have the means to advocate for their children. In such situations, it is important for clinicians to see themselves as advocates for the families they serve. I do not see how one can go wrong if they put the needs of children first, even if it may not be the most popular or the easiest route to take.

• • • •

Numeracy

We often assume that a person who is good at math is not as good at reading, or vice versa, but in fact these skills are often related. For instance, longitudinal research reveals that phonological processing predicts children's number recognition and mathematical performance (Kuzmina, Ivanova, & Kaiky, 2019).

During first grade and second grade, children can usually count to 100, understand the value of coins, predict what comes next in a pattern, and compute addition and subtraction problems. One of the most basic reasoning skill concepts children must grasp as they learn arithmetic is the *inversion concept*, that is, the opposite relationship between addition and subtraction, such as a + b − b = a. Most children understand this concept by 8 or 9 years of age (Ching & Wu, 2019; Robinson, Dubé, & Beatch, 2017).

In third grade, children learn multiplication and division, as well as decimal points. Fourth- and fifth-grade students begin comparing numbers using "greater than" and "less than"; they can calculate long division problems, estimate and round numbers, classify shapes, measure angles, and even apply math to everyday situations such as cooking (Hannula-Sormunen, McMullen, & Lehtiner, 2019; Nanu et al., 2018).

Longitudinal research indicates that children's fifth-grade math achievement is correlated positively with their preschool home learning environment. This environment includes, for example, how often parents engage in literacy activities, the quality of parents' interactions with the child, and children's own spontaneous focus on *numerosity* (the numbers of things). Numerosity may be possible to encourage via modeling, and the availability of learning materials such as books, art materials, and toys that facilitate learning numbers (Hannula-Sormunen, McMullen, & Lehtiner, 2019; Nanu et al., 2018).

In middle school, children learn to use ratios; to graph with coordinates; and to add, subtract, multiply, and divide fractions. They also begin using algebra. However, research indicates that children from low-income homes tend to have poorer math skills; one longitudinal study of low-income children found that their understanding of set sizes and their ability to repeat patterns in preschool predicted their scores on high-stakes math tests in fourth, fifth, and sixth grades (Fyfe, Rittle-Johnson, & Farran, 2019; Garron-Carrier et al., 2018).

Therefore, math skills in elementary school are consistent with the lifelong pattern of development in which development during one stage is predictive of development in a subsequent stage. This tells us that the scaffolding of children's math skills must be taken seriously, and the earlier the better.

Research shows that the relationship between math performance and *math attitudes* (anxiety, confidence) within just the first two years of elementary school is reciprocal, meaning that the early experience of math success lowers any potential math anxiety. This in turn leads to greater math success and a positive snowball trajectory of a virtuous cycle—or vice versa into a vicious cycle—with early math (Gunderson et al., 2018).

So, in addition to preschool preparedness, early low-stakes math activities that are fun (such as linear board games and word problems relevant to children's interests) can propel children toward success. This is especially true of activities that emphasize the intrinsic pleasure of working with numbers rather than emphasizing performance (Gunderson et al., 2018).

The environment really does matter. Some people may describe themselves as "good at math" or "not good at math," with the underlying assumption that mathematical ability is a fixed heritable trait. But environments, and different types of them, certainly play a role—even for children within the same family. Recall the role of nonshared environments that we first encountered in Chapter 3, such as a much more innovation, supportive, and humorous math teacher that one identical twin has but the other twin does not (Larsen et al., 2019).

Cross-cultural differences in math abilities are seen too, and as early as 7 years of age. For example, Chinese children perform significantly better on numerical tasks than children in England (Dowker & Li, 2018). Because these differences are evident as early as the beginning of formal schooling, they may be the result of differences in counting systems (the Chinese counting system is transparent, with 11 being *shi yi* or "ten-one" and 20 being *er shi* or "two ten," whereas the English counting system is much more irregular) and/or context, such as the opportunities that parents do or do not provide their children to practice math concepts (Dowker & Li, 2018).

Once children have progressed in middle school, though, other differences may play a role. For example, Chinese students report their schools' climate more favorably—and report greater emotional engagement in school—as compared to American students (Bear et al., 2018).

Children who struggle to make progress in mathematics may do so because of home and/or cultural influences, but because of cognitive and emotional factors as well. Children who show severe difficulties in math tend to perform more poorly on measures of executive functioning and working memory, so interventions to improve such can help (MacDonald & Berg, 2018).

Such interventions can be specific to working memory, or they can focus on skills that increase working memory, such as bilingual proficiency. Individuals who are literate in and speak two languages are **bilingual**, and those who are literate in and speak more than two languages are **multilingual**.

Bilingual and multilingual children possess greater inhibitory control than monolingual children, perhaps because they must constantly inhibit one language when the situation calls for them to use another language, while also calling upon working memory while shifting tasks and monitoring their attention. This indicates that bilingualism, especially early on, provides children with working memory benefits that pay dividends in other cognitive abilities (Nayak, Salem, & Tarullo, 2020; Swanson, Kong, & Petcu, 2020).

Keep in mind that these benefits may still be available to children who are not by definition fully fluent in two languages. Bilingualism is really a spectrum of experiences that affect both the structure and the function of the brain (DeLuca et al., 2019; Swanson, Kong, & Petcu, 2018). Additional research supports the finding that bilingualism (in Latinx, and other children) *is not a risk to be remedied, but an advantage to be supported.* They offer children greater cultural knowledge as well as opportunities for code-switching that can scaffold executive function (Lee-James & Washington, 2018; Terry, Gatlin, & Johnson, 2018).

Parenting and Schools in the United States

Learning begins in the home. And not just in terms of the role that SES plays, which we have learned about earlier in this chapter. Parents' emotional support matters as well. Children first learn to academically self-regulate in the classroom from behaviors they learn in the home.

For example, parents who support their children's autonomy while interacting with their children when the children are doing their homework have children who are more engaged and on task while doing such homework. This engagement in turn is associated with greater achievement—and in general, perceived support from parents is associated with children being more persistent while doing homework (Doctoroff & Arnold, 2017; Sillinkas & Kikas, 2019).

Clearly, learning exemplifies the multidimensional pattern of development, with emotional support from parents boosting children's cognitive development. Yet the strongest predictor of student achievement may be parents' academic socialization (Day & Dotterer, 2018; Yamamoto & Sonnenschein, 2016). What's this?

Academic socialization occurs in the home when parents discuss learning strategies with children, foster children's educational and occupational aspirations, communicate their values regarding the importance of education, relate children's schoolwork to current events, and help children make plans for the future. The degree to which it occurs is very much a function of context.

As Annette Lareau (2003) points out in her book *Unequal Childhoods: Class, Race, and Family Life*, "America may be the land of opportunity, but it is also a land of inequality" (p. 3). Children from families that adhere to the *accomplishment of natural growth* philosophy that we first encountered in Chapter 8 are less likely to be on the receiving end of what Lareau calls **transmission of differential advantages** or **cultural capital**. These are the cognitive and social advantages that can translate into benefits when applying for jobs and/or navigating the working world: vocabulary, conversational skills, comfort interacting with authority, familiarity with abstract concepts like justice, and knowledge of the arts.

For families that value **concerted cultivation** or the intentional parenting style in which parents and their children participate in extracurricular activities for securing skills as well as for enjoyment, yet cannot afford the demands of such, the arts are both a precursor and an outcome of the aforementioned differential advantages (Vincent & Maxwell, 2016). Besides bringing meaning, pleasure, and culture into our lives, participation the arts can boost literacy. Indeed, a study conducted in New York City public schools by the Guggenheim museum (Korn, 2010) found that fifth-grade students who were asked to discuss a work of art were better able to express themselves verbally, and had better literacy skills, than students not in the program.

Schools certainly matter too. Unlike the schools in many other countries across the globe, schools in the United States are run locally by the states. This means that what a fifth-grader knows, and should know, may depend on the school they attend.

Since the Common Core Standards Initiative (a set of milestones of what children need to know and need to be able to do by the end of each school year) was put into place in 2010, 41 states, the District of Columbia, and four U.S. territories (the American Samoa Islands, Guam, the Northern Mariana Islands, and the U.S. Virgin Islands) have adopted these standards (Common Core State Standards Initiative, 2019). Not only does this mean that students in different communities face unequal expectations and receive unequal support. It also means that the students in Alaska, Florida, Indiana, Nebraska, Oklahoma, Puerto Rico, South Carolina, Texas, Virginia, and Wisconsin may be at greater risk for struggling in the global economy if our varying local standards are not in line with those of other countries (Common Core State Standards Initiative, 2019).

Although there are valid criticisms of the Common Core Standards, such as that they apply a cookie-cutter approach to curriculum that does not allow sufficient attention to children's strengths and weaknesses, and that they may not emphasize the humanities sufficiently, these standards may at least be a step in the right direction if they are implemented fully. They work toward at least equality if not equity, in which everyone is provided with the same tools to ensure that they do their best.

Remember from our discussion of social justice in Chapter 1 that the people's ability to reach their full potential in the societies where they reside requires not just equality, but also equity.

Most public schools in the United States still use an *agrarian calendar*. That calendar is based on children needing to leave school in the afternoon to help out on farms before it becomes dark and needing to spend the entire summer harvesting crops (Pedersen, 2012; 2015). Such a school calendar, tailored to needs that are no longer relevant to current generations, likely contributes to the **summer slide**. This is a decline in academic skills that can occur when children are not attending school (Allington & McGill-Franzen, 2018; McEachin, Augustine, & McCombs, 2018).

The large achievement gaps between students from low-income homes and high-income homes are attributed partially by the unequal financial resources available to their schools as a function of schools' funding being tied to the local tax base, as well as social resources such as the local rates of adult educational attainment (Allington & McGill-Franzen, 2018; Bischoff & Owens, 2019, Owens, 2018). These differences are often overlooked, or at worst they are dismissed, in the dominant individualistic American culture that tends to see each person (and/or their parents) as solely responsible for their outcomes (Freeman, Condron, & Steidl, 2019).

Yet people (especially children) are held personally responsible for their bad luck in not having earlier generations to pass down financial support and/or educational support, while also needing to be preoccupied with survival rather than piano lessons. This is hardly consistent with an ethos of the United States being a land of opportunity in which everyone can obtain a high-quality education regardless of their individual resources, much less their class, race, ethnicity, religion, etc.

Such discrepancies between ideals and practices are especially important when we consider than socioeconomic disadvantage is associated with real concrete differences in the hippocampus and amygdala areas of children's brains (Dufford, Bianco, & Kim, 2018; Freeman, Condron, & Steidl, 2019; Suárez-Orozco, 2017).

Further, the size of the summer slide's loss in skills is often greater for children from low-income homes. Although the data are out there to support the factors that make summer literacy effective in preventing summer reading losses, the political will to extend the school year and provide funding for both summer and regular academic-year needs at equitable levels is not—at least, not yet (Allington & McGill-Franzen, 2018; McDaniel, McLeod, Carter, & Robinson, 2017; McEachin, Augustine, & McCombs, 2018).

Key Terms

Academic Socialization

Accomplishment of Natural Growth

Attention Deficit Hyperactivity Disorder (ADHD)

Balanced Instruction

Bilingual

Biodiversity Hypothesis

Bodily-Kinesthetic

Cognitive Flexibility

Concerted Cultivation

Cultural Capital

Early Maturing

Eyewitness Testimony

Food Desert

Food Insecurity

Food Swamp

g

Goal Setting

Horizontal Décalage

Hygiene Hypothesis

Intelligence

Interpersonal

Intrapersonal

Late Maturing

Linguistic

Literacy

Summary

1. **Outline normative physical development within middle childhood.** Physical growth is asynchronous, meaning that the body's different physical systems grow at different rates. It is near the end of this stage that we begin to see gender differences in physical growth.

2. **Describe the nonnormative changes in physical development within middle childhood.** Children are early maturing if their skeletal age is more than one year *ahead* of their chronological age, late maturing if it is more than one year *behind* their chronological age, and on time if their skeletal and chronological ages are less than one year apart. There is a secular trend in pubertal timing, due to a number of contributing factors, with there being lifelong and multidimensional consequences of early menarche.

   Brain development is polydirectional, with changes in gray matter and white matter found over time. Motor skills improve in middle childhood, and physical activity levels drop. Nonnormative development includes obesity, sleep disturbances, illness, and/or injuries.

3. **Summarize what Piaget's theory can tell us about school-age cognitive development.** Beginning around age 6 or 7, children are no longer so perception-bound, are less egocentric, and are more capable of logical thinking. School-age children are more likely than preschoolers to solve other types of problems, such as class inclusion, seriation, and transitive inference. Among school-age children, operational thought develops along a horizontal décalage or within this stage, so conservation may be understood on some tasks earlier than on other conservation tasks. The understanding of irony is related to social skills and theory of mind.

4. **Identify what cognitive processes are most relevant to middle childhood.** Most of the aspects of executive function that really begin to develop in middle childhood include goal setting, cognitive flexibility, prioritizing and organizing, accessing working memory, and self-monitoring. ADHD is a neurodevelopmental disorder in which individuals show inappropriate levels of inattention, hyperactivity, and impulsivity that can impair functioning at school, at home, or in social situations.

Working memory also improves through middle childhood due to an increase in memory capacity, or the amount of material held within, as well as increases in children's knowledge about memory. For children to be able to testify in court and provide statements under oath in a court of law, they must possess sufficient intelligence, and they must have the ability to observe, recall, and communicate events; to understand what it means to take an oath; and to appreciate the need to tell the truth.

5. **Illustrate how children are smart.** According to the psychometric approach, intelligence is a score on an IQ test, and it reflects the ability to learn, to reason, and to solve problems. This psychometric approach posits that intelligence is made up of "g," a general form of intelligence that includes working memory, control of our attention, mental flexibility, being aware of our mental processes, and making inferences.

   Gardner proposes that rather than a general "g," multiple intelligences exist, and they help us process information in order to solve problems or create things of value within our culture, whether they be abstract engineering designs for a new electronic product, a television series, a sculpture, or a musical piece. Therefore, all children (and adults) possess multiple forms of intelligence, yet we differ in their relative strengths.

6. **Explain how language develops in middle childhood.** Neuroscience research finds that at the beginning of middle childhood, the amount of adult–child conversation in which a child participates is correlated positively with the degree of connections among neurons in the left hemisphere of the child's brain. This tells us that one means of reducing, if not closing, the language gap between children from low-SES and high-SES homes is campaigns and/or interventions directed at parents and care providers about the importance of conversation. Another valuable means is shared book reading. Children's grammar development corresponds to their vocabulary development, and follows a trajectory consistent with the polydirectional pattern of development.

7. **Analyze how literacy and numeracy develop in middle childhood.** The development of literacy is similar to general Cognitive Development in Piaget's theory. Children develop through a series of three stages during middle childhood by interacting with the environment. Reading is best taught with a combination of phonics and whole language instruction, but the balance of the two does not mean devoting equal time to phonics and comprehension, as is often practiced. Instead, instruction must be tailored to where children are developmentally.

   During first and second grade, children can usually count to 100, understand the value of coins, predict what comes next in a pattern, and compute addition and subtraction problems. In third grade, children learn multiplication and division, as well as decimal points. Fourth- and fifth-grade students begin comparing numbers using "greater than" and "less than"; they can calculate long division problems, estimate and round numbers, classify shapes, measure angles, and even apply math to everyday situations such as cooking. In middle school, children learn to use ratios; to graph with coordinates; and to add, subtract, multiply, and divide fractions. They also begin using algebra.

8. **Discuss what is known about parenting and schools in the United States.** Learning begins in the home. And not just in terms of the role that SES plays, which we have learned about earlier in this chapter. Parents' emotional support matters as well. Children first learn to

academically self-regulate in the classroom based on behaviors they learn in the home. Yet the strongest predictor of student achievement may be parents' academic socialization. Schools certainly matter too. Unlike schools in many other countries across the globe, schools in the United States are run locally by the states. This means that what a fifth-grader knows, and should know, may depend on the school they attend.

The Cycle of Science

Research

Why was the study conducted?
The researchers wanted to know about the effectiveness of different behavioral interventions on children's executive function skills (Takacs & Kassai, 2019).

Who participated in the study?
As mentioned earlier in the chapter, this study was a **meta-analysis**, or a review that combines results from multiple studies. This particular meta-analysis reviewed 90 studies, which included data from a total of 8,925 children, all under 12 years of age.

Which type of design was used?
All of the 90 studies were experimental or quasi-experimental. To improve executive function skills, the studies included different interventions, whether it be computer training program, aerobic exercise, cognitive exercises, biofeedback, art activities, music activities, mindfulness meditation, or the teaching of specific self-regulation strategies.

What were the results?
Takacs & Kassai (2019) found that interventions that taught children strategies for self-regulation (such as planning before acting) were best for nontypically developing children, such as those with neurodevelopmental disorders or behavior problems. Mindfulness meditation practices were best for typically developing children. The researchers surmised that mindfulness helped children regulate their attention, as well reduce their stress and anxiety.

Additionally, the researchers found that 15 of the 90 studies did follow-up assessment anywhere from 6 weeks to 1 year after their respective intervention. Most of the studies did not find convincing evidence that the benefits of an intervention remained over time.

Are the results consistent with theory?
We learned earlier in this chapter that children in high-SES homes tend to have better executive function, which suggests that executive function is a function of context. Yet better executive function is most likely a product of multiple interactions among environmental and genetic influences, including interventions such as those reviewed in this meta-analysis (Farah, 2017a; Hartanto, Toh, & Yang, 2018; Lawson, Hook, & Farah, 2018).

How can the results be used to improve our lives?

The results of this meta-analysis (Takacs & Kassai, 2019) tell us that executive function skills are not static but can be improved. The results also indicate that improvement is possible for both typically developing children and nontypically developing children.

Exercises

1. What type of intervention do you think would be most likely to improve children's executive function skills over time? Why?

2. Would the length of the intervention be important, as well as the type of intervention? What length of intervention might be most effective?

3. What pattern of results would you expect if only children from low-SES homes were included in the study? Why?

Helpful Websites

Pediatric Pedestrian Safety in Virtual Reality concerns how virtual reality can be used to study, and prevent, unintentional injuries in children, such as injuries occurring at crosswalks, on playgrounds, and at swimming pools: https://www.uab.edu/cas/psychology/youth-safety-lab/initiatives/pedestrian-safety

Vivid real-life examples of how social class influences our lives in childhood, and later in the lifespan, are the focus of the *UP Series* documentary films, which have followed British children since they were 7 years of age. To find out more, visit the PBS website: http://www.pbs.org/pov/fortynineup/

To learn about how to become a volunteer CASA or volunteer GAL, to advocate in court on behalf of children who have experienced abuse or neglect, explore the CASA/GAL website: https://casaforchildren.org/our-work/the-casa-gal-model/

MindWare sells toys that are entertaining as well as educational. A number of MindWare toys have received awards from the Parents' Choice Foundation, which provides parents with guidance on high-quality children's toys and media. You can learn more about MindWare and the Parents' Choice® Foundation at these two websites:

https://www.mindware.orientaltrading.com

https://www.parentschoice.org

For suggestions on quality apps for learning and the best books for children by age group, including books for children on social media and related topics such as dealing with cyber-bullying and spending engaged and meaningful time offline as well as online, Common Sense Media is a go-to resource: https://www.commonsensemedia.org/book-lists

826 National is a nonprofit organization in a number of cities within the United States that helps underresourced children with their writing, including publishing it. To learn more about this terrific organization and how it helps students, teachers, and communities, point your browser to https://826national.org/about/

Recommended Reading

American Academy of Pediatrics (2018). *Caring for your school-age child* (3rd ed.). New York, NY: Bantam Books.

Atwell, N. (2016). *The reading zone: How to help kids become passionate, skilled, habitual, critical readers* (2nd ed.). New York, NY: Scholastic Teaching Resources.

Hallowell, E. M., & Ratey, J. J. (2011). *Driven to distraction: Recognizing and coping with attention deficit disorder from childhood through adulthood*. New York, NY: Touchstone.

Nisbett, R. E. (2010). *Intelligence and how to get it: Why schools and cultures count*. New York, NY: W. W. Norton.

Emotional Development in Middle Childhood

CHAPTER 11

Snapshot

Wu is 9 years old and a second-generation immigrant. His parents moved to San Francisco's Chinatown, where he was born, after leaving China for a better life. Wu's father died after his parents arrived in the United States. Now his single mother works hard not just to provide for him, but also to be as emotionally responsive as possible to his needs.

In this chapter, we will learn all about emotional development during middle childhood, and the milestones through which children develop, while taking into account issues such as race/ethnicity, class, and family structure such as Wu's.

What Can Erikson's Theory Tell Us About Needs in Middle Childhood?

We first encountered Erikson's (1963) theory of development in Chapter 1. We considered the first two stages of his theory (Trust–Mistrust and Autonomy–Shame and Doubt) in detail in Chapter 7, and his third stage of Initiative–Guilt during the preschool years in Chapter 9.

In this chapter we will explore his fourth stage, Industry–Inferiority, which corresponds to the school years or middle childhood, the stage of development that corresponds to approximately 7 to 12 years of age.

FIG. 11.1   Wu

Copyright © Depositphotos/sirikornt.

Industry–Inferiority

Just as the course of global history has had an "industrial age," the course of individual history has an "industrial" stage.

That is, Erikson proposed the crisis of middle childhood is **Industry–Inferiority**, a struggle between feeling capable and feeling inadequate. If children resolve this stage successfully, meaning they have more experiences of feeling capable and industrious than of feeling inadequate and inferior, they will leave this stage with a sense of competence.

Competence means we have the skills and/or knowledge necessary to do something successfully. If children don't resolve the Industry–Inferiority stage successfully, meaning they have more experiences of feeling inferior than of feeling competent, they will leave this stage with a sense of inertia.

Inertia is a tendency not to act, and to hesitate to try something—even when a person is capable of doing it, and doing it well. So inertia sways a person to give up easily, and competence sustains a person and motivates them to complete difficult projects. Endurance like this has consequences consistent with the multidimensional pattern of development.

For Erikson, if children leave middle childhood without successfully resolving the crisis of this stage because they did not develop mastery of something, they will feel inferior. These emotions then prevent them from using their physical and cognitive strengths, from being productive, and from expressing their true talents and interests.

Notice, too, the relationships here, which are consistent with the lifelong pattern of development: The successful resolution of the stage prior to Industry–Inferiority—that is, Initiative–Guilt—makes successful resolution of Industry–Inferiority more likely. Therefore, children who are curious and explore different play opportunities are more likely to later seek out different competence opportunities. For example, children show better physical health, academic outcomes, and emotional well-being when they participate in extracurricular activities such as sports, music, and art (Meier, Hartmann, & Larson, 2018).

Yet children's opportunities to discover and strengthen their competencies, via extracurricular activities, is unfortunately often a function of their family's resources. Although children from

Learning Goals

- ▸ Identify what Erikson's theory can tell us about school-age children's needs
- ▸ Describe how school-age children's emotion understanding can be best supported
- ▸ Illustrate how self-concept, self-resiliency, and self-esteem develop
- ▸ Explain how to best support gender-nonbinary children's needs
- ▸ Summarize how peers influence development in middle childhood
- ▸ Compare and contrast patterns in family structures during middle childhood
- ▸ Discuss the moral development of distributive justice in middle childhood

low-SES homes benefit most from participating in extracurricular lessons, clubs, and after-school activities, children from middle- and high-SES homes are more likely to participate in such (Heath, Anderson, Turner, & Payne, 2018; Meier, Hartmann, & Larson, 2018; Pew Research Center, 2015).

For example, Wu's mother is looking into an after-school art class for him, given his interest in drawing, especially because he is often on his own after school, riding his bike without supervision while she works as a house cleaner. But so far she hasn't been able to find an art class she can bring him to, much less afford.

Such a socioeconomic class gap is particularly discouraging for children in low resource areas. They are *more likely* to be at risk of participating in delinquent behavior and substance use yet *less likely* to participate in extracurricular activities. That is, although extracurricular activities have the potential to reduce inequalities, if schools and community organizations were better funded, such activities appear to be exacerbating inequalities instead—erring children frustratingly on the risk side of the risk–resilience pattern of development (Eisman et al., 2018; Meier, Hartmann, & Larson, 2018).

And the presence of some environmental factors can cripple competence. Family members and/or

FIG. 11.2   Wu on His Bike

friends may belittle children's initial attempts to gain mastery, perhaps because of their own failures.

Or, as Erikson has pointed out, family life may not have prepared a child for school life—a lack of discipline, reading, and/or of modeling good behavior at home can increase the likelihood that a child fails at school (Erikson, 1959). Indeed, adults must "prepare the child by teaching him things which first of all make him literate, the widest possible basic education for the greatest number of possible careers." (Erikson, 1963, p. 259).

The Nature and the Nurture of Competence

Educational achievement is one form of competence, yet it is not predicted completely by our level of intelligence.

In Chapter 3 we learned that according to behavioral geneticists, *heritability* refers to what portion of the differences among people, such as personality differences, is due to genes. Geneticists then assume that the remaining variation in these differences is due to environmental factors. The symbol used to represent heritability is h^2, and estimates can range from 0 to 1.0; the higher the score, the greater the genetic influence.

In terms of educational achievement during the school years, heritability estimates are approximately 0.60. This means that 60% of the individual differences we see in the school achievement of children are due to inherited differences in their DNA (Melchior & Hebebrand, 2018; Rimfield et al., 2018).

This tells us that these variables of school achievement and heritability are certainly related, but that they don't perfectly predict one another. Other factors (family support, family conflict, relationships with peers and teachers, and choice of interests—as well as exposure to different environments via differences in SES, minority status, and/or immigrant status) certainly come into play, which suggests that intelligence is rather malleable (Ho & Kao, 2018; Sauce & Matzel).

Also, remember that correlations cannot distinguish cause and effect. It may be that more intelligent people seek out more education, that more education and exposure to different experiences increase intelligence scores, or both.

Keep in mind, though, that intelligence tests often measure factors that reflect the test-taker's home or school context, such as whether they have been exposed to discussions of *Hamlet* and have learned the definition of *scintilla*. Although tests measuring such may be called intelligence tests, many of these assessments do not measure **aptitude**, or potential for learning, but measure achievement instead.

And we know that "nature versus nurture" is a false dichotomy because both concepts, and the interactions of the two, are involved in educational attainment and are necessary to development in general (Bates et al., 2018; Kong et al., 2018). The same holds for the roles of talent and practice in achieving competence. That is, children's skills are a result of their talents *interacting* with the extent to which their families have the means to allow them to devote time to deliberate practice in order to develop such talents and interests (N.V. Miller et al., 2018; Olszewski-Kubilius, 2018).

These interactions between genetics and environments take three different forms.

Passive Genetic × Environment (G × E) interactions occur when the family *environment* depends on the genetic parents' heredity. An example would be parents who provide a child with music lessons or books because they themselves have an inclination for playing an instrument or engaging in avid reading and writing, and do so within the home.

Of course, parents who are the genetic parents of their children also pass on their *genes* to the child. So any aspect of child development and adolescent development that is attributed to the environment (an environment created by their families) must also take into consideration the role of the child's genetic tendencies, such as children's own inclinations for playing a music instrument or reading and writing (van Bergen et al., 2017).

An **Evocative G × E interaction** occurs when a child's inclinations evoke a response in the environment, such as when a child shows a talent for singing so that the parents provide singing lessons, or when a child is an effortless storyteller and asks for puppets, causing the home collection of homemade or store-bought puppets to grow (van Bergen et al., 2017).

On the other hand, an **Active G × E interaction** occurs when children spend more time outside the home and actively seek out opportunities in those outside environments to express their genetic tendencies. Examples would be a child who is musically talented and chooses to join the hip-hop club, or a child who is verbally talented and chooses to join a creative writing club and publish their work.

Active G × E interactions are more likely during the school years and beyond. As we grow older, we have more control over the environments in which we place ourselves and the decisions we make within them (Sauce & Matzel, 2018).

Differential exposure to such environments (whether they be different exposures among siblings, among SES groups, across an individual's development, across generations due to immigration from a lower to a higher SES environment) and/or historical changes (such as the advent of the Internet and ready access to information) interact with our genes. This may be why intelligence varies both *among people* and *within people*, and why intelligence is fairly malleable and not completely heritable (Sauce & Matzel, 2018).

How Can School-Age Children's Emotion Understanding Be Best Supported?

Emotion understanding, or expertise in the meaning of emotion, requires both emotion recognition and emotion knowledge (Castro, Cheng, Halberstadt, & Grühn, 2016).

Emotion recognition includes the skills of noticing the emotions of others and of oneself (using visual, auditory, and bodily information, as well as contextual cues) and labeling these emotions.

Emotion knowledge includes comprehending the internal and external causes of emotions, the consequences and functions of emotions, and cultural rules and norms regarding emotions—and managing one's emotions. Recall the idea of *emotional regulation* or what we learned in Chapter 7 is the multidimensional process of modifying our emotional experiences along with the physical reactions that underlie them—in order to transform them into an adaptive state of mind (Castro et al., 2016).

In this section, we discuss both aspects of emotion understanding, along with emotion socialization and emotional competence.

Emotion Recognition

Children tend to learn to recognize emotions from the easiest to noticing the most subtle or indefinite, in a sequence of happy, angry, sad, disgusted, surprised, and scared (Gu et al., 2019; Sidera, Amadó, & Martínez, 2017). This sequence is the same for both typically developing children and children with hearing impairments, although the latter group of children tend to be somewhat delayed in learning the sequence from facial cues (perhaps because of less experience participating in conversations with others and/or impairments in visual processing). More research is needed to better understand if children with hearing impairments need more assistance and what those needs may be (Gu et al., 2019; Sidera, Amadó, & Martínez, 2017).

Experience does make a difference. Data show that the accuracy of recognizing vocal emotions increases from middle childhood to adolescence (Chronaki et al., 2018; Wang, Y., et al., 2019). Interestingly, other research finds that individuals who are deaf signers are *more* accurate at recognizing happy faces than are hearing nonsigners and are *less* accurate at recognizing angry faces than are hearing nonsigners, likely because of deaf signers' lifelong experience of focusing on the mouth region (Dobel et al., 2019).

Children who grow up in poverty show equal accuracy in labeling emotions of high intensity compared to children who did not grow up in poverty. Yet they show less accuracy in labeling emotions of regular intensity, perhaps because the poverty-related adversity (such as needing to move often,

FIG. 11.3   Wu Feeling Sad

not being able to pay bills, being exposed to conflict, going hungry) is a chronic stressor that depletes a child's adrenal glands (Erhart et al., 2019).

Keep in mind that such depletion is magnified given their families' circumstances. This means they may be at greater risk for experiencing parents who may not be as sensitive and emotionally available to them as they would like. Also, they may attend schools of poorer quality that may not teach emotion understanding. All of this puts children more on the risk side of the risk–resilience pattern of development (Erhart et al., 2019).

Emotion recognition, particularly in face-to-face interactions, is difficult for children on the autism spectrum, as it also is for children with intellectual disabilities (such as Down Syndrome), especially when contextual information is provided to them (Golan et al., 2018; Murray et al., 2019). That is, typically developing children are more accurate in recognizing emotions when there is more visual information available, as in an image of a child opening a birthday present and looking happy. Children with intellectual disabilities perform worse when more visual information is available—they are instead more accurate in recognizing emotions from simple line drawings, as in a simple smiley face (Golan et al., 2018; Murray et al., 2019). Such findings are consistent with the multidimensional pattern of development, in which emotional development is interrelated with cognitive development.

Negative correlations between emotion recognition and problem behaviors (such as internalizing and externalizing behaviors) have been found in typically developing school-age children, and a recent longitudinal study was able to distinguish the chicken from the egg in these relationships. That is, researchers established developmental pathways in their data when they found that lower levels of emotion recognition in first grade predicted internalizing behaviors in third grade, and that greater hyperactivity in first grade predicted lower emotion recognition in third grade (Castro et al., 2018). So helping child manage their emotions, along with understanding their emotions, supports their well-being.

For a discussion of if and how apps can help children who are struggling with internalizing disorders such as anxiety, see the *Tech & Media: Apps for Child Anxiety* box.

Tech & Media

Apps for Child Anxiety

Apps for devices such as smartphones and tablets have the potential to increase the reach of mental health care for everyone. Apps that are designed with a game format may be especially helpful to children, particularly those who struggle with issues such as anxiety and who are reluctant or unable to seek help otherwise.

While an abundance of such apps have been industry-developed, not nearly as many have been developed by researchers, nor are many supported with empirical evidence regarding their effectiveness.

In fact, an inventory of the apps for child anxiety that are available on Google Play and Apple Store revealed that few of these apps were evidence-based. This makes their effectiveness questionable (Bry et al., 2018).

However, one app, SmartCAT 2.0—in which children practice cognitive behavioral therapy (CBT) skills outside their sessions with a therapist (who is connected to the app via a portal that allows secure two-way communication within it)—has proven quite effective.

Researchers studied children between 9 and 14 years of age who were diagnosed with some type of anxiety disorder, participated in brief 8-week CBT, and used the app approximately 5 minutes each day. At the end of the 8-week study, the researchers found that children showed better emotion identification, that 67% of the children no longer met the diagnostic criteria for an anxiety disorder, and that this percentage increased to 86% at a 2-month follow-up period.

These findings indicate that a well-designed app has the potential to reach children whose families may not otherwise have access to CBT or other mental health services. More research is needed on whether apps such as this can be as effective without therapy for those who do not have access to such (Silk et al., 2019).

FIG. 11.4   The SmartCAT App

Source: https://www.innovation.pitt.edu/wp-content/uploads/2018/10/4271_smartcat_silk.pdf.

Emotion Knowledge

We know that emotion knowledge—that is, comprehending the internal and external causes of emotions, the consequences and functions of emotions, and cultural rules and norms regarding emotions; and managing one's emotions—is one component of emotion understanding. And we know that it develops over time.

During the preschool years, emotion knowledge in general is related to children having more positive emotions (Ferrier et al., 2018). The correlates of emotion knowledge during the school years are even greater. That is, the stronger a kindergartner's emotion knowledge—in combination with high levels of theory of mind—the greater their social skills, emotional skills, behavioral adjustment, and academic adjustment (Brock et al., 2019).

And there continue to be positive relationships between emotion knowledge and academic performance and peer relationships through age 12, indicating that understanding the causes and consequences of emotions, the cultural norms regarding emotions, and the importance of managing one's emotions continues to be a necessary skill during all of the school years (Voltmer & von Salisch, 2017).

Pan & Zoom

The Role of Culture in the Correlates of Emotion Knowledge

In this box, we pan across or take a brief but wide-angle panoramic view of the role of culture in the correlates of emotion knowledge. Why? Because although emotion knowledge is associated with greater well-being in some children, it isn't associated with such in all children.

Longitudinal research with European American children and immigrant Chinese children in the United States (like Wu) reveals that when children are 3.5 years of age, those with *higher* levels of emotion knowledge show *lower* levels of internalizing problems when they are 7 years of age. But this is only true for European American children. Chinese immigrant children with *higher* levels of emotion knowledge showed *higher* levels of internalizing problems when they were 7 years of age (Doan & Wang, 2018).

Researchers Doan and Wang speculate that a value of European American culture seems to be for parents to coach their children to be emotionally intelligent and for parents to validate their children's emotional expressions. Perhaps this approach is taken to ensure that their children's emotional needs are met, and that the children are better able to discern social situations and/or negotiate interacting with others.

On the other hand, directing children's attention to their inner subjective experiences is contrary to a Chinese value of social harmony and the interests of groups over the interests of individuals. So emotion knowledge in Chinese immigrant children within the United States may put them at risk of social shaming and criticism within their in-culture familial and social groups, which understandably could increase their feelings or depression and/or anxiety (Doan & Wang, 2018).

This study helps us consider the complexity of immigrant children's experiences, but it doesn't tell the entire story. Interindividual differences certainly exist within cultures, in that not everyone adheres to their culture's norm to the same degree. Longitudinal studies that follow children for a greater number of years, as they acclimate to a new culture that values emotion knowledge, will help shed light on whether emotion knowledge is still counterproductive as children become more acculturated or bicultural.

Additionally, much more research is needed on children who aren't European American and/or on children who are immigrants but from cultures other than that of China.

• • • •

How Do Self-Concept, Self-Resiliency, and Self-Esteem Develop?

When asked to describe himself, Wu often talks about being in third grade, how he does okay in school, how he tries to be kind, and how he is either really liked or ignored by others except a few bullies.

Wu's description of himself may or may not be accurate, but it is developmentally consistent with that of a school-age child. Why? Read ahead.

Self-Concept

Self-concept refers to the set of traits we use to describe ourselves. Between 8 and 11 years of age, children begin to describe themselves with fewer physical traits and with more psychological ones, like "athletic," "clumsy," "smart," "dumb," "nice," and "mean." Such changes are consistent with the multidimensional pattern of development in which physical, cognitive, and emotional development are interrelated.

School-age children also are more likely to see themselves in terms of group memberships, so they may name their school, their grade, their race/ethnicity, and/or the language(s) they speak. School-age children's self-concepts are also more realistic than those of preschoolers, likely because of the feedback they receive regarding themselves, such as academic grades and comparisons with peers

FIG. 11.5   Wu Thinking about Himself and Others

at school. Self-concept differentiates into types (such as school, physical appearance, athletic ability, and peer acceptance) with increasing age too.

Competencies that grow in one domain can offset weaknesses in another—if not also improve those weaknesses. For instance, among children who have stronger peer relationships and who are struggling readers at the beginning of the school year, those with greater **resiliency**, or the capacity to adapt despite adversity, show greater academic achievement three years later (Liew et al., 2018; Masten, 2019).

Such a pattern suggests that a component of resilience is the ability to problem-solve and work with others. Classrooms structured to have children learn from one another by working in pairs or in small groups could help move children to the resilience side of the risk–resilience pattern of development. Such classroom structures benefit children academically and socially by first empowering them with problem-solving skills and other necessary ingredients of resiliency.

Remember from Chapter 1, however, that resiliency is not simply a product of individual differences within a child or a teen. Resiliency is a product of that individual child's or teen's genetic tendencies interacting with environmental conditions, including how equitable or inequitable the society is (Burman, 2016; Liew, Cao, Hughes, & Deutz, 2018).

Self-Resiliency (It Takes a Village)

Competence and achievement are often thought to be limited to children's innate differences in intelligence, resiliency, and **grit**—or the inclination to pursue long-term goals with passion and perseverance. However, it is important to remember a proverb from many African cultures: "It takes a village to raise a child" (Park et al., 2018). That is, a child needs others to help them develop intelligence, resiliency, and grit.

The research data support this notion that others are closely involved. For example, self-regulation is transmitted intergenerationally. Thus, a child's genetic inclinations will interact with an environment of chronic stress and therefore interfere with the neurobiological mechanisms that foster the development of their brain's frontal lobe and corresponding executive function (Bridgett et al., 2015; Loe, Adams, & Feldman, 2019).

Dysregulation, or the inability to adjust our physical arousal as caused by strong emotions, is a greater risk for children living in chronic stress and/or with insecure attachment bonds to their parents. This leaves children with a range of negative outcomes associated with the polydirectional and lifelong patterns of development, including greater friendship difficulties, less educational attainment, lower employment, and greater job loss (McQuillan et al., 2018).

In Chapter 8, we discussed the necessity of praising *effort* over *outcome*. This distinction is parallel to whether a family or school context encourages performance goals or mastery goals. Such goals play a role in a child's degree of grit—and therefore their movement toward the risk or the resiliency side of the risk–resilience pattern of development.

What are these two different goals that are children are taught? Well, some children may be encouraged to have **performance goals**, in which they are given messages about valuing primarily others' perceptions of their capability on a task. Others may be encouraged to have **mastery goals**, in which they are given messages about valuing curiosity and learning new things. Children who perceive

FIG. 11.6   Wu's Mother Helping Him with His Homework

Copyright © Depositphotos/sirikornt.

their schools as more mastery-oriented show more grit, and interestingly, higher report card grades over time too (Park et al., 2018).

Longitudinal research reveals outcomes associated with children having these different types of goals as a product of the different types of praise they receive, types that are consistent with Chapter 8's distinction between praising effort and praising outcome. Specifically, children who receive relatively more **process praise**, or praise directed at *the child's behavior* ("You worked hard at this" or "That was the right way to do it"), rather than **person praise**, or praise directed at *the child's intelligence* ("You are smart" or "You are good at this"), are more likely to appreciate that their intelligence is malleable rather than fixed, and subsequently show higher academic achievement (Gunderson et al., 2018).

Remember, resiliency is not merely the resources a child (or an adult) can muster alone by simply "trying harder." Resiliency is a product of interrelated systems of praise—plus other concrete forms of support from families, communities, and national policies.

The resiliency of all people will grow with greater prevention and elimination of inequity, via economic redistribution policies that change the narrative from some children not possessing a coveted personality trait that helps them "beat the odds," to a narrative instead of society "changing the odds" (Masten, 2019; Seccombe, 2004).

For an interactive demonstration of how policy decisions influence outcomes for children and their families, see *Tipping the Scales: The Resilience Game* by Harvard's Center for the Developing Child, listed in the *Helpful Websites* section at the end of this chapter.

Whereas self-concept is domain-specific, **self-esteem**, or one's subjective evaluation of self-worth, is domain-general. It used to be thought that declines in self-esteem occur from early childhood to middle childhood as children begin to make *social comparisons*. That is, unlike preschool age children, school age children begin to evaluate themselves relative to others in school (often via grades or other performance assessments); they gain perspective-taking skills so that they realize their ideal performance on any given task is not their actual performance; and they think hierarchically about global self-worth that supersedes all of their areas of self-concept, such as "I (don't) like myself." (Harter, 2012; Orth, Erol, & Luciano, 2018).

Yet a meta-analysis of longitudinal research studies on self-esteem from ages 4 to 94 indicates that self-esteem indeed *increases* from early childhood to middle childhood, then stabilizes in adolescence—all regardless of ethnicity, gender, country, and generation (Orth, Erol, & Luciano, 2018). While these increases might initially strike us as an age effect or as changes with age, they may really be an example of the cohort or generational difference that we learned about in Chapter 2. That is, people born after 1960 tend to have higher self-esteem and were more likely to experience increases in self-esteem as they aged, perhaps as a function of context, in that U.S. culture began to emphasize self-esteem in recent generations (Twenge, Carter, & Campbell, 2017).

In this section, we have learned about different aspects of the self. Now we will consider how school-age children define themselves in terms of their gender identity.

How Can We Best Support Gender-Nonbinary Children's Needs?

In Chapter 9, we learned quite a bit about gender typing and gender identity, and about *preschool* children who are gender nonbinary and/or transgender. Relatively less is known about *school-age* children who are gender nonbinary and/or transgender. In this section, we consider the most recently available research on these children and their needs.

Compared to cisgender school-age children, gender-nonbinary school-age children are more likely to struggle with depressive disorders and attention-deficit disorders, perhaps related to the distress of their assigned gender at birth not matching their identity, as well as the prejudice and discrimination they often experience (Becerra-Culqui et al., 2018). Such struggles are an unfortunate example of the multidimensional pattern of development in which a child's feeling and thoughts do not match their assigned physical gender.

Research on adults' attitudes toward gender-nonbinary youth is worrisome too, especially given adults' potential as role models and decision-makers. In a study in the United States, adults who were most likely to have negative attitudes toward transgender youth were those who are politically conservative, endorse a belief in a gender binary, and believe that the causes of being transgender are environmental rather than biological (Elischberger et al., 2018).

In comparison, study participants in India who were most likely to have negative attitudes toward transgender youth were those who are religiously conservative and believe that the causes of being transgender are environmental rather than biological. A belief in a gender binary did not play much

FIG. 11.7   Wu and His Friend Peter

Copyright © Depositphotos/sirikornt.

of a role. It is interesting to note that believing in a gender binary was not an issue in this study's sample from India, where they have a *hijra* community of individuals legally recognized as a third gender (Elischberger, Glazier, Hill, & Verduzco-Baker, 2018).

Research on children's attitudes toward gender-nonbinary youth is hopeful. Consistent with the own-gender bias often seen at this age, school-age cisgender children do not strongly dislike their nonbinary peers—instead, they tend to most prefer their cisgender peers who share their gender; then next they most prefer their nonbinary peers who share their gender, such as Wu's friend Peter who was assigned the female gender at birth but prefers to dress as and identifies as a boy (Gülgöz et al., 2018).

One study with children who participated in an arts-based after-school program found that at the end of the program, the children had more positive attitudes towards gender-expansive children (Vilkin et al., 2019). To learn more about the specifics of this particular arts-based program, see the *Cycle of Science* feature at the end of this chapter.

Clearly, peers play a role in the well-being of gender-nonbinary and/or transgender children. Let's consider now, though, how peers generally influence development for all children.

How Do Peers Influence Development in Middle Childhood?

The transition from early childhood to middle childhood means a child's contexts grow in number, and in influence. In this section, we look at peers.

Peer Relationships

A **peer** is an age mate, or a child of approximately the same age. Peer relationships provide children with interpersonal resources, such as emotional support. These relationships may alter the way children treat and are treated by other children, and they may socialize children to develop certain strengths and/or vulnerabilities, such as peer acceptance or bullying. This is especially applicable during a time in which social influences on the attachment bond between the child and their parents broadens (Waters et al., 2015).

Indeed, the more children and adolescents perceive their classmates to be supportive, the less likely they are to be involved in bullying and other forms of violent behavior occur. This protective relationship has been found in various countries, including Estonia, Latvia, Lithuania, Moldova, Russia, and Ukraine (Šmigelskas et al., 2018).

In order to socialize with their peers, school-age children need to be friendly, interact with others, share, and be cooperative—just like preschool-age children. Yet school-age children must also increasingly engage in complex play—with rules that require them to self-regulate, as well as use perspective-taking and think about other individuals. Research shows that compared to the preschool years, the school years are a time when children are more likely to give more to the children they like—and also give more to unlucky others (Flook, Zahn-Waxler, & Davidson, 2019).

We will have more to say about children's thinking in regard to justice in the distribution of resources at the end of this chapter, in the section on distributive justice. For now, let's get back to those whom children like.

In contrast to preschool-age children (who seem to value similarity more), school-age children are more likely to value proximity and loyalty of friends and to value mutual liking. Mutual liking describes a reciprocity that is linked to greater self-worth—along with trust, emotional intimacy, affection, and companionship—as the basis of their friendships (Beazidou & Botsoglou, 2016; Liberman & Shaw, 2019; Maunder & Monks, 2019).

Compared to mutual liking, peer acceptance (as a basis for peer status) is more unilateral and may not be reciprocated (Beazidou & Botsoglou, 2016; Liberman & Shaw, 2019; Maunder & Monks, 2019). We'll address this important topic next.

Peer Status

Sociometric nominations measure children's status among other children, or their peer status. Numerous studies on peer acceptance have confirmed that there are five peer statuses, which are based on how children perceive other children's behavior and how they perceive their teachers to perceive other children's behavior: Popular, Controversial, Rejected, Neglected, and Average (Hendrickx et al., 2017; van der Wilt et al., 2018).

Although these statuses are a common way to measure social competence, keep in mind that they are not the only method. Also, this method has some weaknesses, such as how the paradigm forces children's profiles to fit into mutually exclusive categories and how popular children may also be deviant (Kulawiak & Wilbert, 2019).

Compared to **Average children**, who are liked and also disliked, **Popular children** are very well liked, have superior social problem-solving skills, more often engage in positive peer interactions with strong cooperativeness and supportiveness, and show low aggression (Lonigro et al., 2018; van der Wilt et al., 2018).

Neglected children are neither liked nor disliked, and are not terribly aggressive nor sociable, whereas **Controversial children** are both very much liked and very much disliked in that they are as sociable as Popular children, but are as aggressive as or more aggressive than Rejected children (Kulawiak & Wilbert, 2019; van der Wilt et al., 2018).

Rejected children are not liked, and they can be withdrawn, unsociable, submissive, aggressive, and/or disruptive. They are more likely to be diagnosed with ADHD and/or other difficulties in learning (Grygiel et al., 2018; Krull, Wilbert, & Hennemann, 2018; McDonald & Asher, 2018; van der Wilt et al., 2019). Rejected children are also more likely to show poor communication skills in that they are least likely to anticipate the needs of their listener and are least likely to be able to frame their requests to others in a way that takes into consideration the needs of others (Grygiel et al., 2018; Krull, Wilbert, & Hennemann, 2018; McDonald & Asher, 2018; van der Wilt et al., 2019).

In addition to children with learning difficulties, children with visible physical disabilities (such as needing to use a wheelchair) and children from migrant families are at higher risk of being rejected by peers. Yet research shows that such children are more likely to be socially accepted when teachers respond positively to them. This underscores how important it is for teachers to be mindful of how much positive feedback they give (Huber et al., 2018)

All children can benefit from more opportunities to practice and be praised for prosocial behaviors, especially in light of research showing that children with a low social standing are more at risk for later depression and aggression if their degree of prosocial behavior does not change over time. Research has shown no increased risk of later depression and aggression for those children who are of low social standing but do engage in more prosocial behaviors (inviting other children to play, comforting a crying or sad peer, helping others, etc.) over time (He et al., 2018).

Bullying

Bullying is aggressive behavior that is intended to hurt others. It is a behavior that tends to be engaged in repeatedly, and via a power imbalance in which it is difficult for victims to defend themselves (Ettekal & Ladd, 2017; Smith, 2016).

Not all aggressive behaviors constitute bullying; but because bullying is aggressive, it is a type of aggression. The key distinction between aggression and bullying is the power differential between the bully and the victim, as well as the repetition of the aggressive behavior.

Bullying takes various forms, including *physical, verbal, relational,* and *cyber* or electronic bullying (we will have more to say about cyber bullying in Chapter 13).

These forms are not mutually exclusive, so any child who is engaging in bullying behavior may use more than one form at any given time, and/or over time. Although there are always exceptions, a child who becomes an aggressor will typically use more than one form of bullying. These forms may change with age, so that an early-school-age child who is physically aggressive is likely to become a late-school-age child who is verbally aggressive, and then an adolescent who is relationally, then an adult who bullies family members and/or co-workers (Ettekal & Ladd, 2017; Smith, 2016).

Children who identify as female tend to be victims of *verbal and relational bullying,* as a result of exposure to verbal and relational bullying, and they tend to exhibit internalizing symptoms and negative expectations toward their teachers. Thus, the consequences of being bullied are not negligible; in fact, as we will see in in the next few paragraphs, they can be devastating (Marengo et al., 2019).

Children who identify as male tend to be the victims of *physical bullying*, as a result of exposure to physical bullying, and they tend to exhibit externalizing symptoms as well as conflict with their teachers (Marengo et al., 2019).

Consistent with the polydirectional pattern of development, if children are to engage in bullying, they typically do so by approximately 7 or 8 years of age. This behavior peaks around the time of school transitions in which peer groups are re-evaluated, and it tends to decline in the later school years (Ettekal & Ladd, 2017; Smith, 2016).

Yet with the possibility of their bullying behavior cropping up again in adolescence and adulthood, and because adults are most likely to bully others at the workplace, bullying prevention programs are likely needed at all stages in development (Ettekal & Ladd, 2017; Smith, 2016).

Unfortunately, bullying occurs against others based on group characteristics, such as against children who identify as nonwhite, female, of a sexual minority, gender expansive, or non–English-speaking at home. For instance, children with disabilities are both more likely to become victims of bullying (particularly if the disability with which they struggle is observable), and more likely to become perpetrators, perhaps because their social skills and/or friendships tend to be of lower quality (Smith, 2016).

Children (and adults) who are bullied are at greater risk of depression, anxiety, paranoid thoughts, and other mental health problems, as well as physical and economic problems through adulthood (Arsenault, 2018). Children who are sexual minority and/or gender expansive are at significantly higher risk for cyberbullying, and as a result, are at significantly higher risk for depression, suicidal ideation, suicidal attempt, low self-esteem, isolation, an inability to concentrate at school, and being less likely to receive support from their families when they tell them, as compared to their hetero-sexual peers (Abreu & Kenny, 2017; Singham et al., 2017; Smith, 2016).

To help children err on the resilience side of the risk–resilience pattern of development, bullying prevention programs specific to queer students are especially needed, as well as general bullying prevention programs (Abreu & Kenny, 2017). It has been suggested that involving students in the delivery of antibullying information may increase students' awareness of the problem and simul-taneously decrease bullying behaviors (Abreu & Kenny, 2017). Additionally, pediatricians are in a unique position to foster inclusive and affirming care with their queer patients, and to advocate for developmentally appropriate antibullying prevention programs in all schools—as well as mandates for schools to report and intervene in bullying incidents (Casper & Card, 2017; Earnshaw et al., 2017).

How Are Families Similar To and Different From One Another?

Children's peer networks grow in middle childhood as a result of meeting new children at school and outside activities. But family dynamics still very much influence development during middle childhood.

In this section, we consider different types of families, as well as international similarities and differences among families.

Family Structure

As children move through middle childhood and feel the strengthening influence of peers, the influence of family becomes weaker, but certainly not negligible.

These two contexts are also related, because parents' practices later influence their children's choice of peers and the children's interactions with peers (Dickson et al., 2018). Remember that families come in all shapes and sizes: Some families have multiple children, whereas other families have one child; some families are *extended* or multigenerational, a practice that may be a cultural tradition and/or an economic strategy that allows a family to avoid the costs of care outside the home for members of all ages (Amorim, 2019).

Some families are *single-parent* or are headed by a single parent who may be a biological parent, an adoptive parent, or a grandparent. These families tend to be economically vulnerable.

Like Wu, who sometimes needs to help his mother after work, such single-parent families may teach their children discipline early on. They may also need their children to take on adult responsibilities prematurely in order to contribute to the family income, thereby causing those children to miss out on childhood opportunities (Cancian & Meyer, 2018).

And because the current system of private child support to be paid by a noncustodial parent (who is assumed to be of the middle class and to have a stable job) often leaves children with divorced parents to live in poverty, some have called for a public (rather than private) guarantee of child support (Cancian & Meyer, 2018).

FIG. 11.8   Wu Helping His Mother with Work

Some families are *blended*, in that the children are related genetically to one parent but not necessarily to the other parents. The parents of a blended family may or may not be married to each other yet have formed a new family together as a result of divorce from or the death of their former partner.

Children in blended families may struggle with loss of their other parent, the loss of their former family structure, and/or confusion about their roles if the new blended family has poorly defined boundaries. It is in the best interests of the children in a blended family for all of their parents to establish parenting agreements, with everyone's roles and expectations defined clearly (Kumar, 2017).

Like all families, blended families may benefit from counseling. This is particularly true if a divorce preceded the created of the blended family and the divorce was contentious. Research shows that although children may adjust quite well after a divorce, the divorce experience can be traumatic to them (van der Wal, Finkenauer, & Visser, 2019).

Some families are led by two parents, who may or may not be in a long-term committed relationship, and who may be opposite-sex or same-sex. Children in families with same-sex parents may be biologically related to them or not. Adopted children with same-sex parents are similar to adopted children with opposite-sex parents in that many of their families have regular contact with the birth families (Farr, Ravvina, & Grotevant, 2018b).

Also, whether they were adopted or not, children with same-sex (two mothers or two fathers) parents are highly similar to their peers with opposite-sex parents, and they are no more likely to be queer or gender-nonconforming (Farr et al., 2018a; Golombok et al., 2018; Patterson, 2017). Instead, studies show that children's adjustment is influenced more by *family processes* (such as the quality of the relationship with the parents) than by the *family structure* (Patterson, 2017).

Some families are *immigrant families* in which one or more of a child's parents were not, at the time of their child's birth, citizens of the country in which their child was born. The United States has more immigrants than any other country, and more than 75% of immigrants in the United States are lawful immigrants and citizens. The remainder are unauthorized immigrants or temporary residents—the latter because they are refugees persecuted in their home country for their religious views, political views, or race; because of work; or because of family (Radford, 2019). The top three countries from which immigrants came to the United States in recent years are India, Mexico, and China (Radford, 2019).

In addition to their right to high-quality health care, immigrant children have a right to dignity, to respect, and to not be exposed to conditions that could harm and/or (re-)traumatize them. According to the American Association of Pediatrics, the facilities of the Department of Homeland Security do not meet basic standards of care for children (Linton, Griffin, Shapiro, and Council on Community Pediatrics, 2017; Linton, Kennedy, Shapiro, & Griffin, 2018).

Trauma occurs before migration (especially for children living in countries with violence, war, and genocide), as well as during migration, and these two forms of trauma can further threaten children's health and well-being.

So a zero tolerance immigration policy that separates children from their families upon their entrance the United States—and which keeps them in detention centers for months at a time while making it difficult for relatives to reunite with their children after the U.S. government claims custody of them—has the potential to damage children's physical, cognitive, and emotional well-being throughout their lives. This must be stopped immediately (Linton et al., 2018; Muñiz de la Pēna, Pineda, & Punsky, 2019).

In the meantime, an array of medical, psychological, and legal service providers is needed to help build resilience in these children who have been mistreated—and through no fault of their own. To learn more about an organization dedicated to doing so, and for information on how to get involved, visit the website of Terra Firma, listed in the *Helpful Websites* section at the end of this chapter.

And to learn about a psychologist at Terra Firma who works with unaccompanied immigrant children, see *A Mentor Minute: Cristina Muñiz de la Pēna, PhD*.

Cristina Muñiz de la Pēna, PhD

1) Describe your work, please.

I am a psychologist at the Center for Child Health and Resiliency (CCHR) [in the Bronx, New York City] and mental health director and cofounder of the Terra Firma program. The CCHR is an outpatient healthcare clinic from the Montefiore Medical Center's network that provides primary care and mental health services to the South Bronx Community. As a psychologist in this clinic, I provide psychotherapy to children and adults. The Terra Firma program is an integrated, collocated model of care where unaccompanied immigrant children (UIC) receive medical, mental health, and legal services to help them adjust, heal, and achieve legal status. My role as cofounder and mental health (MH) director is to design and implement psychological inter-ventions that are appropriate and sensitive to the MH needs of UIC and their families in coordination with the medical and legal needs.

FIG. 11.9 Cristina Muñiz de la Pēna, PhD

As part of my role, I provide individual, family, and group psychother-apy which addresses the psycho-social needs associated with resettlement and acculturation while also addressing the present impact of past trauma and the immigration process as a source of chronic stress. In this sense, my role involves assessing and addressing the immigration legal process in session, coordi-nating with the legal team, and providing support in the case of documentation or testimony. Over the years, our unique expertise in working with UIC has led to our involvement in advocacy work outside our program. For example, I have been part of the APA immigration work group; I published a report on UIC with this group; I have provided trainings and consultation to other healthcare professionals, legal agen-cies, the APA, and other institutions that work with UIC; and I testified in Congress about the impact of parent–child separation at the border.

2) How does social justice inform your work?

Social justice is at the basis of all my work. It is the core belief that we are all born deserving love and equal opportunity for and access to resources, and yet we live in a society in which the system is set up so that only some have more access than others. Social justice informs my work in that I am aware of my own privilege and sources of oppression, and it promotes an attitude of ongoing reflection about my power, my minority status, and my level of awareness, all [of which] determine the quality of my work and my impact in the world.

3) How did you become involved in social justice and/or advocacy?

As a graduate student, and also as an international student outside the comfort of my cultural environ-ment, I started learning about myself and the world. I soon became aware of how the serendipity of my being born in Spain as a White, abled, straight, cisgender woman afforded me certain opportunities and privileges and some areas of oppression, which are in no way based on just, reasonable, or earned-based systems. I soon started realizing the injustice of this system and how each of us contributes with our unawareness and inaction. I soon got involved in initiatives to learn and reflect on my own identity and to promote social justice on campus and in the world. I co-created the "multicultural student coalition" with other peers, which aimed at encouraging self-reflection and awareness of power dynamics within our-selves and with others. These experiences were a shift in my understanding of myself and the world, and encouraged me to think about the role I want and can play in this unjust system with an advanced degree in psychology and the power this affords. Therefore, I have henceforward sought out opportunities to use my power to advocate for people's rights, to call out injustices, to empower others, and to promote awareness of these issues. Since graduation, I have worked with underserved children and adults in Spain and the United States. Since the inception of Terra Firma, I have focused my efforts on working with immigrant children and asylum seekers of all ages.

4) What are your thoughts on how social justice can improve child and adolescent development?
Social justice is the necessary lens through which every aspect of society should be organized, because it's the required element that would ensure all children have equal access and opportunity. Since environment plays such a crucial role in development, social justice becomes the required ingredient to allow children to have the necessary resources for the development of their utmost potential.

5) What suggestions do you have for undergraduate students who are interested in making a change in child and adolescent development?
The very first and most important recommendation is to take any opportunity through college and after to get to know themselves, their own developments, their experiences that shaped them to be who they are and, very specifically, the areas of their identities and the social groups they belong to which afforded power and privilege or which led to experiences of oppression and discrimination. One of the most crucial opportunities for me was studying abroad and travelling in general. I did my undergraduate in Spain, my home country, but I studied one year abroad in the Netherlands and had my very first experience outside my comfort zone. This experience was very fun but also very difficult as I sort of lost the safety structure that helped me know who I am and how to behave. After this, I realized I needed/wanted to study abroad more and so I sought out scholarships and programs to help me study abroad again after college. I got a scholarship to study at Wesleyan University in Bloomington, Illinois, for a year, and after that I got accepted to the doctoral program in Counseling Psychology at SUNY in Albany, New York. Once you step out of your cultural context and the immediate structure of your family and support system, you gain a certain perspective and have access to an array of experiences (both hard and wonderful), which help you learn about yourself and the world in ways that you would likely not otherwise, if you remained in your surroundings.

Also, engaging in individual therapy whenever I struggled, or whenever I wanted to challenge myself to grow, has been an ongoing practice to this day. Similarly, any trainings, workshops, classes, and experiences that seemed like opportunities to learn about human beings and about myself have been very important to help me understand what children and human beings need. Certainly, having as many experiences with children as possible will provide a direct perspective to what you then read and learn in the child development textbooks.

• • • •

International Similarities and Differences Among Families

Do parents influence their children in the same ways across different countries? And do children influence their parents in the same ways across different countries? Cross-cultural research can help us answer these questions. One study found that the answer was yes.

That is, the more that parents in China, Colombia, Italy, Jordan, Kenya, the Philippines, Sweden, Thailand, and the United States are accepting of their children (such as agreeing strongly with "I make my child feel wanted and needed" and disagreeing strongly with "My child is a nuisance for me"), the more prosocially their children behave and try to help others (Putnick et al., 2018).

Another study with families from these same countries found that the more that families experience material deprivation (being unable to pay for necessities, such as food and housing), the more parents are likely to engage in psychological aggression and shame, to threaten, or to ignore their children, and their children are therefore more likely to display externalizing behaviors (Schenck-Fontaine et al., 2018).

These patterns are similar for families from high-income countries and families from middle-income and low-income countries. This suggests that the consequences of material deprivation may be universal rather than culture-specific (Schenck-Fontaine et al., 2018).

Also seemingly universal is how children's behavior affects parents.

That is, in these same nine countries, the more that children engage in externalizing or internalizing behaviors, the *less* likely their parents are to be warm and the *more* likely they are to be controlling. This tells us that theories such as Baumrind's (1971), covered in Chapter 9—which posit a major role for parent warmth and control, and the subsequent consequences for children—are relevant across many very different cultural groups (Lansford et al., 2018).

Additionally, research that includes the aforementioned countries along with a host of others (among them Ghana, Australia, Greece, Egypt, Russia, Mexico, Cameroon, Brazil, Poland, and Saudi Arabia) shows that although Authoritarian parenting is more culturally normative in some cultures than in others, Authoritative parenting is best for most children. The Authoritative approach is associated with fewer internalizing and externalizing problems, and this pattern holds true for Asian, African, European, and Hispanic families (Pinquart & Kauser, 2018).

These findings do not mean that cultural differences in caregiving simply do not exist or that they are not important. Still, as some have suggested, so far there is no evidence to suggest that developmental processes function differently between cultures or between dominant and minority groups (Causadias & Cicchetti, 2018; Causadias, Korous, & Cahill, 2018).

How Does the Moral Development of Distributive Justice Occur in Middle Childhood?

Throughout this book, we have considered how inequity, including economic inequity, influences children's development. Yet inequity is also something that children begin to think about carefully.

What is most often considered fair to school-age children seems to be **distributive justice**, which Prilleltensky (2012, p. 6) defines as "the fair and equitable allocation of burdens and privileges, rights and responsibilities, and pains and gains in society" (see also Engelmann & Tomasello, 2019; Ruck, Mistry, & Flanagan, 2019). This understanding varies by children's own backgrounds, though.

Although injustices and *structural causes*, rather than *individual causes*, of inequity are something with which children are increasingly able to grapple as they grow older, children's sense of distributive justice is associated with their background (McLoyd, 2019; Rogers, 2019; Ruck, Mistry, & Flanagan, 2019). That is, children from lower-income homes tend to be less aware of barriers to equal opportunity, while being more likely to attribute poverty, unemployment, and homelessness to *individual causes*, such as insufficient motivation, rather than *structural causes*, such as restricted opportunities (McLoyd, 2019; Rogers, 2019; Ruck, Mistry, & Flanagan, 2019).

Perhaps because their schools tend to be of poorer quality and therefore less able to teach children to think critically about government investments in social programs or lack thereof, the children who are *most* likely to be disadvantaged by restricted opportunities are *least* likely to question such. Yet these restricted opportunities mean their lives tend to err more on the risk side of the risk–resilience pattern of development.

Interestingly, when children are told a hypothetical story in which they can sit on a school bus seat with only one other person—either a child who lives in a rundown house or a child from another school—school-age children compared to preschool-age children feel worse about excluding someone who is disadvantaged than they feel about excluding someone from another school (Dys et al., 2019; Elenbaas & Killen, 2016; Malti et al., 2016).

School-age children are also more likely than preschool-age children to consider the needs of a recipient when allocating resources, and to rectify inequalities in resources between those who are disadvantaged and those who are advantaged (Dys et al., 2019; Elenbaas & Killen, 2016; Malti et al., 2016).

For example, when asked about whom to admit to a hypothetical summer camp, children who perceived wide disparities in access to other special opportunities (such as how often other children have opportunities) were more likely to reason about fair access and to state that opportunities should be distributed equitably, rather than equally, in order to address past inequality. Thus, they might state that only low-income children should be admitted to the special camp if they have been excluded in the past (Elenbaas, 2019).

Key Terms

Active G × E interaction	Emotion Understanding	Person Praise
Aptitude	Evocative G × E Correlation	Popular Children
Average Children	Grit	Process Praise
Bullying	Industry–Inferiority	Rejected Children
Controversial Children	Mastery Goals	Resiliency
Distributive Justice	Neglected Children	Self-Concept
Dysregulation	Passive G × E Correlation	Self-Esteem
Emotion Knowledge	Peer	Sociometric Nominations
Emotion Recognition	Performance Goals	

Summary

1. **Identify what Erikson's theory can tell us about school-age children's needs.** For Erikson, the crisis of middle childhood is one of Industry–Inferiority, in which children must discover the ways in which they are and are not capable. Opportunities for children to discover where their talents lie is unfortunately a process that is likely a function of their family's SES. Yet competence is a product of the interaction between nature and nurture, with such interactions taking at least three different forms.

2. **Describe how school-age children's emotion understanding can be best supported.** Emotion understanding requires emotion recognition and emotion knowledge. As discussed in the chapter, there is some research to indicate that a mental health app available for children struggling with anxiety can reduce such, and improve emotion recognition. Emotion knowledge can be a function of the culture(s) in which a child is raised and immersed, so the culture value of validating children's emotions in the hope of increasing their well-being can backfire in other cultures.

3. **Illustrate how self-concept, self-resiliency, and self-esteem develop.** *Self-concept* refers to how children describe themselves in a domain-general way with various traits, and we see changes in the types of traits stated in middle childhood as compared to early childhood. *Self-resiliency* is often assumed to be a function of nature, such as inherited intelligence. While research shows that there is indeed a genetic component, the environment plays a major role as well, particularly in terms of the types of goals children are taught to value and the types of praise they are given. *Self-esteem*, or a personal evaluation of one's worth, is domain-specific and tends to increase from early childhood to middle childhood, perhaps as a function of cohort or generational differences.

4. **Explain how to best support gender-nonbinary children's needs.** Gender-nonbinary school-age children, as compared to cisgender children, are more likely to struggle with depressive disorders and attention-deficit disorders. Research with adults from the United States and India who have negative attitudes toward transgender youth revealed that there are some cultural differences at play, such as political conservatism versus religious conservatism. Cisgender children appear to have more positive attitudes toward transgender children, and research shows this positive attitude to an even greater extent after children participate in an after-school arts-based program.

5. **Summarize how peers influence development in middle childhood.** School-age children seem to value loyalty more than preschool-age children do. Also, compared to preschool-age children they also establish statuses in which children are deemed Average, Popular, Neglected, Controversial, or Rejected on the basis of how children perceive other children's behavior and how well-liked they are. Research indicates that some children are more at risk for being rejected by their peers, yet teaching children to engage in more prosocial behaviors can help greatly.

    Bullying, a form of aggression, can occur during the school years, and can take many forms, including physical, verbal, relational, and/or cyber/electronic bullying. The consequences of bullying can be devastating and can be long-lasting, so effective prevention programs, especially those for vulnerable populations, are very much needed.

6. **Compare and contrast patterns in family structures during middle childhood.** School-age children develop in many types of family structures, including extended families, single-parent families, blended families, two-parent families that may or may not be in a long-term relationship and may be opposite-sex or same-sex, and immigrant families. Overall, though, research shows that *family processes* (such as the quality of the relationship with the parents) seem to matter more to children's well-being than does the *family structure*. There appear to be many more similarities across countries and cultures in terms of the caregiving behaviors that are associated with children's well-being, in terms of children's prosocial behavior, and in terms of internalizing and externalizing behaviors.

7. **Discuss the moral development of distributive justice in middle childhood.** Distributive justice (or the fair and equitable allocation of burdens and privileges, rights and responsibilities, and pains and gains) varies by children's own backgrounds. For example, although injustices and *structural causes*, rather than *individual causes*, of inequity are something children better appreciate with age, those from lower-income homes tend to be less aware of barriers to equal opportunity, while being more likely to attribute poverty, unemployment, and homelessness to *individual causes*, such as insufficient motivation, rather than *structural causes*, such as restricted opportunities.

Unfortunately then, children who are *most* likely to be disadvantaged by restricted opportunities are *least* likely to question such, perhaps as a result of their schools tending to be of poorer quality and therefore less able to teach them to think critically about government investments in social programs or lack thereof—and these restricted opportunities mean their lives tend to err more on the risk side of the risk–resilience pattern of development.

The Cycle of Science

Research

Why was the study conducted?

The researchers wanted to know what effects a 12-week after-school arts education curriculum had on children if the program embraced an expansive understanding of gender (Vilkin et al., 2019).

Who participated in the study?

The participants were 83 students in kindergarten through fifth grade.

Which type of design was used?

A pretest, posttest design was used in which, after their parents gave permission for them to participate, children were interviewed about their gender, their preferred bathroom use, their beliefs about gender norms, and their beliefs about social norms in general.

Then, once a week for 12 weeks, children participated in developmentally appropriate arts activities with a theme of exploring and deconstructing gender stereotypes. For example, kindergartners learned about animals that are nonbinary or gender-fluid, such as clown fish, Komodo dragons, and sea horses, whereas older children learned about gender-targeted toys and about creating alternatives to such. At the end of the 12-week program, the children were interviewed again.

What were the results?

Out of the 83 students who participated, 3 reported their gender to be gender-expansive prior to participating in the arts program, and 12 reported their gender to be gender-expansive after participating in the arts program. Interestingly, although students' awareness of gender norms increased from the beginning to the end of the 12 weeks, their attitudes toward people who are gender-expansive also increased, indicating that the program promoted acceptance and inclusivity.

Are the results consistent with theory?

Yes. Children tend to have less-negative attitudes toward gender-expansive individuals than do adults.

How can the results be used to improve our lives?

Educational programming involving the arts has the potential to broaden children's experiences, as well as their attitudes, and the consequences of such can greatly improve the health and well-being of gender-nonbinary children—as well as all children—given empathy and perspective-taking improves with such programs.

Exercises

1. What pattern of results would you expect if children had learned only about gender norms, without any opportunity to consider alternatives to such?

2. What pattern of results would you expect if the study had compared children of parents who are politically conservative versus politically liberal?

3. How might a school incorporate a program such as this in its regular curriculum?

Helpful Websites

For an interactive demonstration of how policy decisions influence outcomes for children and their families, see *Tipping the Scales: The Resilience Game*, created by Harvard's Center for the Developing Child: https://developingchild.harvard.edu/resources/resilience-game/

Terra Firma seeks to facilitate the mental health, physical health, and legal needs of immigrant children: http://www.terrafirma.nyc/

For fact sheets, video resources, and tips for children, teens, parents, and educators on cyberbullying, visit the Cyberbullying Research Center: http://www.cyberbullying.us/

The *Kids with Cameras* organization "teaches the art of photography to marginalized children in communities around the world. We use photography to capture the imaginations of children, to empower them, building confidence, self-esteem and hope." To learn more about this fantastic organization, consider watching the Oscar-winning documentary about them by the same name, and visit their website at http://www.kids-with-cameras.org/home/

Recommended Reading

Faber, A., & Mazlish, E. (2012). *How to talk so kids will listen and listen so kids will talk*. New York, NY: Simon & Schuster.

Hall, S. K. (2008). *Raising kids in the 21st century: The science of psychological health for children*. Malden, MA: John Wiley & Sons.

Levin, D. E., & Kilbourne, J. (2008). *So sexy so soon: The new sexualized childhood and what parents can do to protect their kids*. New York, NY: Ballantine Books.

CHAPTER 12

Physical and Cognitive Development in Adolescence

Snapshot

Mona, who is 19 years old, has just told her parents that she now has little interest in becoming a doctor. Mona once wanted to be a doctor, after experiencing excellent care from physicians for sports injuries she had while being on a swim team.

Yet Mona now wants to pursue a career as an entrepreneur. In the last year, she has developed two different projects on Kickstarter, both of which exceeded their funding goals—funding that has allowed her to finish the projects.

Both of Mona's parents were practicing physicians in Syria before they were forced to leave as a result of the civil war. Although they struggled to find equivalent work when they arrived in the United States, they attended a local business incubator program that helped them leverage their early chemistry expertise from med school into launching a successful bakery.

So when Mona first wanted to be a physician, they were excited by and understood this interest of hers. Yet they are also just thrilled by her clear strengths in innovation, and they intend to strongly support this new career interest of hers.

Mona knows she should continue to consider other possibilities before making a commitment to a career as an entrepreneur. But she also feels she would be less stressed about planning for the future if she could just make—and stick with—a decision. Besides, she's really excited about entrepreneurship right now.

FIG. 12.1   Mona

In this chapter, we will learn about how Mona's experiences illustrate some of the changes that are part of physical and cognitive development during adolescence.

How Do Nature and Nurture Shape Our Understanding of Adolescence?

The definition of an *adolescent* or teenager seems fairly simple. It specifies someone who is in *adolescence*, the period of the lifespan that occurs between childhood and adulthood, and one that includes a number of changes within physical development (such as puberty), cognitive development, and emotional development (Dorn et al., 2019).

Yet developmental science's view of adolescence has changed over time, as has our understanding of how nature and nurture interact in this stage of life, during which drastic physical changes occur.

Also, while we will be discussing similarities and differences between two sexes in this chapter, remember from Chapter 9 that not all children and teens identify as such. The data on intersex teens and gender-expansive teens are currently insufficient, which means we are limited to comparisons and contrasts between those assigned the female or male gender at birth (Deardorff et al., 2019; Mendle et al., 2019).

So the use of the terms *female* and *male* in this chapter are not intended to deny the right and need of nonbinary teens to assert their gender (one that may not match their sex at birth) and/or assert themselves as genderqueer, gender nonconforming, and/or transgender. Instead, the terms *female* and *male* in this chapter are intended to reflect the data we now have on physiological changes that occur in adolescence according to sex at birth.

When more data are collected on how these changes may or may not differ for intersex teens and nonbinary teens (such as if they do transition, and if so, whether or not they opted for puberty blockers), such data will be a welcome addition. Adolescence and its corresponding physical changes can be distressing to all teens, but perhaps especially so for those who physical development does not match their gender identity (Crockett et al., 2019).

Learning Goals

- Discuss how nature and nurture shape our understanding of adolescence
- Describe what normative changes in physical growth occur during adolescence
- Illustrate the changes that occur in puberty
- Detail how the brain develops during adolescence
- Specify how physical activity, sports, and sports injuries play a role in motor skills
- Clarify what are some of the major health issues relevant to adolescents
- Explain what Piaget's theory can tell us about adolescent cognitive development
- Recount the factors associated with academic success in adolescence

A Brief History of Adolescence

Despite ages 18 and 21 both having served as conventional markers of the end of adolescence and the beginning of adulthood, there are no dramatic or abrupt changes in the brain that occur at these times (Giedd, 2018). In addition, most 18- and 19-year-olds say they do not feel like adults and are unsure when they will. Some adolescents think it will happen when their age no longer ends in "-teen"; others believe it will occur at around age 21, and some worry it will be at age 25 or even later.

Yet in order to encompass the hormonal changes that set the stage for puberty, as well as the interconnections among various parts of the brain that continue to increase through early adulthood, the largest number of researchers suggest that the transition from childhood to adulthood corresponds to 10 to 24 years of age (Giedd, 2018; Sawyer et al., 2018).

So our views about when adolescence begins and ends have evolved over time, as have our assumptions about what this period of life entails.

G. Stanley Hall, who founded the American Psychological Association in 1892 and served as its first president, proposed in 1904 that adolescence was a time of "storm and stress," that is, a tumultuous period full of passion, conflict, and moodiness. The National Institute of Mental Health (2019) noted that 50% of adolescents struggle with a mental disorder.

Nature and Nurture

If the storm and stress theory characterizes approximately half of all teens, does that mean their tumult is biologically determined, just as the period of adolescence is biologically determined by puberty to some degree? No.

It would be overstating the case to say that strife and confusion are innate and biologically programmed to reveal themselves in the teen years. As we learned in Chapter 3, nature and nurture are always interacting within development; for example, puberty is a product of interactions among genetics, environment, and nutrition (Alotaibi, 2019). So another overstatement is the suggestion that adolescence is solely influenced by nurture.

To learn more about a specific—and beautiful—form of nurture in terms of a Native American coming-of-age ritual for those teens who identity as female, read about a Navajo rite of passage celebration in the *Pan & Zoom: The Kinaaldá Ceremony* feature.

Pan & Zoom

The Kinaaldá Ceremony

In this box, we zoom in on a beautiful cultural ritual. Some rites of spiritual passage are quite well known: Think of the Jewish Bat Mitzvahs for 12-year-olds who identify as female and Bar Mitzvahs for 13-year-olds who identify as male; the Catholic sacrament of confirmation, which generally is given at approximately age 14; and the *quinceañera* ceremony that marks the transition to adulthood at age 15 for those who identify as female and Latinx.

FIG. 12.2   Girl with Corn Pollen at Her Kinaaldá Ceremony

Source: https://www.flickr.com/photos/valonialhardy/2713110832.

Increasingly, the quinceañera ceremony is also embraced and celebrated by those from other and often mixed backgrounds, including Latinx and Black (for a "quinceanegra") and Latinx and Muslim—as well as "quinces" for queer or transgender teens, along with "double quinces" for those who are turning 30 and may not have had a quinceañera at age 15 (Thompson-Hernández, 2019)

For Native Americans, though, some coming-of-age rituals observe the biological changes associated with puberty, such as menarche, and are celebratory in nature. The 4-day Navajo Kinaaldá ceremony, which is based on the creation story of the Navajo's chief deity, Changing Woman, honors a girl's entry into woman-hood with festive social events (Rutter, 2007).

The ceremony begins when a girl experiences her first or second menstruation, and it includes a variety of rituals. As you can see in Figure 12.2, these rituals may include wearing special clothing that visually symbolizes the departure from childhood (as in the blanket wrapped around her), washing jewelry for purification (as in her turquoise necklaces), the grinding of corn (a symbol of fertility and that which is in the basket) to make celebratory cakes, and running during each of the four days of the ceremony. Navajos consider the anticipated length of a girl's lifespan to be determined by the length of her run.

The increases in logical thinking that occur prior to puberty are a requirement for the Kinaaldá ceremony, because for Navajos menarche is not just a physical event. It also represents a psychological evolution of growth and transformation, presenting new roles and expectations.

The extensive preparation required for the Kinaaldá ceremony's dramatic 4 days focuses the entire community on the female in question for the duration. Such activities ease her social separation from childhood and aid in her acclimation to a new adult role.

Coming-of-age ceremonies represent a culture's beliefs regarding the path to adulthood. Whether performed by the elders who conduct the Kinaaldá ceremony in a Navajo tribe, or by the adults at the Department of Motor Vehicles who issue driver's licenses to teens, these rituals impart some type of meaning and they specify acts to occur within the rite.

• • • •

What Normative Changes in Physical Growth Occur During Adolescence?

When we talk about physical growth in any stage of life, remember that we are discussing averages. The growth of any individual adolescent (such as Mona) may occur *earlier* or *later*—as well as *faster* or *slower*—than the average, so any given child's trajectory might not match that of another child (Haywood & Getchell, 2020).

As you can see in Figure 12.3, the average weight for those who identify as female is approximately 102 pounds at 13 years of age and approximately 122 pounds at 18 years of age. Their average height is approximately 61 inches at 13 years of age and approximately 64 inches at 18 years of age. Height in females tapers off at around 14 years of age, and any increases in height after age 16 are usually not noticeable (Haywood & Getchell, 2020).

As you can see in Figure 12.4, the average weight for those who identify as male is approximately 100 pounds at 13 years of age and approximately 145 pounds at 18 years of age. Their average height is approximately 61 inches at 13 years of age and approximately 69 inches at 18 years of age. Height in males tapers off at around 17 years of age, and any increases in height after age 18 are usually not noticeable (Haywood & Getchell, 2020). Indeed, males tend to start out similar to females but gain more inches and pounds over time, likely because they experience a longer growing period.

Average changes in height from infancy through adolescence are consistent with the polydirectional pattern of development. There are rapid gains in infancy, followed by steady growth in childhood, and then eventually another rapid increase in adolescence.

Remember, though, that any individual may change percentiles during their development as a result of rapid gains. They may start out in the 60th percentile in middle childhood and grow to the 90th percentile in adolescence (Haywood & Getchell, 2020).

What Changes Occur in Puberty?

Other than being puzzled that her male-identified cousin, who is the same age as her, seemed to look like an adult much later than she did, Mona has found puberty to be pretty uneventful.

In this section, we consider growth patterns, puberty phases, and maturational timing, all of which could explain some of the differences Mona has noticed.

Growth Patterns

Puberty refers to the gradual physical transition from childhood to adulthood. This transition is very much a process that is consistent with the multidimensional pattern of development (in that it involves emotional development), and also one that is consistent with the risk–resilience pattern of development because differential exposure to advantages or disadvantages has a biological and behavioral impact on teens' developing bodies and minds (Alotaibi, 2019; Mendle et al., 2019; Worthman, Dockray, & Marceau, 2019).

For now, know that visible growth differences among females and males are not uncommon, even for fraternal twins, because females begin to mature earlier than males.

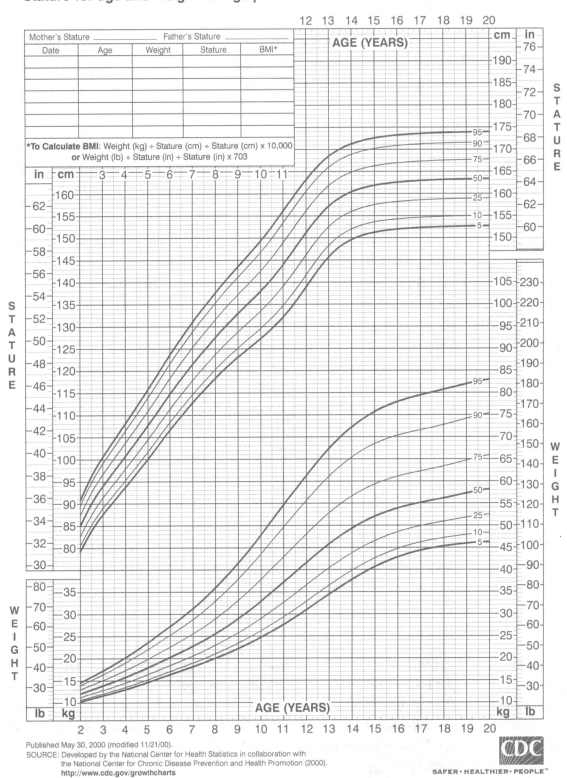

2 to 20 years: Girls
Stature-for-age and Weight-for-age percentiles

NAME _____

RECORD # _____

FIG. 12.3   Stature-for-Age and Weight-for-Age Percentiles for Females

Source: https://www.cdc.gov/growthcharts/data/set1clinical/cj41c022.pdf.

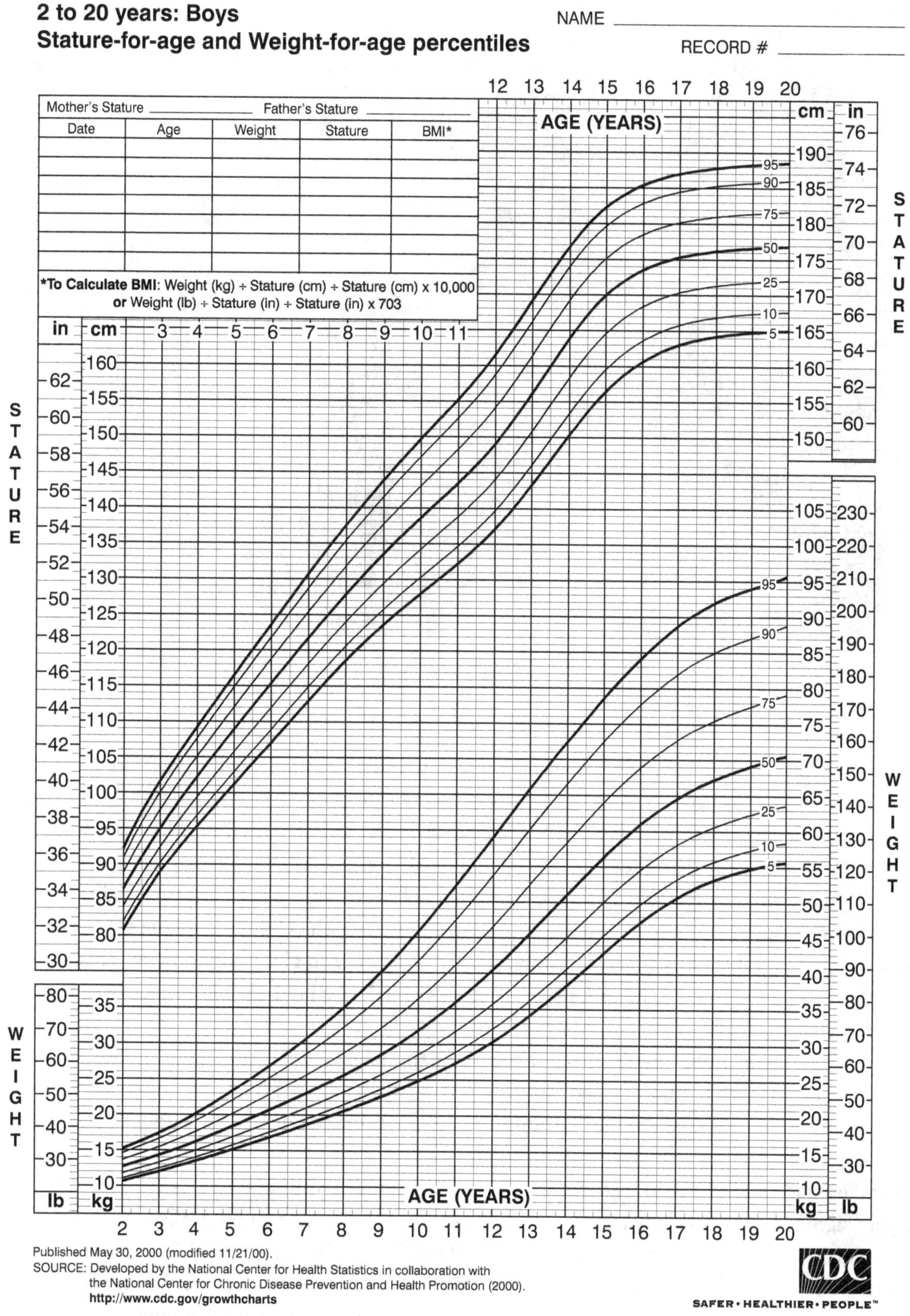

2 to 20 years: Boys
Stature-for-age and Weight-for-age percentiles

NAME _____

RECORD # _____

*To Calculate BMI: Weight (kg) ÷ Stature (cm) ÷ Stature (cm) x 10,000
or Weight (lb) ÷ Stature (in) ÷ Stature (in) x 703

Mother's Stature _____ Father's Stature _____

Date	Age	Weight	Stature	BMI*

AGE (YEARS)

AGE (YEARS)

STATURE

WEIGHT

Published May 30, 2000 (modified 11/21/00).
SOURCE: Developed by the National Center for Health Statistics in collaboration with
the National Center for Chronic Disease Prevention and Health Promotion (2000).
http://www.cdc.gov/growthcharts

CDC
SAFER • HEALTHIER • PEOPLE™

FIG. 12.4   Stature-for-Age and Weight-for-Age Percentiles for Males

Source: https://www.cdc.gov/growthcharts/data/set1clinical/cj41c021.pdf.

FIG. 12.5   Males Start to Be Taller Than Females Around Age 14

Copyright © Depositphotos/monkeybusiness.

The physical changes that mark the onset of puberty result from genetically determined processes that begin as early as age 8 or 9, as we noted in Chapter 10. These internal processes occur *before* the external changes become apparent, but you can see slight differences in the Stature-for-Age and Weight-for-Age growth charts for females and males in Figures 12.3 and 12.4.

Differences between females and males in early adolescence are due to differences in the onset of the **growth spurt**. The growth spurt, or the rapid gain in both height and weight that is the first outward sign of puberty, occurs, on average, two years *earlier* in girls than in boys. This explains why Mona observed that her male cousin of the same age looked like an adult much later than she did (Alotaibi, 2019).

As a result, females are often taller and heavier than males of the same age in adolescence. This difference tends to be temporary, though. As you can see in Figure 12.5, these differences are represented in adolescents' height until around age 14, when males start to grow taller than females (Ambler, 2013).

Females and males differ in their muscle–fat makeup and body proportions as well. Females tend to gain significantly more *fat mass* than males, whereas males tend to gain significantly more *muscle mass* and *bone mass* than females (Ambler, 2013; Handelsman, 2017; Haywood & Getchell, 2020).

Such gains in strength for males coincide with the gender divergence in adolescent athletes that is first noticeable around age 13, when males tend to show greater strength and speed. Mona saw this in her male-identifying fellow swimmers, whom she began to struggle to keep up with a few years ago (Ambler, 2013; Handelsman, 2017; Haywood & Getchell, 2020).

Phase 1 of Puberty: Hormonal Changes

What is it exactly that leads to other changes during puberty, such as how a female's hips widen and a male's voice deepens? Well, puberty is precipitated by two distinct yet overlapping events: adrenarche and gonadarche.

The first phase, **adrenarche**, refers to an awakening of the adrenal glands, at around 6 to 8 years of age, in which the adrenal cortex releases a dramatic increase in androgen hormones (Alotaibi, 2019; Mendle et al., 2019).The hormones that are released do not result in any of the visible changes we associate with puberty, such as the development of the breasts, genitals, and pubic hair. Only later, when hormone levels are high enough during the second phase of puberty, do external changes manifest and become apparent to others.

Interestingly, the earlier the timing of adrenarche, and the higher the levels of hormones secreted, the more children and teens are at risk for internalizing or externalizing problems, perhaps because these hormones play a role in brain development (Byrne et al., 2017).

FIG. 12.6   Mona Confronts the Reality of Sex Differences in Speed

Copyright © Depositphotos/AsierRomeroCarballo.

These hormones secreted by the adrenal glands during adrenarche include *thyroxine* and the *growth hormone*, both of which contribute to increases in body size and maturation of the skeletal system. The pituitary gland secretes hormones essential in sexual maturation, including **estrogen** and **androgens**. It is often assumed that females have estrogen and males have androgens, but this is a misunderstanding.

Females have more estrogen than do males, and males have more androgens than do females, but all genders have both types of these hormones.

Although hormones certainly contribute to development, including emotional functioning such as the prevalence of moodiness, the relationship is bidirectional: Emotional well-being can also influence hormonal functioning, such as when an emotionally arousing experience leads to the release of adrenal hormones, which leads to a cascade of other physiological changes that enhance the consolidation of the memory for this emotional experience (Tyng, Amin, Saad, & Malik, 2017).

Phase 2 of Puberty: Sexual Maturation

The second phase of puberty, in which sexual maturation is manifested as a result of sex steroids released by the gonads, is referred to as **gonadarche** (Alotaibi, 2019). Gonadarche begins at around age 9 or 10 in females, at around age 10 or 11 in males, and can last 4 to 5 years. It consists of two major events (Mendle et al., 2019).

One of these two major events is the development of the gonads. The **gonads** are the reproductive organs—the ovaries in females and the testes in males—and they produce the gametes we learned about in Chapter 3. They also are often referred to as the **primary sexual characteristics**.

The other major event in the second phase of puberty is the development of the outward characteristics of sexual maturity, the **secondary sexual characteristics**, such as the breasts, the genitals, pubic hair, and a deepening voice.

The entire process of sexual maturation takes approximately four years to complete, for both females and males. **Menarche**, a girl's first menstruation, and **spermarche**, a boy's first ejaculation, can occur around the onset of adolescence, but these events can also occur during mid to late puberty, because pubertal processes begin before the adolescent stage of development.

Since the major pubertal changes occur in a relatively standard sequence, the *order* in which these events occur is less variable than the *ages* at which they occur. As a result, the puberty experience is both universal and individual (Mandle et al., 2019).

Maturational Timing

The difference between the growth spurt of Mona and the growth spurt of her male-identified cousin is consistent with the *sex differences* in pubertal onset. However, it may also reflect *individual differences* in pubertal onset.

Maturational timing, or the moment when the cascade of pubertal events begins, varies from adolescent to adolescent. Some adolescents are *early-maturing* (at age 11–12), others are *late-maturing* (14–15), and still others fall in between. There are both precursors to, and consequences of, maturational timing being early or late.

In terms of the precursors to maturational timing being "off," some females may be late-maturing because of genetics, diet, and/or athleticism (Eveleth, 2017). Other females may be early-maturing because of *uncontrollable early chronic stress* (such as poverty, maltreatment, and/or family dysfunction, which we know can interfere with the development of self-regulation). According to an evolutionary perspective we first encountered in Chapter 1, early maturation may be a developmental adaptation that promotes physical survival, as well as reproduction, under adverse circumstances (Ellis & Del Giudice, 2019; Papadimitriou, 2016).

Early-maturing cisgender and heterosexual females with a higher percentage of friends who are cisgender and heterosexual are also at greater risk for dating abuse (being insulted, swore at, pushed/ shoved, and/or threatened). This consequence of maturational timing being off is consistent, unfortunately, with a lifelong pattern of development. It is perhaps due to a maturational mismatch between these females' physical appearance and their brains—a discrepancy that continues to develop at least until early adulthood (Chen, Rothman, & Jaffee, 2017).

Yet maturational timing, in addition to being a precursor or consequence of pathology, is likely also a marker of **allostatic load**, or stress that accelerates aging via wear and tear on the body's immune, metabolic, reproductive, and cardiovascular systems. Allostatic load may very well slow down or stop as teens acquire emotional resilience and as they practice self-regulation skills that reduce stress on the adrenal glands (Joos et al., 2018; Skrove, Lydersen, & Indredavik, 2016).

A secular trend or generational change (that we first learned about in Chapter 8) in the timing of menarche is apparent too, at least for female-identity teens in European countries (although other regions show similar patterns, particularly for those from families who live in rural areas and are financially secure).

As you can see in Figure 12.7, after the Industrial Revolution, when living conditions had deteriorated with unhealthy environments in crowded urban areas, the average age of menarche was 15.5 years of age, whereas in the second half of the 20th century, the average age decreased to 12.5 years and seems to have leveled off in recent years. This generational decrease is a result of vast improvements in public health, hygiene, and nutrition over time (Eveleth, 2017; Papadimitriou, 2016).

Yet there are other contributors to this historical trend, and not all of them are positive. Variations in maturation are now also associated with differences in exposure to endocrine disruptors, health, nutrition, and/or families' SES (Aylwin et al., 2018; Worthman, Dockray, & Marceau, 2019). Therefore, differential access to resources becomes part of teens' lifelong health and well-being—especially because off-time maturation is associated with an increased risk of of conditions that are often preventable, and unfortunately serve as negative examples of the lifelong pattern of development, such as insulin, hypertension, cardiovascular disease, behavioral problems, and/or mental illness (Aylwin et al., 2018; Worthman, Dockray, & Marceau, 2019).

Indeed, females who are overweight or obese are more likely to be early-maturing, and males who are overweight are more likely to be early-maturing. Yet males who are obese are more likely to be late-maturing. So far, the reasons why this opposite pattern occurs for obese males is unclear (Reinehr & Roth, 2019; Werneck et al., 2018).

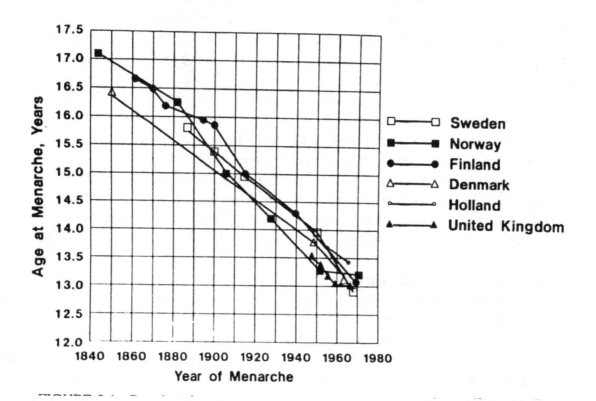

FIG. 12.7   A Secular Trend in Menarche within Europe

Jane Beckman Lancaster and Beatrix A. Hamburg, "A Secular Trend in Menarche with Europe," School-age Pregnancy and Parenthood: Biosocial Dimensions, pp. 44. Copyright © 2008 by Taylor & Francis Group.

The data also indicate that early maturational timing for females and males is associated with outcomes that also unfortunately serve as negative examples of the multidimensional pattern of development too, such as greater substance abuse and emotional distress. Perhaps this is because off-time maturation can increase adolescents' anxiety about their appearance at that time, especially if they are teased about such (Senia, Donnellan, & Neppl, 2018; Zimmer-Gembeck et al., 2018).

Off-time maturation reminds us that puberty in general is a window of opportunity for helping teens err on the resilience side of risk–resilience pattern of development in order to reverse the effects of early life stress—while also improving later health and well-being. Research indicates that such improvements can come about through public investment in prevention and intervention programs that promote positive development. Notably, the successful programs teach skills and knowledge—as well as providing sustained support for families, schools, and communities to foster these skills and knowledge in teens (Crockett et al., 2019; Dorn et al., 2019).

Such support during this stage of development is vital in light of data indicating that puberty may prompt a reorganization of neural activity in the brain (Goddings et al., 2019). The brain is the topic to which we now turn.

How Does the Brain Develop During Adolescence?

Whether due to pubertal hormones and/or to age, brain development during adolescence continues after obvious physical changes have become apparent. This means that the regions of the brain associated with decision-making and the processing emotions are still developing. So teens, even those who mature "on-time," experience a mismatch between physical maturity and emotional maturity in this stage of development—with such incongruity also likely playing a role in adolescent impulsivity (Worthman, Dockray, & Marceau, 2019).

One example of such is the ongoing brain development throughout this stage (and beyond, into early adulthood), particularly in the *prefrontal cortex* (PFC). This plays a major role in impulse control, reasoning, and learning, so the extended time the PFC takes to mature and reach full myelination is likely related to adolescent risk-taking (Galván, 2019; Ziegler et al., 2019).

We learned in Chapter 8 that white matter refers to the myelin that covers axons, and gray matter refers primarily to neurons, synapses, and dendrites. As you can see in Figure 12.8, white matter *increases* during adolescence and at a faster rate in females than males, whereas changes in gray matter are consistent with the polydirectional pattern of development. That is, after increasing throughout childhood, with a peak of gray-matter volume typically occurring before 10 years of age, gray matter gradually *decreases* in adolescence and early adulthood as a result of the elimination of excessive synaptic connections (Crone & Konijn, 2018, Tamnes et al., 2017). Recall that we first read about such changes in Chapter 5.

Upon further inspection of how gray matter increases throughout childhood before decreasing gradually, we can see that it follows an inverted U-shape pattern of development over time. This developmental trend is most significant for those changes that are involved in social understanding and communication, so social interactions that occur in person—or increasingly, via social media—are *especially* influential on brain development during adolescence (Crone & Konijn, 2018; Lee, Hollarek, & Krabbendam, 2018).

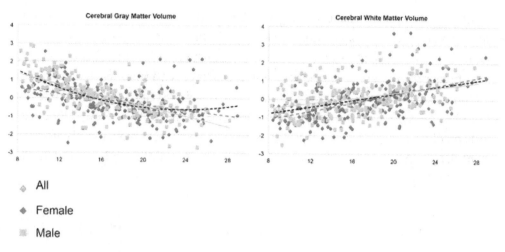

FIG. 12.8   Changes in White Matter and Gray Matter over Time

P. Cédric M.P. Koolschijn and Eveline A. Crone, Changes in white matter and grey matter over time, from "Sex differences and structural brain maturation from childhood to early adulthood," Developmental Cognitive Neuroscience, vol. 5. Copyright © 2013 by Elsevier B.V.

Today, these normative brain changes in adolescents converge with teens' typically increased use of technology relative to earlier stages in their development. This should make us mindful that feeling socially accepted or socially rejected on social media can be a very emotionally intense experience for adolescents, even if such experiences aren't intense for other age groups (Crone & Konijn, 2018; Lee, Hollarek, & Krabbendam, 2018).

Yet there certainly are clear benefits to these brain changes during adolescence. Increased white matter, as a result of greater myelination of axons, corresponds to the faster speed of processing of neural signals and better communication among various areas of the brain (Crone & Konijn, 2018; Galván, 2019; Morgan et al., 2018). As a result, teens now possess both better cognitive processing and better behavioral control (such as the ability to wait, and wait longer, for a reward). Yet those adolescents whose white-matter development is interfered with—perhaps by suboptimal sleep—may end up on the risk side of the risk–resilience pattern of development because they are consequently more likely to experience struggles in the classroom, in externalizing behaviors, and/or with substance abuse (Crone & Konijn, 2018; Galván, 2019; Morgan et al., 2018).

Thinner gray matter is associated with a more mature brain. Research has found that adolescents with larger brain volumes and thicknesses are more irritable, whereas those with a thinner cerebral cortex show more advanced social perspective-taking, akin to the theory of mind tasks we first learned about in Chapter 8 (Dennis et al., 2019; Tamnes et al., 2018).

This is not to say that thinning of the cortex is always beneficial. For instance, accelerated cortical thinning in adolescence (due to early life stress or to ongoing stress in adolescence) is associated with symptoms of ADHD, depression, and antisocial behavior, as well as schizophrenia (Bos et al., 2018; Humphreys et al., 2018; Morgan et al., 2018; Tyborowska et al., 2018).

As we will learn in Chapter 13's discussion of emotions, though, any internalizing or externalizing behaviors that teens may struggle with are not merely the direct result of their brain functioning. Rather, such behaviors relate to how their family environment, school environment, peer environment, health practices, and so on have shaped their brain's structures and functions—*and how the brain is both an outcome and a precursor of functioning* (Fuligni, Dapretto, & Galván, 2018).

For example, although thickness and volume of the gray matter in general decreases during adolescence, the higher the quality of the relationship teens have with their mother (such as the really good one Mona has with her mother now, after a few years of struggle with both developmental changes and the stress of being refugees), the greater the volume of their frontal lobe. This volume subsequently predicts higher levels of adapting to adulthood, as well as higher levels of the personality traits of conscientiousness and emotional stability (Demers et al., 2019; Ferschmann et al., 2018; Tamnes et al., 2017).

How Do Physical Activity, Sports, and Sports Injuries Play a Role in Motor Skills?

Gross motor skills continue to develop into adolescence. Physical activity, sports, and sports injuries, such as those that Mona developed, are also issues that are part of adolescent physical development, and have numerous precursors and outcomes, as we will learn about now.

Physical Activity

According to the 2018 U.S. Physical Activity Guidelines Advisory Committee, adolescents should engage in 60 minutes of moderate to vigorous physical activity each day. Mona certainly engages in this amount, even when the swim team isn't in session, because she loves the stress reduction that swimming gives her (Budd et al., 2019; Corder et al., 2019; Piercy et al., 2018).

Yet 80% of adolescents in the United States are insufficiently active. This is worrisome, since physical activity tends to decline from adolescence to early adulthood, especially for those teens who do not perceive their neighborhood, school, and/or family climate to be supportive of such (Budd et al., 2019; Corder et al., 2019; Piercy et al., 2018).

Unsurprisingly, those teens who show the most daily difference *within* their activity, such as an intense workout early in day with regular movement later in the day, tend to have lower a BMI (Quante et al., 2019).

The benefits of daily physical activity are consistent with the multidimensional pattern of development. Research shows that teens who engage in daily physical activity benefit cognitively. That is, their academic performance is characterized by better grades (especially if they also eat breakfast daily) than those of teens who don't engage in daily physical activity (Biddle et al., 2019; Burns et al., 2018).

Teens also benefit emotionally from daily physical activity: They are less likely to experience depression, and they experience better moods, especially if they also spend time in nature or green spaces (Biddle et al., 2019; Burns et al., 2018).

Schools that want the best for their students' well-being, as well as for their students' test score profiles, could benefit both, and could help teens err on the resilience side of the risk–resilience pattern of development by ensuring that teens have daily opportunities to engage in moderate physical activity of their choice. Research data reveal that students are *less cognitively engaged* after general breaks, but are *more cognitively engaged* after engaging in moderate physical activity—even during challenging math lessons. Also, they are more motivated to engage in this physical activity if it is of their choice, and when they experience a sense of belonging, rather than when they are forced to participate and/or are embarrassed by peers in an activity that not of their choosing (Owen, Parker, Astell-Burt, & Lonsdale, 2018; White et al., 2018).

Sports

Despite popular sentiment, there really is no empirical evidence to support the belief that engaging in sports builds character or leadership traits (Brière et al., 2018; Ransom & Ransom, 2018).

Yet sports participation is correlated negatively with loneliness, social anxiety, and depression, particularly for teens with preexisting psychological difficulties (as was likely the case for Mona when she first arrived in this country after experiencing the traumas of war, the death of loved ones, forced displacement, resettling, discrimination, etc.). This indicates that what may help heal the body may help heal the mind (Brière et al., 2018; Ransom & Ransom, 2018).

An annual survey begun in 1971 shows that the number of teens participating in high school sports has continued to increase, reaching an all-time high in the 2017–2018 school year (the most recent year for which data are available). Females are most likely to participate in (by decreasing order) track and field, volleyball, basketball, soccer, softball, cross country, tennis, swimming/diving, and lacrosse; males are most likely to participate in (by decreasing order) football, track and field, basketball, baseball, cross country, wrestling, tennis, golf, and swimming/diving (National Federation of State High School Associations, 2017).

In terms of college sports participation, participation is not equally supported by gender. With the passage of 1972's Title IX amendment to the 1964 Civil Rights act, the federal government prohibited discrimination in education, including physical education. Title IX allowed for equal opportunity for females and males to participate in athletics.

And according to the National Collegiate Athletic Association's (2017) report to mark the 45th anniversary of the Title IX law, the number of student athletes is at an all-time high. Yet at the same time, those who identify as female represent fewer than 25% of all head coaches, with especially poor representation of minority women. In addition, athletic departments spend twice as much on male athletes in Division I sports than they do on female athletes in Division I sports. This tells us that before addressing how gender-expansive children and teens may be discouraged from even playing sports, true gender equity has yet to be achieved in athletics.

Sports Injuries

Youth sports have potential benefits in terms of both positive and negative outcomes associated with the multidimensional pattern of development, including, cognitive, and emotional well-being, but physical, cognitive, and emotional as well. Prominent examples of such harm are the greater risk of physical, sexual, or psychological abuse from coaches; serious sports injuries (such as Mona's rotator cuff tear, the treatment for which galvanized her initial interest in becoming a physician); and/or nonmedical use of prescription opioids that may be an attempt to cope with injuries (Ford et al., 2018; Lamb et al., 2018; McKay, Cumming, & Blake, 2019).

There seems to be growing public appreciation that these injuries can be grave. For example, teens' participation in football has declined, perhaps because more people are aware of research documenting the serious long-term consequences of having a sports-related concussion, including adult-onset chronic traumatic encephalopathy (CTE), which is associated with changes in personality, such as aggression and depression, as well as dementia (Mez, Daneshvar, & Kiernan, 2017).

Other consequences are devastating as well. Memory impairment, poor impulse control, self-harm, depression, and suicide attempts are all significantly higher in high school students who experience a concussion (Taylor et al., 2018; Yang, Clements-Nolle, Parrish, & Yang, 2019). And concussions are not limited to those who play football.

Teens who participate in baseball, basketball, gymnastics, icy hockey, lacrosse, soccer, track, and weightlifting are more likely to have multiple diagnosed concussions than their peers who do not participate in these sports (Veliz et al., 2019). All 50 states and the District of Columbia require that a student who is suspected of experiencing a concussion must be removed from playing a sport and must be evaluated by a medical professional before returning to play (Halstead, Walter, & Moffatt, 2018). Treatment for a concussion involves either the elimination or the reduction of physical and cognitive activity until a medical professional can attest that the teen's vestibular, somatic, cognitive, emotional, and sleep-related symptoms have subsided (Halstead, Walter, & Moffatt, 2018):

The symptoms of a concussion include the following characteristics, and all parents, coaches, teachers, and peers should be alert to them: headache; nausea; vomiting; neck pain; sensitivity to light and/or noise; problems with vision, hearing, and/or balance; dizziness; confusion; feeling foggy; having difficulty concentrating and/or remembering; answering questions slowly; repeating questions; losing consciousness; showing irritability; being more emotional than usual; sadness; anxiety; drowsiness; fatigue; feeling slowed down; having difficulty falling asleep; and sleeping too much or too little (Halstead, Walter, & Moffatt, 2018).

What Are Some of the Major Health Issues Relevant to Adolescents?

Sports, and adolescent physical health in general, is not necessarily fraught with endless peril, but many teens do find that maintaining their safety and their health becomes increasingly difficult during this period of their lives. New challenges occur every day as they confront decisions about what to eat, whether to conform to popular images of attractiveness, how to manage school schedules that may be out of sync with their biological clocks, and whether to join peers who entice them to experiment with drugs.

Food

Adolescence is a second window of opportunity to improve development, because it has the potential for nurturing the growth spurt. Yet the hormones responsible for a healthy growth spurt are sensitive to undernutrition (especially insufficient protein, calcium, and iron), so anemia and micronutrient deficiencies are common in adolescents (Christian & Smith, 2018; Khanna, Chattu, & Aeri, 2019).

That is, such deficiencies are especially common if parents and/or society make it even more difficult for teens to make good food choices and experience the protective emotional effects of healthy foods, with such effects also illustrating the polydirectional pattern of development. Fried foods, processed foods, and baked products are all associated with an *increased* risk of depression, whereas olive oil, fish nuts, vegetables, and fruit are associated with a *decreased* risk of depression (Christian & Smith, 2018; Khanna, Chattu, & Aeri, 2019).

Most adolescents know about the benefits of good nutrition, as well as the importance of moderation, balance, and variety for healthy eating. Yet many report that they find it difficult to follow known good advice because of a lack of time or because of a lack of healthy food in schools and/or home.

Adolescents have a tendency to make unhealthy food choices. Also, those who live in homes with readily available food products that have known health risks, such as sugar-sweetened beverages (and not just soda, but sports drinks and prepared tea beverages as well), are more likely to consume such foods, compared to adolescents who don't have access to these food products at home. Yet the home environment can also be positive: Adolescents who live in homes with at least one health-oriented food rule make better snack choices (Hess et al., 2019; Wang & Fielding-Singh, 2018; Watts et al., 2018).

One study found that teens are indeed motivated to make good food choices, but they often have *capability gaps* when making those choices. Their nutritional knowledge may be too basic, and they may have major misconceptions about a food's healthfulness (such as grossly underestimating the amount of sugar in many foods and beverages) (Beck et al., 2019).

Teens also often have *opportunity challenges* if their parents regularly purchase high-calorie and low-nutrient food and/or if they have access to unhealthy food products when finding their school lunches unpalatable. So parents' behavior, along with policies that improve the school food environment, could better help teens reach their food and health goals (Beck et al., 2019).

In fact, the relationship between parents and teens is bidirectional. Teens influence their parents' consumption of fruits and vegetables, junk food, and sugar-sweetened beverages and their parents' sedentary screen time and engagement in physical activity—just as parents influence their teens, especially if parents adopt an Authoritative caregiving style (Lenne et al., 2019).

Some teens struggle with an **eating disorder**, which the DSM-5 defines as "a persistent disturbance in eating or eating-related behaviors that results in the altered consumption or absorption of food and that significantly impairs physical health or psychosocial functioning" (American Psychiatric Association, 2013, p. 329). Eating disorders include, but are not limited to, anorexia nervosa, bulimia nervosa, binge eating disorder, and other unspecified eating disorders. Eating disorders can have serious medical consequences, including cardiovascular failure and death. They can have serious precursors as well, in that they are not "just" the result of cultural factors, pressure from peers, and/or media encouragement, but also the product of conflict with parents in general (as well as negative emotional interactions specifically during family mealtime) and trauma (DerMarderosian et al., 2018; Saul & Rodgers, 2018; White, Haycraft, & Meyer, 2019).

Eating disorders are often thought to be conditions that primarily females struggle with, but males struggle with them as well. Males typically are motivated with different forms of body dissatisfaction, such as wanting to be bigger and stronger, rather than to be of a certain weight (Limbers, Cohen, & Gray, 2018). Also, males' needs for treatment are often different from females' needs. Males are less likely to seek treatment for an eating disorder; and when they do see treatment, it is often later in their struggle and when they may be dealing with additional issues such as substance abuse, as in the case of males participating in competitive sports (Limbers, Cohen, & Gray, 2018).

An ecological understanding of eating disorders helps us appreciate that when teens are empowered with skills and have strong relationships with others, their relationship with their bodies are healthier too. How so?

Imagine a female-identifying Black teen who is struggling with binge eating as a result of stress and a limited support system due to her parents' own stressors that take their attention away from her. If she had the opportunity to enroll in a 4-H Positive Youth Development program, such as one that teaches teens to cook healthful and ethnic meals and share them with others, she would learn kitchen skills (Skill-Building under 4-H PYD Inputs in Figure 12.9) from her 4-H mentors to whom she would be able to develop a meaningful relationship and who can express care, challenge growth, provide support, share power, expand possibilities (Long-Term Caring Adult under 4-H PYD Inputs in Figure 12.9), and have opportunities to teach others her family traditions, such as salted cod with fruit from Jamaica (Meaningful Leadership under 4-H PYD Inputs in Figure 12.9).

 Positive youth development programs (PYD), which help teens err on the resilience side of the risk–resilience pattern of development, are based on an ecological systems theory, similar to Bronfenbrenner's (1977).

All of the opportunities that PYD programs provide allow teens, such as the aforementioned Black female-identifying student, to thrive with a sense of confidence, competence, caring, character, and connectedness (as seen in the "Outcomes" section of Figure 12.9). The opportunities provided by PYD programs also allow teens to help their families, community, and society and reduce their risk of engaging in unhealthy behaviors. In the case of our Black female-identifying student, she might lead after-school cooking classes for her peers and the local neighborhood, leading to the 'C' outcomes in Figure 12.9. She might then work with these others to deliver the meals to their community members

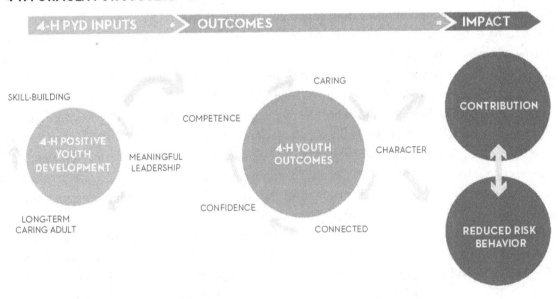

FIG. 12.9 4-H Formula for Success

National 4-H Council, "4_H Formula for Success," The Positive Development of Youth: Comprehensive Findings from the 4-h Study of Positive Youth Development, pp. 3. Copyright © 2013 by Tufts University.

who are in need and express an interest in receiving such, accomplishing both Contribution and Reduced Risk Behavior (as in the Impact section of Figure 12.9) for others. This would give herself newfound interest in cooking as well as less stress and isolation that leads to binging. (Lerner et al., 2005, 2018; Lerner, 2019; Scales & Roehlkepartain, 2018).

Longitudinal research on PYD programs, such as 4-H, indicates that children and teens who participate in them are more likely to contribute to their communities, be civically active, participate in science programs during out-of-school time, and make healthier choices. Additionally, those who participate and identify as female are less likely to be driven for thinness, and those who participate and identify as male are less likely to have body dissatisfaction (Stephens, Bowers, & Lerner, 2018).

One such PYD program involved fifth-grade and sixth-grade students from low-income families. This after-school program was based on physical activities, yet it incorporated lessons on character development and social relationships. See the *Cycle of Science* feature at the end of this chapter to

Mentor Minute

David Tierranegra Meets Jose Hernández

David Tierranegra was 16 years old when he won the National 4-H essay contest that enabled him to travel from his native Texas to the Kennedy Space Center in Florida to meet retired astronaut Jose Hernández.

At that time, David had already been participating in a local 4-H PYD program: the Juntos 4-H program, which specializes in helping Latinx youth and their families, so that these young people obtain the skills and knowledge they need to further their education.

David reported that his experiences with the Juntos 4-H included opportunities to visit college campuses—to gain a sense of what college life can be like, as well as to meet new people and build relationships with them (Schattenberg, 2018).

David is an aspiring engineer. For him, winning the National 4-H essay contest meant not only that he flew on an airplane for the first time in his life, but also that he got to meet retired astronaut Jose Hernández. Hernández is an engineer as well as an astronaut, and he shared with David that before he was accepted by NASA, he was rejected 11 times. The lesson for him: Perseverance is vital to reaching one's goals (Schattenberg, 2018).

Astronaut Hernández also took David on a tour of the Kennedy Space Center and had him participate in space stimulation training. You can watch that visit here: https://www.youtube.com/watch?v=gVgWLqM7fzU

• • • •

find out how it helped teens.

For an example of a young person who participated in a PYD program, then won an essay contest that helped him meet retired astronaut Jose Hernández, see the *Mentor Minute: David Tierranegra Meets Jose Hernández* box.

In addition to body image pressures from the media and/or peers, the difficulty of making good food choices, and the danger of eating disorders, other food issues relevant to adolescents are frequent family meals. Such gatherings are a great way for families like Mona's to connect emotionally, via planning and preparing healthy meals, as well as to talk and listen to one another.

Research shows that family meals are associated with teens having better health outcomes and behavior outcomes too. Yet families face many obstacles in this regard, including time issues, work issues, and distractions in the home environment—as well as the simple yet devastating inability to have home-cooked family meal due to homelessness or food insecurity (Jones, 2018; Niemeier & Fitzpatrick, 2019).

Sharing frequent family meals assumes that families have access to food.

Food insecurity can be psychologically damaging, especially for teens who view healthy eating as morally superior, with healthy eating being a behavior in which few teens from low-SES homes can engage, while many teens from middle-SES and high-SES may take such a privilege for granted. Children from middle-SES and high-SES homes may not have had the experience of their self-worth being damaged by their family's SES, and their corresponding food opportunities being moralized (Fielding-Singh, 2019).

Teens who live in food-insecure homes suffer from additional heartbreaking outcomes associated with the multidimensional and lifelong patterns of development. These include inequalities in the ability to learn, since hunger disrupts focus; subsequent lower verbal scores as well as math scores; and a greater (and understandable) risk of anxiety. Such teens are also likely to have significantly more biological children once they reach early adulthood (Aurino, Fledderjohann, & Vellakkal, 2019; Heflin, Kukla-Acevedo, & Darolia, 2019; Maynard, Perlman, & Kirkpatrick, 2019).

Sleep

Mona obtains ample exercise, but she does not get enough sleep. She isn't unusual in this regard.

Adolescent sleep is a public health concern. Teens need 9–10 hours of sleep each night to maintain their health, yet more than 70% of adolescents average less than 8 hours of sleep per night—indicating an epidemic of insufficient sleep in young people and a troubling mass erring on the risk side of the risk–resilience pattern of development, often a result of evening use of electronic media with blue light that disrupts circadian rhythms (Touitou, Touitou, & Reinberg, 2016; Weaver, Barger, & Malone, 2018).

As you can see from Figure 12.10, insufficient sleep can have perilous consequences, with research data indicating that sleep duration in adolescence is correlated negatively with risk-taking behaviors, and that the odds of teenagers engaging in drug use and self-harm are especially high for those who sleep fewer than 6 hours per night (Weaver, Barger, & Malone, 2018). Other

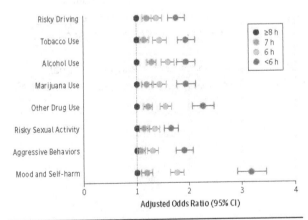

Estimated odds ratios are from weighted logistic regression models adjusted for age, sex, race/ethnicity, and year of survey.

FIG. 12.10   Associations between Sleep Duration and Risk-Taking Behaviors

Source: https://www.doversherborn.org/uploaded/District_Administration/Superintendent/School_Start_Times_Info/2018_Weaver_et_al_Dose-Dependent_Associations_Between_Sleep_and_Risky_Behaviors_JAMA_Ped.pdf.

research indicates that teens who do not obtain sufficient sleep are at greater risk for depression (Berger, Wahlstrom, & Windome, 2019).

These data beg the question of why teens do not obtain enough sleep. Yet insufficient sleep during adolescence may be a result of "perfect storm" factors, including biological changes associated with puberty, academic and/or extracurricular demands, and lifestyle choices (American Academy of Pediatrics, 2014; Crowley et al., 2018).

Indeed, the more screen time teens engage in (particularly with portable devices), the less they sleep. Some teens even report that they feel pressured to communicate at night, via phone (Godsell & White, 2019; Mazzer, Baudacco, & Boersma, 2018; Twenge, Hisler, & Krizan, 2019).

Yet teens such as Mona—whose parents engage in parental monitoring of her behavior at home, with friends, and at school—are more likely to engage in healthful behaviors, including obtaining sufficient sleep. Perhaps this is because of the structure and security that parental monitoring and positive family dynamics foster. Conversely, negative family dynamics in a teen's life are associated with poor sleep and cardiovascular risk, such as hypertension and later heart disease (Gunn et al., 2019; Gunn & Eberhardt, 2019).

In addition to parental monitoring, national and international secondary-school start times of 8:30 a.m. or later are needed as a public health and safety measure (American Academy of Pediatrics, 2014; Blake et al., 2019). Why? Because after the onset of puberty, our internal clock shifts so that teens are typically not sleepy until much later than they were as children.

The data show that later school start times are associated with better academic performance, as well as lower rates of behavioral problems, lower teen-driver motor vehicle crash rates, and reduced substance abuse and delinquency. Better sleep promotes better self-control and more participation in school activities later in the day, compared to unstructured activities with peers (Foss, Smith, & O'Brien, 2019; Semenza et al., 2019).

Substance Abuse

We just learned that sleep problems are a risk factor for substance abuse in adolescence, and the data indicate that this relationship continues over time. So prevention of substance abuse in adulthood might start with measures to ensure that teens get sufficient sleep (Nguyen-Louie et al., 2018).

Additionally, 90% of adults with a substance abuse issue began using substances before age 18. Depending how early a teen starts, the risk of later serious substance abuse issues can double or triple (Hadland, 2019; Levy, Schizer, & Green, 2019).

So early detection can help prevent substance abuse—as well as death during adolescence. Substance use plays a major role in unintentional injuries (motor vehicle crashes), homicide, and suicide—the three leading causes of teen death (Hadland, 2019; Levy, Schizer, & Green, 2019).

Having a brain that is still under construction is also a general risk factor for substance abuse, because the teen brain underestimates risks and overestimates pleasures (Debenham et al., 2019). The nucleus accumbens, the brain's reward center, experiences a surge of growth in preadolescence and early adolescence, and the result is that what satisfies a teen as a reward is no longer toys as in childhood, but something that brings much larger rewards, such as risk-taking (Levy, Schizer, & Green, 2019).

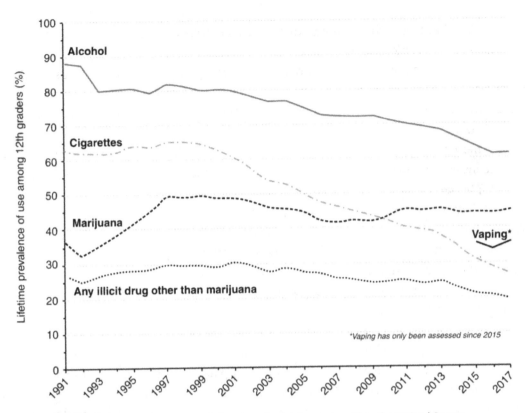

FIG. 12.11   Trends in the Use of Common Substances in Adolescents within the United States

Justine W. Welsh, Scott E. Hadland, "Trends in the use of common substances in adolescents within the U.S.," *Treating Adolescent Substance Use: A Clinician's Guide*, pp. 4. Copyright © 2019 by Springer Nature.

This forceful change in the brain's reward center, in combination with the slow-maturing change in the brain's prefrontal cortex, helps explain why teens are inclined toward risk-taking. This is especially the case for teens who experience failure at school; who struggle with ADHD, depression, or anxiety; who have a risk-taking personality, who associate with peers who use substances, who live amidst family dysfunction, who have parents who don't engage in much parental monitoring, and/ or who have parents who abuse substances themselves (Levy, Schizer, & Green, 2019).

In terms of what substances adolescents are using, the data show trend associated with the polydirectional pattern of development over time with increases, stability, and decreases. As you can see in Figure 12.11, the use of alcohol and combustible cigarettes has declined substantially, with slight declines as well in the use of any illicit drug other than marijuana. On the other hand, since the introduction of e-cigarettes, vaping has grown, as has marijuana use given recent changes in U.S. policy regarding such (Hadland, 2019).

In general, substance abuse in adolescence has costly consequences. For example, alcohol use can result in injury, vomiting, hangover, and memory lapses; nicotine can cause "rewiring" and structural changes that make the immature brain create more nicotine receptors that crave the drug (Wicki et al., 2018; Zeller, 2019).

Discouragingly, teens who have experienced these negative consequences are often willing to experience them again in the future (perhaps due to their being see as a necessary evil to attain the positive consequences). This suggests that prevention efforts that emphasize learning the facts and making rational choices may be ineffective with at least some teens; the rewiring of teens' brains doesn't always render them open to rational decision-making (Wicki et al., 2018; Zeller, 2019).

A review of drug prevention programs targeting adolescents indicates that some of these programs are fact-based, some include skill-training, some address the family, and yet others incorporate technology—but very few profile their intended audience before the programs are delivered (Demant & Schierff, 2019). To help teens err on the resilience side of the risk–resilience pattern of development, prevention of substance abuse may be best approached by profiling teens with certain needs and motivations.

For example, to be more effective, programs may wish to obtain a better understanding of the personalities of those teens who see negative consequences of substance use as a necessary evil (such as in order to obtain a thrill) rather than a deterrent. From there, the programs could find and practice alternatives to obtaining the positive consequences, such as identifying a community pool where teens can engage in intense exercise and experience a subsequent high" from endorphins, as Mona began to do when struggling with extreme postmigration stress (Demant & Schierff, 2019; Wicki et al., 2018).

Seeing the consequences of substance use in tangible visual form may help too. Research shows that the rates of teens who begin smoking went down after the Food and Drug Administration (FDA) began its youth-specific public health media campaign, "The Real Cost." The campaign emphasized the cosmetic consequences of smoking (loss of teeth), the loss of control as a result of addiction, and the way the body becomes a chemistry experiment after inhaling toxic chemicals (Farrelly et al., 2017).

In 2018, the FDA launched "The Real Cost" again, this time to address the use of e-cigarettes. Research indicates that teens tend to mistakenly believe that e-cigarettes are addictive but that they are not otherwise harmful. Ads dispelling this mistaken belief are delivered in schools and on social media channels such as Instagram, YouTube, Facebook, as well as Pandora and Spotify. The results are forthcoming (Zeller, 2019).

What Can Piaget's Theory Tell Us About Adolescent Cognitive Development?

Although the stage of adolescence is universal, the experience of it is not. Different countries, cultures, and subcultures provide varying degrees of support for exploration and experimentation. For example, a teen's culture may have views on roles regarding who can and cannot do science—attitudes that will guide the teen's educational choices, career goals, beliefs, and values, regardless of their cognitive or intellectual capabilities.

For instance, Native Americans are underrepresented in science, technology, engineering, and mathematics (STEM) fields, and research reveals that 67% of Native American students would take more science classes if such classes were respectful of tribal taboos, such as against dissection (Ricci & Riggs, 2019; Williams & Shipley, 2018).

All teens' opportunities to participate in STEM fields must be supported. In order for such to occur, many things need to happen. For example, if Native American teens' opportunities to participate in STEM and to become tribal science leaders are to grow, their cultural concerns need be addressed, their history of having their lands exploited by scientists and engineers needs be remembered and

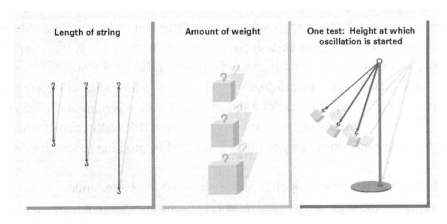

Length of string	Amount of weight	One test: Height at which oscillation is started

FIG. 12.12   Piaget's Pendulum Problem

Joan Littlefield Cook and Greg Cook, "Piaget's Pendulum Problem," Child Development: Principles and Perspectives. Copyright © 2003 by Pearson Education, Inc.

respected, and their high degree of valuing nature means that outdoor and field experiences must be included in the curriculum (Ricci & Riggs, 2019; Williams & Shipley, 2018).

Piaget's Theory

Piaget proposed that the **Formal Operational** stage, in which we possess the ability to reason abstractly, begins at approximately 11 years of age (Inhelder & Piaget, 1958). As a result of developing such abstract thinking, teens are better able than children to appreciate not only what *is*, but also what *is possible*. For example, a teenager such as Mona is equipped to consider seriously that a man or a nonbinary person can be a nurse and that a woman or a nonbinary person can be a software engineer. Adolescents who are capable of engaging in formal operational thinking no longer need concrete objects in order to think logically; they can now engage in internal mental operations (Inhelder & Piaget, 1958). In addition, formal operational thinkers can engage in *scientific reasoning*, which consists of testing hypotheses by isolating the effects of each variable individually, while holding other variables constant.

For example, imagine Mona is tutoring a friend about physics, and asks them what is responsible for the speed at which a pendulum swings by testing the length of the string, the weight of the pendulum, the point at which the pendulum is released, and/or the amount of impetus or pressure that is exerted on it—as illustrated in Figure 12.12 (Inhelder & Piaget, 1958). Her friend still uses concrete operational thinking, so they tend to start by immediately picking up the materials and trying different combination of variables by trial and error, such as a medium length-string with a heavy weight and then a short-length string with a light weight, rather than trying them systematically via hypothesis testing (Piaget & Inhelder, 2000). Her friend therefore has not yet considered testing one variable at a time while controlling all others.

Mona suggests they instead use one length of string to start (such as the shortest) and test it with one amount of weight (such as the lightest), then consider these two constant variables in combination with each and every height at which the oscillation is started. Mona helps her friend through this process, a systematic way of thinking they have never seen before.

By the time they are finished experimenting with each height, her friend has a lightbulb go off in their head and exclaims that they want to now control the length of the string and height at which the oscillation is started and vary the amount of weight.

Formal operational thinking does not develop in the same way for all teens, though—nor does it appear at any specific time during adolescence. The evidence that formal operational thinking develops more continuously and less universally than Piaget proposed falls into three categories: There are differences *within* any one adolescent in the ages at which different types of formal operational thinking begin; there are differences *between* different teens in the age at which formal operational thinking begins; and there are differences both within and between adolescents on measures of formal operational thinking, depending on how the tasks are measured—with teens and adults being more likely to show evidence of formal operational thinking in the areas in which they are most curious, in their college major, and/or in their career interests (Molitor & Hsu, 2019).

Civic Participation

Adolescents are certainly able to think about what is possible in society and engage in **civic participation,** or work to sustain a democratic society.

For instance, the survivors of the 2018 high school massacre in Parkland, Florida, organized March for Our Lives, a demonstration in Washington, DC (with additional events at different locations around the world), attended by 1 million to 2 million people, to protest gun violence. This grassroots political movement was mobilized with help from social media, and it received the 2018 International Children's Peace Prize from antiapartheid and human rights activist Desmond Tutu (Yammine et al., 2018).

Other forms of civic participation that teens engage in include, but are not limited to, participating in public protests, contacting the media to express an opinion, volunteering (for example, at a local soup kitchen, hospital, childcare center, or nursing home), tutoring, contacting a government official, signing a petition, and mentoring youth at a community center (Daiute, 2018).

Civic participation in adolescence is consistent with the multidimensional pattern of development, in terms of both the precursors and the outcomes. That is, it requires achievement of *cognitive developmental milestones* (such as prosocial moral reasoning and future orientation) and *emotional developmental milestones* (such as empathy and emotional regulation). Research indicates that teens with greater emotional regulation and/or greater prosocial moral reasoning are more likely to engage in informal helping; have greater perspective taking, conflict negotiation, and civic skills (such being more likely to contact someone in a leadership position); show more environmental behavior, such as limiting water and paper use; and have greater social responsibility values in which they believe it is important to consider the needs of others (Daiute, 2018; Metzger et al., 2018).

Additionally, teens who vote and volunteer are less likely to engage in risky health behaviors in adulthood. Also, they are less likely to experience symptoms of depression, perhaps because these civic opportunities can also serve as opportunities to voice and exercise personal control. Teens who vote, volunteer, and engage in activism also achieve significantly higher levels of education and income in adulthood, as compared to teens who do not engage in these civic activities (Ballard, Hoyt, & Pachucki, 2019).

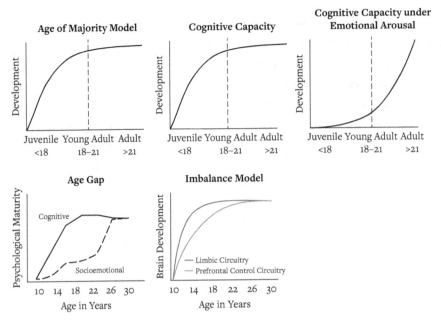

FIG. 12.13   Legal, Psychological, and Brain-Based Accounts of When an Adolescent Is an Adult

Decision-Making and Risk-Taking

In many countries, 18 years of age is considered the age of majority, or when citizens become legal adults (Icenogle et al., 2019). Yet as we learned earlier in this chapter, no dramatic or abrupt changes in the brain occur at this time (Giedd, 2018). And there is no single age at which we become competent decision-makers with mature cognitive capacities.

Within the U.S. legal system, people are considered either children or adults. Such a position is inconsistent with the empirical research evidence indicating that teens resemble children in some ways but adults in other ways. That is, cross-cultural data reveal that teens in numerous diverse countries experience a "maturity gap" in that typically they possess *cognitive capacity abilities*, such as logical reasoning, at approximately age 16, whereas typically they do not possess *psychosocial maturity abilities*, such as the ability to restrain themselves in the face of emotional arousal, until their 20s (Icenogle et al., 2019).

As you can see in Figure 12.13, examples of the polydirectional pattern of development abound here, starting with how the legal age of Majority model in Panel A and the Cognitive Capacity model in Panel B assume very different levels of development than do the more empirically based information presented in the other panels. Panel C shows the Cognitive Capacity Under Emotional Arousal model, as when teens are interacting with the very legal system that deems them to be adults at age 18. Panel D shows the Age Gap model, in which adolescents' cognitive abilities (verbal fluency, memory) mature faster than their emotional abilities (risk perception, impulse control). Panel E shows the Imbalance Model, in which teens' prefrontal cortex takes time to catch up with the highly reactive emotional limbic circuitry of the teen brain (Casey, 2019).

Teens are less able than adults to self-regulate when experiencing strong emotions. They tend to make decisions similar to those of adults in neutral situations, but they tend to make more risky decisions in situations that are emotionally arousing. This is related to the surge of growth in their nucleus accumbens—the brain's reward center that we learned about earlier in this chapter (Casey, 2019; Levy, Schizer, & Green, 2019).

Cross-cultural research on teens in China, Columbia, Cyprus, India, Italy, Jordan, Kenya, the Philippines, Sweden, Thailand, and the United States shows that risk-taking is higher in late adolescence than at any other stage (Duell et al., 2018; McCormick, Gates, & Telzer, 2019).

In terms of different types of risks, though, trends indicative of the polydirectional pattern of development are apparent when we compare these types. *Antisocial risks* (such as shoplifting) are highest in mid-to-late adolescence, then decline in early adulthood. *Health risks* (such as binge drinking) increase significantly throughout adolescence, reaching a peak and then plateauing in early adulthood, with such a pattern particularly true for teens in countries such as the United States where drinking is not legally condoned until age 21, unlike normative adolescent drinking in countries as diverse as China and those in Europe (Duell et al., 2018; McCormick, Gates, & Telzer, 2019).

Other research suggests that the adolescent *increase* and peak in risk-taking may be present only when risk-taking is measured on certain tasks. For example, a Stoplight task found that the level of risk is stable over time, but the level of emotional arousal (arousal that we learned earlier in this chapter inclines teens to make more risky decisions) increases over time. More specifically, this Stoplight task is a virtual-reality driving game that participants can win by reaching their destination in the shortest amount of time (so that emotional arousal increases as an individual plays and time runs out). Participants are required to make decisions at multiple intersections where the light turns yellow, so that speeding ahead may or may not lead to getting in an accident and consequently losing the game (Lee, Hollarek, & Krabbendam, 2018; Lorenz & Kray, 2019; van Hoorn et al., 2018).

Compared to their performance on the Stoplight task, unless teens rate high on measures of impulsivity, teen risk-taking appears to *decrease* with age. This was shown on a Treasure Hunting task in which participating teens could choose either a sure gain with only a small loss, or the option of winning money with the possibility of no loss of money or a large loss of money (Lorenz & Kray, 2019; van den Bos & Hertwig, 2017).

These particular declines in risk-taking with increasing age are consistent with other research showing that teens become increasing averse to taking risks over time when they anticipate potential losses (Lorenz & Kray, 2019; van den Bos & Hertwig, 2017).

In addition to *age differences* and *task differences* in risk-taking, the research data indicate that there are likely *individual differences* in risk-taking as well. Teens who experience early life stress demonstrate *less activity* in their prefrontal cortex and *more activity* in their amygdala. This leaves them with weaker cognitive control along with intense emotional arousal—likely leading to more impulsive behavior as a result of earlier risk (Gee et al., 2018). Yet a review of the research on risky decision-making reveals that there is no one brain region that distinguishes teens who make risky decisions from teens who do not. This suggests that future research on risk-taking in adolescence should conduct studies that investigate the activation of teens' entire brains (Sherman, Steinberg, & Chein, 2018).

There are some data from fMRI research showing that teens may make more risky decisions (such as dangerous driving and/or delinquent behavior) with their peers than with their parents, because different parts of their brain are active in these different social contexts. That is, teens experience

FIG. 12.14   Mona Feeling Confident About Her Academic Success

Copyright © Depositphotos/AsierRomeroCarballo.

greater integration of emotional and cognitive control regions while making decisions in the presence of parents—for example, whether to go through a yellow light in a game similar to the aforementioned Stoplight task (Lee, Hollarek, & Krabbendam, 2018; Rosenbaum et al., 2017; van Hoorn et al., 2018).

Driving games may seem frivolous, yet they may be anything but. For reducing risk-taking, interventions that are based on conveying information may be beneficial during adolescence. In particular, virtual-reality interventions show promise for helping teens, especially older adolescents, err on the resilience side of the risk–resilience pattern of development in that they allow teens to emotionally "experience" the negative consequences of their choices within a safe laboratory environment (Rosenbaum, Venkatraman, Steinberg, & Chein, 2018).

How Can Adolescents' Academic Success Be Best Supported?

A variety of factors may detract from or enhance the academic success of teens such as Mona. Let's consider them now.

Memory Strategies

Memory strategies are techniques that move information from working memory to long-term memory, and they can vary by age. Information in short-term memory that is not acted on will be lost forever. This explains why, for example, we need to keep repeating a new phone number to ourselves to avoid forgetting it before we enter it into our phone.

This *rehearsal*, or repeating information to be remembered, is a memory strategy. Adolescent and school-age children are more likely than kindergarteners to spontaneously use rehearsal, but there is evidence that kindergarteners and even preschoolers use some other memory strategies (Flavell, Beach, & Chinsky, 1966; Schneider & Ornstein, 2019). Another memory strategy is *organization*, which refers to a structure imposed on the material to be learned, either by the learner or by another.

The effective use of memory strategies doesn't occur overnight, however. It grows over time and with experience, beginning with the elementary school years and moving into the high school years (Schneider & Ornstein, 2019).

For instance, a *meditational deficiency*—in which we don't use memory strategies spontaneously and even don't use them when instructed how to do so—is seen in preschoolers. On the other hand, cross-sectional research also reveals a *production deficiency*, in which older children do not

Tech & Media

Tech & Media in Our Lives: Monotasking Over Multitasking

Monotasking is engaging in one cognitive activity at a time (Szumowska, Poplawska-Boruc, & Kossowska, 2018). Monotasking gives the subject of our attention utmost respect. The subject might be a friend whom we are looking at and really hearing because we put down our phone; or it might be a project we are working on and are in the flow with, knowing it's going to be good because of the loving attention we have given it.

The temptation to check an electronic device while we're in the flow of a project or a face-to-face interaction may still be there when we are monotasking—but that temptation recedes because of how rewarding the task itself has become, and because we know we will allow ourselves to devote time to the reward once we complete our task, or meet our next mini-deadline on the task.

What is quite different from monotasking—in terms of both the experience and the consequences—is multitasking. *Multitasking* is engaging in more than one cognitive activity at a time.

It is an illusion that multitasking is effective when our attention is required to complete a task. It's understandable that teens (and adults) may be tempted to multitask because of the amount of work they have to complete. But in trying to do more than one thing at a time, a person often ends up operating under a productivity illusion in which their performance (including their grades, as we will learn in the following paragraphs) is actually *diminished* rather than *improved* (Srna, Schrift, & Zauberman, 2018; Tang & Patrick, 2018; Watson et al., 2016).

Multitasking is not effective when we try to engage in more than one activity requiring attention. The *task-switching* that multitasking really entails (shifting from, say, reading this paragraph to responding to text messages, then back to this paragraph, then back to one's phone) typically leads us to perform *worse* on both activities (May & Elder, 2018; Srna, Schrift, & Zauberman, 2018; Uzun & Kilis, 2019).

The research data on multitasking in teens indicates that it is associated with worse reading comprehension, note-taking, self-regulation, test performance, and GPA, as well as feelings of dissatisfaction and frustrated. Being annoyed and agitated is understandable when we realize that we missed out on something important in a lecture and didn't fully comprehend what our friend posted on Instagram about us either (May & Elder, 2018; Srna, Schrift, & Zauberman, 2018; Uzun & Kilis, 2019).

So it is not surprising that multitasking during academic activities is associated with subsequent difficulties paying attention during academic activities. But what may not be as well appreciated is that multitasking during real-life social interactions also results in lower social success—a clearly remedial situation and one that illustrates one of the unfortunate aspects of the multidimensional pattern of development: that is, how poor cognitive control of attention decreases our emotional well-being, and quality of our relationships (van der Schuur et al., 2019; Xu, Wang, & David, 2016).

Media multitasking in seventh-graders is associated with sleep problems too. <u>But for teens who drive, multitasking while doing so is especially worrisome. It greatly increases the risk of teens erring on the risk side of the risk–resilience pattern of development. Specifically, it greatly increases the risk of injury and death—for the teens themselves, their passengers, people in other vehicles, and pedestrians</u> (Stavrinos et al., 2019; van der Schuur et al., 2018).

For those of us still feel compelled to multitask while driving (or studying), it may be helpful to remember that we have control over ourselves, even if we may not feel like it at times.

The choices we make—starting with the smallest attempt—accumulate and lead to change. Practice strengthens monotasking, via allowing ourselves to check our phone only after we complete a certain amount of studying.

Monotasking is also easiest when we listen to a guided imagery recording before we start a task and/or binaural beats during the task, as well as if we engage regularly in meditation so our mind is in the habit of returning our attention, again and again, to our breath when it wanders. Some other ideas for monotasking: taking out a sketchbook and noticing the details of something well enough to draw it; wearing a sleep mask and having a friend present us with a piece of food and having us try to guess what it is by focusing on its texture, shape, smell, and taste.

• • • •

spontaneously use strategies on their own, but will do so when taught *how* to use them. And once children begin to use strategies such as organization, their recall likely improves, although children may still use ineffective strategies alongside effective ones (Schlagmüller & Schneider, 2002; Schneider & Ornstein, 2019).

Yet even when children and teens begin to spontaneously use an appropriate strategy, some don't always benefit from it, a situation referred to as a *utilization deficiency* (Schneider et al., 2004; Stone et al., 2016). Rather than a universal stage that all must pass through, the utilization deficiency is more likely a phase that some children and teens experience depending on their age, their level of executive function, and the nature of the task. Most children become competent at using strategies by the end of elementary school (Schneider & Ornstein, 2019; Schwenck, Bjorklund, & Schneider, 2007).

How do children and teens learn strategies in the first place?

Well, they are more likely to be exposed to strategy use when their home environment is stimulating, and although some teachers and schools provide explicit instruction in memory strategies, not all do. Children begin to use new strategies when they realize they are faster and lead to improved accuracy, and/or when they have been taught how to use them (Schneider & Ornstein, 2019; Siegler & Svetina, 2006).

It could be argued that learning how to monotask is a strategy that needs to be taught in school—perhaps not as a memory strategy but at least as an attention strategy. To learn more, check out the *Tech & Media in Our Lives: Monotasking Over Multitasking* box.

Reading and Mathematics

In Chapter 10, we began to learn about literacy—one aspect being that it develops in stages. In that chapter, we ended our discussion with Stage 3, in which children and teens approximately ages 9 to 13 read for learning.

In *Stage 4: Multiple Viewpoints*, adolescents gain experience with numerous diverse points of view on a regular basis in school; for example, some history books fortunately now even consider past events from different points of view. These multiple viewpoints are easier to acquire once a basic viewpoint has been acquired in Stage 3, which indicates how hierarchical the stages of reading can be.

Adolescents need to practice reading works that offer multiple points of view, whether it be from history textbooks, in-depth newspaper coverage of events, newspaper editorials, and/or more sophisticated fiction than (hopefully) they were reading in Stage 3. Fiction stories have benefits illustrating the multidimensional pattern of development too. It is mostly from fiction that we obtain multiple perspectives on something—a powerful habit of mind that develops not only our cognitive skills but also our emotional skills. A regular appreciation of multiple views of one situation or person, including ourselves, helps us interact more maturely in real life with others.

Notice how appreciating multiple points of view in a novel is easier if adolescents are already in the habit of reading simpler fiction with one point of view. Mona is pretty sure that mastering English, which is not her first language, by reading children's books and then young-adult (YA) novels helped her emotional well-being as well as her vocabulary.

In *Stage 5: World View*, adolescents and adults enter the most advanced stage of reading. In this stage, individuals have learned to read as much or as little as they choose for their purpose, whether it be gaining facts or reading stories for pleasure. And they develop the most sophisticated view of the world in this stage, since they have learned to appreciate multiple viewpoints on any given topic, whether it be music or taxes.

Despite the importance of this cognitive ability, Chall (1983) pointed out there is no guarantee that adults reach this World View stage, even after four years of college. Unfortunately, that seems to have become disturbingly true in recent years for even earlier grades; 48% of fourth-graders from higher-income homes in the United States cannot read at grade level—and 79% of fourth-graders from lower-income homes in the United States cannot read at grade level (Children's Defense Fund, 2017).

How has this happened? Likely, there are multiple factors. Longitudinal research shows that the greater the quality of children's pre-K classrooms, the greater children's vocabularies are in elementary school—especially so for children with high quality home learning environments in which their parents scaffold their learning (Han, O'Connor, & McCormick, 2019). Other research finds that the more parents read to their children when they are between 1 and 2.5 years of age, the greater their children's intrinsic motivation to read, reading comprehension, and vocabularies in elementary school (Demir-Lira, Applebaum, Golden-Meadow, & Levine, 2019).

International Comparisons

Every three years, the Programme for International Student Assessment (PISA) determines if 15-year-old students across the globe have acquired the skills and knowledge they will need to participate fully in society once they leave school.

The 2015 results indicate that students from the United States score at levels not significantly different from the average for reading and science, but at levels significantly *lower* than average for mathematics. U.S. students score significantly *higher* than average across all countries when it comes to the differences in resources (such as staff) between advantaged schools and disadvantaged schools. This means that students in more advantaged schools within the United States receive, on average, 30 more hours of instruction in science per year than students in disadvantaged schools (OECD, 2016a, 2016b).

Related to such discrepancies within the United States is how **intergenerational social mobility**—or the ability to go beyond the educational, occupational, and/or income level of one's family and have a higher standard of living than one's parents—is becoming more scarce in the United States. This is likely a result of a lack of shared prosperity and an unequal distribution of growth in our country (Narayan et al., 2018).

Also, while intergenerational social mobility becomes more *scarce* in the United States, intergenerational social mobility is becoming more *frequent* in other industrialized countries in which there is more tax revenue due to progressive taxation. For example, the number of adults with more education than their parents is significantly higher in Canada than in the United States. Without intergenerational mobility, the social contract of trust in society is damaged; and social cohesion declines too, as people increasingly compete for a slice of a decreasing economic pie (Narayan et al., 2018).

Work

Theorists from G. Stanley Hall onward have considered adolescence to be a time of exploring one's identity, beliefs, values, talents, and interests. Contemporary research data seem to confirm this. For instance, a meta-analysis of exploratory changes in adolescents' career interests indicates polydirectional of development. That is, in just about all types of careers, teens' interest tends to be low or to decrease before age 14, and then either continue to decrease, remain stable, or increase from 14 to 18. Perhaps this is due to changes in school environments and corresponding exposure to new topics and peers—as in the case of Mona who, with the help of teachers, discovered she has the creativity for entrepreneurial innovation (Hoff, Briley, Wee, & Rounds, 2018).

When it comes to type of careers, though, older adolescents' interest in *Realistic* careers (careers involving tools and materials, such as physical labor) seems to not change over time. However, older adolescents become *decreasingly* interested in *Investigative* careers (those involving research) and *Conventional* careers (those involving manipulation of data, such as accountant), while becoming *increasingly* interested in *Artistic* careers (those involving creativity and self-expression), *Social* careers (those involving helping and nurturing), and *Enterprising* careers (those involving selling and influencing within a business context) as Mona did.

Remember that these trends are averages, and individual teens may not follow these averages. These data also represent adolescents who went on to college. Research on teens who do not go to college may show different patterns, perhaps revealing more interest in *Realistic* careers as a function of more exposure to such—exposure that is not typically part of a college curriculum (Hoff, Briley, Wee, & Rounds, 2018).

In terms of working *during* adolescence, two noteworthy generational trends are apparent. Compared to two decades ago, significantly fewer high school seniors work and significantly fewer high school seniors work intensively, that is, an average of more than 20 hours per week (Staff, Mortimer, & Johnson, 2018).

Such changes can have benefits. Research indicates that youth employment, especially for more than 20 hours a week, is associated with more substance abuse (especially for teens from low-SES homes), delinquency, exposure to sexual harassment, mental health problems, physical injuries, school misconduct, negative attitudes toward working, school dropout, and/or diminished educational attainment. Not working allows teens more time to complete school assignments, study for exams, prepare for college entrance exams, and engage in extracurricular activities (Rocheleau, 2018; Sears & Papini, 2019; Staff, Mortimer, & Johnson, 2018).

Keep in mind that some teens also engage in unpaid work, such as taking care of family members. Such responsibilities can take time away from scholarly activities and from the simple developmental needs that teens have for unstructured time of their own (Verma, 2018; Wikle, Jensen, & Hoagland, 2018).

Rather than discouraging teens from working altogether, or encouraging them to work but only for less than 20 hours a week, alternatives (in addition to national paid-time-off policies for adults to care for family members) could be made available to teens. One possibility is the ability to obtain high school course credit for meaningful work (perhaps with professionals in the community with whom teachers could partner) in which the teens could also earn money and develop work readiness skills. Another possibility after high school is apprenticeships, similar to those in Germany, that provide a full-time position and for which individuals do not need a college degree yet are qualified to sit for an interview after graduation, given their apprenticeship experience (Staff, Mortimer, & Johnson, 2018).

The Social Class Achievement Gap

The consequences of school performance become more serious in early adolescence, because these consequences begin to set the stage for later career and personal opportunities. The effects of school therefor have outcomes illustrating the lifelong and multidimensional patterns of development: They begin to define individual identity as well as scaffold cognitive development.

Most advanced countries endorse the goal of a fair society, with an individual's social position being determined by their merit, rather than the social class of their parents.

Yet research reveals a **social class achievement gap** in which students from low-SES families perform worse than students from high-SES families. This may be caused by the schools' tracking of students into different programs that may or may not prepare students for future success. Such tracking is the antithesis of providing equal opportunity and social mobility (Autin, Batruch, & Butera, 2019; Croizet et al., 2017).

What do we mean by tracking? Well, **academic tracking** streams students into different types of classes based on their *performance*, which is not the same thing as grouping by *ability*.

Remember from Chapter 1 that a level playing field might establish *equality*, in which everyone is provided with the same thing to ensure they do their best. But it doesn't guarantee *equity*, in which everyone is provided with what they need to ensure they do their best.

It has been suggested that school actions such as tracking do not simply create an uneven playing field. In fact, they are a kind of *symbolic violence* that undermines students from underprivileged homes, because tracking perpetuates social inequalities and unnecessarily positions some teens on the risk side of the risk–resilience pattern of development (Batruch et al., 2019; Croizet et al., 2017).

For those who are skeptical that systematic school policies are symbolic violence, it is worth noting that psychologists have suggested that the individualistic culture of mainstream U.S. society not only tends to encourage people to believe in a *just world* and focus on *individual causes of behavior* (such that if someone works hard enough, they will be successful) but also encourages *economic inequality blindness* by hiding *structural causes of behavior* (Fisher, O'Donnell, & Oyserman, 2017; Goudeau & Croizet, 2017; Z. Li et al, 2018; Markus & Stephens, 2017; Piff, Kraus, & Keltner, 2018; Shafir, 2017).

These structural causes of behavior include a lack of a social safety net for working families; insufficient funding of libraries and schools in low-income neighborhoods; predatory banking and rental housing practices that can also lead to financial and residential unpredictability; and an unpredictability that is associated with greater difficulty functioning well academically and socially (Fisher, O'Donnell, & Oyserman, 2017; Goudeau & Croizet, 2017; Z. Li et al., 2018; Markus & Stephens, 2017; Piff, Kraus, & Keltner, 2018; Shafir, 2017).

The cultural encouragement of *focusing on* individual causes of behavior and *not focusing on* structural causes of behavior leads many people to incorrectly infer that class and/or racial differences in achievement reflect character differences, rather what are instead consequences of the aforementioned differences in structure (Fisher, O'Donnell, & Oyserman, 2017; Goudeau & Croizet, 2017; Marks & Coll, 2018; Markus & Stephens, 2017; Shafir, 2017).

These consequences of the aforementioned differences in structure include scarcity mindsets, cumulative disadvantage, threat orientations, racism, and oppression. They also bring chronic stress, which depletes the attention and cognitive resources that parents could give their children even if they are unable to give them much in the way of preparing them for academic culture, material resources, or even food (Fisher, O'Donnell, & Oyserman, 2017; Goudeau & Croizet, 2017; Marks & Coll, 2018; Markus & Stephens, 2017; Shafir, 2017).

Interventions to close the social class achievement gap must therefore address three factors: individual, construal, and structural (Dittman & Stephens, 2017).

Individual factors are those that help children and teens (especially, but not exclusively, those from lower-SES families who may not have had access to high-quality early education) engage in more effective self-regulation, as well as specific academic skills and abilities.

Construal factors are those that help change how students from low-income homes construe, or make sense of, their experiences. For example, a student might repeatedly attend poor-quality schools so that by the time they attend college, the student believes they don't belong in college and therefore are not be aware of, much less make use of, the college's or university's support services, such as mentoring and tutoring (Dittman & Stephens, 2017).

We all have implicit theories of what it means to be smart, and these theories of intelligence influence whether and how we learn. These theories could address construal factors as well (For instance, individuals who emphasize *performance goals* are more concerned with proving their intelligence via performance on tests.)

We call them **entity theories**, because whether people who believe such theories are conscious of it or not, they assume that intelligence is a fixed entity they either have or do not have. Therefore, they attribute any poor performance on their part to a lack of ability—rather than a lack of effort—and then often disengage from a task when they feel their weaknesses are exposed (Costa & Faria, 2018; Dweck, 1999). Such entity theories tend to be held by those individuals who focus most on performance goals, rather than mastery goals, which we learned about in Chapter 11.

Incremental theories, on the other hand, emphasize *mastery goals*, and people who hold them are more concerned with acquiring knowledge. Again, whether they are conscious of such or not, those who believe these theories have a **growth mindset** in that they assume intelligence can be acquired incrementally—so they are therefore more resilient in the face of failure because they attribute any poor performance on their part to a lack of effort rather than a lack of ability (Costa & Faria, 2018; Dweck, 1999).

Cross-cultural data reveal that students in Asia and Australia who hold incremental beliefs show higher achievement, whereas students in Europe who hold entity beliefs show higher achievement. Students in the United States who hold entity beliefs show worse achievement in general (Costa & Faria, 2018).

Yet a growth mindset can be acquired, and doing so reaps benefits for students in the United States. For example, the National Study of Learning Mindsets taught students about what a growth mindset means—that intellectual abilities can be developed—via an online intervention that lasted less than an hour (Yeager et al., 2019). The researchers found that this intervention improved grades and enrollment in an advanced mathematics course among a nationally representative sample of over 12,000 ninth-grade lower-achieving public school students in the United States. Even more impressive was that the effects of the intervention were sustained over time, especially when a growth mindset—and a sense of the importance of seeking out challenges—became the norm among students. This continued success may be due at least in part to the fact that taking on intellectual challenges in front of others is safer with supportive peers (Yeager et al., 2019).

Interventions that address construal factors—such as mindset or *grit*, or the willingness to sustain interest in and effort toward challenging goals over time (an inclination associated with mastery goals)—are likely necessary. But the interventions are not sufficient unless they also address structural factors (Dittman & Stephens, 2017; Duckworth, Peterson, Matthews, & Kelly, 2007; Park et al, 2018).

Structural factors are those that would provide as many material resources, as much access to high-quality teachers, and as many opportunities within schools in low-income neighborhoods as there are material resources, access to high-quality teachers, and opportunities within schools in high-income neighborhoods (Dittman & Stephens, 2017; Sawyer & Patton, 2018). Such changes would likely help close the social class achievement gap, and a social class health gap as well; those with more educational opportunities tend to live longer and healthier lives.

Interventions that include objective change in situations, via structural factors, are especially necessary. The emphasis on individual or construal factors in our culture of inequality blindness can isolate the source of problems as primarily residing in individual shortcomings—rather than take notice of the need for school reform, the political will to make such reform happen, and the necessary changes in the tax structure (Dittman & Stephens, 2017; Kirchgasler, 2018; Piff, Kraus, & Keltner, 2018; Walton & Wilson, 2018).

Organized Activities

Teens who spend their time out of school unsupervised and with peers are more likely to engage in risky behaviors such as missing school or selling drugs, as well as externalizing behaviors, whereas teens who participate in sports or who work show an increased positive identity, with a sense of knowing where their interests lie (K. T. H. Lee et al., 2018).

On the other hand, participation in extracurricular activities (arts, sports, community service, etc.) helps teens err on the resilience side of the risk–resilience pattern of development. This participation is associated with lower dropout rates, as well as outcomes revealing a positive example of the lifelong pattern of development, such as higher levels of educational attainment eight years after high school (Denault & Poulin, 2019; Haghighat & Knifsend, 2019; Neely & Vaquera, 2017). This latter finding about educational attainment is especially strong if adolescents continue to participate in extracurricular activities after high school (Denault & Poulin, 2019; Haghighat & Knifsend, 2019; Neely & Vaquera, 2017).

These positive outcomes are likely not just for the white middle class either. For instance, male teens who live in low-safety neighborhoods but who have access to youth-serving institutions (such as a YMCA) experience more friend support, perhaps because regular interaction with others promotes a sense of connectedness (Anderson et al., 2018).

Research also indicates that teens who live among neighborhood violence but whose parents engage in high levels of supervision are more likely to be involved in organized activities. Further, longitudinal work with Black teens in an urban disadvantaged community shows that the more these teens participate in organized activities at their school or church and/or in their community, the lower their substance use and the greater their life satisfaction when they are young adults (Anderson, Bohnert, & Governale, 2018; Eisman et al., 2017).

Additional longitudinal research reveals that teens who participate in a greater overall number of extracurricular activities show *more* career exploration and *less* career indecision. Such findings suggest that if teens are concerned about committing to a career choice prematurely, participating in extracurricular activities may help their later job satisfaction (Denault et al., 2019).

And it isn't merely the number of activities in which teens engage, despite how frequent such participation may be. Researchers have found that the greater the *variety* of extracurricular activities that teens participate in at the transition to high school, the less likely they are to experience decreases in their general self-concept, as well as their academic self-concept (Modecki et al., 2018).

This may be what has been occurring for Mona: She has been an ongoing member of swim teams and a Muslim American club. And in the last two years of high school she started contributing to a school-sponsored literary magazine given her love of reading, got involved in theater set design given her love of drawing, and participated in an innovation challenge.

After Mona graduated high school, the summer before she started college she volunteered at a local hospital, thinking it would mesh with her interests in becoming a physician. But her experiences in high school with the innovation challenge, in which students were to identify a societal problem and design a solution, stuck with her. It has her really excited about how engineering could be "the" college major for her, now that she sees the field's humanitarian impacts.

Other specific benefits of organized activities include the opportunity to take on roles (such as cameraperson, committee chair, or activity leader) that give adolescents a sense of purpose and a sense of being accountable to others. They also learn to think strategically, fulfill their need to contribute meaningfully, and persevere in the face of initial failure (Fuligni, 2018; Larson et al. 2019; Raffaelli et al., 2018).

The role possibilities of organized activities take on special importance in modern society too, especially when we consider that the household roles of working on the family farm or taking care of siblings are not as universal as they once were. Also, the responsibilities that come from role opportunities via organized activities transfer to more responsibility at home, with teens doing more chores and errands (Fuligni, 2018; Larson et al. 2019; Raffaelli et al., 2018).

Organized activities may also provide teens with psychological meaning, and interviews with students, parents, teachers, activity leaders, and school administrators reveal that such meaning can vary by the SES of a teen's family.

For instance, interviews of adolescents from higher-SES families indicate that organized activities (called "cocurricular activities") provide these teens with the opportunity to maximize their talents and devote time to their passion with ample equipment, facilities and full-time staff. Interviews of adolescents from lower-SES families indicate that organized activities (called "extracurricular activities") provide these teens with an opportunity to overcome challenges and obstacles (Guest, 2018). The latter group's being able to overcome challenges and obstacles with limited equipment, facilities, and staff is indeed an opportunity.

Yet it can also represent disproportionate demands that burden lower-income teens.

An example of such disproportionate demands occurs when the success of a low-income group of teens' basketball team is deemed to be a matter of hard work—and this hard work requires not just the same practice that higher-income teens need engage in, but also that the team members arrive at a community gym (because of the school's lack of a regulation gym) by 5:15 a.m., with some students needing public transportation to and from this off-campus gym.

So a deficit-based orientation of extracurricular activities providing teens with such opportunities is also an unfair burden—and an unfair source of stress—when healthy development is not a privilege, but a right, and a right we learned about in Chapter 1, to be supported with government policies and funding that provides adequate availability and quality of services without disproportionate and unfair demands on adolescents (Banati & Lansford, 2018; Casey, 2019; Guest, 2018).

Key Terms

Academic Tracking	Entity Theories	Growth Mindset
Adrenarche	Estrogens	Growth Spurt
Allostatic Load	Formal Operational	Incremental Theories
Androgens	Gonadarche	Intergenerational Social Mobility
Civic Participation	Gonads	Maturational Timing
Eating Disorder	Grit	Memory Strategies

Summary

1. **Discuss how nature and nurture shape our understanding of adolescence.** Adolescence refers to the period of the human lifespan that occurs between childhood and adolescence. Despite ages 18 and 21 having served as conventional markers of adulthood, no dramatic or abrupt changes in the brain occur at this time. The interconnections among various parts of the brain continue to increase through early adulthood, so our understanding of when adolescence begins and ends continues to evolve over time.

2. **Describe what normative changes in physical growth occur during adolescence.** Males tend to start out similar to females but gain more inches and pounds over time, likely because they experience a longer growing period. Height in females tapers off at around 14 years of age, and any increases in height after age 16 are usually not noticeable; height in males tapers off at around 17 years of age, and any increases in height after age 18 are usually not noticeable.

3. **Illustrate the changes that occur in puberty.** Puberty refers to the gradual physical transition from childhood to adulthood, a process that involves two events: adrenarche and gonadarche. Visible growth differences among the sexes are not uncommon. These differences in early adolescence are due to differences in the onset of the growth spurt, or the rapid gain in both height and weight that is the first outward sign of puberty. Maturational timing, which refers to the moment when the cascade of pubertal events begins, varies from adolescent to adolescent, with additional secular changes apparent over generations and within-group differences in teens; some teens experience maturation on-time and some experience it off-time.

4. **Detail how the brain develops during adolescence.** Puberty likely prompts a reorganization of neural activity in the brain, a process that continues after obvious external physical changes are apparent in teens, and then into adulthood. Changes include those to the prefrontal cortex, white matter, and gray matter.

5. **Specify how physical activity, sports, and sports injuries play a role in motor skills.** Teens should engage in 60 minutes of moderate to vigorous physical activity each day, yet most do not meet this health standard. Schools could benefit students by ensuring that teens have daily opportunities to engage in moderate physical activity of their choice. Students are less cognitively engaged after breaks, but more cognitively engaged after engaging in moderate physical activity.

    Sports participation is correlated negatively with psychological difficulties, indicating that what may help heal the body may also help heal the mind. Yet sports also have the potential for physical, cognitive, and emotional harm; there is the risk of physical, sexual, or psychological abuse from coaches, from serious sports injuries, and/or from nonmedical use of prescription opioids perhaps as an attempt to cope with such injuries.

6. **What are some of the major health issues relevant to adolescents?** New challenges occur every day as adolescents confront decisions about what to eat; some struggle with eating disorders. They also must deal with whether to conform to popular images of attractiveness, how to manage school schedules that may be out of sync with their biological clocks, and whether to join peers who entice them to experiment with drugs and other substances illicitly.

   Teens who participate in positive youth development programs experience multiple benefits, including making healthier physical choices and also being more likely to contribute to their communities, to be civically active, and to participate in science programs during out-of-school time. Females in such groups feel less driven to thinness, and males in such groups are less likely to have body dissatisfaction.

7. **Explain what Piaget's theory can tell us about adolescent cognitive development.** Piaget's theory of Formal Operational Thinking refers to the ability to reason abstractly. Because they are capable of Formal Operational Thinking, teens are better able than children to appreciate not only what *is*, but also what *is possible*, and they no longer need concrete objects in order to think logically. They can now engage in internal mental operations as well as *scientific reasoning*, which consists of testing hypotheses by isolating the effects of each variable individually while holding other variables constant.

   Adolescents are certainly able to think about what is possible in society and to engage in civic participation or work to sustain a democratic society. There is no single age at which teens become competent decision-makers with mature cognitive capacities. Teens experience a maturity gap in that they typically possess *cognitive capacity abilities* before they possess *psychosocial maturity abilities*.

8. **Recount the factors associated with academic success in adolescence.** Memory strategies are techniques that move information from working memory to long-term memory. Teens have the potential to progress through two stages of literacy. Students from the United States score at levels that are not significantly different from average for reading and science, but they score at levels significantly lower than average for mathematics. The U.S. system scores significantly higher than the average across all countries when it comes to the differences in resources (such as staff) between advantaged schools and disadvantaged schools.

   Intergenerational Social Mobility is becoming more scarce in the United States. There is also a social class achievement gap in the Unites States; that is, students from low-SES families perform worse than students from high-SES families. Our country's tendency toward *economic inequality blindness* hides structural causes of behavior, leading people to incorrectly infer that class and/or racial differences in achievement reflect character differences. Students who adopt incremental theories of intelligence and growth are therefore more resilient in the face of failure. There are many positive benefits of teens participating in organized activities.

The Cycle of Science

Research

Why was the study conducted?

The researchers wanted to examine the effectiveness of an after-school positive youth development (PYD) program that followed the 4-H model yet was based on physical activities, that incorporated lessons on character development and social relationships, and that took place in an urban environment (Riciputi et al., 2019).

Who participated in the study?

The Black, Asian American, European American, Latinx, Native American, or multiracial participants included fifth-grade and sixth-grade students at one particular urban school in the Midwest. Of the participants, 75% were from low-income families and qualified for free lunches. The leaders were trained educators at the school and had previous experience with 4-H programs.

Which type of design was used?

The researchers had participants report on their experiences in the after-school program via semistructured interviews. These are akin to the clinical interviews we learned about in the section on self-report methods in Chapter 2; participants are asked a limited number of questions, with the intent of allowing them to guide the direction the interview takes.

The semistructured interviews of the student participants took approximately 30 minutes each. The researchers' questions, which participants answered and elaborated on, concerned *if and what the participants learned in the after-school program*, as well as their *interactions with peers*, such as how the program helped them get to know the other kids better than they knew them before.

The researchers also interviewed the leaders for approximately 60 minutes each about their experiences delivering the program. The interviews included questions on the program's strengths (such as the main benefits for the participants) as well as its challenges (such as in implementing the curriculum and training the staff). The leaders were asked to answer the questions and to elaborate on their answers with examples.

The researchers also collected observational data, then coded these data, along with the data from both sets of interviews.

What were the results?

The researchers found that even though the participants initially resisted some activities, each of the activities ended with full participation. The participants were also very engaged and found the program to be fun, especially those activities that involved team competitions or uniqueness (such as Sumo wrestling in inflatable body suits), so that they were exercising without realizing it. They least preferred the activities that were similar to those in their school environment, in which they were required to follow lengthy instructions and/or wait their turn.

The participants reported that they learned about responsibility via group activities, about making better choices than simply doing what usually feels good, about the option of making other positive changes in their lives, and about learning to interact with other kids more than they usually do. Leaders reported that, in general, the participants came to accept each other's differences and engaged in positive peer pressure to help one another make good choices. Also, the electing of student officers helped these participants serve as role models for others.

Are the results consistent with theory?

Yes. PYD programs such as this one help teens err on the resilience side of the risk–resilience pattern of development. They are based on the ecological systems theory (which we learned about in Chapter 1). This theory holds that of the various contexts in which we develop, each has a unique influence on us, and each context interacts with the other contexts. The behavior of the participants in this study was likely a function of their mesosystems—that is, the interactions among their various microsystems (for example, sharing different school activities with different peers, as well with as the leaders)—interacting with one another (Bronfenbrenner, 1977).

How can the results be used to improve our lives?

Interventions such as these can provide adolescents with after-school programs, supervised by adults, where they are given opportunities to exercise physically; to practice teamwork; and to learn emotional skills such as initiating interactions with others with whom one does not usually socialize as well as getting along with others who are different.

Exercises

1. What pattern of results would you expect if the participants were older?

2. What pattern of results would you expect if the study focused on team competitions under high emotional arousal, so teens could practice making safer choices in such situations?

3. How might graduates of programs such as these get involved to serve as mentors?

Helpful Websites

The National Sleep Foundation provides advocacy tips for changing school start times: http://www.sleepfoundation.org/hottopics/index.php?secid=18&id=205

The American Psychological Association provides answers to common questions about transgender people, gender identity, and gender expression, including ways to support them: https://www.apa.org/topics/lgbt/transgender

Information about different types of birth control is available here: http://www.plannedparenthood.org/birth-control-pregnancy/birth-control.htm

The Internet is influencing all of our lives, especially the lives of adolescents. To see how, watch PBS's online program, "Growing Up Online": http://www.pbs.org/wgbh/pages/frontline/kidsonline/

To learn more about Positive Youth Development programs, including how to incorporate them into local communities and programs, visit https://www.hhs.gov/ash/oah/adolescent-development/positive-youth-development/index.html

Recommended Reading

Jensen, F. E., & Nutt, A. E. (2015). *The teenage brain: A neuroscientist's survival guide to raising adolescents and young adults*. New York, NY: HarperCollins.

Mooney, N. (2008). *Not keeping up with our parents: The decline of the professional middle class*. Boston, MA: Beacon Press.

Nisbett, R. E. (2010). *Intelligence and how to get it: Why schools and culture count*. New York, NY: W. W. Norton.

Payne, K. (2017). *The broken ladder: How inequality affects the way we think, live, and die*. New York, NY: Viking Press.

Robinson, A. (1993). *What smart students know: Maximum grades. Optimum learning. Minimum time*. New York, NY: Three Rivers Press.

Siegel, D. J. (2014). *Brainstorm: The power and purpose of the teenage brain*. New York, NY: Jeremy P. Tarcher/Penguin.

CHAPTER 13

Emotional Development in Adolescence

Snapshot

Sequoia, whose assigned gender at birth was male, identifies as *Two-Spirit*, meaning they represent a third gender in Native American communities.

Sequoia is also a high school senior, and is both excited about upcoming graduation, yet they have many concerns about their future, especially as being someone with an intersectional identity struggling with multiple forms of oppression and worried about discrimination in the various colleges and careers they are contemplating. These stresses run alongside more normative issues such as wishing to be able to spend more time with friends and family while wanting to say involved in numerous student activities, working part-time, and volunteering one day a week.

How can we ensure that all teenagers, both similar to and different from Sequoia, will thrive?

What Can Erikson's Theory Tell Us About Needs in Adolescence?

In Erikson's theory, the development of self intensifies to a crisis in adolescence, partly as a result of the multidimensional cascade of biological and cognitive changes associated with puberty.

Such changes can alter a teen's view of their gender, physical abilities, sexuality, and/or appearance, as well as increase their capacity to think hypothetically about not only who they are,

FIG. 13.1　Sequoia

but also who they could be—a process not unknown to Sequoia—especially as they ponder which college will be most supportive of them and their desire to discover who they are and fulfill their potential, as well as prepare for a career (Roshandel & Hudley, 2018).

Erikson called the crisis of adolescence *identity–role confusion* (Erikson, 1965).

Identity–Role Confusion

During the adolescent crisis of **Identity–Role Confusion**, either we are able to "maintain inner sameness and continuity of one's meaning for others'" or we are unable to do so (Erikson, 1963, p. 261).

As with the other crises hypothesized in each stage of Erikson's theory that we have discussed in prior chapters, this crisis of Identity–Role Confusion is a period of increased conflict—but also of high growth potential (Erikson, 1959). Our identity does reflect some continuity over time. In fact, our identity is our accrued confidence in our ability to maintain this inner sameness and continuity, an integration of all that we have resolved up to the present day—a process that is clearly consistent with the lifelong pattern of development (Erikson, 1959).

For example, self-esteem results not from praise, but from the strengths we acquire by mastering the crises of each life stage, such as the Industry–Inferiority crisis of middle childhood. These gains, achieved during our relatively long human childhood, are required to prepare us for the tasks of adulthood. Our increasing sense of identity is then experienced as emotional well-being and a sense of knowing where we are going.

That is, if and when individuals do resolve the crisis of each stage in Erikson's theory, they gain that stage's *ego strength* or virtue. The virtue of the adolescent identity–role confusion is **Fidelity**, or the ability to be loyal or faithful to someone or something (Erikson, 1964). What encourages fidelity?

Well, secure emotional attachments likely support the processes of *exploring* diverse ways of being and then *committing* to our own unique identity among such ways of being, whereas inhabiting the

Learning Goals

▶ Discuss what Erikson's theory can tell us about needs in adolescence

▶ Compare and contrast models of identity

▶ Explain Intersectionality

▶ Recount what is known about teens' families and the relationships within them

▶ Recount what is known about teens' relationships outside the family

▶ Detail some common emotional problems that teens struggle with

▶ Identify how empathy and prosocial behavior develop in adolescence

▶ Clarify what makes effective interventions for and with adolescents

life story given to or expected of us likely does not foster fidelity, perhaps because the processes of exploration and commitment are too psychologically risky without secure bonds to others (Erikson, 1968; Kerpelman & Pittman, 2018; Skarstein et al., 2018).

Attaining the virtue of fidelity eases the conflicts in later stages, though.

Indeed, the holistic approach to Erikson's theory reveals between-stage relationships, in which the conflict of any given stage is related to conflicts in other stages, and reveals the relational nature of identity (Kroger, 2018; Schachter & Galliher, 2018). For example, how the *Identity–Role Confusion* crisis of adolescence is resolved will likely have implications for how the *Intimacy–Isolation* crisis of early adulthood is resolved, so that a change in a person's identity may lead to a change in the person's romantic relationship and vice versa (Erikson, 1959; Kerpelman & Pittman, 2018).

So the process of identity development is dynamic and indeed relational: It involves continuity between who we perceive ourselves to be and who we perceive others to see in us, and expect of us (Erikson, 1968; Kerpelman & Pittman, 2018; Schwartz, Luyckx, & Crocetti, 2015).

Although the community in which a person develops may experience initial mistrust at a newly emerging individual in adolescence, those individuals who mirror and accept the evolving identity in a teen will take pleasure in becoming acquainted with this person. The person who is "becoming" also, in turn, acknowledges the community by wishing to be recognized.

For Erikson, community interactions may include feelings of rejection and/or vengeance when either party exhibits a lack of recognition or care, as in, say, the case of a teen who is rejected by their family.

FIG. 13.2   Identity

Unfortunately, this is consistent with attachment research findings that show a relationship among an anxious attachment style, a need to belong, and rejection sensitivity (Erikson, 1959; Kerpelman & Pittman, 2018; Sato, Fonagy, & Luyten, 2019).

Models of Identity

So how can we study identity? Well, one popular classic approach to understanding how individuals resolve the *Identity–Role Confusion* crisis is the **Status Model of Identity** (Marcia, 1966).

As you can see in Figure 13.3, the identity statuses in this model are based on the extent to which an individual has engaged in the process of Identity Exploration—that is, has considered different identity-related possibilities in terms of race, ethnicity, gender, sexuality, religion, spirituality, career, etc. This classic Identity Status model also diagrams the extent to which an individual has engaged in the process of Identity Commitment, that is, has made decisions regarding the aforementioned possibilities (Marcia, 1966).

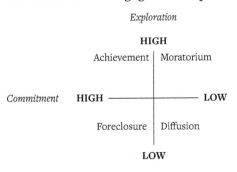

FIG. 13.3   Identity Statuses

Source: https://www.researchgate.net/figure/Marcias-1966-original-identity-status-model-Marcias-model-has-since-been-expanded-by_fig1_328997161.

Out of these two processes come the four statuses. The **Identity Diffusion** status is one in which the individual has engaged in little or no exploration, and little or no commitment, such as an early adolescent who has not begun to think seriously about potential careers.

On the other hand, the individual in the **Identity Foreclosure** status has engaged in little or no exploration, yet possesses high levels of commitment (which may be quite rigid and therefore render a person less resilient later on in the face of life challenges compared to a person who has achieved high levels of commitment alongside high levels of exploration). An example would be an adolescent who plans on pursuing the career their parents prefer (Ferrer-Wreder & Kroger, 2020).

One form of Foreclosure is a **negative identity**, in which an individual simply adheres to roles that oppose the expectations of parents and/or society, a process that errs on the risk side of the risk–resilience pattern of development. This status understandably might be embarked on by teens whose parents don't acknowledge their individuality and instead demand their teen full a role the parents have chosen for them, and/or by marginalized teens who experience discrimination against themselves, their family members, and/or community members and therefore have fewer opportunities, role models, and guidance in developing a **positive identity** or one based on developing their individual needs, talents, values, etc. (Hihara, Sugimura, & Syed, 2018).

The **Identity Moratorium** status is opposite that of the Identity Foreclosure status, in that the individual has engaged in high levels of exploration but has low levels of commitment. This status might apply to an adolescent who doesn't plan on pursuing the career their parents prefer they do, and is currently exploring their own path of possibilities.

The **Identity Achievement** status is the opposite of the Identity Diffusion status, in that the individual has gone through extensive levels of both the exploration process and commitment process. Keep in mind, however, that the identity of these individuals, as well as those in the other three statuses, may change because identity is dynamic and open to revision——so that we are always "in process" (Kerpelman & Pittman, 2018; Schwartz, Luyckx, & Crocetti, 2015).

Sequoia is likely in an Identity Moratorium in some ways, such as their career, yet in an Identity Achievement in other ways, such as their gender identity.

Sequoia's Identity Moratorium may continue for some time, as they graduate high school, attend college, and prepare for whatever work they choose—yet it may also eventually subside. This is because longitudinal research indicates that from age 18 to 35, young people's scores on the Foreclosure and Moratorium statuses (when measured continuously rather than dichotomously) tend to decline, whereas their scores on the Achievement status tend to increase (Cramer, 2017; Ferrer-Wreder & Kroger, 2020).

Changes over time such as these polydirectional patterns of development point to identity status development indeed being a process, and one that occurs over an extended period of time including adolescent and early adulthood, if not also stages beyond (Cramer, 2017; Ferrer-Wreder & Kroger, 2020).

More recent research provides evidence for a **Dual-Cycle Model of Identity** of commitment formation and commitment evaluation. These two ongoing cycles include other developmental dimensions, which may include *ruminative exploration* (such as repetitively deliberating over one's options, and in a passive manner without being able to decide, a process that is associated with poorer emotional adjustment); *exploration in breadth* (such as investigating a range of college majors) and making a commitment (such as choosing a college major); *exploration in depth* (looking further into one's career possibilities with a major in psychology); *identifying with a commitment* (such sensing that the choice of a psychology major will really suit the person (Beyers & Luyckx, 2016; van Doeselaar et al., 2019).

The **Three Factor Model of Identity** maintains the commitment of the Identity Status Model, as well as the exploration in depth of the Dual-Cycle Model of Identity. This model also includes *commitment reconsideration*, which involves comparing one's current commitments—which are no longer satisfying to the person—to alternative possible commitments. Research shows that commitment reconsideration is both a predictor, and an outcome, of poorer-quality relationships between adolescents and their parents (Crocetti, Rubini, & Meeus, 2008; Crocetti et al., 2013, 2017; Sznitman, Zimmermann, & Van Petegm, 2019).

When this reconsideration of commitment is incorporated into the traditional Identity Status Model, a *Searching Moratorium* status can be distinguished, in which an adolescent shows high levels of exploration, but high levels of commitment and reconsideration of commitment as well (Crocetti, 2018). Teens in this Searching Moratorium status tend to show higher levels of psychological adjustment than do those in the Moratorium status, likely because the commitment they have made serves as a secure base—a base that the teens in the Moratorium status do not (yet) have (Crocetti, 2018).

There are additional models of identity besides the Status, Dual-Cycle, and Three Factor models. One of these is the Narrative approach, which focuses on a person's story of how they came to be the person they are becoming; this model focuses primarily on identity in adults (McAdams, 2018).

For the purposes of adolescent identity, know that across the three identity models covered here, commitment is generally associated with lower anxiety and depression, greater psychological adjustment and well-being (including a sense of mastery, self-esteem, and life satisfaction), and greater perceived family climate (Becht et al., 2019; Schwartz, Luyckx, & Crocetti, 2015; van Doeselaar et al., 2018). On the other hand, low levels of commitment, commitment reconsideration, and ruminative exploration are both associated with less optimal functioning, including greater internalizing and externalizing problems over time (Becht et al., 2019; Schwartz, Luyckx, & Crocetti, 2015; van Doeselaar et al., 2018).

Societal Investment in Identity

We learned a moment ago that identity development occurs over an extended period of time. And although an identity crisis may be *prolonged*, *severe* (in that it is overwhelming to the person), and/or *aggravated* (in that repeated attempts to resolve the crisis are not successful), an identity crisis need not be a catastrophe either, but instead a normative state, a growth opportunity, and an invitation for adolescents to engage actively and lead a self-determined life (Erikson, 1968; Côté, 2018).

Identity development that is especially prolonged may be a voluntary opportunity (such as for teens who can find a way to afford to take a gap year after high school or college). But it may be imposed burden, such for teens who suffer from high levels of anxiety and find it difficult to develop a stable identity, and/or because economic factors may make it difficult to take time specifically to muse about one's ideal options, especially in the face of limited educational and occupational opportunities.

But exploration can (and should) be possible, particularly when schools have flexible curriculums to allow teens to discover where their strengths and interests lie. There are also community organizations that provide the positive youth development programs we learned about in Chapter 12—programs that help teens err on the resilience side of the risk–resilience pattern of development (Arnold, 2017; Côté, 2019; Crocetti, 2018; Ferrer-Wreder & Kroger, 2020).

Universal preschool and equitably funded public schools that scaffold self-regulation from the early years will also better serve society by fostering identity development in young people (Becht et al., 2018; Pfeifer & Berkman, 2018).

Indeed, research data indicate that identity development exhibits characteristics associated with the multidimensional pattern of development. That is, the volume of brain's nucleus accumbens (which is associated with the processing of reward and the motivation to pursue long-term goals) and the brain's prefrontal cortex (which is associated with information-seeking and cognitive control) are both greater in adolescents with stronger commitments and reflections on such commitments (Becht et al., 2018; Pfeifer & Berkman, 2018).

So it is imperative that society scaffold such opportunities, particularly when only approximately 25% of young people engage in the proactive identity formation that requires the critical thinking, moral reasoning, self-regulation, and self-reflection to explore significant life choices (and the viability of such choices). They need to do this ahead of time while also developing skills and knowledge in the face of numerous modern-day distractions (Côté, 2019).

The aforementioned percentage is particularly worrisome given adolescents' eventual choices (or lack thereof, whether due to a lack of support, to anxiety, to taking the path of least resistance, and/or to following a consumer model of impression management and pleasure-seeking rather than the discomfort of personal growth). Such choices can have enduring consequences that are difficult to reverse later on in their lives—especially for young people who have limited personal and/or family resources to act as a safety net and help redirect them (Côté, 2019).

Although many universities are providing excellent service helping students cope with valid emotional struggles, many of the students report high levels of anxiety and depression as a result of a society that assumes everyone is well-suited for college. In addition, their prior schooling experiences may have left them underprepared, academically and emotionally, for the demands of higher education. In such cases, the current "college for all" context contributes to anxiety and depression (Côté, 2018; 2019; Lerner et al., 2018; Pinquart & Pfeiffer, 2018).

Underprepared students might want to consider that these emotional states (and perhaps even any diagnoses they receive or may come to identify for themselves) are a function of the United States' failure to provide viable alternatives to college (such as the apprenticeship-to-work models found in other countries that we learned about in Chapter 12) that curtail young people's developmental

FIG. 13.4 A Stressed Student

Copyright © Depositphotos/Wavebreakmedia.

need to establish an identity (Côté, 2018, 2019; Lerner et al., 2018; Pinquart & Pfeiffer, 2018).

Critics who are opposed to funding the societal investment in young people's identities might want to take note that a mature identity is associated not only with more goal-directed behavior, lower delinquency, and higher well-being but also with greater social responsibility as well as more volunteering and civic engagement—behaviors that contemporary unstructured and complex societies seek from young people and therefore must nurture (Arnold, 2017; Camilletti & Banati, 2018; Crocetti, 2018).

Intersectionality

Intersectionality refers to how multiple aspects of identity (such as nationality, language(s), religion, culture, class or socioeconomic status, race, ethnicity, gender identity, affectional orientation, ability, body size, and age) shape our experiences and life chances. These intersecting systems of equality and inequality often self-perpetuate for better or worse, as a result of privilege or the intersection of multiple forms of oppression such as classism, racism, heterosexism, and ableism (Crenshaw, 1989; Nadan & Korbin, 2018; Santos & Toomey, 2018; Schwartz, Luyckx, & Crocetti, 2015).

As you can see in Figure 13.5, each of these 12 systems of equality and inequality is nonbinary, and each serves as a prism through which the other 11 systems are seen (deVries, 2015).

For example, with regard to race, someone may have an identity of being "mixed" given they have Black, European American, and Asian ancestry, but they are often perceived and legally classified by others as Black as a result of their physical attributes. Additionally, through this lens of race, the person's social positions on other systems are viewed, so that a Christian Black male may be understood differently and perhaps not viewed as legitimately as a Christian European American male, since the latter group is the beneficiary of existing power structures (deVries, 2015).

In regards to how this prism can better help us understand intersectionality, imagine a student who identifies as Black (*race* in Figure 13.5) and who speaks Spanish (*language* in Figure 13.5). Although we each have unique life experiences, this student tends to have a different set of experiences compared to a student who identifies as European-American (*race*) and who speaks Spanish—intersectionalities that become more complex when we consider citizenship (*nationality* in Figure 13.5, on a different plane), such as the former student identifying as Dominican and on a student visa and the latter student as identifying as North American.

So although developmental science researchers have created excellent interventions that help marginalized teens err of the resilience side of the risk–resilience pattern of development by fostering their developmental task of forming their ethnic–racial identity (which leads to valuable improvements in their emotional outcomes), advocacy work informed by intersectionality is sorely needed.

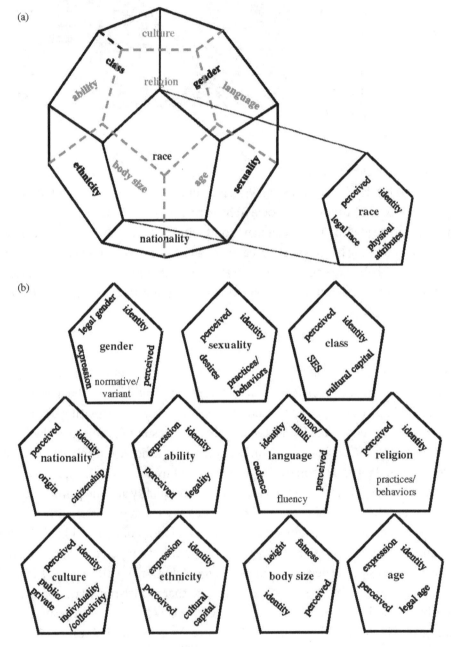

FIG. 13.5   A Prism of Intersectionality

This is because researchers can only do so much. Interventions do tremendous work, but can't necessarily eradicate structural oppression in the face of prejudice and/or discriminatory policies.

As another example, consider how policies in the United States prevent undocumented immigrants (including those who were brought to the United States as children) from working. This sends a message to these immigrants that they are unwelcome, and the policies severely restrict their quality of life and their ability to fulfill their potential (Schwartz et al., 2018; Syed & Fish, 2018; Umaña-Taylor et al., 2018; Umaña-Taylor et al., 2018).

Unfortunately, it isn't difficult to imagine that the aforementioned lack of opportunity is likely even magnified for those with other marginalized identities, such as Sequoia. Or imagine the effect on a working-class Latinx teen who was brought here as a child, has become fully fluent in both Spanish and English, has excelled as a student, and who wishes to pursue their talent in science—but who is not always taken seriously by some others in the university's chemistry lab and cannot even be employed in the lab as a work-study student (Goldberg & Allen, 2018; Schwartz et al., 2018).

An intersectional view of development not only provides us with a richer understanding of the lives of children and teens, but also helps us work for greater equity (including prevention and intervention efforts, as well as social justice advocacy) to improve the lives of children and teens over their lifespan.

Adopting an intersectional view is a very important charge for developmental science, and one that is consistent with the lifelong pattern of development. Current generations of young people face *expanding* income inequality, yet *shrinking* access to opportunities that may very well have consequences for their futures if changes are not soon made soon, as well as dismaying levels of continued marginalization and oppression against themselves or others close to them (deVries, 2015; Mays & Ghavani, 2018; Rogers, 2019; Santos & Toomey, 2018; Schachter & Galliher, 2018).

To learn more about intersectionality and the researcher who proposed the aforementioned prism model, see *A Mentor Minute: Kylan DeVries, PhD*.

Mentor Minute

Kylan DeVries, PhD

1) Describe your work, please.

I'm an associate professor with a joint appointment in Sociology and Gender, Sexuality, and Women's Studies. My particular areas of expertise include intersectionality, transgender studies, queer studies, queer of color theory, critical race studies, critical mixed race studies, sociology of gender, social psychology (with emphasis on identity, collective identity, and symbolic interactionism), and qualitative research methods.

My current institution is a liberal arts organization that focuses on teaching. Most of my time is spent teaching, and I'm lucky enough to have a lot of say in what classes I teach. For instance, I will be teaching a new course examining how trans people experience and assert agency in or in relation to various social institutions such as prison, ICE, education, and families. One key aspect of the courses I teach is to address social change and the ways individuals and groups are attempting to create equity and inclusion. This sometimes includes critiques of social justice organizations that do not approach problems intersectionally, and we address what we might learn from that.

FIG. 13.6   Kylan DeVries, PhD

I consider myself an intersectional and critical scholar, which means social justice is infused in my research, scholarship, and teaching. The work of Black women scholars, such as Hooks, Crenshaw, and Hill Collins, has had a profound influence on my thinking and action both as an activist and as a scholar. Much of my research has focused on the experiences of transgender people of color, although I later critique that terminology. Bringing intersectionality to my work was a bit of a challenge, as many sociologists viewed it as an additive approach and only address marginalized identities and social locations. I wanted to highlight how normative identities, such as Whiteness, were just as important to consider as marginalized identities. I attempted to do that by creating an intersectional model, which I now often use in my classes.

2) How does social justice inform your work?

One thing that drew me to the field of sociology, before going to graduate school, was how some scholars were working toward social change and engaging in social justice work through their research, teaching, and/or service. It was inspiring. As I thought about going to graduate school and what I might research, my goal was to bring change to academe and broader communities. I was particularly bothered by the White normativity of queer and trans spaces and wanted my research to address and challenge that.

Two of my mentors in graduate school modeled different ways of connecting scholarship and activism. One of my mentors in graduate school was Robert D. Benford, whose work focused on social movements. He was also engaged in local activism. He challenged me to think about how my research could inform activism. My mentor and dissertation chair was Jennifer L. Dunn; some of her work includes the books *Judging Victims: Why We Stigmatize Survivors and How They Reclaim Respect* and *Courting Disaster: Intimate Stalking, Culture, and Criminal Justice*. She was also inspiring in thinking about how research could inform the work of advocacy groups and create institutional social change. She really encouraged me to connect symbolic interactionism (the examination of individual interactions) with social institutions.

3) How did you become involved in social justice and/or advocacy?

My activism, which I later understood as social justice, began before my academic career. It infused my friend groups, jobs, and volunteer work. I'm a first-generation student and took a slow road through academe. Before moving to graduate school, I held a number of jobs. What was missing for me was the ability to create any real social change. While I could sometimes help contribute to small change, it increasingly felt meaningless (a little defeatist, I know). When I saw sociologists engaging in activism, it seemed to have broader ramifications. That is when I decided I wanted to go to graduate school, so that my teaching and research could have a broader influence on social change.

I'd also add that I grew up in British Columbia (although I was born in the USA) in a White bicultural home (my mom is Canadian and my dad Dutch). My dad's, and his family's, sharing of experiences of during and post WWII in the Netherlands significantly influenced my perceptions of the world and what was ethically and morally right, sometimes in contrast to what was "legal." During my school years, the BC government implemented cultural diversity education classes. If I remember correctly, I was part of one of the first classes to take this. The multicultural stance also influenced how I thought about the world and what was "just," although in later years I learned to critique the use of "multiculturalism" and "diversity" as problematically used by institutions and organizations without real change.

My queer and trans (and formerly lesbian) identities and experiences have also shaped my involvement in social justice. When I came out in my early 20's as a lesbian, it was in the early 1990s, and I encountered a lot of homophobia. Some of my first advocacy work was around what we then called GLB issues (later I would use the term *queer* and include additional identities). I now identify as trans masculine, and this has also shaped my trans activism in social justice.

4) What are your thoughts on how social justice can improve child and adolescent development?

In reflecting back, it was social justice work by others that influenced the Canadian government to implement cultural diversity education. This education helped me better understand the importance of differences, the problems with "us versus them" thinking, and how personal growth within social justice entails lifelong learning and self-reflection. I then think about how my own social justice work might influence the next generation to further critically engage with our world, the ways of knowing (and how this is political), and how to create social change.

My partner and I are also implementing social justice work in how we raise our child. We decided to raise our child with a gender-inclusive approach, and we are using *they/them/theirs* pronouns for our child until they tell us differently. We also feel it's very important to have conversations with our child about social justice. We are very deliberate in including diverse representations in the many books we read to our child, including diversity of race and ethnicity, gender, sexuality, dis/ability, body size, and other types of difference. In doing this, we've also had many conversations with other parents. We bring our child to many campus and community events, often social justice–related. Our hope is that our child will also be social justice–oriented and have the tools to create the change they want for the world.

5) What suggestions do you have for undergraduate students who are interested in making a change in child and adolescent development?

It is much easier for children to think outside of our institutional boxes, and I would encourage students interested in child and adolescent development to promote more student-centered learning rather than attempting to make children conform. Yes, children need to become functional and active members in our society, but do they really need to keep things as they are? Especially given where we are headed? I look at the many children and youth engaged in social justice work today. I am truly inspired by them. I think the best we can do is give children the skills to create change and teach them resiliency.

• • • •

What Do We Know About Teens' Families and the Relationships Within Them?

Family structures refer to the people a teen resides with, as well as the legal and/or biological relationships among the adults in the home and their legal and/or biological relationships to the teen.

Although married, two-parent heterosexual families are a statistical minority, they are often assumed to be ideal, whether they are or not. They become the referent against which other families (often deemed "alternative," despite being the statistical majority) are compared, consciously or not (Murry & Lippold, 2018).

Yet the empirical research data indicate that the *quality of relationships* among family members is a stronger predictor of adolescents' well-being than is the *particular structure* of their specific family. This is consistent with what we learned in Chapter 9 about one type of family—that is, children with GBQTIA+ parents.

What are some other family structures, including but not limited to those that may be marginalized yet stable, as well as foster and adoptive? We learned about some of the various structures in Chapter 11, but here we consider most of them.

Family Structures

Some adolescents grow up in extended families with relatives; with a single parent who is a single parent out of choice or because of the departure or death of their partner; opposite-sex but unmarried parents; separated or divorced parents; parents who remarry; same-sex parents; parents who may be nonbinary; parents of races and/or ethnicities that are different from that of the other parent and perhaps the children; stepfamilies; families in which a parent and/or a teen has physical limitations, special needs, and/or mental health issues; families who are part of the working poor; families created through foster care, adoption, reproductive technologies, or surrogacy; families who have many or few economic resources and/or support; families in which a parent is incarcerated; families with custodial grandparents; immigrant families, and/or refugee families (Demir-Dagdas et al., 2017; Murry & Lippold, 2018). Obviously, the variations are many.

Some structures—such as when there is only one parent or when the structure is undergoing transition, particularly when it involves an economic downturn (perhaps as a result of parental death, divorce, and/or stepfamily creation)—show more inconsistent parenting. This increases the risk—but does not guarantee—that teens will perform worse academically, socially, and emotionally (Hua, Bugeja, & Maple, 2019; Lin et al., 2019; Murry & Lippold, 2018; Schaan et al., 2019).

Other work, with children and teens who are in foster care—in which they are (ideally temporarily) removed from their homes by child welfare services as a result of maltreatment—shows that they are more likely to have mental health issues than are children who live with their biological parents (Xu & Bright, 2018).

There is some evidence that children in *kinship care*, living with kin such as a grandparent or other relative or a close friend of the family (as is the case of Sequoia's best friend, whose parents both died when he was young as a result of a lack of medical care to treat complications of diabetes) experience fewer problems than those in nonkinship care, although it likely depends on other factors, especially the quality of care (Xu & Bright, 2018).

Elected officials in Arizona and Georgia have passed laws that caring for a child or a teen for at least 9 months in a foster family is equal to kinship care (Levin, 2019). Individuals in Ohio are pressing their elected officials to do the same, especially in light of how one county in Ohio—which has long been considered the origin of Ohio's opioid epidemic—as of 2019 had 200 children in foster care (with approximately half of these children being removed from their home as a result of parents' drug use) but only 49 registered foster homes (Levin, 2019).

To learn more about foundations that provide direct services to improve the quality of foster care, to ensure the transition from foster care to adulthood is successful, and work with both child welfare services and policymakers to provide, improve, and eventually prevent the need for foster care, see the website of the Casey Philanthropies in the *Helpful Websites* section at the end of this chapter.

No matter teens' reasons for being in foster care or adopted and/or otherwise different from the married two-parent heterosexual statistical minority family, these teens may feel different and/or may be concretely stigmatized by peers, other families, employment settings, housing options, and/or school systems. This can be devastating and can have a negative effect on their development across the lifespan.

Some parents in such families socialize their children with perspective-taking, empathy, a sense of the value of diversity, and an appreciation for how their families are similar to, as well as different from, all sorts of other families. By actions such as these, they are adding to their teens' empowerment, and increasing the likelihood their teen errs on the resilience side of the risk-reslience pattern of development, particularly if they also prepare the teens for encountering and responding to bias (Murry & Lippold, 2018; Prendergast & MacPhee, 2018; Wang et al., 2019).

By knowing that bias may occur, and preparing their teens for how to respond to it, parents can *decrease* the likelihood that teens will struggle with externalizing problems and can *increase* the likelihood that teens with have a positive perception of themselves and engage in high-quality interpersonal relationships (Murry & Lippold, 2018; Prendergast & MacPhee, 2018; Wang et al., 2019).

Parent–Adolescent Relationship Quality

In Chapter 9, we learned about parenting styles for children. The influence of each style tends to reveal similar influences for the parents of adolescents (King, Boyd, & Pragg, 2018; Lippold et al., 2019; Murry & Lippold, 2018).

That is, teens usually fare best and err on the resilience side of the risk–resilience pattern of development when they feel a sense of *family belonging* (such as feelings of being included, being paid attention to, being understood by the family) regardless of their family's structure; when their parents are high in demands as well as warmth; when their parents are involved in their lives; and when their parents, like Sequoia's parents, engage in mindful parenting. Mindful parenting includes the practice of parents listening with their full attention, emotional awareness of themselves and their teen, self-regulation in their own behavior, nonjudgmental acceptance of themselves and their teen, and compassion for themselves and their teen (King, Boyd, & Pragg, 2018; Lippold et al., 2019; Murry & Lippold, 2018).

Yet teens differ from children in their experience of parenting styles in that they take a more active role in their development, so they may or may not perceive their parents' style as legitimate.

For example, teens are more likely to comply with parents' rules and are more likely to disclose their activities to their parents if their parents' authority does not interfere with their privacy, bodily control, and personal preferences—so that their own autonomy is respected (Pinquart, 2017; Smetana, 2017). On the other hand, teens are more likely to struggle with externalizing problems when their parents use *harsh control*, such as yelling and intrusiveness, and/or *psychological control*, such as shame, guilt, and/or conditional love (Pinquart, 2017; Smetana, 2017).

Other work confirms that the more parents meet their teens' emotional needs (such as for autonomy), the more likely it is that they contribute to their teens' psychological health. Also, teens will be more likely to identify with their parents' guidelines, be intrinsically motivated and curious about the world, be open in social relationships, and be resilient in the face of distress and adversity (Soenens, Deci, & Vansteenkiste, 2017).

Yet some increases in parental hostility and decreases in parental warmth are developmentally typical fluctuations that occur as teens individuate and psychologically separate from their parents. Such ups and downs in parents' hostility and warmth are known as *lability*—a behavior that is different from *conflict*, which refers to interactions between a parent and a teen (Lippold et al., 2018).

Although lability is normative (and consistent with the polydirectional pattern of development), more extreme degrees of it in parents are associated with teens being at a greater risk of engaging in delinquent behaviors such as stealing or physically fighting with others. These teens may be at a greater risk for substance use (Lippold et al., 2018).

So adolescence is a developmental window that includes many challenges but also opportunities to continue—or reset—a teen's developmental progress to a more positive one during (and beyond) adolescence (Suleiman & Dahl, 2019).

For instance, many internalizing and externalizing behaviors begin in adolescence as teens' developmental needs change. This is a function of the cascade of changes they experience as a result of puberty (Ebbert, Infurna, & Luthar, 2018; Mastrotheodoros et al., 2019; Suleiman & Dahl, 2019).

This is particularly true if a family is unable to reorganize and adapt to a teen's needs.

Research confirms that the more likely a teen is to perceive a lack of trust with a parent and the less likely a family as a unit is to show *flexibility* (trying new ways of dealing with problems), *cohesion* (being supportive of one another, especially during difficulty times), and *communication* (calmly discussing problems with one another), the greater their teens' erring on the risk side of the risk-resilience pattern of development by manifesting internalizing and externalizing problems (Ebbert, Infurna, & Luthar, 2018; Mastrotheodoros et al., 2019; Suleiman & Dahl, 2019).

Perhaps unsurprisingly, other work confirms that teens also fare poorly when their parents are struggling with psychopathology, substance abuse, and/or accumulated adversities during their adolescence and/or earlier when they were children (McKinney & Franz, 2019; Pitkänen et al., 2019; Taher, Damer, & Wong, 2019).

Parent-Adolescent Conflict Management

In the transition to adolescence, teens may become more aware of parents' weaknesses, may no longer idealize them as much (or at all), and may question the parents' dominance. The gains in adolescents' abstract reasoning also prompt them to push for more egalitarian relationships that can pose a challenge to some parents and can lead to conflict.

Empirical research on adolescents' reports of the intensity of these conflicts shows that the conflicts increase from early adolescence to mid-adolescence, then become stable from mid-adolescence to late adolescence. Interestingly, parents' reports of the intensity of these conflicts state that the conflicts are initially stable. (Mastrotheodoros et al., 2019).

As for if and how conflict affects the quality of relationships among teens and their parents, most disagreements between parents and adolescents do not constitute serious conflict or a threat to the relationship, so conflict isn't necessarily detrimental. If anything, conflicts can be a growth opportunity if the members engaged in the conflict learn how to *respond* and adapt flexibly to the needs of the other, rather than to *react* rigidly (Branje, 2018).

Research indicates that teens who experience major conflict with their parents are more at risk for depression later on, while those who experience minor conflict with their parents are not at such risk, nor for other problems, such as anxiety, substance abuse, nor suicidal behavior; conflicted disagreements between parents and teens that also include *parent negativity* (such as scolding, punishment,

FIG. 13.7   A Teen and His Father After Resolving a Conflict

Copyright © Depositphotos/pixelheadphoto.

arguing), are associated with adolescent anxiety and depression though (Alaie et al., 2019; Samek et al., 2018).

Additionally, although parents' **behavioral control**—such as consistently structuring family life to scaffold teens' competent and responsible behavior (such as via parental monitoring), along with communicating high expectations to their teens—can be highly beneficial to teens, psychological control is not (Smetana, 2017).

Research on **psychological control** (such as parental love withdrawal, parental guilt induction, and parental intrusiveness that leads to more teen secret-keeping and less mutual trust) indicates that it leads to both internalizing and externalizing behaviors, likely because such control is highly disrespectful—and can backfire and lead to more adolescent withdrawal and avoidance even when teens are doing nothing wrong (Frijns, Keijsers, & Finkenauer, 2020; Rote & Smetana, 2018; Smetana, 2017).

On the other hand, longitudinal work over the course of four years shows that the more teens engage in positive problem-solving when they have conflicts with their parents, the fewer conflicts they have later on (Missotten et al., 2017). And the conflict resolution styles that teens use matter as well.

Research with Dutch-speaking families in Belgium has found that the more supportive parents are (in that they use little psychological control but do support their teens' autonomy and respond warmly when their teens are distress), the more their teens use positive problem-solving, such as trying to find solutions they agree upon, instead of less adaptive behaviors such as compliance, withdrawal, and/or escalated conflict (Missotten et al., 2018).

Research with Turkish teens reveals that the conflict resolution styles they use with their parents are those they are most likely use when they have conflicts with their best friends as well, with the most frequent style they use being problem-solving—a style that is also associated with more life satisfaction (Dost-Gözkan, 2019).

Other work with Latinx teens in the United States finds that teens are more likely to use constructive problem-solving with their parents if their parents engage in communication with their teens that is characterized by hope (in that they help their teens establish long-term goals); help them develop the means for meeting such goals; and tell them that they are doing well and are prepared for the future (Daigle & Hoffman, 2018; Merolla & Kam, 2018).

Speaking of hope, it is unfortunately not surprising but understandable that teens (no matter their race or ethnicity) who have been violently victimized have lower expectations for the future. Perhaps this is because having had an experience in which they were robbed of self-control leads them to *incorrectly* infer that they have no self-efficacy (Daigle & Hoffman, 2018; Merolla & Kam, 2018).

Violent victimization during adolescence can have a range of consequences, including depression, substance use issues, criminal offenses, suicidality, and/or repeat victimization. Yet all of these consequences of victimization tend to exert less power over teens who have high-quality relationships with their families and schools (Turanovic & Pratt, 2017).

For Native American adolescents—like Sequoia, who has been beaten up at school—research shows that violent victimization against these teens is associated with a smaller range of outcomes, such as depression and poor health, but not suicidality. This should remind us that what is known about one group of teens must not lead us to make assumptions about other groups—particularly when they need our help (Turanovic & Pratt, 2017).

Parent–Teen Communication

During adolescence, teens spend increasing amounts of time away from and not supervised by their parents. Also, they are less likely to share information with their parents than when they were children, due to their developmental needs for privacy, autonomy, and differentiation (Dietvorst et al., 2018; Lionetti et al., 2019).

Parents ideally support these needs of their teens, while balancing such with their own needs to monitor their teens—so that they can be a source of support and guidance, while also maintaining emotional connectedness and respect.

Sequoia's parents have been great in doing so, which has likely contributed to Sequoia having such clarity about who they are, at least in terms of their gender identity, if not yet in terms of their career and other aspects of their identity.

What does communication between adolescents and their parents look like during this time? Well, **parent–teen communication** includes parental monitoring and adolescent information management, both of which influence one another, so that parent knowledge of their teens is truly bidirectional—and teens truly take an active role in their own socialization (Darling & Tilton-Weaver, 2019; Dishion & McMahon, 1998; Lionetti et al., 2019).

Parental monitoring refers to whether and how parents pay attention to and track their teen's well-being, activities, whereabouts, and friends. Parents needs to apply *active strategies* by setting rules about what they must share or *solicitation strategies* by asking teens for information (Darling & Tilton-Weaver, 2019; Dishion & McMahon, 1998; Lionetti et al., 2019).

Adolescent information management refers to teens sharing accurate information with their parents via *revealing strategies* in which they provide information voluntarily, because they are asked to do so, and/or via *concealing strategies* in which they hide information by lying or obscuring information (Darling & Tilton-Weaver, 2019; Dishion & McMahon, 1998; Lionetti et al., 2019).

The greater the parents' propensity to monitor via psychological control, the *more* their teens tend to keep secrets and engage in relational aggression or delinquency and the *less* likely their teens are to engage in prosocial behavior (Darling & Tilton-Weaver, 2019; Padilla-Walker et al., 2019).

On the other hand, the greater the parents' propensity to monitor via behavioral control and the more supportive they are of their teens' autonomy, the *more* their teens are likely to use revealing strategies and the *less* likely they are to use concealing strategies (Padilla-Walker & Son, 2019; Wuyts et al., 2018). For instance, the more the parents ask the teens their opinion and expect them to follow rules, the more information their teens are to disclose (including about their media use) and the less likely they are to keep secrets (including about their media use). And when parents show warmth in conversations when teens do disclose, it builds trust and understanding. Research also indicates that such conditions increase teens' prosocial behavior toward family members (Padilla-Walker & Son, 2019).

Other data indicate that teens also are more likely to subsequently disclose when their parents express *validation*, such as expressing understanding and recognizing teens' perspectives, and express *interest*, such as asking open-ended questions (Disla et al., 2018; Main et al., 2018). Some work also reveals that parental expressions of negative emotions do not necessarily shut down teen disclosure, at least for older adolescents (Disla et al., 2018; Main et al., 2018). And adolescents learn different lessons from when they disclose versus lie to their parents, with teens showing more psychological growth with new insights about themselves when they disclose, and more negative self-conclusions with a poorer self-image when they lie (Smetana et al., 2019).

Adolescent information management may change over time with increasing age, and in ways reflecting the polydirectional pattern of development. For example, a longitudinal study that had children and teens complete surveys every year from age 12 to age 18 found that most (82%) participants showed changes in

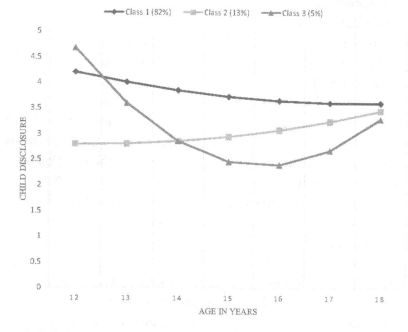

FIG. 13.8 Trajectories of Teens' Disclosure to Parents

Laura M. Padilla-Walker, Daye Son, and Larry J. Nelson, Trajectories of Teens' Disclosure to Parents, from "A Longitudinal Growth Mixture Model of Child Disclosure to Parents Across Adolescence," Journal of Family Psychology, Vol. 32, No. 4, pp. 479. Copyright © 2017 by American Psychological Association.

adolescents' information management over time, such as declines in their disclosure to parents with increasing age (Padilla-Walker, Son, & Nelson, 2018).

As you can see in Figure 13.8, though, another group (13%) showed relatively consistent low levels of disclosure over time, and this group had the highest levels of substance use and delinquency along with the lowest levels of prosocial behavior. A third group (5%) began with high levels of disclosure, followed by a steep decline and then a rebound from age 16 to age 18; this third smallest group differed from the second group of low and stable disclosure in that their parents initially showed somewhat higher levels of maternal warmth. Yet they also may have demonstrated such with higher levels of control, hence the decline in teen disclosure (Padilla-Walker, Son, & Nelson, 2018).

Interestingly, although parents' self-reports indicate that they engage in less solicitation over time, teens' reports of such in their parents do not indicate less solicitation. Perhaps the discrepancy in perception is because parental solicitation has more negative and more pronounced effects as teens grow older, so any solicitation begins to feel like too much solicitation (Lionetti et al., 2019).

On a related note, parents tend to report more similar monitoring of siblings than their siblings report experiencing, and siblings tend to report even less similar styles of information management from one another (Darling & Tilton-Weaver, 2019).

Sibling Relationships

Research has also documented discrepancies in how parents and their teens perceive differential treatment of siblings, with ill effects. For instance, longitudinal data indicate that when mothers and their firstborn children have greater discrepancies in their perception of affection from parents, these mothers and their firstborn children experience greater conflict the following year (Jensen & McHale, 2017).

Keep in mind that differential treatment from parents is not necessarily a bad thing, given teens are different people and have different needs. Instead, it is *unfair* differential treatment that seems to be problematic.

Yet hostility among siblings can increase when their parents' conflict results in their using **triangulation**, or the attempt of one parent to form a coalition with a child or a teen that excludes or undermines the other parent (Ruff, Durtschi, & Day, 2017). Such triangulation not only results in differential treatment of siblings but also disrupts the functioning of a family and prevents them from working out their differences (Ruff, Durtschi, & Day, 2017).

Other work confirms that differential treatment of siblings can be a product of parents' individual stressors (such as role overload and/or depression), as well as conflict between parents or among step-parents (Padilla et al., 2018).

Does this mean that single children such as Sequoia are better off than teens who have siblings? Not necessarily. It is often assumed that (children and) teens with siblings have better social skills—but social skills are not a product of whether or not teens have siblings. Instead, it is the quality of teens' relationships with their sibling(s) that determines their ability to maintain relationships with other individuals who are not family members (Yucel, Bobbitt-Zeher, & Downey, 2018).

For example, high-quality relationships with favorable levels of warmth, closeness, and problem-solving among siblings do protect teens from the insecurity (such as worry that the parents will go their separate ways) they understandably feel when parents are in conflict, with their siblings helping to reduce the anxiety they feel about such conflict (Davies et al., 2018). Regarding any maltreatment from parents, whether it involves neglect, emotional abuse, physical abuse, and/or sexual abuse, siblings can also play a protective role (Katz & Hamama, 2016).

Teens with siblings who have health and/or behavioral issues may experience anxiety of their own, though. For instance, teens with a sibling on the autism spectrum report that although they sometimes worry about their sibling's behavior, the disruptions to family relationships, the disruptions to their social lives, and their sibling's long-term well-being, they also report that they are more tolerant and caring as a result. Very few of these siblings show clinical levels of internalizing or externalizing problems (Moss et al., 2019; Tudor, Rankin, & Lerner, 2018).

Research on the siblings of children with cancer show somewhat similar patterns, but the studies also point to their even greater unmet needs and limited parental support. These outcomes are worse for teens from families of color, those who live in poverty, those who have poorer overall functioning, and those who have limited social support (Long et al., 2018). Qualitative research with siblings of teens with a chronic condition (such as cystic fibrosis, diabetes, or muscular dystrophy) also points to the need these siblings have for coping strategies and their anxiety about how others might negatively treat their siblings (Deavin, Greasley, & Dixon, 2018).

To learn about an online intervention that supports the needs of teens with siblings with a chronic condition, see *the Cycle of Science* feature at the end of this chapter.

Trouble in the nest does occur, though. Siblings can protect one another, but some may victimize one another too. The data show that those teens who identify as male, those who are first-born, and those who grow up in larger households are most likely to bully their siblings. This last characteristic is consistent with an evolutionary theory explanation that attempts at social dominance increase when there is greater competition for limited resources (Dantchev & Wolke, 2019).

Sibling victimization is not to be taken lightly. The research data indicate that such victimization is associated with increased mental health problems as well as delinquency—and that these outcomes are even stronger for teens who are maltreated by their parents, a heartbreaking situation given that the teens are being victimized within two primary relational contexts (van Berkel, Tucker, & Finkelhor, 2018).

In addition, teens who are victimized by their siblings, whether it be physically (such as being hit), in terms of their property (such as having their things taken or broken intentionally), and/or psychologically (such as being told mean things) are more likely to be victimized by their peers. This is especially true for those teens who are <u>chronically</u> victimized by their siblings (Tucker, Finkelhor, & Turner, 2018).

So sibling relationships can, at times, be a training ground for problematic relationships.

If, and how, parents intervene in sibling bullying matters (Plamondon, Bouchard, & Lachance-Grzela, 2018). That is, siblings are *more likely to be victimized* when their parents ignore their conflicts, solve the conflict problem for the siblings, and/or punish the siblings for fighting (Plamondon, Bouchard, & Lachance-Grzela, 2018).

On the other hand, siblings are *less likely to be victimized* when their parents explain the siblings' feelings to one another and/or give advice on solving the problem (Plamondon, Bouchard, & Lachance-Grzela, 2018). Sibling relationships are not necessarily problematic, though, nor are they static.

As teens need greater autonomy from their family and as peer relationships become increasingly important to them, teen siblings tend to spend less time together—while also demanding more equal treatment from parents. So siblings conflict tend to show a trend reflective of the polydirectional pattern of development, that is, conflicts tend to increase in early adolescence, then typically decrease through the remainder of the teen years (Lindell & Campione-Barr, 2017).

Siblings with poorer-quality relationships tend to experience greater egalitarian relationships over time, due to a decline in power struggles, perhaps because of their increasing focus on peers. Those with higher-quality relationships don't experience a decline in their siblings' relative power over them (Lindell & Campione-Barr, 2017). Yet warmth in sibling relationships, as early as middle childhood, promotes modeling of one another over time, and even predicts similarity in their college completion (Sun, McHale, & Updegraff, 2019).

In this section, we have examined what developmental science knows about teens' families and the relationships within them. In the next section, we consider what developmental science knows about teens' relationships outside the family.

What Do We Know About Teens' Relationships Outside the Family?

Relationships, as well as how children and teens understand them, are crucial drivers of development. Relationships can provide major assets and/or major risks to our well-being, to the well-being of those around us, and to the well-being of future generations (Osher et al., 2018).

Such relationships, and the power of them, extend beyond the family, especially now. Peers become increasingly important during the adolescent years, as teens begin to spend less time with their families and more time with age mates. These relationships also become more complex and include mutual antipathies or dislikes, bully–victim relationships, friendships, romantic relationships, and/or sexual relationships.

Friendships in particular can be a resource that provides teens with social capital that has consequences consistent with the lifelong pattern of development. That is, the research data indicate that friends can boost teen's academic performance and can encourage them to have greater educational aspirations (Ahlborg et al., 2019; Borowski, Zeman, & Braunstein, 2018; Wentzel, Jablansky, & Scalise, 2018).

Friends also help teens practice and improve their emotional regulation skills during times of conflict and heightened emotions. Teens with social anxiety (such as being afraid to invite others out because they might say no) may be at risk for missing out on these formative experiences unless, perhaps with the aid of a school counselor or a therapist, they work to stop what could be a self-fulfilling prophecy (Ahlborg, et al., 2019; Borowski, Zeman, & Braunstein, 2018; Wentzel, Jablansky, & Scalise, 2018).

Teens on the autism spectrum (who tend to show *a lack of positive behaviors*, such as prosocial actions) and/or with attention deficit disorder (who tend to show *a presence of negative behaviors*, such as impulsive interactions and/or overreactivity) are at risk for being socially impaired. With therapy, however, they can participate meaningfully in friendships as well, and can do so with a lower risk of social rejection (Mikami, Miller, & Lerner, 2019).

Whether teens are atypical or typical in their development, it is important to keep in mind something we learned about in Chapter 12 that is consistent with the multidimensional pattern of development: The changes in the brain's gray matter that occur during adolescence are associated with changes in social understanding and communication; therefore, social influences (whether they be in person and/or via social media) are especially influential on brain development during adolescence. So any

FIG. 13.9   Sequoia After a Negative Experience on Social Media

social acceptance or social rejection on social media can be a very emotionally intense experience for adolescents compared to adults—intense negative experiences that Sequoia has experienced personally and that contributed to their choice to stay off social media for awhile while still being close friends with a few others (Crone & Konijn, 2018; Lee, Hollarek, & Krabbendam, 2018).

The consequences of being interested in maintaining close friendships during adolescence are consistent with the lifelong pattern of development too. Longitudinal research reveals that 15-year-olds who value developing intimate emotional relationships with peers have better adjustment and a better stress response while still adolescents, along with greater self-worth, as well as lower anxiety and depression, by the time they are in early adulthood.

On the other hand, 15-year-olds who value being popular and liked by their peers are more likely to struggle with social anxiety by the time they are in early adulthood. Thus, close friendships serve a *protective function* in dealing with the difficulty of negative life events, and a *promotional function* of sorts in fostering the development of skills such as attending closely to another, providing emotional support tailored to another's needs, and problem-solving in terms of conflict resolution (Narr et al., 2019).

The preference for *quality* of friendships rather than *quantity* of friendships may be considered more developmentally normative too. Compared to school-age children, teens tend to lose more friends from their social network over time (due partially to experiencing more school transitions), and this is especially true for those teens for whom the friendship is not reciprocal, so that the end result is consistent with the polydirectional pattern of development. That is, the *quantity of teens' friends tends to decrease* over adolescence, whereas the *quality tends to increase* over adolescence (Felmlee et al., 2018).

And when greater quality is present, teens have an opportunity to develop a secure attachment to a peer outside their family as well, which can lead a self-fulfilling prophecy with long-term consequences, in which teens begin to expect, and therefore set in motion, more positive peer and romantic relationships over time (Narr, Allen, Tan, & Loeb, 2019). Additional longitudinal work confirms this, with the data revealing that when teens establish positive expectations and the capacity for assertiveness, along with social competence and the ability to maintain close friendships, they are more satisfied with their romantic life in early adulthood (Allen et al., 2019).

Interestingly, as teens develop into late adolescence and into early adulthood, their attitudes shift: They have more positive attitudes and fewer negative attitudes about being alone, likely as a result of having already established social connections and support from peers by that time. They also become increasingly independent, so they realize the benefits of solitude (Danneel et al., 2018).

Findings such as this are a reminder that the benefits of close friends are indeed vital to well-being—and that teens who also wish to be alone, especially in late adolescence, are not showing signs of pathology. In fact, as you can see in Figure 13.10, the negative implications of being unsociable or preferring solitude are age-related and therefore consistent with the polydirectional pattern of development. There are age-related expectations for greater social interactions from early childhood through early adolescence, so that solitary play in preschool is normative and even encouraged (Coplan, Ooi, & Baldwin, 2019).

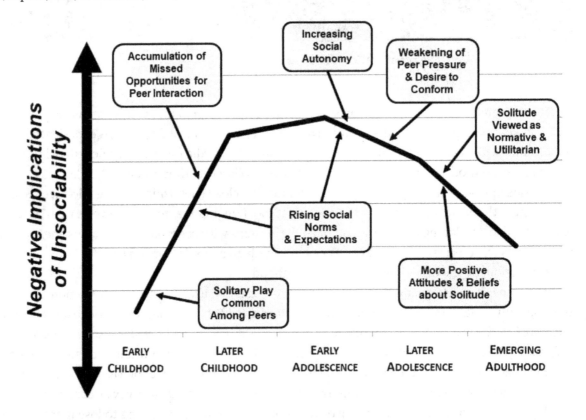

FIG. 13.10 Changes in the Negative Implications of Unsociability Over Time

Robert J. Coplan, Laura L. Ooi, and Danielle Baldwin, Changes in the Negative Implications of Unsociability Over Time, from "Does it Matter When We Want to Be Alone? Exploring Developmental Timing Effects in the Implication of Unsociability," New Ideas in Psychology, vol. 53, pp. 50. Copyright © 2019 by Elsevier B.V.

Over time, however, school-age children who choose to spend time alone are missing out on opportunities for peer interactions, including building and maintaining close relationships, practicing emotional regulation in the face of conflict, and practicing conflict resolution and problem-solving (Coplan, Ooi, & Baldwin, 2019).

By early to mid-adolescence, teens begin to feel less pressure to conform to others' expectations. They begin to appreciate that time spent alone may serve as a refuge from social demands, an opportunity to work through strong emotions, time for creative pursuits that reflect their identity, a chance for self-care, and an occasion for leisure (Coplan, Ooi, & Baldwin, 2019). So it should come as little surprise that by early adulthood, those emerging adults who choose to spend more time alone show less stress, which indicates that solitude is also restorative (Nguyen, Ryan, & Deci, 2018).

Yet teens who are chronically lonely over long periods of time are *more likely* to use maladaptive strategies to regulate their emotions (such as catastrophizing or blowing negative experiences out of proportion and/or blaming themselves when things go wrong). Also, they are *less likely* to accept social invitations (Vanhalst et al., 2018).

Even when they are motivated to accept social invitations, teens who are chronically lonely usually do so because they feel pressure from others (or themselves), rather than any intrinsic motivation. This is perhaps a result of giving up and feeling helpless about being able to change their situation, in terms of either finding others with whom they have something in common, or being able to change their behavior (Vanhalst et al., 2018).

Some teens are indeed spending less time with others in person. This absence of real-time interactions means that teens are forfeiting opportunities to attend to the body language and facial gestures of others, an absence of interactions—in combination with more social media use—is associated with greater *loneliness*, or the experience of a discrepancy between one's actual and desired social interactions (Leon-Moreno et al., 2019; Twenge, Spitzberg, & Campbell, 2019; Vanhalst et al., 2018).

Teens who experience peer victimization are also likely to report high levels of loneliness, which is worrisome but understandable given the breach of trust that has occurred in their social bonds with others (Leon-Moreno et al., 2019; Twenge, Spitzberg, & Campbell, 2019; Vanhalst et al., 2018).

Peer Status in Adolescence

In Chapter 11, we learned about the sociometric peer statuses of childhood: Average, Popular, Neglected, Controversial, and Rejected. Remember that these statuses are derived by asking children (and teens) whom they like the most, and whom they like the least.

Teens high in *sociometric popularity* or the sociometric nominations we first learned about in Chapter 11 are those who receive the highest number of liked-most nominations and the lowest number of liked-least nominations. Sociometric popularity is akin to "likeability," is consistent with teens' personal feelings of acceptance regarding peers, and reflects those teens who engage in positive peer interactions with strong cooperativeness and supportiveness, as well as low aggression (Lonigro et al., 2018; van der Wilt et al., 2018).

On the other hand, **perceived popularity** concerns a teen's reputation in terms of being socially dominant, being visible, having prestige, and being able to control resources. **Admiration** refers to teens whom others admire, respect, or want to be like (Zhang et al., 2018a). Teens who rate high in all three forms of peer status (that is, sociometric popularity, perceived popularity, and admiration) may be especially powerful agents of socialization given their influence on peers.

There also appear to be somewhat universal characteristics of high peer status, yet more research in different regions of the globe is needed. For now, though, we do know that prosocial behaviors (such as kindness and a willingness to help others) predict all forms of peer status in early adolescence—and peer status *over the course of* adolescence—for teens in both China and the United States, but especially in China, where interdependence tends to be more highly regarded (Zhang et al., 2018a).

Consistent with such cultural differences, Zhang et al. also found cultural specifics. That is, in the United States, when it comes to just the perceived popularity peer status, prosocial behavior is less likely to play a role than is likeability—perhaps because early adolescents with high perceived popularity in the United States tend to be more likely to exhibit both positive and negative traits, such as being sociable but also being manipulative (Zhang et al., 2018a).

Data also indicate that moderate levels of risk-taking in U.S. teens who identify as male are associated with greater popularity, as is the ability to inspire others (such as persuading others that something is a good idea) for both males and females (Rebellon et al., 2019; Vermande et al., 2018).

Additional work reveals that early adolescents whose peer status is high in terms of likability as well as perceived popularity, but not admiration, are significantly more likely to show greater academic engagement over time, in terms of their *academic behavior* (such as working hard), their *academic cognitions* (such as trying to understand what they are learning), and their *academic emotions* (such as being interested). This is true in both China and the United States to an equal extent (Zhang et al., 2018b).

Yet academic engagement can happen only in a school context of emotional safety. School environments in which the norm is one of *popularity = high aggression and low prosocial behavior*—versus the opposite equation of *popularity = low aggression and high prosocial behavior*—likely render safety inadequate while increasing students' aggression. Depending on the context, aggression can be contagious (Dumas, Davis, & Ellis, 2019; Jung, Busching, & Krahé, 2019; Laninga-Wijnen et al., 2019).

FIG. 13.11   We'wha: A Celebrated Weaver in the Zuni Tribe

Source: https://en.wikipedia.org/wiki/File:Wewha1.gif.

Affectional Orientation

Affectional orientation, sometimes also known as *sexual identity* or *sexual orientation*, refers to with whom we prefer to have an intimate relationship.

We rarely ask people with a heterosexual affectional orientation when they knew they were straight. But we often want to know when queer people realized they were not straight—and unfortunately we make assumptions about what such may or may not mean.

Some Native American tribes have had a history of honoring individuals who are male-bodied yet take on female roles, such as We'wha, who was from the Zuni tribe. Contemporary Native American tribes often now honor individuals like We'wha, who they now refer to as Two-Spirit individuals, who represent a third gender.

Some but not all Two-Spirit individuals, such as Sequoia whose assigned gender at birth was male, may identify as transgender, part of the *queer* or **LGBTQIA+** (lesbian, gay, bisexual, transgender, questioning, intersex) community. And some but not all Two-Spirit individuals may identify as gender expansive, that is, as we learned in Chapter 9 and further discussed in Chapter 12, someone whose expression of their gender identity does not match their sex at birth.

So teens who identify as transgender may or may not identify as nonbinary, genderqueer, gender variant, and/or gender-nonconforming.

Therefore, it is important to be mindful that we don't always know if and how others may be different from and/or similar to us. Consequently, it is important not to make assumptions about adolescents' identities—nor assumptions that their identities match their romantic attraction and/or sexual behavior, which they indeed often do not.

For instance, research shows that not all teens who identify as heterosexual have sexual partners of a different gender—and that some teens who identify as heterosexual have sexual partners of the same gender (Ybarra, Price-Feeney, & Mitchell, 2019). Additionally, sexuality is fluid, as teens' (and adults') affectional orientations can change over time (Kaestle, 2019).

Although adolescents today live in a climate in which there are laws protecting same-sex marriage in all 50 states, major inequalities still exist, injustices that place teens on the risk side of the risk–resilience pattern of development. Indeed, there is no federal law that prohibits students from discrimination on the basis of affectional orientation or gender identity, nor is there any federal law that prohibits employment discrimination or housing discrimination on the basis of affectional orientation or gender identity.

So unlike prior generations, sexual minority teens may very well see affirming messages about the queer community from celebrities in the media but, paradoxically, also see hostile messages from society about the rights of the queer community. And they may experience the same negative messages or even worse from those close to home.

Pediatricians and others who work with teens must be alert to child maltreatment and/or family violence with all adolescents, but especially sexual minority teens given these disparities in experiencing adversity—adversity that can increase the risk for later health problems consistent with the lifelong pattern of development. These include the emotional issues that queer teens are at greater risk for, such as substance abuse, mental health such as depression and self-harm, and/or sexual health as a result of not having access to supportive providers (Baams, 2018; Russell & Fish, 2019).

Research with queer adolescents like Sequoia indicates that compared to heterosexual adolescents, queer teens are at greater risk of bullying, harassment, and violence from peers, as well as psychological and physical abuse from their parents. Teens who identify as nonbinary and/or transgender are also significantly more likely to be psychologically and physically abused by their parents than are cisgender adolescents (Baams, 2018; Gayles & Garofalo, 2019; Martin-Storey & Baams, 2019).

Queer high school students are also more at risk for binge drinking and suicide ideation, yet less so if they have someone with whom they can speak and who is supportive, such as a school nurse. Sexual minority teens of color report that they not only need someone to have their back, but also need their school environment to be safe (Craig, McInroy, & Austin, 2018; Goodin, Elswick, & Fallin-Bennett, 2019; Russell & Fish, 2019).

Unfortunately, school policies, community resources, and faith communities have instead often turned their backs on such teens. Also, federal efforts as recently as 2019 have attempted to invalidate prior recommendations for transgender teens' safety in school (Craig, McInroy, & Austin, 2018; Goodin, Elswick, & Fallin-Bennett, 2019; Russell & Fish, 2019).

Romantic Relationships in Adolescence

Romantic relationships are very important to teens. The salience of such in their minds is not to be dismissed. The more an adolescent experiences negative feelings about their romantic relationships (such as being doubtful or jealous) and/or conflict within these relationships, the more likely they are to feel upset, distressed, nervous, or irritable (A. A. Rogers et al., 2018).

The direction of the connection between teens and romantic relationships is unclear as of now. But longitudinal research may want to examine the connection more closely. They may find that teens' long-term well-being is a function of daily romantic experiences—experiences that could be improved upon with interventions in order to benefit long-term well-being (A. A. Rogers et al., 2018).

Romantic relationships can have long-term benefits consistent with the lifelong pattern of development, not "just" in reducing loneliness if the quality of those relationships is strong, but also because high-quality romantic relationships in adolescence can be considered assets. They have been found to reduce externalizing behaviors and predict greater well-being over time (Gómez-López, Viejo, & Ortega-Ruiz, 2019; Kansky & Allen, 2018).

Romantic relationships, which often begin in some form during early to middle adolescence, are a developmental milestone that marks a transition from age mates consisting solely of one's peers to age mates consisting of one's peers, as well as romantic prospects or romantic partners (Chang & Rosenthal, 2018). So when exactly might these relationships start? Research on heterosexual teens in the United States indicates that within a sample of 15-year-olds, 9% *abstain* from participating in any form of romantic relationship, 20% *socialize with relationships* (meaning they engage in romantic socializing, such as going to activities with both same-sex and opposite-sex teens present, as well as dating), 21% *socialize with dating* (meaning they engage in romantic socializing, as well as serious romantic relationships), and 50% engage in *romantic socializing* (Beckmeyer & Malacane, 2018).

Yet this participation should be limited, given that engaging in dating or serious romantic relationships in middle adolescence increases the likelihood that a teen will engage in risk-taking behaviors, perhaps because these activities are associated with *less parental supervision* as well as *more pressure* to make choices that teens may not yet feel ready to make and/or don't have the hope about the future to make well. Speaking of hope, data indicate that teens who identify as male are more likely to use condoms consistently if they have optimistic expectations for the future (Beckmeyer & Malacane, 2018; Knowles et al., 2019).

Research with heterosexual adolescents in the Netherlands found that these teens report entering their first serious romantic relationship at age 16 on average. Also, the more these teens had opposite-gender peers and the more they were perceived as popular by these opposite-gender peers, the earlier the timing of their first romantic relationship (Savickaité et al., 2019). Indeed, while more research with teens around the globe, and with teens who are not heterosexual, is clearly needed, the 2019 study by Savickaité and colleagues is valuable for identifying the role of friendships and popularity in the onset of romantic relationships.

Additionally, a remarkable 13-year longitudinal study with French Canadian adolescents, albeit only with cisgender and middle-class teens, established patterns of romantic relationships from mid-adolescence to early adulthood that are associated with characteristics of teens' relationships with family and friends at 12 years of age. The patterns—*Intense, Frequent, Long-Term, Sporadic,* and *Later*—form a continuum. *Intense* (characterized by continuous involvement in romantic relationships and with frequent partner changes) is at one end, *Frequent* (characterized by partner changes but not as frequent as Intense, with *Long-Term* (which is characterized by maintaining relationships over time) is in the middle, and *Sporadic* (characterized by some involvement in romantic relationships) and *Later* (characterized by late entry into romantic relationships) are at the other end. The researchers also found that those who identify as female were overly represented in the patterns associated with high levels of involvement, such as *Intense, Frequent,* and *Long-Term,* and that those who identify as male were overly represented in the patterns associated with low levels of involvement, such as *Sporadic* and *Later* (Boisvert & Poulin, 2016).

In terms of precursors of these patterns, that is, the participants' characteristics that predicted their later patterns, those in the *Intense* pattern reported *more conflict* with their parents at age 12. This is consistent with other research that shows that teens' problem-solving and conflict style with their friends and romantic partners mirrors that of the problem-solving and conflict style they learn from their parents (Boisvert & Poulin, 2016; Staats et al., 2017).

Those in both the *Intense* and *Long-Term* patterns reported being *more well-liked* by their peers at age 12, whereas those in the *Later* pattern reported being *least liked* by their peers at age 12. Those in the *Long-Term* pattern reported being *least withdrawn* at age 12, whereas those in the *Later* pattern reported being *most withdrawn* at age 12 (Boisvert & Poulin, 2016; Staats et al., 2017). So a teen's family of origin seems to set the stage for later patterns of communication with others (Chang & Rosenthal, 2018).

Additionally, those in the *Frequent* pattern reported *more closeness* in their friendships at age 12, whereas those in the *Later* pattern reported the *least closeness* in their friendship at age 12. Those in the *Intense* and *Frequent* patterns reported *having the most opposite-sex friends* at age 12, whereas those in the *Later* pattern reported *having the least opposite-sex friends* at age 12 (Boisvert & Poulin, 2016).

The researchers speculate that the social withdrawal of teens in the *Later* pattern may lead to their being excluded by peers, which leads to difficulties forming and maintaining friendships. This in turn restricts opportunities to develop closeness with others, as well as to develop relationships with opposite-sex peers (Boisvert & Poulin, 2016).

More data are needed, including data with more economically diverse, ethnically diverse, atypically developing (for example, teens with ADHD tend to have more romantic partners), and queer teens, as well as nonbinary teens. The queer and nonbinary groups deserve to be understood in their own right and could represent a segment of teens in the *Later* pattern, like Sequoia (Boisvert & Poulin, 2016; Loeb et al., 2018; Rokeach & Wiener, 2018). That is, given the difficulty of coming out for some and nonbinary teens, they are more likely to experience early insecure attachment relationships with their parents that contributed to negative expectations regarding relationships. They are also more likely to experience trauma and to struggle with psychological issues such as depression (Boisvert & Poulin, 2016; Loeb et al., 2018; Rokeach & Wiener, 2018).

All teens who experience more competent parenting and who also experience a generally more positive family climate show greater self-regulation, more effective problem-solving skills, greater social competence, more secure attachment over time into early adulthood, and lower violence in their romantic relationships (Allen et al., 2018; Chang & Rosenthal, 2018; Moilanen & Manuel, 2017; Xia et al., 2018). Teens also make healthier sexual choices when their parents participate regularly in conversations with them about romantic relationships and sexual decision-making. This suggests that parents should continue or begin to do so, and that pediatricians can also play a role in initiating such conversations with teens (Allen et al., 2018; Chang & Rosenthal, 2018; Moilanen & Manuel, 2017; Xia et al., 2018).

Follow-up work on the aforementioned patterns of romantic relationships also indicates that from ages 16 to 22, teens in the *Frequent* pattern and teens in the *Sporadic* pattern experience *increases* in intimacy with their best friends, while teens in the *Long-Term* pattern report *no changes* in the emotional support, intimacy, or conflict with best friends, whereas those in the *Later* pattern report *increases* in conflict with their best friends over this time period (Camirand & Poulin, 2019). It could be that changes in teens' friendship quality may vary according to their relationship involvement—so that friends and romantic partners may serve similar emotional needs for teens, since they reflect fairly similar patterns of emotional well-being (Camirand & Poulin, 2019).

Sexual Activity in Adolescence

Sequoia, like most teens, became sexually active while in high school. In the United States, most young people have sex for the first time at age 17; "having sex" can mean vaginal intercourse, oral sex, and/or anal sex (Guttmacher Institute, 2017).

Hooking up refers to a sexual encounter, anywhere from kissing to penetration, that is "uncommitted" in the sense that the individuals involved neither have a current relationship nor express any desire for such after hooking up (Garcia et al., 2019; James-Kangal et al., 2018). Teens who engage in hooking up relationships are just as likely to expect to be in committed relationships in the future as are teens who don't engage in hooking up, contrary to the worries of some who are concerned about declining marriage rates (Garcia et al., 2019; James-Kangal et al., 2018).

The failure to acknowledge the reality of adolescent sexuality reduces the ability of parents to inform their teens' choices, perhaps unwittingly directing teens to the risk side of the risk–resilience pattern of development. This failure is also relevant to adolescents with physical, cognitive, and/or emotional disabilities, who are often subject to an additional societal stigma that views them as asexual.

Such denial of their sexuality not only infantilizes teens with disabilities, but it may preclude any parental and or educator discussions regarding sexuality.

Failure to discuss sexuality with these teens can also increase their risk of contracting sexually transmitted infections (STIs) and/or of having an unwanted pregnancy—issues whose consequences are consistent with the lifelong pattern of development in the difficulties that teens face every day. In light of such, it is imperative that parents and those working with these teens support their emotional development by addressing interpersonal skills; establishing and maintaining friendships; addressing self-esteem and image concerns; teaching assertiveness, including the ability to say "no"; and providing them with adequate and age-appropriate sex education. This last item is especially important because, depending on the type of impairment, they can be as sexually active as teens without such impairments (Shandra, 2018; Wienholz et al., 2016).

Regardless of whether or not they have impairments or disabilities, all teens deserve the respect of being able to discuss sexual behavior with their parents. However, parents may not always feel comfortable doing so and/or they may not know how to initiate such conversations in a way that will be inviting and productive for teens (Ford et al., 2019). With this in mind, researchers designed an intervention that coaches parents on how to talk to adolescents about sex (and drug use) while their teen is at their well-child visit with the pediatrician; the data indicate that these coaching interventions do indeed increase parent–adolescent communication. To learn more about the study, visit *The Cycle of Science* feature at the end of this chapter (Ford et al., 2019).

This parent–teen communication is sorely needed, because teens really do have sex. Research indicates that by the time adolescents are in 12th grade, 57% of them have been sexually active—with most, but not all, using some form of contraception (Witwer, Jones, & Lindberg, 2018). In fact, contraceptive use (including but not limited to condoms) among teens has greatly increased over time, and teen pregnancies have been at record lows in recent years (Guttmacher Institute, 2017).

Yet only 28% of males and 42% of females have completed the three-dose regime of vaccination against human papillomavirus (HPV), which accounts for 66% of **sexually transmitted infections (STIs)** in teens and has consequences that unfortunately illustrate a negative example of the lifelong pattern of development. For example, if untreated, HPV can cause cervical cancer—the risk which is made even higher given that HPV is asymptomatic (Guttmacher Institute, 2017).

Racial disparities are great among teen STI rates, with Black adolescents being 5 times more likely to be diagnosed with chlamydia and 14 times more likely to be diagnosed with gonorrhea than European American teens (Guttmacher Institute, 2017).

When asked "Would you ever not go for sexual or reproductive health care because your parents might find out?" 18% of 15- to 17-year-olds and 9% of 18- to 25-year-olds report saying yes (Fuentes et al., 2018). Among those with confidentiality concerns, sexually experienced females are less likely to have received any contraceptive services in the past year, which suggests that in order for adolescents to practice healthy sexual behavior, they need better access to confidential reproductive services so they are not deterred from obtaining contraception (Fuentes et al., 2018).

Intimate partner violence during adolescence includes violence that can be *verbal*, such as insults; *relational*, such as bringing up something bad the partner had done in the past; *physical*, such as pushing, shoving, or shaking; and/or *sexual*, such as forcing the other to participate in a sexual act when they don't want to do so (Espelage et al., 2019).

Research shows that teens are least likely to perpetrate dating violence when they have more empathy for others, feel more social support from family and friends, experience more parental monitoring, and feel that they belong to and are respected at their school. This indicates that in order to prevent intimate partner violence, schools would be well advised to increase a sense of belonging, especially for teens with limited social support (Espelage et al., 2019).

Notably, 1 out of every 10 adolescents experiences intimate partner violence, with teens who are female-identifying, of color, and/or queer being significantly more likely to be victims of such, and with females becoming pregnant as a result of the assault (Charlton et al., 2019; Whitton et al., 2019; Witwer, Jones, & Lindberg, 2018). These disturbing findings indicate that in order for teens to err on the resilience side of the risk–resilience pattern of development and to have healthy relationships and healthy lives, all young people need comprehensive, medically accurate, and unbiased sexual education that also addresses the necessity of sexual consent and respect (Charlton et al., 2019; Whitton et al., 2019; Witwer, Jones, & Lindberg, 2018).

Other research distinguishing between physical violence and sexual violence in adolescents has found that the former is more prevalent, with 1 in 5 teens reporting physical violence, compared to 1 in 10 teens reporting sexual violence (Wincentak, Connolly, & Card, 2017).

FIG. 13.12   An Absence of Positive Interactions During a Disagreement

So, when adolescent romantic partners disagree with, get mad at, and argue with one another, what determines if the conflict will escalate? The data indicate that the *absence of positive interactions* (such as listening actively to the other person, positively structuring what is being heard, engaging in sensitive physical touching, smiling, and appropriately using humor) increases the likelihood that a conflict will escalate (Ha, Kim, & McGill, 2019).

Are there characteristics that increase the risk of violence in romantic relationships before conflicts occur? Yes, there are—and knowing what they are can help prevent further violence. In terms of the precursors, researchers have found that teens who show higher levels of bullying, depression, and/or anxiety are more at risk for perpetrating later dating violence, and the victims of bullying are more at risk of being victims of dating violence (Farrell & Vaillancourt, 2019; Yu et al., 2018; Zych et al., 2019).

Additionally, the developmental timeline shows that poor self-regulation in early adolescence predicts bullying in middle adolescence, which in turn predicts dating violence in late adolescence (Farrell & Vaillancourt, 2019; Yu et al., 2018; Zych et al., 2019).

Other factors that predict the perpetration of intimate partner violence include having experienced interparental aggression during childhood, currently experiencing relationship insecurity, and currently engaging in social-information processing biases (such as making hostile attributions in ambiguous situations, a tendency we will discuss further later in this chapter). These factors increase the likelihood that teens and young adults will be physically violent toward their partner (Fuligni, Dapretto, & Galván, 2018; Heinze et al., 2018; Saint-Eloi Cadely et al., 2018).

Studies confirm what we know about the heightened sensitivity of teens' brains to peers. However, strong attachments to friends can help mitigate some of these outcomes, especially the depression and anxiety that often result after exposure to violence (Fuligni, Dapretto, & Galván, 2018; Heinze et al., 2018; Saint-Eloi Cadely et al., 2018).

Such findings make it clear that interventions based on cognitive behavioral therapy (which help reframe perceptions so that individuals can see things more clearly without jumping to incorrect conclusions about others' seemingly hostile attributions) can help such teens, along with earlier interventions with families that disrupt interparental aggression and help parents practice effective communication and problem-solving strategies (Saint-Eloy Cadely, Mrug, & Windle, 2019; Zucchelli & Ugazio, 2019).

These interventions are especially needed in light of other research which shows that being exposed to violence in the home during adolescence—either as an observer or as a victim—is a strong predictor of perpetrating intimate partner violence in late adolescence. Such exposure interferes with the development of inhibitory control, theory of mind, and empathy (Saint-Eloy Cadely, Mrug, & Windle, 2019; Zucchelli & Ugazio, 2019).

What Are Some Common Problems That Teens Struggle With?

Adolescence is a time when many disorders begin to emerge, such as depression, anxiety, eating disorders, substance abuse, personality disorders, and/or psychosis. This is likely a result of variations in the maturational changes that occur in the brain at this time.

Contemporary research on these multidimensional patterns of development includes addressing how differences in teens' brain activity that occur in response to rewards (such as a blunted response after a monetary gain) or differences in teens' brain activity that occur in response to low-social-status words (such as *loser*, *disliked*, or *ignored*) are associated with a great risk of concurrent or future depression (Giedd, Keshavan, & Paus, 2008; K. H. Lee et al., 2018; B. D. Nelson et al., 2018).

Internalizing Problems

Internalizing problems include anxiety and depression. Both anxiety and depression tend to *decrease* throughout the school years up until age 12. This age is a **developmental knot**, or a point at which trajectories change course, because both anxiety and depression begin to *increase* in early adolescence (Cohen, Andrews, Davis, & Rudolph, 2018; Kohli et al., 2015).

When we consider them separately, we see that adolescent anxiety is predicted by childhood anxiety; on the other hand, depression is more complex because both anxiety and depression in childhood increase the risk of depression in adolescence. Yet neither anxiety nor depression is necessary, because other factors increase the risk of depression in adolescence without a teen having preexisting anxiety or depression (Cohen, Andrews, Davis, & Rudolph, 2018).

These other factors that contribute to depression in adolescence represent a wide range of variables. Unfortunately, this means that there are multiple ways a teen's emotional development might be disrupted during adolescence, and perhaps even beyond.

Such disruption can occur because depression during this time of life—when teens are learning how to build healthy relationships, explore their interests, acquire skills, and eventually transition into the labor force—can interfere with interpersonal relationships, as well as with later socioeconomic well-being.

A meta-analysis of the research on teens with and without depression during adolescence revealed that for teens struggling with depression, the outcomes of such were consistent with the lifelong pattern of development: Such teens were *more likely* to struggle with unintended pregnancy/parenthood, failure to complete high school, and unemployment, while they were also *less likely* to enter college (Clayborne, Varin, & Colman, 2019).

The findings are also consistent with the polydirectional pattern of development, and they aren't surprising when we consider that unaddressed depression during adolescence doesn't just increase the risk of later depression and anxiety in adulthood. It also impairs a teen's ability to attend school, to understand and complete schoolwork even when the teen is able to attend school, to maintain stable friendships, and to be part of a social community (Clayborne, Varin, & Colman, 2019; Johnson et al., 2018).

Let's look again at what those multiple contributing factors to depression in adolescence are.

In Chapter 12, we learned that accelerated cortical thinning in adolescence (due to early life stress or ongoing stress in adolescence), insufficient sleep, and poor food choices are *correlated positively with symptoms of depression*, whereas sports participation, daily physical activity, healthful food choices, and civic participation in the forms of volunteering and voting are *correlated negatively with symptoms of depression* (Ballard, Hoyt, & Pachucki, 2019; Berger, Wahlstrom, & Windome, 2019; Biddle et al., 2019; Bos et al., 2018; Brière et al., 2018; Rice et al., 2019).

Such outcomes indicate that depression is also consistent with the multidimensional patterns of development, particularly with how physical factors (including a genetic risk for depression, especially early-onset depression that is evident by the beginning of adolescence) contribute to the emotional struggle of depression (Ballard, Hoyt, & Pachucki, 2019; Berger, Wahlstrom, & Windome, 2019; Biddle et al., 2019; Bos et al., 2018; Brière et al., 2018; Rice et al., 2019).

Other factors that may amplify depression during adolescence include the following: environmental influences (such as exposure to violence during the teens years); substance use (such as tobacco, sedatives, amphetamines, cannabis, cocaine, and hallucinogens); higher expressions of irritability and anger; insecure attachment to one's parents; having parents who have *low depression literacy* or understanding of teen depression; having parents who hold stigmatized views of depression (such as that depression is a weakness and can be "snapped out of"); having parents who are depressed themselves, and/or are critical, overprotective, distressed, withdrawn, and unsupportive in the face of a teen's depression (Galambos, Johnson, & Krahn, 2018; Johnco & Rapee, 2018; Khan et al., 2019; Walters et al., 2018).

With regard to the role of the family in teen depression, some studies also suggest there are sex differences in the trajectories or paths of how depression may develop from adolescence to emerging early adulthood. More data on nonbinary teens such as Sequoia are very much needed. Sequoia experienced a temporary increase in anxiety and depression around 14 years of age, which then declined, perhaps because they "came out" to their parents about their gender identity, and the parents were very supportive of such—it is important to know if their experience is or is not similar to other nonbinary teens, and why or why not.

That is, teens who identify as female are less likely to be depressed when they are better able to communicate with their parents and have greater peer support. Teens who identify as male are less likely to be depressed when they have greater peer support, yet they are more likely to be depressed in the face of sibling hostility (Finan, Ohannessian, & Gordon, 2018).

And for teens of both of these genders, depression tends to decline over time into emerging early adulthood, when they have greater communication with their same-sex parent. But these declines are less steep for teens in the face of sibling hostility, indicating that relationships are paramount in understanding depression in adolescents (Finan, Ohannessian, & Gordon, 2018).

Other research confirms the protective role that familial support, as well as active coping and planning, play in keeping depression at bay from adolescence to early adulthood, whereas venting and denial are associated with greater depression (Vannucci, Flannery, & Ohannessian, 2018).

Help for depression is available, though—and it can be quite effective. There is empirical evidence on the benefits of various programs to deal with

FIG. 13.13   Generational Changes in the Precursors to Depression

Copyright © Depositphotos/mtkang.

depression, verifying that such programs do indeed help teens err on the resilience side of the risk-resilience pattern of development.

Such programs include the positive youth development (PYD) programs we learned about in Chapter 12, which prevent depression (and substance use); psychoeducational programs that can increase parent understanding of depression; school-based prevention programs that can increase knowledge of depression as well as reduce depression and anxiety; behavioral sleep interventions that can reduce depression; and even single-session interventions that reduce depression over the long term (Blake, Trinder, & Allen, 2018; R. B. Jones et al., 2018; Taubman et al., 2019; Werner-Seidler et al., 2017; Travers & Mahalik, 2019).

Although these interventions for teen depression are effective, they seem to have become less effective in recent years (perhaps because of generational changes in the precursors to depression, such as increasing academic pressure and bullying via social media; these societal forces do not yet have interventions tailored to the needs of contemporary teens). Prevention strategies are especially welcome—and important in the first place in order to reduce the suffering and burden on teens, their families, and society (Schleider, Abel, & Weisz, 2019; Thomas, 2019; Weisz et al., 2018).

Externalizing Problems in Adolescence

Externalizing behaviors include aggression and rule-breaking (Zondervan-Zwijnenburg et al., 2019).

In general, teens who show greater externalizing behaviors tend to also show traits such as a lack of empathy, a lack of guilt, manipulation of others for one's own benefit, and indifference to rules as a result of believing that ethical codes do not apply to oneself (Ciucci et al. 2018; Sijtsema et al., 2019).

Teens who have poor self-regulation and who experience little positive affect (such as feeling excited, interested, or proud) are also at greater risk for externalizing behaviors (Brieant et al., 2018). In terms of aggression, in particular, teens are aggressive for a number of reasons, ranging from a genetic predisposition to a lack of community support (Vitaro, Boivin, & Poulin, 2018).

In the first part of this section, we will focus on factors associated with aggression (including bullying) in teens: Among these factors are cognitive biases, personality traits, peer influences (including peer norms for what is acceptable, as well as how peers may instigate aggression, support aggressors, and/or defend victims of aggression), the social injustice of income inequality, sex differences, gender roles, and parenting behaviors.

One factor that is associated with greater aggression in teens is cognitive biases, such as a **hostile attribution bias**, or the tendency to assume that others' ambiguous behavior is hostile. An example of this would be one peer walking by a second peer without saying hello—an event that could have occurred for an assortment of reasons, some of which are unrelated to the second peer—and the second peer interpreting it as hostility and consequently assuming unequivocally that they were being snubbed. Other factors include the personality traits of preferring to be popular rather than liked and of having low levels of honesty and humility. These factors indicate a self-importance that leads aggressive individuals to *coerce others* rather than *cooperate with* them (Garandeau & Lansu, 2019; Martinelli et al., 2018; Volk et al., 2019).

Teens who have a cognitive bias of interpreting others' behavior as hostile, in addition to having greater daily levels of anger, are more likely to engage in *reactive aggression*; this is conduct that tends

FIG. 13.14   Bullies, Followers, and a Victim

to occur as a function of their frustration or perceived threat, as well as perhaps poor impulse control (Martinelli et al., 2018; Moore et al., 2018; Perino, Moreira, & Telzer, 2019).

Reactive aggression is "emotionally hot" in that it is impulsive. *Proactive aggression* is "emotionally cool" in that it is more premeditated; also, the perpetrator assumes that it is positive because it enables them to reach a goal of theirs (Martinelli et al., 2018; Moore et al., 2018; Perino, Moreira, & Telzer, 2019).

A developmental factor that contributes to the rise of aggression over time is the role of peer influences. These influences include the greater value placed on popularity during adolescence than in childhood, with *bullies* (those who attack, humiliate, and/or exclude others—that is, their victims) and their *followers* tending to be rewarded with more social status in secondary school than in primary school, and therefore representing a greater percentage of roles over increasing grade levels (Pouwels, Lansu, & Cillessen, 2018; Pouwels et al., 2018a).

Note the other roles associated with bullying: *defenders*, those who try to stop the bullying and/or comfort the victims (likely as a result of a family climate in which their parents encouraged empathy); *outsiders*, those who do not side with either the bully or the victim; the *victims*; and *those with no clear role* (Pouwels, van Noorden, & Caravita, 2019; Valdés-Cuervo, Alcántar-Nieblas, Martínez-Ferrer, & Parra-Pérez, 2018).

Teens who are victims of aggression tend to have experienced great income inequality compared to other teens. Perhaps a lack of early resources contributes to decreased social trust as well as greater discrimination, teasing, shame, trauma, and mental health problems (Elgar et al., 2019).

Research on whether social status and behavior in middle childhood predicts participation in bullying confirms that indeed they do. The data reveals that bullies show above-average popularity and high aggression in middle childhood (Pouwels et al., 2018b).

Interestingly, defenders tend to show above-average popularity in middle childhood as well, yet in combination with low levels of aggression and average levels of prosocial behavior. Outsiders show low aggression and average prosocial behavior, while victims tend to show low levels of both popularity and likeability (Pouwels et al., 2018b).

Other work finds that teens who are perceived as emotionally competent but also extraverted are considered more likeable, raising questions for future research about whether teens who are emotionally competent but also introverted are more likely to be the victims of bullying (Szczygiel & Mikolajczak, 2018).

A combination of high aggression and high prosocial behavior also needs be discussed. According to *resource control theory*, individuals who are both coercive and prosocial—that is, *bistrategic* rather than simply antisocial or prosocial—are better able to control resources (Ciarrochi et al., 2019; Hartl et al., 2019).

Yet the data indicate that although bistrategic teens tend to be popular, they are also regarded as angry and disruptive, and they show relatively poorer well-being in terms of self-esteem and mental health compared to prosocial teens. Perhaps acquiring friends as resources is less satisfying than developing and maintaining genuine emotional connections to others (Ciarrochi et al., 2019; Hartl et al., 2019).

Although there appear to be some gender differences in aggression type during adolescence, data on nonbinary teens is very much needed. Until then, we at least know that teens who identify as male and teens who identify as female are equally likely to be bullying victims of *relational aggression* (such as spreading lies, threatening to end a friendship, and/or excluding peers). Only teens who identify as male are likely to be bullying victims of *physical aggression* (such as kicking, hitting, and/or using one's body to intimidate); being the victim of this type of aggression depends on many factors, including pubertal timing and the aforementioned popularity (Carter, Halawah, & Trinh, 2018; Casper & Card, 2017; Voulgaridou & Kokkinos, 2015).

That is, some research has found that teens who are at risk for being rejected and experiencing relational aggression from their peers are those teens who identify as female and who are not popular but *wish to be popular*. This may be because females who are of low social status may engage in behaviors associated with high-social-status females (such as snobbery and meanness) but without the resources of high-status females, such as material goods, information, and/or social attention, leading them to simply be disliked and mistreated instead (Bresland et al., 2018).

This same research study found that teens who identify as male and who are not popular and who also *do not wish to be popular* are at risk for these negative consequences. Such differences between these two genders may be that status-seeking and the desire for social dominance are more normative for those who identify as male, so that their absence is deemed questionable. Yet some have begun to suggest that dominance over others may be a sign of what can be thought of as *toxic masculinity* in contemporary mainstream society, or that dominance over others as normative is questionable (Berke, Reidy, & Zeichner, 2018; Jenney & Exner-Cortens, 2018).

Traditional gender norms for teens who identify as male also tend to include a requisite that they be "tough," whereas gender norms for teens who identify as female also tend to include a requisite that they be "nice." This double standard may explain why prosocial behavior in those who identify as male *increases* their risk of being the victim of relational aggression, while prosocial behavior in those who identify as female *decreases* their risk of being the victim of relational aggression (Closson & Watanabe, 2018). Other polydirectional patterns of development are found over time too.

Bullying and related roles change over time though, as bullies are sometimes victimized, victims are sometimes aggressive, and involved teens sometimes become bullies or victims (Zych et al., 2018).

It could be that changes in these roles are related to changes in parents' behaviors. Greater positive parenting, including monitoring and supervision, is associated with less bullying and less **cyberbullying**, which includes posting humiliating and/or threatening pictures and videos without another person's permission, as well as harassing, intimidating, and/or threatening another via electronic forms of contact (Extremera et al., 2018; Zych, Farrington, & Ttofi, 2019).

Yet personality traits such as high levels of empathy, self-esteem, and academic performance are also associated with less involvement in bullying and cyberbullying (Extremera et al., 2018; Zych, Farrington, & Ttofi, 2019).

Because cyberbullying includes posting humiliating and/or threatening pictures and videos without another person's permission, this suggests that **sexting**, or the sending of sexually explicit images of oneself, may, along with cyberbullying, heighten a teen's risk for subsequently being a victim of online sexual solicitations. The research data indicate that this is indeed the case—so teens can benefit not only from bullying prevention programs, but also from cyberbullying and sexting prevention programs (Gámez-Guadix & Mateos-Pérez, 2019; Van Ouystel et al., 2019).

We have discussed aggression and bullying quite a bit here. In terms of the rule-breaking aspect of externalizing behaviors, we now consider the roles of depression, school environments, and family environments.

To begin, research on French Canadian teens has distinguished between *nonviolent delinquency* (such as stealing from a store) and *violent delinquency* (such as beating up someone who hasn't done anything to). The data reveal that those teens who had conduct problems in childhood, including kicking or hitting people their age, were more likely to struggle with depression in middle adolescence, which then led to greater acts of both types of delinquency by the end of adolescence (Fontaine et al., 2019). These findings suggest that depression is both a *precursor to* and an *outcome of* behavior challenges, so that any intervention that hopes to prevent or reduce delinquency in children and teens needs to address depression and other emotional struggles as well (Fontaine et al., 2019).

Schools are ideally agents of social justice, but unfortunately can perpetuate discrimination.

That is, research shows that students of color are more likely to be disciplined—and even more so when they engage in the very same extracurricular sports activities that European American teens do, but for which European American teens receive lower discipline rates. This means that racial and ethnic disparities in school-based discipline continue even when teens of color conform to a school's values regarding athletics, both as an opportunity to serve as role models of discipline and as a chance to engage in teamwork and social bonding (Latimore et al., 2018).

Research has found that Mexican American teens who perceive their school to have a hostile environment (in terms of discrimination and violence) experience more brain reactivity to social exclusion. This is a multidimensional pattern of development. It contributes to their being at greater risk for *deviance* or engaging in both risky and antisocial behavior, unless they feel emotionally connected to their families (C. R. Rogers et al., 2018; Schriber et al., 2018).

Results such as these remind us that behavior is a product of complex variables, some of which are risk factors but need not be (if schools were of better quality), and some of which are protective factors, such as support and love from one's family and closeness to one's siblings. Interestingly, closeness to one's siblings has been shown to increase activation in areas of the brain associated with safer choices and less externalizing behaviors (C. R. Rogers et al., 2018; Schriber et al., 2018).

Latinx children and teens not only struggle with discrimination, as do Black and Native American children and teens (and after legacies of slavery and genocide), but also may also struggle with a gap between themselves and their parents in terms of **acculturation**. This is the process of adopting not only the language but also the values and behaviors of their host country (Kim et al., 2018; Nair, Roche, & White, 2018).

The greater this acculturation gap, in which teens are more acculturated than their parents, the less harmonious their family relations tend to be. Also, the teens' subsequent performance in school tends to be worse, whether they were born in the host country or elsewhere (Kim et al., 2018; Nair, Roche, & White, 2018).

Latinx and other immigrant teens may also struggle with immigration and acculturation stress, such as serving as interpreters for their parents. This practice is associated with better academic performance if it mainly involves interpreting in low-stakes situations, such appliance instructions and entertainment media, and with worse academic performance if it mainly involves interpreting in high-stakes situations, such as those concerning the family's health and safety (Anguiano, 2018).

Regardless of the racial and ethnic configuration of a family, though, other research indicates that teens are at greater risk of being aggressive and having substance abuse issues if they were especially high in impulsivity as toddlers; if their parents are rejecting (engaging in critical and hostile comments as well as critical and hostile tone and mannerisms); and/or if there is aggression within their family, such as between their parents and/or between themselves and their parents (Hentges, Shaw, & Wang, 2018; Saxbe et al., 2018).

Tech & Media

Internet Addiction during Adolescence

Adolescence is a stage during which teens must continue to develop their self-regulation, a task made even more difficult in recent generations with the unparalleled rise of the Internet. The Internet has led to increasing opportunities (such as seeking help when in danger; monitoring one's health; and online learning, especially for those who may have been unable to access education in the past) as well as increasing dangers (such being stalked, distracted driving, and compulsive use of the Internet). These are opportunities and dangers whose influences on the developing brains of teens we have yet to still fully comprehend (Yan, 2018).

Internet Addiction refers to excessive Internet use that interferes with the user's well-being (Lu et al., 2019; Pace, D'Urso, & Zapulla, 2019; Stavropoulos et al., 2018). Anyone can develop Internet Addiction, yet teens with ADHD are even more prone to developing such, especially those with poor frustration tolerance. Longitudinal research also indicates that even teens without ADHD but who have difficulties in self-regulation in early adolescence are at risk for internalizing problems in middle adolescence. These difficulties then increase the risk of Internet Addiction during the teens' late adolescence (Lu et al., 2019; Pace, D'Urso, & Zapulla, 2019; Stavropoulos et al., 2018).

Other work indicates that teens with poor self-regulation are also more likely to engage in problematic mobile phone use (Fumero et al., 2018; Liu et al., 2019). Therefore, those who are interested in designing preventions and interventions to help children and teens may want to focus on strengthening their self-regulation skills—particularly those teens with greater hostility, depression, anxiety, and/or family functioning, as well as poorer social skills—since they are at greater risk of Internet Addiction (Fumero et al., 2018; Liu et al., 2019).

Research with Greek adolescents indicates that those who report the most *online* flow, or feelings of being so absorbed by their activity that they lose self-consciousness, are those most likely to manifest Internet Addiction symptoms. For example, their school and/or work performance may suffer because of their Internet use (Stavropoulos et al., 2018). Information such as this can help professionals design interventions to improve family functioning; it can also be used to help teens discover opportunities for *offline* flow experiences that are meaningful to them, via creative and/or physical activities they enjoy.

Such offline flow activities will then become self-reinforcing, but will likely not interfere as easily with the teens' lives as online flow does. Offline flow activities may even provide other means of reducing the anxiety and isolation that Internet Addiction causes, perhaps via attending a regular art, music, or exercise class (Baldry, Sorrentino, & Farrington, 2019; Brighi et al., 2019; Stavropoulos et al., 2018).

Engaging in offline flow activities also means that teens' opportunities to avoid dealing with their sadness and anger are limited, given they therefore have both more healthy outlets to channel their feelings, and fewer opportunities for easy anonymous cyberbullying and abusive scapegoating of others, as well other antisocial behaviors (Baldry, Sorrentino, & Farrington, 2019; Brighi et al., 2019; Stavropoulos et al., 2018).

· · · ·

Interestingly, externalizing behaviors tend to be correlated negatively with parent age, indicating that although delayed childbearing may be associated with some increased risks to children, there are also benefits (Zondervan-Zwijnenburg et al., 2019). Older parents tend to have fewer mental health issues of their own, fewer substance abuse issues, and greater life experience. They often are in a more stable socioeconomic position than younger parents, which helps them create a more favorable environment in which their children and teens can develop fully (Duncan et al., 2018; Zondervan-Zwijnenburg et al., 2019).

Teens with older parents are less likely to engage in externalizing behaviors. The data also indicate that for each year a mother delays a first birth, the greater the school achievement and the lower the problem behaviors in her children and teens (Duncan et al., 2018; Zondervan-Zwijnenburg et al., 2019).

At this point, we have discussed internalizing and externalizing issues as two of the common emotional problems with which teens struggle. Next we will consider nonsuicidal self-injury. But before we do that, another problem that can occur in adolescence (and adulthood) needs our consideration: Internet Addiction. To learn more about which teens are more at risk for such, and how we can better help them, see the *Tech & Media: Internet Addiction during Adolescence* box.

At the beginning of this section on problems in development, we learned that differences in teens' brain activity in response to rewards (such as a *blunted response* after a monetary gain) are associated with a greater risk of depression.

Yet early adolescents who show a *heightened response* to a reward such as a monetary gain are more at risk of engaging in **nonsuicidal self-injury** (**NSSI**), or inflicting harm on oneself (such as cutting, hair-pulling, and bruising) without suicidal intent (B. D. Nelson et al., 2018; Poon et al., 2019). Rather than being a diagnosis on its own, NSSI is more a symptom of other disorders, such as ADHD, depression, borderline personality disorder, and/or PTSD.

In addition to having a greater sensitivity to reward, teens who may be at greater risk for thinking of and perhaps even engaging in NSSI are those who have been bullied by peers and/or siblings during childhood; have parents who are struggling with psychopathology, substance abuse, and/or accumulated adversities; and have parents who use harsh punishment and low monitoring. They also likely have a poor-quality attachment to their parent(s), a weakened bond that may disrupt identity development and emotional regulation, so that NSSI becomes a way to manage affect when one lacks support from others in doing so (Dantchev et al., 2019; Esposito, Bacchini, & Affuso, 2019; Gandhi et al., 2019; Pitkänen et al., 2019; Victor et al., 2019).

Although studies that examine brain activation in response to rewards look at different outcomes, such as depression and NSSI, these outcomes are linked. For example, *alexithymia*, or the inability to understand and describe one's feelings, is related to both depression and self-harm (Hemming et al., 2019). Interestingly, some researchers have found that depression and NSSI co-occur, and that they are predicted by a combination of peer victimization, having negative experiences while drinking, and low self-esteem (Tilton-Weaver, Marshall, & Svensson, 2019).

Heightened brain activation in response to rewards during early adolescence, followed by blunted brain activation in response to rewards in mid-adolescence (a time during which NSSI peaks and depression increases), suggests a polydirectional pattern of development and a timeline of changes within brain activation that future research may want to address (Tilton-Weaver, Marshall, & Svensson, 2019).

It could be that heightened reward systems in teens, together with low levels of coping skills and high levels of stressors, are a combination of factors that increase the risk of NSSI thoughts.

Then, if NSSI behaviors are engaged in and repeated, the rewards (of reducing negative affect and increasing positive affect after inflicting pain on oneself) alter the brain's reward circuitry. This leads to brain activation becoming blunted and desensitized to such rewards over time (B. D. Nelson et al., 2018; Poon et al., 2019).

So, providing teens with other tools to regulate their emotions is critical to helping them err on the resilience side of the risk–resilience pattern of development.

Research shows that thoughts of NSSI are associated with a greater risk of engaging in NSSI behaviors. Engaging in NSSI behaviors is associated with a greater risk of psychiatric disorders (including depression, eating disorders, and borderline personality disorder), as well as suicide and early death from all causes, including accidental death (Andrewes, 2017; Poon et al., 2019; Stead, Boylan, & Schmidt, 2019; Townsend, 2019; Wilkinson et al., 2018).

It is important to keep in mind that it is neither the frequency nor the severity of NSSI that predicts suicide attempt frequency; rather, depression and impulsivity are the predictors. So suicide interventions must address these two latter traits in teens as well. Additionally, the *randomness* of NSSI should be considered: Research shows that *habitual* patterns of NSSI are associated with fewer suicide attempts, whereas *random* patterns of NSSI are high-risk, especially for teens who struggle with borderline personality symptoms (Andrewes et al., 2017, 2018).

More than 90% of teens who attempt suicide also report NSSI. Other factors that increase the risk of teen suicide are mental disorders (such as substance abuse; anorexia nervosa; borderline personality disorder; depression, and its precursor of increasing irritability during childhood) in teens themselves as well as in their parents (Bilsen, 2018; Björkenstam et al., 2018; Duarte et al., 2019; Koyanagi et al., 2019; Orri et al., 2019).

Additional factors that increase the risk of teen suicide include previous suicide attempts, certain personality traits (such as passivity, impulsivity, black-and-white thinking, and poor problem-solving), poor family communication and high family conflict, housing instability, parental poverty, being convicted of a violent crime as a teen, peer bullying, peer rejection, romantic breakups, the loss of a friend, a desire to imitate suicidality of others in one's peer group or the media, and the availability of means (Bilsen, 2018; Björkenstam et al., 2018; Duarte et al., 2019; Koyanagi et al., 2019; Orri et al., 2019).

Teens who are Native American and/or nonbinary transgender are at a higher risk of suicide too. Yet the data show that having positive relationships with adults in their home protects teens against this risk, a protection with which Sequoia—who is both Native American and transgender—has thrived (Fullerton et al., 2019; Toomey, Syvertsen, & Shramko, 2018).

What works best for preventing suicide are interventions in clinical settings (such as hospitals) to reduce the frequency of suicide ideation, along with screenings and psychoeducational programs in school settings (Levi-Belz, et al., 2018; Robinson et al., 2018).

However, screenings that rely on teens' disclosure of their suicide ideation to researchers may not be entirely effective unless the screenings address how to help teens communicate better with others. In fact, research indicates that teens who admit to researchers (but to no one else up until then) that they have attempted suicide in the past show higher levels of current suicide ideation and distress (Levi-Belz et al., 2018; Robinson et al., 2018).

Disclosing their suicidality can ensure that teens get help and can strengthen their relationships with those in whom they confide. However, developmental scientists who design interventions need to understand that such disclosures can also result in the teens experiencing negative reactions, such as feeling stigma and shame (Sheehan et al., 2019).

Interventions to prevent suicide also need to address factors such as race, ethnicity, and religion. Most interventions have been designed for middle-class European American teens, yet the data show, for example, that the discrimination Black teens experience—for example, being individually excluded from activities at school and/or overhearing negative comments about Blacks—is understandably associated with greater depression, a factor that is associated with greater risk of suicide (Bluehen-Unger et al., 2017; Dotterer & James, 2018; Miller & Prinstein, 2019).

Additional research indicates that training programs for teachers and parents *do* increase their knowledge of suicide and increase their confidence to intervene. But such programs *do not* increase their ability to identify young people who are at risk of suicide, nor their ability to refer them to mental health services (Karnik & Winiarski, 2019; Torok et al., 2019).

More research is very much needed to determine how to help adults help teens, particularly in determining what to ask, and how to provide concrete resources in the moment, when teens need them most (Karnik & Winiarski, 2019; Torok et al., 2019).

How Do Empathy and Prosocial Behavior Develop in Adolescence?

Longitudinal research indicates that empathy generally increases from adolescence through late adulthood, likely because perspective-taking continues to improve as the brain develops (Oh, Chopik, Konrath, & Grimm, 2019).

Moral development is clearly consistent with the multidimensional pattern of development, with environmental factors playing a role as well. That is, the more parents provide their teens with social rewards such as praise (versus providing material rewards such a physical gift), say, when their teen helps others in need, the greater their teen's perspective-taking, prosocial moral reasoning (which we first learned about in Chapter 11), and empathy—all of which are associated with greater prosocial behavior (Davis & Carlo, 2018).

Other work indicates that empathy, in combination with *self-compassion* (an appreciation of the shared nature of human suffering, so that individuals high in self-compassion are more likely to recognize when they are suffering from their flaws and when others are suffering from their flaws) in ninth grade predicts increases in prosocial behavior over the course of high school as rated by teens' peers (Marshall et al., 2019).

These findings suggest that the more warmth, care, and love we can extend to ourselves, the more mindful and compassionate, as well as less reactive and judgmental, we may be of others. These traits are very conducive to constructive problem-solving during moments of interpersonal conflict.

So empathy and prosocial behavior can change over time. Yet what factors are correlated with them?

A review of over 150 different research studies conducted in the United States, Italy, the Netherlands, China, Spain, the UK, Canada, Germany, other European countries, other Asian countries, Central and South American countries, African countries, and Australia found a host of variables that were correlated positively with empathy and prosocial behavior in teens. These variables included greater self-regulation, resiliency, self-esteem, prosocial values, Authoritative parenting, parent role modeling of empathic behavior, parent income, parent education, teen–parent attachment, positive peer relationships, democratic school norms, school support and counseling availability, residential stability

FIG. 13.15　An Environmental Activist Teen

neighborhood cohesion, exposure to prosocial media content (as opposed to violent media content), a religious or spiritual practice, and membership in a group or club (Silke et al., 2018).

Additional reviews of research on greater empathy during adolescence point to high-quality relationships between teens and their parents, and they point especially to high-quality relationships between teens and their peers (Boele et al., 2019).

Empathy is not limited to other humans. The human relationship with the natural environment is one of reciprocal dependence, and environmental education can illuminate this relationship to children and teens with discussions about what can be done to change our behaviors and how we can work toward sustainability in the face of climate change, the depletion of the ozone layer, the destruction of forests, the pollution of oceans, etc. (Musitu-Ferrer et al., 2019).

Appreciating and internalizing this reciprocal relationship between human behavior and environmental well-being is strengthened by some parents, including Sequoia's, and by many others across the globe. For instance, research on teens in Spain has found that teens with more *empathy for nature* (indicated by their feeling better in natural environments that are well cared for and by their efforts to understand why others might engage in behaviors that harm the environment) and with more feelings of connectedness to nature tend to have parents who engage significantly more of either the Authoritative or the Indulgent parenting style behaviors, which we first read about in Chapter 9, and significantly less of either the Authoritarian or the Neglectful parenting styles (Musitu-Ferrer et al., 2019).

Prosocial behavior, the outcome variable in many of the aforementioned studies, is consistent with the polydirectional pattern of development, particularly when researchers study it through a gendered lens. Although research on nonbinary teens is still needed, for now we know that although empathy increases from adolescence onward, prosocial behavior is more complex: Those identifying as female increase in their prosocial behavior from 13 to 16 years of age, then decrease; those identifying as male remain stable in their prosocial behavior from 13 to 14 years of age, then increase until 17 years of age, then decrease (Van der Graff et al., 2018).

Why? Researchers speculate that these patterns likely reflect how brain development is more rapid in females than in males. Also, those who identify as female are exposed to more socialization efforts for them to be nurturing and supportive of others, whereas those who identify as male are exposed to more socialization efforts for them to be assertive and competitive (Van der Graff et al., 2018).

These same researchers also found that *empathic concern* (such as feelings of sorrow or concern for others) was a greater predictor of prosocial behavior than was perspective-taking. This

FIG. 13.16   Sequoia After His Shift as a Youth Mentor

The Needs of Refugee Children, Teens, and Their Families

In this box, we pan across or take a panoramic wide-angle view of the experiences and needs of refugee children and teens. Refugees tend to be quite resilient, particularly postmigration; they also tend to experience low stigma and discrimination, as well as high levels of cohesion and adaptability within their own families, and high levels of social support—opportunities to participate economically as well as socially (Hodes, Anagnostopoulos, & Skokauskas, 2018; Sara & Brann, 2018; Yaylaci, 2018).

Yet as refugees—after experiencing violence, organized conflict, war, the death of loved ones, and frequently dangerous journeys of crossing national borders; after being detained in settlements or refugee camps that often have harsh living conditions and treatment; after forced displacement and resettling in a host country whose citizens may be hostile to them or may simply not have the social services to ease their transition even if they are welcoming—children and teens, especially unaccompanied minors, are often at an increased risk of externalizing and/or internalizing symptoms (Bryant et al., 2018; Hodes, 2019; Nielsen et al., 2019; Vossoughi et al., 2018).

For instance, even if parents survive the aforementioned conflicts and show no post-traumatic stress disorder (PTSD) symptoms, their children and teens may experience insecure attachment to their parents as well as harsher parenting, and exhibit emotional and behavioral problems themselves (Bryant et al., 2018; Hodes, 2019; Hodes, Anagnostopoulos, & Skokauskas, 2018; Nielsen et al., 2019).

Findings such as these indicate a need for social services to include culturally sensitive mental health services for all family members—especially in order to support these teens and increase the likelihood that subsequent generations of their families are not at increased risk of being burdened by a legacy of transgenerational mental health problems (Bryant et al., 2018; Hodes, 2019; Hodes, Anagnostopoulos, & Skokauskas, 2018; Nielsen et al., 2019).

Ideal services include those that address the impact of trauma exposure and acculturation stress on the health and well-being of children, teens, and their families—with resettlement agencies and volunteers (including teens) providing assistance in cultural adjustment; mentoring; organizing of leisure activities; interpreting; language instruction; tutoring; assistance with seeking employment; housing and transportation to access these services; and advocacy in schools and health care settings. These sorely needed services should be provided by culturally competent service providers who are able to provide a continuation of services regardless of political factors (Forrest-Bank, Held, & Jones, 2019).

• • • •

indicates that efforts to increase prosocial behavior in adolescence may be more effective when *moral emotions* are emphasized rather than *moral cognitions*—a distinction consistent with other research showing that empathy and perspective-taking involve different parts of the brain (Stietz et al., 2019; Van der Graff et al., 2018).

Before we transition to the next section, on interventions for and with adolescents, let's consider the needs of refugee children, teens, and their families—including how adolescents can take prosocial action with regard to refugees, perhaps via volunteering in order to help with their resettlement and adjustment postmigration. This critical topic is explored in the *Pan & Zoom: The Needs of Refugee Children, Teens, and Their Families* box.

Whether it be with refugees or with others, adolescence is an ideal time for volunteering, given teens' ability to consider the needs, concerns, and perspectives of others increases through adolescence (Hussong, Jones, & Jensen, 2018). Working with others who are different from themselves also gives teens another opportunity for *diversity socialization* in an increasingly complex and multicultural world. In this way, teens can become *interculturally mature* and retain their own cultural identities while recognizing and respecting the identities of others (Hussong, Jones, & Jensen, 2018).

Adolescents' *need to contribute* (or their desire to provide resources and support to others in their community, schools, peer group, and/or family) grows as they desire more autonomy in making choices consistent with their unique developing identities, as is the case of Sequoia, who chooses to volunteer one afternoon a week (Fuligni, 2018).

What Makes for Effective Interventions for, and with, Adolescents?

Intervention efforts that are successful with school-age children, whether they increase children's prosocial behavior or otherwise, are not always successful with teens if these interventions aren't designed with the specific needs of adolescents. These needs include the need for *status*, or affirming one's rank in the social hierarchy, and *respect*, or being granted the rights that one expects to be granted in society (Dahl et al., 2018; Yeager, Dahl, & Dweck, 2018).

Such needs are a priority for all teens, but especially at this point in history—when social changes (such as technological breakthroughs, earlier onset of puberty, entering adult roles later as a result of increasing demand for higher education, and economic policies than favor the wealthy rather than fully funding education for all, a "gig" economy in the face of full-time employment scarcity, etc.) are affecting adolescents in ways that we have yet to understand and that can either *intensify their vulnerabilities*, such as exploitation or radicalization, or *intensify their opportunities*, such as learning, innovation, and social connections (Dahl et al., 2018).

And those interventions with teens that *are* designed with teens' needs for respect and status are more effective.

Consider this alternative to "reminding" teens about unhealthy junk food with a heavy-handed lecture that provides information teens already possess: Instead, researchers have designed an intervention that includes an exposé of food industry practices (such as how scientists are hired by food companies so they can engineer food to be more addictive; how food company executives won't let their own children eat the food they market to others; and how every time a teen buys junk food, they inadvertently give money to wealthy shareholders, who may also hope teens don't know any better), provided quotes from high-status peers who vowed not to eat such food, and assigned students to write an essay persuading future students to rebel against these food companies by eating healthful food (Yeager, Dahl, & Dweck, 2018).

Additionally, out of respect for their own decision-making, the students in this intervention weren't required to believe their own attempt at persuasion. The essay exercise also provided teens with an opportunity to engage in prosocial behavior—and it gave them the social status of being able to share with other teens the specific wisdom that they (unlike adults) have about being a teenager under pressure.

The results showed that when offered a snack later on, teens chose a more healthful snack. This suggests that wisely designed interventions like this one not only help teens err on the resilience side of the risk–resilience pattern of development, but also are consistent with the recognition that interventions with teens are most effective when the teens are treated with the status and respect they deserve (Bryan et al., 2016; Yeager, Dahl, & Dweck, 2018).

Key Terms

Acculturation

Admiration

Adolescent Information Management

Affectional Orientation

Behavioral Control

Cyberbullying

Developmental Knot

Dual-Cycle Model of Identity

Fidelity

Hostile Attribution Bias

Identity Achievement

Identity Diffusion

Identity Foreclosure

Identity Moratorium

Identity–Role Confusion

Internet Addiction

Intersectionality

Intimate Partner Violence

LGBTQIA+

Negative Identity

Nonsuicidal Self-Injury (NSSI)

Parent–Teen Communication

Parental Monitoring

Perceived Popularity

Positive Identity

Psychological Control

Sexting

Sexually Transmitted Infections

Status Model of Identity

Three Factor Model of Identity

Triangulation

Summary

1. **Discuss what Erikson's theory can tell us about needs in adolescence.** Adolescence is a period of heightened conflict, as well as high growth potential, in which adolescents must work to obtain an inner sameness and continuity that is personally meaningful to them.

2. **Compare and contrast the models of identity.** The Identity Status model concerns the extent to which individuals have engaged in Identity Exploration and Identity Commitment. Both of these processes can be thought of as a continuum to create four statuses from low and high levels of exploration and commitment: Diffusion, Foreclosure, Moratorium, and Achievement. The Dual-Cycle Model of Identity addresses the extent to which individuals engage in exploration in breadth and making a commitment, then exploration in depth and identifying with a commitment. The Three Factor Model of Identity also addresses the process of commitment reconsideration, in which individuals compare their current commitments to alternative possible commitments.

3. **Explain Intersectionality.** *Intersectionality* refers to how multiple aspects of identity (such as citizenship, acculturation, language(s) spoken, socioeconomic status, gender identity, race, ethnicity, affectional orientation, ability, and immigrant status) shape the experiences and life chances of teens, via intersecting systems of equality and inequality that often self-perpetuate, for better or worse.

4. **Recount what is known about families and the relationships within them.** Although there are a variety of different family structures in which a teen may development, the quality of relationships among family members is a stronger predictor of adolescents' well-being than is the particular structure of their specific family. Communication between teens and their parents includes parents' monitoring of their teens, teens' management of how they share information with their parents, and how both of the aspects of communication influence one another. In terms of teens' relationships with siblings, it is often assumed that (children and) teens with siblings have better social skills. But what matters is not whether teens have siblings. Instead, the quality of their relationship with their sibling(s) determines their ability to maintain relationships with other individuals who are not family members.

5. **Recount what is known about teens' relationships outside the family.** Sociometric popularity, along with perceived popularity and admiration, all constitute forms of peer status, which can have profound effects on teens themselves and on their peers. Teens may develop a *queer* affectional orientation, so it is important not to make assumptions about adolescents' identities or to assume that their identities match their romantic attraction and/or sexual behavior. Researchers have identified common patterns of romantic relationships from mid-adolescence to early adulthood. The failure to acknowledge the reality of adolescent sexuality reduces the ability of parents to influence their teen's choices. This failure is also relevant to adolescents with physical and/or cognitive disabilities, who are often subject to an additional societal stigma that views them as asexual.

6. **Detail some of the common emotional problems that teens struggle with.** Adolescence is a time during which many disorders begin to emerge (such as depression, anxiety, eating disorders, substance abuse, personality disorders, and/or psychosis), likely as a result of variations in the maturational changes that occur in the brain at this time. Anxiety and depression tend to decrease throughout the school years up until age 12. At this point, trajectories change course—so that both begin to increase in early adolescence.

   Teens are aggressive for a number of reasons, ranging from a genetic predisposition to a lack of community support. Such aggression includes involvement in bullying, cyberbullying, relational aggression, and/or physical aggression. Differences in teens' brain activity are related to an increased risk of engaging in nonsuicidal self-injury or inflicting harm on oneself (such as cutting, hair-pulling, and bruising) without suicidal intent, in early adolescence. Nonsuicidal self-injury is a risk factor for suicide, but other risk factors play a role as well—factors that can be addressed in prevention and intervention efforts.

7. **Identify how empathy and prosocial behavior develop in adolescence.** Empathy generally increases from adolescence through late adulthood, as perspective-taking continues to improve as the brain develops. Other factors that contribute to empathy and prosocial behavior include greater self-regulation, resiliency, self-esteem, prosocial values, Authoritative parenting, parent role-modeling of empathic behavior, parent income, parent education, teen–parent attachment, positive peer relationships, democratic school norms, school support and counseling availability, residential stability, neighborhood cohesion, exposure to prosocial media

content, a religious or spiritual practice, membership in a group or club, and high-quality relationships between teens and their parents, and as well as between teens and their peers.

Adolescence is an ideal time for volunteering. Teens are able to consider the needs, concerns, and perspectives increases through adolescence. Also, they can see that working with others who are different from themselves provides another opportunity for diversity socialization in an increasingly complex and multicultural world.

8. **Clarify what makes effective interventions for and with adolescents.** Effective interventions take into account teens' need for status, or recognition of one's rank in the social hierarchy, and teens' need for respect, or being granted the rights one expects in society.

The Cycle of Science

Research

Why was the study conducted?
The researchers wanted to know about the effectiveness of an intervention that coaches parents on how to talk to adolescents about sex (and drug use) while their teen is at their well-child visit with the pediatrician (Ford et al., 2019).

Who participated in the study?
After researchers contacted the parents of 14- and 15-year-old teens with a scheduled annual well-child visit at a primary care pediatric practice, they screened 196 parent–teen dyad participants for their eligibility. Out of these 196 dyads, some were ineligible, some were unavailable, some declined to participate, some withdrew, and some did not participate, leaving the researchers with 118 dyad participants who provided parent informed consent and adolescent assent.

Which type of design was used?
An experimental research study was conducted in which dyads were assigned randomly to a sexual health intervention group, an alcohol prevention group, or a control group. The intervention groups were asked to come to their well-child visit 15 minutes early, and the parents were then taken to a quiet area in the waiting room away from their teen so they could receive the intervention materials. Parents later joined their teens in the examination room.

Two weeks after this visit, research assistants contacted the parents to discuss information not addressed in the first visit, and to give parents a survey. The research assistants also discussed with parents how they could use the materials they were given in order to have a conversation with their teen about the intervention topic, if they had not already done so within the past two weeks since their visit. Then, four weeks after the initial well-child visit, parents and their teens completed a final survey.

Out of the 118 dyad participants who provided parent informed consent and adolescent assent, 99 dyads completed the study, with 25 dyads in the sexual health intervention group, 36 dyads in the alcohol prevention intervention group, and 38 dyads in the control group.

What were the results?

The data indicate that the coaching interventions did indeed increase parent–adolescent communication, with adolescents reporting significantly greater parent–teen discussions about both sexual health and alcohol prevention for up to four months after the initial well-child visit. Interestingly, parents did not report significantly greater parent–teen discussions about either sexual health or alcohol prevention, so they may have perceived their interactions with their teens about these topics differently than did the teens.

The discrepancies may reflect differences in self-report. Or parents may have set a higher bar for themselves than they were able to reach regarding such sensitive topics. Their teens were glad to have any increased communication at all, with the sensitivity of the topic being a real possibility, given that communication about sexual health was less frequent than communication about alcohol prevention.

Are the results consistent with theory?

Yes. Although professionals recommend clinical preventive services for adolescents and young adults, the actual delivery of such is less than desired. This study shows that it is both possible and feasible to deliver a preventative intervention program (Harris et al., 2017).

How can the results be used to improve our lives?

Interventions that can prevent adolescent pregnancy, sexually transmitted infections, alcohol abuse, alcohol-related injuries, and other problems that can harm teens' health and well-being seem to be both effective and feasible, at least within this sample. Future research should conduct similar studies with other and diverse populations. It is also necessary to determine if the increases in parent–child communication translate into changes in adolescents' choices, confidence, level of assertiveness in the face of peer pressure, and other communication with parents.

Exercises

1. What pattern of results would you expect if parents had discussed the materials they were given within a group of other parents before meeting their teen in the examination room?

2. What pattern of results would you expect if the study had an intervention to address the use of e-cigarettes?

3. How might pediatricians' offices incorporate a program such as this in their regularly scheduled visits? What practical barriers would there be, and how can they be addressed?

Helpful Websites

To learn more about several foundations that provide direct services to improve the quality of foster care, that work to ensure that the transition from foster care to adulthood is successful, and that join with both child welfare services and policy makers to provide, improve, and eventually prevent the need for foster care, see the Casey Philanthropies website. The website provides detailed information and useful links to these foundations: https://www.aecf.org/about/the-casey-philanthropies-a-legacy-of-service-to-children-and-families/

Your Life, Your Voice has tips for teens on dealing with tough situations, including how to talk to parents. Teens can get help by calling, texting, chatting, emailing, and/or using their app: http://www.yourlifeyourvoice.org/Pages/home.aspx

Teens Against Bullying helps teens better understand bullying, advocate for themselves, advocate for others, and take action against bullying: https://pacerteensagainstbullying.org

Loveisrespect educates and empowers young people to prevent, as well as end, abusive relationships. The website includes Healthy Relationships 101 resources, as well as help in English and Spanish via chat, email, and/or text: https://www.loveisrespect.org/

For information on suicide, including the prevention of teen suicide, visit the American Psychological Association's website: https://www.apa.org/helpcenter/

To learn about volunteer opportunities for teens, and the possibility of scholarships for service, visit the website of Volunteennation: http://www.volunteennation.org

Recommended Reading

Faber, A., & Mazlish, E. (2005). *How to talk so teens will listen & listen so teens will talk.* New York, NY: HarperCollins.

Lohmann, R. C., & Taylor, J. V. (2013). *The bullying workbook for teens: Activities to help you deal with social aggression and cyberbullying.* Oakland, CA: New Harbinger Publications.

Rayne, K. (2017). *GIRL: Love, sex, romance and being you.* Washington, DC: Magination Press.

Rayne, K., & Gonzales, K. (2019). *Trans+: Love, sex, romance, and being you.* Washington, DC: Magination Press.

Siegel, D. J. (2013). *Brainstorm: The power and purpose of the teenage brain.* New York, NY: Penguin.

Smiler, A. P. (2016). *Dating and sex: A guide for the 21st century teen boy.* Washington, DC: Magination Press.

Toner, J. B., & Freeland, C. A. B. (2016). *Depression: A teen's guide to survive and thrive.* Washington, DC: Magination Press.

References

Ablewhite, J., Peel, I., McDaid, L., Hawkins, A., Goodenough, T., Deave, T., Stewart, J., & Kendrick, D. (2015). Parental perceptions of barriers and facilitators to preventing child unintentional injuries within the home: A qualitative study. *BMC Public Health, 15,* 280. https://doi.org/10.1186/s12889-015-1547-2

Abramson, L., Paz, Y., & Knafo-Noam, A. (2018). From negative reactivity to empathic responding: Infants high in negative reactivity express more empathy later in development, with the help of regulation. *Developmental Science 22*(3), e12766. https://doi.org/10.1111/desc.12766

Abreu, R. L., & Kenny, M. C. (2018). Cyberbullying and LGBTQ youth: A systematic literature review and recommendations for prevention and intervention. *Journal of Child & Adolescent Trauma, 11,* 81–97. https://doi.org/10.1007/s40653-017-0175-7

Adams, B. N. & Grunebaum, A. (2014). Does "pink all over" accurately describe an APGAR score of 2 in newborns of color? *Obstetrics & Gynecology, 123*(36S). https:// 10.1097/01.AOG.0000447310.59592.32

Adams-Price, C. E., et al. (2018). The creative benefits scale: Connecting generativity to life satisfaction. *The International Journal of Aging and Human Development, 86*(3), 242–265. https://doi.org/10.1177/0091415017699939

Addabbo, M., et al. (2018). Dynamic facial expressions of emotions are discriminated at birth. *PLOS ONE, 13*(3): e0193868. https://doi.org/10.1371/journal.pone.0193868

Adolph, K. E., & Hoch, J. E. (2019). Motor development: Embodied, embedded, enculturated, and enabling. *Annual Review of Psychology, 70,* 141–164. https://doi.org/10.1146/annurev-psych-010418-102836

Adolph, K. E., Hoch, J. E., & Cole, W. G. (2018). Development (of walking): 15 suggestions. *Trends in Cognitive Sciences, 22*(8), 699–711. https://doi.org/10.1016/j.tics.2018.05.010

Adolph, K. E., Kretch, K. S., & LoBue, V. (2014). Fear of heights in infants? *Current Directions in Psychological Science, 23*(1), 60–66. https//doi.org/10.1177/0963721413498895

Adolph, K. E. & Robinson, S. R. (2013). The road to walking: What learning to walk tells us about development. In P. Zelazo (Ed.), *Oxford handbook of developmental psychology, Vol 1,* 403–443. Oxford, UK: Oxford University Press.

Adolph, K. E., Robinson, S. R., Young, J. W., Gill-Alvarez, F. (2008). What is the shape of developmental change? *Psychological Review, 115*(3), 527–543. https://doi.org/ 10.1037/0033-295X.115.3.527

Aeschlimann, E. A., Voelke, A. E., & Roebers, C. M. (2017). Short-term storage and executive working memory processing predict fluid intelligence in primary school children. *Journal of Intelligence, 5*(2), 17. https://doi.org/10.3390/jintelligence5020017

Aggensteiner, P-M., et al. (2019). Slow cortical potentials neurofeedback in children with ADHD: Comorbidity, self-regulation, and clinical outcomes six months after treatment in a multicenter randomized controlled trials. *European Child & Adolescent Psychiatry,* 1–9. https://doi.org/10.1007/s00787-018-01271-8

Agodoa, I., et al. (2018). Societal costs of sickle cell disease in the United States. *Blood, 132* (Suppl. 2), 4706. https://doi.org/10.1182/blood-2018-99-119420

Ahern, S. M., Caton, S. J., Blundell-Birtill, P., & Hetherington, M. M. (2019). The effects of repeated exposure and variety on vegetable intake in preschool children. *Appetite, 132,* 37–43. https://doi.org/10.1016/j.appet.2018.10.001

Ahlborg, M. G., et al. (2019). Into the realm of social capital for adolescents: A latent profile analysis. *PLOS ONE, 14*(2), e0212564. https://doi.org/10.1371/journal.pone.0212564

Ahmed, F., Ahmed, N., Pissarides, C. & Stiglitz, J. (2020). Why inequality could spread COVID-19. *Lancet Public Health.* https://doi.org/10.1016/ S2468-2667(20)30085-2

Ainsworth, M. D. S. (1967). *Infancy in Uganda: Infant care and the growth of love.* Baltimore: Johns Hopkins University Press.

Ainsworth, M. D. S., Blehar, M. C., Waters, E. & Wall, S. (1978). *Patterns of attachment: A psychological study of the strange situation.* Hillsdale, NJ: Lawrence Erlbaum.

Akbari, E., et al. (2018). Kangaroo mother care and infant biopsychosocial outcomes in the first year: A meta-analysis. *Early Human Development, 122*, 22–31. https://doi.org/10.1016/j.earlhumdev.2018.05.004

Alaie, I., Läftman, S. B., Jonsson, U., & Bohman, H. (2019). Parent–youth conflict as a predictor of depression in adulthood: A 15-year follow-up of a community-based cohort. *European Child & Adolescent Psychiatry*, 1–10. https://doi.org/10.1007/s00787-019-01368-8

Albott, C. S., Forbes, M. K., & Anker, J. J. (2018). Association of childhood adversity with differential susceptibility of transdiagnostic psychopathology to environmental stress in adulthood. *JAMA Network Open, 1*(7), e185354. https://doi.org/10.1001/jamanetworkopen.2018.5354

Alegret, I. A., et al. (2018). Influence of communicative openness on the psychological adjustment of internationally adopted adolescents. *Journal of Research on Adolescence*, 1–12. https://doi.org/10.1111/jora.12464

Alemdar, D. K. (2018). Effect of recorded maternal voice, breast milk odor, and incubator cover on pain and comfort during peripheral cannulation in preterm infants. *Applied Nursing Research, 40*, 1–6. https://doi.org/10.1016/j.apnr.2017.12.001

Alexandre-Silva, G. M., et al. (2018). The hygiene hypothesis at a glance: Early exposures, immune mechanism and novel therapies. *Acta Tropica, 188*, 16–26. https://doi.org/10.1016/j.actatropica.2018.08.032

Allen, J. P., Grande, L., Tan, J., & Loeb, E. (2018). Parent and peer predictors of attachment security from adolescence to adulthood. *Child Development, 89*(4), 112011–32. https://doi.org/10.1111/cdev.12840

Allen, J. P., Narr, R. K., Kansky, J., & Szwedo, D. E. (2019). Adolescent peer relationship qualities as predictors of long-term romantic life satisfaction. *Child Development*, 1–14. https://doi.org/10.1111/cdev.13193

Allington, R. L. & McGill-Franzen, A. (2013). *Summer reading: Closing the rich-poor reading achievement gap*. New York, NY: Teachers College Press.

Alotaibi, M. F. (2019). Physiology of puberty in boys and girls and pathological disorders affecting its onset. *Journal of Adolescence, 71*, 63–71. https://doi.org/10.1016/j.adolescence.2018.12.007

Alston, J. M., & Okrent, A. M. (2017). Causes of obesity: External influences. In *The Effects of Farm and Food Policy on Obesity in the United States*. Palgrave Studies in Agricultural Economics and Food Policy. Palgrave Macmillan. https://doi.org/10.1057/978-1-137-47831-3_5

Al-Shawaf, L., Conroy-Beam, D., Asao, K., & Buss, D. M. (2016). Human emotions: An evolutionary psychological perspective. *Emotion Review, 8*(2), 173–186. https://doi.org/10.1177/1754073914565518

Ambler, G. (2013). Normal physical development and growth at puberty (pp. 1–14). In K. Steinbeck & M. R. Kohn (Eds.), *A clinical handbook in adolescent medicine: A guide for health professionals who work with adolescents and young adults*. World Scientific Publishing.

American Academy of Pediatrics (2019). Organized Sports for Children and Preadolescents. *Pediatrics*. 128, e748. https://doi.org/ https://doi.org/10.1542/peds.2019-0997

American Academy of Pediatrics (2012a). Male circumcision. *Pediatrics, 130*(3), e756-e785. https://doi.org/10.1542/peds.2012-1990

American Academy of Pediatrics (2012b). Breastfeeding and the use of human milk. *Pediatrics, 129*(3), e827-e841. https://doi.org/10.1542/peds.2011-3552

American Academy of Pediatrics. (2014). Policy statement: School start times for adolescents. *Pediatrics, 134*, 642–649. https://doi.org/10.1542/peds.2014-1697

American Academy of Pediatrics Council on Communications and Media. (2016). Media and young minds. *Pediatrics, 138*(5), e20162591.

American Academy of Pediatrics (2020). *Swaddling: Is it safe?* Retrieved from: https://www.healthychildren.org/English/ages-stages/baby/diapers-clothing/Pages/Swaddling-Is-it-Safe.aspx

American Academy of Pediatric Dentistry (2018). *Predictive model for caries risk based on determinants of health available to primary care providers*. Retrieved from: https://www.aapd.org/assets/1/7/DentaQuest-RE-4dig.pdf

American Psychiatric Association. (2013). *Diagnostic and statistical manual of mental Disorders* (5th ed). https://doi.org/10.1176/appi.books.9780890425596

American Psychological Association (2015). Guidelines for psychological practice with transgender and gender nonconforming people. *American Psychologist, 70*(9), 832–864. http://dx.doi.org/10.1037/a0039906

American Public Health Association. (2018). *Health in all policies*. Retrieved from https://www.apha.org/topics-and-issues/health-in-all-policies

American Society for Reproductive Medicine. (2018). *Quick facts about infertility*. Retrieved from https://www.reproductivefacts.org/faqs/quick-facts-about-infertility/

Aminimanesh, A., Ghazavi, Z., & Merhrabi, T. (2019). Effectiveness of the puppet show and storytelling methods on children's behavioral problems. *Iranian Journal of Nursing and Midwifery Research, 24*(1), 61–65. https://doi.org/10.4103/ijnmr.IJNMR_115_15

Amorim, M. (2019). Are grandparents a blessing or a burden? Multigenerational coresidence and child-related spending. *Social Science Research, 80*, 132–144. https://doi.org/10.1016/j.ssresearch.2019.02.002

Amsterdam, B. (1972), Mirror self-image reactions before the age of two. *Developmental Psychobiology, 5*, 297–305. https://doi.org/ https://doi.org/10.1002/dev.420050403

Anastasi, A. (1958). Heredity, environment, and the question "how?" *Psychological Review, 65*, 197–208. https://doi.org/10.1037/h0044895

Anderson, C., & Cacola, P. (2017). Implications of preterm birth for maternal mental health and infant development. *MCN, The American Journal of Maternal/Child Nursing, 42*(2), 108–114. https://doi.org/10.1097/NMC.0000000000000311

Anderson, M., & Jiang, J. (2018). Teens, social media, & technology 2018. Retrieved from https://www.pewinternet.org/2018/05/31/teens-social-media-technology-2018/

Anderson, N. A., Bohnert, A. M., & Governale, A. (2018). Organized activity involvement among urban youth: Understanding family- and neighborhood-level characteristics as predictors of involvement. *Journal of Youth and Adolescence, 47*, 1697–1711. https://doi.org/10.1007/s10964-018-0823-8

Anderson, S., et al. (2018). Youth-serving institutional resources and neighborhood safety: Ties with positive youth development. *American Journal of Orthopsychiatry, 88*(1), 78–87. http://dx.doi.org/10.1037/ort0000220

Andrade, C. (2018). Risk of major congenital malformations associated with the use of methylphenidate or amphetamines in pregnancy. *The Journal of Clinical Psychiatry, 79*(1). https://doi.org/10.4088/JCP.18f12108

Andrewes, H. E., et al. (2017). Relationships between the frequency and severity of non-suicidal self-injury and suicide attempts in youth with borderline personality disorder. *Early Intervention in Psychiatry, 13*(2), 194–201. https://doi.org/10.1111/eip.12461

Andrewes, H. E., et al. (2018). Patterns of non-suicidal self-injury and their relationship with suicide attempts in youth with borderline personality disorder. *Archives of Suicide Research, 22*, 465–478. https://doi.org/10.1080/13811118.2017.1358226

Andreyeva, T., & Henderson, K. E. (2018). Center-reported adherence to nutrition standards of the child and adult care food program. *Childhood Obesity, 14*(6). https://doi.org/10.1089/chi.2018.0076

Anglin, J. M., Miller, G. A., & Wakefield, P. C. (1993). Vocabulary development: A morphological analysis. *Monographs of the Society for Research in Child Development, 58*(10), 1–186. https://doi.org/10.2307/1166112

Anguiano, R. M. (2018). Language brokering among Latino immigrant families: Moderating variables and youth outcomes. *Journal of Youth and Adolescence, 47*, 222–242. https://doi.org/10.1007/s10964-017-0744-y

Ansari, A., & Pianta, R. C. (2018). Variation in the long-term benefits of child care: The role of classroom quality in elementary school. *Developmental Psychology, 54*(10), 1854–1867. http://dx.doi.org/10.1037/dev0000513

Anvari, S., et al. (2017). Evolution of guidelines on peanut allergy and peanut introduction in infants: A review. *JAMA Pediatrics, 171*(1), 77–82. https://doi.org/10.1001/jamapediatrics.2016.2552

Anzures, G., et al. (2013). Developmental origins of the other-race effect. *Current Directions in Psychological Science, 22*(3), 173–178. https://doi.org/10.1177/0963721412474459

Arnett, K., Roach, A., Elzy, M., & Jelsone-Swain, L. (2018). Childhood emotional invalidation and right hemispheric mu suppression during a pain empathy task: An EEG study. *Social Neuroscience, 14*(2), 236–250. https://doi.org/10.1080/17470919.2018.1441905

Arnold, M. E. (2017). Supporting adolescent exploration and commitment: Identity formation, thriving, and positive youth development. *Journal of Youth Development, 12*(4). https://doi.org/10.5195/jyd.2017.522

Arsalidou, M., & Pascual-Leone, J. (2016). Constructivist developmental theory is needed in developmental neuroscience. *npj Science of Learning, 1*, 16016. https://doi.org/10.1038/npjscilearn.2016.16

Arsenault, L. (2018). Annual research review: The persistent and pervasive impact of being bullied in childhood and adolescence: Implications for policy and practice. *The Journal of Child Psychology and Psychiatry, 59*(4), 405–421. https://doi.org/10.1111/jcpp.12841

Artukoglu, B. B., & Bloch, M. H. (2018). Editorial: Can omega-3 fatty acids improve executive functioning? Will this reduce ADHD and depression? *Journal of Child Psychology and Psychiatry, 59*(6), 615–617. https://doi.org/10.1111/jcpp.12932

Aurino, E., Fledderjohann, J., & Vellakkal, S. (2019). Inequalities in adolescent learning: Does the timing and persistence of food insecurity at home matter? *Economics of Education Review, 70*, 94–108. https://doi.org/10.1016/j.econedurev.2019.03.003

Austin, J. E., Doering, J. J., & Davies, W. H. (2018). Using technology to teach parents to create a safe infant sleep space. *Clinical Practice in Pediatric Psychology, 6*(3), 211–222. http://dx.doi.org/10.1037/cpp0000241

Autin, F., Batruch, A., & Butera, F. (2019). The function of selection of assessment leads evaluators to artificially create the social class achievement gap. *Journal of Educational Psychology, 111*(4), 717–735. http://dx.doi.org/10.1037/edu0000307

Aylwin, C. F., Toro, C. A., Shirtcliff, E., & Lomniczi, A. (2018). Emerging genetic and epigenetic mechanisms underlying pubertal maturation in adolescence. *Journal of Research on Adolescence, 29*(1), 54–79. https://doi.org/10.1111/jora.12385

Azañón, E., Camacho, K., Morales, M., & Longo, M. R. (2017). The sensitive period for tactile remapping does not include early infancy. *Child Development.* https://www.ncbi.nlm.nih.gov/pubmed/28452406

Baams, K. (2018). Disparities for LGBTQ and gender nonconforming adolescents. *Pediatrics, 141*(5), e20173004. https://doi: 10.1542/peds.2017-3004

Babar, A., et al. (2019). Changes in endothelial function, arterial stiffness and blood pressure in pregnant women after consumption of high-flavanol and high-theobromine chocolate: A double blind randomized clinical trial. *Hypertension in Pregnancy, 37*(2), 68–80. https://doi.org/10.1080/10641955.2018.1446977

Baddock, S. A., et al. (2019). The influence of bed-sharing on infant physiology, breastfeeding, and behaviour: A systematic review. *Sleep Medicine Reviews, 43*, 106–117. https://doi.org/10.1016/j.smrv.2018.10.007

Bach, J-F. (2018). The hygiene hypothesis in autoimmunity: The role of pathogens and commensals. *Nature Reviews Immunology, 18*, 105–120. https://doi.org/10.1038/nri.2017.111

Baillargeon, R. (1987). Object permanence in 3 ½ and 4 ½ month old infants. *Developmental Psychology, 23*(5), 655–664. https://doi.org/10.1037/0012-1649.23.5.655

Baillargeon, R. (2008). Innate ideas revisited: For a principle of persistence in infants' physical reasoning. *Perspectives on Psychological Science, 3*, 2–13. https://doi.org/10.1111/j.1745-6916.2008.00056.x

Balart, P., Oosterveen, M., & Webbink, D. (2018). Test scores, noncognitive skills and economic growth. *Economics of Education Review, 63*, 134–153. https://doi.org/10.1016/j.econedurev.2017.12.004

Baldry, A. C., Sorrentino, A., & Farrington, D. P. (2019). Cyberbullying and cybervictimization versus parental supervision, monitoring, and control of adolescents' online activities. *Children and Youth Services Review, 96*, 302–307. https://doi.org/10.1016/j.childyouth.2018.11.058

Baldwin, J. M. (1895/1998). *Mental development in the child and the race.* Thoemmes Press: Bristol, U.K.

Ballard, P. J., Hoyt, L. T., & Pachucki, M. C. (2019). Impacts of adolescent and young adult civic engagement on health and socioeconomic status in adulthood. *Child Development, 90*(4), 1138–1154. https://doi.org/10.1111/cdev.12998

Ballesteros, M. F., et al. (2018). The epidemiology of unintentional and violence-related injury morbidity and mortality among children and adolescents in the United States. *International Journal of Environmental Research and Public Health, 15*(4), 616. https://doi.org/10.3390/ijerph15040616

Banati, P., & Lansford, J. E. (2018). Introduction: Adolescence in a global context. In J. E. Lansford & P. Banati (Eds.), *Handbook of adolescent development research and its impact on global policy* (pp. 1–23). Oxford University Press.

Baranowski, T., Diep, C., & Baranowski, J. (2013). Influences on children's dietary behavior, and innovative attempts to change it. *Annals of Nutrition & Metabolism, 62*(3), 38–46. https://doi.org/10.1159/000351539

Barone, L., Carta, A., & Ozturk, Y. (2018). Social-emotional functioning in planned lesbian families: Does biological versus non-biological mother status matter? An Italian pilot study. *Attachment & Human Development, 22*(2), 143–156. https://doi.org/10.1080/14616734.2018.1528620

Barrouillet, P. (2015). Theories of cognitive development: From Piaget to today. *Developmental Review, 38*, 1–12. https://doi.org/10.1016/j.dr.2015.07.004

Bar, S., Milanaik, R., & Adesman, A. (2016). Long-term neurodevelopmental benefits of breastfeeding. *Current Opinion in Pediatrics, 28*(4), 559–566. https://doi.org/10.1097/MOP.0000000000000389

Barquero, B., Robinson, E. & Thomas, G. (2003). Children's ability to attribute different interpretations of ambiguous drawings to a naive vs. a biased observer. *International Journal of Behavioral Development, 27*(5), 445–456. https://doi.org/10.1080/01650250344000064

Bartick, M., Tomori, C., & Ball, H. L. (2018). Babies in boxes and the missing links on safe sleep: Human evolution and the cultural revolution. *Maternal & Child Nutrition, 14*(2), e12544. https://doi.org/10.1111/mcn.12544

Barton, A. L. & Hirsch, J. K. (2015). Permissive parenting and mental health in college students: Mediating effects of academic entitlement. *Journal of American College Health.* https://doi.org/10.1080/07448481.2015.1060597

Basgul, S. , Uneri, O. , Akkaya, G. , Etiler, N. & Coskun, A. (2011). Assessment of drawing age of children in early childhood and its correlates. *Psychology, 2*, 376–381. https://doi.org/10.4236/psych.2011.24059

Bass, P. F., & Bauer, N. (2018). Parental postpartum depression: More than "baby blues." *Contemporary Pediatrics, 35*(9). https://www.contemporarypediatrics.com/neonatalperinatology/parental-postpartum-depression-more-baby-blues

Bassock, D., Gibbs, C. R., & Latham, S. (2018). Preschool and children's outcomes in elementary school: Have patterns changed nationwide between 1998 and 2010? *Child Development 90*(6), 1875–1897. https://doi.org/10.1111/cdev.13067

Bates, T. C., et al. (2018). The nature of nurture: Using a virtual-parent design to test parenting effects on children's educational attainment in genotyped families. *Twin Research and Human Genetics, 21*(2), 73–83. https://doi.org/10.1017/thg.2018.11

Bathelt, J., Gathercole, S. E., Johnson, A., & Astle, D. (2018). Differences in brain morphology and working memory across childhood. *Developmental Science, 21*, e12579. https://doi.org/10.1111/desc.12579

Bathory, E., et al. (2016). Infant sleep and parent health literacy. *Academic Pediatrics, 16*(6), 550–557. https://doi.org/10.1016/j.acap.2016.03.004

Batruch, A., Autin, F., Bataillard, F., & Butera, F. (2019). School selection and the social class divide: How tracking contributes to the reproduction of inequalities. *Personality and Social Psychology Bulletin, 45*(3), 477–490. https://doi.org/10.1177/0146167218791804

Battersby, L. (2015, September 29). Millions of social media photos found on child exploitation sharing sites. *The Sydney Morning Herald*, https://www.smh.com.au/national/millions-of-social-media-photos-found-on-child-exploitation-sharing-sites-20150929-gjxe55.html

Bauer, J-R., & Booth, A. E. (2019). Exploring potential cognitive foundations of scientific literacy in preschoolers: Causal reasoning and executive function. *Early Childhood Research Quarterly, 46*, 275–284. https://doi.org/10.1016/j.ecresq.2018.09.007

Bauer, L. (2020). *The COVID-19 crisis has already led too many children hungry in America.* Retrieved from: https://www.hamiltonproject.org/blog/the_covid_19_crisis_has_already_left_too_many_children_hungry_in_america

Bauminger-Zviely, N. (2013). False-belief task (p. 1249). In I. B. Harris (Ed), *Encyclopedia of Autism Spectrum Disorders.* New York, NY: Springer.

Bazzi, M., et al. (2018). The effects of obesity on male fertility. *Fertility and Sterility, 110*(4), e162–e163. https://doi.org/10.1016/j.fertnstert.2018.07.482

Bassok, D., Gibbs, C. R., & Latham, S. (2018). Preschool and children's outcomes in elementary school: Patterns changed nationwide between 1998 and 2010? *Child Development.* https://doi-org.scsu.idm.oclc.org/10.1111/cdev.13067

Bathory, E., & Tomopoulos, S. (2017). Sleep regulation, physiology and development, sleep duration and patterns, and sleep hygiene in infants, toddlers, and preschool-age children. *Current Problems in Pediatric and Adolescent Health Care, 47*(2), 29–42. https://doi.org/10.1016/j.cppeds.2016.12.001

Bauer, P. J. (2015). A complementary processes account of the development of childhood amnesia and a personal past. *Psychological Review, 122*(2), 204–231. https//doi.org/ 10.1037/a0038939.

Baumrind, D. (1971). Current patterns of parental authority. *Developmental Psychology, 4*(1, Pt.2), 1–103. https://doi.org/10.1037/h0030372

Baumrind, D. (2012). Differentiating between confrontive and coercive kinds of parental power-assertive disciplinary practices. *Human Development, 55*(2), 35–51. https://doi.org/ 0.1159/000337962

Bear, G. G., Yang, C., Chen, D., He, X., Xie, J.-S., & Huang, X. (2018). Differences in school climate and student engagement in China and the United States. *School Psychology Quarterly, 33*(2), 323–335. https://doi.org/10.1037/spq0000247

Beazidou, E., & Botsoglou, K. (2016). Peer acceptance and friendship in early childhood: The conceptual distinctions between them. *Early Child Development and Care, 186*(10), 1615–1631. https://doi.org/10.1080/03004430.2015.1117077

Becerra-Culqui, T. A., et al. (2018). Mental health of transgender and gender nonconforming youth compared with their peers. *Pediatrics, 141*(5), e20173845.

Becht, A. I., et al. (2018). Goal-directed correlates and neurobiological underpinnings of adolescent identity: A multimethod multisample longitudinal approach. *Child Development, 89*(3), 823–836. https://doi.org/10.1111/cdev.13048

Becht, A. I., et al. (2019). Linking identity and depressive symptoms across adolescence: A multisample longitudinal study testing within-person effects. *Developmental Psychology, 55*(8), 1733–1742. http://dx.doi.org/10.1037/dev0000742

Beck, A. L., et al. (2019). Barriers and facilitators to healthy eating among low-income Latino adolescents. *Appetite, 138*, 215–222. https://doi.org/10.1016/j.appet.2019.04.004

Beckmeyer, J., & Malacane, M. J. (2018). Patterns of adolescents' romantic activities: Associations with psychosocial adjustment. *Journal of Child and Family Studies, 27*(8), 2394–2403. https://doi.org/10.1007/s10826-018-1108-2

Bell, A. F., Andersson, E., Goding, K., & Vonderheid, S. C. (2018). The birth experience and maternal caregiving attitudes and behavior: A systematic review. *Sexual & Reproductive Healthcare, 16*, 67–77. https://doi.org/10.1016/j.srhc.2018.02.007

Bell, G., et al. (2018). Behavioral outcomes of infant colic in toddlerhood: A longitudinal study. *The Journal of Pediatrics, 201*, 154–159. https://doi.org/10.1016/j.jpeds.2018.05.010

Bell, L. K. (2018). Poor dietary patterns at 1–5 years of age are related to food neophobia and breastfeeding duration but not age of introduction to solids in a relatively advantaged sample. *Eating Behaviors, 31*, 28–34. https://doi.org/10.1016/j.eatbeh.2018.06.005

Belsky, J. & deHaan, M. (2011). Annual Research Review: Parenting and children's brain development: the end of the beginning. *Journal of Child Psychology and Psychiatry, 52*(4), 409–428. https://doi.org/10.1111/j.1469-7610.2010.02281.x

Bendezú, J. J., et al. (2018). Longitudinal relations among parental monitoring strategies, knowledge, and adolescent delinquency in a racially diverse at-risk sample. *Journal of Clinical Child and Adolescent Psychiatry, 47*(Supp. 1), S21–S34. https://doi.org/10.1080/15374416.2016.1141358

Benish-Weisman, M., Daniel, E., Sneddon, J., & Lee, J. (2019). The relations between values and prosocial behavior among children: The moderating role of age. *Personality and Individual Differences, 141*, 241–247. https://doi.org/10.1016/j.paid.2019.01.019

Bennett, M., Webster, A. A., Goodall, E., & Rowland, S. (2019). Challenging the public's perception of life on autism spectrum: The impact of the vaccination myth. *Life on the Autism Spectrum*, 37–60.

Berger, A. T., Wahlstrom, K. L., & Widome, R. (2019). Relationships between sleep duration and adolescent depression: A conceptual replication. *Sleep Health, 5*(2), 175–179. https://doi.org/10.1016/j.sleh.2018.12.003

Berger, S. E., Theuring, C., & Adolph, K. E. (2007). How and when infants learn to climb stairs. *Infant Behavior & Development, 30*, 36–49. https://doi.org/10.1016/j.infbeh.2006.11.002

Bergey, M. R., & Conrad, P. (2018). The rise and transformation of ADHD in the United States. In M. R. Bergey, A. M. Filipe, P. Conrad, & I. Singh (Eds.), *Global perspectives on ADHD: Social dimensions of diagnosis and treatment in sixteen countries* (pp. 9–33). Johns Hopkins Press.

Berke, D. S., Reidy, D., & Zeichner, A. (2018). Masculinity, emotion regulation, and psychopathology: A critical review and integrated model. *Clinical Psychology Review, 66*, 106–116. https://doi.org/10.1016/j.cpr.2018.01.004

Bernard, K., Hostinar, C. E., & Dozier, M. (2019). Longitudinal association between attachment quality in infancy, C-reactive protein in early childhood, and BMI in middle childhood: Preliminary evidence from a CPS-referred sample. *Attachment & Human Development, 21*(1), 5–22. https://doi.org/10.1080/14616734.2018.1541513

Berzenski, S. R., Madden, A. R., & Yates, T. M. (2019). Childhood emotional abuse characteristics moderate associations with adult psychopathology and caregiving. *Child Abuse & Neglect, 87*, 77–87. https://doi.org/10.1016/j.chiabu.2018.06.004

Beyers, W., & Luyckx, K. (2016). Ruminative exploration and reconsideration of commitment as risk factors for suboptimal identity development in adolescence and emerging adulthood. *Journal of Adolescence, 47*, 169–178. https://doi.org/10.1016/j.adolescence.2015.10.018

Berzoff, J. (2016). Psychosocial ego development: The theory of Erik Erikson. In J. Berzoff, L. M. Flanagan, & P. Hertz (Eds.), *Inside out and outside in: Psychodynamic clinical theory and psychopathology in contemporary multicultural contexts* (pp. 100–122). Rowman & Littlefield.

Bhat, S., Beilin, L., Robinson, M., Burrows, S., & Mori, T. (2018). Maternal smoking and low family income during pregnancy as predictors of the relationship between depression and adiposity in young adults. *Journal of Developmental Origins of Health and Disease, 9*(5), 552–560. https://doi.org/10.1017/S2040174418000533

Bialystock, E., & Werker, J. F. (2017). Editorial: The systematic effects of bilingualism on children's development. *Developmental Science* (20)1, e12535. https://doi.org/10.1111/desc.12535

Biddle, S. J. H., Ciaccioni, S., Thomas, G., & Vergeer, I. (2019). Physical activity and mental health in children and adolescents: An updated review of reviews and an analysis of causality. *Psychology of Sport and Exercise, 42*, 146–155. https://doi.org/10.1016/j.psychsport.2018.08.011

Bilsen, J. (2018). Suicide and youth: Risk factors. *Frontiers in Psychiatry*. https://doi.org/10.3389/fpsyt.2018.00540

Binder, A. M., et al. (2018). Childhood and adolescent phenol and phthalate exposure and the age of menarche in Latina girls. *Environmental Health, 17*(32). https://doi.org/10.1186/s12940-018-0376-z

Birdsong, D. (2018). Plasticity, variability and age in second language acquisition and bilingualism. *Frontiers in Psychology*. https://doi.org/10.3389/fpsyg.2018.00081

Birmingham, R. S., Bub, K. L., & Vaughn, B. E. (2017). Parenting in infancy and self-regulation in preschool: An investigation of the role of attachment history. *Attachment & Human Development, 19*(2). https://doi.org/10.1080/14616734.2016.1259335

Bischoff, K., Owens, A. (2019). The segregation of opportunity: Social and financial resources in the educational contexts of lower- and higher-income children, 1990–2014. *Demography 56*, 1635–1664. https://doi.org/10.1007/s13524-019-00817-y

Björkenstam, E., Hjern, A., Björkenstam, C., & Kosidou, K. (2018). Association of cumulative childhood adversity and adolescent violent offending with suicide in early adulthood. *JAMA Psychiatry, 75*(2), 185–193. https://doi.org/10.1001/jamapsychiatry.2017.3788

Bjorklund, D. F. (2018a). A metatheory for child development (or "Piaget is Dead" revisited). *Child Development 89*(6), 2288–2302. https://doi.org/10.1111/cdev.13019

Bjorklund, D. F. (2018b). Behavioral epigenetics: The last nail in the coffin of genetic determinism. *Human Development, 61*, 54–59. https://doi.org/10.1159/000481747

Bjorklund, D. J. & Causey, K. B. (2018). *Children's thinking: Cognitive development and individual differences* (6ᵗʰ Ed.). LosAngeles, CA: Sage Publications.

Black, M. M., et al. (2017). Advancing early childhood development: From science to scale 1. *Lancet, 389*(10064), 77–90. https://doi.org/10.1016/S0140-6736(16)31389-7

Blake, M. J., Latham, M. D., Blake, L. M., & Allen, N. B. (2019). Adolescent-sleep-intervention research: Current state and future directions. *Current Directions in Psychological Science 28*(5), 475–482. https://doi.org/10.1177/0963721419850169

Blake, M. J., Trinder, J. A., & Allen, N. B. (2018). Mechanisms underlying the association between insomnia, anxiety, and depression in adolescence: Implications for behavioral sleep interventions. *Clinical Psychology Review, 63*, 25–40. https://doi.org/10.1016/j.cpr.2018.05.006

Blizard, R. A., & Shaw, M. (2019). Lost-in-the-mall: False memory or false defense? *Journal of Child Custody 16*(1), 20–41. https://doi.org/10.1080/15379418.2019.1590285

Bloom, P. (2000b). *How children learn the meanings of words*. Cambridge, MA: MIT Press.

Bluehen-Unger, R. G., et al. (2017). An exploration of culturally grounded youth suicide prevention programs for Native American and Black youth. *International Journal of Learning, Teaching, and Educational Research, 16*(2), 48–61.

Bocknek, E. L., et al. (2018). Sleep moderates the association between routines and emotion regulation for toddlers in poverty. *Journal of Family Psychology, 32*(7), 966–974. https://doi.org/10.1037/fam0000433

Bodri, D., et al. (2018). Shared motherhood IVF: High delivery rates in a large study of treatments for lesbian couples using partner-donated eggs. *Reproductive BioMedicine Online, 36*(2), 130–136. https://doi.org/10.1016/j.rbmo.2017.11.006

Boele, S., et al. (2019). Linking parent–child and peer relationship quality to empathy in adolescence: A multilevel meta-analysis. *Journal of Youth and Adolescence, 48*(6),1033–1055. https://doi.org/10.1007/s10964-019-00993-5

Bohn-Gettler, C. M. & Pellegrini, A. D. (2014). Recess in primary school: The disjuncture between educational policy and scientific research (pp. 313–336). In B. H. Bornstein & R. L. Wiener (Eds.), *Justice, Conflict, and Wellbeing*. New York, NY: Springer. https://doi.org/10.1007/978-1-4939-0623-9_12

Boisvert, S., & Poulin, F. (2016). Romantic relationship patterns from adolescent to emerging adulthood: Association with family and peer experiences in early adolescence. *Journal of Youth & Adolescence, 45*, 945–958. https://doi.org/10.1007/s10964-016-0435-0

Bowlby, J. (1969). *Attachment and loss: Vol 1: Attachment*. New York: Basic Books, Inc.

Bowlby, J. (1976). *Attachment and loss: Vol. 2: Separation: Anxiety and Anger*. New York, NY: Basic Books, Inc.

Bombard, J. M., et al. (2018). Vital signs: Trends and disparities in infant safe sleep practices—United States, 2009–2015. *Morbidity and Mortality Weekly Report, 67*(1), 39–46. https://doi.org/10.15585/mmwr.mm6701e1

Bonilla-Silva, E. (2015). The structure of racism in color-blind, "post-racial" America. *American Behavioral Scientist, 59*(11), 1358–1376. https://doi.org/10.1177/0002764215586826

Booth, F. W., Roberts, C. K., Thyfault, J. P., Ruegsegger, G. N., & Toedebusch, R. G. (2017). Role of inactivity in chronic diseases: Evolutionary insight and pathophysiological mechanisms. *Physiological Reviews 97*(4), 1351–1402. https://doi.org/10.1152/physrev.00019.2016

Booton, R. D., Iwasa, Y., Marshall, J. A. R., & Childs, D. Z. (2017). Stress-mediated Allee effects can cause the sudden collapse of honey bee colonies. *Journal of Theoretical Biology, 420*, 213–219. https://doi.org/10.1016/j.jtbi.2017.03.009

Borman, G. D., et al. (2018). Self-affirmation effects are produced by school context, student engagement with the intervention, and time: Lessons from a district-wide implementation. *Psychological Science, 29*(11), 1773–1784. https://doi.org/10.1177/0956797618784016

Börnert-Ringleb, M., & Wilbert, J. (2018). The association of strategy use and concrete-operational thinking in primary school. *Frontiers in Education*. https://doi.org/10.3389/feduc.2018.00038

Bornstein, M. H., Putnick, D. L., Garstein, M. A., Hahn, C-S., Auestad, N., & O'Connor, D. L. (2015). Infant temperament: Stability by age, gender, birth order, term status, and socioeconomic status. *Child Development, 86*(3), 844–863. https//doi.org/10.1111/cdev.12367

Borowski, S. K., Zeman, J., & Braunstein, K. (2018). Social anxiety and socioemotional functioning during early adolescence: The mediating role of best friend emotion socialization. *Journal of Early Adolescence, 38*(2), 238–260. https://doi.org/10.1177/0272431616665212

Borst, G., Poirel, N., Pineau, A., Cassotti, M., & Houdé, O. (2013). Inhibitory control efficiency in a Piaget-like class-inclusion task in school-age children and adults: A developmental negative priming study. *Developmental Psychology, 49*(7), 1366–1374. http://dx.doi.org/10.1037/a0029622

Bos, M. G. N., et al. (2018). Emerging depression in adolescence coincides with accelerated frontal cortical thinning. *The Journal of Child Psychology and Psychiatry, 59*(9), 994–1002. https://doi.org/10.1111/jcpp.12895

Bosquet Enlow, M., Bollati, V., Sideridis, G., Flom, J. D., Hoxha, M., Hacker, M. R., & Wright, R. J. (2018). Sex differences in effects of maternal risk and protective factors in childhood and pregnancy on newborn telomere length. *Psychoneuroendocrinology, 95*, 74–85. https://doi.org/10.1016/j.psyneuen.2018.05.025

Bouchard, G., Plamondon, A., & Lachance-Grzela, M. (2019). Parental intervention style and adult sibling conflicts: The meditating role of involvement in sibling bullying. *Journal of Social and Personal Relationships, 36*(8), 2585–2602. https://doi.org/10.1177/0265407518793227

Bourgeron, T. (2015). From the genetic architecture to synaptic plasticity in autism spectrum disorder. *Nature Reviews Neuroscience, 16*, 551–563. https://doi.org/10.1038/nrn3992

Boutwell, B. B., Young, J. T. N., & Meldrum, R. C. (2018). On the positive relationship between breastfeeding & intelligence. *Developmental Psychology, 54*(8), 1426–1433. http://dx.doi.org/10.1037/dev0000537

Bowlby, J. (1969). Attachment. *Attachment and Loss* (Vol. 1). Basic Books.

Bowling, A. (2019, November 22). The parents passed a drug test. Should they get their children back? *The New York Times*, https://www.nytimes.com/2019/11/22/us/opioids-foster-care-ohio.html

Braeken, M. A. K. A., et al. (2017). Potential benefits of mindfulness during pregnancy on maternal autonomic nervous system function and infant development. *Psychophysiology, 54*(2), 279–288. https://doi.org/10.1111/psyp.12782

Braham, E. J., Libertus, M. E., & McCrink, K. (2018). Children's spontaneous focus on number before and after guided parent–child interactions in a children's museum. *Developmental Psychology, 54*(8), 1492–1498. http://dx.doi.org/10.1037/dev0000534

Brainerd, C. J., Reyna, V. F., & Holliday, R. E. (2018). Developmental reversals in false memory: Development is complementary, not compensatory. *Developmental Psychology, 54*(9), 1773–1784. http://dx.doi.org/10.1037/dev0000554

Brand, R. J., Escobar, K., Patrick, A. M. (2020). Coincidence of cascade? The temporal relation between locomotor behaviors and the emergence of stranger anxiety. *Infant Behavior and Development, 58*. https://doi.org/10.1016/j.infbeh.2020.101423

Brandt, J. S., Cruz Ithier, M. A., Rosen, T., & Ashkinadze, E. (2018). Advanced paternal age, infertility, and reproductive risks: A review of the literature. *Prenatal Diagnosis, 39*(2), 81–87. https://doi.org/10.1002/pd.5402

Branje, S. (2018). Development of parent–adolescent relationships: Conflict interactions as a mechanism of change. *Child Development Perspectives, 12*(3), 171–176. https://doi.org/10.1111/cdep.12278

Brassell, A. A., Rosenberg, E., Parent, J., Rough, J. N., Fondacaro, K., & Seehuus, M. (2016). Parent's psychological flexibility: Associations with parenting and child psychosocial well-being. *Journal of Contextual Behavioral Science, 5*(2), 111–120. https://doi.org/10.1016/j.jcbs.2016.03.001

Brantley, M. D., et al. (2018). *Report from nine maternal mortality review committees*. Retrieved from http://reviewtoaction.org/sites/default/files/national-portal-material/Report%20from%20Nine%20MMRCs%20final_0.pdf

Bratberg, E., Davis, J., Mazumder, B., Nyborn, M., Schnitzlein, D. D., & Vaage, K. (2018). A comparison of intergenerational mobility curves in Germany, Norway, Sweden, and the U.S. *The Scandinavian Journal of Economics, 119*(1), 72–101. https://doi.org/10.1111/sjoe.12197

Bratsberg, B., & Rogeberg, O. (2017). Childhood socioeconomic status does not explain the IQ-mortality gradient. *Intelligence, 62*, 148–154. https://doi.org/10.1016/j.intell.2017.04.002

Braarud, H. C. (2018). Maternal DHA status during pregnancy has a positive impact on infant problem solving. A Norwegian prospective observation study. *Nutrients, 10*(5), 529. https://doi.org/10.3390/nu10050529

Bredin-Oja, S. L. & Fey, M. E. (2014). Children's responses to telegraphic and grammatically complete prompts to imitate. *American Journal of Speech-Language Pathology, 23*, 15–26. DOI: 10.1044/1058-0360(2013/12-0155

Bremner, J. G., Slater, A. M., & Johnson, S. P. (2015) Perception of object permanence in infancy. *Child Development Perspectives, 9*(1), 7–13. https//doi.org/10.1111/cdep.12098

Bresland, N. L., Shoulberg, E. K., McQuade, J. D., & Murray-Close, D. (2018). Social costs for wannabes: Moderating effects of popularity and gender on the links between popularity goals and negative peer experiences. *Journal of Youth and Adolescence, 47*, 1894–1906. https://doi.org/10.1007/s10964-018-0810-0

Briana, D. D., & Malamitsi-Puchner, A. (2017). Developmental origins of adult health and disease: The metabolic role of BDNF from early life to adulthood. *Metabolism, 81*, 45–51. https://doi.org/10.1016/j.metabol.2017.11.019

Bridgett, D. J., Burt, N. M., Edwards, E. S., & Deater-Deckard, K. (2015). Intergenerational transmission of self-regulation: Multidisciplinary review and integrative conceptual framework. *Psychological Bulletin, 141*(3), 602–654. https://doi.org/10.1037/a0038662

Brieant, A., et al. (2018). Positive and negative affect and adolescent adjustment: Moderation effects of prefrontal functioning. *Journal of Research on Adolescence, 28*(1), 40–55. https://doi.org/10.1111/jora.12339

Brière, F. N., et al. (2018). Prospective associations between sport participation and psychological adjustment in adolescents. *Journal of Epidemiology & Community Health,72*(7), 575–581. http://dx.doi.org/10.1136/jech-2017-209656

Brighi, A., Menin, D., Skrzypiec, G., & Guarini, A. (2019). Young, bullying and connected. Common pathways to cyberbullying and problematic Internet use in adolescence. *Frontiers in Psychology, 10,* 1467. https://doi.org/10.3389/fpsyg.2019.01467

Brinchmann, E. I., Braeken, J., & Halaas Lyster, S-A. (2019). Is there a direct relation between the development of vocabulary and grammar? *Developmental Science, 22*(1), e12709. https://doi.org/10.1111/desc.12709

Brillo, E., & Di Renzo, G. C. (2015). Chocolate and other cocoa products: Effects on human reproduction and pregnancy. *Journal of Agricultural and Food Chemistry, 63*(45), 9927–993. https://doi.org/10.1021/acs.jafc.5b01045

Brittian, A. S. et al. (2015). Do dimensions of ethnic identity medicate the associate between perceived ethnic group discrimination and depressive symptoms? *Cultural Diversity and Ethnic Minority Psychology, 21*(1), 41–53. https://doi.org/10.1037/a0037531

Brock, L. L., et al. (2019). Theory of mind, directly and indirectly, facilitates kindergarten adjustment via verbal ability, executive function, and emotion knowledge. *Psychology in the Schools, 56*(2), 176–193. https://doi.org/10.1002/pits.22216

Bronfenbrenner, U. (1977). Toward an experimental ecology of human development. *American Psychologist, 32*(7), 513–531. https://doi.org/10.1037/0003-066X.32.7.513

Bronfenbrenner, U., & Morris, P.A. (2006). The bioecological model of human development. In W. Damon & R. M. Lerner (Series Eds.) & R. M. Lerner (Vol. Ed.), *Handbook of child psychology. Vol. 1: Theoretical models of human development* (6th ed., pp. 793–828). John Wiley & Sons.

Brooker, R. J., Buss, K. A., Lemery-Chalfant, K., Aksan, N., Davidson, R. J., & Goldsmith, H. H. (2013). The development of stranger fear in infancy and toddlerhood: Normative development, individual differences, antecedents, and outcomes. *Developmental Science, 16*(6), 864–878. https//doi.org/10.1111/desc.12058

Brooks, R. & Meltzoff, A. N. (2013). Gaze following: A mechanism for building social connections between infants and adults. In M. Mikulincer & P. R. Shaver (Eds.), *Nature and development of social connections: From brain to group.* Washington, D.C.: American Psychological Association.

Brooks, R. & Meltzoff, A. N. (2015). Connecting the dots from infancy to childhood: A longitudinal study connecting gaze following, language, and explicit theory of mind. *Journal of Experimental Child Psychology, 130,* 67–78. https//doi.org/10.1016/j.jecp.2014.09.010

Brown, A. C. (Ed.). (2016). *Between families and schools: Creating meaningful relationships* (2nd ed.). Teaching for Change. https://www.teachingforchange.org/between-families-relationships

Brown, T. T. & Jernigan, T. L. (2012). Brain development during the preschool years. *Neuropsychology Review, 22*(4), 313–333. https://doi.org/10.1007/s11065-012-9214-1.

Brubacher, S. P., et al. (2019). How children talk about events: Implications from eliciting and analyzing eyewitness reports. *Developmental Review, 51,* 70–89. https://doi.org/10.1016/j.dr.2018.12.003

Bruck, M. & Ceci, S. J. (2015). Children's testimony: A scientific framework for evaluating the reliability of children's statements. In A. Thapar, D. S. Pine, J. F. Leckman, S. Scott, M. J. Snowling, & E. A. Taylor (Eds.), *Rutter's Child and Adolescent Psychiatry* (pp. 250–260). West Sussex, UK: John Wiley & Sons, Ltd. https://doi.org/10.1002/9781118381953.ch20

Brunamonti, E., et al. (2017). Evaluation of relational reasoning by a transitive inference task in attention-deficit/hyperactivity disorder. *Neuropsychology, 31*(2), 200–208. http://dx.doi.org/10.1037/neu0000332

Bruner, J. (1974). Toward a theory of instruction. Cambridge, MA: Belknap Press.

Brusdal, R. & Frønes, I. (2014). Well-being and children in a consumer society. In A. Ben-Arieh, F. Casas, I. Frønes, & J. E. Korbin (Eds.), *Handbook of Child Well-Being* (pp. 1427–1443). New York, NY: Springer. https://doi.org/10.1007/978-90-481-9063-8_58

Bry, L. J., Chou, T., Miguel, E., & Comer, J. S. (2018). Consumer smartphone apps marketed for child and adolescent anxiety: A systematic review and content analysis. *Behavior Therapy, 49*(2), 249–261. https://doi.org/10.1016/j.beth.2017.07.008

Bryan, C. J., Yeager, D. S., Hinojosa, C. P., Chabot, A. M., Bergen, H., Kawamura, M., & Steubing, F. (2016). Harnessing adolescent values to reduce unhealthy snacking. *Proceedings of the National Academy of Sciences, USA, 113*(39), 10830–10835. https://doi.org/10.1073/pnas.1604586113

Bryant, R. A., et al. (2018). The effect of post-traumatic stress disorder on refugees' parenting and their children's mental health: A cohort study. *The Lancet Public Health, 3*(5), e249–e258. https://doi.org/10.1016/S2468-2667(18)30051-3

Budd, E. L., et al. (2018). The role of physical activity enjoyment in the pathways from the social and physical environments to physical activity of early adolescent girls. *Preventative Medicine, 111,* 6–13. https://doi.org/10.1016/j.ypmed.2018.02.015

Burchinal, M. (2018). Measuring early care and education quality. *Child Development Perspectives, 12*(1), 3–9. https://doi.org/10.1111/cdep.12260

Burke, E. E., & Bribiescas, R. G. (2018). A comparison of testosterone and cortisol levels between gay fathers and non-fathers: A preliminary investigation. *Physiology & Behavior, 193*(Part A), 69–81. https://doi.org/10.1016/j.physbeh.2018.03.011

Burman, E. (2016). *Deconstructing developmental psychology* (3rd Ed.). London, UK: Routledge.

Burnett, A. C., et al. (2018). Trends in executive functioning in extremely preterm children across three birth eras. *Pediatrics, 141*(1), e20171958. https://doe.org/10.1542/peds.2017-1958

Burns, R. D., et al. (2018). Relationships among physical activity, sleep duration, diet, and academic achievement in a sample of adolescents. *Preventative Medicine Reports, 12*, 71–74. https://doi.org/10.1016/j.pmedr.2018.08.014

Bustamante, A. S., & Hindman, A. H. (2019). Classroom quality and academic school readiness outcomes in Head Start: The indirect effect of approaches to learning. *Early Education and Development, 30*(1). https://doi.org/10.1080/10409289.2018.1540249

Byrne, M. L., et al. (2017). A systematic review of adrenarche as a sensitive period in neurobiological development and mental health. *Developmental Cognitive Neuroscience, 25*, 12–28. https://doi.org/10.1016/j.dcn.2016.12.004

Caballero, T. M., Johnson, S. B., Buchanan, C. R. M., & DeCamp, L. R. (2017). Adverse childhood experiences among Hispanic children in immigrant families versus US-native families. *Pediatrics, 140*(5), e20170297. https://doi.org/10.1542/peds.2017-0297

Cabell, S. Q., et al. (2019). Prekindergarten interactive book reading quality and children's language and literacy development: Classroom organization as a moderator. *Early Education and Development, 30*(1). https://doi.org/10.1080/10409289.2018.1514845

Callaghan, T. & Corbit, J. (2015). The Development of Symbolic Representation. *Handbook of Child Psychology and Developmental Science, 2*(7), 1–46. https://doi.org/10.1002/9781118963418.childpsy207

Cadima, J., et al. (2019). Bidirectional associations between vocabulary and self-regulation in preschool and their interplay with teacher–child closeness and autonomy support. *Early Childhood Research Quarterly, 46*(1), 75–86. https://doi.org/10.1016/j.ecresq.2018.04.004

Camilletti, E., & Banati, E. (2018). Making strategic investments in adolescent well-being. In J. E. Lansford & P. Banati (Eds.), *Handbook of adolescent development research and its impact on global policy* (pp. 299–318). Oxford University Press.

Camirand, E., & Poulin, F. (2019). Changes in best friendship quality between adolescence and emerging adulthood: Considering the role of romantic involvement. *International Journal of Behavioral Development, 43*(3), 231–237. https://doi.org/10.1177/0165025418824995

Cancian, M., & Meyer, D. R. (2018). Reforming policy for single-parent families to reduce child poverty. *The Russell Sage Foundation Journal of the Social Sciences, 4*(2), 91–112. https://doi.org/10.7758/RSF.2018.4.2.05

Capaldi, D. M., Tiberio, S. S., Pears, K. C., & Kerr, D. C. R. (2019). Intergenerational associations in physical maltreatment: Examination of mediation by delinquency and substance use, moderated mediation by anger. *Development and Psychopathology, 31*(1), 73–82. https://doi.org/10.1017/S0954579418001529

Capone, G. T. et al. (2018). Co-occurring medical conditions in adults with Down syndrome: A systematic review toward health care guidelines. *American Journal of Medical Genetics Part A, 176*(1). https://doi.org/10.1002/ajmg.a.38512

CAPTA Reauthorization Act (2010). Child Abuse Prevention and Treatment Act. Pub. L. No. 111–320. https://www.govinfo.gov/content/pkg/PLAW-111publ320/pdf/PLAW-111publ320.pdf

Carlin, R., & Moon, R. Y. (2018). Learning from national and state trends in sudden unexpected infant death. *Pediatrics, 141*(3), e20174083. https://doi.org/10.1542/peds.2017-4083

Carlo, G., et al. (2018). Longitudinal relations among parenting styles, prosocial behaviors, and academic outcomes in U.S. Mexican adolescents. *Child Development, 89*(2), 577–592. https://doi.org/10.1111/cdev.12761

Carolan, M., & Wright, R. J. (2017). Miscarriage at advanced maternal age and the search for meaning. *Death Studies, 41*(3). https://doi.org/10.1080/07481187.2016.1233143

Carr, A., et al. (2018). Mind the children: A longitudinal study of mental state talk, theory of mind, and behavioral adjustment from the age of 3 to 10. *Social Development, 27*(4), 826–840. https://doi.org/10.1111/sode.12315

Carrick, N., Sawaya, S., & Palisoc, J. (2018). Witches, fire, and fairies: Parent–child conversations during fantastic and real emotionally charged stories. *Infant and Child Development, 27*(6), e2111. https://doi.org/10.1002/icd.2111

Carson, V., et al. (2019). Physical activity and sedentary behavior across three time-points and associated with social skills in early childhood. *BMC Public Health, 19*(27), https://doi.org/10.1186/s12889-018-6381-x

Carstairs, S. A., et al. (2018). Can reduced intake associated with downsizing a high energy dense meal be offset by increased vegetable variety in 3–5-year-old children? *Nutrients, 10*(12), 1879. https://doi.org/10.3390/nu10121879

Carter, R., Halawah, A., & Trinh, S. L. (2018). Peer exclusion during the pubertal transition: The role of social competence. *Journal of Youth and Adolescence, 47*, 121–134. https://doi.org/10.1007/s10964-017-0682-8

Carver, R. B., Castéra, J., Gericke, N., Evangelista, N. A. M., & El-Hani, C. N. (2017) Young adults' belief in genetic determinism, and knowledge and attitudes towards modern genetics and genomics: The PUGGS questionnaire. *PLOS ONE, 12*(1), e0169808. https://doi.org/10.1371/journal.pone.0169808

Casey, B. J. (2019). Healthy development as a human right: Lessons from developmental science. *Neuron, 102*(4), 724–727. https://doi.org/10.1016/j.neuron.2019.03.035

Casper, D. M., & Card, N. A. (2017). Overt and relational victimization: A meta-analytic review of their overlap and associations with social-psychological adjustment. *Child Development, 88*(2), 466–483. https://doi.org/10.1111/cdev.12621

Castles, A., Rastle, K., & Nation, K. (2018). Ending the reading wars: Reading acquisition from novice to expert. *Psychological Science in the Public Interest, 19*(1), 5–51. https://doi.org/10.1177/1529100618772271

Castro, V. L., Cheng, Y., Halberstadt, A. G., & Grühn, D. (2016). EUReKA! A conceptual model of emotion understanding. *Emotion Review, 8*(3), 258–268. https://doi.org/10.1177/1754073915580601

Castro, V. L., Cooke, A. N., Halberstadt, A. G., & Garrett-Peters, P. (2018). Bidirectional linkages between emotion recognition and problem behaviors in elementary school children. *Journal of Nonverbal Behavior, 42*(2), 155–178. https://doi.org/10.1007/s10919-017-0269-9

Causadias, J. M., & Cicchetti, D. (2018). Cultural development and psychopathology. *Development and Psychopathology, 30*, 1549–1555. https://doi.org/10.1017/S0954579418001220

Causadias, J. M., Korous, K. M., & Cahill, K. M. (2018). Are Whites and minorities more similar than different? Testing the cultural similarities hypothesis on psychopathology with a second order meta-analysis. *Development and Psychopathology, 30*, 2009–2027. https://doi.org/10.1017/S0954579418000895

Cavalera, C., et al. (2018). Negative social emotions and cognition: Shame, guilt and working memory impairments. *Acta Psychologica, 188*, 9–15. https://doi.org/10.1016/j.actpsy.2018.05.005

Caye, A., Swanson, J. M., Coghill, D., & Rohde, L. A. (2019). Treatment strategies for ADHD: An evidence-based guide to select optimal treatment. *Molecular Psychiatry, 24*, 390–408. https://doi.org/10.1038/s41380-018-0116-3

Cazzola, M., et al. (2018). How does race/ethnicity influence pharmacological response to asthma therapies? *Expert Opinion on Drug Metabolism & Toxicology, 14*(4), 435–446. https://doi.org/10.1080/17425255.2018.1449833

Centers for Disease Control and Prevention (2017). *Ten leading causes of death and injury.* U.S. Department of Health and Human Services. Retrieved from https://www.cdc.gov/injury/wisqars/LeadingCauses.html

Centers for Disease Control and Prevention (2019a). *Childhood obesity facts.* U.S. Department of Health and Human Services. Retrieved from https://www.cdc.gov/obesity/data/childhood.html

Centers for Disease Control and Prevention (2019b). *Physical activity guidelines for Americans* (2nd ed.). U.S. Department of Health and Human Services, https://health.gov/paguidelines/second-edition/pdf/Physical_Activity_Guidelines_2nd_edition.pdf#page=46

Centers for Disease Control and Prevention (2019c). *Asthma in children.* U.S. Department of Health and Human Services. Retrieved from https://www.cdc.gov/vitalsigns/childhood-asthma/index.html

Centers for Disease Control and Prevention (2019d). *Ten leading causes of injury deaths by age group highlighting unintentional injury death, United States—2017.* U.S. Department of Health and Human Services. Retrieved from https://www.cdc.gov/injury/images/lc-charts/leading_causes_of_death_by_age_group_unintentional_2017_1100w850h.jpg

Chaddock, L. et al. (2018). Physical activity increases white matter microstructure in children. *Frontiers in Neuroscience, 12*(950). https://doi.org/10.3389/fnins.2018.00950

Chae, D.H., et al. (2015). Association between an Internet-based measure of area racism and black mortality. *PLOS ONE, 10*(4), e0122963. https://doi.org/10.1371/journal.pone.0122963

Chae, D. H., et al. (2018). Area racism and birth outcomes among Blacks in the United States. *Social Science & Medicine, 199*, 49–55. https://doi.org/10.1016/j.socscimed.2017.04.019

Chall, Jeanne. 1983. *Stages of Reading Development.* New York: McGraw Hill

Chambers, D.W. (1983). Stereotypic images of the scientist: The Draw a Scientist test. *Science Education, 67*(2): 255–265. doi:10.1002/sce.3730670213

Chang, J., & Rosenthal, S. L. (2018). Let's talk about dating—Promoting discussion about adolescent dating and early romantic relationships. *JAMA Pediatrics, 172*(7), 611–612. https://doi.org/10.1001/jamapediatrics.2018.0392

Charlop, M. H., Lang R., & Rispoli, M. (2018). All children can play: Prompting and modeling procedures to teach play to children with autism spectrum disorder. In *Play and social skills for children with autism spectrum disorder.* Evidence-based practices in behavioral health. Springer.

Charlton, B. M., Nava-Coultier, B., Coles, M. S., & Katz-Wise, S. L. (2019). Teen pregnancy experiences of sexual minority women. *Journal of Pediatric & Adolescent Gynecology, 32*(5), 499–505. https://doi.org/10.1016/j.jpag.2019.05.009

Chawarska, K., Macari, S. L., Volkmar, F. R., Kim, H., & Shic, F. (2014). ASD in infants and toddlers. *Handbook of Autism and Pervasive Developmental Disorders, Volume 1.* Hoboken, NJ: John Wiley & Sons, Inc.

Chen, F. R., Rothman, E. F., & Jaffee, S. R. (2017). Early puberty, friendship group characteristics, and dating abuse in US girls. *Pediatrics, 139*(6), e20162847. https://doi.org/10.1542/peds.2016-2847

Chen, I., Young, L., & Schneider, B. (2019). Friends are resources too: Examining college-going aspirations in stable and newly established friendships among urban and rural low-income students. *American Educational Research Association,* https://par.nsf.gov/biblio/10065764

Chen, J-Q., & Gardner, H. (2018). Assessment from the perspective of multiple-intelligences theory. In D. P. Flanagan & E. M. McDonough (Eds.), *Contemporary intellectual assessment: Theories, tests, and issues* (pp. 164–173). Guilford Press.

Chen, L-W., et al. (2018). Association of maternal caffeine intake with birth outcomes: Results from the Lifeways Cross Generation Cohort Study. *The American Journal of Clinical Nutrition, 108*(6), 1301–1308. https://doi.org/10.1093/ajcn/nqy219

Chen, Z-Y., & Liu, R. X. (2014). Comparing adolescent only children with those who have siblings on academic related outcomes and psychosocial adjustment. *Child Development Research, 2014,* Article ID 578289. http://dx.doi.org/10.1155/2014/578289

Chern, A., Tillmann, B., Vaughn, C., & Gordon, R. L. (2018). New evidence of a rhythmic priming effect that enhances grammaticality judgments in children. *Journal of Experimental Child Psychology, 173,* 371–379. https://doi.org/10.1016/j.jecp.2018.04.007

Chess, S. & Thomas, A. (1999). *Goodness of fit: Clinical applications, from infancy through adult life.* New York, NY: Routledge.

Chetty, R., & Hendren, N. (2018). The impacts of neighborhoods on intergenerational mobility I: Childhood exposure effects. *The Quarterly Journal of Economics, 133*(3), 1107–1162. https://doi.org/10.1093/qje/qjy007

Child Care Aware America (2017). *Parents and the high cost of child care.* Retrieved from: https://www.childcareaware.org/wp-content/uploads/2017/12/2017_CCA_High_Cost_Report_FINAL.pdf

Child Welfare Information Gateway (2016). *Definitions of child abuse and neglect.* https://www.childwelfare.gov/pubpdfs/define.pdf

Children's Defense Fund (2017). *The state of America's children.* Retrieved from: https://www.childrensdefense.org/wp-content/uploads/2018/06/2017-soac.pdf

Ching, B. H.-H., & Wu, X. (2019). Concreteness fading fosters children's understanding of the inversion concept in addition and subtraction. *Learning and Instruction, 61,* 148–159. https://doi.org/10.1016/j.learninstruc.2018.10.006

Chopik, W. J., Moore, A. C., & Edelstein, R. S. (2014). Maternal nurturance predicts decreases in attachment avoidance in emerging adulthood. *Journal of Research in Personality, 53,* 47–53. https://doi.org/10.1016/j.jrp.2014.08.004

Chow, J., & Wehby, J. H. (2018). Associations between language and problem behavior: A systematic review and correlational meta-analysis. *Educational Psychology Review, 30*(1) 61–82. https://doi.org/10.1007/s10648-016-9385-z

Christakis, D. A., Benedikt Ramirez, J. S., Ferguson, S. M., Ravinder, S., & Ramirez, J. M. (2018). How early media exposure may affect cognitive function: A review of results from observations in humans and experiments in mice. *PNAS, 115*(40), 9851–9858. https://doi.org/10.1073/pnas.1711548115

Christakis, E. (2016). *The importance of being little: What preschoolers really need from grownups.* Viking Press.

Christensen, D. L., et al. (2018). Prevalence and characteristics of autism spectrum disorder among children aged 8 years—Autism and developmental disabilities monitoring network, 11 sites, United States, 2012. *MMWR Surveillance Summaries, 65*(13), 1–23. https://doi.org/10.15585/mmwr.ss6513a1

Christian, P., & Smith, E. R (2018). Adolescent undernutrition: Global burden, physiology, and nutritional risks. *Annals of Nutrition & Metabolism, 72,* 316–328. https://doi.org/10.1159/000488865

Chronaki, G., Wigelsworth, M., Pell, M. D., & Kotz, S. A. (2018). The development of cross-cultural recognition of vocal emotion during childhood and adolescence. *Scientific Reports, 8,* 8659. https://doi.org/10.1038/s41598-018-26889-1

Ciarrochi, J., Sahdra, B. K., Hawley, P. H., & Devine, E. K. (2019). The upsides and downsides of the dark side: A longitudinal study in the role of prosocial and antisocial close friendship formation. *Frontiers in Psychology.* https://doi.org/10.3389/fpsyg.2019.00114

Cimadomo, D., Fabozzi, G., Vaiarelli, A., Ubaldi, N., Ubaldi, F. M., & Rienzi, L. (2018). Impact of maternal age on oocyte and embryo competence. *Frontiers in Endocrinology, 9,* 237. https://doi.org/10.3389/fendo.2018.00327

Ciucci, E., et al. (2018). Attentional orienting to emotional faces moderates the association between callous-unemotional traits and peer-nominated aggression in young adolescent school children. *Journal of Abnormal Child Psychology, 46,* 1011–1019. https://doi.org/10.1007/s10802-017-0357-7

Claes, M., et al. (2018). Parental control and conflicts in adolescence: A cross-national comparison of the United States, Canada, Mexico, France, and Italy. *Journal of Family Issues, 39*(16), 3857–3879. https://doi.org/10.1177/0192513X18800123

Clayborne, Z. M., Varin, M., & Colman, I. (2019). Systematic review and meta-analysis: Adolescent depression and long-term psychosocial outcomes. *Journal of the American Academy of Child & Adolescent Psychiatry, 58*(1), 72–79. https://doi.org/10.1016/j.jaac.2018.07.896

Clegg, J. M., Wen, N. J., & Legare, C. H. (2017). Is non-conformity WEIRD? Cultural variation in adults' beliefs about children's competency and conformity. *Journal of Experimental Psychology: General, 146*(3), 428–441. http://dx.doi.org/10.1037/xge0000275

Closson, L. M., & Watanabe, L. (2018). Popularity in the peer group and victimization within friendship cliques during early adolescence. *Journal of Early Adolescence, 38*(3), 327–351. https://doi.org/10.1177/0272431616670753

Cohen, L., & Billard, A. (2018). Social babbling: The emergence of symbolic gestures and words. *Neural Networks, 106*, 194–204. https://doi.org/10.1016/j.neunet.2018.06.016

Cohen, J. R., Andrews, A. R., Davis, M. M., & Rudolph, K. D. (2018). Anxiety and depression during childhood and adolescence: Testing theoretical models of continuity and discontinuity. *Journal of Abnormal Child Psychology, 46*(6), 1295–1308. https://doi.org/10.1007/s10802-017-0370-x

Cohen, S., et al. (2018). Effects of yoga on attention, impulsivity, and hyperactivity in preschool-aged children with attention-deficit hyperactivity disorder symptoms. *Developmental & Behavioral Pediatrics, 39*(3), 200–209. https://doi.org/10.1097/DBP.0000000000000552

Cole, P. M., Bendezú, J. J., Ram, N., & Chow, S-M. (2017). Dynamical systems modeling of early childhood self-regulation. *Emotion, 17*(4), 684–699. https://doi.org/10.1037/emo0000268

Cole, P. M., & Hollenstein T., eds. (2018). *Emotion Regulation: A Matter of Time.* Routledge.

Colston, H. L. (2019). Figurative language acquisition and development. In A. Bar-On & D. Ravid (Eds.), *Handbook of communication disorders: Theoretical, empirical, and applied linguistic perspectives* (pp. 117–136). Mouton De Gruyter. https://doi.org/10.1515/9781614514909

Common Core State Standards Initiative (2019). *Standards in your state.* Retrieved from: http://www.corestandards.org/standards-in-your-state/

Common Sense Media (2018). *The common sense census: Media use by kids age zero to eight 2017*: https://www.commonsensemedia.org/research/the-common-sense-census-media-use-by-kids-age-zero-to-eight-2017

Congdon, P. (2019). Obesity and urban environments. *International Journal of Environmental Research and Public Health, 16*(3), 464. https://doi.org/10.3390/ijerph16030464

Connelly, J-A., Champagne, M., & Manningham, S. (2018). Early childhood educators' perceptions of children's physical activity: Do we need to clarify expectations? *Journal of Research in Childhood Education, 32*(3), 283–294. https://doi.org/10.1080/02568543.2018.1464979

Conrad, M., & Stricker, S. (2017). Personality and labor: A retrospective study of the relationship between personality traits and birthing experiences. *Journal of Reproductive and Infant Psychology, 36*(5), 1–14. https://doi.org/10.1080/02646838.2017.1397611

Conradt, E. (2017). Using principles of behavioral epigenetics to advance research on early life stress. *Child Development Perspectives.* https://doi-org.scsu.idm.oclc.org/10.1111/cdep.12219

Cook, J. L., et al. (2016). Fetal alcohol spectrum disorder: A guideline for diagnosis across the lifespan. *CMAJ, 188*(3), 191–197. https://doi.org/10.1503/cmaj.141593

Cooke, J. E., et al. (2018). Parent–child attachment and children's experience and regulation of emotion: A meta-analytic review. *Emotion.* 19(6), 1103–1126 http://dx.doi.org/10.1037/emo0000504

Cooksey-Stowers, K., Schwartz, M. B., & Brownell, K. D. (2017). Food swamps predict obesity rates better than food deserts in the United States. *International Journal of Environmental Research and Public Health, 14*(11), 1366. https://doi.org/10.3390/ijerph14111366

Coplan, R. J., Ooi, L. L., & Baldwin, D. (2019). Does it matter when we want to be alone? Exploring developmental timing effects in the implications of unsociability. *New Ideas in Psychology, 53*, 47–57. https://doi.org/10.1016/j.newideapsych.2018.01.001

Corder, K., et al. (2019). Change in physical activity from adolescence to early adulthood: A systematic review and meta-analysis of longitudinal cohort studies. *British Journal of Sports Medicine, 53*, 496–503. http://dx.doi.org/10.1136/bjsports-2016-097330

Cornelius, D. C. (2018). Preeclampsia: From inflammation to immunoregulation. *Clinical Medicine Insights: Blood Disorders, 11*. https://doi.org/10.1177/1179545X17752325

Costa, A., & Faria, L. (2018). Implicit theories of intelligence and academic achievement: A meta-analytic review. *Frontiers in Psychology, 9*, 829. https://doi.org/10.3389/fpsyg.2018.00829

Côté, J. E. (2018). The enduring usefulness of Erikson's concept of the identity crisis in the 21st century: An analysis of student mental health concerns. *Identity: An International Journal of Theory and Research, 18*(4), 251–263. https://doi.org/10.1080/15283488.2018.1524328.

Côté, J. E. (2019). *Youth development in identity societies: Paradoxes of purpose.* Routledge.

Cottini, M., Basso, D., & Palladino, P. (2018). The role of declarative and procedural metamemory in event-based prospective memory in school-aged children. *Journal of Experimental Child Psychology, 166*, 17–33. https://doi.org/10.1016/j.jecp.2017.08.002

Coven, J. & Gupta, A. (2020). Disparities in mobility responses to COVID-19. Retrieved from: https://static1.squarespace.com/static/56086d00e4b0fb7874bc2d42/t/5e99ade697b58449042cf36d/1587129833215/DemographicCovid.pdf

Cowan, C. P., & Cowan, P. A. (2000). *When partners become parents: The big life change for couples.* Lawrence Erlbaum Associates Publishers.

Cowan, C. P., & Cowan, P. A. (2018). Prevention: Intervening with couples at challenging family transition points. In A. Balfour (Ed.), *How couple relationships shape our world: Clinical Practice, Research, and Policy Perspectives* (pp.1–14). Routledge.

Cowan, N. (2014). Working memory underpins cognitive development, learning, and education. *Educational Psychology Review, 26*(2), 197–223. https://doi.org/10.1007/s10648-013-9246-y

Cowan, N., Li, Y., Glass, B., & Saults, J. S. (2018). Development of the ability to combine visual and acoustic information in working memory. *Developmental Science, 21*(5), e12635. https://doi.org/10.1111/desc.12635

Coyle, E. F., & Liben, L. S. (2018). Gendered packaging of a STEM toy influences children's play, mechanical learning, and mothers' play guidance. *Child Development, 91*(1), 43–62. https://doi.org/10.1111/cdev.13139

Craig, S. L., McInroy, L. B., & Austin, A. (2018). "Someone to have my back": Exploring the needs of racially and ethnically diverse lesbian, gay, bisexual, and transgender high school students. *Children & Schools, 40*(4), 231–239. https://doi.org/10.1093/cs/cdy016

Cramer, P. (2017). Identity change between adolescence and adulthood. *Personality and Individual Differences, 104*, 538–543. http://dx.doi.org/10.1016/j.paid.2016.08.044

Cremone, A., et al. (2017). Sleep tight, act right: Negative affect, sleep and behavior problems during early childhood. *Child Development, 89*(2), e42–e59. https://doi.org/10.1111/cdev.12717

Crenshaw, K. W. (1989). Demarginalizing the intersection of race and sex: A Black feminist critique of antidiscrimination doctrine, feminist theory and antiracist politics. *University of Chicago Legal Forum, 140*, 139–167. Retrieved from http://chicagounbound.uchicago.edu/uclf/vol1989/iss1/8

Crespo-Llado, M. M., Vanderwert, R., Roberti, E., & Geangu, E. (2018). Eight-month-old infants' behavioral responses to peers' emotions as related to the asymmetric frontal cortex activity. *Scientific Reports, 8*, e17152.

Creswell, J. W. (2014). *Research design: Qualitative, quantitative, and mixed method approaches.* Thousand Oaks, CA: Sage Publications, Inc.

Crisp, J. (2017, December 20). Take five months parental leave, Swedish fathers told. *The Telegraph*, https://www.telegraph.co.uk/news/2017/12/19/take-five-months-parental-leave-swedish-fathers-told/

Crocetti, E., et al. (2017). Identity processes and parent–child and sibling relationships in adolescence: A five-wave multi-informant longitudinal study. *Child Development, 88*(1), 210–228. https://doi.org/10.1111/cdev.12547

Crocetti, E. (2018). Identity dynamics in adolescence: Processes, antecedents, and consequences. *European Journal of Developmental Psychology, 15*(1), 11–23. https://doi.org/10.1080/17405629.2017.1405578

Crocetti, E., Rubini, M., & Meeus, W. (2008). Capturing the dynamics of identity formation in various ethnic groups: Development and validation of a three-dimensional model. *Journal of Adolescence, 31*, 207–222. http://dx.doi.org/10.1016/j.adolescence.2007.09.002

Crocetti, E., et al. (2013). Impact of early adolescent externalizing problem behaviors on identity development in middle to late adolescence: A prospective 7-year longitudinal study. *Journal of Youth and Adolescence, 42*, 1745–1758. https://doi.org/10.1007/s10964-013-9924-6

Crockett, L. J., et al. (2019). Puberty education in a global context: Knowledge gaps, opportunities and implications for policy. *Journal of Research on Adolescence, 29*(1), 177–195. https://doi.org/10.1111/jora.12452

Croizet, J.-C., Goudeau, S., Marot, M., & Millet, M. (2017). How do educational contexts contribute to the social class achievement gap: Documenting symbolic violence from a social psychological point of view. *Current Opinion in Psychology, 18*, 105–110. http://dx.doi.org/10 .1016/j.copsyc.2017.08.025

Crone, E. A., & Konijn, E. A. (2018). Media use and brain development during adolescence. *Nature Communications, 9*(588). https://doi.org/10.1038/s41467-018-03126-x

Crowder, M. D., Cools, K. S., Kucera, K. L., Thomas, L. C., Hosokawa, Y., Casa, D. J., Lee, S., & Schade Willis, T. M. (2018). Sudden death in high school athletes: A case series examining the influence of sickle cell trait. *Pediatrics, 142*(1). https://doi.org/10.1542/peds.142.1_MeetingAbstract.414

Crowley, S. J., Wolfson, A. R., Tarokh, L., & Carskadon, M. A. (2018). An update on adolescent sleep: New evidence informing the perfect storm model. *Journal of Adolescence, 67*, 55–65. https://doi.org/10.1016/j.adolescence.2018.06.001

Cunningham, C., et al. (2018). Does Kangaroo care affect the weight of preterm/low birth-weight infants in the neonatal setting of a hospital environment? *Journal of Neonatal Nursing, 24*(4), 189–195. https://doi.org/10.1016/j.jnn.2017.10.001

Curtin, S. C., Heron, M., Miniño, A. M., & Warner, M. (2018). Recent increases in injury mortality among children and adolescents aged 10–19 years in the United States: 1999–2016. *National Vital Statistics Reports, 67*(4), 1–16.

Curtis, P. R., Kaiser, A. P., Estabrook, R., & Roberts, M. Y. (2019). The longitudinal effects of early language intervention on children's problem behaviors. *Child Development, 90*(2), 576–592. https://doi.org/10.1111/cdev.12942

Dagan, O., & Sagi-Schwartz, A. (2017). Early attachment network with mother and father: An unsettled issue. *Child Development Perspectives, 12*(2), 115–121. https://doi-org.scsu.idm.oclc.org/10.1111/cdep.12272

Dahir, A. L. (2019, November 21). Arabic-language version of "Sesame Street" will debut three new muppets. *New York Times*, https://www.nytimes.com/2019/11/21/arts/television/sesame-street-middle-east-trauma.html

Dahl, A., & Killen, M. (2018). A developmental perspective on the origins or morality in infancy and early childhood. *Frontiers in Psychology, 9*, 1736. https://doi.org/10.3389/fpsyg.2018.01736

Dahl, R. E., Allen, N. B., Wilbrecht, L., & Suleiman, A. B. (2018). Importance of investing in adolescence from a developmental science perspective. *Nature, 554*, 441–450. https://doi.org/10.1038/nature25770

Daigle, L. E., & Hoffman, C. Y. (2018). Violent victimization and future expectations: Results for a longitudinal study of at-risk youth. *Victims & Offenders, 13*(6), 798–813. https://doi.org/10.1080/15564886.2018.1479909

Daiute, C. (2018). Adolescent civic engagement in contemporary political and technological realities. In J. E. Lansford & P. Banati (Eds.), *Handbook of Adolescent Development Research and Its Impact on Global Policy* (pp. 84–103). Oxford University Press.

Dalimonte-Merckling, M., & Brophy-Herb, H. E. (2018). A person-centered approach to child temperament and parenting. *Child Development, 90*(5), 1–16. https://doi.org/10.1111/cdev.13046

Dandurand, F., & Shultz, T. R. (2011). A fresh look at vocabulary spurts. In C. Hoelscher, T. F. Shipley, & L. Carlson (Eds.), *Proceedings of the 33rd Annual Conference of the Cognitive Science Society* (pp. 1134–1139). Boston, MA: Cognitive Science Society.

Danneel, S., et al. (2018). Developmental change in loneliness and attitudes towards aloneness in adolescence. *Journal of Youth and Adolescence, 47*, 148–161. https://doi.org/10.1007/s10964-017-0685-5

Dantchev, S., & Wolke, D. (2019). Trouble in the nest: Antecedents of sibling bullying victimization and perpetration. *Developmental Psychology, 55*(5), 1059–1071. http://dx.doi.org/10.1037/dev0000700

Dantchev, S., et al. (2019). The independent and cumulative effects of sibling and peer bullying in childhood on depression, anxiety, suicidal ideation, and self-harm in adults. *Frontiers in Psychology.* https://doi.org/10.3389/fpsyt.2019.00651

Darling, N., & Steinberg, L. (2017). Parenting style as context: An integrative model. In B. Laursen & R. Zukauskiene (Ed.), *Interpersonal Development* (pp. 487–496). Routledge.

Darling, N., & Tilton-Weaver, L. (2019). All in the family: Within-family differences in parental monitoring and adolescent information management. *Developmental Psychology, 55*(2), 402. http://dx.doi.org/10.1037/dev0000641

Darnon, C., Jury, M., & Aelenei, C. (2018). Who benefits from mastery-approach and performance-approach goals in college? Students' social class as a moderator of the link between goals and grade. *European Journal of Psychology of Education, 33*(4), 713–726. https://doi.org/10.1007/s10212-017-0351-z

Darwin, C. (1877). A biographical sketch of an infant. Mind, 2(7), 285–294. Retrieved from: https://www.jstor.org/stable/2246907

Daubert, E. N., & Ramani, G. B. (2019). Math and memory in bilingual preschoolers: The relations between bilingualism, working memory, and numerical knowledge. *Journal of Cognition and Development, 20*(3). https://doi.org/10.1080/15248372.2019.1565536

Davies, P. T., et al. (2018). Children's vulnerability to interparental conflict: The protective role of sibling relationship quality. *Child Development, 90*(6), 1–17. https://doi.org/10.1111/cdev.13078

Davis, A. N., & Carlo, G. (2018). The roles of parenting practices, sociocognitive/emotive traits and prosocial behaviors in low-income adolescents. *Journal of Adolescence, 62*, 140–150. https://doi.org/10.1016/j.adolescence.2017.11.011

Davis, E. E., Carlin, C. C., Kraft, C., & Forry, N. D. (2018). Do child care subsidies increase employment in low-income parents? *Journal of Family and Economic Issues, 39*(4), 622–682. https://doi.org/10.1007/s10834-018-9582-7

Davis, E. S. & Pereira, J. K. (2014). Child-centered play therapy: A creative approach to culturally competent counseling. *Journal of Creativity in Mental Health, 9*(2), 262–274. https://doi.org/10.1080/15401383.2014.892863

Davis, P. E., Meins, E. & Fernyhough, C. (2014). Children with imaginary companions focus on mental characteristics when describing their real-life friends. *Infant and Child Development, 23*(6), 622–633. https://doi.org/10.1002/icd.1869

Day, E., Dotterer, A.M. (2018). Parental involvement and adolescent academic outcomes: Exploring differences in beneficial strategies across racial/ethnic groups. *J Youth Adolescence, 47*, 1332–1349. https://doi.org/10.1007/s10964-018-0853-2

de Bruijn, A. G. M., et al. (2018). Exploring the relations among physical fitness, executive functioning, and low academic achievement. *Journal of Experimental Child Psychology, 167*, 204–221. https://doi.org/10.1016/j.jecp.2017.10.010

de Chanville, A. B., et al. (2017). Analgesic effect of maternal human milk odor on premature neonates: A randomized controlled trial. *Journal of Human Lactation, 33*(2), 300–308. https://doi.org/10.1177/0890334417693225

de Greeff, J. W., et al. (2018). Effects of physical activity on executive functions, attention and academic performance in preadolescent children: A meta-analysis. *Journal of Science and Medicine Sport, 21*(5), 501–507. https://doi.org/10.1016/j.jsams.2017.09.595

de Hevia, M. D., Izard, V., Coubart, A., Spelke, E. S. & Streri, A. (2014). Representations of space, time, and number in neonates. *PNAS, 111*(13), 4809–4813. https://:doi.org/10.1073/pnas.1323628111

de Kat, A. C., & Broekmans, F. J. M. (2018) Female age and reproductive chances. In D. Stoop (Ed.), *Preventing age related fertility loss*. Springer. https://doi.org/10.1007/978-3-319-14857-1_1

de Lemos, M. M. (2019). The development of spatial concepts in Zulu children. In J. W. Berry & P. R. Dasen (Eds.), *Culture and cognition: Readings in cross-cultural psychology* (pp. 367–380). Routledge.

de Vries, K. M. (2015). Transgender people of color at the center: Conceptualizing a new intersectional model. *Ethnicities, 15*(1), 3–27. https://doi.org/10.1177/1468796814547058

Deák, G. O., Krasno, A. M., Jasso, H., & Triesch, J. (2018). What leads to shared attention? Maternal cues and infant responses during object play. *Infancy, 23*(1), 4–28. https://doi.org/10.1111/infa.12204

Dean, D. C., III et al. (2015). Characterizing longitudinal white matter development during early childhood. *Brain Structure and Function, 220*(4), 1921–1933. https://doi.org/ 10.1007/s00429-014-0763-3

Deardorff, J., Hoyt, L. T., Carter, R., & Shirtcliff, E. A. (2019). Next steps in puberty research: Broadening the lens toward understudied populations. *Journal of Research on Adolescence, 29*(1), 133–154. https://doi.org/10.1111/jora.12402

Deavin, A., Greasley, P., & Dixon, C. (2018). Children's perspectives on living with a sibling with a chronic illness. *Pediatrics, 142*(2), e201174151.

Debenham, J., Newton, N., Birrell, L., & Askovic, M. (2019). Alcohol and other drug prevention for older adolescents: It's a no brainer. *Drug and Alcohol Review, 38*(4), 327–330. https://doi.org/10.1111/dar.12914

Deckert, M., Schoeger, M., Schaunig-Busch, & Willinger, U. (2018). Metaphor processing in middle childhood and at the transition to early adolescence: The role of chronological age, mental age, and verbal intelligence. *Journal of Child Language, 46*(2), 334–367. https://doi.org/10.1017/S0305000918000491

DeCasper, A. J. & Spence, M. J. (1986). Prenatal maternal speech influences newborns' perception of speech sounds. *Infant Behavior and Development, 9*, 13–150. https://doi.org/ https://doi.org/10.1016/0163-6383(94)90051-5

DeClercq, E., Cabral, H., & Ecker, J. (2017). The plateauing of cesarean rates in industrialized countries. *American Journal of Obstetrics & Gynecology, 216*(3), 322–323. https://doi.org/10.1016/j.ajog.2016.11.1038

DeFlorio, L., et al. (2019). A study of the developing relations between self-regulation and mathematical knowledge in the context of an early math intervention. *Early Childhood Research Quarterly, 46*, 33–48. https://doi.org/10.1016/j.ecresq.2018.06.008

del Río, M. F., Susperreguy, M. I., Strasser, K., & Salinas, V. (2017). Distinct influence of mothers and fathers on kindergartners' numeracy performance: The role of math anxiety, home numeracy practices, and numeracy expectations. *Early Education and Development, 28*(8). https://doi.org/10.1080/10409289.2017.1331662

Del-Ponte, B., et al. (2019). Dietary patterns and attention deficit/hyperactivity disorder (ADHD): A systematic review and meta-analysis. *Journal of Affective Disorders, 252*, 160–173. https://doi.org/10.1016/j.jad.2019.04.061

Delalibera, B. R., & Ferreira, P. C. (2019). Early childhood education and economic growth. *Journal of Economic Dynamics and Control, 98*, 82–104. https://doi.org/10.1016/j.jedc.2018.10.002

DelGiudice, M. (2018). Middle childhood: An evolutionary-developmental synthesis. In N. Halfon, C. B. Forrest, R. M. Lerner, & E. M. Faustman (Eds.), *Handbook of life course health development* (pp. 95–107). Springer.

DeLoache, J. S. (1987). Rapid change in the symbolic functioning of very young children. *Science, 238*(4833), 1556–1557. https://doi.org/10.1126/science.2446392

Demant, J., & Schierff, L. M. (2019). Five typologies of alcohol and drug prevention programmes. A qualitative review of the content of alcohol and drug prevention programmes targeting adolescents. *Drugs: Education, Prevention and Policy, 26*(1). https://doi.org/10.1080/09687637.2017.1347147

Demers, L. A., et al. (2019). Childhood maltreatment disrupts brain-mediated pathways between adolescent maternal relationship quality and positive adult outcomes. *Child Maltreatment, 24*(4), 424–434. https://doi:10.1177/1077559519847770

Demetriou, A., et al. (2018a). Mapping the dimensions of general intelligence: An integrated differential-developmental theory. *Human Development, 61*, 4–42. https://doi.org/10.1159/000484450

Demetriou, E. A., et al. (2018b). Autism spectrum disorders: A meta-analysis of executive function. *Molecular Psychiatry, 23*, 1198–1204. https://doi.org/10.1038/mp.2017.75

Demir-Lira, Ö. E., Applebaum, L. R., Goldin-Meadow, S., & Levine, S. C. (2018). Parents' early book reading to children: Relation to children's later language and literacy outcomes controlling for other parent language input. *Developmental Science, 22*(3), e12764. https://doi.org/10.1111/desc.12764

Demir-Dagdas, T., Isik-Ercan, Z., Intepe-Tingir, S., & Cava-Tadik, Y. (2017). Parental divorce and children from diverse backgrounds: Multidisciplinary perspectives on mental health, parent–child relationships, and educational experiences. *Journal of Divorce & Remarriage, 59*(6). https://doi.org/10.1080/10502556.2017.1403821

Demirci, J., Caplan, E., Murray, N., & Cohen, S. (2018). "I just want to do everything right:" Primaparous women's accounts of early breastfeeding via an App-based diary. *Journal of Pediatric Health Care, 32*(2), 163–172. https://doi.org/10.1016/j.pedhc.2017.09.010

Denault, A-A., & Poulin, F. (2019). Trajectories of participation in organized activities and outcomes in young adulthood. *Applied Developmental Science, 23*(1), 74–89. http://dx.doi.org/10.1080/10888691.2017.1308829

Denault, A-S., Ratelle, C. F., Duchense, S., & Guay, F. (2019). Extracurricular activities and career indecision: A look at the mediating role of vocational exploration. *Journal of Vocational Behavior, 110*(A), 43–53. https://doi.org/10.1016/j.jvb.2018.11.006

Denham, S. A., Bassett, H. H., & Miller, S. L. (2017). Early childhood teachers' socialization of emotion: Contextual and individual contributors. *Child & Youth Care Forum, 46*(6), 805–824. https://doi.org/10.1007/s10566-017-9409-y

Dennis, E. L., et al. (2019). Irritability and brain volume in adolescents: Cross-sectional and longitudinal associations. *Social Cognitive and Affective Neuroscience, 14*(7), 687–698. https://doi.org/10.1093/scan/nsz053

DerMarderosian, D., Chapman, H. A., Tortolani, C., & Willis, M. D. (2018). Medical considerations in children and adolescents with eating disorders. *Child & Adolescent Psychiatric Clinics, 27*(1), 1–14. https://doi.org/10.1016/j.chc.2017.08.002

Desmond, R. (2001). Free reading: Implications for child development. In D. G. Singer, & J. L. Singer (Eds.), Handbook of children and the media (pp. 29–45). Thousand Oaks, CA: Sage Publications, Inc.

Dias, C. C., Figueiredo, B., Rocha, M., & Field, T. (2018). Reference values and changes in infant sleep–wake behavior during the first 12 months of life: A systematic review. *Journal of Sleep Research, 27*(5), e12654. https://doi.org/10.1111/jsr.12654

Dickson, D. J., et al. (2018). Parent contributions to friendship stability during the primary school years. *Journal of Family Psychology, 32*(2), 217–228. https://doi.org/10.1037/fam0000388

Dietvorst, E., Hiemstra, M., Hillegers, M. H. J., & Keijsers, L. (2018). Adolescent perceptions of parental privacy invasion and adolescent secrecy. *Child Development, 89*(6), 2081–2090. https://doi.org/10.1111/cdev.13002

Dillon, M. R., & Spelke, E. S. (2018). From map reading to geometric intuitions. *Developmental Psychology, 54*(7), 1304–1316. http://dx.doi.org/10.1037/dev0000509

Dirks, M. A., Persram, R., Recchia, H. E., & Howe, N. (2015). Sibling relationships as sources of risk and resilience in the development and maintenance of internalizing and externalizing problems during childhood and adolescence. *Clinical Psychology Review, 42*, 145–155. https://doi.org/10.1016/j.cpr.2015.07.003

Dirks, M. A., et al. (2018). Differentiating typical from atypical perpetration of sibling-directed aggression during the preschool years. *Journal of Child Psychology and Psychiatry, 60*(3), 267–276. https://doi.org/10.1111/jcpp.12939

Dishion, T. J., & McMahon, R. J. (1998). Parental monitoring and the prevention of child and adolescent problem behavior: A conceptual and empirical formulation. *Clinical Child and Family Psychology Review, 1*(1), 61–75. https://doi.org/10.1023/A:1021800432380

Disla, J., Main, A., Kashi, S., & Boyajian, J. (2018). The effect of mothers' emotion-related responses to adolescent disclosures and adolescent perspective taking on the timing of future disclosures. *Social Development, 28*(3), 657–673. https://doi.org/10.1111/sode.12360

Dittman, A. G., & Stephens, N. M. (2017). Interventions aimed at closing the social class achievement gap: Changing individuals, structures, and construals. *Current Opinion in Psychology, 18*, 111–116. https://doi.org/10.1016/j.copsyc.2017.07.044

Doan, S. N., & Wang, Q. (2018). Children's emotion knowledge and internalizing problems: The moderating role of culture. *Transcultural Psychiatry, 55*(5), 689–709. https://doi.org/10.1177/1363461518792731

Dobel, C., et al. (2019). Deaf signers outperform hearing non-signers in recognizing happy facial expressions. *Psychological Research*, 1–10. https://doi.org/10.1007/s00426-019-01160-y

Dobewall, H., et al. (2018). Gene-environment correlations in parental emotional warmth and intolerance: Genome-wide analysis over two generations of the Young Finns Study. *Journal of Child Psychology and Psychiatry, 60*(3):277–285. https://doi.org/10.1111/jcpp.12995

Doctoroff, G. L., & Arnold, D. H. (2017). Doing homework together: The relation between parenting strategies, child engagement, and achievement. *Journal of Applied Developmental Psychology, 48,* 103–113. https://doi.org/10.1016/j.appdev.2017.01.001

Dodgson, J. E. (2018). The intersection of power, social justice and lactation. *Journal of Human Lactation, 34*(3), 411–412. https://doi.org/10.1177/0890334418776983

Donovan, G. H., Gatziolis, D., Longley, I., & Douwes, J. (2018). Vegetation diversity protects against childhood asthma: Results from a large New Zealand birth cohort. *Nature Plants, 4,* 358–364. https://doi.org/10.1038/s41477-018-0151-8

Dorn, L. D., Hostinar, C. E., Susman, E. J., & Pervanidou, P. (2019). Conceptualizing puberty as a window of opportunity for impacting health and well-being across the life span. *Journal of Research on Adolescence, 29*(1), 155–176. https://doi.org/10.1111/jora.12431

Dost-Gözkan, A. (2019). Adolescents' conflict resolution with their best friends: Links to life satisfaction. *Journal of Child and Family Studies, 28*(10), 2854–2866. https://doi.org/10.1007/s10826-019-01465-x

Dotterer, A. M., & James, A., Jr. (2018). Can parenting microprotections buffer against adolescents' experiences of racial discrimination? *Journal of Youth and Adolescence, 47,* 38–50. https://doi.org/10.1007/s10964-017-0773-6

Dowd, J. B. & Renson, A. (2018). "Under the skin" and into the gut: Social epidemiology of the microbiome. *Social Epidemiology, 5,* 432–441. https://doi.org/10.1007/s40471-018-0167-7

Dowker, A. & Li, A. M. (2019). English and Chinese children's performance on numerical tasks. *Frontiers in Psychology.* https://doi.org/10.3389/fpsyg.2018.02731

Downes, M., et al. (2018). Visual attention control differences in 12-month-old preterm infants. *Infant Behavior and Development, 50,* 180–188. https://doi.org/10.1016/j.infbeh.2018.01.002

Driessnack, M. (2009). Children and nature-deficit disorder. *Journal for Specialists in Pediatric Nursing, 14*(1), 73–75. https://doi.org/10.1111/j.1744-6155.2009.00180.x

Du Toit, G., et al. (2018). Food allergy: Update on prevention and tolerance. *Journal of Allergy and Clinical Immunology, 141*(1), 30–40. https://doi.org/10.1016/j.jaci.2017.11.010

Duarte, T. A., et al. (2019). Self-harm as a predisposition for suicide attempts: A study of adolescents' deliberate self-harm, suicide ideation, and suicide attempts. *Psychiatry Research, 287.* https://doi.org/10.1016/j.psychres.2019.112553

Dubé, E., Vivion, M., & MacDonald, N. E. (2015). Vaccine hesitancy, vaccine refusal and the anti-vaccine movement: Influence, impact and implications. *Expert Review of Vaccines, 14*(1), 99–117. https://doi.org/10.1586/14760584.2015.964212

Duckworth, A. L. (2016). *Grit: The power of passion and perseverance*. Scribner.

Duckworth, A. L., Peterson, C., Matthews, M. D., & Kelly, D. R. (2007). Grit: Perseverance and passion for long-term goals. *Journal of Personality and Social Psychology, 92*(6), 1087–1101. https://doi.org/10.1037/0022-3514.92.6.1087

Duell, N., et al. (2018). Age patterns in risk taking around the world. *Journal of Youth and Adolescence, 47*(5), 1052–1072. https://doi.org/10.1007/s10964-017-0752-y

Duff, D., Tomblin, J. B., & Catts, H. (2015). The influence of reading on vocabulary growth: A case for a Matthew effect. *Journal of Speech, Language, and Hearing Research, 58*(3), 853–864. https://doi.org/10.1044/2015_JSLHR-L-13-0310

Dumas, T. M., Davis, J. P., & Ellis, W. E. (2019). Is it good to be bad? A longitudinal analysis of adolescent popularity motivations as a predictor of engagement in relational aggression and risk behaviors. *Youth & Society, 51*(5), 659–679. https://doi.org/10.1177/0044118X17700319

Duncan, G. J., Lee, K. T. H., Rosales-Rueda, M., & Kalil, A. (2018). Maternal age and child development. *Demography, 55*(6), 2229–2255. https://doi.org/10.1007/s13524-018-0730-3

Dunham, Y., & Olson, K. R. (2016). Beyond discrete categories: Studying multiracial and transgender children will strengthen developmental science. *Journal of Cognition and Development, 17*(4), 642–655. https://doi.org/10.1080/15248372.2016.1195388

Dunn, E. C., Wang, Y., Tse, J., et al. (2017). Sensitive periods for the effect of childhood interpersonal violence on psychiatric disorder onset among adolescents. *The British Journal of Psychiatry*, 211(6): 365–372. https://doi.org/10.1192/bjp.bp.117.208397

Durwood, L., McLaughlin, K., & Olson, K. R. (2017). Mental health and self-worth in socially transitioned transgender youth. *Journal of the American Academy of Child & Adolescent Psychiatry, 56*(2), 116–123. https://doi.org/10.1016/j.jaac.2016.10.016

Dutil, C., et al. (2018). Influence of sleep on developing brain functions and structures in children and adolescents: A systematic review. *Sleep Medicine Reviews, 42*, 184–201. https://doi.org/10.1016/j.smrv.2018.08.003

Dvash, J. & Shamay-Tsoory, S. G. (2014). Theory of mind and empathy as multidimensional constructs: Neurological foundations. *Topics in Language Disorders, 34*(4), 282–295. https://doi.org/10.1097/TLD.0000000000000040

Dweck, C. S. (1999). *Self-theories: Their role in motivation, personality, and development.* Psychology Press.

Dys, S. P., Peplak, J., Colasante, T., & Malti, T. (2019). Children's sympathy and sensitivity to excluding economically disadvantaged pers. *Developmental Psychology, 55*(3), 482–487. http://dx.doi.org/10.1037/dev0000549

Earnshaw, V. A., et al. (2017). LGBTQ bullying: Translating research to action in pediatrics. *Pediatrics, 140*(4), e20170432. https://doi.org/10.1542/peds.2017-0432

Eastmand, C. J., & Zimmerman, M. B. (2018). The iodine deficiency disorders. In L. J. DeGroot et al. (Eds.), *Endotext.* Retrieved from https://www.ncbi.nlm.nih.gov/books/NBK285556/

Ebbert, A. M., Infurna, F. J., & Luthar, S. S. (2018). Mapping developmental changes in perceived parent-adolescent relationship quality throughout middle school and high school. *Development and Psychopathology, 31*(4), 1541–1556. https://doi.org/10.1017/S0954579418001219

Eisenberg, M. L., & Meldrum, D. (2017). Effects of age on fertility and sexual function. *Fertility and Sterility, 107*(2), 301–304. https://doi.org/10.1016/j.fertnstert.2016.12.018

Eisman, A. B., et al. (2017). Trajectories of organized activity participation among urban adolescents: Associations with young adult outcomes. *Journal of Community Psychology, 45*, 513–527. https://doi.org/10.1002/jcop.21863

Eisman, A. B., et al. (2018). More than just keeping busy: The protective effects of organized activity participation on violence and substance use among urban youth. *Journal of Youth and Adolescence, 47*(1), 2231–2242. https://doi.org/10.1007/s10964-018-0868-8.

Ekelund, U., et al. (2018). Do the associations of sedentary behaviour with cardiovascular disease mortality and cancer mortality differ by physical activity level? A systematic review and harmonised meta-analysis of data from 850 060 participants. *British Journal of Sports Medicine, 53*(14), 886–894. https://doi.org/10.1136/bjsports-2017-098963

El Marroun, H., et al. (2018). Preconception and prenatal cannabis use and the risk of behavioural and emotional problems in the offspring; A multi-informant prospective longitudinal study. *International Journal of Epidemiology, 48*(1), 287–296. https://doi.org/10.1093/ije/dyy186

Eldesouky, L., & English, T. (2018). Regulating for a reason: Emotion regulation goals are linked to spontaneous strategy use. *Journal of Personality, 87*(5), 948–961. https://doi.org/10.1111/jopy.12447

Elenbaas, L. (2019). Perceptions of economic inequality are related to children's judgments about access to opportunities. *Developmental Psychology, 55*(3), 471–481. http://dx.doi.org/10.1037/dev0000550

Elenbaas, L., & Killen, M. (2016). Children rectify inequalities for disadvantaged groups. *Developmental Psychology, 52*, 1318–1329. https://doi.org/10.1037/dev0000154

Elgar, F. J., et al. (2019). Association of early-life exposure to income inequality with bullying in adolescence in 40 countries. *JAMA Pediatrics, 173*(7), e191181. https://doi.org/10.1001/jamapediatrics.2019.1181

Elischberger, H. B., Glazier, J. J., Hill, E. D., & Verduzco-Baker, L. (2018). Attitudes toward and beliefs about transgender youth: A cross-cultural comparison between the United States and India. *Sex Roles, 78*, 142–160. https://doi.org/10.1007/s11199-017-0778-3

Ellis, B. J., & Del Guidice, M. (2019). Developmental adaptation to stress: An evolutionary perspective. *Annual Review of Psychology, 70*, 111–139. https://doi.org/10.1146/annurev-psych-122216-011732

Elmlinger, S. L., Schwade, J. A., & Goldstein, M. H., (2019). The ecology of prelinguistic vocal learning: Parents simplify the structure of their speech in response to babbling. *Journal of Child Language, 46*(5), 998–1011. https://doi.org/10.1017/S0305000919000291

El-Sheikh, M., & Kelly, R. J. (2017). Family functioning and children's sleep. *Child Development Perspectives, 11*(4), 264–269. https://doi.org/10.1111/cdep.12243

El-Sheikh, M., et al. (2019). What does a good night's sleep mean? Nonlinear relations between sleep and children's cognitive functioning and mental health. *Sleep, 42*(3). https://doi.org/10.1093/sleep/zsz078

Engelhardt, L. E., Church, J. A., Harden, K. P., & Tucker-Drob, E. M. (2018). Accounting for the shared environment in cognitive abilities and academic achievement with measured socioecological contexts. *Developmental Science, 22*(1), e12699. https://doi.org/10.1111/desc.12699

Engelmann, J. M., & Tomasello, M. (2019). Children's sense of fairness as equal respect. *Trends in Cognitive Sciences, 23*(6), 454–463. https://doi.org/10.1016/j.tics.2019.03.001

Enlow, M. B., King, L., Schreier, H. M. C., Howard, J. M., Rosenfield, D., Ritz, T., & Wright, R. J. (2014). Maternal sensitivity and infant autonomic and endocrine stress responses. *Early Human Development, 90*(7), 377–385. https//:doi.org/10.1016/j.earlhumdev.2014.04.007

Enriquez-Geppert, S., Smit, D., Garcia Pimenta, M., & Arns, M. (2019). Neurofeedback as a treatment intervention in ADHD: Current evidence and practice. *Current Psychiatry Reports, 21*(46). https://doi.org/10.1007/s11920-019-1021-4

Erhart, A., Dimitreva, J., Blair, R. J. & Kim, P. (2019). Intensity, not emotion: The role of poverty in emotion labeling ability in middle childhood. *Journal of Experimental Psychology, 180,* 131–140. https://doi.org/10.1016/j.jecp.2018.12.009

Erikson, E. (1959). *Identity and the life cycle.* New York, NY: W. W. Norton & Company, Inc.

Erikson, E. (1963). *Childhood and society* (2ⁿᵈ edition). New York, NY: W. W. Norton & Company, Inc.

Erikson, E. (1964). *Insight and Responsibility.* New York, NY: W. W. Norton & Company, Inc.

Erikson, E. (1968). *Identity: Youth and crisis.* New York, NY: W. W. Norton & Company, Inc.

Erikson, E. H. (1993). *Childhood and society.* New York, NY: W. W. Norton & Company.

Erikson, E. H. (1997). *The life cycle completed: Extended version with new chapters on the ninth stage of development by Joan M. Erikson.* New York, NY: W. W. Norton & Company.

Eshraghi, A. A., et al. (2018). Epigenetics and autism spectrum disorder: Is there a correlation? *Frontiers in Cellular Neuroscience.* https://doi.org/10.3389/fncel.2018.00078

Espelage, D. L., et al. (2019). Teen dating violence perpetration: Protective factor trajectories from middle to high school among adolescents. *Journal of Research on Adolescence, 30*(1), 170–188. https://doi.org/10.1111/jora.12510

Esposito, C., Bacchini, D., & Affuso, G. (2019). Adolescent non-suicidal self-injury and its relationship with school bullying and peer rejection. *Psychiatry Research, 274,* 1–6. https://doi.org/10.1016/j.psychres.2019.02.018

Esposito, G., Azhari, A., & Borelli, J. L. (2018). Gene × environment interaction in developmental disorders: Where do we stand and what's next? *Frontiers in Psychology, 9,* 2036. https://doi.org/10.3389/fpsyg.2018.02036 Esteban-Guitart, M. (2018). The biosocial foundation of the early Vygotsky: Educational psychology before the zone of proximal development. *History of Psychology, 21*(4), 384–401. http://dx.doi.org/10.1037/hop0000092

Etel, E., & Slaughter, V. (2019). Theory of mind and peer cooperation in two play contexts. *Journal of Applied Developmental Psychology, 60,* 87–95. https://doi.org/10.1016/j.appdev.2018.11.004

Ettekal, I., & Ladd, G. W. (2017). Developmental continuity and change in physical, verbal, and relational aggression and peer victimization from childhood to adolescence. *Developmental Psychology, 53*(9), 1709–1721. http://dx.doi.org/10.1037/dev0000357

Eun, B. (2019). The zone of proximal development as an overarching concept: A framework for synthesizing Vygotsky's theories. *Educational Philosophy and Theory, 51*(1). https://doi.org/10.1080/00131857.2017.1421941

Eveleth, P. B. (2017). Timing of menarche: Secular trend and population differences. In J. B. Lancaster & B. A. Hamburg (Eds.), *School-age pregnancy and parenthood: Biosocial dimensions* (pp. 39–52). Transaction Publishers.

Extremera, N., Quintana-Orts, C., Mérida-López, S., & Rey, L. (2018). Cyberbullying victimization, self-esteem, and suicidal ideation in adolescence: Does emotional intelligence play a buffering role? *Frontiers in Psychology.* https://doi.org/10.3389/fpsyg.2018.00367

Fabiano, G. A., & Caserta, A. (2018). Future directions in father inclusion, engagement, retention, and positive outcomes in child and adolescent research. *Journal of Clinical Child & Adolescent Psychology, 47*(5), 847–862. https://doi.org/10.1080/15374416.2018.1485106

Facompré, C. R., Bernard, K., & Waters, T. E. A. (2018). Effectiveness of interventions in preventing disorganized attachment: A meta-analysis. *Development and Psychopathology, 20*(1), 1–11. https://doi.org/10.1017/S0954579417000426

Fandakova, Y., et al. (2019). Neural specificity of scene representations is related to memory performance in childhood. *NeuroImage, 199,* 105–113. https://doi.org/10.1016/j.neuroimage.2019.05.050

Fang, Z., et al. (2017). Post-conventional moral reasoning is associated with increased ventral striatal activity at rest and during task. *Scientific Reports, 7,* 7105. https://doi.org/10.1038/s41598-017-07115-w

Fantz, R. L. (1964). Visual experience in infants: Decreased attention to familiar patterns relative to novel ones. *Science, 146*(3644), 668–670. https://doi.org10.1126/science.146.3644.668

Farah, M. J. (2017a). The neuroscience of socioeconomic status: correlates, causes, and consequences. *Neuron, 96*(1), 56–71. https://doi.org/10.1016/j.neuron.2017.08.034

Farah, M. J. (2017b). Socioeconomic status and the brain: Prospects for neuroscience-informed policy. *Nature Reviews Neuroscience, 19,* 428–438. https://doi.org/10.1038/s41583-018-0023-2

Farkas, C., et al. (2018). Maternal mental state language during storytelling versus free-play contexts and its relation to child language and socioemotional outcomes at 12 and 30 months of age. *Cognitive Development, 47,* 181–197. https://doi.org/10.1016/j.cogdev.2018.06.009

Farr, R. H., Bruun, S. T., Doss, K. M., & Patterson, C. J. (2018a). Children's gender-types behavior from early to middle childhood in adoptive families with lesbian, gay, and heterosexual parents. *Sex Roles, 78*(7–8), 528–541. https://doi.org/10.1007/s11199-017-0812-5

Farr, R. H., Ravvina, Y., & Grotevant, H. D. (2018b). Birth family contact experiences among lesbian, gay, and heterosexual adoptive parents with school-age children. *Family Relations, 67*(1), 132–146. https://doi.org/10.1111/fare.12295

Farran, L. K., Lee, C-C., Yoo, H., & Oller, D. K. (2016). Cross-cultural register differences in infant-directed speech: An initial study. *PLOS ONE, 11*(3), e0151518. https://doi.org/10.1371/journal.pone.0151518

Farrell, A. H., & Vaillancourt, T. (2019). Temperament, bullying, and dating aggression: Longitudinal associations for adolescents in a romantic relationship. *Evolutionary Psychology, 17*(2), 1–13. https://doi.org/10.1177/1474704919847450

Farrelly, M. C., et al. (2017). Association between the real cost media campaign and smoking initiation among youths—United States, 2014–2016. *Morbidity and Mortality Weekly Report, 66*(2), 47–50. https://doi.org/10.15585/mmwr.mm6602a2

Fast, A. A., & Olson, K. R. (2018). Gender development in transgender preschool children. *Child Development, 89*(2), 620–637. https://doi.org/https://doi.org/10.1111/cdev.12758

Federal Office for Migration and Refugees (2019). *Child benefit and other benefits.* Retrieved from http://www.bamf.de/EN/Willkommen/KinderFamilie/Kindergeld/kindergeld-node.html

Fedewa, A. L., Black, W. W., & Ahn, S. (2015). Children and adolescents with same-gender parents: A meta-analytic approach in assessing outcomes. *Journal of GLBT Family Studies, 11*(1), 1–34. https//doi.org/10.1080/1550428X.2013.869486

Feldmann, R., Schallert, M., Nguyen, T., Och, U., Rutsch, F., & Weglage, J. (2018). Children and adolescents with phenylketonuria display fluctuations in their blood phenylalanine levels. *Acta Pædiatrica 108*(3), 541–543. https://doi.org/10.1111/apa.14517

Felmlee, D. H., McMillan, C., Rodis, P. I., & Osgood, D. W. (2018). The evolution of youth friendship networks from 6th to 12th grade: School transitions, popularity and centrality. In D. F. Alwin, D. H. Felmlee, & D. A. Kreager (Eds.), *Social networks and the life course* (pp. 161–184). Springer.

Ferrer-Wreder, K., & Kroger, J. (2020). *Identity in adolescence* (4th ed.). Routledge.

Ferrier, D. E., Karalus, S. P., Denham, S. A., & Bassett, H. H. (2018). Indirect effects of cognitive self-regulation on the relation between emotion knowledge and emotionality. *Early Child Development and Care, 188*(7), 966–979. https://doi.org/10.1080/03004430.2018.1445730

Ferschmann, L., et al. (2018). Personality traits are associated with cortical development across adolescence: A longitudinal structural MRI study. *Child Development, 89*(3), 811–822. https://doi.org/10.1111/cdev.13016

Field, T. (2017). Infant sleep problems and interventions: A review. *Infant Behavior and Development, 47*, 40–53. https://doi.org/10.1016/j.infbeh.2017.02.002

Field, T. (2018). Paternal prenatal, perinatal, and postpartum depression: A narrative review. *Journal of Anxiety & Depression, 1*(1), 102.

Fielding-Singh, P. (2019). You're worth what you eat: Adolescents beliefs about healthy eating, morality and socioeconomic status. *Social Science & Medicine, 220*, 41–48. https://doi.org/10.1016/j.socscimed.2018.10.022

Finan, L. J., Ohannessian, C. M., & Gordon, M. (2018). Trajectories of depressive symptoms from adolescence to emerging adulthood: The influence of parents, peers, and siblings. *Development al Psychology, 54*(8), 1555–1567. https://doi.org/10.1037/dev0000543

Finch, J. E., Johnson, A. D., & Phillips, D. A. (2015). Is sensitive caregiving in child care associated with children's effortful control skills? An exploration of linear and threshold effects. *Early Childhood Research Quarterly, 31*(2nd Quarter 2015), 125–134. https//doi.org/ 10.1016/j.ecresq.2014.12.007

Fink, E., Begeer, S., Peterson, C. C., Slaughter, V., & de Rosnay, M. (2015). Friendlessness and theory of mind: A prospective longitudinal study. *British Journal of Developmental Psychology, 33*(1), 1–17. https://doi.org/10.1111/bjdp.12060

Fink, E., Patalay, P., Sharpe, H., & Wolpert, M. (2018). Child- and school-level predictors of children's bullying behavior: A multilevel analysis in 648 primary schools. *Journal of Educational Psychology, 110*(1), 17–26. https://doi.org/0.1037/edu0000204

Finson, K. D. (2002). Drawing a scientist: What we do and do not know after fifty years of drawings. *School Science and Mathematics, 102*, 335–345. https://doi.org/10.1111/j.1949-8594.2002.tb18217.x

Firk, C., et al. (2018). Down-regulation of amygdala response to infant crying: A role for distraction in maternal emotion regulation. *Emotion, 18*(3), 412–423. http://dx.doi.org/10.1037/emo0000373

Fish, J. N., Baams, L., Wojciak, A. S., & Russell, S. T. (2019). Are sexual minority youth overrepresented in foster care, child welfare, and out-of-home placement? Findings from nationally representative data. *Child Abuse & Neglect, 89*, 203–211. https://doi.org/10.1016/j.chiabu.2019.01.005

Fisher, O., O'Donnell, S. C., & Oyserman, D. (2017). Social class and identity-based motivation. *Current Opinion in Psychology, 18*, 61–66. https://doi.org/10.1016/j.copsyc.2017.07.035

Fitzgerald, R. J. & Price, H. L. (2015). Eyewitness identification across the life span: A meta-analysis of age differences. *Psychological Bulletin.* https://doi.org/10.1037/bul0000013

Flavell, J. H. (1963). *The developmental psychology of Jean Piaget.* New York: Van Nostrand. https://doi.org/doi:10.1037/11449-000

Flavell, J. H. (1979). Metacognition and cognitive monitoring: A new area of cognitive–developmental inquiry. *American Psychologist, 34*(10), 906–911. https://doi.org/10.1037/0003-066X.34.10.906

Flavell, J. H., Beach, D. R., & Chinsky, J. M. (1966). Spontaneous verbal rehearsal in a memory task as a function of age. *Child Development, 37*(2), 283–299. https://doi.org/10.2307/1126804

Fleming-Milici, F., Harris, J. L., & Liu, S. (2018). Race, ethnicity, and other factors predicting U.S. parents' support for policies to reduce food and beverage marketing to children and adolescents. *Health Equity, 2*(1). https://doi.org/10.1089/heq.2018.0048

Flensborg-Madsen, T., & Mortensen, E. L. (2018). Associations of early developmental milestones with adult intelligence. *Child Development, 89*(2), 638–648. https://doi.org/10.1111/cdev.12760

Fletcher, K. L., & Reese, E. (2005). Picture book reading with young children: A conceptual framework. *Developmental Review, 25*, 64–103. https://doi.org/10.1016/j.dr.2004.08.009

Flook, L., Zahn-Waxler, C., & Davidson, R. J. (2019). Developmental differences in prosocial behavior between preschool and late elementary school. *Frontiers in Psychology.* https://doi.org/10.3389/fpsyg.2019.00876

Fogarty, M., et al. (2018). Delayed vs early umbilical cord clamping for preterm infants: A systematic review and meta-analysis. *American Journal of Obstetrics and Gynecology, 218*(1), 1–18. https://doi.org/10.1016/j.ajog.2017.10.231

Folkvord, F., & van't Riet, J. (2018). The persuasive effect of advergames promoting unhealthy foods among children: A meta-analysis. *Appetite, 129*, 245–251. https://doi.org/10.1016/j.appet.2018.07.020

Fombonne, E. (2018). Editorial: The rising prevalence of autism. *The Journal of Child Psychology and Psychiatry, 59*(7), 717–720. https://doi.org/10.1111/jcpp.12941

Fontaine, N. M. G., et al. (2019). Longitudinal associations between delinquency, depression and anxiety symptoms in adolescence: Testing the moderating effect of sex and family and socioeconomic status. *Journal of Criminal Justice, 62*, 58–65. https://doi.org/10.1016/j.jcrimjus.2018.09.007

Ford, C. A. et al. (2019). Effect of Primary Care Parent-Targeted Interventions on Parent-Adolescent Communication About Sexual Behavior and Alcohol Use. *JAMA Network Open, 2* (8): e199535 https://doi.org/10.1001/jamanetworkopen.2019.9535

Ford, J. A., et al. (2018). Sports involvement, injury history, and non-medical use of prescription opioids among college students: An analysis with a national sample. *The American Journal on Addictions, 27*, 15–22. https://doi.org/10.1111/ajad.12657

Forrest-Bank, S. S., Held, M. L., & Jones, A. (2019). Provider perspectives of services addressing the mental health needs of resettled refugee youth. *Child and Adolescent Social Work Journal, 36*(6), 669–684. https://doi.org/10.1007/s10560-019-00602-1

Foss, R. D., Smith, R. L., & O'Brien, N. P. (2019). School start times and teenage driver motor vehicle crashes. *Accident Analysis & Prevention, 126*, 54–63. https://doi.org/10.1016/j.aap.2018.03.031

Fox, N. A., Snidman, N., Hass, S. A., Degnan, K. A., & Kagan, J. (2015). The relations between reactivity at 4 months and behavioral inhibition in the second year: Replication across three independent samples. *Infancy, 20*(1), 98–114. https://doi.org/10.1111/infa.12063

Franck, L. S., et al. (2018). A novel method for involving women of color at high risk for preterm birth in research priority setting. *Journal of Visualized Experiments, 131*, 56220. https://doi.org/10.3791/56220

Franz, A. P., et al. (2018). Attention-deficit/hyperactivity disorder and very preterm/very low birthweight: A meta-analysis. *Pediatrics, 141*(1), e20171645. https://doi.org/10.1542/peds.2017-1645

Frederiksen, L., et al. (2018). Risk of adverse pregnancy outcomes at advanced maternal age. *Obstetrics & Gynecology, 131*(3), 457–463. https://doi.org/10.1097/AOG.0000000000002504

Freeman, K. J., Condron, D. J., & Steidl, C. R., (2019). Structures of stratification: Advancing a sociological debate over culture and resources. *Critical Sociology, 46*(2), 191–206. https://doi.org/10.1177/0896920518823888

Freitas-Simoes, T-M., Ros, E., & Sala-Vila, A. (2018). Telomere length as a biomarker of accelerated aging: Is it influenced by dietary intake? *Current Opinion in Clinical Nutrition & Metabolic Care, 21*(6), 430–436. https://doi.org/10.1097/MCO.0000000000000506

Frew, J. W. (2019). The hygiene hypothesis, old friends, and new genes. *Frontiers in Immunology.* https://doi.org/10.3389/fimmu.2019.00388

Frey, S., et al. (2018). Prenatal alcohol exposure is associated with adverse cognitive effects and distinct whole-genome DNA methylation patterns in primary school children. *Frontiers in Behavioral Neuroscience.* https://doi.org/10.3389/fnbeh.2018.00125

Frias-Lassere, D., Villagra, C. A., & Guerrero-Bosangna, C. (2018). Stress in the educational system as a potential source of epigenetic influences on children's development and behavior. *Frontiers in Behavioral Neuroscience.* https://doi.org/10.3389/fnbeh.2018.00143

Friedman-Krauss, A. H., Barnett, W. S., Weisenfeld, G. G., Kasmin, R., DiCrecchio, N., & Horowitz, M. (2018). *The State of Preschool 2017: State Preschool Yearbook.* National Institute for Early Education Research.

Friedrich, M., Mölle, M., Friederici, A. D., & Born, J. (2018). The reciprocal relation between sleep and memory in infancy: Memory-dependent adjustment of sleep spindles and spindle-dependent improvement of memories. *Developmental Science, 22*(2), e12743. https://doi.org/10.1111/desc.12743

Frijns, T., Keijsers, L., & Finkenauer, C. (2020). Keeping secrets from parents: On galloping horses, prancing ponies and pink unicorns. *Current Opinion in Psychology, 31,* 49–54. https://doi.org/10.1016/j.copsyc.2019.07.041

Fuentes, L., Ingerick, M., Jones, R., & Lindberg, L. (2018). Adolescents' and young adults' reports of barriers to confidential health care and receipt of contraceptive services. *Journal of Adolescent Health, 62*(1), 36–43. https://doi.org/10.1016/j.jadohealth.2017.10.011

Fujii, K. (2017). Re-verification with regard to Scammon's growth curve proposal of Fujimmon's growth curve as a tentative idea. *American Journal of Sport Science, 5*(3), 14–20. https//doi.org/10.11648/j.ajss.20170503.11

Fuligni, A. J. (2018). The need to contribute during adolescence. *Perspectives on Psychological Science, 14*(3), 331–343. https://doi.org/10.1177/1745691618805437

Fuligni, A. J., Dapretto, M., & Galván, A. (2018). Broadening the impact of developmental neuroscience on the study of adolescence. *Journal of Research on Adolescence, 28*(1), 150–153. https//doi.org/10.1111/jora.12373

Fullerton, L., et al. (2019). Suicide attempt resiliency in American Indian, Hispanic and Anglo youth in New Mexico: The influence of positive adult relationships. *Family & Community Health, 42*(3), 171–179. https//doi.org/10.1097/FCH.0000000000000223

Fumero, A., Marrero, R. J., Voltes, D., & Peñate, W. (2018). Personal and social factors involved in internet addiction among adolescents: A meta-analysis. *Computers in Human Behavior, 86,* 387–400. https://doi.org/10.1016/j.chb.2018.05.005

Funk, C., & Parker, K. (2018). *Diversity in the STEM workforce varies widely across jobs.* Retrieved from http://www.pewsocialtrends.org/2018/01/09/diversity-in-the-stem-workforce-varies-widely-across-jobs/

Furman, L. (2018). *Breast is best again and again.* Retrieved from http://www.aappublications.org/news/2018/09/27/breast-is-best-again-and-again-pediatrics-9-27-18

Fyfe, E. R., Rittle-Johnson, B., & Farran, D. C. (2019). Predicting success on high-stakes math tests from preschool math measures among children from low-income homes. *Journal of Educational Psychology, 111*(3), 402–413. https://doi.org/10.1037/edu0000298

Galambos, N. L., Johnson, M. D., & Krahn, H. J. (2018). The anger-depression connection: Between-persons and within-in-person associations from late adolescence to midlife. *Developmental Psychology, 54*(10), 1940–1953. http://dx.doi.org/10.1037/dev0000568

Galinsky, E., Bezos, J., McClelland, M., Carlson, S. M., & Zelazo, P. D. (2017). Civic science for public use: Mind in the Making and Vroom. *Child Development, 88*(5), 1409–1418. https//doi.org/10.1111/cdev.12892

Gallop, G. G., Jr. (1970). Chimpanzees: Self-recognition. *Science, 167,* 86–87. https://doi.org/10.1126/science.167.3914.86

Galván, A. (2019). The unrested adolescent brain. *Child Development Perspectives, 13*(3), 141–146. https//doi.org/10.1111/cdep.12332

Gámez-Guadix, M., & Mateos-Pérez, E. (2019). Longitudinal and reciprocal relationships between sexting, online sexual solicitations, and cyberbullying among minors. *Computers in Human Behavior, 94,* 70–76. https://doi.org/10.1016/j.chb.2019.01.004

Gandhi, A., et al. (2019). Maternal and peer attachment, identity formation, and non-suicidal self-injury: A longitudinal mediation study. *Child and Adolescent Psychiatry and Mental Health, 13*(7). https://doi.org/10.1186/s13034-019-0267-2

Gansen, H. M. (2019). Push-ups versus clean-up: Preschool teachers' gendered beliefs, expectations for behavior, and disciplinary practices. *Sex Roles, 80,* 393–408. https://doi.org/10.1007/s11199-018-0944-2

Gao, W., et al. (2019). A review of neuroimaging studies of genetic and environmental influences on brain development. *Neuroimage, 185,* 802–812. https//doi.org/10.1016/j.neuroimage.2018.04.032

Gao, Y., Wilson, G. R., Bozaglou, K., Elefanty, A. G., Stanley, E. G., Dottori, M., & Lockhart, P. J. (2018). Generation of RAB39B knockout isogenic human embryonic stem cell lines to model RAB39B-mediated Parkinson's disease. *Stem Cell Research, 28*, 161–164. https//doi.org/10.1016/j.scr.2018.02.015

Garandeau, C. F., & Lansu, T. A. M. (2019). Why does decreased likeability not deter adolescent bullying perpetrators? *Aggressive Behavior, 45*, 348–359. https//doi.org/10.1002/ab.21824

Garcia, T. A., et al. (2019). Growing up, hooking up, and drinking: A review of uncommitted sexual behavior and its association with alcohol use and related consequences among adolescents and young adults in the United States. *Frontiers in Psychology, 22*. https://doi.org/10.3389/fpsyg.2019.01872

Gardner, H. (2011). *Frames of mind: the theory of multiple intelligences, 30th year edition*. Basic Books.

Gardner, H. (2017). Taking a multiple intelligences (MI) perspective. *Behavioral and Brain Sciences, 40*, e203. https://doi.org/10.1017/S0140525X16001631

Garfield, C. F. (2018). Toward better understanding of how fathers contribute to their offspring's health. *Pediatrics, 141*(1), e20173461. https//doi.org/10.1542/peds.2017-3461

Garg, B. D., Kabra, N. S., & Balasubramanian, H. (2018). Role of massage therapy on the reduction of neonatal hyperbilirubinemia in term and preterm neonates: A review of clinical trials. *The Journal of Maternal-Fetal & Neonatal Medicine, 32*(2), 301–309. https://doi.org/10.1080/14767058.2017.1376316

Gargaro, B. A., et al. (2018). Attentional mechanisms in autism, ADHD, and autism–ADHD using a local–global paradigm. *Journal of Attention Disorders, 22*(14), 1320–1332. https://doi.org/10.1177/1087054715603197

Garon-Carrier, G. et al. (2018). Early developmental trajectories of number knowledge and math achievement from 4 to 10 years: Low-persistent profile and early-life predictors. *Journal of School Psychology, 68*, 84–98. https://doi.org/10.1016/j.jsp.2018.02.004.

Garrett-Peters, P., et al. (2019). Early student (dis)engagement: Contributions of household chaos, parenting, and self-regulatory skills. *Developmental Psychology, 55*(7), 1480–1492. http://dx.doi.org/10.1037/dev0000720

Gartzia, L., Pizarro, J., & Baniandres, J. (2018). Emotional androgyny: A preventative factor of psychosocial risks at work? *Frontiers in Psychology, 9*, 2144. https//doi.org/10.3389/fpsyg.2018.02144

Gash, A., & Raiskin, J. (2018). Parenting without protection: How legal status ambiguity affects gay parenthood. *Law & Social Inquiry, 43*(1), 82–118. https://doi.org/10.1111/lsi.12233

Gartstein, M. A., & Skinner, M. K. (2018). Prenatal influences on temperament development: The role of environmental epigenetics. *Development and Psychopathology, 30*, 1269–1303. https//doi.org/10.1017/S0954579417001730

Gayles, T. A., & Garofalo, R. (2019). Exploring the health issues of LGBT adolescents. In J. S. Schneider, V. M. B. Silenzio, & L. Erickson-Schroth (Eds.), *The GLMA handbook on LGBT health* (pp. 133–154). ABC-CLIO.

Geary, D. C., & van Marle, K. (2018). Growth of symbolic number knowledge accelerates as children understand cardinality. *Cognition, 177*, 69–78. https://doi.org/10.1016/j.cognition.2018.04.002

Gee, D. G., et al. (2018). Neurocognitive development of motivated behavior: Dynamic changes across childhood and adolescence. *The Journal of Neuroscience, 38*(44), 9433–9445. https://doi.org/10.1523/JNEUROSCI.1674-18.2018

Genovese, J. E. C. (2018). Evidence of a Flynn effect in children's human figure drawings (1902–1968). *The Journal of Genetic Psychology, 179*(4), 176–182. https://doi.org/10.1080/00221325.2018.1469113

Gerber, M., & Johnson, A. (2012). *Your self-confident baby: How to encourage your child's natural abilities—from the very start*. John Wiley & Sons.

Gerhardt, S. (2004). *Why love matters: How affection shapes a baby's brain*. Brunner-Routledge.

Gershoff, E. T., et al. (2018). The strength of the causal evidence against physical punishment of children and its implications for parents, psychologists, and policymakers. *American Psychologist, 73*(5), 636–638. https//doi.org/10.1037/amp0000327

Gervain, J. (2018). The role of prenatal experience in language development. *Current Opinion in Behavioral Sciences, 21*, 62–67. https://doi.org/10.1016/j.cobeha.2018.02.004

Gesell, A., Halverson, H. M., Thompson, H. Ilg, F. L., Castner, B. M., Ames, L. B., & Amatruda, C. S. (1940). *The first five years of life: A guide to the study of the preschool child*. New York: Harper & Row.

Ghosh, R., & Tabrizi, S. J. (2018). Huntington Disease. In D. H. Geschwind, H. L. Paulson, & C. Klein (Eds.), *Neurogenetics, Part 1: Handbook of Clinical Neurology* (pp. 255–278). Elsevier, https//doi.org/10.1016/B978-0-444-63233-3.00017-8

Gibson, J. J. (1979). *The ecological approach to visual perception*. Hillsdale, J: Lawrence Erlbaum Associates.

Gibson, E. J. (1997). An ecological psychologist's prolegomena for perceptual development: A functional approach. In C. Dent-Read & P. Zukow-Goldring (Eds.), *Evolving explanation of development* (pp. 23–45). Washington, D. C.: American Psychological Association.

Gibson, E. J. (2000). Perceptual learning in development: Some basic concepts. *Ecological Psychology, 12*(4), 295–302. https://doi.org/10.1207/S15326969ECO1204_04

Gibson, E. J., & Walk, R. D. (1960). The visual cliff. *Scientific American, 202*, 67–71.

Giedd, J. N. (2018). A ripe time for adolescent research. *Journal of Research on Adolescence, 28*(1), 157–159. https//doi.org/10.1111/jora.12378

Giedd, J. N., Keshavan, M., & Paus, T. (2008). Why do many psychiatric disorders emerge during adolescence? *Nature Reviews Neuroscience, 9*(12), 947–957. https://doi.org/10.1038/nrn2513

Gill, M., Koleilat, M., & Whaley, S. E. (2018). The impact of food insecurity on the home emotional environment among low-income mothers of young children. *Maternal and Child Health Journal, 22*(8), 1146–1153. https://doi.org/10.1007/s10995-018-2499-9

Gingrey, J. P. (2020). Maternal mortality: A U.S. public health crisis. *American Journal of Public Health, 110*(4), 462–464. https://doi.org/ 10.2105/AJPH.2019.305552

Gilmore, J. H., Knickmeyer, R. C., & Gao, W. (2018). Imaging structural and functional brain development in early childhood. *Nature Reviews Neuroscience, 19*, 123–137. https://doi.org/10.1038/nrn.2018.1

Gleason, J. B. (1958). "The child's learning of English morphology." *WORD* 14(2–3): 150–177. https://doi.org/10.1080/00437956.1958.11659661

Gleicher, N., et al. (2018). Older women using their own eggs? Issue framed with two oldest reported IVF pregnancies and a live birth. *Reproductive BioMedicine Online, 37*(2), 172–177. https://doi.org/10.1016/j.rbmo.2018.05.010

Glenn, A. L. (2019). Early life predictors of callous-unemotional and psychopathic traits. *Infant Mental Health Journal, 40*(1), 39–53. https://doi.org/10.1002/imhj.21757

Goddings, A-L., et al. (2019). Understanding the role of puberty in structural and functional development of the adolescent brain. *Journal of Research on Adolescence, 29*(1), 32–53. https//doi.org/10.1111/jora.12408

Godsell, S., & White, J. (2019). Adolescent perceptions of sleep and influences on sleep behavior: A qualitative study. *Journal of Adolescence, 73*, 18–25. https//doi.org/10.1016/j.adolescence.2019.03.010

Golan, O., Gordon, I., Fichman, K., & Keinan, G. (2018). Specific pattern of emotion recognition from faces in children with ASD: Results of a cross-modal matching paradigm. *Journal of Autism and Developmental Disorders, 48*(3), 844–852. https://doi.org/10.1007/s10803-017-3389-5

Goldberg, A. E., & Allen, K. R. (2018). Teaching undergraduates about LGBTQ identities, families, and intersectionality. *Family Relations, 67*, 176–191. https//doi.org/10.1111/fare.12224

Goldstein, T. R., Lerner, M. D., & Winner, E. (2017). The arts as a venue for developmental science: Realizing a latent opportunity. *Child Development, 88*(5). https://doi.org/10.1111/cdev.12884

Goldstein, J., & Ruch, W. (2018). Paul McGhee and humor research. *Humor: International Journal of Humor Research, 31*(2), 169–181. https://doi.org/10.1515/humor-2018-0031

Golinkoff, R. M., Can, D. D., Soderstrom, M., & Hirsh-Pasek, K. (2015). (Baby)talk to me: The social context of infant-directed speech and its effects on early language acquisition. *Current Directions in Psychological Science, 24*(5), 339–344. https//doi.org/10.1177/0963721415595345

Golinkoff, R. M., Hirsh-Pasek, K., Grob, R., & Schlesinger, M. (2017). "Oh, the Places You'll Go" by bringing developmental science into the world! *Child Development, 88*(5), 1403–1408. https//doi.org/10.1111/cdev.12929

Golinkoff, R. M., et al. (2018). Language matters: Denying the existence of the 30-million-word gap has serious consequences. *Child Development, 90*(3), 985–992. https//doi.org/10.1111/cdev.13128

Golombok, S., et al. (2018). Parenting and the adjustment of children born to gay fathers through surrogacy. *Child Development, 89*(4), 1223–1233. https//doi.org/10.1111/cdev.12728

Gómez-López, M., Viejo, C., & Ortega-Ruiz, R. (2019). Psychological well-being during adolescence: Stability and association with romantic relationships. *Frontiers in Psychology.* https://doi.org/10.3389/fpsyg.2019.01772

Gonzalez, et al. (2017). Latino maternal literacy beliefs and practices mediating socioeconomic status and maternal education effects in predicting child receptive vocabulary. *Early Education and Development, 28*(1), 78–95. https://doi.org/10.1080/10409289.2016.1185885

Goodin, A., Elswick, A., & Fallin-Bennett, A. (2019). Mental health disparities and high-risk alcohol use among non-heterosexual high school students. *Perspectives in Psychiatric Care, 55*(4), 570–575. https://doi.org/10.1111/ppc.12394

Goodman, J. B., Freeman, E. E., & Chalmers, K. A. (2018). The relationship between early life stress and working memory in adulthood: A systematic review and meta-analysis. *Memory, 27*(6). https://doi.org/10.1080/09658211.2018.1561897

Gottesman, I. I. (1963). Heritability of personality: A demonstration. *Psychological Monographs: General and Applied, 77*(9), 1–21. https://doi.org/10.1037/h0093852

Gottlieb, G. (1992). Individual development and evolution: The genesis of novel behavior. Oxford University Press.

Gottlieb, G. (2007). Probabilistic epigenesis. *Developmental Science, 10*(1). https://doi.org/10.1111/j.1467-7687.2007.00556.x

Gottman, J., & DeClaire, D. (1998). *Raising an emotionally intelligent child: The heart of parenting.* Simon & Schuster.

Gottschling , J., Hahn, E., Beam, C. R., Spinath, F. M., Carroll, S., & Turkheimer, E. (2019). Socioeconomic status amplifies genetic effects in middle childhood in a large German twin sample. *Intelligence, 72*, 20–27. https//doi.org/10.1016/j.intell.2018.11.006

Goudeau, S., & Croizet, J-C. (2017). Hidden advantages and disadvantages of social class: How classroom settings reproduce social inequality by staging unfair comparisons. *Psychological Science, 28*(2), 162–170. https//doi.org/10.1177/0956797616676600

Granger, K. L., Hanish, L. D., Kornienko, O., & Bradley, R. H. (2017). Preschool teachers' facilitation of gender and gender-neutral activities during free play. *Sex Roles, 76*, 498–510. https//doi.org/10.1007/s11199-016-0675-1

Green, E. L. (2019, November 6). Flint's children suffer in class after years of drinking the lead-poisoned water. *New York Times,* https://www.nytimes.com/2019/11/06/us/politics/flint-michigan-schools.html

Grenell, A., et al. (2019). Individual differences in the effectiveness of self-distancing for young children's emotion regulation. *British Journal of Developmental Psychology, 37*(1), 84–100. https://doi.org/10.1111/bjdp.12259

Greve, W., & Thomsen, T. (2016). Evolutionary advantages of free play during childhood. *Evolutionary Psychology, 14*(4), 1–9. https//doi.org/10.1177/1474704916675349

Gross, J. J. (Ed.). (2014). *Handbook of emotion regulation* (2nd ed.). Guilford Press.

Gross, J. J. (2015). Emotion regulation: Current status and future prospects. *Psychological Inquiry, 26*, 1–26. https//doi.org/10.1080/1047840X.2014.940781

Grossmann, T., & Jessen, S. (2017). When in infancy does the "fear bias" develop? *Journal of Experimental Child Psychology, 153*, 149–154. https://doi.org/10.1016/j.jecp.2016.06.018

Grossmann, T., Missana, M., & Krol, K. M. (2018). The neurodevelopmental precursors of altruistic behavior in infancy. *PLOS Biology, 16*(9), e2005281. https//doi.org/10.1371/journal.pbio.2005281

Groussard, M., Viader, F., Landeau, B., Desgranges, B., Eustache, F., & Platel, H. (2014). The effects of musical practice on structural plasticity: The dynamics of grey matter changes. *Brain and Cognition, 90*, 174–180. https://doi.org/10.1016/j.bandc.2014.06.013

Grygiel, P., et al. (2018). Peer rejection and perceived quality of relations with schoolmates among children with ADHD. *Journal of Attention Disorders, 22*(8), 738–751. https://doi.org/10.1177/1087054714563791

Gu, H et al. (2019). Facial emotion recognition in deaf children: Evidence from event-related potentials and event-related spectral perturbation analysis. *Neuroscience Letters, 703*, 198–204. https://doi.org/10.1016/j.neulet.2019.01.032

Gudmundsdottir, H., & Trehub, S. (2018). Adults recognize toddlers' song renditions. *Psychology of Music, 46*(2), 281–291. https://doi.org/10.1177/0305735617711762

Guest, A. M. (2018). The social organization of extracurricular activities: Interpreting developmental meanings in contrasting high schools. *Qualitative Psychology, 5*(1), 41–58. http://dx.doi.org/10.1037/qup0000069

Guglielmo, D., et al. (2018). Racial/ethnic sleep disparities in US school-aged children and adolescents: A review of the literature. *Sleep Health, 4*(1), 68–80. https://doi.org/10.1016/j.sleh.2017.09.005

Guilbert, T., et al. (2019). Racial disparities in asthma-related health outcomes in children with severe/difficult-to-treat asthma. *The Journal of Allergy and Clinical Immunology: In Practice, 7*(2), 568–577. https://doi.org/10.1016/j.jaip.2018.07.050

Guilliland, K., & Dixon, L. (2017). Re: women and babies need protection from the dangers of normal birth ideology. *BJOG: An International Journal of Obstetrics and Gynecology, 125*(3), 390–391. https://doi.org/10.1111/1471-0528.14945

Gülgöz, S., Gomez, E. M., DeMeules, M. R., & Olson, K. R. (2018). Children's evaluation and categorization of transgender children. *Journal of Cognition and Development, 19*(4), https://doi.org/10.1080/15248372.2018.1498338

Gunderson, E. A., et al. (2018). Parent praise to toddlers predicts fourth grade academic achievement via children's incremental mindsets. *Developmental Psychology, 54*(3), 397–409. http://dx.doi.org/10.1037/dev0000444

Gündoğan, A. (2018). Oh no monster! Do imaginative fears trigger creative imagination? *Early Child Development and Care.* https://doi.org/10.1080/03004430.2018.1523154

Gunn, H. E., et al. (2019). Young adolescent sleep is associated with parental monitoring. *Sleep Health, 5*(1), 58–63. https://doi.org/10.1016/j.sleh.2018.09.001

Gunn, H.E., & Eberhardt, K.R. (2019). *Current Hypertension Reports, 21*(39). https://doi.org/10.1007/s11906-019-0944-9

Gupta, A. P. & Lewontin, R. C. (1982). A study of reaction norms in natural populations of drosophilia pseudoosbcura. *Evolution, 36*(5), 934–948. https://doi.org/ 10.1111/j.1558-5646.1982.tb05464.x.

Gutierrez-Galve, L., Stein, A., & Hanington, L. (2018). Association of maternal and paternal depression in the postnatal period with offspring depression at age 18 years. *JAMA Psychiatry, 76*(3), 290–296. https//doi.org/10.1001/jamapsychiatry.2018.3667

Guttmacher Institute (2017). *Adolescent sexual and reproductive health in the United States*. Retrieved from https://www.guttmacher.org/fact-sheet/american-teens-sexual-and-reproductive-health

Guyer, A. E., Pérez-Edgar, K., & Crone, E. A. (2018). Opportunities for neurodevelopmental plasticity from infancy through early adulthood. *Child Development*. https://doi-org.scsu.idm.oclc.org/10.1111/cdev.13073

Ha, T., Kim, H., & McGill, S. (2019). When conflict escalates into intimate partner violence: The delicate nature of observed coercion in adolescent romantic relationships. *Development and Psychopathology, 31*(5), 1729–1739. https//doi.org/10.1017/S0954579419001007

Haahtela, T. (2019). A biodiversity hypothesis. *Allergy, 74*(8), 1445–1456. https://doi.org/10.1111/all.13763

Hadders-Algra, M. (2018). Early human brain development: Starring the subplate. *Neuroscience & Biobehavioral Reviews, 92*, 276–290. https://doi.org/10.1016/j.neubiorev.2018.06.017

Hadland, S. E. (2019). Epidemiology and historical drug use patterns. In J. Welsh & S. Hadland (Eds.), *Treating Adolescent Substance Use* (pp. 3–14). Springer.

Haghighat, M. D., & Knifsend, C. A. (2019). The longitudinal influence of 10th grade extracurricular involvement: Implications for 12th grade academic practices and future educational attainment. *Journal of Youth and Adolescence, 48*, 609–619. https://doi.org/10.1007/s10964-018-0947-x

Halim, M. L., et al. (2014). Pink frilly dressed and avoidance of all things "girly": Children's appearance rigidity and cognitive theories of gender development. *Developmental Psychology, 50*(4), 1091–1101. https//doi.org/10.1037/a0034906

Halim, M. L. D., et al. (2018). The roles of self-socialization and parent socialization in toddlers' gender-typed appearance. *Archives of Sexual Behavior, 47*(8), 2277–2285. https://doi.org/10.1007/s10508-018-1263-y

Halstead, M. E., Walter, K. D., & Moffatt, K. (2018). Sport-related concussion in children and adolescents. *Pediatrics, 142*(6), e20183074. https://doi.org/10.1542/peds.2018-3074

Han, J. & Neuharth-Pritchett, S. (2014). Parents' interactions with preschoolers during shared book reading: Three strategies for promoting quality interactions. *Childhood Education, 90*(1), 54–60. https://doi.org/10.1080/00094056.2014.872516

Hammond, S. I. (2014). Children's early helping in action: Piagetian developmental theory and early prosocial behavior. *Frontiers in Psychology, 5*, 759. https://doi.org/10.3389/fpsyg.2014.00759

Han, J., O'Connor, E. E., & McCormick, M. P. (2019). The role of elementary school and home quality in supporting sustained effects of pre-K. *Journal of Educational Psychology*. Advance online publication. https://doi.org/10.1037/edu0000390

Handelsman, D. J. (2017). Sex differences in athletic performance coincide with the onset of male puberty. *Clinical Endocrinology, 87*, 68–72. https//doi.org/10.1111/cen.13350

Hanno, E., & Surrain, S. (2019). The direct and indirect relations between self-regulation and language development among monolinguals and dual language learners. *Clinical Child and Family Psychology Review, 22*(1), 75–89. https://doi.org/10.1007/s10567-019-00283-3

Hannula-Sormunen M.M., McMullen J., Lehtinen E. (2019) Everyday Context and Mathematical Learning: On the Role of Spontaneous Mathematical Focusing Tendencies in the Development of Numeracy. In A. Fritz, V. Haase, & P. Räsänen (Eds.) *International Handbook of Mathematical Learning Difficulties*. Cham, CH: Springer.

Hanson, J. L., et al. (2018). A family focused intervention influence hippocampal-prefrontal connectivity through gains in self-regulation. *Child Development*. https://doi-org.scsu.idm.oclc.org/10.1111/cdev.13154

Hantman, G. B. (2011). Holophrases. *Encyclopedia of Child Behavior and Development, 746*. New York, NY: Springer.

Hardy, S., Ng, C., Cunningham, S., & Kramer, M. (2019). Abstract 036: Contemporary estimates of obesity incidence in the United States. *Circulation, 139*(1), A036. https://doi.org/10.1161/circ.139.suppl_1.036

Hardy, T. M., et al. (2018). Exploring the ovarian reserve within health parameters: A latent class analysis. *Western Journal of Nursing Research, 40*(12), 1903–1918. https://doi.org/10.1177/0193945918792303

Harley, K. G. et al. (2019). Association of phthalates, parabens, and phenols found in personal care products with pubertal timing in girls and boys. *Human Reproduction, 34*(1), 109–117. https://doi.org/10.1093/humrep/dey337

Harlow, H. (1958). The nature of love. *American Psychologist, 13*, 678–685.

Harris, S. K. et al. (2017). Research on clinical preventive services for adolescents and young adults: Where are we and where to we need to go? *Journal of Adolescent Health, 60*(3), 249–260. https://doi.org/10.1016/j.jadohealth.2016.10.005

Harris, T. S. & Ramsey, M. (2015). Paternal modeling, household availability, and paternal intake as predictors of fruit, vegetable, and sweetened beverage consumption among Black children. *Appetite, 85*, 171–177. https//doi.org/10.1016/j.appet.2014.11.008

Harrison, F. et al. (2017). Weather and children's physical activity: How and why do relationships vary between countries?. *International Journal of Behavioral Nutrition and Physical Activity, 14*(74). https://doi.org/10.1186/s12966-017-0526-7

Hart, B. & Risley, T. R. (2003). The early catastrophe: The 30 million word gap by age 3. *American Educator*. Retrieved from: http://www.aft.org/pubs-reports/american_educator/spring2003/catastrophe.html

Hartanto, A., Toh, W. X., & Yang, H. (2018). Bilingualism narrows socioeconomic disparities in executive functions and self-regulatory behaviors during early childhood: Evidence from the early childhood longitudinal study. *Child Development.* https://doi-org.scsu.idm.oclc.org/10.1111/cdev.13032

Harter, S. (2012). *The construction of the self: Development and sociocultural foundations* (2nd ed.). Guilford Press.

Harter, S. (2016). I-self and me-self processes affecting developmental psychopathology and mental health. In D. Cicchetti (Ed.), *Developmental psychopathology: Theory and method* (pp. 470–526). John Wiley & Sons.

Hartl, A. C., Laursen, B., Cantin, S., & Vitaro, F. (2019). A test of the bistrategic control hypothesis of adolescent popularity. *Child Development.* https://doi.org/10.1111/cdev.13269

Harville, E. W., Myers, L., Shu, T., Wallace, M. E., & Bazzano, L. A. (2018). Pre-pregnancy cardiovascular risk factors and racial disparities in birth outcomes: The Bogalusa Heart Study. *BMC Pregnancy and Childbirth, 18*(339). https//doi.org/10.1186/s12884-018-1959-y

Hashemipour, M., Kelishadi, R., Medhi Amin, M. M., & Ebrahim, K. (2018). Is there any association between phthalate exposure and precocious puberty in girls? *Environmental Science and Pollution Research, 25*(14), 13589–13596. https://doi.org/10.1007/s11356-018-1567-4

Hassinger-Das, B., Hirsh-Pasek, K., & Golinkoff, R. M. (2017). The case of brain science and guided play: A developing story. *Young Children, 72*(2), 45–50.

Hay, D. F., et al. (2018). Seven-year-olds' aggressive choices in a computer game can be predicted in infancy. *Developmental Science, 21*(3), e12576. https://doi.org/10.1111/desc.12576

Hayes, J. F., Eichen, D. W., Barch, D. M., & Wilfley, D. E. (2018). Executive function in childhood obesity: Promising intervention strategies to optimize treatment outcomes. *Appetite, 124*, 10–23. https://doi.org/10.1016/j.appet.2017.05.040

Haywood, K. M., & Getchell, N. (2020). *Life span motor development* (7th ed). Human Kinetics.

Healey-Stoffel, M., & Levant, B. (2018). N-2 (Omega-3) fatty acids: Effects on brain dopamine systems and potential role in the etiology and treatment of neuropsychiatric disorders. *CNS & Neurological Disorders, 17*(3), 216–232. https://doi.org/10.2174/1871527317666180412153612

Heath, R. D., Anderson, C., Turner, A. C., & Payne, C. M. (2018). Extracurricular activities and disadvantaged youth: A complicated—but promising—study. *Urban Education.* https://doi.org/10.1177/0042085918805797

Heckman, J. J. (2011). The economics of inequality: The value of early childhood education. *American Educator, 35*(1), 31–35.

Hedges, S. H., Shea, V., & Mesibov, G. B. (2018). Age-related issues in the assessment of autism spectrum disorder. In S. Goldstein & S. Ozonoff (Eds.), *Assessment of autism spectrum disorder* (2nd ed., pp. 130–146). Guilford Press.

He, J., Koot, H. M., Buil, J. M., & van Lier, P. A. C. (2018). Impact of low social preference on the development of depressive and aggressive symptoms: Buffering by children's prosocial behavior. *Journal of Abnormal Child Psychology, 46*(7), 1497–1507. https://doi.org/10.1007/s10802-017-0382-6

Hee, P. J., Yu, X., & Krieg, A. (2017). Validation of the head-toes-knees-shoulders tasks in Native Hawaiian and non-Hawaiian children. *Early Childhood Research Quarterly, 44*(3), 192–205. https://doi.org/10.1016/j.ecresq.2017.12.007

Heflin, C., Kukla-Acevedo, S., & Darolia, R. (2019). Adolescent food insecurity and risky behaviors and mental health during the transition to adulthood. *Children and Youth Services Reviews, 105.* https://doi.org/10.1016/j.childyouth.2019.104416

Heilmann, J. J., Moyle, M. J., & Rueden, A. M. (2018). Using alphabet knowledge to track the emergent literacy skills of children in Head Start. *Topics in Early Childhood Special Education, 38*(2), 118–128. https://doi.org/10.1177/0271121418766636

Heinze, J. E., et al. (2018). Friendship attachment style moderates the effect of adolescent exposure to violence on emerging adult depression and anxiety trajectories. *Journal of Youth and Adolescence, 47*, 177–193. https//doi.org/10.1007/s10964-017-0729-x

Hellemans, A. & Bryan, B. (1988). *The timetables of science: A chronology of the most important people and events in science.* New York, NY: Simon & Schuster. https://doi.org/10.1177/027046768900900473

Hemming, L., Haddock, G., Shaw, J., & Pratt, D. (2019). Alexithymia and its associations with depression, suicidality, and aggression: An overview. *Frontiers in Psychiatry.* https://doi.org/10.3389/fpsyt.2019.00203

Hendrickx, M. M. H. G., et al. (2017). Teacher behavior and peer liking and disliking: The teacher as a social referent for peer status. *Journal of Educational Psychology, 109*(4), 546–558. http://dx.doi.org/10.1037/edu0000157

Henrich, J., Heine, S. J., & Norenzayan, A. (2010). The weirdest people in the world? *Behavioral and Brain Sciences, 2–3*, 61–83. https://doi-org.scsu.idm.oclc.org/10.1017/S0140525X0999152X

Hentges, R. F., Shaw, D. S., & Wang, M-T. (2018). Early childhood parenting and child impulsivity as precursors to aggression, substance use, and risky sexual behavior in adolescence and early adulthood. *Development and Psychopathology, 30*(4), 1305–1319. https//doi.org/10.1017/S0954579417001596

Hernandez, D. J. (2012). *Double jeopardy: How third-grade reading skills and poverty influence high school graduation.* Annie E. Casey Foundation. Retrieved from http://www.aecf.org/resources/ double-jeopardy/

Hess, J. M., Lilo, E. A., Cruz, T. H., & Davis, S. M. (2019). Perceptions of water and sugar-sweetened beverage consumption among teens, parents and teachers in the rural south-western USA. *Public Health Nutrition, 22*(8), 1376–1387. https://doi.org/10.1017/S1368980019000272

Hidalgo, M. A., & Chen, D. (2019). Experiences of gender minority stress in cisgender parents of transgender/gender-expansive prepubertal children: A qualitative study. *Journal of Family Issues, 40*(7), 865–886. https//doi.org/o0r.g1/107.171/0717/90215921531X3X1919882299502

Hihara, S., Sugimura, K., & Syed, M. (2018). Forming a negative identity in contemporary society: Shedding light on the most problematic identity resolution. *Identity: An International Journal of Theory and Research, 18*(4), 325–333. https://doi.org/10.1080/15283488.2018.1524329

Hill, S. (2013). *The myth of low-tax America: Why Americans are not getting their money's worth.* Retrieved from: https://www.theatlantic.com/business/archive/2013/04/the-myth-of-low-tax-america-why-americans-arent-getting-their-moneys-worth/274945/

Hiniker, A., Schoenebeck, S. Y., & Kientz, J. A. (2016). *Not at the dinner table: Parents' and children's perspectives on family technology rules.* CSCW '16: Proceedings of the 19th AMC Conference on Computer-Supported Cooperative Work & Social Computing. http://dx.doi.org/10.1145/2818048.2819940

Hinkley, T., Brown, H., Carson, V., & Teychenne, M. (2018). Cross sectional association of screen time and outdoor play with social skills in preschool children. *PLOS ONE, 13*(4), e0193700. https://doi.org/10.1371/journal.pone.0193700

Hjetland, H. N., et al. (2018). Pathways to reading comprehension: A longitudinal study from 4 to 9 years of age. *Journal of Educational Psychology, 111*(5), 751–763. http://dx.doi.org/10.1037/edu0000321

Ho, P., & Kao, G. (2018) Educational achievement and attainment differences among minorities and immigrants. In B. Schneider (Ed.), *Handbook of the sociology of education in the 21st century.* Handbooks of sociology and social research. Springer, https://doi.org/10.1007/978-3-319-76694-2_5

Hoare, C. H. (2005). Erikson's general and adult developmental revisions of Freudian thought: "Outward, forward, and upward". *Journal of Adult Development, 12*(1), 19–31.

Hodes, M. (2019). New developments in the mental health of refugee children and adolescents. *Evidence Based Mental Health, 22,* 72–76. http://dx.doi.org/10.1136/ebmental-2018-300065

Hodes, M., Anagnostopoulos, D., & Skokauskas, N. (2018). Challenges and opportunities in refugee mental health: Clinical, service, and research considerations. *European Child & Adolescent Psychiatry, 27*(4), 385–388. https://doi.org/10.1007/s00787-018-1115-2

Hoff, E. (2006). Language experience and language milestones during early childhood. In (K. McCartney & D. Phillips (Eds.), *Blackwell Handbook of Early Childhood Development* (p. 233–251). Malden, MA: Blackwell Publishing.

Hoff, E. (2013). Interpreting the early language trajectories of children from low-SES and language minority homes: Implications for closing achievement gaps. *Developmental Psychology, 49*(1), 4–14. https//doi.org/10.1037/a0027238

Hoff, E. (2014). *Language development* (5th ed.). Cengage Learning.

Hoff, E. (2018). Lessons from the study of input effects on bilingual development. *International Journal of Bilingualism, 24*(1), 82–88. https://doi.org/10.1177/1367006918768370

Hoff, K. A., Briley, D. A., Wee, C. J. M., & Rounds, J. (2018). Normative changes in interests from adolescence to adulthood: A meta-analysis of longitudinal studies. *Psychological Bulletin, 144*(4), 426–451. http://dx.doi.org/10.1037/bul0000140

Hofstee, P., McKeating, D. R., Perkins, A. V., & Cuffe, J. S. M. (2018). Placental adaptation to micronutrient dysregulation in the programming of chronic disease. *Clinical and Experimental Pharmacology and Physiology, 45*(8), 871–884. https://doi.org/10.1111/1440-1681.12954

Hogan, C. M., et al. (2018). Parental perceptions, risks, and incidence of pediatric unintentional injuries. *Journal of Emergency Nursing, 44*(3), 267–273. https://doi.org/10.1016/j.jen.2017.07.017

Hollander, J., McNivens, M., Pautassi, R.M, & Nizhnikov, M.E (2018). Offspring of male rats exposed to binge alcohol exhibit heightened ethanol intake at infancy and alterations in T-maze performance. *Alcohol, 76,* 65–71. https//doi.org/10.1016/j.alcohol.2018.07.013

Holley, C. E., Haycraft, E., & Farrow, C. (2018). Predicting children's fussiness with vegetables: The role of feeding practices. *Maternal & Child Nutrition, 14*(1), e12442. https://doi.org/10.1111/mcn.12442

Holmes, J. (1993). *John Bowlby and attachment theory.* London: Routledge.

Hooker, G. W., Babu, D., Myers, M. F., Zierhut, H., & McAllister, M. (2017). Standards for the reporting of genetic counseling interventions in research and other studies (GCIRS): An NGSC Task Force report. *Journal of Genetic Counseling, 26*(3), 355–360. https//doi.org/10.1007/s10897-017-0076-9

Hooley, J. M., & Franklin, J. C. (2018). Why do people hurt themselves? A new conceptual model of nonsuicidal self-injury. *Clinical Psychological Science, 6*(3), 428–451. https://doi.org/10.1177/2167702617745641

Hooven, J. T., Fogel, B. N., Waxmonsky, J G., & Sekhar, D. L. (2018). Exploratory study of barriers to successful office contacts for attention deficit hyperactivity disorder. *ADHD Attention Deficit and Hyperactivity Disorders, 10*, 237–243. https//doi.org/10.1007/s12402-017-0246-5

Horm, D. M., et al. (2018). Associations between continuity of care in infant-toddler classrooms and child outcomes. *Early Childhood Research Quarterly, 42*, 105–118. https://doi.org/10.1016/j.ecresq.2017.08.002

Horst, J. S., & Houston-Price, C. (2015). Editorial: An open book: What young children learn from picture and story books. *Frontiers in Psychology.* https://doi.org/10.3389/fpsyg.2015.01719

Horta, B. L., de Sousa, B. A., & de Mola, C. L. (2018). Breastfeeding and neurodevelopmental outcomes. *Current Opinion in Clinical Nutrition and Metabolic Care, 21*(3), 174–178. https://doi.org/10.1097/MCO.0000000000000453

Hoskovec, J. M., et al. (2018). Projecting the supply and demand for certified genetic counselors: A workforce study. *Journal of Genetic Counseling, 27*(1), 16–20. https//doi.org/10.1007/s10897-017-0158-8

Housman, D. K., Denham, S. A., & Cabral, H. (2018). Building young children's emotional competence and self-regulation from birth: The begin to … ECSEL approach. *International Journal of Emotion Education, 10*(2), 5–25. http://oaji.net/articles/2017/4987-1543496038.pdf

Howe, M. L. (2019). Unravelling the nature of early (autobiographical) memory. *Memory, 27*(1). https://doi.org/10.1080/09658211.2019.1537140

Howe, N. & Recchia, H. (2014). Sibling relationships as a context for learning and development. *Early Education and Development, 25*(2), 155–159. https://doi.org/10.1080/10409289.2014.857562

Howell, E. (2018). Reducing disparities in severe maternal morbidity and mortality. *Clinical Obstetrics and Gynecology, 61*(2), 387–399. https//doi.org/10.1097/GRF.0000000000000349

Howell, E. A., Hebert, P. L. & Zeitlin, J. (2019). Racial segregation and inequality of care in neonatal intensive care units in unacceptable. *JAMA Pediatrics, 173*(5), 420–421. https://doi.org/ 10.1001/jamapediatrics.2019.0240

Hoyniak, C. P., Bates, J. E, Staplese, A. D., Rudasill, K. M., Molfese, D. L., & Molfese, V. J. (2018). Child sleep and socioeconomic context in the development of cognitive abilities in early childhood. *Child Development.* https://doi-org.scsu.idm.oclc.org/10.1111/cdev.13042

Hritz, A. C., Royer, C. E., Helm, R. K., Burd, K. A., Ojeda, K., & Ceci, S. J. (2015). Children's suggestibility research: Things to know before interviewing a child. *Anuario de Psicología Jurídica, 25*(1), 3–12. https://doi.org/10.1016/j.apj.2014.09.002

Hua, P., Bugeja, L., & Maple, M. (2019). A systematic review on the relationship between childhood exposure to external cause parental death, including suicide, on subsequent suicidal behavior. *Journal of Affective Disorders, 257*, 723–734. https://doi.org/10.1016/j.jad.2019.07.082

Huang, S-F., Oi, M., & Taguchi, A. (2015). Comprehension of figurative language in Taiwanese children with autism: The role of theory of mind and receptive vocabulary. *Clinical Linguistics & Phonetics, 29*(8–10), 764–775. https://doi.org/10.3109/02699206.2015.1027833

Huber, C., Gerullis, A., Gebhardt, M., & Schwab, S. (2018). The impact of social referencing on social acceptance of children with disabilities and migrant background: An experimental study in primary school settings. *European Journal of Special Needs Education, 33*(2), 269–285. https://doi.org/10.1080/08856257.2018.1424778

Huber, E., Donnelly, P. M., Rokem, A., & Yeatman, J. D. (2018). Rapid and widespread white matter plasticity during an intensive reading intervention. *Nature Communications, 9*, 2260. https://doi.org/10.1038/s41467-018-04627-5

Hughes, C., & Devine, R. T. (2019). For better or worse?: Positive and negative parental influences on young children's executive function. *Child Development.* https://doi-org.scsu.idm.oclc.org/10.1111/cdev.12915

Hughes, C., McHarg, G., & White, N. (2018). Sibling influences on prosocial behavior. *Current Opinion in Psychology, 20*, 96–101.

Hughes, H. K., et al. (2017). Pediatric asthma health disparities: Race, hardship, housing, and asthma in a national survey. *Academic Pediatrics, 17*(2), 127–134. https://doi.org/10.1016/j.acap.2016.11.011

Humble, J. J., et al. (2018). Child-centered play therapy for youths who have experienced trauma: A systematic literature review. *Journal of Child & Adolescent Trauma, 12*, 365–375. https://doi.org/10.1007/s40653-018-0235-7

Humpal, M. (2015). Music therapy for developmental issues in early childhood (pp. 265–276). In B. L. Wheeler (Ed.), *Music therapy handbook.* New York, NY: The Guilford Press.

Humphreys, K. L., et al. (2018). Stressful life events, ADHD symptoms, and brain structure in early adolescence. *Journal of Abnormal Child Psychology, 47,* 421–432. https://doi.org/10.1007/s10802-018-0443-5

Huntsinger, C. S. Jose, P., Krieg, D. B., & Luo, Z. (2010). Cultural differences in Chinese American and European American children's drawing skills over time. *Early Childhood Research Quarterly, 26*(1), 134–145. https://doi.org/10.1016/j.ecresq.2010.04.002

Huppert, E., et al. (2018). The development of children's preferences for equality and equity across 13 individualistic and collectivistic cultures. *Developmental Science, 22*(2), e12729. https://doi.org/10.1111/desc.12729

Hurrell, K. & Stack, M. (2017). Initiative versus guilt. In V. Zeigler-Hill & T. Shackelford (Eds.), *Encyclopedia of personality and individual differences.* Cham, CH: Springer. https://doi.org/10.1007/978-3-319-28099-8_597-1

Hurrell, K. E., Houwing, F. L., & Hudson, J. L. (2017). Parental meta-emotion philosophy and emotion coaching in families of children and adolescents with an anxiety disorder. *Journal of Abnormal Child Psychology, 45*(3), 569–582.

Hussong, A. M., Jones, D. J., & Jensen, M. (2018). Synthesizing a Special Issue on Parenting Adolescents in an Increasingly Diverse World. *Journal of Research on Adolescence, 28*(3), 665–673. https//doi.org/10.1111/jora.12397

Hutton, J. S., et al. (2017). Shared reading and television across the perinatal period in low-SES households. *Clinical Pediatrics, 57*(8), 904–912. https://doi.org/10.1177/0009922817737077

Hyde, J. S., et al. (2019). The future of sex and gender in psychology: Five challenges to the gender binary. *American Psychologist, 74*(2), 171–193. http://dx.doi.org/10.1037/amp0000307

Icenogle, G., et al. (2019). Adolescents' cognitive capacity reaches adult levels prior to their psychosocial maturity: Evidence for a 'maturity gap' in a multinational, cross-sectional sample. *Law and Human Behavior, 43*(1), 69–85. http://dx.doi.org/10.1037/lhb0000315

Ilgaz H., Hassinger-Das B., Hirsh-Pasek K., Golinkoff R.M. (2018). Making the case for playful learning. In M. Fleer & B. van Oers (Eds.), *International handbook of early childhood education.* Springer International Handbooks of Education. Springer, https://doi.org/10.1007/978-94-024-0927-7_64

Inhelder, B., & Piaget, J. (1958). *An essay on the construction of formal operational structures. The growth of logical thinking: From childhood to adolescence* (A. Parsons & S. Milgram, Trans.). Basic Books. https://doi.org/10.1037/10034-000

Inhelder, B., & Piaget, J. (1964). *The early growth of logic in the child: Classification and seriation.* Harper & Row.

Inhorn, M. C. (2018). Elective egg freezing and its underlying socio-demography: A binational analysis with global implications. *Reproductive Biology and Endocrinology, 16*(70). https://doi.org/10.1186/s12958-018-0389-z

International Society for Stem Cell Research (2016). Guidelines for stem cell research and clinical translation. Retrieved from: https://www.isscr.org/docs/default-source/all-isscr-guidelines/guidelines-2016/isscr-guidelines-for-stem-cell-research-and-clinical-translationd67119731dff6ddbb37cff0000940c19.pdf?sfvrsn=4

Irwin, J., & Turcios, J. (2017). Teaching and learning guide for audiovisual speech perception: A new approach and implications for clinical populations. *Language and Linguistics Compass, 11*(3), 92–97. https//doi.org/10.1111/lnc3.12238

Isaacs, D. (2018). Perplexing perinatal practices. *Child Health, 54*(2), 113–114. https//doi.org/10.1111/jpc.13839

Ispa, J. M., Carlo, G., Palermo, F., Su-Russell, C., Harmeyer, E., & Streit, C. (2015). Middle childhood feelings toward mothers: Predictions from maternal directiveness at the age of two and respect for autonomy cruelty. *Social Development.* https://doi.org/:10.1111/sode.12108

Jabagchourian, J. J., Sorkhabi, N., Quach, W., & Strage, A. (2014). Parenting styles and practices of Latino parents and Latino fifth graders' academic, cognitive, social, and behavioral outcomes. *Hispanic Journal of Behavioral Sciences, 36*(2), 175–194. https://doi.org/10.1177/0739986314523289

Jabès, A. & Nelson, C. A. (2015). 20 years after "The ontogeny of human memory: A cognitive neuroscience perspective" where are we? *International Journal of Behavioral Development.* https//doi.org/10.1177/0165025415575766

Jaeger, E. L. (2016). Negotiating complexity: A bioecological systems perspective on literacy development. *Human Development, 59,* 163–187. https://doi.org/10.1159/000448743

Jager, J. J., Putnick, D. L., & Bornstein, M. H. (2017). More than just convenient: The scientific merits of homogenous convenience samples. *Monographs of the Society for Research in Child Development, 82*(2), 13–30. https://doi.org/10.1111/mono.12296

Jahdi, F., et al. (2017). Yoga during pregnancy: The effects of labor pain and delivery outcomes (A randomized controlled trial). *Complementary Therapies in Clinical Practice, 27,* 1–4. https://doi.org/10.1016/j.ctcp.2016.12.002

Jambon, M., et al. (2018). The development of empathic concern in siblings: A reciprocal influence model. *Child Development, 90*(5), 1598–1613. https://doi.org/10.1111/cdev.13015

Jambon, M., & Smetana, J. G. (2018). Self-reported moral emotions and physical and relational aggression in early childhood: A social domain approach. *Child Development, 91*(1), e92–e107. https//doi.org/10.1111/cdev.13174

James, W. (1890/1998). *The principles of psychology, Vol. 1.* New York, NY: Henry Holt.

James-Kangal, N., Weitbrecht, E. M., Francis, T. E., & Whitton, S. W. (2018). Hooking up and emerging adults' relationship attitudes and expectations. *Sexuality & Culture, 22*(3), 706–723. https://doi.org/10.1007/s12119-018-9495-5

Jamieson, A., and Radick, G. (2017). Genetic determinism in the genetics curriculum: An exploratory study of the effects of Mendelian and Weldonian emphases. *Science and Education, 26*(10), 1261–1290. https://doi.org/10.1007/s11191-017-9900-8

Janecka, M., et al. (2018). Advanced paternal age effects in neurodevelopmental disorders—Review of potential underlying mechanisms. *Translational Psychiatry, 7*, e1019. https://doi.org/10.1038/tp.2016.294

Janevic, T., et al. (2018). Association of race/ethnicity with very preterm neonatal morbidities. *JAMA Pediatrics, 172*(11), 1061–1069. https://doi.org/10.1001/jamapediatrics.2018.2029

Jankowska, D.M., & Omelańczuk, I. (2019) Imaginative play, socio-emotional competence, and sociometric status in preschool children: Common methodological problems and new research directions. In I. Lebuda & V. Glǎveanu (Eds.), *The Palgrave handbook of social creativity research* (pp. 76–90). Palgrave Studies in Creativity and Culture. Palgrave Macmillan, https://doi.org/10.1007/978-3-319-95498-1_6

Jarraya, S., Wagner, M., Jarraya, M., & Engel, F. A. (2019). 12 weeks of kindergarten-based yoga practice increases visual attention, visual-motor precision and decreases behavior of inattention and hyperactivity in 5-year-old children. *Frontiers in Psychology.* https://doi.org/10.3389/fpsyg.2019.00796

Jenney, A., & Exner-Cortens, D. (2018). Toxic masculinity and mental health in young women: An analysis of 13 reasons why. *Affilia: Journal of Women and Social Work, 33*(3), 410–417. https://doi.org/10.1177/0886109918762492

Jennings, M. O., Owen, R. C., Keefe, D., & Kim, E. D. (2017). Management and counseling of the male with advanced paternal age. *Fertility and Sterility, 107*(2), 324–328. https://doi.org/10.1016/j.fertnstert.2016.11.018

Jensen, A. C. & McHale, S. M. (2017). Mothers', fathers', and siblings' perceptions of parents' differential treatment of siblings: Links with family relationship qualities. *Journal of Adolescence, 60*, 119–129. https://doi.org/10.1016/j.adolescence.2017.08.002

Jeon, L., Kwon, K-A., & Choi, J. Y. (2018). Family child care providers' responsiveness toward children: The role of professional support and perceived stress. *Children and Youth Services Review, 94*, 500–510. https://doi.org/10.1016/j.childyouth.2018.08.023

Jewett, C., & Luthra, S. (2018). Defendants in diapers? Immigrant toddlers ordered to appear in court alone. *Kaiser Health News.* Retrieved from https://khn.org/news/defendants-in-diapers-immigrant-toddlers-ordered-to-appear-in-court-alone/

Jeynes, W. H. (2017). A meta-analysis: The relationship between parental involvement and Latino student outcomes. *Education and Urban Society, 49*(1), 4–28. https://doi.org/10.1177/0013124516630596

Jin, K-S., et al. (2018). Young infants expect an unfamiliar adult to comfort a crying baby: Evidence from a standard violation-of-expectation task and a novel infant-triggered task. *Cognitive Psychology, 102*, 1–20. https://doi.org/10.1016/j.cogpsych.2017.12.004

Jolley, R. P. (2010). *Children & pictures: Drawing and understanding.* Wiley-Blackwell.

Johansson, A., et al. (2019). Epigenome-wide association study for lifetime estrogen exposure identifies and epigenetic signature associated with breast cancer risk. *Clinical Epigenetics, 11*(66). https://doi.org/10.1186/s13148-019-0664-7

Johnco, C., & Rapee, R. M. (2018). Depression literacy and stigma influence how parents perceive and respond to adolescent depressive symptoms. *Journal of Affective Disorders, 241*, 599–607. https://doi.org/10.1016/j.jad.2018.08.062

Johnson, A. M., et al. (2017). Emotion socialization and child conduct problems: A comprehensive review and meta-analysis. *Clinical Psychology Review, 54*, 65–80. http://dx.doi.org/10.1016/j.cpr.2017.04.001

Johnson, D., et al. (2018). Adult mental health outcomes of adolescent depression: A systematic review. *Depression & Anxiety, 35*(8), 700–716. https://doi.org/10.1002/da.22777

Johnson, R. C. & Jackson, C. K. (2019). Reducing inequality Inequality through dynamic complementarity: Evidence from Head Start and public school spending." *American Economic Journal: Economic Policy,* 11 (4): 310–49. https://doi.org/10.1257/pol.20180510

Jonas, K., & Kochanska, G. (2018). An imbalance of approach and effortful control predicts externalizing problems: Support for extending the dual-systems model in early childhood. *Journal of Abnormal Child Psychology, 46*(8), 1573–1583. https://doi.org/10.1007/s10802-018-0400-3

Jones, B. L. (2018). Making time for family meals: Parental influences, home eating environments, barriers and protective factors. *Physiology & Behavior, 193*(Part B), 248–251. https://doi.org/10.1016/j.physbeh.2018.03.035

Jones, J. D., et al. (2018). Stability of attachment style in adolescence: An empirical test of alternative developmental processes. *Child Development, 89*(3). https://doi.org/10.1111/cdev.12775

Jones, R. B., et al. (2018). Psychoeducational interventions in adolescent depression: A systematic review. *Patient Education and Counseling, 101*(5), 804–816. https://doi.org/10.1016/j.pec.2017.10.015

Joos, C. M., Wodzinski, A. M., Wadsworth, M. E., & Dorn, L. D. (2018). Neither antecedent nor consequence: Developmental integration of chronic stress, pubertal timing, and conditionally adapted stress response. *Developmental Review, 48,* 1–23. https://doi.org/10.1016/j.dr.2018.05.001

Joseph, R. M., et al. (2018). Maternal educational status at birth, maternal educational advancement, and neurocognitive outcomes at age 10 years among children born extremely preterm. *Pediatric Research, 83*(4), 767–777. https://doi.org/10.1038/pr.2017.267

Juang, L. P., Hou, Y., Bayless, S. D., & Kim, S. Y. (2018). Time-varying associations of parent–adolescent cultural conflict and youth adjustment among Chinese American families. *Developmental Psychology, 54*(5), 938–949. http://dx.doi.org/10.1037/dev0000475

Jung, J., Busching, R., & Krahé, B. (2019). Catching aggression from one's peers: A longitudinal multilevel analysis. *Social and Personality Psychology Compass, 13*(2), 12433. https://doi.org/10.1111/spc3.12433

Justice, L., et al. (2018). Modeling the nature of grammar and vocabulary trajectories from prekindergarten to third grade. *Journal of Speech, Language, and Hearing Research, 61*(4), 910–923. https://doi.org/10.1044/2018_JSLHR-L-17-0090

Justice, L. M., Jiang, H., & Strasser, K. (2018). Linguistic environment of preschool classrooms: What dimensions support children's language growth? *Early Childhood Research Quarterly, 42,* 79–92. https://doi.org/10.1016/j.ecresq.2017.09.003

Kaestle, C. E. (2019). Sexual orientation trajectories based on sexual attractions, partners, and identity: A longitudinal investigation from adolescence through young adulthood using a U.S. representative sample. *The Journal of Sex Research. 56*(7), 811–826. https://doi.org/10.1080/00224499.2019.1577351

Kagan, J. (2007). *What is emotion?: History, measures, and meaning.* New Haven: Yale University Press.

Kagan, J. (2012). The biography of behavioral inhibition (pp. 69–82). In M. Zentner & R. L. Shiner (Eds.), *Handbook of temperament.* New York, NY: The Guilford Press.

Kagan, J. (2018). Perspectives on two temperamental biases. *Philosophical Transactions of the Royal Society B: Biological Sciences, 373*(*1744*). https://doi.org/10.1098/rstb.2017.0158

Kagan, J., & Snidman, N. (2004). *The long shadow of temperament.* Cambridge, MA: Harvard University Press.

Kalandadze, T., Norbury, C., Nærland, T., & Næss, K-A. B. (2018). Figurative language comprehension in individuals with autism spectrum disorder: A meta-analytic review. *Autism, 22*(2), 99–117. https://doi.org/10.1177/1362361316668652

Kalb, G. & van Ours, J. C. (2014). Reading to young children: A head-start in life? *Economics of Education Review, 40,* 1–24. https://doi.org/10.1016/j.econedurev.2014.01.002

Kamens, S. R., Constandinides, D., & Flefel, F. (2016). Drawing the future: Psychosocial correlates of Palestinian children's drawings. *International Perspectives in Psychology: Research, Practice, Consultation, 5*(3), 167–183. http://dx.doi.org/10.1037/ipp0000054.supp

Kansky, J., & Allen, J. P. (2018). Long-terms risks and possible benefits associated with late adolescent romantic relationship quality. *Journal of Youth and Adolescence, 47*(7), 1531–1544. https//doi.org/10.1007/s10964-018-0813-x

Karnik, N. S., & Winiarski, D. A. (2019). Editorial: Bullying and suicide risk: Restructuring prevention, identification, and treatment to address a global mental health crisis. *Journal of the American Academy of Child & Adolescent Psychiatry, 58*(9), 851–852. https://doi.org/10.1016/j.jaac.2019.04.007

Kassai, R., Futo, J., Demetrovics, Z., & Takacs, Z. K. (2019). A meta-analysis of the experimental evidence on the near- and far-transfer effects among children's executive function skills. *Psychological Bulletin, 145*(2), 165–188. https://doi.org/10.1037/bul0000180

Katelaris, C. H., & Beggs, P. J. (2018). Climate change: Allergens and allergic disease. *Internal Medicine Journal, 48*(2), 129–134. https//doi.org/10.1111/imj.13699

Katz, C., & Hamama, L. (2016). The sibling relationship in the context of child maltreatment: What do we know? What are the directions for the future? *Trauma, Violence, & Abuse, 19*(3), 343–351. https//doi.org/10.1177/1524838016659878

Katziari, M. A., et al. (2017). Stress management during the second trimester of pregnancy. *International Journal of Stress Management, 26*(1), 102–105. http://dx.doi.org/10.1037/str0000078

Keating, L., Muller, R. T., & Classen, C. C. (2017). Changes in attachment organization, emotion dysregulation, and interpersonal problems among women in treatment for abuse. *Journal of Trauma & Dissociation, 19*(2). https://doi.org/10.1080/15299732.2017.1331946

Keller, K. L., et al. (2018). Brain responses to food cues varying in portion size is associated with individual differences in the portion size effect in children. *Appetite, 125,* 139–151. https://doi.org/10.1016/j.appet.2018.01.027

Kelly, R. J., & El-Sheikh, M. (2018). Reciprocal relations between parental problem drinking and children's sleep: The role of socioeconomic adversity. *Child Development.* https://doi-org.scsu.idm.oclc.org/10.1111/cdev.13074

Kenny, M. C., et al. (2018). Counselors' mandated responsibility to report child maltreatment: A review of U.S. laws. *Journal of Counseling & Development, 96*(4), 372–387. https://doi.org/10.1002/jcad.12220

Kerpelman, J. L., & Pittman, J. F. (2018). Erikson and the relational context of identity: Strengthening connections with attachment theory. *Identity: An International Journal of Theory and Research, 18*(4), 306–314. https://doi.org/10.108 0/15283488.2018.1523726

Kessel, E. M., et al. (2018). Hurricane Sandy exposure alters the development of neural reactivity to negative stimuli in children. *Child Development, 89*(2), 339–348. https//doi.org/10.1111/cdev.12691

Khan, F., et al. (2019). Developmental trajectories of attachment and depressive symptoms in children and adolescents. *Attachment & Human Development.* https://doi.org/10.1080/14616734.2019.1624790

Killen, M., Rutland, A., & Yip, T. (2016). Equity and justice in developmental science; Discrimination, social exclusion, and intergroup attitudes. *Child Development, 87*(5), 1317–1336. https://doi.org/10.1111/cdev.12593

Kim, S., & Kochanska, G. (2019). Evidence for the childhood origins of conscientiousness: Testing a developmental path from toddler age to adolescence. *Developmental Psychology, 55*(1), 196–206. https://doi.org/10.1037/dev0000608

Kim, S. Y., et al. (2018). Profiles of language brokering experiences and contextual stressors: Implications for adolescent outcomes in Mexican immigrant families. *Journal of Youth and Adolescence, 47*(8), 1629–1648. https://doi.org/10.1007/s10964-018-0851-4

Kimura, R., Yoshizaki, K., & Osumi, N. (2018) Risk of neurodevelopmental disease by paternal aging: A possible influence of epigenetic alteration in sperm. In T. Kubota & H. Fukuoka (Eds.), *Developmental Origins of Health and Disease (DOHaD)* (Vol. 1012). *Advances in Experimental Medicine and Biology.* Advances in Experimental Medicine and Biology. Springer, https://doi.org/10.1007/978-981-10-5526-3_8.

King, V., Boyd, L. M., & Pragg, B. (2018). Parent–adolescent closeness, family belonging, and adolescent well-being. *Journal of Family Issues, 39*(7), 2007–2036. https://doi.org/10.1177/0192513X17739048

Kinser, P. A., et al. (2017). Physical activity and yoga-based approaches for pregnancy-related low back and pelvic pain. *Journal of Obstetric, Gynecologic & Neonatal Nursing, 46*(3), 334–346. https://doi.org/10.1016/j.jogn.2016.12.006

Klahr, A. M., Burt, A., Leve, L. D., Shaw, D. S., Ganiban, J. M., Reiss, D., & Neiderhiser, J. M. (2017). Birth and adoptive parent antisocial behavior and parenting: A study of evocative gene-environment correlation. *Child Development, 88*(2), 505–513. https://doi.org/10.1111/cdev.12619

Kelin, M. R., et al. (2018). Temperament, mothers' reactions to children's emotional experiences, and emotion understanding predicting adjustment in preschool children. *Social Development, 27*(2), 351–365. https://doi.org/10.1111/sode.12282

Kelly, B., Vandevijvere, S., Freeman, B., & Jenkin, G. (2015). New media but same old tricks: Food marketing to children in the Digital Age. *Current Obesity Reports, 4*(1), 37–45. https://doi.org/10.1007/s13679-014-0128-5

Kenney, S. R., Lac, A., Hummer, J. F., Grimaldi, E. M., LaBrie, J. W. (2015). Pathways of parenting style on adolescents' college adjustment, academic achievement, and alcohol risk. *Journal of College Student Retention: Research, Theory, & Practice, 17*(2), 186–203. https://doi.org/10.1177/1521025115578232

Kersh, R., & Elbel, B. (2019). Childhood obesity: Can public policy make a difference? In D. Bagchi (Ed.), *Global Perspectives on Childhood Obesity: Current Status, Consequences and Prevention* (2nd ed., pp. 239–246). Academic Press.

Khanna, P., Chattu, V. K., & Aeri, B. T. (2019). Nutritional aspects of depression in adolescents—A systematic review. *International Journal of Preventative Medicine, 10*(1), 42. https://doi.org/10.4103/ijpvm.IJPVM_400_18

Kim, Y., Cubbin, C., & Oh, S. (2019). A systematic review of neighbourhood economic context on child obesity and obesity-related behaviours. *Obesity Reviews, 20*(3), 420–431. https://doi.org/10.1111/obr.12792

Kimmes, J. G., & Heckman, S. J. (2017). Parenting styles and college enrollment: A path analysis of risky human capital decisions. *Journal of Family and Economic Issues, 38*, 614–627. https://doi.org/10.1007/s10834-017-9529-4

Kirchgasler, C. (2018). True grit? Making a scientific object and pedagogical tool. *American Educational Research Journal, 55*(4), 693–720. https://doi.org/10.3102/0002831217752244

Kivnick, H. Q. & Wells, C. K. (2013). Untapped richness in Erik H. Erikson's rootstock. *The Gerontologist, 54*(1), 40–50. https//doi.org/10.1093/geront/gnt123

Klein, M. R. et al. (2018). Temperament, mothers' reactions to children's emotional experiences, and emotion understanding adjustment in preschool children. *Social Development, 27*(2), 351–365. https://doi.org/10.1111/sode.12282

Knoop-van Campen, C. A. N., Segers, E., & Verhoeven, L. (2018). How phonological awareness mediates the relation between working memory and word reading efficiency in children with dyslexia. *Dyslexia, 24*(2), 156–169. https://doi.org/10.1002/dys.1583

Knowles, A., et al. (2019). Risky sexual behavior among arrest adolescent males: The role of future expectations and impulse control. *Journal of Research on Adolescence, 30*(S2), 562–579. https://doi.org/10.1111/jora.12499

Koback, R., & Bosmans, G. (2019). Attachment and psychopathology: A dynamic model of the insecure cycle. *Current Opinion in Psychology, 25*, 76–80. https://doi.org/10.1016/j.copsyc.2018.02.018

Kochanska, G., Boldt, L. J., & Goffin, K. C. (2018). Early relational experience: A foundation for the unfolding dynamics of parent–child socialization. *Child Development Perspectives, 13*(1), 41–47. https://doi.org/10.1111/cdep.12308

Kochanska, G., Murray, K. T., & Harlan, E. (2000). Effortful control in early childhood: Continuity and change, antecedents, and implications for social development. *Developmental Psychology, 36*(2), 220–232. http://dx.doi.org/10.1037/0012-1649.36.2.220

Kohlberg, L. (1966). A cognitive-developmental analysis of children's sex- role concepts and attitudes. In E. E. Maccody (Ed.), *The development of sex differences.* Stanford, CA: Stanford University Press.

Kohlberg, L. (1969). Stage and sequence: The cognitive-developmental approach to socialization. In D. A. Goslin (Ed.), *Handbook of socialization theory and research.* Chicago: Rand McNally.

Kohlberg, Lawrence (1981). *Essays on Moral Development, Vol I. I: The Philosophy of Moral Development.* San Francisco, CA: Harper & Row.

Kohlberg, L. (1984). *The psychology of moral development.* San Francisco, CA: Harper & Row.

Köhler, S. et al. (2019). Expansion of the human phenotype ontology (HPO) knowledge base and resources. *Nucleic Acids Research, 47*(D1), D1018-1027. doi.org/10.1093/nar/gky1105

Kohli, N., Hughes, J., Wang, C., Zopluoglu, C., and Davison, M. L. (2015). Fitting a linear–linear piecewise growth mixture model with unknown knots: a comparison of two common approaches to inference. *Psychological Methods, 20*(2), 259–275. https://doi.org/10.1037/met0000034

Kollmayer, M., et al. (2018). Parents' judgments about the desirability of toys for their children: Associations with gender role attitudes, gender-typing of toys, and demographics. *Sex Roles, 79*, 329–341. https://doi.org/10.1007/s11199-017-0882-4

Komesaroff, L., Komesaroff, P. A., & Hyde, M. (2015). Ethical issues in cochlear implantation. In J. Clausen & N. Levy (Eds.), *Handbook of Neuroethics.* Springer Netherlands.

Kong, A., et al. (2018). The nature of nurture: Effects of parental genotypes. *Science, 359*(6374), 424–428. https://doi.org/10.1126/science.aan6877

Kopala-Sibley, D. C., Hayden, E. P., Singh, S. M., Sheikh, H. I., Kryski, K. R., & Klein, D. N. (2018). Gene-environment correlations in the cross-generational transmission of parenting: Grandparenting moderates the effect of child 5-HTTLPR genotype on mothers' parenting. *Social Development, 26*, 724–739. https://doi.org/10.1111/sode.12221

Koren, A., Kahn-D'Angelo, L., Reece, S. M., & Gore, R. (2019). Examining childhood obesity from infancy: The relationship between tummy time, infant BMI-z, weight gain, and motor development—An exploratory study. *Journal of Pediatric Health Care, 33*(1), 80–91. https://doi.org/10.1016/j.pedhc.2018.06.006

Korn, R. (2010). *The art of problem-solving.* Retrieved from: https://www.guggenheim.org/wp-content/uploads/2015/11/guggenheim-research-aps-executivesummary.pdf

Koster, J. B. (2009). *Growing artists: Teaching the arts to young children.* Clifton Park, NY: Delmar Learning.

Kostyrka-Allchorne, K., Cooper, N. R., & Simpson, A. (2017). The relationship between television exposure and children's cognition and behaviour: A systematic review. *Developmental Review, 44*, 19–58. https://doi.org/10.1016/j.dr.2016.12.002

Kourassanis-Velasquez, J., & Jones, E.A. (2018). Increasing joint attention in children with autism and their peers. *Behavior Analysis in Practice, 12*, 78–94. https://doi.org/10.1007/s40617-018-0228-x

Kovaniemi, S., et al. (2018). How are socio-emotional and behavioral competences and problems at 1 year of age associated with infant motor development? A general population study. *Infant Behavior and Development, 51*, 1–14. https://doi.org/10.1016/j.infbeh.2018.02.007

Koyanagi, A., et al. (2019). Bullying victimization and suicide attempt among adolescents aged 12–15 years from 48 countries. *Journal of the American Academy of Child & Adolescent Psychiatry, 58*(9), 907–918. https://doi.org/10.1016/j.jaac.2018.10.018

Kracht, C. L., et al. (2018). Difference in objectively measured physical activity and obesity in children with and without sibling. *Human Kinetics Journals, 31*(3), 348–355. https://doi.org/10.1123/pes.2018-0184

Kral, T. R. A., et al. (2018). Impact of short- and long-term mindfulness meditation training on amygdala reactivity to emotional stimuli. *NeuroImage, 181*, 301–313. https://doi.org/10.1016/j.neuroimage.2018.07.013

Kravitz-Wirtz, N., et al. (2018). Early-life pollution exposure, neighborhood poverty, and childhood asthma in the United Status, 1990–2014. *International Journal of Environmental Research and Public Health, 15*(6), 1114. https://doi.org/10.3390/ijerph15061114

Kroger, J. (2018). The epigenesist of identity—What does it mean? *Identity: An International Journal of Theory and Research, 18*(4), 334–342. https://doi.org/10.1080/15283488.2018.1523730

Krull, J., Wilbert, J., & Hennemann, T. (2018). Does social exclusion by classmates lead to behaviour problems and learning difficulties or vice versa? A cross-lagged panel analysis. *European Journal of Special Needs Education, 33*(2). https://doi.org/10.1080/08856257.2018.1424780

Kubin, L. (2019). Is there a resurgence of vaccine preventable diseases? *Journal of Pediatric Nursing, 44*, 115–118. https://doi.org/10.1016/j.pedn.2018.11.011

Kucharczyk, S., et al. (2018). Supporting parent use of evidence-based practices for infants and toddlers with autism spectrum disorder. In M. Siller & L. Morgan (Eds.), *Handbook of parent-implemented interventions for very young children with autism.* Autism and child psychopathology series. Springer, https://doi.org/10.1007/978-3-319-90994-3_25

Kulawiak, P. R., & Wilbert, J. (2019). Introduction of a new method for representing the sociometric status within the peer group: The example of sociometrically neglected children. *International Journal of Research & Method in Education, 43*(2). https://doi.org/10.1080/1743727X.2019.1621830

Kumar, K. (2017). The blended family life cycle. *Journal of Divorce & Remarriage, 58*(2), 110–125. https://doi.org/10.1080/10502556.2016.1268019

Kuntoro, I. A., Dwiputri, G., & Adams, P. (2018). The contribution of parenting style and theory of mind to the understanding of morally relevant theory of mind in Indonesian children. In A. Ariyanto et al. (Eds.), *Diversity in unity: Perspectives from psychology and behavioral sciences* (pp. 83–89). Routledge.

Kuppens, S., et al. (2019). The enduring effects of parental alcohol, tobacco, and drug use on child well-being: A multilevel meta-analysis. *Development and Psychopathology*, 1–14. https://doi.org/10.1017/S0954579419000749

Kuvalanka, K. A., et al. (2017). Trans and gender-nonconforming children and their caregivers: Gender presentations, peer relations, and well-being at baseline. *Journal of Family Psychology, 31*(7), 889–899. http://dx.doi.org/10.1037/fam0000338

Kuwertz-Bröking, E., & von Gontard, A. (2018). Clinical management of nocturnal enuresis. *Pediatric Nephrology, 33*(7), 1145–1154. https://doi.org/10.1007/s00467-017-3778-1

Kuzmina, Y., Ivanova, A., & Kaiky, D. (2019). The effect of phonological processing on mathematics performance in elementary school varies for boys and girls: Fixed-effects longitudinal analysis. *British Educational Research Journal, 45*(3), 650–661. https://doi.org/10.1002/berj.3518

Labat, H., Vallet, G., Magnan, A., & Ecalle, J. (2015). Facilitating effect of multisensory letter encoding on reading and spelling in five-year0old children. *Applied Cognitive Psychology, 29*(3), 381–391. https:/doi.org/10.1002/acp.3116

Labouvie-Vief, G. (2015). Cognitive-emotional development in infants. *Integrating Emotions and Cognition Throughout the Lifespan.* New York, NY: Springer Publishing.

Lamb, C. (2014). Growing up in the gay shadow: The impact of heterosexual privilege on children with same-sex parents. *Canadian Journal of Family and Youth, 6*(1). https://doi.org/ https://doi.org/10.29173/cjfy21489

Lamb, M., Kuhn, A., LaBotz, M., & Diamond, A. B. (2018). Safeguarding the child and adolescent athlete. *Current Sports Medicine Reports, 17*(12), 419–424. https://doi.org/10.1249/JSR.0000000000000538

Lamb, M. E., Malloy, L. C., Hershkowitz, I., & La Rooy, D. (2015). Children and the law (pp. 1–49). *Handbook of Child Psychology and Developmental Science.*

Langian, J., Tee, L., & Brandreth, R. (2019). Childhood obesity. *Medicine, 47*(3), 190–194. https://doi.org/10.1016/j.mpmed.2018.12.007

Laninga-Wijnen, L., et al. (2019). Classroom popularity hierarchy predicts prosocial and aggressive popularity norms across the school year. *Child Development, 90*(5), e637–e653. https://doi.org/10.1111/cdev.13228

Lansbury, J. (2014). *No bad kids: Toddler discipline without shame.* JLML Press.

Lansford, J. E., et al. (2018). Bidirectional relations between parenting and behavioral problems from age 8 to 13 in nine countries. *Journal of Research on Adolescence, 28*(3), 571–590. https://doi.org/10.1111/jora.12381

Lareau, A. (2011). *Unequal childhoods: Class, race, and family life* (2nd ed.). Berkeley, CA: University of California Press.

Largo-Wight, E., et al. (2018). Nature contact at school: The impact of an outdoor classroom on children's well-being. *International Journal of Environmental Health Research, 28*(6), 653–666. https://doi.org/10.1080/09603123.2018.1502415

Larson, R. W., et al. (2019). The important (but neglected) developmental value of roles: Findings from youth programs. *Developmental Psychology, 55*(5), 1019–1033. http://dx.doi.org/10.1037/dev0000674

Latif, R. (2018). Maternal and fetal effects of chocolate consumption during pregnancy: A systematic review. *Journal of Maternal-Fetal & Neonatal Medicine, 32*(17), 2915–2927. https://doi.org/10.1080/14767058.2018.1449200

Latimore, T. L., et al. (2018). School-based activities, misbehavior, discipline, and racial and ethnic disparities. *Education and Urban Society, 50*(5), 403–434. https://doi.org/10.1177/0013124517713603

Latuskie, K. A., Leibson, T., Andrews, N. C. Z., Motz, M., Pepler, D. J., & Ito, S. (2018). Substance use in pregnancy among vulnerable women seeking addiction and parenting support. *International Journal of Mental Health and Addiction, 17*, 137–150. https://doi.org/10.1007/s11469-018-0005-7

Laurita, A. C., Hazan, C., & Spreng, R. N. (2018). Neural signature of chronic accessibility in parent–adult child attachment bonds. *Social Neuroscience, 14*(4), 462–469. https://doi.org//10.1080/17470919.2018.1494037

Lavi, I., et al. (2019). Broken bonds: A meta-analysis of emotional reactivity and regulation in emotionally maltreating parents. *Child Abuse & Neglect, 88,* 376–388. https://doi.org/10.1016/j.chiabu.2018.11.016

Law, F., Mahr, T., Schneeberg, A., & Edwards, J. (2017). Vocabulary size and auditory word recognition in preschool children. *Applied Psycholinguistics, 38*(1), 89–125, https://doi.org/10.1017/S0142716416000126

Lawson, G. M., Hook, C. J., & Farah, M. J. (2018). A meta-analysis of the relationship between socioeconomic status and executive function performance among children. *Developmental Science, 21*(2). https://doi.org/10.1111/desc.12529

Leaper, C. (2015). Gender and social-cognitive development. *Handbook of Child Psychology and Developmental Science* (pp. 1–48). Hoboken, NJ: John Wiley & Sons, Inc.

LeBarton, E. S., & Landa, R. J. (2019). Infant motor skill predicts later expressive language and autism spectrum disorder diagnosis. *Infant Behavior and Development, 54,* 37–47. https://doi.org/10.1016/j.infbeh.2018.11.003

Le-Ha, C., et al. (2018). Age at menarche and childhood body mass index as predictors of cardio-metabolic risk in young adulthood: A prospective cohort study. *PLOS ONE, 13*(12), e0209355. https://doi.org/10.1371/journal.pone.0209355

Lebel, C., et al. (2019). Developmental trajectories of white matter structure in children with and without reading impairments. *Developmental Cognitive Neuroscience, 36.* https://doi.org/10.1016/j.dcn.2019.100633

Lebel, C., & Deoni, S. (2018). The development of brain white matter microstructure. *Neuroimage, 182,* 207–218. https://doi.org/10.1016/j.neuroimage.2017.12.097

Lee, K. H., et al. (2018). Prefrontal cortical response to negative social words links social risk to depressive symptoms in adolescence. *Journal of Research on Adolescence, 28*(1), 87–102. https://doi.org/10.1111/jora.12360

Lee, K. T. H., Lewis, W., Kataoka, S., Schenke, K., & Vandell, D. (2018). Out-of-school time and behaviors during adolescence. *Journal of Research on Adolescence, 28*(2), 284–293. https://doi.org/10.1111/jora.12389

Lee, N. C., Hollarek, M., & Krabbendam, L. (2018). Neurocognitive development during adolescence (pp. 46–67). In J. E. Lansford & P. Banati (Eds.), *Handbook of Adolescent Development Research and Its Impact on Global Policy.* Oxford University Press.

Lee, Y. Y., et al. (2018). Gut microbiota in early life and its influence on health and disease: A position paper by the Malaysian Working Group on Gastrointestinal Health. *Journal of Paediatrics and Child Health, 53*(12), 1152–1158. https://doi.org/10.1111/jpc.13640

Lee-James R., Washington J. A. (2018). Language skills of bidialectal and bilingual children: Considering a strengths-based perspective. *Topics in Language Disorders, 38*(1), 5–26. https://doi.org/10.1097/TLD.0000000000000142

Leerkes, E. M., & Zhou, N. (2018). Maternal sensitivity to distress and attachment outcomes: Interactions with sensitivity to nondistress and infant temperament. *Journal of Family Psychology, 32*(6), 753–761. http://dx.doi.org.scsu.idm.oclc.org/10.1037/fam0000420

Lenne, R. L., et al. (2019). Parenting styles moderate how parent and adolescent beliefs shape each other's eating and physical activity: Dyadic evidence from a cross-sectional, U.S. National Survey. *Journal of Experimental Social Psychology, 81,* 76–84. https://doi.org/10.1016/j.jesp.2018.06.003

Leon-Moreno, C., Martínez-Ferrer, B., Moreno-Ruiz, D., & Musitu-Ferrer, D. (2019). Forgiveness and loneliness in peer-victimized adolescents. *Journal of Interpersonal Violence,* 1–22. Advance online publication. https://doi.org/10.1177/0886260519869078

Leonard, J. A., et al. (2019). Associations between cortical thickness and reasoning differ by socioeconomic status in development. *Developmental Cognitive Neuroscience, 36.* https://doi.org/10.1016/j.dcn.2019.100641

Lerner, R. M. (2019). Frontiers in theory-predicated research in youth development: A commentary. *Journal of Youth Development, 14*(1), https://doi.org/10.5195/jyd.2019.739

Lerner, R. M., et al. (2005). Positive youth development, participation in community youth development programs, and community contributions of fifth-grade adolescents: Findings from the first wave of the 4-H study of positive youth development. *The Journal of Early Adolescence, 25*(1), 17–71. https://doi.org/10.1177/0272431604272461

Lerner, R. M., Batanova, M., Ettekal, A. V., & Hunter, C. (2015). When the stars align: On the contributions of Gilbert Gottlieb and Peter C. M. Molenaar to developmental science theory and method. *International Journal of Developmental Science, 9*(1), 11–14. https://doi.org/10.3233/DEV-14159

Lerner, R. M., et al. (2018). Studying positive youth development in different nations. In J. E. Lansford & P. Banati (Eds.), *Handbook of adolescent development research and its impact on global policy* (pp. 68–83). Oxford University Press.

Leslie, T. F., Delamater, P. L., & Yang, T. T. (2018). It could have been much worse: The Minnesota measles outbreak. *Vaccine, 36*(14), 1808–1810. https://doi.org/10.1016/j.vaccine.2018.02.086

Levi-Belz, Y., et al. (2018). Psychosocial factors correlated with undisclosed suicide attempts to significant others: Findings from the adolescence SEYLE study. *Suicide and Life-Threatening Behavior, 49*(3), 759–773. https://doi.org/10.1111/sltb.12475

Levin, D. (2019). The parents passed a drug test. Should they get their children back? *The New York Times*. Retrieved from: https://www.nytimes.com/2019/11/22/us/opioids-foster-care-ohio.html

Levine, D., Pace, A., Luo, R., Golinkoff, R. M., de Villiers, J., Hirsh-Pasek, K., & Wilson, M. S. (2019). Evaluating SES gaps in preschoolers' vocabulary, syntax, and language-learning process skills with the Quick Interactive Language Screener (QUILS). *Early Childhood Research Quarterly, 50*(Part 1), 114–128. https://doi.org/10.1016/j.ecresq.2018.11.006

Levy, S., Schizer, M. A., & Green, L. S. (2019). Developmental perspectives and risk factors for substance use. In J. Welsh & S. Hadland (Eds.), *Treating Adolescent Substance Use* (pp. 7–25). Springer.

Lewis, H. B. (1971). *Shame and guilt in neurosis*. New York, NY: International Universities Press.

Lewis, J. D., et al. (2017). The emergence of network inefficiencies in infants with autism spectrum disorder. *Biological Psychiatry, 82*(3), 176–185. https://doi.org/10.1016/j.biopsych.2017.03.006

Lewontin, R. (2000). *The triple helix: Gene, organism, and environment*. Cambridge, MA: Harvard University Press.

Liberman, Z., & Shaw, A. (2019). Children use similarity, propinquity, and loyalty to predict which people are friends. *Journal of Experimental Child Psychology, 184*, 1–17. https://doi.org/10.1016/j.jecp.2019.03.002

Lick, D. J., Patterson, C. J., & Schmidt, K. M. (2013). Recalled social experiences and current psychological adjustment among adults reared by gay and lesbian parents. *Journal of GLBT Family Studies, 9*(3), 230–253. https://doi.org/10.1080/1550428X.2013.781907

Li, D., et al. (2018). Moving beyond the neighborhood: Daily exposure to nature and adolescents' mood. *Landscape and Urban Planning, 173*, 33–43. https://doi.org/10.1016/j.landurbplan.2018.01.009

Li, G., et al. (2018). The wisdom of honeybee defenses against environmental stresses. *Frontiers in Microbiology, 9*, 722. https://doi.org/10.3389/fmicb.2018.00722

Li, J. C., & Danese, A. (2018). Biological embedding of child maltreatment through inflammation. In J. Noll & I. Shalev (Eds.), *The Biology of Early Life Stress*. Child maltreatment solutions network. Springer, https://doi.org/10.1007/978-3-319-72589-5_1

Li, W., Farkas, G., Duncan, G. J., Burchinal, M. R., & Vandell, D. L. (2013). Timing of high-quality child care and cognitive, language, and preacademic development. *Developmental Psychology 49*(8), 1440–1451. https://doi.org/10.1037/a0030613

Li, Y-C., Kwan, M. Y. W., King-Dowling, S., & Cairney, J. (2015). Determinants of physical activity during early childhood: A systematic review. Advances in Physical Education, 5, 116–127. https://doi.org/10.4236/ape.2015.52015

Li, Z., Liu, S., Hartman, S., & Belsky, J. (2018). Interactive effects of early-life income harshness and unpredictability on children's socioemotional and academic functioning in kindergarten and adolescence. *Developmental Psychology, 54*(11), 2101–2112. http://dx.doi.org/10.1037/dev0000601

Liben, L. S., & Bigler, R. S. (2002). The developmental course of gender differentiation: Conceptualizing, measuring, and evaluating constructs and pathways. *Monographs of the Society for Research in Child Development, 67*(2), vii–viii. http://dx.doi.org/10.1111/1540-5834.t01-1-00187

Lickliter, R., & Witherington, D. C. (2017). Towards a truly developmental epigenesis. *Human Development, 60*, 124–138. https://doi.org/10.1159/000477996

Liew, J., Cao, Q., Hughes, J. N., & Deutz, M. H. F. (2018). Academic resilience despite early academic adversity: A three-wave longitudinal study on regulation-related resiliency, interpersonal relationships, and achievement in first to third grade. *Early Education and Development, 29*(5), 762–779. https://doi.org/10.1080/10409289.2018.1429766

Liew, J., Carlo, G., Streit, C., & Ispa, J. M. (2018). Parenting beliefs and practices in toddlerhood as precursors to self-regulatory, psychosocial, and academic outcomes in early and middle childhood in ethnically diverse low-income families. *Social Development, 27*(4), 891–909. doi:https://doi.org/10.1111/sode.12306

Lima, R. A., Pfeiffer, K., Larsen, L. R., & Bugge, A. (2017). Physical activity and motor competence present a positive reciprocal longitudinal relationships across childhood and early adolescence. *Human Kinetics Journal, 14*(6), 440–447. https://doi.org/10.1123/jpah.2016-0473

Limbers, C. A., Cohen, L. A., & Gray, B. A. (2018). Eating disorders in adolescent and young adult males: Prevalence, diagnosis, and treatment strategies. *Adolescent Health, Medicine and Therapeutics, 9*, 111–116. https://doi.org/10.2147/AHMT.S147480

Lindberg, S., Linkersdörfer, J., Lehmann, M., Hasselhorn, M., & Lonnemann, J. (2013). Individual different in children's early strategy behavior in arithmetic tasks. *Journal of Educational and Developmental Psychology, 3*(1). https://doi.org/10.5539/jedp.v3n1p192

Lindell, A. K., & Campione-Barr, N. (2017). Relative power in sibling relationships across adolescence. *New Directions for Child and Adolescent Development, 2017*(156), 49–66. https://doi.org/10.1002/cad.20201

Lin, Q, et al. (2018). Chinese children's imaginary companions: Relations with peer relationships and social competence. *International Journal of Psychology, 53*(5), 388–396. https://doi.org/10.1002/ijop.12392

Lin, Y-C., Washington-Nortey, P-M., Hill, O. W., & Serpell, Z. N. (2019). Family functioning and not family structure predicts adolescents' reasoning and math skills. *Journal of Child and Family Studies, 28*(10), 2700–2707. https://doi.org/10.1007/s10826-019-01450-4

Lindsey, E. W. (2019). Emotions expressed with friends and acquaintances and preschool children's social competence with peers. *Early Childhood Research Quarterly, 47*(2), 373–384. https://doi.org/10.1016/j.ecresq.2019.01.005

Lindsey, E. W. & Colwell, M. J. (2013). Pretend and physical play: Links to preschoolers' affective social competence. *Merrill Palmer Quarterly, 59*(3), 330–360. https://doi.org/10.1353/mpq.2013.0015

Linnavalli, T., et al. (2018). Music playschool enhances children's linguistic skills. *Scientific Reports, 8*(8767). https://doi.org/10.1038/s41598-018-27126-5

Linton, J. M., Griffin, M., Shapiro, A. J., & Council on Community Pediatrics (2017). Detention of immigrant children. *Pediatrics, 139*(5), e20170483. https://doi.org/10.1542/peds.2017-0483

Linton, J. M., Kennedy, E., Shapiro, A., & Griffin, M. (2018). Unaccompanied children seeking safe haven: Providing care and supporting well-being of a vulnerable population. *Child and Youth Services Review, 92*, 122–132. https://doi.org/10.1016/j.childyouth.2018.03.043

Lionetti, F., et al. (2019). The development of parental monitoring during adolescence: A meta-analysis. *European Journal of Developmental Psychology, 16*(5), 552–580. https://doi.org/10.1080/17405629.2018.1476233

Lippold, M. A., Hussong, A., Fosco, G. M., & Ram, N. (2018). Lability in the parent's hostility and warmth toward their adolescent: Linkages to youth delinquency and substance use. *Developmental Psychology, 54*(2), 348–361. https://doi.org/10.1037/dev0000415

Lippold, M. A., et al. (2019). Mindful parenting, parenting cognitions, and parent–youth communications: Bidirectional linkages and meditational processes. *Mindfulness.* https://doi.org/10.1007/s12671-019-01119-5

Listl, S. et al. (2018). Childhood socioeconomic conditions and teeth in older adulthood: Evidence from SHARE wave 5. *Community Dentistry and Oral Epidemiology, 46*(1), 78–87. https://doi.org/10.1111/cdoe.12332

Liu, R-D., et al. (2019). Psychological distress and problematic mobile phone use among adolescents: The mediating role of maladaptive cognitions and the moderating role of effortful control. *Frontiers in Psychology, 10*, 1589. https://doi.org/10.3389/fpsyg.2019.01589

Loe, I. M., Adams, J. N., & Feldman, H. M. (2019). Executive function in relation to white matter in preterm and full term children. *Frontiers in Pediatrics.* https://doi.org/10.3389/fped.2018.00418

Loeb, E. L., et al. (2018). Getting what you expect: Negative social expectations in early adolescence predict hostile romantic partnerships and friendships into adulthood. *Journal of Early Adolescence, 38*(4), 475–496. https://doi.org/10.1177/0272431616675971

Loizou, E. (2017). Towards play pedagogy: Supporting teacher play practices with a teacher guide about socio-dramatic and imaginative play. *European Early Childhood Education Research Journal, 25*(5), 784–795. https://doi.org/10.1080/1350293X.2017.1356574

Loizou, E., Michaelides, A., & Georgiou, A. (2019). Early childhood teacher involvement in children's socio-dramatic play: Creative drama as a scaffolding tool. *Early Child Development and Care, 189*(4), 600–612. https://doi.org/10.1080/03004430.2017.1336165

Long, K. A., et al. (2018). Psychosocial functioning and risk factors among siblings of children with cancer: An updated systematic review. *Psycho-Oncology, 27*(6), 1467–1479. https://doi.org/10.1002/pon.4669

Longo L.D. (2018) Epigenetics and the fetal origins of adult health and disease. In *The rise of fetal and neonatal physiology.* Perspectives in physiology. Springer, https://doi.org/10.1007/978-1-4939-7483-2_16

Lonigro, A., Baiocco, R., Pallini, S., & Kaghi, F. (2018). Theory of mind and sociometric peer status: The mediating role of social conduct. *Frontiers in Psychology.* https://doi.org/10.3389/fpsyg.2018.02191

Lopéz, G., Ruiz, N. G., & Patten, E. (2017). *Key facts about Asian American, a diverse and growing population.* Retrieved from http://www.pewresearch.org/fact-tank/2017/09/08/key-facts-about-asian-americans/

Lorente-Pozo, S. et al. (2018). Influence of sex on gestational complications, fetal-to-neonatal transition, and postnatal adaptation. *Frontiers in Pediatrics.* https://doi.org/10.3389/fped.2018.00063

Lorenz, C., & Kray, J. (2019). Are mid-adolescents prone to risky decisions? The influences of task setting and individual differences in temperament. *Frontiers in Psychology.* https://doi.org/10.3389/fpsyg.2019.01497

Louis-Jacques, A., & Stuebe, A. (2018). Long-term maternal benefits of breastfeeding. *Contemporary Ob/Gyn, 64*(7). Retrieved from http://www.contemporaryobgyn.net/breast-health/long-term-maternal-benefits-breastfeeding.

Loy, M., Masur, E. F., & Olson, J. (2018). Developmental changes in infants' and mothers' pathways to achieving joint attention episodes. *Infant Behavior and Development, 50*, 264–273. https://doi.org/10.1016/j.infbeh.2018.02.001

Lu, W-H, et al. (2019). Correlates of Internet addiction severity with reinforcement sensitivity and frustration intolerance in adolescents with attention-deficit/hyperactivity disorder: The moderating effect of medications. *Frontiers in Psychiatry.* https://doi.org/10.3389/fpsyt.2019.00268

Lucca, K., & Wilbourne, M. P. (2018). Communicating to learn: Infants' pointing gestures result in optimal learning. *Child Development, 89*(3), 941–960. https://doi.org/10.1111/cdev.12707

Lucca, K., & Wilbourn, M. P. (2019). That what and the how: Information-seeking pointing gestures facilitates learning labels and functions. *Journal of Experimental Child Psychology, 178,* 417–436. https://doi.org/10.1016/j.jecp.2018.08.003

Lu, S., Perez, L., Leslein, A., & Hatsu, I. (2019). The relationship between food insecurity and symptoms of attention-deficit hyperactivity disorder in children: A summary of the literature. *Nutrients, 11*(3), 659. https://doi.org/10.3390/nu11030659

Lyle, R. R. (2011). Developmental neuroscience. In S. Goldstein & J. A. Naglieri (Eds.), *Encyclopedia of child behavior and development.* Springer, https://doi.org/10.1007/978-0-387-79061-9_1963.

Lynch, B. A., et al. (2018). The impact of positive contextual factors on the association between adverse family experiences and obesity in a National Survey of Children. *Preventative Medicine, 116,* 81–86. https://doi.org/10.1016/j.ypmed.2018.09.002

Ma, X., Jin, Y., Luo, B., Zhang, G., Wei, R., & Liu, D. (2015). Giant pandas failed to show mirror self-recognition. *Animal Cognition, 18*(3), 713–721. https://doi.org/10.1007/s10071-015-0838-4

Majumder, M. A. (2016). The impact of parenting style on children's educational outcomes in the United States. *Journal of Family and Economic Issues 37,* 89–98. https://doi.org/10.1007/s10834-015-9444-5

Malchiodi, C. A. (1998). *Understanding children's drawings.* Guilford Press.

Malina, R. M., Bouchard, C. & Bar-Or, O. (2004). *Growth, maturation, and physical activity* (2nd Ed.). Champaign, IL. Human Kinetics.

Marks, A. K., & Coll, C. G. (2018). Education and developmental competencies of ethnic minority children: Recent theoretical and methodological advances. *Developmental Review, 50*(A), 90–98. https://doi.org/10.1016/j.dr.2018.05.004

Masten, A. S. (2019). Resilience from a developmental systems perspective. *World Psychiatry, 18*(1), 101–102. https://doi.org/10.1002/wps.20591

Mastrotheodoros, S., et al. (2019). Family functioning and adolescent internalizing and externalizing problems: Disentangling between-, and within-family associations. *Journal of Youth and Adolescence, 49,* 804–817. https://doi.org/10.1007/s10964-019-01094-z

Maunder, R., & Monks, C. P. (2019). Friendships in middle childhood: Links to peer and school identification, and general self-worth. *British Journal of Developmental Psychology, 37,* 211–229. https://doi.org/10.1111/bjdp.12268

Maynard, M. S., Perlman, C. M., & Kirkpatrick, S. I. (2019). Food insecurity and perceived anxiety among adolescents: An analysis of data from the 2009–2010 National Health and Nutrition Examination Survey (NHANES). *Journal of Hunger & Environmental Nutrition, 14*(3), 339–351. https://doi.org/10.1080/19320248.2017.1393363

M'hamdi, H. I., de Beaufort, I., Jack, B., & Steegers, E. A. P. (2018). Responsibility in the age of developmental origins of health and disease (DOHaD). *Journal of Developmental Origins of Health and Disease, 9*(1), 58–62. https://doi.org/10.1017/S2040174417000654

Ma, F., et al. (2018). Generalized trust predicts young children's willingness to delay gratification. *Journal of Experimental Child Psychology, 169,* 118–125. https://doi.org/10.1016/j.jecp.2017.12.015

Määttä, S., et al. (2019). Children's physical activity and the preschool physiological environment: The moderating role of gender. *Early Childhood Research Quarterly, 47*(2), 39–48. https://doi.org/10.1016/j.ecresq.2018.10.008

MacNeill, L. A., Ram, N., Bell, M. A., Fox, N. A., & Pérez-Edgar, K. (2018). Trajectories of infants' biobehavioral development: Timing and rate of A-not-B performance gains and EEG maturation. *Child Development.* https://doi org.scsu.idm.oclc.org/10.1111/cdev.13022

MacPhee, D., & Prendergast, S. (2019). Room for improvement: Girls' and boys' home environments are still gendered. *Sex Roles, 80*(5–6), 332–346. https://doi.org/10.1007/s11199-018-0936-2

Madigan, S., Browne, D., & Racine, N. (2019). Association between screen time and children's performance on a developmental screening test. *JAMA Pediatric, 173*(3), 244–250. https://doi.org/10.1001/jamapediatrics.2018.5056

Madigan, S., et al. (2018). A meta-analysis of maternal prenatal depression and anxiety on child socioemotional development. *Journal of the American Academy of Child & Adolescent Psychiatry, 57*(9), 645–657. https://doi.org/10.1016/j.jaac.2018.06.012

Maguire, M. J. et al. (2018). Vocabulary knowledge mediates the link between socioeconomic status and word learning in grade school. *Journal of Experimental Child Psychology, 166,* 679.675. https://doi.org/10.1016/j.jecp.2017.10.003

Mahdi, S., et al. (2017). An international qualitative study of ability and disability in ADHD using the WHO–ICF framework. *European Child & Adolescent Psychiatry, 26*(10), 1219–1231. https://doi.org/10.1007/s00787-017-0983-1

Mahdi, S., et al. (2018). An international clinical study of ability and disability in ADHD using the WHO–ICF framework. *European Child & Adolescent Psychiatry, 27*(10), 1305–1319. https://doi.org/10.1007/s00787-018-1124-1

Maher, G. M., et al. (2018). A perspective on pre-eclampsia and neurodevelopmental outcomes in the offspring: Does maternal inflammation play a role? *International Journal of Developmental Neuroscience, 77*(1), 69–76. https://doi.org/10.1016/j.ijdevneu.2018.10.004

Mahler, M. S. (1974). Symbiosis and individuation: The psychological birth of the human infant. *The Psychoanalytic Study of the Child, 29*(1), 89–106. https://doi.org/10.1080/00797308.1974.11822615

Main, A., Lougheed, J., P., Disla, J., & Kashi, S. (2018). Timing of adolescent emotional disclosures: The role of maternal emotions and adolescent age. *Emotion, 9*(5), 829–840. http://dx.doi.org/10.1037/emo0000483

Malti, T., Gummerum, M., Ongley, S. F., Chaparro, M. P., Nola, M., & Bae, N. Y. (2016). "Who is worthy of my generosity?" Recipient characteristics and the development of children's sharing. *International Journal of Behavioral Development, 40,* 31–40. http://dx.doi.org/10.1177/0165025414567007

Marceau, K., et al. (2019). Longitudinal associations of sleep duration, morning and evening cortisol, and BMI during childhood. *Obesity, 27*(4), 645–652, https://doi.org/10.1002/oby.22420

Marcelo, A. K. & Yates, T. M. (2014). Prospective relations among preschoolers' play, coping, and adjustment as moderated by stressful events. *Journal of Applied Developmental Psychology, 35*(3), 223–233. https://doi.org/10.1016/j.appdev.2014.01.001

Marcia, J. E. (1966). Development and validation of ego–identity status. *Journal of Personality and Social Psychology, 3*(5), 551–558. https://doi.org/10.1037/h0023281

Marengo, D., et al. (2019). Exploring the dimensional structure of bullying victimization among primary and lower-secondary school students: Is one factor enough, or do we need more? *Frontiers in Psychology, 10,* 770. https://doi.org/10.3389/fpsyg.2019.00770

Mariotti V., Palumbo S., Pellegrini S. (2019) Prenatal and early postnatal Influences on neurodevelopment: The role of epigenetics. In A. Pingitore, F. Mastorci, & C. Vassalle (Eds.), *Adolescent Health and Wellbeing.* Cham, CH: Springer.

Markus, H. R., & Stephens, N. M. (2017). Editorial overview: The psychological and behavioral consequences of inequality and social class: A theoretical integration. *Current Opinion in Psychology, 18,* iv–xii. http://dx.doi.org/10.1016/j.copsyc.2017.11.001

Marshall, S. L., Ciarrochi, J., Parker, P. D., & Sahdra, B. K. (2019). Is self-compassion selfish? The development of self-compassion, empathy, and prosocial behavior in adolescence. *Journal of Research on Adolescence*, 30(S2), 472–484. https://doi.org/10.1111/jora.12492

Martarelli, C. S., Mast, F. W., Läge, D., & Roebers, C. M. (2015). The distinction between real and fictional worlds: Investigating individual differences in fantasy understanding. *Cognitive Development, 36,* 111–126. http://dx.doi.org/10.1016/j.cogdev.2015.10.001

Martin-Storey A., & Baams L. (2019). Gender nonconformity during adolescence: Links with stigma, sexual minority status, and psychosocial outcomes. In H. Fitzgerald, D. Johnson, D. Qin, F. Villarruel, & J. Norder (Eds.), *Handbook of children and prejudice.* Springer.

Martinelli, A., et al. (2018). Hostile attribution bias and aggression in children and adolescents: A systematic literature review on the influence of aggression subtype and gender. *Aggression and Violent Behavior, 39,* 25–32. https://doi.org/10.1016/j.avb.2018.01.005

Masapollo, M., Polka, L., & Ménard, L. (2015). When infants talk, infants listen: Pre- babbling infants prefer listening to speech with infant vocal properties. *Developmental Science.* https://doi.org/10.1111/desc.12298

Mason, G. M., Kirkpatrick, F., Schwade, J. A., & Goldstein, M. H. (2018). The role of dyadic coordination in organizing visual attention in 5-month-old infants. *Infancy, 24*(2), 162–186. https://doi.org/10.1111/infa.12255

Masten, A. S (2018). Resilience theory and research on children and families: Past, present, and promise. *Journal of Family Theory & Review, 10,* 12–31. https://doi.org/10.1111/jftr.12255

Masten, A. S., & Barnes, A. J. (2018). Resilience in children: Developmental perspectives. *Children, 5*(7), 98. https://doi.org/10.3390/children5070098

Mastrotheodoros, S., et al. (2019). Parent–adolescent conflict across adolescence: Trajectories of informant discrepancies and associations with personality types. *Journal of Youth and Adolescence,* 1–17. https://doi.org/10.1007/s10964-019-01054-7

Masur, E. F., Flynn, V., & Olson, J. (2016). Infants' background television exposure during play: Negative relations and quality of mothers' speech and infants' vocabulary acquisition. *First Language, 36*(2), 109–123. https://doi.org/10.1177/0142723716639499

Mathes, E. W. (2019). An evolutionary perspective on Kohlberg's theory of moral development. *Current Psychology*, 1–14. https://doi.org/10.1007/s12144-019-00348-0

Matsui, T. (2019). *Food allergy is linked to season of birth, sun exposure, and vitamin d.* Allergology International, 68(2). https://doi.org/10.1016/j.alit.2018.12.003

Mattson, M. P. (2019). An evolutionary perspective on why food overconsumption impairs cognition. *Trends in Cognitive Sciences, 23*(3), 200–212. https://doi.org/10.1016/j.tics.2019.01.003

May, K. E., & Elder, A. D. (2018). Efficient, helpful, or distracting? A literature review of media multitasking in relation to academic performance. *International Journal of Educational Technology in Higher Education, 15*, Article 13. https://doi.org/10.1186/s41239-018-0096-z

Maykel, C., Bray, M., & Rogers, H. J. (2018). A classroom-based physical activity intervention for elementary student on-task behavior. *Journal of Applied School Psychology, 34*(3), 259–274. https://doi.org/10.1080/15377903.2017.1403402

Mayo, A. & Siraj, I. (2015). Parenting practices and children's academic success in low-SES families. *Oxford Review of Education, 41*(1), 47–63. https://doi.org/10.1080/03054985.2014.995160

Mayo-Gamble, T. L., Barnes, P. A., Erves, J. C., Middlestat, S. E., & Lin, H-C. (2018). 'It means everyone should know their status': Exploring lay conceptions of sickle cell trait and sickle cell trait screening among Blacks within middle reproductive age. *Ethnicity & Health, 23*(7). https://doi.org/10.1080/13557858.2017.1295135

Mays, V. M., & Ghavami, N. (2018). History, aspirations, and transformations of intersectionality: Focusing on gender. In C. B. Travis, J. W. White, A. Rutherford, W. S. Williams, S. L. Cook, & K. F. Wyche (Eds.), *APA handbooks in psychology®. APA handbook of the psychology of women: History, theory, and battlegrounds* (pp. 541–566). American Psychological Association, http://dx.doi.org/10.1037/0000059-028

Mazzer, K., Baudacco, S., Linton, S. J., & Boersma, K. (2018). Longitudinal associations between time spent using technology and sleep duration among adolescents. *Journal of Adolescence, 66*, 112–119. https://doi.org/10.1016/j.adolescence.2018.05.004

McAdams, D. P. (2018). Narrative identity: What is it? What does it do? How do you measure it? *Imagination, Cognition and Personality: Consciousness in Theory, Research, and Clinical Practice, 37*(3), 359–372. https://doi.org/10.1177/0276236618756704

McBride, D. L. (2019). Life-threatening allergic reactions increasing among children. *Journal of Pediatric Nursing, 44*, 127–129. https://doi.org/10.1016/j.pedn.2018.05.013

McClatchey, T., et al. (2018). Missed opportunities: Unidentified genetic risk factors in prenatal care. *Prenatal Diagnosis* 38 (1), 75–79. https://doi.org/10.1002/pd.5048

McClelland, M. M., et al. (2014). Predictors of early growth in academic achievement: The head-toes-knees-shoulders task. *Frontiers in Psychology.* https://doi.org/10.3389/fpsyg.2014.00599

McCormick, E. M., Gates, K. M., & Telzer, E. H. (2019). Model-based network discovery of developmental and performance-related differences during risky decision-making. *NeuroImage, 188*, 456–464. https://doi.org/10.1016/j.neuroimage.2018.12.042

McDaniel, B. T., & Radesky, J. S. (2018). Technoconference: Longitudinal associations between parent technology use, parenting stress, and child behavior problems. *Pediatric Research, 84*, 210–218.

McDaniel, S. C., McLeod, R., Carter, C. L. & Robinson, C. (2017). Supplemental summer literacy instruction: Implications for preventing summer reading loss. *Reading Psychology, 38*(7), 673–686. https://doi.org/10.1080/02702711.2017.1333070

McDermott, C. L. et al. (2019). Longitudinally mapping child socioeconomic status associations and subcortical morphology. *Journal of Neuroscience, 39*(8), 1365–1373. https://doi.org/10.1523/JNEUROSCI.1808-18.2018

McDonald, K., & Asher, S. R. (2018). Peer acceptance, peer rejection, and popularity: Social-cognitive and behavioral perspectives. In W. M. Bukowski, B. Laursen, & K. H. Rubin (Eds.), *Handbook of peer interactions, relationships and groups* (pp. 429–446). Guilford Press.

McDonald, P. A., & Berg, D. H. (2018). Identifying the nature of impairments in executive functioning and working memory of children with severe difficulties in arithmetic. *Child Neuropsychology: A Journal of Normal and Abnormal Development in Childhood and Adolescence, 24*(8), 1047–1062. https://doi.org/10.1080/09297049.2017.1377694

McEachin, A., Augustine, C. H. & McCombs, J. (2018). Effective summer programming: What educators and policymakers should know. *American Educator, 42*(1), 10–11.

McGhee, P. E. (1974). Cognitive mastery and children's humor. *Psychological Bulletin, 81*(1), 721–730. https://doi.org/10.1037/h0037015

McKay, C. D., Cumming, S. P., & Blake, T. (2019). Youth sport: Friend or foe? *Best Practice & Research Clinical Rheumatology, 33*(1), 141–157. https://doi.org/10.1016/j.berh.2019.01.017

McKinney, C., & Franz, A. O. (2019). Latent profiles of perceived parental psychopathology: Associations with emerging adult psychological problems. *Child Psychiatry & Human Development, 50*(3), 411–424. https://doi.org/10.1007/s10578-018-0851-3

McLemore, M. R., et al. (2018). Healthcare experiences of pregnant, birthing and postnatal women of color at risk for preterm birth. *Social Science & Medicine, 201,* 127–135. https://doi.org/10.1016/j.socscimed.2018.02.013

McLeod, B. A., Johnson, W. E., Jr., Cryer-Coupet, & Mincy, R. B. (2019). Examining the longitudinal effects of paternal incarceration and coparenting relationships on sons' educational outcomes: A mediation analysis. *Child and Youth Services Review, 100,* 362–375. https://doi.org/10.1016/j.childyouth.2019.03.010

McLoyd, V. C. (2019). How children and adolescents think about, make sense of, and respond to economic inequality: Why does it matter? *Developmental Psychology, 55*(3), 592–600. http://dx.doi.org/10.1037/dev0000691

McMullen J., Chan J.YC., Mazzocco M.M.M., Hannula-Sormunen M.M. (2019). Spontaneous mathematical focusing tendencies in mathematical development and education. In A. Norton & M. Alibali (Eds.), *Constructing number: Research in mathematics education.* Springer, https://doi.org/10.1007/978-3-030-00491-0_4

McQuillan, M. E. (2018). Dysregulation in children: Origins and implications from age 5 to 28. *Development and Psychopathology, 30*(2), 695–713. https://doi.org/10.1017/S0954579417001572

McRae, D.N., et al. (2018). Reduced prevalence of small-for-gestational-age and preterm birth for women of low socioeconomic position: A population-based cohort study comparing antenatal midwifery and physician models of care. *BMJ Open, 8*(10), e022220. https://doi.org/10.1136/bmjopen-2018-022220

Meakings, S., Coffey, A., & Shelton, K. H. (2017). The influence of adoption on sibling relationships: Experiences and support needs of newly adopted families. *British Journal of Social Work, 47,* 1781–1799. https://doi.org/10.1093/bjsw/bcx097

Meier, A., Hartmann, B. S., & Larson, R. (2018). A quarter century of participation in school-based extracurricular activities: Inequalities by race, class, gender and age? *Journal of Youth and Adolescence, 47,* 1299–1316. https://doi.org/10.1007/s10964-018-0838-1

Meixner, J., et al. (2019). The relation between executive function and reading comprehension in primary-school students: A cross-lagged-panel analysis. *Early Childhood Research Quarterly, 46*(1), 62–74. https://doi.org/10.1016/j.ecresq.2018.04.010

Mejeur, J., & Poppe, J. (2014). Family leave with pay. *State Legislatures, 40*(6), 11. https://www.questia.com/magazine/1G1-371687127/family-leave-with-pay

Melchers, M., Plieger, T., Montag, C., Reuter, M., Spinath, F. M., & Hahn, E. (2018). The heritability of response styles and its impact on heritability estimates of personality: A twin study. *Personality and Individual Differences, 134,* 16–24. https://doi.org/10.1016/j.paid.2018.05.023

Melchior, M., & Hebebrand, J. (2018). Unraveling genetic factors involved in intelligence, educational attainment and socioeconomic standing: What are the implications for childhood mental health care professionals? *European Child & Adolescent Psychiatry, 27*(5), 545–552. https://doi.org/10.1007/s00787-018-1142-z

Melnitchouk, N., Scully, R. E., & Davids, J. S. (2018). Barriers to breastfeeding for U.S. physicians who are mothers. *JAMA Internal Medicine, 178*(8), 1130–1132. https://doi.org/10.1001/jamainternmed.2018.0320

Meltzer, L. (2018). Creating strategic classrooms and schools: Embedding executive function strategies in the curriculum. In L. Meltzer (Ed.), *Executive function in education: From theory to practice* (2nd ed., pp. 263–299). Guilford Press.

Meltzoff, A. N., & Marshall, P. J. (2018). Human infant imitation as a social survival circuit. *Current Opinion in Behavioral Sciences, 24,* 130–136. https://doi.org/10.1016/j.cobeha.2018.09.006

Mendle, J., Beltz, A. M., Carter, R., & Dorn, L. D. (2019). Understanding puberty and its measurement: Ideas for research in a new generation. *Journal of Research on Adolescence, 29*(1), 82–96. https://doi.org/10.1111/jora.12371

Mendle, J., Ryan, R. M., & McKone, K. M. P. (2019). Early menarche and internalizing and externalizing in adulthood: Explaining the persistence of effects. *Journal of Adolescent Health, 65*(5), 500–606. https://doi.org/10.1016/j.jadohealth.2019.06.004

Mennella, J. A., Daniels, L. M., & Reiter, A. R. (2017). Learning to like vegetables during breastfeeding: A clinical trial of lactating mothers and infants. *The American Journal of Clinical Nutrition, 106*(1), 67–76. https://doi.org/10.3945/ajcn.116.143982

Merolla, A. J., & Kam, J. A. (2018). Parental hope communication and parent–adolescent constructive conflict management: A multilevel longitudinal analysis. *Journal of Family Communication, 18*(1), 32–50. https://doi.org/10.1080/15267431.2017.1385461

Merz, E. C., Landry, S. H., Montroy, J., & Williams, J. M. (2017). Bidirectional association between parental responsiveness and executive function during early childhood. *Social Development, 26*(3), 591–609. https://doi.org/10.1111/sode.12204

Metcalfe, J. J., et al. (2018). Family food involvement is related to healthier dietary intake in preschool-age children. *Appetite, 126*, 195–200. https://doi.org/10.1016/j.appet.2018.03.021

Metzger, A., et al. (2018). The intersection of emotional and sociocognitive competencies with civic engagement in middle childhood and adolescence. *Journal of Youth and Adolescence, 47*, 1663–1668. https://doi.org/10.1007/s10964-018-0842-5

Meyer, S. et al. (2014). Parent emotion representations and the socialization of emotion regulation in the family. *International Journal of Behavioral Development, 38*(2), 164–173. https://doi.org/10.1177/0165025413519014

Mez, J., Daneshvar, D. H., & Kiernan, P. T. (2017). Clinicopathological evaluation of chronic traumatic encephalopathy in players of American football. *JAMA, 318*(4), 360–370. https://doi.org/10.1001/jama.2017.8334

Michl, P. et al. (2014). Neurobiological underpinnings of shame and guilt: A pilot fMRI study. *Social Cognitive and Affective Neuroscience, 9*(2), 150–157. https://doi.org/*10.1093/scan/nss114*

Mikami, A. Y., Miller, M., & Lerner, M. D. (2019). Social functioning in youth with attention-deficit/hyperactivity disorder and autism spectrum disorder: Transdiagnostic commonalities. *Clinical Psychology Review, 68*, 54–70. https://doi.org/10.1016/j.cpr.2018.12.005

Mikulincer, M., & Shaver, P. R. (2019). Attachment orientations and emotion regulation. *Current Opinion in Psychology, 25*, 6–10. https://doi.org/10.1016/j.copsyc.2018.02.006

Miljkovitch, R., et al. (2018). Borderline personality disorder in adolescence as a generalization of disorganized attachment. *Frontiers in Psychology, 9*. https://doi.org/10.3389/fpsyg.2018.01962

Miller, A. B., & Prinstein, M. J. (2019). Adolescent suicide as a failure of acute stress-response systems. *Annual Review of Clinical Psychology, 7*(15), 425–450. https://doi.org/10.1146/annurev-clinpsy-050718-095625

Miller, D. I., Nolla, K. M., Eagly, A. H., & Uttal, D. H. (2018). The development of children's gender stereotypes: A meta-analysis of five decades of U.S. Draw-A-Scientist studies. *Child Development, 89*(6), 1943–1955. https://doi.org/10.1111/cdev.13039

Miller, M. M., et al. (2018). Sleep duration and incidence of obesity infants, children, and adolescents: Systematic review and meta-analysis of prospective studies. *Sleep, 41*(4). https://doi.org/10.1093/sleep/zsy018

Miller, N. V., et al. (2018). Infant temperament reactivity and early maternal caregiving: Independent and interactive links to later childhood attention-deficit/hyperactivity disorder symptoms. *Journal of Child Psychology and Psychiatry, 60*(1), 43–53. https://doi.org/10.1111/jcpp.12934

Miller, P. H., & Aloise-Young, P. (2018). Revisiting young children's understanding of the psychological causes of behavior. *Child Development, 89*(5), 1441–1461. doi:10.1111/cdev.12891

Miller, A. L., Seifer, R., Crossin, R. and Lebourgeois, M. K. (2015), Toddler's self-regulation strategies in a challenge context are nap-dependent. *Journal of Sleep Research, 24*: 279–287. https//doi.org/10.1111/jsr.12260

Miller, S. D., et al. (2018). To be or not to be (an expert)? Revisiting the role of deliberate practice in improving performance. *High Ability Studies.* https://doi.org/10.1080/13598139.2018.1519410

Milojevich, H. M., Quas, J. A., & Yano, J. Z. (2016). Children's participation in legal proceedings: Stress, coping, and consequences. In M. Miller & B. Bornstein (Eds.), *Advances in psychology and law* (Vol. 1). Springer, https://doi.org/10.1007/978-3-319-29406-3_6

Mindell, J. A., Lee, C. I., Leichman, E. S., & Rotella, K. N. (2018). Massage-based bedtime routine: Impact of sleep and mood in infants and mothers. *Sleep Medicine, 41*, 51–57. https://doi.org/10.1016/j.sleep.2017.09.010

Mindell, J. A., Leichman, E. S., DuMond, C., & Sadeh, A. (2017). Sleep and social-emotional development in infants and toddlers. *Journal of Clinical Child & Adolescent Psychology, 46*(2), 236–246. https://doi.org/10.1080/15374416.2016.1188701

Mindell, J. A., & Moore, M. (2018). Does sleep matter? Impact on development and functioning in infants. *Pediatrics, 142*(6), e20182589. https://doi.org/10.1542/peds.2018-2589

Mischel, W. et al. (2011). 'Willpower' over the life span: Decomposing self-regulation. *Social Cognitive and Affective Neuroscience, 6*(2), 252–256. DOI: *10.1093/scan/nsq081*

Mischel, W. (2012). Self-control theory. In P. A. M. Van Lange, A. W. Kruglanski, & E. T. Higgins (Eds.), *The handbook of theories of social psychology, Volume 2* (pp. 1–22). London, UK: Sage Publications. http://dx.doi.org/10.4135/9781446249222.n26

Mischel, W., Ebbesen, E. B., & Zeiss, A. M. (1972). Cognitive and attentional mechanisms in delay of gratification. *Journal of Personality and Social Psychology, 21*, 204–218. https://doi.org/ 10.1037/h0032198

Mischel, W., Shoda, Y., & Rodriquez, M. L. (1989). Delay of gratification in children. *Science, 244*, 933–938.

Misri, S. K. (2018). History of postpartum psychiatric disorders: Don't forget the dads. In *Paternal Postnatal Psychiatric Illnesses.* Springer, https://doi.org/10.1007/978-3-319-68249-5_1

Missotten, L. C., Luyckx, K., Branje, S., Hale, W. W., III, & Meeus, W. H. (2017). Examining the longitudinal relations among adolescents' conflict management with parents and conflict frequency. *Personality and Individual Differences, 117,* 37–41. http://dx.doi.org/10.1016/j.paid.2017.05.037

Missotten, L. C., Luyckx, K., Branje, S., & Van Petegem, S. (2018). Adolescents' conflict management styles with mothers: Longitudinal associations with parenting and reactance. *Journal of Youth & Adolescence, 47,* 260–274. https://doi.org/10.1007/s10964-017-0634-3

Modabbernia, A., et al. (2018). APGAR score and risk of autism. *European Journal of Epidemiology, 34,* 105–114. https://doi.org/10.1007/s10654-018-0445-1

Modecki, K. L., Blomfield Neira, C., & Barber, B. L. (2018). Finding what fits: Breadth of participation at the transition to high school mitigates declines in self-concept. *Developmental Psychology, 54*(10), 1954–1970. http://dx.doi.org/10.1037/dev0000570

Mohammed, R. (2018). *Creative learning in the early years: Nurturing the characteristics of creativity.* Routledge.

Moilanen, K. L., & Manuel, M. L. (2017). Parenting, self-regulation and social competence with peers and romantic partners. *Journal of Applied Developmental Psychology, 49,* 46–54. http://dx.doi.org/10.1016/j.appdev.2017.02.003

Mol, S. E. & Bus, A. G. (2011). To read or not to read: A meta-analysis of print exposure from infancy to early adulthood. *Psychological Bulletin, 137*(2), 267–296. https://doi.org/10.1037/a0021890

Molenaar, D. et al. (2013). Genotype by environment interactions in cognitive ability: A survey of studies from four countries covering four age groups. *Behavior Genetics, 43,* 208–219. https://doi.org/10.1007/s10519-012-9581-7

Molitor, A., & Hsu, H-C. (2019). Child development across cultures. In K. D. Keith (Ed.), *Cross-cultural psychology: Contemporary themes and perspectives* (2nd ed., pp. 153–188). John Wiley & Sons.

Mongan, D., et al. (2018). Childhood adversity and psychotic experiences in the general population: What is the predictive role of resilience, coping style and social support? *Schizophrenia Bulletin, 44*(1), S317. https://doi.org/10.1093/schbul/sby017.773

Montoya, J. G. (2018). Systematic screening and treatment for toxoplasmosis during pregnancy: Is the glass half full or half empty? *American Journal of Obstetrics & Gynecology, 219*(4), 315–319. https://doi.org/10.1016/j.ajog.2018.08.001

Moon, C. (2017) Prenatal experience with the maternal voice. In M. Filippa, P., Kuhn, & B. Westrup (Eds.), *Early vocal contact and preterm infant brain development* (pp. 25–37). Springer, https://doi.org/10.1007/978-3-319-65077-7_2

Moon, C., Zernzach, R. C., & Kuhl, P. K. (2015). Mothers say "baby" and their newborns do not choose to listen: A behavioral preference study to compare with ERP results. *Frontiers in Human Neuroscience, 9,* 153. https//doi.org/10.3389/fnhum.2015.00153

Moore, C. C., Hubbard, J. A., Bookhout, M. K., & Mlawer, F. (2018). Relations between reactive and proactive aggression and daily emotions in adolescents. *Journal of Abnormal Child Psychology, 47,* 1495–1507. https://doi.org/10.1007/s10802-019-00533-6

Moore, C., Mealiea, J., Garon, N., & Povinelli, D. (2007). The development of body self-awareness. *Infancy, 11*(2), 157–174. https://doi.org/10.1111/j.1532-7078.2007.tb00220.x

Moore, D. S. (2015). *The developing genome: An introduction to behavioral epigenetics.* Oxford University Press.

Moore, R. M. (2014). Anxiety in toddlers-Role of social referencing at onset. *Journal of Developmental and Behavioral Pediatrics, 35*(3), 230. https://doi.org/ 10.1111/j.1467-8624.1988.tb01492.x

Mora, L., van Sebille, K., & Neill, L. (2018). An evaluation of play therapy for children and young people with intellectual disabilities. *Research and Practice in Intellectual and Developmental Disabilities, 5*(2), 178c191. https://doi.org/10.1080/23297018.2018.1442739

Moradi, S., et al. (2018). Food insecurity and the risks of under-nutrition complications among children and adolescents: A systematic review and meta-analysis. *Nutrition, 62,* 52–60. https://doi.org/10.1016/j.nut.2018.11.029

Morales, D. R., Slattery, J., Evans, S., & Kurz, X. (2018). Antidepressant use during pregnancy and risk of autism spectrum disorder and attention deficit hyperactivity disorder: Systematic review of observational studies and methodological considerations. *BMC Medicine, 16*(6). https://doi.org/10.1186/s12916-017-0993-3

Morawska, A., Dittman, C. K., & Rusby, J. C. (2019). Promoting self-regulation in young children: The role of parenting interventions. *Clinical Child and Family Psychology Review, 22,* 43–51. https://doi.org/10.1007/s10567-019-00281-5

Moreau, J., Gatimel, N., Cohade, C., Parinaud, & Léandri, R. (2018). Mother's age at menopause but not own age at menarche has an impact on ovarian reserve. *Gynecological Endocrinology, 34*(8), 664–665. https://doi.org/10.1080/09513590.2018.1428300

Moreno, S., Lee, Y., Janus, M., & Bialystock, E. (2015). Short-term second language and music training induces lasting functional brain changes in early childhood. *Child Development, 86*(2), 394–406. https://doi.org/10.1111/cdev.12297

Morgan, S. E., White, S. R., Bullmore, E. T., & Vértes, P. E. (2018). A network neuroscience approach to typical and atypical brain development. *Cognitive Neuroscience and Neuroimaging, 3*(9), 754–766. https://doi.org/10.1016/j.bpsc.2018.03.003

Moriguchi, Y., & Todo, N. (2018). Prevalence of imaginary companions in children: A meta-analysis. *Merrill-Palmer Quarterly, 64*(4), 459–482.

Morris, A. S., Cui, L., Criss, M. M., & Simmons, W. K. (2018). Emotional regulation dynamics during parent–child interactions: Implications for research and practice. In M. Cole & T. Hollenstein (Eds.), *Emotion regulation: A matter of time.* Routledge.

Morton, S. U., & Brodsky, D. (2016). Fetal physiology and the transition to extrauterine life. *Clinics in Perinatology, 43*(3), 395–407. https://doi.org/10.1016/j.clp.2016.04.001

Moss, P., Eirinaki, V., Savage, S., & Howlin, P. (2019). Growing older with autism—The experiences of adult siblings of individuals with autism. *Research in Autism Spectrum Disorders, 63*, 42–51. https://doi.org/10.1016/j.rasd.2018.10.005

Muenks, K., Wigfield, A., & Eccles, J. (2018). I can do this! The development and calibration of children's expectations for success and competence beliefs. *Developmental Review, 48*, 24–39. https://doi.org/10.1016/j.dr.2018.04.001

Muhle, R. A., Reed, H. E., & Stratigos, K. A. (2018). The emerging clinical neuroscience of autism spectrum disorder. *JAMA Psychiatry, 75*(5), 514–523. https://doi.org/10.1001/jamapsychiatry.2017.4685

Mueller, E., & Blaser, M. (2018). Breast milk, formula, the microbiome and overweight. *Nature Reviews Endocrinology, 14*, 510–511. https://doi.org/10.1038/s41574-018-0066-5

Muller, C., Sampson, R. J., & Winter, A. S. (2018). Environmental inequality: The social causes and consequences of lead exposure. *Annual Review of Sociology, 44*, 263–282. https://doi.org/10.1146/annurev-soc-073117-041222

Muñiz de la Pēna, C., Pineda, L., & Punsky, B. (2019). Working with parents and children separated at the border: Examining the impact of the Zero Tolerance Policy and beyond. *Journal of Child & Adolescent Trauma, 12*(2), 153–164. https://doi.org/10.1007/s40653-019-00262-4

Muris, P. & Meesters, C. (2014). Small or big in the eyes of the other: On the developmental psychopathology of self-conscious emotions as shame, guilt, and pride. *Clinical Child and Family Psychology Review, 17*(1), 19–40. https://doi.org/10.1007/s10567-013-0137-z

Murray, G., et al. (2019). The impact of contextual information on the emotion recognition of children with an intellectual disability. *Journal of Applied Research in Intellectual Disabilities, 32*(1), 152–158. https://doi.org/10.1111/jar.12517

Murry, V. M., & Lippold, M. A. (2018). Parenting practices in diverse family structures: Examination of adolescents' development and adjustment. *Journal of Research on Adolescence, 28*(3), 65—664. https://doi.org/10.1111/jora.12390

Musitu-Ferrer, D., et al. (2019). Relationships between parental socialization styles, empathy, and connectedness with nature: The implications in environmentalism. *International Journal of Environmental Research and Public Health, 16*(14), 2461. https://doi.org/10.3390/ijerph16142461

Nadan, Y., & Korbin, J. (2018). Cultural context, intersectionality, and child vulnerability. *Childhood Vulnerability Journal, 1*(1–3), 5–14. https://doi.org/10.1007/s41255-019-00003-7

Nagayama Hall, G. C. N., Yip, T., & Zárate, M. A. (2016). On becoming multicultural in a monocultural research world: A conceptual approach to studying ethnocultural diversity. *American Psychologist, 71*(1), 40–51. https://doi.org/10.1037/a0039734

Nair, R. L., Roche, K. M., & White, R. M. B. (2018). Acculturation gap distress among Latino youth: Prospective links to family processes and youth depressive symptoms, alcohol use, and academic performance. *Journal of Youth and Adolescence, 47*, 105–120. https://doi.org/10.1007/s10964-017-0753-x

Nanu, C. E., et al. (2018). Spontaneous focusing on numerosity in preschool as a predictor of mathematical skills and knowledge in fifth grade. *Journal of Experimental Child Psychology, 169*, 42–58. https://doi.org/10.1016/j.jecp.2017.12.011

Napoletano, A., Elgar, F. J., Saul, G., Dirks, M., & Craig, W. (2015). The view from the bottom: Relative deprivation and bullying victimization in Canadian adolescents. *Journal of Interpersonal Violence, 31*(20), 3443–3463. http://dx.doi.org/10.1177/0886260515585528

Narayan, A., et al. (2018). *Fair progress? Economic mobility across generations around the world.* Retrieved from https://www.worldbank.org/en/topic/poverty/publication/fair-progress-economic-mobility-across-generations-around-the-world

Narr, R. K., Allen, J. P., Tan, J. S., & Loeb, E. L. (2019). Close friendship strength and broader peer group desirability as differential predictors of adult mental health. *Child Development, 90*(1), 298–313. https://doi.org/10.1111/cdev.12905

Nasiri, S., Akbari, H., Tagharrobi, L., & Tabatabaee, A. S. (2018). The effect of progressive muscle relaxation and guided imagery on stress, anxiety, and depression of pregnant women referred to health centers. *Journal of Education and Health Promotion, 7*(41). https://doi.org/10.4103/jehp.jehp_158_16

Nassar, R., et al. (2019). Gestational age is dimensionally associated with structural brain network abnormalities across development. *Cerebral Cortex, 29*(5), 2102–2114. https://doi.org/10.1093/cercor/bhy091

National Collegiate Athletic Association. (2017). *45 years of Title IX: The status of women in intercollegiate athletics.* http:// www.ncaa.org/sites/default/files/TitleIX45-295-FINAL_WEB.pdf

National Federation of State High School Associations (2017). *High school sports participation increases for the 29th consecutive year.* Retrieved from https://www.nfhs.org/articles/high-school-sports-participation-increases-for-29th-consecutive-year/

National Institute of Dental and Craniofacial Research. (2020). Dental caries (tooth decay) in children 2 to 11. Retrieved from: https://www.nidcr.nih.gov/research/data-statistics/dental-caries/children

National Institute of Mental Health (2019). *Mental illness.* Retrieved from https://www.nimh.nih.gov/health/statistics/mental-illness.shtml

National Sleep Foundation (2019). *How much sleep do we really need?* Retrieved from https://www.sleepfoundation.org/how-sleep-works/how-much-sleep-do-we-really-need

Nayak, S., Salem, H. Z., & Tarullo, A. R. (2020). Neural mechanisms of response-preparation and inhibition in bilingual and monolingual children: Lateralized readiness Potentials (LRPs) during a nonverbal Stroop task. Developmental Cognitive Neuroscience, 41, https://doi.org/10.1016/j.dcn.2019.100740

Nazanin, M., et al., (2018). Is ovarian reserve associated with body mass index and obesity in reproductive aged women? A meta-analysis. *Menopause, 25*(9), 1046–1055. https://doi.org/10.1097/GME.0000000000001116

Neelon, S. E. B., Finkelstein, J., Neelon, B., & Gillman, M. W. (2017). Evaluation of physical activity regulation for child care in Massachusetts. *Childhood Obesity, 13*(1), 36–43. https://doi.org/10.1089/chi.2016.0142

Neely, S. R., & Vaquera, E. (2017). Making it count: Breadth and intensity of extracurricular engagement and high school dropout. *Sociological Perspectives, 60*(6), 1039–1062. https://doi.org/10.1177/0731121417700114

Nelson, B. D., et al. (2018). Time-frequency reward-related delta prospectively predicts the development of adolescent-onset depression. *Biological Psychiatry: Cognitive Neuroscience and Neuroimaging, 3*(1), 41–49. http://dx.doi.org/10.1016/j.bpsc.2017.07.005

Nelson, C., Paul, K., Johnston, S. S., & Kidder, J. E. (2017). Use of a creative dance intervention package to increase social engagement and play complexity of young children with autism spectrum disorder. *Education and Training in Autism and Developmental Disabilities, 52*(2), 170–185.

Nelson, E. L., et al. (2019). The home handedness questionnaire: Pilot data from preschoolers. *Laterality: Asymmetries of Brain, Behaviour, and Cognition, 24*(4), 482–503. https://doi.org/10.1080/1357650X.2018.1543313

Nesbitt, K. T., Fuhs, M., W., & Farran, D. C. (2019). Stability and instability in the co-development of mathematics, executive function skills, and visual-motor integration from prekindergarten to first grade. *Early Childhood Research Quarterly, 46*(1), 262–274. https://doi.org/10.1016/j.ecresq.2018.02.003

Nestle, M. (2018). Perspective: Challenges and controversial issues in the dietary guidelines for Americans, 1980–2015. *Advances in Nutrition, 9*(2), 148–150. https://doi.org/10.1093/advances/nmx022

Nettle, D., et al. (2019). Opportunistic food consumption in relation to childhood and adult food insecurity: An exploratory correlational study. *Appetite, 132,* 222–229. https://doi.org/10.1016/j.appet.2018.07.018

Neuman, S. B., & Kaefer, T. (2018). Developing low-income children's vocabulary and content knowledge through a shared book reading program. *Contemporary Educational Psychology, 52,* 15–24. https://doi.org/10.1016/j.cedpsych.2017.12.001

Neuman, S. B., & Moland, N. (2016). Book deserts: The consequences of income segregation on children's access to print. *Urban Education, 54*(1), 126–147. https://doi.org/10.1177/0042085916654525

Newcombe, N. (2013). Cognitive development: Changing view of cognitive change. *Wiley Interdisciplinary Reviews: Cognitive Science, 4*(5), 479–491. https://doi.org10.1002/wcs.1245

Newland, R. P., & Crnic, K. A. (2017). Developmental risk and goodness of fit in the mother–child relationship: Links to parenting stress and children's behavior problems. *Infant and Child Development, 26*(2), e1980. https://doi.org/10.1002/icd.1980

Ng, F. F., Pomerantz, E. W., Lang, S-F., & Deng, C. (2019). The role of mothers' child-based worth in their affective responses to children's performance. *Child Development, 90*(1), e165–e181. https://doi.org/10.1111/cdev.12881

Nguyen, T. T., Ryan, R. M., & Deci, E. L. (2018). Solitude as an approach to affective self-regulation. *Personality and Social Psychology Bulletin, 44*(1), 92–106. https://doi.org/10.1177/0146167217733073

Nguyen-Louie, T. T., et al. (2018). Effects of sleep on substance use in adolescents: A longitudinal perspective. *Addiction Biology, 23*(2), 750–760. https://doi.org/10.1111/adb.12519

Nichols, J et al. (2019). The role of data type and recipient in individuals' perspectives on sharing passively collected smartphone data for mental health: Cross-sectional questionnaire study. *JMIR Mhealth and Uhealth, 7*(4), e12578. https://doi.org/10.2196/12578

Nicholson, A., Whalen, J. M., & Pexman, P. M. (2013). Children's processing of emotion in ironic language. *Frontiers in Psychology.* https://doi.org/10.3389/fpsyg.2013.00691

Niedźwiecka, A., Ramotowska, S., & Tomalski, P. (2018). Mutual gaze during early mother–infant interactions promotes attention control development. *Child Development, 89*(6), 2230–2244. https://doi.org/10.1111/cdev.12830

Nielsen, M., Haun, D. Kärtner, J., & Legare, C. H. (2017). The persistent sampling bias in developmental psychology: A call to action. *Journal of Experimental Child Psychology, 162*, 31–38. https://doi:10.1016/j.jecp.2017.04.017

Nielsen, M. B., et al. (2019). Risk of childhood psychiatric disorders in children of refugee parents with post-traumatic stress disorder: A nationwide, register-based cohort study. *The Lancet Public Health, 4*(7), e353–e359. https://doi.org/10.1016/S2468-2667(19)30077-5

Niemeier, J., & Fitzpatrick, K. M. (2019). Examining food insecurity among high school students: A risks and resources model. *Appetite, 135*, 20–27. https://doi.org/10.1016/j.appet.2018.12.028

Norman, J., et al. (2018). Sustained impact of energy-dense TV and online food advertising on children's dietary intake: A within-subject, randomised, crossover, counter-balanced trial. *International Journal of Behavioral Nutrition and Physical Activity, 15*(37). https://doi.org/10.1186/s12966-018-0672-6

Oberle, E., & Schonert-Reichl, K. A. (2016). Stress contagion in the classroom? The link between classroom teacher burnout and morning cortisol in elementary school students. *Social Sciences & Medicine, 159,* 30–37. https://doi.org/10.1016/j.socscimed.2016.04.031

O'Connor, R. J., Lindsay, S., Mather, E., & Riggs, K. J. (2019). Why would a special FM process exist in adults, when it does not appear to exist in children? *Cognitive Neuroscience, 10*(4), 221–222. https://doi.org/10.1080/17588928.2019.1574260

O'Driscoll, D. N., McGovern, M., Greene, C. M., & Molloy, E. J. (2018). Gender disparities in preterm neonatal outcomes. *Acta Pædiatrica, 107*(9), 1494–1499. https://doi.org/10.1111/apa.14390

OECD. (2016a). PISA 2015 results in focus. *PISA in Focus, No. 67.* OECD Publishing, https://doi.org/10.1787/aa9237e6-en

OECD. (2016b). *PISA 2015 results (Vol. I): Excellence and equity in education.* OECD Publishing, http://dx.doi.org/10.1787/9789264266490-en

OECD. (2018). *Engaging young children: Lessons from research about quality in early child care education, starting strong.* OECD Publishing, https://doi.org/10.1787/9789264085145-en

Ogi, H., et al. (2018). Associations between parents' health literacy and sleeping hours in children: A cross-sectional study. *Healthcare, 6*(2), 32. https://doi.org/10.3390/healthcare6020032

Oh, J., Chopik, W. J., Konrath, S., & Grimm, K. J. (2019). Longitudinal changes in empathy across the life span in six samples of human development. *Social Psychological and Personality Science, 11*(2), 244–253. https://doi.org/10.1177/1948550619849429

O'Farrelly, C., Doyle, O., Vitory, G., & Palamaro-Munsell, E. (2018). Shared reading in infancy and later development: Evidence from an intervention. *Journal of Applied Developmental Psychology, 54*, 69–83. DOI: https://doi.org/10.1016/j.appdev.2017.12.001

O'Keefe, L. (2014). Parents who read to their children nurture more than literacy skills. *AAP News: The Official Newsmagazine of the American Academy of Pediatrics.* https://doi.org 10.1542/aapnews.20140624-2

O'Keefe, L. M., et al. (2019). Puberty timing and adiposity change across childhood and adolescence: Disentangling cause and consequence. *BioRxiv.* https://doi.org/10.1101/578005

Olson, K. R., & Enright, E. A. (2018). Do transgender children (gender) stereotype less than their peers and siblings? *Developmental Science, 21*(4), e12606. https://doi.org/10.1111/desc.12606

Olson, K. R., Key, A. C., & Eaton, M. R. (2015). Gender cognition in transgender children. *Psychological Science, 26*(4), 467–474. https://doi.org/10.1177/0956797614568156

Olson, S. L., Choe, D. E., & Sameroff, A. J. (2018). Trajectories of externalizing problems between age 3 and 10 years: Contributions of children's early effortful control, theory of mind, and parenting experiences. *Development and Psychopathology, 29*(4), 1333–1351. https://doi.org/10.1017/S095457941700030X

Olszewski-Kubilius, P. (2018). The role of the family in talent development. In S. Pfeiffer (Ed.), *Handbook of giftedness in children.* Springer, https://doi.org/10.1007/978-3-319-77004-8_9

Ong, J. S. Y., Soundappan, S. V., Adams, S., & Adams, S. (2018). Helmet use in bicycles and non-motorised wheeled recreational vehicles in children. *Journal of Paediatrics and Child Health, 54*(9), 968–974. https://doi.org/10.1111/jpc.13925

Oosterman, M., Schuengel, C., Forrer, M. L., & De Moor, M. H. M. (2019). The impact of childhood trauma and psychophysiological reactivity on at-risk women's adjustment to parenthood. *Development and Psychopathology, 31*(1), 127–141. https://doi.org/10.1017/S0954579418001591

Orri, M., et al. (2019). Pathways of association between childhood irritability and adolescent suicidality. *Journal of the American Academy of Child & Adolescent Psychiatry, 58*(1), 99–107. https://doi.org/10.1016/j.jaac.2018.06.034

Orth, U., Erol, R. Y., & Luciano, E. C. (2018). Development of self-esteem from age 4 to 94 years: A meta-analysis of longitudinal studies. *Psychological Bulletin, 144*(10), 1045–1080. http://dx.doi.org/10.1037/bul0000161

Osher, D., Cantor, P., Berg, J., Steyer, L., & Rose, T. (2018). Drivers of human development: How relationships and context shape learning and development. *Applied Developmental Science, 24*(1), 6–36. https://doi.org/10.1080/10888691.2017.1398650

Osterhaus, C., Koerber, S., & Sodian, B. (2016). Scaling of advanced theory-of-mind tasks. *Child Development, 87*(6), 1971–1991. https://doi.org/10.1111/cdev.12566

Ótuari, G., Kolling, T., & Knopf, M. (2018). Developmental trend towards exact imitation in the second year: Evidence from a longitudinal study. *International Journal of Behavioral Development, 42*(4), 388–395. https://doi.org/10.1177/0165025417713727

Owen, K. B., et al. (2016). Physical activity and school engagement in youth: A systematic review and meta-analysis. *Educational Psychology, 51*(2), 129–145. https://doi.org/10.1080/00461520.2016.1151793

Owen, K. B., Parker, P. D., Astell-Burt, T., & Lonsdale, C. (2018). Effects of physical activity and breaks on mathematics engagement in adolescents. *Journal of Science and Medicine in Sport, 21*(1), 63–68. https://doi.org/10.1016/j.jsams.2017.07.002

Owen, L. H., Kennedy, O. B., Hill, C., & Houston-Price, C. (2018). Peas, please! Food familiarization through picture books helps parents introduce vegetables into preschoolers' diets. *Appetite, 128*, 32–43. https://doi.org/10.1016/j.appet.2018.05.140

Owens, A. (2017). Income segregation between school districts and inequality in students' achievement. *Sociology of Education, 91*(1), 1–27. https://doi.org/10.1177/0038040717741180

Ozernov-Palchik, O., et al. (2019). The relationship between socioeconomic status and white matter microstructure in pre-reading children: A longitudinal investigation. *Human Brain Mapping, 40*(3), 741–754. https://doi.org/10.1002/hbm.24407

Pace, U., D'Urso, G., & Zappulla, C. (2018). Negative eating attitudes and behaviors among adolescents: The role of parental control and perceived peer support. *Appetite, 121*, 77–82. https://doi.org/10.1016/j.appet.2017.11.001

Pace, U., D'Urso, G., & Zappulla, C. (2019). Internalizing problems as a mediator in the relationship between low effortful control and internet abuse in adolescence: A three-wave longitudinal study. *Computers in Human Behavior, 92*, 47–54. https://doi.org/10.1016/j.chb.2018.10.030

Padilla, J., et al. (2018). Longitudinal course and correlates of parents' differential treatment of siblings in Mexican-origin families. *Family Process, 57*(4), 979–995. https://doi.org/10.1111/famp.12328

Padilla-Walker, L. M., et al. (2019). Associations between parental media monitoring style, information management, and prosocial and aggressive behavior. *Journal of Social and Personal Relationships, 31*(1), 180–200. https://doi.org/10.1177/0265407519859653

Padilla-Walker, L. M., & Son, D. (2019). Longitudinal associations among routine disclosure, parent-child relationship, and adolescents' prosocial and delinquent behaviors. *Journal of Social and Personal Relationships, 36*(6), 1853–1871. https://doi.org/10.1177/0265407518773900

Padilla-Walker, L. M., Son, D., & Nelson, L. J. (2018). A longitudinal growth model of child disclosure to parents across adolescence. *Journal of Family Psychology, 32*(4), 475–483. http://dx.doi.org/10.1037/fam0000369

Pahigiannis, K., & Glos, M. (2018). Peer influences in self-regulation development and interventions in early childhood. *Early Child Development and Care.* https://doi.org/10.1080/03004430.2018.1513923

Palacios-Barrios, E. E., & Hanson, J. L. (2019). Poverty and self-regulation: Connecting psychosocial processes, neurobiology, and the risk of psychopathology. *Comprehensive Psychiatry, 90*, 52–64. https://doi.org/10.1016/j.comppsych.2018.12.012

Pallini et al. (2018). The relation of attachment security status to effortful self-regulation: A meta-analysis. *Psychological Bulletin, 144*(5), 501–531. http://dx.doi.org/10.1037/bul0000134

Paniagua, C., et al. (2019). Under the same label: Adopted adolescents' heterogeneity in well-being and perception of social contexts. *Youth & Society,* https://doi.org/10.1177/0044118X19828081

Pantell, R. H. (2017). The child witness in the courtroom. *Pediatrics, 139*(3), e20164008. https://doi.org/10.1542/peds.2016-4008

Papadimitriou, A. (2016). The evolution of the age at menarche from prehistorical to modern times. *Journal of Pediatric & Adolescent Gynecology, 29*(6), 527–530. https://doi.org/10.1016/j.jpag.2015.12.002

Parent, J., McKee, L. G., & Forehand, R. (2015). Seesaw discipline: The interactive effect of harsh and lax discipline on youth psychological adjustment. *Journal of Child and Family Studies.* https://doi.org/10.1007/s10826-015-0244-1

Park, D., et al. (2018). Fostering grit: Perceive school goal-structure predicts growth in grit and grades. *Contemporary Educational Psychology, 55*, 120–128. https://doi.org/10.1016/j.cedpsych.2018.09.007

Partanen, E., Kujala, T., Tervaniemi, M., & Huotilainen, M. (2013). Prenatal music exposure induces long-term neural effects. *PLoS ONE, 8*(10), e78946. https://doi.org/10.1371/journal.pone.0078946

Parten, M. B. (1932). Social participation among pre-school children. *The Journal of Abnormal and Social Psychology, 27*(3), 243–269. https://doi.org/10.1037/h0074524

Pärtty, A., Rautava, S., & Kalliomäki, M. (2018). Probiotics on pediatric functional gastrointestinal disorders. *Nutrients, 10*(12), 1836. https://doi.org/10.3390/nu10121836

Pascual-Leone, J. (2012). Piaget as a pioneer of dialectical constructivism: Seeking dynamic processes for human science (pp. 15–42). In E. Martí & C. Rodríguez (Eds.), *After Piaget*. New Brunswick, NJ: Transaction Publishers.

Pate, R. R., et al. (2019). Change in children's physical activity: Predictors in the transition from elementary to middle school. *American Journal of Preventative Medicine, 56*(3), e65–e73. https://doi.org/10.1016/j.amepre.2018.10.012

Pateman, H., & Vincent, J. (2010). *Public libraries and social justice*. Routledge.

Patterson, C. J. (2017). Parents' sexual orientation and children's development. *Child Development Perspectives, 11*(1), 45–49. https://doi.org/10.1111/cdep.12207

Patterson, L., Stutey, D. M., & Dorsey, B. (2018). Play therapy with Black children exposed to adverse childhood experiences. *International Journal of Play Therapy, 27*(4), 215–226. http://dx.doi.org/10.1037/pla0000080

Pattison, K. L., et al. (2019). Breastfeeding initiation and duration and child health outcomes in the first baby study. *Preventative Medicine, 118*, 1–6. https://doi.org/10.1016/j.ypmed.2018.09.020

Paul, K. C., Schulz, J., & Bronstein, J. M. (2018). Association of polygenetic risk score with cognitive decline and motor progression in Parkinson disease. *JAMA Neurology, 75*(3), 360–366. https://doi.org/10.1001/jamaneurol.2017.4206

Paulus, M. (2019). Is young children's helping affected by helpees' need? Preschoolers, but not infants selectively help needy others. *Psychological Research*, 1–11. https://doi.org/10.1007/s00426-019-01148-8

Paz-Alonso, P. M., & Goodman, G. S. (2016). Developmental differences across middle childhood in memory and suggestibility for negative and positive events. *Behavioral Sciences and the Law, 34*(1), 30–46. https://doi.org/10.1002/bsl.2239

Peachey, A. A., Wenos, J., & Baller, S. (2017). Trait emotional intelligence related to bullying in elementary school children and to victimization in boys. *OTJR: Occupation, Participation and Health, 37*(4), 178–187. https://doi.org/10.1177/1539449217715859

Pearl, A. M., French, B. F., Dumas, J. E., Moreland, A. D., & Prinz, R. (2014). Bidirectional effects of parenting quality and child externalizing behavior in predominantly single parent, under-resourced Black families. *Journal of Child and Family Studies, 23*(2), 177–188. https://doi.org/10.1007/s10826-012-9692-z

Pedersen, J. (2012). The history of school and summer vacation. *Journal of Inquiry & Action in Education, 5*(1). Retrieved from: https://files.eric.ed.gov/fulltext/EJ1134242.pdf

Pedersen, J. (2015). *Summer versus school: The possibilities of the year-round school*. Lanham, MD: The Rowman & Littlefield Publishing Group, Inc.

Penkler, M., Hanson, M., Biesma, R. & Müller, R. (2019). DOHaD in science and society: Emerging opportunities and novel responsibilities. *Journal of Developmental Origins of Health and Disease, 10*(3), 268–273. https://doi.org/10.1017/S2040174418000892

Perkins, N. H., & Barry, J. E. (2019). Should failure to protect laws include physical and emotional sibling violence? *Child & Family Social Work*. https://doi.org/10.1111/cfs.12643

Perino, M. T., Moreira, J. F. G., & Telzer, E. H. (2019). Links between adolescent bullying and neural activation to viewing social exclusion. *Cognitive, Affective, & Behavioral Neuroscience, 19*, 1467–1478. https://doi.org/10.3758/s13415-019-00739-7

Perone, S., Almy, B., & Zelazo, P. D. (2018). Toward an understanding of the neural basis of executive function development. In R. Gibb & B. Kolb (Eds.), *The Neurobiology of Brain and Behavioral Development* (pp. 291–314). Elsevier/Academic Press, http://dx.doi.org/10.1016/B978-0-12-804036-2.00011-X

Perone, S., Palanisamy, J., & Carlson, S. M. (2018). Age-related change in brain rhythms from early to middle childhood: Links to executive function. *Developmental Science, 21*(6). https://doi.org/10.1111/desc.12691

Perry, N. B., et al. (2018). Childhood self-regulation as a mechanism through which early overcontrolling parenting is associated with adjustment in preschool. *Developmental Psychology, 54*(8), 1542–1554. http://dx.doi.org/10.1037/dev0000536

Petersen, E. E. et al. (2019). Racial/ethnic disparities in pregnancy-related deaths—United States, 2007–2016. *MMWR and Morbidity and Mortality Weekly Report 68*, 762–765. http://dx.doi.org/10.15585/mmwr.mm6835a3

Petscher, Y., Justice, L. M., & Hogan, T. (2018). Modeling the early language trajectory of language development when the measures change and its relation to poor reading comprehension. *Child Development, 89*(6), 2136–2156. https://doi.org/10.1111/cdev.12880

Pew Research Center (2015). *Parenting in America: Outlook, worries, aspirations are strongly linked to financial situation.* Retrieved from https://www.pewsocialtrends.org/2015/12/17/5-childrens-extracurricular-activities/

Pezzella, F. S., Thornberry, T. P., & Smith, C. A. (2016). Race socialization and parenting styles: Links to delinquency for Black and white adolescents. *Youth Violence and Juvenile Justice, 14*(4), 448–467. https://doi.org/10.1177/1541204015581390

Pfeifer, J. H., & Berkman, E. T. (2018). The development of self and identity in adolescence: Neural evidence and implications for a value-based choice perspective on motivated behavior. *Child Development Perspectives, 12*(3), 158–164. https://doi.org/10.1111/cdep.12279

Philbrook, L. E., Shimizu, M., Buckhalt, J. A., & El-Sheikh, M. (2018). Sleepiness as a pathway linking race and socioeconomic status with academic and cognitive outcomes in middle childhood. *Sleep Health, 4*(5), 405–412. https://doi.org/10.1016/j.sleh.2018.07.008

Phinney, J. S. (1996). When we talk about American ethnic groups, what do we means? *American Psychologist, 51*(9), 918–927. https://doi.org/ 10.1037/0003-066X.51.9.918

Piaget, J., (1941). *The child's conception of number.* Routledge and Kegan Paul.

Piaget, J., (1952). *The origins of intelligence in children* (M. Cook, Trans.). International Universities Press.

Piaget, J. (1977). *The moral judgment of the child.* Harcourt, Brace.

Piaget, J., & Inhelder, B. (1948). *The child's conception of space.* W. W. Norton & Company.

Piaget, J. & Inhelder, B. (2000). *The psychology of the child.* New York, NY: Basic Books.

Piccolo, L. R., et al. (2019). School climate is associate with cortical thickness and executive function in children and adolescents. *Developmental Science, 22*(1), e12719. https://doi.org/10.1111/desc.12719

Piercy, K. L., et al. (2018). The physical activity guidelines for Americans. *JAMA, 320*(19), 2020–2028. https://doi.org/10.1001/jama.2018.14854

Piff, P. K., Kraus, M. W., & Keltner, D. (2018). Unpacking the inequality paradox: The psychological roots of inequality and social. In J. M. Olson (Ed.), *Advances in experimental social psychology* (Vol. 57, pp. 53–124). Elsevier, https://doi.org/10.1016/bs.aesp.2017.10.002

Pinquart, M. (2017). Associations of parenting dimensions and styles with externalizing problems of children and adolescents: An updated meta-analysis. *Developmental Psychology, 53*(5), 873–932. http://dx.doi.org/10.1037/dev0000295

Pinquart, M., & Kauser, R. (2018). Do the associations of parenting styles with behavior problems and academic achievement vary by culture? Results from a meta-analysis. *Cultural Diversity and Ethnic Minority Psychology, 24*(1), 75–100. http://dx.doi.org/10.1037/cdp0000149

Pinquart, M., & Pfeiffer, J. P. (2018). Longitudinal associations of the attainment of developmental tasks with psychological symptoms in adolescence: A meta-analysis. *Journal of Research on Adolescence, 30*(S1), 4–14. https://doi.org/10.1111/jora.12462

Piqueras, J. A., Mateu-Martínez, O., Cejudo, J., & Pérez-González, J-C. (2019). Pathways into psychosocial adjustment in children: Modeling the effects of trait emotional intelligence, social-emotional problems, and gender. *Frontiers in Psychology.* https://doi.org/10.3389/fpsyg.2019.00507

Pitkänen, J., Remes, H., Aaltonen, M., & Martikainen, P. (2019). Experience of maternal and paternal adversities in childhood as determinants of self-harm in adolescence and young adulthood. *Journal of Epidemiology and Community Health 73*(11), 1040–1046. https://doi.org/10.1136/jech-2019-212689

Plamondon, A., Bouchard, G., & Lachance-Grzela, M. (2018). Family dynamics and young adults' well-being: The mediating role of sibling bullying. *Journal of Interpersonal Violence.* Advance online publication. https://doi.org/10.1177/0886260518800313

Plomin, R., DeFries, J. C., & Loehlin, J. C. (1977). Genotype-environment interaction and correlation in the analysis of human behavior. *Psychological Bulletin, 84*(2), 309–322. https://doi.org/10.1037/0033-2909.84.2.309

Plomin, R., & von Stumm, S. (2018). The new genetics of intelligence. *Nature Reviews Genetics, 19*, 148–159. https://doi.org/10.1038/nrg.2017.104

Plotka, R., & Busch-Rossnagel, N. A. (2018). The role of length of maternity leave in supporting mother–child interactions and attachment security among American mothers and their infants. *International Journal of Child Care and Education Policy, 12*(2). https://doi.org/10.1186/s40723-018-0041-6

Plutchik, R. (2003). *Emotions and life: Perspectives from psychology, biology, and evolution.* Washington, DC: American Psychological Association.

Pomeranz, J. L., et al. (2018). Legal and administrative feasibility of a federal junk food and sugar-sweetened beverage tax to improve diet. *American Journal of Public Health, 108*(2), 203–209. https://doi.org/0.2105/AJPH.2017.304159

Pomerantz, E. M., Ng, F. F., Cheung, C. S., & Qu, Y. (2014). Raising happy children who succeed in school: Lessons from China and the United States. *Child Development Perspectives, 8*(2), 71–76. https://doi.org/10.1111/cdep.12063

Poon, J. A., Thompson, J. C., Forbes, E. E., & Chaplin, T. M. (2019). Adolescents' reward-related neural activation: Links to thoughts of nonsuicidal self-injury. *Suicide and Life-Threatening Behavior, 49*(1), 76–89. https://doi.org/10.1111/sltb.12418

Pons, F., Bosch, L., & Lewkowicz, D. J. (2019). Twelve-month-old infants' attention to the eyes of a talking face is associated with communication and social skills. *Infant Behavior and Development, 54*, 80–84. https://doi.org/10.1016/j.infbeh.2018.12.003

Pontzer, H., Wood, B. M., & Raichlen, D. A. (2018). Hunter-gatherers as models in public health. *Obesity Reviews, 19*(S1), 24–35. https://doi.org/10.1111/obr.12785

Porter, R. M., et al. (2018). A review of modifiable risk factors for severe obesity in children ages 5 and under. *Childhood Obesity, 14*(7), 468–476. https://doi.org/10.1089/chi.2017.0344

Posner, M. I., & Rothbart, M. K. (2018). Temperament and brain networks of attention. *Philosophical Transactions of the Royal Society B: Biological Sciences, 373*(1744). https://royalsocietypublishing.org/doi/full/10.1098/rstb.2017.0254

Post, P. B., Phipps, C. B., Camp, A. C., & Grybush, A. L. (2019). Effectiveness of child-centered play therapy among marginalized children. *International Journal of Play Therapy, 28*(2), 88–97. http://dx.doi.org/10.1037/pla0000096

Potharst, E.S., Zeegers, M., & Bögels, S.M. (2018). Mindful with your toddler group training: Feasibility, acceptability, and effects on subjective and objective measure. *Mindfulness.* https://doi.org/10.1007/s12671-018-1073-2

Pouwels, J. L., Lansu, T. A. M., & Cillessen, A. H. (2018a). A developmental perspective on popularity and the group process of bullying. *Aggression and Violent Behavior, 43*, 64–70. https://doi.org/10.1016/j.avb.2018.10.003

Pouwels, J. L., et al. (2018b). Predicting adolescents' bullying participation from developmental trajectories of social status and behavior. *Child Development, 89*(4), 1157–1176. https://doi.org/10.1111/cdev.12794

Pouwels, J. L., van Noorden, T. H. J., & Caravita, S. C. S. (2019). Defending victims of bullying in the classroom: The role of moral responsibility and social costs. *Journal of Experimental Social Psychology, 84*, 103831. https://doi.org/10.1016/j.jesp.2019.103831

Pouwels, J. L., van Noorden, T. H. J., Lansu, T. A. M., & Cillessen, A. H. N. (2018). The participant roles of bullying in different grades: Prevalence and social status profiles. *Social Development, 27*(4), 732–747. https://doi.org/10.1111/sode.12294

Powell, K. K., Heymann, P., Tsatsanis, K. D., & Chawarska, K. (2018). Assessment and diagnosis of infants and toddlers with autism spectrum disorder. In S. Goldstein & S. Ozonoff (Eds.), *Assessment of autism spectrum disorder* (2nd ed., pp. 96–129). Guilford Press.

Pozzi, M., et al. (2018). Adverse drug events related to mood and emotion in paediatric patients treated for ADHD: A meta-analysis. *Journal of Affective Disorders, 238*, 161–178. https://doi.org/10.1016/j.jad.2018.05.021

Preckel, K., Kanske, P., & Singer, T. (2018). On the interaction of social affect and cognition: Empathy, compassion, and theory of mind. *Current Opinion in Behavioral Sciences, 19*, 1–6. https://doi.org/10.1016/j.cobeha.2017.07.010

Prehn, K., Korczkowski, M., Rao, H., Fang, Z., Detre, J. A., & Robertson, D. C. (2015). Neural correlates of post-conventional moral reasoning: A voxel-based morphometry study. *PLoS ONE.* https://doi.org/10.1371/journal.pone.0122914

Prendergast, S., & MacPhee, D. (2018). Family resilience amid stigma and discrimination: A conceptual model for families headed by same-sex parents. *Family Relations, 67*(1), 26–40. https://doi.org/10.1111/fare.12296

Presmanes, A., Zuckerman, K. E., & Fombonne, E. (2014). Epidemiology of autism spectrum disorders. In F. R. Volkmar, R. Paul, S. J. Rogers, & K. A. Pelphrey (Eds.) *Handbook of autism and pervasive developmental disorders, 2 Volume Set, 4th Edition.* Hoboken, NJ: John Wiley & Sons, Inc.

Preston, S. H., Vierboom, Y. C., & Stokes, A. (2018). The role of obesity in exceptionally slow US mortality improvement. *PNAS, 115*(5), 957–961. https://doi.org/10.1073/pnas.1716802115

Price, J., & Kalil, A. (2018). The effect of mother–child reading time on children's reading skills: Evidence from natural within-family variation. *Child Development, 90*(6), e688-e702. https://doi.org/10.1111/cdev.13137

Prilleltensky, I. (2012). Wellness as fairness. *American Journal of Community Psychology, 49*, 1–21. http://dx.doi.org/10.1007/s10464-011-9448-8

Protzko, J., Aronson, J., & Blair, C. (2013). How to make a young child smarter: Evidence from the database of raising intelligence. *Perspectives on Psychological Science, 8*(1), 25–40. https://doi.org/10.1177/1745691612462585

Proulx, M-F. & Poulin, F. (2013). Stability and change in kindergartners' friendships: Examination of links with social functioning. *Social Development, 22*(1), 111–125. https://doi.org/10.1111/sode.12001

Providence Talks (2019). *Pilot findings and next steps.* Retrieved from: http://www.providencetalks.org/wp-content/uploads/2015/10/Providence-Talks-Pilot-Findings-Next-Steps.pdf

Psouni, E., et al. (2019). Together I can! Joint attention boosts 3- to 4-year-olds performance in a verbal false-belief test. *Child Development, 90*(1), 35–50. https://doi.org/10.1111/cdev.13075

Psychogiou, L., et al. (2018). Children's emotion understanding in relation to attachment to mother and father. *British Journal of Developmental Psychology, 36*(4), 557–572. https://doi.org/10.1111/bjdp.12239

Ptomey, L. T., et al., (2018). Changes in cognitive function after a 12-week exercise intervention in adults with Down syndrome. *Disability and Health Journal, 11*(3), 486–490. https://doi.org/10.1016/j.dhjo.2018.02.003

Putnick, D. L., et al. (2018). Parental acceptance–rejection and child prosocial behavior: Developmental transactions across the transition to adolescence in nine countries, mothers and fathers, girls and boys. *Developmental Psychology, 54*(10), 1881–1890. http://dx.doi.org/10.1037/dev0000565

Pyle, A., & Danniels, E. (2017). A continuum of play-based learning: The role of the teacher in play-based pedagogy and the fear of hijacking play. *Early Education and Development, 28*(3), 274–289. https://doi.org/10.1080/10409289.2016 .1220771

Quante, M., et al. (2019). Association of daily rest-activity patterns with adiposity and cardiometabolic risk measures in teens. *Journal of Adolescent Health, 65*(2), 224–231. https://doi.org/10.1016/j.jadohealth.2019.02.008

Quesnel-Vallières, M., et al. (2018). Autism spectrum disorder: Insights into convergent mechanisms from transcriptomics. *Nature Reviews Genetics, 20*, 51–63. https://doi.org/10.1038/s41576-018-0066-2

Quinn, P. C., Lee, K., & Pascalis, P. (2018). Perception of face race by infants: Five developmental changes. *Child Development Perspectives, 12*(3), 204–209. https://doi.org/10.1111/cdep.12286

Raby, K. L., & Dozier, M. (2019). Attachment across the lifespan: Insight from adoptive families. *Current Opinion in Psychology, 25*, 81–85. https://doi.org/10.1016/j.copsyc.2018.03.011

Radford, J. (2019). Key findings about U.S. immigrants. *Pew Research Center.* Retrieved from https://www.pewresearch. org/fact-tank/2019/06/17/key-findings-about-u-s-immigrants/

Raffaelli, M., Simpkins, S. D., Tran, S. P., & Larson, R. W. (2018). Responsibility development transfers across contexts: Reciprocal pathways between home and afterschool programs. *Developmental Psychology, 54*(3), 559–570. http:// dx.doi.org/10.1037/dev0000454

Rajeh, A., Amanullah, S., Shivakumar, K., & Cole, J. (2017). Interventions in ADHD: A comparative review of stimulant and behavioral therapies. *Asian Journal of Psychiatry, 25*, 131–135. https://doi.org/10.1016/j.ajp.2016.09.005

Raju, T. N. K. (2014). Reasonable break time for nursing mothers: A provision enacted through the Affordable Care Act. *Pediatrics, 134*(3). https://doi.org/10.1542/peds.2014-0762

Raman, S. R., et al. (2018). Trends in attention-deficit hyperactivity disorder medication use: A retrospective observational study using population-based databases. *The Lancet Psychiatry, 5*(10), 824–835. https://doi.org/10.1016/ S2215-0366(18)30293-1

Ramey, D. M. (2018). The social construction of child social control via criminalization and medicalization: Why race matters. *Sociological Forum, 33*(1), 139–164. https://doi.org/10.1111/socf.12403

Ramirez, N. F., & Kuhl, P. (2017). Bilingual baby: Foreign language intervention in Madrid's infant education centers. *Mind, Brain, and Education, 11*(3), 133–143. https://doi.org/10.1111/mbe.12144

Ramírez-Esparza, N., García-Sierra, A., & Kuhl, P. K. (2014). Look who's talking: Speech style and social context in language input to infants are linked to concurrent and future speech development. *Developmental Science, 17*(6), 880–891. https//doi.org: 10.1111/desc.12172

Ramon, I., Chattopadhyay, S. K., Barnett, W. S., & Hahn, R. A. (2018). Early childhood education to promote health equity: A community guide economic review. *Journal of Public Health Management and Practice, 24*(1), e8–e15. https://doi. org/10.1097/PHH.0000000000000557

Ranjit, A., et al. (2018). Outcomes of mothers and children at five years after cesarean versus vaginal delivery. *Obstetrics & Gynecology, 131*, 58S. https://doi.org/10.1097/01.AOG.0000533041.89071.b7

Ransom, M. R., & Ransom, T. (2018). Do high school sports build or reveal character? Bounding causal estimates of sports participation. *Economics of Education Review, 64*, 75–89. https://doi.org/10.1016/j.econedurev.2018.04.002

Rasheed, S. (2018). Male circumcision and human immunodeficiency virus infection: An update on randomized controlled trails and molecular evidences. *International Journal of Health Sciences, 12*(1), 1–3. Retrieved from https://ijhs.org.sa/ index.php/journal/article/view/3142

Rasmussen, E. E., et al. (2016). Relation between active mediation, exposure to *Daniel Tiger's Neighborhood*, and US preschoolers' social and emotional development. *Journal of Children and Media, 10*(4), 443–461. https://doi.org/10.1 080/17482798.2016.1203806

Rasmussen, E. E., et al. (2018). Promoting preschoolers' emotional competence through prosocial tv and mobile app use. *Media Psychology, 22*(1), 1–22. https://doi.org/10.1080/15213269.2018.1476890

Rasmussen, L. J. H., et al. (2019). Cumulative childhood risk is associated with a new measure of chronic inflammation in adulthood. *The Journal of Child Psychology and Psychiatry, 60*(2), 199–208. https://doi.org/10.1111/jcpp.12928

Ray, A., Oliver, T. R., Halder, P., Pal., U., Sarkar, S., Dutta, S., & Ghosh, S. (2018). Risk of Down syndrome birth: Consanguineous marriage associated with maternal meiosis-II nondisjunction at younger age and without any detectable recombination. *American Journal of Medical Genetics, 176*(11), 2342–2349. https://doi.org/10.1002/ajmg.a.40511

Raz, N., et al. (2018). Cumulative pregnancy and live birth rates through assisted reproduction in women 44–45 years of age: Is there any hope? *Journal of Assisted Reproduction and Genetics, 35*(3), 441–447. https://doi.org/10.1007/s10815-017-1094-0

Razza, R. A., Bergen-Cico, D., & Raymond, K. (2015). Enhancing preschoolers' self-regulation via mindful yoga. *Journal of Child and Family Studies, 24*, 372–385. https://doi.org/10.1007/s10826-013-9847-6

Read, K., & Quirke, J. (2018). Rhyme and word placement in storybooks support high-level verb mapping in 3- to 5-year-olds. *Frontiers in Psychology, 9*, 889. https://doi.org/10.3389/fpsyg.2018.00889

Rebellon, C. J., Trinker, R., Van Gundy, K. T., & Cohn, E. S. (2019). No guts, no glory: The influence of risk-taking on adolescent popularity. *Deviant Behavior, 40*(12). https://doi.org/10.1080/01639625.2018.1519128

Reed, J., Hirsch-Pasek, K., & Golinkoff, R. M. (2017). Learning on hold: Cell phones sidetrack parent–child interactions. *Developmental Psychology, 53*(8), 1428–1436. https://doi.org/10.1037/dev0000292

Reiß, M., Krüger, M., & Krist, H. (2017). Theory of mind and the video deficit effect: Video presentation impairs children's encoding and understanding false belief. *Media Psychology, 22*(1), 23–28. https://doi.org/10.1080/15213269.2017.1412321

Reichle, J. (2018). Explicit joint attention interventions for young children with autism spectrum disorders are successful: But determining a specific strategy requires further evidence. *Evidence-Based Communication Assessment and Intervention, 12*(1–2), 1–6. https://doi.org/10.1080/17489539.2018.1459161

Reijman, S., et al. (2016). Baseline functioning and stress reactivity in maltreating parents and at-risk adults: Review and meta-analyses of autonomic nervous system studies. *Child Maltreatment, 21*(4), 327–342. https://doi.org/10.1177/1077559516659937

Reinehr, T., & Roth, C. L. (2019). Is there a causal relationship between obesity and puberty? *The Lancet Child & Adolescent Health, 3*(1), 44–54. https://doi.org/10.1016/S2352-4642(18)30306-7

Reinisch, B., Krell, M., Hergert, S., Gogolin, S., & Krüger, D. (2017). Methodical challenges concerning Draw-A-Scientist Test: A critical view about the assessment and evaluation of learners' conceptions of scientists. *International Journal of Science Education, 39*(14), 1952–1975. https://doi.org/10.1080/09500693.2017.1362712

Reisz, S., Duschinsky, R., & Siegel, D. J. (2017). Disorganized attachment and defense: Exploring John Bowlby's unpublished reflections. *Attachment & Human Development, 20*(2), 107–134. https://doi.org/10.1080/14616734.2017.1380055

Reisz, S., Jacobvitz, D. & George, C. (2015. Birth and motherhood: Childbirth experience and mother's perceptions of themselves and their children. Infant Mental Health Journal, 36(2), 167–178. https://doi.org/10.1002/imhj.21500

Ren, L., & Edwards, C. P. (2017). Chinese parents' expectations and child preacademic skills: The indirect role of parenting and social competence. *Early Education and Development, 28*(8), 1052–1071. https://doi.org/10.1080/10409289.2017.1319784

Resch, C., et al. (2019). Age-dependent differences in the impact of paediatric traumatic brain injury on executive functions: A prospective study using susceptibility-weighted imaging. *Neuropsychologia, 124*, 236–245. https://doi.org/10.1016/j.neuropsychologia.2018.12.004

Reyes, M. L. (2019). Cultural moderators of the influence of environmental affordances and provisions on children's subjective well-being. *Child Indicators Research, 12*(1), 71–98. https://doi.org/10.1007/s12187-017-9520-5

Reynolds, G. D., & Roth, K. C. (2018). The developmental of attention biases for faces in infancy: A developmental systems perspective. *Frontiers in Psychology.* https://doi.org/10.3389/fpsyg.2018.00222

Reynolds, J. L., et al. (2017). Caregiving experience and its relation to perceptual narrowing of face gender. *Developmental Psychology, 53*(8), 1437–1446. http://dx.doi.org/10.1037/dev0000335

Reynolds, S. A., et al. (2017). Disparities in children's vocabulary and height in relation to household wealth and parental schooling: A longitudinal study in four low- and middle-income countries. *SSM—Population Health, 3*, 767–786. https://doi.org/10.1016/j.ssmph.2017.08.008

Rhoades, M. & Brandone, A. C. (2014). Three-year-olds' theories of mind in actions and words. *Frontiers in Psychology.* https://doi.org/10.3389/fpsyg.2014.00263

Rhoads, J. M., et al. (2018). Infant colic represents gut inflammation and dysbiosis. *The Journal of Pediatrics, 203*, 55–61. https://doi.org/10.1016/j.jpeds.2018.07.042

Ribner, A., Fitzpatrick, C., & Blair, C. (2017). Family socioeconomic status moderates associations between television viewing and school readiness skills. *Journal of Developmental & Behavioral Pediatrics, 38*(3), 233–239. https://doi.org/10.1097/DBP.0000000000000425

Rice, F., et al. (2019). Characterizing developmental trajectories and the role of genetic risk variants in early-onset depression. *JAMA Psychiatry, 77*(3), 306–313. https://doi.org/10.1001/jamapsychiatry.2018.3338

Riciputi, S., Boyer, P., McDonough, M. H., & Snyder, F. J. (2019). Formative evaluation of a pilot afterschool physical activity-based positive youth development program. *Health Promotion Practice, 20*(2), 269–281. https://doi.org/10.1177/1524839918759956

Ricci, J. L., & Riggs, E. M. (2018). Making a connection to field geoscience for Native American youth through culture, nature, and community. *Journal of Geoscience Education, 67*(4), 487–504. https://doi.org/10.1080/10899995.2019.1616273

Rideout, V. (2017). *The common sense census: Media use by kids zero to eight.* Retrieved from: https://www.commonsense-media.org/sites/default/files/uploads/research/csm_zerotoeight_fullreport_release_2.pdf

Rimfield, K., et al. (2018). The stability of educational achievement across school years is largely explained by genetic factors. *npj Science of Learning, 3,* Article 16. https://doi.org/10.1038/s41539-018-0030-0

Rindermann, H., & Ceci, S. J. (2018). Parents' education is more important than their wealth in shaping their intelligence: Results of 19 samples in seven countries at different developmental levels. *Journal for the Education of the Gifted, 41*(4), 298–326. https://doi.org/10.1177/0162353218799481

Rittle-Johnson, B., Zippert, E. L., & Boice, K. L. (2019). The roles of patterning and spatial skills in early mathematics development. Early *Childhood Research Quarterly, 46*(1), 166–178. https://doi.org/10.1016/j.ecresq.2018.03.006

Robertson, N., Yim, B., & Paatsch, L. (2018). Connections between children's involvement in dramatic play and the quality of early childhood environments. *Early Child Development and Care, 190*(3), 376–389. https://doi.org/10.1080/03004430.2018.1473389

Robinson, J., et al. (2018). What works in youth suicide prevention? A systematic review and meta-analysis. *EClinicalMedicine, 4,* 52–91. https://doi.org/10.1016/j.eclinm.2018.10.004

Robinson, K. M., Dubé, A. K., & Beatch, J.-A. (2017). Children's understanding of additive concepts. *Journal of Experimental Child Psychology, 156,* 16–28. https://doi.org/10.1016/j.jecp.2016.11.009

Robins, S., Ghosh, D., Rosales, N., & Treiman, R. (2014). Letter knowledge in parent-child conversations: Differences between families differing in socio-economic states. *Frontiers in Psychology.* https://doi.org/10.3389/fpsyg.2014.00632

Rocheleau, G. C. (2018). Long-term relationships between adolescent intense work and deviance: Are there differences by social class? *Advances in Life Course Research, 37,* 69–78. https://doi.org/10.1016/j.alcr.2018.08.002

Rochester, J. & Bolden, R. (2015). Bisphenol S and F: A systematic review and comparison of the hormonal activity of bisphenol A substitutes. *Environmental Health Perspectives, 123*(7), 643–650. http://dx.doi.org/10.1289/ehp.1408989.

Rogers, A. A., Ha, T., Updegraff, K. A., & Iida, M. (2018). Adolescents' daily romantic experiences and negative mood: A dyadic, intensive longitudinal study. *Journal of Youth and Adolescence, 47*(5), 1517–1530. https://doi.org/10.1007/s10964-017-0797-y

Rogers, C. R., et al. (2018). Neural correlates of sibling closeness and association with externalizing behavior in adolescence. *Social Cognitive and Affective Neuroscience, 13*(9), 977–988. https://doi.org/10.1093/scan/nsy063

Rogers, L. O. (2019). Commentary on economic inequality: "What" and "who" constitutes research on social inequality in developmental science? *Developmental Psychology, 55*(3), 586–591. http://dx.doi.org/10.1037/dev0000640

Rogoff, B., Dahl, A., & Callanan, M. (2018). The importance of understanding children's lived experience. *Developmental Review, 50*(Part A), 5–15. https://doi.org/10.1016/j.dr.2018.05.006

Rokeach, A., & Wiener, J. (2018). The romantic relationships of adolescents with ADHD. *Journal of Attention Disorders, 22*(1), 35–45. https://doi.org/10.1177/1087054714538660

Romeo, R. R., et al. (2018). Language exposure relates to structural neural connectivity in childhood. *The Journal of Neuroscience, 38*(36), 7870–7877. https://doi.org/10.1523/JNEUROSCI.0484-18.2018

Ronfard, S., Chen, E. E., & Harris, P. L. (2018). The emergence of the empirical stance: Children's testing of counterintuitive claims. *Developmental Psychology, 54*(3), 482–493. https://doi.org/10.1037/dev0000455

Rooney, M., Hinshaw, S., McBurnett, K., & Pfiffner, L. (2018). Parent adherence in two behavioral treatment strategies for the predominantly inattentive presentation of ADHD. *Journal of Clinical Child & Adolescent Psychology, 47*(S1), S233–S241. https://doi.org/10.1080/15374416.2016.1236341

Ropars, S., Tessier, R., Charpak, N., & Uriza, L. F. (2018). The long-term effects of the Kangaroo Mother Care intervention on cognitive functioning: Results from a longitudinal study. *Developmental Neuropsychology, 43*(1), 82–91. https://doi.org/10.1080/87565641.2017.1422507

Rosen, M. L., et al. (2018). Socioeconomic disparities in academic achievement: A multi-modal investigation of neural mechanisms in children and adolescents. *NeuroImage, 173,* 298–310. https://doi.org/10.1016/j.neuroimage.2018.02.043

Rosenbaum, G. M., et al. (2017). Working memory training in adolescents decreases laboratory risk taking in the presence of peers. *Journal of Cognitive Enhancement, 1*(4), 513–525. https://doi.org/10.1007/s41465-017-0045-0

Rosenbaum, G. M., Venkatraman, V., Steinberg, L., & Chein, J. M. (2018). The influences of described and experienced information on adolescent risky decision-making. *Developmental Review, 47,* 23–43. https://doi.org/10.1016/j.dr.2017.09.003

Rosenbaum, L. (2017). *Tooth decay: An epidemic in America's poorest children*. Retrieved from http://sitn.hms.harvard.edu/flash/2017/tooth-decay-epidemic-americas-poorest-children/

Roshandel, S., & Hudley, C. (2018). Role of teachers in influencing the development of adolescents' possible selves. *Learning Environments Research, 21*(2), 211–228. https://doi.org/10.1007/s10984-017-9247-8

Roskam, I. (2018). Externalizing behavior from early childhood to adolescence: Prediction from inhibition, language, parenting, and attachment. *Development and Psychopathology, 31*(2), 587–599. https://doi.org/10.1017/S0954579418000135

Ross, J., et al. (2017). Cultural differences in self-recognition: The early development of autonomous and related selves? *Developmental Science, 20*(3), e12387. https://doi.org/10.1111/desc.12387

Rossant, J., & Tam, P. P. L. (2018). Exploring early human embryo development. *Science, 360*(6393), 1075–1076. http://science.sciencemag.org.scsu.idm.oclc.org/content/360/6393/1075.full

Rossi, A., et al. (2018). Music reduces pain perception in healthy newborns: A comparison between different music tracks and recorded heartbeat. *Early Human Development, 124,* 7–10. https://doi.org/10.1016/j.earlhumdev.2018.07.006

Rossi, N. (2018). Commentary on same-sex and different-sex parent households and child health outcomes: Additional sources of same-sex parenting stress to consider. *Journal of Developmental & Behavioral Pediatrics, 39*(2), 180. https://doi.org/10.1097/DBP.0000000000000542

Rote, W. M., & Smetana, J. G. (2018). Within-family dyadic patterns of parental monitoring and adolescent information management. *Developmental Psychology, 54*(12), 2302–2315. http://dx.doi.org/10.1037/dev0000615

Rothbart, M. K. (2011). *Becoming who we are: Temperament and personality development.* New York, NY.

Rothbart, M. K. (2015). The role of temperament in conceptualizations of mental disorder (pp. 133–149). In B. Probst (Ed.), *Critical Thinking in Clinical Assessment and Diagnosis: Essential Clinical Social Work Series.* New York, NY: Springer, Inc.

Roubinov, D. S., & Boyce, W. T. (2017). Parenting and SES: Relative values or enduring principles? *Current Opinion in Psychology, 15,* 162–167. https://doi.org/10.1016/j.copsyc.2017.03.001

Rovee-Collier, C. (1999). The development of infant memory. *Current Directions in Psychological Science, 8*(3), 80–85. https://doi.org/10.1111/1467-8721.00019

Rovee-Collier, C. & Cuevas, K. (2009). Multiple memory systems are unnecessary to account for infant memory development: An ecological model. *Developmental Psychology, 45*(1), 160–174. https//doi.org/10.1037/a0014538.

Rowe, A., et al. (2019). Interventions targeting working memory in 4–11 year olds within their everyday contexts: A systematic review. *Developmental Review, 52,* 1–23. https://doi.org/10.1016/j.dr.2019.02.001

Rowe, M. L., & Leech, K. A. (2018). A parent intervention with a growth mindset approach improves children's early gesture and vocabulary development. *Developmental Science 22*(4), e12792. https://doi.org/10.1111/desc.12792

Ruben, R. J. (2018). Language development in the pediatric cochlear implant patient. *Otology, Neurotology, and Neuroscience, 3*(3), 209–213. https://doi.org/10.1002/lio2.156

Rubenstein, E., Young, J.C., Croen, L.A., et al. (2018). Brief Report: Maternal Opioid Prescription from Preconception Through Pregnancy and the Odds of Autism Spectrum Disorder and Autism Features in Children. *Journal of Autism and Developmental Disorders, 49,* 376–382. https://doi.org/10.1007/s10803-018-3721-8

Ruck, M. D., Mistry, R. S., & Flanagan, C. A. (2019). Children's and adolescents' understanding and experiences of economic inequality: An introduction to the special section. *Developmental Psychology, 55*(3), 449–456. http://dx.doi.org/10.1037/dev0000694

Ruff, S. C., Durtschi, J. A., & Day, R. D. (2017). Family subsystems predicting adolescents' perceptions of sibling relationship quality over time. *Journal of Marital and Family Therapy, 44*(3), 527–542. https://doi.org/10.1111/jmft.12265

Russell, S. J., Croker, H., & Viner, R. M. (2018). The effect of screen advertising on children's dietary intake: A systematic review and meta-analysis. *Obesity Reviews, 20*(4), 554–568. https://doi.org/10.1111/obr.12812

Russell, S. T. (2015). Human developmental science for social justice. *Research in Human Development, 12*(3–4), 274–279. https://doi.org/10.1080/15427609.2015.1068049

Russell, S. T., & Fish, J. N. (2019). Sexual minority youth, social change, and health: A developmental collision. *Research in Human Development, 16*(1), 5–20. https://doi.org/10.1080/15427609.2018.1537772

Rutter, V. B. (2007). The archetypal paradox of feminine initiation in analytic work. In T. Kirsch, V. B. Rutter, & T. Singer (Eds.), *Initiation: The living reality of an archetype* (pp. 41–62). Routledge.

Rysavy, M. A. et al. (2015). Between-hospital variation in treatment and outcomes of extremely preterm infants. *New England Journal of Medicine, 372*:1801-1811. https://doi.org/ 10.1056/NEJMoa1410689

Saban-Bezalel, R., Dolfin, D., Laor, N., & Mashal, N. (2019). Irony comprehension and mentalizing ability in children with and without Autism Spectrum Disorder. *Research in Autism Spectrum Disorders, 58,* 30–38. https://doi.org/10.1016/j.rasd.2018.11.006

Sabol, T. J., Bohlmann, & N. L. Downer, J. T. (2018). Low-income ethnically diverse children's engagement as a predictor of school readiness above preschool classroom quality. *Child Development, 89*(2), 556–576. https://doi.org/10.1111/cdev.12832

Saffran, J. R., & Kirkham, N. Z. (2018). Infant statistical learning. *Annual Review of Psychology, 69,* 181–203. https://doi.org/10.1146/annurev-psych-122216-011805

Sage, C., & Burgio, E. (2018). Electromagnetic fields, pulsed radiofrequency radiation, and epigenetics: How wireless technologies may affect childhood development. *Child Development, 89*(1), 129–136. https://doi.org/10.1111/cdev.12824

Saint-Eloi Cadely, H., et al. (2018). Predicting patterns of intimate partner violence perpetration from late adolescence to young adulthood. *Journal of Interpersonal Violence.* https://doi.org/10.1177/0886260518795173

Saint-Eloy Cadely, H., Mrug, S., & Windle, M. (2019). Comparisons of types of exposure to violence within and across contexts in predicting the perpetration of dating aggression. *Journal of Youth and Adolescence, 48,* 2377–2390. https://doi.org/10.1007/s10964-019-01102-2

Salam, M. (2018, January 11). For Serena Williams, childbirth was a harrowing ordeal. She's not alone. *New York Times,* https://www.nytimes.com/2018/01/11/sports/tennis/serena-williams-baby-vogue.html

Salganicoff, A. (2018). The importance of strengthening workplace and health policies to support breastfeeding. *Breastfeeding Medicine, 13*(8), 532–534. http://doi.org/10.1089/bfm.2018.0122

Salo, V. C., Rowe, M. L., & Reeb-Sutherland, B. C. (2018). Exploring infant gesture and joint attention as related constructs and as predictors of later language. *Infancy, 23*(3), 432–452. https://doi.org/10.1111/infa.12229

Saltz, J. B., Bell, A. M., Flint, J., Gomulkiewicz, R., Hughes, K. A., & Keagy, J. (2018). Why does the magnitude of genotype-by-environment interaction vary? *Ecology and Evolution, 8*(12), 6342–6353. https://doi.org/10.1002/ece3.4128

Saltzman, J. A., Fiese, B. H., Bost, K. K., & McBride, B. A. (2018). Development of appetite self-regulation: Integrating perspectives from attachment and family systems theory. *Child Development Perspectives, 12*(1), 51–57. https://doi.org/10.1111/cdep.12254

Samek, D. R., Wilson, S., McGue, M., & Iacono, W. G. (2018). Genetic and environmental influences on parent–child conflict and child depression through late adolescence. *Journal of Clinical Child & Adolescent Psychiatry, 47*(Sup 1), S5–S20. https://doi.org/10.1080/15374416.2016.1141357

Sampson, R. J., & Winter, A. (2016).The racial ecology of lead poisoning: Toxic inequality in Chicago neighborhoods, 1995–2013. *Du Bois Review: Social Science Research, 13,* 261–283. https://doi.org/10.1017/S1742058X16000151

Santos, C. E., & Toomey, R. B. (2018). Integrating an intersectionality lens in theory and research in developmental science. *New Directions for Child and Adolescent Development, 2018*(161), 7–15. https://doi.org/10.1002/cad.20245

Sara, G., & Brann, P. (2018). Understanding the mechanisms of transgenerational mental health impacts in refugees. *The Lancet Public Health, 3*(5), PE211–E212. https://doi.org/10.1016/S2468-2667(18)30067-7

Saracho, O. N. (2013). Theory of mind: Children's understanding of mental states. *Early Child Development and Care, 184*(6), 949–961. https://doi.org/10.1080/03004430.2013.821985

Saravillo, S. J., & Agapinan-Alfonso, M. L. (2018). Effects of a community-based reach out and read program among low-income families with young children. *Pediatrics, 142*(1). https://doi.org/10.1542/peds.142.1_MeetingAbstract.517

Sardi, L. & Livingston, K. (2015). Parental decision making in male circumcision. MCN: *The American Journal of Maternal Child Nursing, 40*(2), 110–115. https://doi.org/ 10.1097/NMC.0000000000000112

Sasnett, S. (2014). Are the kids alright? A qualitative study of adults with gay and lesbian parents. *Journal of Contemporary Ethnography, 44*(2), 196–222. https://doi.org/ 10.1177/0891241614540212

Sata, F. (2019). Developmental Origins of Health and Disease (DOHaD) Cohorts and Interventions: Status and Perspective. In F. Sata, H., Fukuoka, & M. Hanson (Eds.), *Pre-emptive medicine: Public health aspects of developmental origins of health and disease.* Current Topics in Environmental Health and Preventive Medicine. Springer, https://doi.org/10.1007/978-981-13-2194-8_4

Sato, M., Fonagy, P., & Luyten, P. (2019). Rejection sensitivity and borderline personality disorder features: The mediating roles of attachment anxiety, need to belong, and self-criticism. *Journal of Personality Disorders.* Advance online publication. https://doi.org/10.1521/pedi_2019_33_397

Sauce, B., & Matzel, L. D. (2018). The paradox of intelligence: Heritability and malleability coexist in hidden gene-environment interplay. *Psychological Bulletin, 144*(1), 26–47. https://doi.org/10.1037/bul0000131

Saul, J. S., & Rodgers, R. F. (2018). Adolescent eating disorder risk and the online world. *Child & Adolescent Psychiatric Clinics, 27*(2), 221–228. https://doi.org/10.1016/j.chc.2017.11.011

Saulle, L. B., Lagana, J., Crawford, R., & Duffield, B. (2018). Community-based art programs, collaborative partnerships, and community resources for at-risk students. In A. D. Hunter, D. Heise, & B. H. Johns (Eds.), *Art for children experiencing psychological trauma: A guide for art educators and school-based professionals* (pp. 248–270). Routledge, https://doi.org/10.4324/9781315301358

Savickaité, R., et al. (2019). Friendships, perceived popularity, and adolescent romantic relationship debut. *Journal of Early Adolescence, 40*(3), 377–399. https://doi.org/10.1177/0272431619847530

Sawyer, S. M., Azzopardi, P. S., Wickremarathne, D., & Patton, G. C. (2018). The age of adolescence. *The Lancet Child & Adolescent Health, 2*(3), 223–228. https://doi.org/10.1016/S2352-4642(18)30022-1

Sawyer, S. M., & Patton, G. C. (2018). Health and well-being in adolescence. In J. E. Lansford & P. Banati (Eds.), *Handbook of adolescent development research and its impact on global policy* (pp. 27–45). Oxford University Press.

Saxbe, D., et al. (2018). Longitudinal associations between family aggression, externalizing behavior, and the structure and function of the amygdala. *Journal of Research on Adolescence, 28*(1), 134–149. https://doi.org/10.1111/jora.12349

Sayal, K., et al. (2018). ADHD in children and young people: Prevalence, care pathways, and service provision. *The Lancet Psychiatry, 5*(2), 175–186. https://doi.org/10.1016/S2215-0366(17)30167-0

Scales, P. C., & Roehlkepartain, E. C. (2018). The contribution of nonfamily adults to adolescent well-being. In J. E. Lansford & P. Banati (Eds.), *Handbook of adolescent development research and its impact on global policy* (pp. 150–170). Oxford University Press.

Schattenberg, P. (2018, August 16). For Juntos 4-H "Day in the Life" contest winner, the sky's the limit. *AgriLifeToday*, Retrieved from https://agrilifetoday.tamu.edu/2018/08/16/for-juntos-4-h-day-in-the-life-contest-winner-the-skys-the-limit/

Schachter, E. P., & Galliher, R. V. (2018). Fifty years since "Identity Youth and Crisis": A renewed look at Erikson's writings on identity. *Identity: An International Journal of Theory and Research, 18*(4), 247–250. https://doi.org/10.1080/15283488.2018.1529267

Schaan, V. K., Schulz, A., Schächinger, H., & Vögele, C. (2019). Parental divorce is associated with an increased risk to develop mental disorders in women. *Journal of Affective Disorders, 257*, 91–99. https://doi.org/10.1016/j.jad.2019.06.071

Schaars, M. M. H., Segers, E., & Verhoeven, L. (2017) Predicting the integrated development of word reading and spelling in the early primary grades.

Schaefer, C. E., & Drewes, A. A. (2018). Fundamental concepts and practices of puppet play therapy. In A. A. Drewes & C. E. Schaefer (Eds.), *Puppet play therapy: A practical guidebook* (pp. 3–16). Routledge/Taylor & Francis Group.

Schenck-Fontaine, A., et al. (2018). Associations between perceived material deprivation, parents' discipline practices, and children's behavior problems: An international perspective. *Child Development, 91*(1), 307–326. https://doi.org/10.1111/cdev.13151

Schlagmüller, M., & Schneider, W. (2002). The development of organizational strategies in children: Evidence from a microgenetic longitudinal study. *Journal of Experimental Child Psychology, 81*(3), 298–319. https://doi.org/10.1006/jecp.2002.2655

Schleider, J. L., Abel, M. R., & Weisz, J. R. (2019). Do immediate gains predict long-term symptom change? Findings from a randomized trial of a single-session intervention for youth anxiety and depression. *Child Psychiatry & Human Development, 50*, 868–881. https://doi.org/10.1007/s10578-019-00889-2

Schleider, J. L., & Weisz, J. R. (2019). A single-session growth mindset intervention for adolescent anxiety and depression: 9-month outcomes of a randomized trial. *The Journal of Child Psychology and Psychiatry, 59*(2), 160–170. https://doi.org/10.1111/jcpp.12811

Schmitt, S. A., et al. (2019). Self-regulation as a correlate of weight status in preschool children. *Early Child Development and Care, 189*(1), 68–78. https://doi.org/10.1080/03004430.2017.1299715

Schneider, W., & Ornstein, P. A. (2019). Determinants of memory development in childhood and adolescence. *International Journal of Psychology, 54*(3), 307–315. https://doi.org/10.1002/ijop.12503

Schriber, R. A., et al. (2018). Do hostile school environments promote social deviance by shaping neural responses to social exclusion? *Journal of Research on Adolescence, 28*(1), 103–120. https://doi.org/10.1111/jora.12340

Schroeder, R. D. & Mowen, T. J. (2014). Parenting style transitions and delinquency. *Youth & Society, 46*(2), 228–254. https://doi.org/10.1177/0044118X12469041

Schuhmacher, M., Köster, M., & Kärtner, J. (2018). Modeling prosocial behavior increases helping in 16-month-olds. *Child Development, 90*(5), 789–1801. https://doi.org/10.1111/cdev.13054

Schwarz, E. R. (2017). Consequences of perinatal infections with rubella, measles, and mumps. *Current Opinion in Virology, 27*, 71–77. https://doi.org/10.1016/j.coviro.2017.11.009

Schwartz, S., Luyckx, K., & Crocetti, E. (2015). What have we learned since Schwartz (2001)? A reappraisal of the field of identity development. In K.C. McLean, M. Syed (Eds.), *The Oxford handbook of identity development* (pp. 539–561). Oxford University Press, https://doi.org/10.1093/oxfordhb/9780199936564.013.028

Schwartz, S. J., et al. (2018). Identity development in immigrant youth. *European Psychologist, 23*(4), 336–349. https://doi.org/10.1027/1016-9040/a000335

Schweinhart, K. J. (2019). Lessons on sustaining early gains from the life-course study of Perry preschool. In A. J. Reynolds & J. A. Temple (Eds.), *Sustaining early childhood learning gains: Program, school, and family influences* (pp. 254–265). Cambridge University Press.

Szczygiel, D., & Mikolajczak, M. (2018). Is it enough to be an extrovert to be liked? Emotional competence moderates the relationship between extraversion and peer-rated likeability. *Frontiers in Psychology, 9*, 804. https://doi.org/10.3389/fpsyg.2018.00804

Sears, K. L., & Papini, D. R. (2019). Psychosocial maladjustment arising from workplace sexual behaviors directed at adolescent workers. *Health Psychology and Behavioral medicine, 7*(1), 308–327. https://doi.org/10.1080/21642850.2019.1653188

Seccombe, K. (2004). "Beating the odds" versus "changing the odds": Poverty, resilience, and family policy. *Journal of Marriage and Family, 64*(2), 384–394. https://doi.org/10.1111/j.1741-3737.2002.00384.x

Segrin, C., & Flora, J. (2019). Fostering social and emotional intelligence: What are the best current strategies in parenting? *Social and Personality Psychology Compass, 13*(3), e12439. https://doi.org/10.1111/spc3.12439

Selzam, S., et al. (2018). Evidence for gene-environment correlation in child feeding: Links between common genetic variation for BMI in children and parental feeding practices. *PLOS Genetics.* https://doi.org/10.1371/journal.pgen.1007757

Semenza, D. C., et al. (2019). School start times, delinquency, and substance use: A criminological perspective. *Crime & Delinquency, 66*(2), 163–193. https://doi.org/10.1177/0011128719845147

Senia, J. M., Donnellan, M. B., & Neppl, T. K. (2018). Early pubertal timing and adult adjustment outcomes: Persistence, attenuation, or accentuation? *Journal of Adolescence, 65*, 85–94. https://doi.org/10.1016/j.adolescence.2018.03.003

Senter, L., Bennett, R. L., Madeo, A. C., Noblin, S., Ormond, K. E., Schneider, K. W., Swan, K., & Virani, A. (2018). National society of genetic counselors code of ethics: Explication of 2017 revisions. *Journal of Genetic Counseling, 27*(1), 9–15. https://doi.org/10.1007/s10897-017-0165-9

Setoodeh, R. (2009, March 13). Books: Eric Carle's Very Hungry Caterpillar. *Newsweek,* https://www.newsweek.com/books-eric-carles-very-hungry-caterpillar-76541

Shafir, E. (2017). Decisions in poverty contexts. *Current Opinion in Psychology, 18*, 131–136. https://doi.org/10.1016/j.copsyc.2017.08.026

Shai, D. (2019). The inconsolable doll task: Prenatal coparenting behavioral dynamics under stress predicting child cognitive development at 18 months. *Infant Behavior and Development, 56*, 101254. https://doi.org/10.1016/j.infbeh.2018.04.003

Shandra, C. L. (2018). Research on adolescent sexuality should be inclusive of disability. *Journal of Adolescent Health, 62*(3), 253–254. https://doi.org/10.1016/j.jadohealth.2017.12.007

Shaweesh, A. I. & Al-Batayneh, O. B. (2018). Association of weight and height with timing of deciduous tooth emergence. *Archives of Oral Biology, 87*, 168–171. https://doi.org/10.1016/j.archoralbio.2017.12.030

Sheehan, L., et al. (2019). Benefits and risks of suicide disclosure. *Social Science & Medicine, 223*, 16–23. https://doi.org/10.1016/j.socscimed.2019.01.023

Sherman, L., Steinberg, L., & Chein, J. (2018). Connecting brain responsivity and real-world risk taking: Strengths and limitations of current methodological approaches. *Developmental Cognitive Neuroscience, 33*, 27–41. http://dx.doi.org/10.1016/j.dcn.2017.05.007

Shlafer, R. J., et al. (2018). Intention and initiation of breastfeeding among women who are incarcerated. *Nursing for Women's Health, 22*(1), 64–78. https://doi.org/10.1016/j.nwh.2017.12.004

Sharp, G. C., Lawlor, D. A., & Richardson, S. S. (2018). It's the mother!: How assumptions about the casual primacy of maternal effects influence research on the developmental origins of health and disease. *Social Science & Medicine, 213*, 20–27. https://doi.org/10.1016/j.socscimed.2018.07.035

Shearer, W. T., et al. (2018). Cord blood banking for potential future transplantation. *Pediatrics, 140*(5). e20172695. https://doi.org/10.1542/peds.2017-2695

Shiffrin, R. M., & Atkinson, R. C. (1969). Storage and retrieval processes in long-term memory. *Psychological Review, 76*(2), 179–193. https://doi.org/10.1037/h0027277

Shormani, M. Q. (2014). The nature of language acquisition: Where L1 and L2 meet? *Journal of Literature, Languages, and Linguistics, 4*, 24–34.

Short, M. A., et al. (2018). Cognition and objectively measured sleep duration in children: A systematic review and meta-analysis. *Sleep Health, 4*(3), 292–300. https://doi.org/10.1016/j.sleh.2018.02.004

Shtulman, A. & Yoo, R. I. (2015). Children's understanding of physical possibility constrains their belief in Santa Claus. *Cognitive Development, 34*, 51–62. https://doi.org/10.1016/j.cogdev.2014.12.006

Sicherer, S. H. & Sampson, H. A. (2014). Food allergy: Epidemiology, pathogenesis, diagnosis, and treatment. *Journal of Allergy and Clinical Immunology, 133*(2), 291–307. https://doi.org/ 10.1016/j.jaci.2013.11.020

Sicherer, S. H., Sampson, H. A., Eichenfield, L. F., & Rotrosen, D. (2017). The benefits of new guidelines to prevent peanut allergy. *Pediatrics, 139*(6), e20164293. https://doi.org/10.1542/peds.2016-4293

Sidera, F., Amadó, A., & Martínez, L. (2017). Influences on facial emotion recognition in children. *The Journal of Deaf Studies and Deaf Education, 22*(2), 164–177. https://doi.org/10.1093/deafed/enw072

Siegler, R. S. (2002). Microgenetic studies of self-explanation. In N. Granott & J. Parziale (Eds.), *Microdevelopment: Transition processes in development and learning* (pp. 31–58). Cambridge, UK: Cambridge University Press.

Siegler, R. S. (2016). Continuity and change in the field of cognitive development and in the perspectives of one cognitive developmentalist. *Child Development Perspectives, 10*(2), 128–133. https://doi.org/10.1111/cdep.12173

Siegler, R. S., & Svetina, M. (2006). What leads children to adopt new strategies? A microgenetic/cross-sectional study of class inclusion. *Child Development, 77*(4), 997–1015.

Sijtsema, J. J., Garofalo, C., Jansen, K., & Klimstra, T. A. (2019). Disengaging from evil: Longitudinal associations between the dark triad, moral disengagement, and antisocial behavior in adolescence. *Journal of Abnormal Child Psychology, 47*(8), 1351–1365. https://doi.org/10.1007/s10802-019-00519-4

Silk, J. S., et al. (2019). Using a smartphone app and clinician portal to enhance brief cognitive behavioral therapy for childhood anxiety disorders. *Behavior Therapy, 51*(1), 69–84. https://doi.org/10.1016/j.beth.2019.05.002

Silke, C., Brady, B., Boyla, C., & Dolan, P. (2018). Factors influencing the development of empathy and pro-social behavior among adolescents: A systematic review. *Children and Youth Services Review, 94*, 421–436. https://doi.org/10.1016/j.childyouth.2018.07.027

Silkenbeumer, J. R., Schiller, E-M., & Kärtner, J. (2018). Co- and self-regulation of emotions in the preschool setting. *Early Childhood Research Quarterly, 44*(3), 72–81. https://doi.org/10.1016/j.ecresq.2018.02.014

Silinskas, G. & Kikas, E. (2019). Parental involvement in math homework: Links to children's performance and motivation. *Scandinavian Journal of Educational Research, 63*(1). https://doi.org/10.1080/00313831.2017.1324901

Simonato, I., Janosz, M., Archambault, I., & Pagani, L. S. (2018). Prospective associations between toddler televiewing and subsequent lifestyle habits in adolescence. *Preventative Medicine, 110*, 24–30. https://doi.org/10.1016/j.ypmed.2018.02.008

Singham, T., et al. (2017). Concurrent and longitudinal contribution of exposure to bullying in childhood to mental health. *JAMA Psychiatry, 74*(11), 1112–1119. https://doi.org/10.1001/jamapsychiatry.2017.2678

Skalická, V., et al. (2019). Screen time and the development of emotion understanding from age 4 to age 8: A community study. *British Journal of Developmental Psychology, 37*(3), 427–443. https://doi.org/10.1111/bjdp.12283

Skalická, V. et al. (2019). Screen time and the development of emotion understanding from age 4 to age 8: A community study. *British Journal of Developmental Psychology, 37*(3). https://doi.org/10.1111/bjdp.12283

Skarstein, S., Lagerløv, P., Kvarme, L., & Helseth, S. (2018). Pain the development of identity in adolescents who frequently use over-the-counter analgesics: A qualitative study. *Journal of Clinical Nursing, 27*(19–20), 3583–3591.

Skerry, A. E. & Spelke, E. S. (2014). Preverbal infants identify emotional reactions that are Incongruent with goal outcomes. *Cognition, 130*(2), 204–216. https//doi.org/ 10.1016/j.cognition.2013.11.002

Skibbe, L. E., Montroy, J. J., Bowles, R. P., & Morrison, F. J. (2019). Self-regulation and the development of literacy and language achievement from preschool through second grade. *Early Childhood Research Quarterly, 46*(1), 240–251. https://doi.org/10.1016/j.ecresq.2018.02.005

Skinner, A. L., & Meltzoff, A. N. (2019). Childhood experiences and intergroup biases among children. *Social Issues and Policy Review, 13*(1), 211–240. https://doi.org/10.1111/sipr.12054

Skjothaug, T., Smith, L., Wentzel-Larsen, T., and Moe, V. (2018). Does fathers' prenatal mental health bear a relationship to parenting stress at 6 months? *Infant Mental Health Journal, 39*(5), 537–551. https://doi.org/10.1002/imhj.21739

Skrove, M., Lydersen, S., & Indredavik, M. S. (2015). Resilience factors may moderate pubertal timing, body mass and emotional symptoms in adolescence. *Acta Pædiatrica, 105*(1), 96–104. https://doi.org/10.1111/apa.13171

Slater, A., Riddell, P. Quinn, P. Pascalis, O., Lee, K., & Kelly, D. J. (2010). Visual perception. In J. G. Bremner & T. D. Wachs (Eds.), *Wiley-Blackwell handbook of infant development: Vol. 1 Basic research* (2nd ed., pp. 40–80). Chichester, UK: Wiley-Blackwell.

Slaughter, V., Imuta, K., Peterson, C. C., & Henry, J. D. (2015). Meta-analysis of theory of mind and peer popularity in the preschool and early school years. *Child Development*. https://doi.org/ 10.1111/cdev.12372

Smetana, J. G. (2017). Current research on parenting styles, dimensions, and beliefs. *Current Opinion in Psychology, 15*, 19–25. https://doi.org/10.1016/j.copsyc.2017.02.012

Smetana, J. G., & Ball, C. L. (2017). Young children's moral judgments, justifications, and emotion attributions in peer relationship contexts. *Child Development, 89*(6), 2245–2263. https://doi.org/10.1111/cdev.12846

Smetana, J., Robinson, J., Bourne, S.V., & Wainryb, C. (2019). "I didn't want to, but then I told": Adolescents' narratives regarding disclosure, concealment, and lying. *Developmental Psychology, 55*(2), 403–414. http://dx.doi.org/10.1037/dev0000646

Šmigelskas, K., et al. (2018). Sufficient social support as a possible preventative factor against fighting and bullying in school children. *International Journal of Environmental Research and Public Health, 5*(15), 870. https://doi.org/10.3390/ijerph15050870

Smith, C. A. (2018). The effect of complementary medicines and therapies on maternal anxiety and depression in pregnancy: A systematic review and meta-analysis. *Journal of Affective Disorders, 245,* 428–439. https://doi.org/10.1016/j.jad.2018.11.054

Smith, P. H. (2018). Social justice at the core of breastfeeding protection, promotion, and support: A conceptualization. *Journal of Human Lactation, 34*(2), 220–225. https://doi.org/10.1177/0890334418758660

Smith, P. K. (2016). Bullying: Definition, types, causes, consequences, and intervention. *Social and Personality Psychology Compass, 10*(9), 519–532. https://doi.org/10.1111/spc3.12266

Snarey, J. & Samuelson, P. L. (2014). Lawrence Kohlberg's revolutionary ideas. In L. Nucci, D. Narvaez, & T. Krettenauer (Eds.), *Handbook of moral and character education, 2ⁿᵈ edition* (pp. 61–83). New York, NY: Routledge.

Snyder, K., et al. (2018). Workplace breastfeeding support varies by employment type: The service workplace disadvantage. *Breastfeeding Medicine, 13*(1), 23–27. http://doi.org/10.1089/bfm.2017.0074

Soenens, B. Deci, E. L., & Vansteenkiste, M. (2017). How parents contribute to children's psychological health: The critical role of psychological need support. In L. Wehmeyer, T. D. Little, S. J. Lopez, K. A. Shogren, & R. Ryan (Eds.), *Development of self-determination through the life-course* (pp. 171–187). Springer.

Sokol, R. L., Qin, B., & Poti, J. M. (2017). Parenting styles and body mass index: A systematic review of prospective studies of among children. *Obesity Reviews, 18*(3), 281–292. https://doi.org/10.1111/obr.12497

Son, S-H. C., & Chang, Y. E. (2018). Childcare experiences and early school outcomes: The mediating role of executive functions and emotionality. *Infant and Child Development, 27*(4), e2087. https://doi.org/10.1002/icd.2087

Sontag, K. C., Song, B., Lee, N., Jung, J. H., Cha, Y., Leblanc, P., Neff, C., Kong, S. W., Carter, B. S., Schweitzer, J., & Kim, K. S. (2018). Pluripotent stem cell-based therapy for Parksinson's disease: Current status and future prospects. *Progress in Neurobiology, 168,* 1–20. https://doi.org/10.1016/j.pneurobio.2018.04.005

Sorge, G. B., Toplak, M. E., & Bialystock, E. (2017). Interactions between levels of attention ability and bilingualism in children's executive functioning. *Developmental Science, 20*(1), e12408. https://doi.org/10.1111/desc.12408

Sorrells, S. F., et al. (2018). Human hippocampal neurogenesis drops sharply in children to undetectable levels in adult. *Nature, 555,* 377–381. https://doi.org/10.1038/nature25975

Spearman, C.E. (1927). *The Abilities of Man.* London: Macmillan.

Specht, I. O., Rohde, J. F., Olsen, N. J., & Heitmann, B. L. (2018). Duration of exclusive breastfeeding may be related to eating behavior and dietary intake in obesity prone normal children. *PLOS ONE, 13*(7), e0200388. https://doi.org/10.1371/journal.pone.0200388

Sperry, D. E., Sperry, L. L., & Miller, P. J. (2018). Language does matter: But there is more to language than vocabulary and directed speech. *Child Development, 90*(3), 993–997. https://doi.org/10.1111/cdev.13125

Spinelli, M., Fasolo, M., & Mesman, J. (2017). Does prosody make a difference? A meta-analysis on relations between prosodic aspects of infant-directed speech and infant outcomes. *Developmental Review, 44,* 1–18. https://doi.org/10.1016/j.dr.2016.12.001

Spinosa, J., et al. (2019). From socioeconomic disadvantage to obesity: The mediating role of psychological distress and emotional eating. *Obesity, 27*(4), 559–564. https://doi.org/10.1002/oby.22402

Spinner, L., Cameron, L., & Calogero, R. (2018). Peer toy play as a gateway to children's gender flexibility of (counter) stereotypic portrayals of peers in children's magazines. *Sex Roles, 79,* 314–328. https://doi.org/10.1007/s11199-017-0883-3

Spinrad, T. L., & Eisenberg, N. (2017). Prosocial behavior and empathy-related responding: Relations to children's well-being. In M. Robinson & M. Eid (Eds.), *The happy mind: Cognitive contributions to well-being* (pp. 331–347). Springer, https://doi.org/10.1007/978-3-319-58763-9_18

Srna, S., Schrift, R. Y., & Zauberman, G. (2018). The illusion of multitasking and its positive effect on performance. *Psychological Science, 29*(12), 1942–1955. https://doi.org/10.1177/0956797618801013

Staff, J., Mortimer, J. T., & Johnson, M. K. (2018). Work intensity and academic success. In B. Schneider (Ed.), *Handbook of the sociology of education in the 21st century* (pp. 335–357). Handbooks of Sociology and Social Research. Springer.

Stahl, A. E., & Feigenson, L. (2015). Observing the unexpected enhances infants' learning and exploration. *Science, 348*(6230), 91–94. https://doi.org/10.1126/science.aaa3799

Stahl, A. E., & Feigenson, L. (2018). Violations of core knowledge shape early learning. *Topics in Cognitive Science, 11*(1), 136–153. https://doi.org/10.1111/tops.12389

Staiano, A. E., et al. (2018). Screen-time policies and practices in early care and education centers in relationship to child physical activity. *Childhood Obesity, 14*(6), 341–348. https://doi.org/10.1089/chi.2018.0078

Stanford, J. B. (2018). What kind of policies for fertility treatments would improve affordability and outcomes for individuals and the public? *Paediatric and Perinatal Epidemiology, 31*(5), 449–451. https://doi.org/10.1111/ppe.12411

Stark, E., Shim, J., Ross, C., & Miller, E. S. (2018). The impact of perinatal depression on breastfeeding rates. *Obstetrics & Gynecology, 131*, 122S–123S. https://doi.org/10.1097/01.AOG.0000533518.70477.73

Staats, S., van der Valk, I. E., Meeus, W. H. J., & Branje, S. J. T. (2017). Longitudinal transmission of conflict management style across inter-parental and adolescent relationships. *Journal of Research on Adolescence, 28*(1), 169–185. https://doi.org/10.1111/jora.12324

Stavrinos, D., McManus, B., Underhill, A. T., & Lechtreck, M. T. (2019). Impact of adolescent media multitasking on cognition and driving safety. *Human Behavior and Emerging Technologies, 1*(2), 161–168. https://doi.org/10.1002/hbe2.143

Stavropoulos, V., et al. (2018). Flow on the Internet: A longitudinal study of Internet addiction symptoms during adolescence. *Behaviour & Information Technology, 37*(2), 159–172. https://doi.org/10.1080/0144929X.2018.1424937

Stead, V. E., Boylan, K., & Schmidt, L .A. (2019). Longitudinal associations between non-suicidal self-injury and borderline personality disorder in adolescents: A literature review. *Borderline Personality Disorder and Emotion Dysregulation, 6*, Article 3. https://doi.org/10.1186/s40479-019-0100-9

Steele, E. H., & McKinney, C. (2018). Emerging adult psychological problems and parenting style: Moderation by parent–child relationship quality. *Personality and Individual Differences, 146*, 201–208. https://doi.org/10.1016/j.paid.2018.04.048

Steele, H. (2017). Emotional development in the first year of life. In D. Skuse, H. Bruce, & L. Dowdney (Eds.), *Child psychology and psychiatry: Frameworks for clinical training and practice* (3rd ed.). John Wiley & Sons, https://doi.org/10.1002/9781119170235.ch6

Steiner A.Z., et al. (2017). Association between biomarkers of ovarian reserve and infertility among older women of reproductive age. *JAMA, 318*(14), 1367–1376. https://doi.org/10.1001/jama.2017.14588

Stenseng, F., Belsky, J., Skalicka, V., & Wichstrøm, L. (2015). Social exclusion predicts impaired self-regulation: A 2-year longitudinal panel study including the transition from preschool to school. *Journal of Personality, 83*(2), 212–220. https://doi.org/10.1111/jopy.12096

Stensvold, H. J., et al. (2018). Neonatal morbidity and one-year survival of extremely preterm infants. *Pediatrics, 139*(3), e20161821. https://doi.org/10.1542/peds.2016-1821

Stephens, G. & Matthews, D. (2014). The communicative infant from 0–18 months: The social- cognitive foundations of pragmatic development (pp. 13–35). In D. Matthews (Ed.), *Pragmatic development in first language acquisition.* Amsterdam, Netherlands: John Benjamins Publishing Company.

Stephens, L. E., Bowers, E. P., & Lerner, J. V. (2018). Positive youth development and adolescent eating disorder symptomatology: The role of natural mentors. *Journal of Community Psychology, 46*(4), 473–488. https://doi.org/10.1002/jcop.21952

Stern, J. A., & Cassidy, J. (2018). Empathy from infancy to adolescence: An attachment perspective on the development of individual differences. *Developmental Review, 47*, 1–22. https://doi.org/10.1016/j.dr.2017.09.002

Sternberg, R. J. (2012). Intelligence. *Wiley Interdisciplinary Reviews: Cognitive Science, 3*(5), 501–511. https//doi.org.10.1002/wcs.1193

Sternberg, R. J. (2018). Successful intelligence in theory, research, and practice. In R. J. Sternberg (Ed.), *The nature of human intelligence* (pp. 308–322). Cambridge University Press.

Sternberg, R. J. (Ed.). (2018). *The nature of human intelligence.* Cambridge University Press.

Stevenson, J. et al. (2018). Language and reading comprehension in middle childhood predicts emotional and behaviour difficulties in adolescence for those with permanent childhood hearing loss. *The Journal of Child Psychology and Psychiatry, 59*(2), 180–190. https://doi.org/10.1111/jcpp.12803

Stewart, K. E., et al. (2019). Preventing juvenile sexual offending through parental monitoring: A comparison study of youth's experience of supervision. *Journal of Sexual Aggression, 25*(1), 16–30. https://doi.org/10.1080/13552600.2018.1528796

Stiemsma, L. T. & Michels, K. B. (2018). The role of the microbiome in the developmental origins of health and disease. *Pediatrics, 141*(4), https://doi.org/ 10.1542/peds.2017-2437

Stietz, J., Jauk, E., Krach, S., & Kanske, P. (2019). Dissociating empathy from perspective-taking: Evidence from intra- and inter-individual differences research. *Frontiers in Psychiatry.* https://doi.org/10.3389/fpsyt.2019.00126

Stirrups, R. (2018). The storm and stress in the adolescent brain. *The Lancet Neurology, 17*(5), 404. http://doi.org/10.1016/S1474-4422(18)30112-1

Stolzenberg, S. N., McWilliams, K., & Lyon, T. D. (2017). The effects of the hypothetical putative confession and negatively valenced yes/no questions on maltreated and nonmaltreated children's disclosure of a minor transgression. *Child Maltreatment, 22*(2), 167–173. http://doi.org/10.1177/1077559516673734

Stone, M. M., Blumberg, F. C., Blair, C., & Cancelli, A. A. (2016). The "EF" in deficiency: Examining the linkages between executive function and the utilization deficiency observed in preschoolers. *Journal of Experimental Child Psychology, 152*, 367–375. https://doi.org/10.1016/j.jecp.2016.07.003

Strehl, U., et al. (2019). Neurofeedback of slow cortical potentials in children with attention-deficit/hyperactivity disorder: A multicenter randomized trial controlling for unspecific effects. *Frontiers in Human Neuroscience, 11*(135). https://doi.org/10.3389/fnhum.2017.00135

Strouse, G. A., & Ganea, P. A., (2017) Parent–toddler behavior and language differ when reading electronic and print picture books. *Frontiers in Psychology.* https://doi.org/10.3389/fpsyg.2017.00677

Strouse, G. A., Nyhout, A., & Ganea, P. A. (2018). The role of book features in young children's transfer of information from picture books to real-world contexts. *Frontiers in Psychology.* https://doi.org/10.3389/fpsyg.2018.00050

Suarez-Rivera, C., Smith, L. B., & Yu, C. (2019). Multimodal parent behaviors within joint attention support sustained attention in infants. *Developmental Psychology, 55*(1), 96–109. http://dx.doi.org/10.1037/dev0000628

Suglia, S. F., et al. (2017). Childhood and adolescent adversity and cardiometabolic outcomes: A scientific statement from the American Heart Association. *Circulation, 137*(5), e15–e28. https://doi.org/10.1161/CIR.0000000000000536

Suizzo, M.A. (2004). Mother-child relationships in France : Balancing autonomy and affilitation in everyday interactions. Ethos, 32(3), 293–323. https://doi.org/10.1525/eth.2004.32.3.293

Suleiman, A. B., & Dahl, R. (2019). Parent–child relationships in the puberty years: Insights from developmental neuroscience. *Family Relations: Interdisciplinary Journal of Applied Family Science, 68*(3), 279–287. https://doi.org/10.1111/fare.12360

Sullivan, J., Moss-Racusin, C., Lopez, M., & Williams, K. (2018). Backlash against gender stereotype-violating children. *PLOS ONE, 13*(4), e0195503. https://doi.org/10.1371/journal.pone.0195503

Sullivan, M. W., & Lewis, M. (2003). Emotional expressions of young infants and children. *Infants and Young Children, 16*(2), 120–142.

Suddendorf, T. & Butler, D. L. (2013). The nature of visual self-recognition. *Trends in Cognitive Sciences, 17*(3), 121–127. https://doi.org/10.1016/j.tics.2013.01.004

Sun, X., McHale, S. M., & Updegraff, K. A. (2019). Sibling experiences in middle childhood predict sibling differences in college graduation. *Child Development, 90*(1), 25–34. https://doi.org/10.1111/jmft.12175

Sung, H., Siegel, R. L., Rosenberg, P. S., & Jemal, A. (2019). Emerging cancer trends among young adults in the USA: Analysis of population-based cancer registry. *The Lancet, 4*(3), e137–e147. https://doi.org/10.1016/S2468-2667(18)30267-6

Susman E.J. (2019) Stress, biomarkers, and resilience in childhood and adolescence: Advances in the last few decades. In: A. Harrist & B. Gardner (Eds.), *Biobehavioral Markers in Risk and Resilience Research. Emerging Issues in Family and Individual Resilience.* Springer, Cham. https://doi.org/10.1007/978-3-030-05952-1_6

Suttie, J. (2016, September 15). How to protect kids from nature-deficit disorder. *Greater Good Magazine*, Retrieved from https://greatergood.berkeley.edu/article/item/how_to_protect_kids_from_nature_deficit_disorder

Suurland, J., van der Heijden, K. B., Huijbregts, S. C. J., van Goozen, S. H. M., & Swaab, H. (2018). Infant parasympathetic and sympathetic activity during baseline, stress, and recovery: Interactions with prenatal adversity predict physical aggression in toddlerhood. *Journal of Abnormal Child Psychology, 46*, 755–768. https://doi.org/10.1007/s10802-017-0337-y

Swanson, H. L., Kong, J., & Petcu, S. D. (2020). Math problem-solving and cognition among emerging bilingual children at risk and not at risk for math difficulties. *Child Neuropsychology, 26*(4), 489–517. https://doi.org/10.1080/09297049.2019.1674268

Syed, M., & Fish, J. (2018). Revising Erik Erikson's legacy on culture, race, and ethnicity. *Identity: An International Journal of Theory and Research, 18*(4), 274–283. https://doi.org/10.1080/15283488.2018.1523729

Syed, M., Santos, C., Yoo, H. C., & Juang, L. (2018). Invisibility of racial/ethnic minorities in developmental science: Implications for research and institutional practices. *American Psychologist, 73*(6), 812–826. https://doi.org/0.1037/amp0000294

Szatmari, P. (2017). Risk and resilience in autism spectrum disorder: A missed translation opportunity? *Developmental Medicine & Child Neurology, 60*(3), 225–229. https://doi.org/10.1111/dmcn.13588

Szepsenwol, O., & Simpson, J. A. (2019). Attachment within life history theory: An evolutionary perspective on individual differences in attachment. *Current Opinion in Psychology, 25*, 65–70. https://doi.org/10.1016/j.copsyc.2018.03.005

Sznitman, G. A., Zimmermann, G., & Van Petegm, S. (2019). Further insight into adolescent personal identity statuses: Differences based on self-esteem, family climate, and family communication. *Journal of Adolescence, 71*, 99–109. https://doi.org/10.1016/j.adolescence.2019.01.003

Szumowska, E., Poplawska-Boruc, A., & Kossowska, M. (2018). How many things do you (like to) do at once? The relationship between need for closure and multitaking preference and behavior. *Personality and Individual Differences, 134,* 222–231. https://doi.org/10.1016/j.paid.2018.06.023

Taheri, P. A., et al. (2018). The effect of a short course of moderate pressure sunflower massage oil on the weight gain velocity and length of NICU stay in preterm infants. *Infant Behavior and Development, 50,* 22–27. https://doi.org/10.1016/j.infbeh.2017.11.002

Taher, T., Damer, A., & Wong, M. (2019). Commentary: Parental depressive symptoms as a predictor of outcome in the treatment of child internalizing and externalizing problems. *Frontiers in Psychiatry, 10,* 533. https://doi.org/10.3389/fpsyt.2019.00533

Takacs, Z. K., & Kassai, R. (2019). The efficacy of different interventions to foster children's executive function skills: A series of meta-analyses. *Psychological Bulletin, 145*(7), 653–697. http://dx.doi.org/10.1037/bul0000195

Tal, R., & Seifer, D. B. (2017). Ovarian reserve testing: A user's guide. *American Journal of Obstetrics and Gynecology, 217*(2), 129–140. https://doi.org/10.1016/j.ajog.2017.02.027

Tamnes, C. K., et al. (2017). Development of the cerebral cortex across adolescence: A multisample study of inter-related longitudinal changes in cortical volume, surface area, and thickness. *The Journal of Neuroscience, 37*(12), 3402–3412. https://doi.org/10.1523/JNEUROSCI.3302-16.2017

Tamnes, C. K., et al. (2018). Social perspective taking is associated with self-reported prosocial behavior and regional cortical thickness across adolescence. *Developmental Psychology, 54*(9), 1745–1757. http://dx.doi.org/10.1037/dev0000541

Tang, S., & Patrick, M. E. (2018). Technology and interactive social media use among 8th and 10th graders in the U.S. and associations with homework and school grades. *Computers in Human Behavior, 86,* 34–44. https://doi.org/10.1016/j.chb.2018.04.025

Tangney, J. P. (1995). Recent advances in the empirical study of shame and guilt. *American Behavioral Scientist, 38*(8), 11-32-1145. https://doi.org/10.1177/0002764295038008008

Taubman, D. S., Parikh, S. V., Christensen, H., & Scott, J. (2019). Using school-based interventions for depression education and prevention. In A. Javed & K. Fountoulakis (Eds.), *Advances in Psychiatry.* Springer.

Taylor, K. M., et al. (2018). Concussion history and cognitive function in a large cohort of adolescent athletes. *The American Journal of Sports Medicine, 46*(13), 3262–3270. https://doi.org/10.1177/0363546518798801

Taylor, R. W., Williams, S. H., Farmer, V. L., & Taylor, B. J. (2013). Changes in physical activity over time in young children: A longitudinal study using accelerometers. *PLoSONE, 8*(11), e81567. https://doi.org/10.1371/journal.pone.0081567

Tebes, J. K., & Thai, N. D. (2018). Interdisciplinary team science and the public: Steps toward participatory team science. *American Psychologist, 73*(4), 549–562. http://dx.doi.org/10.1037/amp0000281

Tenesa, A., & Haley, C. S. (2013). The heritability of human disease: Estimation, uses and abuses. *Nature Reviews Genetics, 14,* 139–149. https://doi.org/10.1038/nrg3377

Terr, L. (2000). *Beyond love and work: Why adults need to play.* New York, NY: Touchstone.

Terry, N. P., Gaitlin, B., & Johnson, L. (2918). Same or different: How bilingual readers can help us understand bidialectical readers. *Topics in Language Disorders, 38*(1), 50–65. https://doi.org/10.1097/TLD.0000000000000141

Teymoori, A., Côté, S. M., & Jones, B. L. (2018). Risk factors associated with boys' and girls' developmental trajectories of physical aggression from early childhood through early adolescence. *JAMA Network Open, 1*(8), e186364. https://doi.org/10.1001/jamanetworkopen.2018.6364

Thomas, G. (2019). Universal mental health prevention for adolescents: Real-world implications. *Pediatrics, 144*(2), e20190937. https://doi.org/10.1542/peds.2019-0937

Thomas, A., & Chess, S. (1977). *Temperament and development.* Brunner/Mazel.

Thompson, R. A. (2013). Attachment theory and research: Précis and prospect (pp. 191–216). In

P. D. Zelazo (Ed.), *The Oxford Handbook of Developmental Psychology, Vol. 2: Self and Other.* New York, NY: Oxford University Press.

Thompson, R. A. & Nelson, C. A. (2001). Developmental science and the media. *American Psychologist, 56*(1), 5–15.

Thompson-Hernández, W. (2019, November 12). The quinceañara, redefined. *New York Times,* https://www.nytimes.com/2019/11/12/style/quinceaera-genz-millennial.html

Tian, S., & Liu, Z. (2020). Emergence of income inequality: Origin, distribution and possible policies. *Physica A: Statistical Mechanics and its Applications, 537,* 122767. https://doi.org/10.1016/j.physa.2019.122767

Tilton-Weaver, L., Marshall, S. K., & Svensson, Y. (2019). Depressive symptoms and non-suicidal self-injury in adolescence: Latent patterns of short-term stability and change. *Journal of Adolescence, 75,* 163–174. https://doi.org/10.1016/j.adolescence.2019.07.013

Timpson, N. J., Greenwood, C. M. T., Soranzo, N., Lawson, D. J., & Richards, J. B. (2018). Genetic architecture: The shape of genetic contribution to human traits and disease. *Nature Reviews Genetics, 19*(2), 110–124. https://doi.org/10.1038/nrg.2017.101

Tippett, N., & Wolke, D. (2015). Aggression between siblings: Association with the home environment and peer bullying. *Aggressive Behavior, 41*(4), 14–24. https://doi.org/10.1002/ab.21557

Titlestad, A. & Pooley, J. A. (2014). Resilience in same-sex-parented families: The lived experience of adults with gay, lesbian, or bisexual parents. *Journal of GLBT Family Studies, 10*(4), 329–353. https://doi.org/10.1080/1550428X.2013.833065

Tiwari, A., et al. (2018). Effects of an evidence-based parenting program on biobehavioral stress among at-risk mothers for child maltreatment: A pilot study. *Social Work in Health Care, 57*(3), 137–163. https://doi.org/10.1080/00981389.2017.1371096

Tobias, N. E. (2018). Managing enuresis in primary care: Part 2. *Contemporary Pediatrics, 35*(10).

Toda, K. & Platt, M. L. (2015). Animal cognition: Monkeys pass the mirror test. *Current Biology, 25*(2), R64-R66. https//doi.org/10.1016/j.cub.2014.12.005

Tompkins, V., Benigno, J. P., Lee, B. K., & Wright, B. M. (2018). The relation between parents' mental state talk and children's social understanding: A meta-analysis. *Social Development, 27*(2), 223–246. https://doi.org/10.1111/sode.12280

Toomela, A. (2002). Drawing as a verbally mediated activity: A study of relationships between verbal, motor, and visuospatial skills and drawing in children. *International Journal of Behavioral Development, 26*(3), 234–247. https://doi.org/10.1080/01650250143000021

Toomey, R. B., Syvertsen, A. K., & Shramko, M. (2018). Transgender adolescent suicide behavior. *Pediatrics, 142*(4), e20174218. https://doi.org/10.1542/peds.2017-4218

Torok, M., et al. (2019). Preventing adolescent suicide: A systematic review of the effectiveness and change mechanisms of suicide prevention gatekeeping training programs for teachers and parents. *Journal of Adolescence, 73*, 100–112. https://doi.org/10.1016/j.adolescence.2019.04.005

Torppa, M., et al. (2019). Leisure reading (but not any kind) and reading comprehension support each others—A longitudinal study across grades 1 and 9. *Child Development.* Advance online publication. https://doi.org/10.1111/cdev.13241

Toth, S. L., & Manly, J. T. (2019). Developmental consequences of child abuse and neglect: Implications for intervention. *Child Development Perspectives, 13*(1), 59–64. https://doi.org/10.1111/cdep.12317

Touitou, Y., Touitou, D., & Reinberg, A. (2016). Disruption of adolescents' circadian clock: The vicious circle of media use, exposure to light at night, sleep loss and risk behaviors. *Journal of Physiology-Paris, 110*(4, Part B), 467–479. https://doi.org/10.1016/j.jphysparis.2017.05.001

Tourva, A., Spanoudies, G., & Demetriou, A. (2016). Cognitive correlates of developing intelligence: The contribution of working memory, processing speed and attention. *Intelligence, 54*, 136–146. https://doi.org/10.1016/j.intell.2015.12.001

Townsend, E. (2019). Time to take self-harm in young people seriously. *The Lancet Psychiatry, 6*(4), 279–280. https://doi.org/10.1016/S2215-0366(19)30101-4

Trahan, M. H. (2017). Paternal self-efficacy and father involvement; A bi-directional relationship. *Psychology of Men & Masculinity, 19*(4), 624–634. http://dx.doi.org/10.1037/men0000130

Travers, A. S. M., & Mahalik, J. R. (2019). Positive youth development as a protective factor for adolescents at risk for depression and alcohol use. *Applied Developmental Science.* Advance online publication. https://doi.org/10.1080/10888691.2019.1634569

Trawick-Smith, J., et al. (2017). Block play and mathematics learning in preschool: The effect of building complexity, peer and teacher interactions in the block areas, and replica play materials. *Journal of Early Childhood Research, 15*(4), 433–448. https://doi.org/10.1177/1476718X16664557

Trehub, S. E., & Cirelli, L. K. (2018). Precursors to the performing arts in infancy and early childhood. In J. R. Christensen & A. Gomila (Eds.), *Progress in brain research: The arts and the brain* (pp. 225–242). Academic Press, https://doi.org/10.1016/bs.pbr.2018.03.008

Treiman, R., Decker, K., Robins, S., & Ghosh, D. (2018). Parent–child conversations about literacy: A longitudinal, observational study. *Journal of Child Language, 45*(2), 511–525. https://doi.org/10.1017/S0305000917000307

Trevarthen, C., & Delafield-Butt, J. (2017). Intersubjectivity in the imagination and feelings of the infant: Implications for education in the early years. In E. White & C. Dalli (Eds.), *Under-three year olds in policy and practice.* Policy and pedagogy with under-three year olds: Cross-disciplinary insights and innovations. Springer.

Triandis, H. C. (2001). Individualism-collectivism and personality. *Journal of Personality, 69*(6), 907–924. https://doi.org/10.1111/1467-6494.696169

Tsotsi, S., et al. (2019). Maternal parenting stress, child exuberance, and preschoolers' behavior problems. *Child Development, 90*(1), 136–146. https://doi.org/10.1111/cdev.13180

Tucker, C. J., & Finkelhor, D. (2015). The state of interventions for sibling conflict and aggression: A systematic review. *Trauma, Violence, & Abuse, 18*(4), 396–406. https://doi.org/10.1177/1524838015622438

Tucker, C. J., Finkelhor, D., & Turner, H. (2018A). Patterns of sibling victimization as predictors of peer victimization in childhood and adolescence. *Journal of Family Violence, 34,* 745–755. https://doi.org/10.1007/s10896-018-0021-1

Tudor, M. E., Rankin, J., & Lerner, M. D. (2018). A model of family and child functioning in siblings of youth with autism spectrum disorder. *Journal of Autism & Developmental Disorders, 48,* 1210–1227. https://doi.org/10.1007/s10803-017-3352-5

Tully, K. P., & Sullivan, C. S. (2018). Parent–infant room-sharing is complex and important for breastfeeding. *Evidence-Based Nursing 21*(1). http://dx.doi.org/10.1136/eb-2017-102801

Tully, L. A., & Hunt, C. (2017). A randomized controlled trial of a brief versus standard group parenting program for toddler aggression. *Aggressive Behavior, 43*(3), 291–303. https://doi.org/10.1002/ab.21689

Tulving E. (1972). Episodic and semantic memory (pp. 382–403). In E. Tulving & W. Donaldson (Eds.), *Organization of Memory.* New York: Academic Press.

Turanovic, J. J., & Pratt, T. C. (2017). Consequences of violent victimization for Native American youth in early adulthood. *Journal of Youth and Adolescence, 46,* 1333–1350. https://doi.org/10.1007/s10964-016-0587-y

Turiel, E., Chung, E., & Carr, J. A. (2016). Struggles for equal rights and social justice as unrepresented and represented in psychological research. *Advances in Child Development and Behavior, 50,* 1–29. https://doi.org/10.1016/bs.acdb.2015.11.004

Turkheimer, E., Beam, C. E., & Davis, D. W. (2015). The Scarr–Rowe interaction in complete seven-year WISC data from the Louisville twin study: Preliminary report. *Behavioral Genetics, 45,* 635–639. https://doi.org/10.1007/s10519-015-9760-4

Turnbull, J. L., Adams, H. N., & Gorard, D. A. (2015). Review article: The diagnosis and management of food allergies and food intolerances. *Alimentary Pharmacology & Therapeutics, 41,* 3–25. https://doi.org/10.1111/apt.12984

Twenge, J. M., Carter, N. T., & Campbell, W. K. (2017). Age, time period, and birth cohort differences in self-esteem: Reexamining a cohort-sequential longitudinal study. *Journal of Personality and Social Psychology, 112*(5), e9–e17. https://doi.org/10.1037/pspp0000122

Twenge, J. M., Hisler, G. C., & Krizan, Z. (2019). Associations between screen time and sleep duration are primarily driven by portable electronic devices: Evidence from a population-based study of U.S. children ages 0–17. *Sleep Medicine, 56,* 211–218. https://doi.org/10.1016/j.sleep.2018.11.009

Twenge, J., Spitzberg, B. H., & Campbell, W. K. (2019). Less in-person social interaction with peers among U.S. adolescents in the 21st century and links to loneliness. *Journal of Social and Personal Relationships, 36*(6), 1892–1913. https://doi.org/10.1177/0265407519836170

Tyborowska, A., et al. (2018). Early-life and pubertal stress differentially module grey matter development in human adolescents. *Scientific Reports, 8,* 9201. https://doi.org/10.1038/s41598-018-27439-5

Tyng, C. M., Amin, H. U., Saad, M. N. M., & Malik, A. S. (2017). The influences of emotion on learning and memory. *Frontiers in Psychology, 8,* 1454. https://doi.org/10.3389/fpsyg.2017.01454 Uchino, E. & Watanabe, S. (2014). Self-recognition in pigeons revisited. *Journal of the Experimental Analysis of Behavior, 102*(3), 327–334. https://doi.org/10.1002/jeab.112

Uhls, Y. T., Michikyan, M., Morris, J., Garcia, D., Small, G. W., Zgourou, E., & Greenfield, P. (2014). Five days at outdoor education camp without screens improves preteen skills with nonverbal emotion cues. *Computers in Human Behavior, 39,* 387–392. https://doi.org/10.1016/j.chb.2014.05.036

Umaña-Taylor, A. J. (2018). Intervening in cultural development: The case of ethnic-racial identity. *Development and Psychopathology, 30*(5), 1907–1922. https://doi.org/10.1017/S0954579418000974

Umaña-Taylor, A. J., Kornienko, O., Bayless, S. D., & Updegraff, K. A. (2018). A universal intervention program increases ethnical-racial identity exploration and resolution to predict adolescent psychosocial functioning one year later. *Journal of Youth and Adolescence, 47,* 1–15. https://doi.org/10.1007/s10964-017-0766-5

UNHCR. (2019). *Syria refugee crisis explained.* Retrieved from https://www.unrefugees.org/news/syria-refugee-crisis-explained/

UNICEF. (2018). *What is the Convention on the Rights of the Child?* https://www.unicef.org/crc/index_30160.html

United Nations Expert Group Meeting on Policy Responses to Low Fertility. (2015). *The influence of family policies on fertility in France.* http://www.un.org/en/development/desa/population/events/pdf/expert/24/Policy_Briefs/PB_France.pdf

United Nations Office of the High Commissioner for Human Rights. (2016). *Free & equal campaign fact sheet: Intersex.* https://www.unfe.org/wp-content/uploads/2017/05/UNFE-Intersex.pdf

U.S. Department of Health and Human Services (2019), *Physical activity guidelines for Americans* (2nd Ed.). Retrieved from: https://health.gov/sites/default/files/2019-09/Physical_Activity_Guidelines_2nd_edition.pdf

U. S. Department of Education (2016). *Fact sheet: Troubling pay gap for early childhood teachers.* Retrieved from https://www.ed.gov/news/press-releases/fact-sheet-troubling-pay-gap-early-childhood-teachers

Uscianowski, C., Almeda, V., & Ginsburg, H. P. (2018). Differences in the complexity of math and literacy questions parents pose during storybook reading. *Early Childhood Research Quarterly, 50*(Part 3), 40–50. https://doi.org/10.1016/j.ecresq.2018.07.003

Usher, E. L., Li, C. R., Butz, A. R., & Rojas, J. P. (2018). Perseverant grit and self-efficacy: Are both essential for children's academic success? *Journal of Educational Psychology.* Advance online publication. http://dx.doi.org/10.1037/edu0000324

Uzun, A. M., & Kilis, S. (2019). Does persistent involvement in media and technology lead to lower academic performance? Evaluating media and technology use in relation to multitasking, self-regulation and academic performance. *Computers in Human Behavior, 90*, 196–203. https://doi.org/10.1016/j.chb.2018.08.045

Vaish, A. (2018). The prosocial functions of early social emotions: The case of guilt. *Current Opinion in Psychology, 20*, 25–29. https://doi.org/10.1016/j.copsyc.2017.08.008

Valcan, D. S., Davis, H., & Pino-Pasternak, D. (2018). Parental behaviours predict early childhood executive functions: A meta-analysis. *Educational Psychology Review, 30*(3), 607–649. https://doi.org/10.1007/s10648-017-9411-9

Valdés-Cuervo, A., Alcántar-Nieblas, C., Martínez-Ferrer, B., & Parra-Pérez, L. (2018). Relations between restorative parental discipline, family climate, parental support, empathy, shame, and defenders in bullying. *Children and Youth Services Review, 95*, 152–159. https://doi.org/10.1016/j.childyouth.2018.10.015

van Bergen, E., van Zuijen, T., Bishop, D., & de Jong, P. F. (2017). Why are home literacy environment and children's reading skills associated? What parental skills reveal. *Reading Research Quarterly, 52*(2), 147–160. https://doi.org/10.1002/rrq.160

van Bergen, E., et al. (2018). Why do children read more: The influence of reading ability on voluntary reading practices. *The Journal of Child Psychology and Psychiatry, 59*(11), 1205–1214. https://doi.org/10.1111/jcpp.12910

van Berkel, S. R., Tucker, C. J., & Finkelhor, D. (2018). The combination of sibling victimization and parental child maltreatment on mental health problems and delinquency. *Child Maltreatment, 23*(3), 244–253. https://doi.org/10.1177/1077559517751670

van den Bos, W., and Hertwig, R. (2017). Adolescents display distinctive tolerance to ambiguity and to uncertainty during risky decision-making. *Scientific Reports, 7*, 40962. https://doi.org/10.1038/srep40962

van der Schuur, W. A., Baumgartner, S. E., Sumter, S. R., & Valkenburg, P. M. (2018). Media multitasking and sleep problems: A longitudinal study among adolescents. *Computers in Human Behavior, 81*, 316–324. https://doi.org/10.1016/j.chb.2017.12.024

van der Schuur, W. A., Baumgartner, S. E., Sumter, S. R., & Valkenburg, P. M. (2018). Exploring the long-term relationship between academic media multitasking and adolescents' academic achievement. *New Media & Society, 22*(1), 140–158. https://doi.org/10.1177/1461444819861956

van der Ven, S. H. G., Boom, J., Kroesbergen, E. H., & Leseman, P. P. M. (2012). Microgenetic patterns of children's multiplication learning: Confirming the overlapping waves model by latent growth modeling. *Journal of Experimental Child Psychology, 113*(1), 1–19. https://doi.org/10.1016/j.jecp.2012.02.001

van der Wal, R. C., Finkenauer, C., & Visser, M. M. (2019). Reconciling mixed findings on children's adjustment following high-conflict divorce. *Journal of Child and Family Studies, 28*(2), 468–478. https://doi.org/10.1007/s10826-018-1277-z

van der Wilt, F., van der Veen, C., van Kruistum, C., & van Oers, B. (2018). Popular, rejected, neglected, controversial or average: Do young children of different sociometric groups differ in their level of oral communicative competence? *Social Development, 27*(4), 793–807. https://doi.org/10.1111/sode.12316

van der Wilt, F., van der Veen, C., van Kruistum, C., & van Oers, B. (2019). Why do children become rejected by their peers? A review of studies into the relationship between oral communicative competence and sociometric status in childhood. *Educational Psychology Review, 31*, 699–724. https://doi.org/10.1007/s10648-019-09479-z

van Dijk, M. & van Geert, P. (2015). The nature and meaning of intraindividual variability in development in the early life span. In M. Diehl, K. Hooker, & M. J. Sliwinski (Eds.), Handbook of Intraindividual Variability Across the Life Span (pp. 37–58). New York, NY: Routledge.

van Doeselaar, L., et al. (2018). The role of identity commitments in depressive symptoms and stressful life events in adolescence and young adulthood. *Developmental Psychology 54*(5), 950962. http://dx.doi.org/10.1037/dev0000479

van Doeselaar, L., et al. (2019). Adolescents' identity formation: Linking the narrative and dual-cycle approach. *Journal of Youth and Adolescence, 49*, 818–835. https://doi.org/10.1007/s10964-019-01096-x

van Dorn, A., Cooney, R. E., & Sabin, M. L. (2020). COVID-19 exacerbating inequalities in the U.S. *Lancet World Report, 395*(10232), 1243–1244. https://doi.org/10.1016/S0140-6736(20)30893-X

van Dyck, L. I., & Morrow, E. M. (2017). Genetic control of postnatal human growth. *Current Opinion in Neurology, 30*(1), 11–124. https://doi.org/10.1097/WCO.0000000000000405

van Hoorn, J., et al. (2018). Differential effects of parent and peer pressure on neural correlates of risk taking in adolescence. *Social Cognitive and Affective Neuroscience, 13*(9), 945–955. https://doi.org/10.1093/scan/nsy071

Vance, A., McGrath, J., & Brandon, D. (2018). Where you are born really does matter: Why birth hospital and quality of care contribute to racial/ethnic disparities. *Advances in Neonatal Care, 18*(2), 81–82. https://doi.org/10.1097/ANC.0000000000000480

Van der Graff, J., et al. (2018). Prosocial behavior in adolescence: Gender differences in development and links with empathy. *Journal of Youth and Adolescence, 47*(5), 1086–1099. https://doi.org/10.1007/s10964-017-0786-1

Van Doren, J. et al. (2019). Sustained effects of neurofeedback in ADHD: a systematic review and meta-analysis. *European Child & Adolescent Psychiatry, 28*, 293–305. https://doi.org/10.1007/s00787-018-1121-4

Van Maele-Fabry, G., Garnet-Payrastre, L., & Lison, D. (2019). Household exposure to pesticides and risk of leukemia in children and adolescents: Updated systematic review and meta-analysis. *International Journal of Hygiene and Environmental Health, 222*(1), 49–67. https://doi.org/10.1016/j.ijheh.2018.08.004

Van Ouystel, J., et al. (2019). Longitudinal associations between sexting, cyberbullying, and bullying among adolescents: Cross-lagged panel analysis. *Journal of Adolescence, 73*, 36–41. https://doi.org/10.1016/j.adolescence.2019.03.008

Vandell, D. L., Burchinal, M., & Pierce, K. (2016). Early child care and adolescent functioning at the end of high school: Results from the NICHD study of early child care and youth development. *Developmental Psychology, 52*(10), 1634–1645. http://doi.org/10.1037/dev0000169

Vandell, D. L., Lee, K. T. H., Whitaker, A. A., & Pierce, K. M. (2018). Cumulative and differential effects of early child care and middle childhood out-of-school time on adolescent functioning. *Child Development 91*(1), 129–144. https://doi-org.scsu.idm.oclc.org/10.1111/cdev.13136

Vanderbilt D., Mirzaian C., Schifsky K. (2018) Environmental risks to NICU outcomes. In H., Needelman & B., Jackson (Eds.), *Follow-up for NICU graduates*. Springer, https://doi.org/10.1007/978-3-319-73275-6_10

Vanhalst, J., Luyckx, K., Van Petegem, S., & Soenens, B. (2018). The detrimental effects of adolescents' chronic loneliness on motivation and emotion regulation in social situations. *Journal of Youth and Adolescence, 47*, 162–176. https://doi.org/10.1007/s10964-017-0686-4

Vannucci, A., Flannery, K. M., & Ohannessian, C. M. (2018). Age-varying associations between coping and depressive symptoms throughout adolescence and emerging adulthood. *Development and Psychopathology, 30*(2), 665–681. https://doi.org/10.1017/S0954579417001183

Varner, F. A., et al. (2018). Racial discrimination experiences and Black youth adjustment: The role of parenting profiles based on racial socialization and involved-vigilant parenting. *Cultural Diversity and Ethnic Minority Psychology, 24*(2), 173–186. http://dx.doi.org/10.1037/cdp0000180

Vasilevsky, N. A., et al. (2018). Plain-language medical vocabulary for precision diagnosis. *Nature Genetics, 50*(4), 474–476. https://doi.org/10.1038/s41588-018-0096-x

Vaziri, F., et al. (2018). Lavender oil aromatherapy on infant colic and maternal mood: A double blind randomized clinical trial. *Pharmaceutical Sciences, 24*(1), 38–43. https://doi.org/10.15171/PS.2018.07

Vélez-Agosto, N. M., et al. (2017). Bronfenbrenner's bioecological theory revision: Moving culture from the macro into the micro. *Perspectives on Psychological Science, 12*(5), 900–910. https://doi.org/10.1177/1745691617704397

Veliz, P., Eckner, J. T., Zdroik, J., & Schulenberg, J. E. (2019). Lifetime prevalence of self-reported concussion among adolescents involved in competitive sports: A national U.S. study. *Journal of Adolescent Health, 64*(2), 272–275. https://doi.org/10.1016/j.jadohealth.2018.08.023

Verhage, C. L., Gillebaart, M., van der Veek, S. M. C., & Vereijken, C. M. J. L. (2018). The relation between family meals and health of infants and toddlers: A review. *Appetite, 127*, 97–109. https://doi.org/10.1016/j.appet.2018.04.010

Verma, S. (2018). Social protection, adolescent well-being, and development in low- and middle-income countries. In J. E. Lansford & P. Banati (Eds.), *Handbook of adolescent development research and its impact on global policy* (pp. 319–340). Oxford University Press.

Vermande, M. M., et al. (2018). Is inspiring group members an effective predictor of social dominance in early adolescence? Direct and moderated effects of behavioral strategies, social skills, and gender on resource control and popularity. *Journal of Youth and Adolescence, 47*(9), 1813–1829. https://doi.org/10.1007/s10964-018-0830-9

Véronneau, M-H., Hiatt Racer, K., Fosco, G. M., & Dishion, T. J. (2014). The contribution of adolescent effortful control to early adult educational attainment. *Journal of Educational Psychology, 106*(3), 730–743. https://doi.org/10.103/a00358317

Vértes, P. E. & Bullmore, E. T. (2015). Annual research review: Growth connectomics—the organization and reorganization of brain networks during normal and abnormal development. *The Journal of Child Psychology and Psychiatry, 56*(3), 299–320. https://doi.org/ 10.1111/jcpp.12365

Vickery, B., Ebisawa, M., Shreffler, W. G., & Wood, R. A. (2019). Current and future treatment of peanut allergy. *The Journal of Allergy and Clinical Immunology: In Practice, 7*(2), 357–365. https://doi.org/10.1016/j.jaip.2018.11.049

Victor, S. E., Hipwell, A. E., Stepp, S. D., & Scott, L. N. (2019). Parent and peer relationships as longitudinal predictors of adolescent non-suicidal self-injury onset. *Child and Adolescent Psychiatry and Mental Health, 13*, 1. https://doi.org/10.1186/s13034-018-0261-0

Vilkin, E., et al. (2019). Elementary students' gender beliefs and attitudes following a 12-week arts curriculum focused on gender. *Journal of LGBT Youth, 17*(1), 70–88. https://doi.org/10.1080/19361653.2019.1613282

Vincent, C. & Maxwell, C. (2015). Parenting priorities and pressures: Furthering understanding of 'concerted cultivation'. *Discourse: Studies in the Cultural Politics of Education.* https://doi.org/10.1080/01596306.2015.1014880

Vitaro, F., Boivin, M., & Poulin, F. (2018). The interface of aggression and peer relations in childhood and adolescence. In W. M. Bukowski, B. Laursen, & K. Rubin, K. (Eds.), *Handbook of peer interactions, relationships, and groups* (2nd ed., pp. 284–301). Guilford Press.

Vitello, P. (2014, October 23). Carolyn Rovee-Collier, who said babies have clear memories, is dead at 72. *New York Times,* https://www.nytimes.com/2014/10/23/us/carolyn-rovee-collier-who-said-babies-have-clear-memories-is-dead-at-72.html

Vöhringer, I. A., et al. (2018). The development of implicit memory from infancy to childhood: On average performance levels and interindividual differences. *Child Development, 89*(2), 370–382. https://doi.org/10.1111/cdev.12749

Volk, A. A., et al. (2019). Personality and bullying: Pathways to adolescent social dominance. *Current Psychology*, 1–12. https://doi.org/10.1007/s12144-019-00182-4

Voltaire, S. T., & Teti, D. M. (2018). Early nighttime parental interventions and infant sleep regulation across the first year. *Sleep Medicine, 52*, 107–115. https://doi.org/10.1016/j.sleep.2018.07.013

Voltmer, K., & von Salisch, M. (2017). Three meta-analyses of children's emotion knowledge and their school success. *Learning and Individual Differences, 59*, 107–118. https://doi.org/10.1016/j.lindif.2017.08.006

Vossoughi, N., Jackson, Y., Gusler, S., & Stone, K. (2018). Mental health outcomes for youth living in refugee camps: A review. *Trauma, Violence, & Abuse, 19*(5), 528–542. https://doi.org/10.1177/1524838016673602

Voulgaridou, I., & Kokkinos, C. M. (2015). Relational aggression in adolescents: A review of theoretical and empirical research. *Aggression and Violent Behavior, 23*, 87–97. https://doi.org/10.1016/j.avb.2015.05.006

Wallace, W. B., & Kelsey, T. W. (2010). Human ovarian reserve from conception to the menopause. *PLoS One, 5* (1), e8772. https://doi.org/ 10.1371/journal.pone.0008772.

Wikle, J. S., Jensen, A. C., & Hoagland, A. M. (2018). Adolescent caretaking of younger siblings. *Social Science Research, 71*, 72–84. https://doi.org/10.1016/j.ssresearch.2017.12.007

Wilson, D. M., & Gross, D. (2018). Parents' executive function and involvement in their children's education: An integrated literature review. *Journal of School Health, 88*(4), 322–329. https://doi.org/10.1111/josh.12612

Winnicott, D. (1953). Transitional objects and transitional phenomena, *International Journal of Psychoanalysis, 34*:89-97. https://doi.org/10.1093/med:psych/9780190271367.003.0034

Won, S., & Yu, S. L. (2018). Relations of perceived parental autonomy support and control with adolescents' academic time management and procrastination. *Learning and Individual Differences, 61*, 205–215. https://doi.org/10.1016/j.lindif.2017.12.001

Yan, Z. (2018). Child and adolescent use of mobile phones: An unparalleled complex developmental phenomenon. *Child Development, 89*(1), 5–16. https://doi.org/10.1111/cdev.12821

Yogman, M., Garner, A., Hutchinson, J., Hirsh-Pasek, K., Golinkoff, R. M., COMMITTEE ON PSYCHOSOCIAL ASPECTS OF CHILD AND FAMILY HEALTH, & AAP COUNCIL ON COMMUNICATIONS AND MEDIA. (2018). The power of play: A pediatric role in enhancing development in young children. *Pediatrics, 142*(3): e20182058. https://doi.org/10.1542/peds.2018-2058

Yoshinaga-Itano, C., Sedey, A., Wiggin, M., & Mason, C. A. (2018). Language outcomes improved through early hearing detection and earlier cochlear implantation. *Otology & Neurotology, 29*(10), 1256–1263. https://doi.org/10.1097/MAO.0000000000001976

Yu, R., et al. (2018). Internalizing symptoms and dating violence perpetration in adolescence. *Journal of Adolescence, 69*, 88–91. https://doi.org/10.1016/j.adolescence.2018.09.008

Wade, M., et al. (2018). Cumulative psychosocial risk, parental socialization, and child cognitive functioning: A longitudinal cascade model. *Developmental Psychology, 54*(6), 1038–1050. http://dx.doi.org/10.1037/dev0000493

Wagner, I. V., Sabin, M., & Kiess, W. (2015). Influences of childhood obesity on pubertal development. *Pediatric and Adolescence Medicine, 19*, 110–125. https://doi.org/ 10.1159/000368112

Wakefield, A. J. et al. (1998). Ileal-lymphoid-nodular hyperplasia, non-specific colitis, and pervasive developmental disorder in children. *Lancet, 351*(9103):637–41. https://doi.org/ 10.1016/s0140-6736(97)11096-0

Wally, M. K., Brunner Huber, L. R., Issel, L. M., & Thompson, M. E. (2018). The association between preconception care receipt and the timeliness and adequacy of prenatal care: An examination of multistate data from pregnancy risk assessment monitoring system (PRAMS) 2009–2011. *Maternal and Child Health, 22*(10), 41–50. https://doi.org/10.1007/s10995-017-2352-6

Walter, J., & O'Mahoney, L. (2019). The importance of social networks—An ecological and evolutionary framework to explain the role of microbes in the aetiology of allergy and asthma. *Allergy, 74*(11), 2248–2251. https://doi.org/10.1111/all.13845

Walters, K. S., et al. (2018). Substance use, anxiety, and depressive symptoms among college students. *Journal of Child & Adolescent Substance Abuse, 27*(2), 103–111. https://doi.org/10.1080/1067828X.2017.1420507

Walton, G. M., & Wilson, T. D. (2018). Wise interventions: Psychological remedies for social and personal problems. *Psychological Review, 125*(5), 617–655. http://dx.doi.org/10.1037/rev0000115.supp

Wang, J. & Candy, T. R. (2010). The sensitivity of the 2- to 4-month-old human infant accommodation system. *Investigative Opthalmology & Visual Science, 51*(6), 3309–3317. https://doi.org: 10.1167/iovs.09-4667

Wang, J., & Fielding-Singh, P. (2018). How food rules at home influence independent adolescent food choices. *Journal of Adolescent Health, 63*(2), 219–226. https://doi.org/10.1016/j.jadohealth.2018.02.010

Wang, J., Morgan, G. A., & Birigen, Z. (2014). Mother-toddler affect exchanges and children's mastery behaviours during the preschool years. *Infant and Child Development, 23*(2), 139–152. https://doi.org/10.1002/icd.1825

Wang, M-T., et al. (2019). Parental ethnic-racial socialization practices and children of color's psychosocial and behavioral adjustment: A systematic review and meta-analysis. *American Psychologist, 75*(1), 1–22. http://dx.doi.org/10.1037/amp0000464

Wang, Y., et al. (2019). Characteristics of emotion recognition in primary school children: Relationships with peer status and friendship quality. *Child Indicators Research, 12*(4), 1369–1388. https://doi.org/10.1007/s12187-018-9590-z

Wang, Y., Palonen, T., Hurme, T-R., & Kinos, J. (2019). Do you want to play with me today? Friendship stability among preschool children. *European Early Childhood Education Research Journal, 27*(2), 170–184. https://doi.org/10.1080/1350293X.2019.1579545

Wange, J-Y., et al. (2018). More effective consolidation of episodic long-term memory in children than adults—Unrelated to sleep. *Child Development, 89*(5), 1720–1734. https://doi.org/10.1111/cdev.12839

Wanzek, J., Petscher, Y., Al Otaiba, S., & Donegan, R. E. (2019). Retention of reading intervention effects from fourth to fifth grade for students with reading difficulties. *Reading & Writing Quarterly, 35*(3), 277–288. https://doi.org/10.1080/10573569.2018.1560379

Warmingham, J. M., Handley, E. D., Rogosch, F. A., Manley, J. T., & Cicchetti, D. (2019). Identifying maltreatment subgroups with patterns of maltreatment subtype and chronicity: A latent class analysis approach. *Child Abuse & Neglect, 87,* 28–39. https://doi.org/10.1016/j.chiabu.2018.08.013

Warren, C. M. et al. (2015). Differences in empowerment and quality of life among parents of children with food allergy. *Annals of Allergy, Asthma & Immunology, 114*(2), 117–125.e3. https://doi.org/10.1016/j.anai.2014.10.025

Warriner, S., Crane, C., Dymond, M., & Krusche, A. (2018). An evaluation of mindfulness-based childbirth and parenting courses for pregnant women and prospective fathers/partners within the UK NHS. *Midwifery, 64,* 1–10. https://doi.org/10.1016/j.midw.2018.05.004

Waters, T. E. A., et al. (2015). Secure base representations in middle childhood across two Western cultures: Associations with parental attachment representations and maternal reports of behavior problems. *Developmental Psychology, 51*(8), 1013–1025. https://doi.org/10.1037/a0039375

Watson, E. J., Banks, S., Coates, A. M., & Kohler, M. J. (2017). The relationship between caffeine, sleep, and behavior in children. *Journal of Clinical Sleep Medicine, 13*(4), 533–543. http://dx.doi.org/10.5664/jcsm.6536

Watson, J. M., et al. (2016). On working memory and a productivity illusion in distracted driving. *Journal of Applied Research in Memory and Cognition, 5*(4), 445–453. https://doi.org/10.1016/j.jarmac.2016.06.008

Watts, A. W., et al. (2018). Multicontextual correlates of adolescent sugar-sweetened beverage intake. *Eating Behaviors, 30,* 422–48. https://doi.org/10.1016/j.eatbeh.2018.04.003

Watts, T. W., Duncan, G. J., Clements, D. H., & Sarama, J. (2018). What is the long-run impact of mathematics during preschool? *Child Development, 89*(2), 539–555. https://doi.org/10.1111/cdev.12713

Watts, T. W., Duncan, G. J., & Quan, H. (2018). Revisiting the marshmallow test: A conceptual replication investigating early delay of gratification and later outcomes. *Psychological Science, 29*(7), 1159–1177. https://doi.org/10.1177/0956797618761661

Waytz, A., & Gray, K. (2018). Does online technology make use more or less sociable? A preliminary review and a call for research. *Perspectives on Psychological Science, 13*(4), 473–491. https://doi.org/10.1177/1745691617746509

Weaver, M. D., Barger, L. K., & Malone, S. K. (2018). Dose-dependent association between sleep duration and unsafe behaviors among US high school students. *JAMA Pediatrics, 172*(12), 1187–1189. https://doi.org/10.1001/jamapediatrics.2018.2777

Webb, A. R., Heller, H. T., Benson, C. B., & Lahav, A. (2015). Mother's voice and heartbeat sounds elicit auditory plasticity in the human brain before full gestation. *PNAS, 112*(1), 3152–3157. https//doi.org/ 10.1073/pnas.1414924112

Weininger, E. B., Lareau, A., & Conley, D. (2015). What money doesn't buy: Class resources and children's participation in organized extracurricular activities. *Social Forces.* https://doi.org/10.1093/sf/sov071

Weisgram, E. S. (2018). Gender typing of toys in historical and contemporary contexts. In E. S. Weisgram & L. M. Dinella (Eds.), *Gender typing of children's toys: How early play experiences impact development.* American Psychological Association.

Weisz, J. R., et al. (2018). Are psychotherapies for young people growing stronger? Tracking trends over time for youth anxiety, depression, attention-deficit/hyperactivity disorder, and conduct problems. *Perspectives of Psychological Science, 14*(2), 216–237. https://doi.org/10.1177/1745691618805436

Weller, C. (2018, February 18). *Silicon Valley parents are raising their kids tech-free and it should be a red flag.* Retrieved from https://www.businessinsider.com/silicon-valley-parents-raising-their-kids-tech-free-red-flag-2018-2

Welty, S. (2019). Challenging the gestational age for the limit of viability: Proactive care. *Journal of Perinatology, 39*(1), 1–3. https://doi.org/10.1038/s41372-018-0271-z

Wentzel, K. R., Jablansky, S., & Scalise, N. R. (2018). Do friendships afford academic benefits? A meta-analytic study. *Educational Psychology Review, 30*(4), 1241–1267. https://doi.org/10.1007/s10648-018-9447-5

Werneck, A. O., et al. (2018). Body adiposity from childhood to adolescence in boys: Interaction with somatic maturity. *American Journal of Human Biology, 30*(5), 23151. https://doi.org/10.1002/ajhb.23151

Werner-Seidler, A., et al. (2017). School-based depression and anxiety prevention programs for young people: A systematic review and meta-analysis. *Clinical Psychology Review, 51*, 30–47. http://dx.doi.org/10.1016/j.cpr.2016.10.005

Wessel, M. A., Cobb, J. C., Jackson, E. B., Harris Jr, G. S., & Detwiler, A. C. (1954). Paroxysmal fussing in infancy, sometimes called colic. *Pediatrics, 14*(5), 421–35. https://doi.org/10.1056/NEJM195707042570104

Westby, C. & Robinson, L. (2014). A developmental perspective for promoting theory of mind. *Topics in Language Disorders, 34*(4), 362–382. https://doi.org/10.1097/TLD.0000000000000035

White, A. S., et al. (2018). (2018) Children's temperament and the transition to kindergarten: A question of "fit." In A. Mashburn, J. LoCasale-Crouch, & K. Pears (Eds.), *Kindergarten transition and readiness.* Springer, https://doi.org/10.1007/978-3-319-90200-5_10

White, H. J., Haycraft, E., & Meyer, C. (2019). Family mealtime negativity and adolescent binge-eating: A replication and extension study in a community sample. *Eating Behaviors, 34*, 101306. https://doi.org/10.1016/j.eatbeh.2019.101306

White, K. (2014). Attachment theory and the John Bowlby Memorial Lecture 2013: A short history (pp. 1–10). In R. Gill (Ed.), *Addictions from an Attachment Perspective.* London, UK: Karnac Books.

White, R. E., & Carlson, S. M. (2016). What would Batman do? Self-distancing improves executive function in young children. *Developmental Science, 19*(3), 419–426. https://doi.org/10.1111/desc.12314

White, R. L., et al. (2018). A qualitative investigation of the perceived influence of adolescents' motivation on relationships between domain-specific physical activity and positive and negative affect. *Mental Health and Physical Activity, 14*, 113–120. https://doi.org/10.1016/j.mhpa.2018.03.002

White-Traut, R. C., et al. (2018). Relationship between mother–infant mutual dyadic responsiveness and premature infant development as measured by the Bayley III at six weeks corrected age. *Early Human Development, 121*, 21–26. https://doi.org/10.1016/j.earlhumdev.2018.04.018

Whitehurst, G. J. (2018). *What is the market price of daycare and preschool?* Retrieved from https://www.brookings.edu/research/what-is-the-market-price-of-daycare-and-preschool/

Whitton, S. W., Dyar, C., Mustanski, B., & Newcomb, M. E. (2019). Intimate partner violence experiences of sexual assault and gender minority adolescents and young adults assigned female at birth. *Psychology of Women Quarterly, 43*(2), 232–249. https://doi.org/10.1177/0361684319838972

WHO Multicentre Growth Reference Study Group (2006). WHO motor development study: Windows of achievement for six gross motor development milestones. *Acta Paediatrica, 450*, 86–95. Wicki, M., Mallett, K. A., Delgrande Jordan, M., Reavy, R., Turrisi, R., Archimi, A., & Kuntsche, E. (2018). Adolescents who experienced negative alcohol-related consequences are willing to experience these consequences again in the future. *Experimental and Clinical Psychopharmacology, 26*(2), 132–137. http://dx.doi.org/10.1037/pha0000184

Widener, M. J. (2018). Spatial access to food: Retiring the food desert metaphor. *Physiology & Behavior, 193*, 257–260. https://doi.org/10.1016/j.physbeh.2018.02.032

Wienholz, S., et al. (2016). Sexual experiences of adolescents with and without disabilities: Results from a cross-sectional study. *Sexuality and Disability, 34*(2), 171–182. https://doi.org/10.1007/s11195-016-9433-0

Wilkinson, P. O., et al. (2018). Sporadic and recurrent non-suicidal self-injury before age 14 and incident onset of psychiatric disorders by 17 years: Prospective cohort study. *The British Journal of Psychiatry, 212*(4), 222–226. https://doi.org/10.1192/bjp.2017.45

Williams, A. S., et al. (2018). Socioeconomic status and other factors associated with childhood obesity. *Journal of the American Board of Family Medicine, 31*(4), 514–521. https://doi.org/10.3122/jabfm.2018.04.170261

Williams, D. H., & Shipley, G. P. (2018). Cultural taboos as a factor in the participation rate of Native Americans in STEM. *International Journal of STEM Education, 5*, 17. https://doi.org/10.1186/s40594-018-0114-7

Williams, N. A. & Hankey, M. (2015). Support and negativity in interpersonal relationships impact caregivers' quality of life in pediatric food allergy. *Quality of Life Research, 24*(6), 1369–1378. https://doi.org/10.1007/s11136-014-0862-x

Wilson, B. D. M., & Kastanis, A. A. (2015). Sexual and gender minority disproportionality and disparities in child welfare: A population-based study. *Children and Youth Services Review, 58*, 11–17. https://doi.org/10.1016/j.childyouth.2015.08.016

Wilson, D. A. et al. (2015). Earlier menarche is associated with lower insulin sensitivity and increased adiposity in young adult women. *PLoS One, 10*(6), e0128427. https://doi.org/10.1371/journal.pone.0128427

Wincentak, K., Connolly, J., & Card, N. (2017). Teen dating violence: A meta-analytic review of prevalence rates. *Psychology of Violence, 7*(2), 224–241. http://dx.doi.org/10.1037/a0040194

Winnicott, D. (1953). Transitional objects and transitional phenomena, *International Journal of Psychoanalysis, 34*:89-97. https://doi.org/10.1093/med:psych/9780190271367.003.0034

Winstanley, M., Webb, R. T., & Conti-Ramsden, G. (2019). Psycholinguistic and socioemotional characteristics of young offenders: Do language abilities and gender matter? *Legal and Criminological Psychology, 24*(2), 195–214. https://doi.org/10.1111/lcrp.12150

Winter, A. S., & Sampson, R. J. (2017). From lead exposure in early childhood to adolescent health: A Chicago birth cohort. *American Journal of Public Health, 107*(9), 1496–1501. https://doi.org/10.2105/AJPH.2017.303903

Witherington, D. C., & Lickliter, R. (2017). Transcending the nature–nurture debate through epigenetics: Are we there yet? *Human Development, 60*, 65–68. https://doi.org/10.1159/000478796

Witwer, E., Jones, R., & Lindberg, L. (2018). *Sexual behavior and contraceptive and condom use among U.S. high school students, 2013–2017.* Retrieved from https://www.guttmacher.org/report/sexual-behavior-contraceptive-condom-use-us-high-school-students-2013-2017

Wolf, A. B. (2017). Embracing our values: Ending the "birth wars" and improving women's satisfaction with childbirth. *International Journal of Feminist Approaches to Bioethics, 10*(2), 31–41. https://doi.org/10.3138/ijfab.10.2.31

Wolke, D. (2018). Preterm birth: High vulnerability and no resiliency? Reflections on van Lieshout et al. (2018). *The Journal of Child Psychology and Psychiatry, 59*(11), 1201–1204. https://doi.org/10.1111/jcpp.12971

Wolff, K., & Stapp, A. (2019). Investigating early childhood teachers' perceptions of a preschool yoga program. *SAGE Open, 9*(1). https://doi.org/10.1177/2158244018821758

World Entertainment News Network (2006). *Beyoncé thrilled by first dance teacher.* Retrieved from http://www.contactmusic.com/beyonce-knowles/news/beyonce-thrilled-by-first-dance-teacher_1007391

Worthman, C. M., Dockray, S., & Marceau, K. (2019). Puberty and the evolution of developmental science. *Journal of Research on Adolescence, 29*(1), 9–31. https://doi.org/10.1111/jora.12411

Wren, T. E. (2013). Moral development. *The International Encyclopedia of Ethics.* https://doi.org/ 10.1002/9781444367072.wbiee770

Wrulich, M., Stadler, G., Brunner, M., Keller, U., & Martin, R. (2015). Childhood intelligence predicts premature mortality: Results from a 40-year population-based longitudinal study. *Journal of Research in Personality.* https://doi.org/10.1016/j.jrp.2015.06.003

Wuyts, D., Soenens, B., Vansteenkiste, M., & Van Petegem, S. (2018). The role of observed autonomy support, reciprocity, and need satisfaction in adolescent disclosure about friends. *Journal of Adolescence, 65*, 141–154. https://doi.org/10.1016/j.adolescence.2018.03.012

Wyman, J., et al. (2019). The efficacy of free-recall, cognitive load, and closed-ended questions when children are asked to falsely testify about a crime. *Applied Cognitive Psychology, 33*(4), 544–560. https://doi.org/10.1002/acp.3494

Xia, M., Fosco, G. M., Lippold, M. A., & Feinberg, M. E. (2018). A developmental perspective on young adult romantic relationships: Examining family and individual factors in adolescence. *Journal of Youth and Adolescence, 47*(7), 1499–1516. https://doi.org/10.1007/s10964-018-0815-8

Xia, R., et al. (2018). Association between parental alcohol consumption before conception and anogenital distance of the offspring. *Alcoholism: Clinical & Experimental Research, 42*(4), 735–742. https://doi.org/10.1111/acer.13595

Xiao, S. X., Cook, R. E., & Martin, C. L., & Nielson, M. G. (2019). Characteristics of preschool gender enforcers and peers who associate with them. *Sex Roles, 81,* 671–685. https://doi.org/10.1007/s11199-019-01026-y

Xiao, S. X., Spinrad, T. L., & Carter, D. B. (2018). Parental emotion regulation and preschoolers' prosocial behavior: The mediating roles of warmth and inductive discipline. *The Journal of Genetic Psychology, 179*(5), 246–255. https://doi.org/10.1080/00221325.2018.1495611

Xiao, S. X., Spinrad, T. L., & Risenberg, N. (2018). Longitudinal relations of preschoolers' dispositional and situational anger to their prosocial behavior: The moderating role of shyness. *Social Development, 28*(2), 383–397. https://doi.org/10.1111/sode.12346

Xiao, Y., et al. (2019). Neural correlates of developing theory of mind competence in early childhood. *NeuroImage, 184,* 707–716. https://doi.org/10.1016/j.neuroimage.2018.09.079

Xie, W., Mallin, B. M., & Richards, J. E. (2019). Development of brain functional connectivity and its relation to infant sustained attention in the first year of life. *Developmental Science, 22*(1), e12730. https://doi.org/10.1111/desc.12703

Xu, S., Wang, Z., & David, P. (2016). Media multitasking and well-being of university students. *Computers in Human Behavior, 55A,* 242–250. https://doi.org/10.1016/j.chb.2015.08.040

Xu, Y., & Bright, C. L. (2018). Children's mental health and its predictors in kinship and non-kinship foster care: A systematic review. *Children and Youth Services Review, 89,* 243–262. https://doi.org/10.1016/j.childyouth.2018.05.001

Yackobovitch-Gavan et al. (2017). Randomised study found that improved nutritional intake was associated with better sleep patterns in prepubertal children who were both short and lean. *Acta Pædiatrica, 107*(4), 666–671. https://doi.org/10.1111/apa.14205

Yamamoto, Y. & Sonnenschein, S. (2016). Family contexts of academic socialization: The role of culture, ethnicity, and socioeconomic status. *Research in Human Development, 13*(3), 183–190. https://doi.org/10.1080/15427609.2016.1194711

Yammine, S. Z., Liu, C., Jarreau, P. B., & Coe, I. R. (2018). Social media for social change in science. *Science, 360*(6385), 162–163. https://doi.org/10.1126/science.aat7303

Yan, Z. (2018). Child and adolescent use of mobile phones: An unparalleled complex developmental phenomenon. *Child Development, 89*(1), 5–16. https://doi.org/10.1111/cdev.12821

Yancy, C. W. (2020). COVID-19 and Blacks. *JAMA.* https://doi: 10.1001/jama.2020.6548

Yang, L. & Colditz, G. A. (2014). An active lifestyle for cancer prevention. *Journal of the National Cancer Institute, 106*(7), dju135. https://doi.org/10.1093/jnci/dju135

Yang, M. N., Clements-Nolle, K., Parrish, B., & Yang, W. (2019). Adolescent concussion and mental health outcomes: A population-based study. *American Journal of Health Behavior, 43*(2), 258–265. https://doi.org/10.5993/AJHB.43.2.3

Yavuz, H. M., & Selcuk, B. (2018). Predictors of obesity and overweight in preschoolers: The role of parenting style and feeding practices. *Appetite, 120,* 491–499. https://doi.org/10.1016/j.appet.2017.10.001

Yaylaci, F. T. (2018). Trauma and resilient functioning among Syrian refugee children. *Development and Psychopathology, 30*(5), 1923–1936. https://doi.org/10.1017/S0954579418001293

Ybarra, M. L., Price-Feeney, M., & Mitchell, K. J. (2019). A cross-sectional study examining the (in)congruency of sexual identity, sexual behavior, and romantic attraction among adolescents in the US. *The Journal of Pediatrics, 214,* 201–208. https://doi.org/10.1016/j.jpeds.2019.06.046

Yeager, D. S., Dahl, R. E., & Dweck, C. S. (2018). Why interventions to influence adolescent behavior often fail but could succeed. *Perspectives on Psychological Science, 13*(1), 101–122. https://doi.org/10.1177/1745691617722620

Yeager, D. S., Hanselman, P., Walton, G.M., et al. (2019). A national experiment reveals where a growth mindset improves achievement. *Nature, 573,* 364–369. https://doi.org/10.1038/s41586-019-1466-y

Yeager, M., & Yeager, D. (2013). *Executive function and child development.* W. W. Norton & Company.

Yogman, M., et al. (2018). The power of play: A pediatric role in enhancing development. *Pediatrics, 142*(3), E20182058. https://doi.org/10.1542/peds.2018-2058

Yu, C., Suanda, S. H., & Smith, L. B. (2019). Infant sustained attention but not joint attention to objects at 9 months predicts vocabulary at 12 and 15 months. *Developmental Science, 22*(1), e12735. https://doi.org/10.1111/desc.12735

Yu, R. et al. (2018). Internalizing symptoms and dating violence perpetration in adolescence. *Journal of Adolescence, 69,* 88–91. https://doi.org/10.1016/j.adolescence.2018.09.008

Yucel, D., Bobbitt-Zeher, D., & Downey, D. B. (2018). Quality matters: Sibling relationships and friendship nominations among adolescents. *Child Indicators Research 11*(2), 523–539. https://doi.org/10.1007/s12187-017-9448-9

Zajac, L., Bookhout, M. K., Hubbard, J. A., Carlson, E. A., & Dozier, M. (2018). Attachment disorganization in infancy: A developmental precursor to maladaptive social information processing at age 8. *Child Development.* https://doi-org.scsu.idm.oclc.org/10.1111/cdev.13140

Zajacova, A., & Lawrence, E. M. (2018). The relationship between education and health: Reducing disparities through a contextual approach. *Annual Review of Public Health, 39*, 273–289. https://doi.org/10.1146/annurev-publhealth-031816-044628

Zarate-Garza, P. P., Biggs, B. K., Croarkin, P. E., Morath, B., Leffler, J., Cuellar-Barboza, A., & Tye, S. J. (2017). How well do we understand the long-term health implications of childhood bullying? *Harvard Review of Psychiatry, 25*(2), 89–95. https://doi.org/10.1097/HRP.0000000000000137

Zarrett, N., et al. (2018). Promoting physical activity within under-resourced afterschool programs: A qualitative investigation of staff experiences and motivational strategies for engaging youth. *Applied Developmental Science, 22*(1), 58–73 https://doi.org/10.1080/10888691.2016.1211482

Zavala, C., et al. (2018). Attained SES as a moderator of adult cognitive performance: Testing gene-environment interaction in various cognitive domains. *Developmental Psychology, 54*(12), 2356–2370. https://doi.org/10.1037/dev0000576

Zeller, M. (2019). Evolving "The Real Cost" campaign to address the rising epidemic of youth e-cigarette use. *American Journal of Preventative Medicine, 56*(2S1), S76–S78. https://doi.org/10.1016/j.amepre.2018.09.005

Zhang, D-W., et al. (2017). Atypical interference control in children with AD/HD with elevated theta/beta ratio. *Biological Psychology, 128*, 82–88. https://doi.org/10.1016/j.biopsycho.2017.07.009

Zhang, M., & Hudson, J. A. (2019). The development of temporal concepts: Linguistic factors and cognitive processes. *Frontiers in Psychology.* https://doi.org/10.3389/fpsyg.2018.02451

Zhang, S., Su, F., Li, J., & Chen, W. (2018). The analgesic effects of maternal milk odor on newborns: A meta-analysis. *Breastfeeding Medicine, 13*(5), 327–334. https://doi.org/10.1089/bfm.2017.0226

Zhang, X., et al. (2018a). Characteristics of likability, perceived popularity, and admiration in the early adolescent peer system in the United States and China. *Developmental Psychology, 54*(8), 1568–1581. http://dx.doi.org/10.1037/dev0000544

Zhang, X., et al. (2018b). Early adolescent social status and academic engagement: Selection and influence processes in the United States and China. *Journal of Educational Psychology, 111*(7), 1300–1316. http://dx.doi.org/10.1037/edu0000333

Zhang, Y., et al. (2019). Neonate and infant brain development from birth to 2 years assessed using MRI-based quantitative susceptibility mapping. *Neuroimage, 185*, 349–360. https://doi.org/10.1016/j.neuroimage.2018.10.031.

Zheng, Y., Ley, S. H., & & Hu, F. B. (2018). Global aetiology and epidemiology of type 2 diabetes mellitus and its complications. *Nature Reviews Endocrinology, 14*, 88–99. https://doi.org/10.1038/nrendo.2017.151

Zhu, R., et al. (2018). The effect of shame on anger at others: Awareness of the emotion-causing events matter. *Cognition and Emotion, 33*(4), 696–708. https://doi.org/10.1080/02699931.2018.1489782

Zhu, R., et al. (2019). Differentiating guilt and shame in an interpersonal context with univariate activation and multivariate pattern analysis. *NeuroImage, 186*, 476–486. https://doi.org/10.1016/j.neuroimage.2018.11.012

Ziegler, G., et al. (2019). Compulsivity and impulsivity traits linked to attenuated developmental frontostriatal myelination trajectories. *Nature Neuroscience, 22*, 992–999. https://doi.org/10.1038/s41593-019-0394-3

Zigler, E., Marsland, K, & Lord, H. (2009). *The tragedy of childcare in America.* Yale University Press.

Zigler, E., & Styfco, S. J. (2001). Can early childhood intervention prevent delinquency? A real possibility. In A. C. Bohart & D. J. Stipek (Eds.), *Constructive & destructive behavior: Implications for family, school, & society* (p. 231–248). American Psychological Association. https://doi.org/10.1037/10433-011

Zimmer-Gembeck, M. J., Webb, H. J., Farrell, L. J., & Waters, A. M. (2018). Girls' and boys' trajectories of appearance anxiety from age 10 to 15 years are associated with earlier maturation and appearance-related teasing. *Development and Psychopathology, 30*(1), 337–350. https://doi.org/10.1017/S0954579417000657

Zimmermann, P., & Iwanski, A. (2018). Development and timing of developmental changes in emotional reactivity and emotional regulation during adolescence. In P. M. Cole & T. Hollenstein (Eds.), *Emotion regulation: A matter of time* (pp. 135–137). Routledge.

Ziv, Y., & Hotam, Y. (2015). Theory and measure in the psychology field: The case of attachment theory and the strange situation procedure. *Theory & Psychology, 25*(3), 274–291. https://doi.org/10.1177/0959354315577970

Zondervan-Zwijnenburg, M. A. J., et al. (2019). Parental age and offspring childhood mental health: A multi-cohort, population-based investigation. *Child Development*, 1–19. Advance online publication. https://doi.org/10.1111/cdev.13267

Zuccarini, M., et al. (2018). Does early object exploration support gesture and language development in extremely preterm infants and full-term infants? *Journal of Communication Disorders, 76*, 91–100. https://doi.org/10.1016/j.jcomdis.2018.09.004

Zucchelli, M. M., & Ugazio, G. (2019). Cognitive-emotional and inhibitory deficits as a window to moral decision-making difficulties related to exposure to violence. *Frontiers in Psychology.* https://doi.org/10.3389/fpsyg.2019.01427

Zuckerman, B. & Khandekar, A. (2010). Reach Out and Read: Evidence based approach to promoting early child development. *Current Opinion in Pediatrics, 22*, 1–6. https://doi.org: 10.1097/MOP.0b013e32833a4673

Zych, I., et al. (2018). A longitudinal study on stability and transitions among bullying roles. *Child Development, 91*(2), 527–545. https://doi.org/10.1111/cdev.13195

Zych, I., Farrington, D. P., & Ttofi, M. M. (2019). Protective factors against bullying and cyberbullying: A systematic review of meta-analyses. *Aggression and Violent Behavior, 45*, 4–19. https://doi.org/10.1016/j.avb.2018.06.008

Zych, I., Viejo, C., Vila, E., & Farrington, D. P. (2019). School bullying and dating violence in adolescents: A systematic review and meta-analysis. *Trauma, Violence, & Abuse*, 1–16. Advance online publication. https://doi.org/10.1177/1524838019854460

Zvara, B. J., Macfie, J., Cox, M., Mills-Koonce, R., & The Family Life Project (2018). Mother–child role confusion, child adjustment problems, and the moderating roles of child temperament and sex. *Developmental Psychology, 54*(10), 1891–1903. https://doi.org/10.1037/dev0000556

Index

chromosomes, 50–51
autosomes, 52
sex, 51–52
chronic preexisting hypertension, 85
circular reactions, 136–137
coordination of secondary, 136
primary, 136
secondary, 136
tertiary, 137
cisgender, 245–246
civic participation, 353
classical conditioning, 13
class-inclusion task, 210
clinical interviews, 32
cochlear implants, 126
Code of Ethics (National Society of Genetic Counselors), 58
cognitive development in adolescents, 351–365
academic success, 356–366
civic participation, 353
decision-making and risk-taking, 354–356
formal operational thinking, 352–353
Piaget's theory, 352–353
cognitive development in early childhood, 208–221
egocentrism, 208–209
eyewitness testimony, 216
intelligence, 216
lack of conservation, 210–211
lack of hierarchical classification, 209–210
language development, 217–221
literacy, 218–219
numeracy, 221

overlapping waves of strategy use, 213
symbolic thought, 211–212
theory capabilities, 213–215
cognitive development in infancy and toddlerhood, 133–156
affordances, 141
attention, 142–144
autism spectrum disorders (ASD), 156–157
childcare effects, 146–147
Core Knowledge theory, 140–141
dishabituation, 138
habituation, 138
infantile amnesia, 146
joint attention, 143–144
language, 149–155
memory, 145–147
Piaget's theory, 134–137
six substages of Sensorimotor stage, 135–137
violation-of-expectation method, 138–140
cognitive development in middle childhood, 276–295
ADHD, 282–284
concrete operations, 277–279
executive function, 281–283
eyewitness testimony, 286–287
intelligence, 287–289
language, 289–290
literacy, 290–292
memory, 286–287
numeracy, 290–291, 294–295
Piaget's theory, 276–280
theory of mind, 279–281
cognitive flexibility, 281

cognitive theories of development, 15–18
Information-Processing theories, 17
Piaget's theory, 16–17
Vygotsky's theory, 17–18
cohort difference, 40–41
colic, 110–111
colic carry, 110
collectivistic cultures, 170
color blind, 30
colostrum, 94
Common Core Standards, 296
comparison group, 39
competency, children and, 305–307
conception. *See* fertilization
concerted cultivation, 296
concerted cultivation approach, 222
concrete operations in middle childhood, 277–279
confidentiality, 44
confirmation and fluency, 291–292
confounding variables, 41
conservation, 210
lack of, 210–211
constructivist theories, 134–135
contemporary theories of development, 18–22
developmental neuroscience, 21–22
Ecological Systems theory, 18–19
ethological theory, 20–21
evolutionary theory, 20–21
Controlled Scribbling, 199
controversial children, 317
Conventional Reasoning, 259–260

government investments, for early childhood development, 223–226

CRC, 226

government policies, 223–224

parental investment, 222

grit, 312

gross motor milestones, 119–120

gross motor skills

early childhood, 198

infants and toddlers, 119

growth, 4

growth mindset, 363–364

growth spurt, 336

guardian ad litem (GAL), 287

guided participation, 17

guilt

initiative and, 232–233

shame vs., 233–234

H

habituation, 138

Hall, G. Stanley, 360

Harlow, Harry, 177

Harrison, Barbara, 60–61

health data, 33

health issues, adolescents and, 344–351

food, 344–347

sleep, 348–349

substance abuse, 349–351

health literacy, 111

hearing, in infants/toddlers, 126–127

hereditary influences, 56

heritability, 62

Hernández, Jose, 347

heterosexual families, parenting inequality and, 86–87

heterozygous pair, 52

hierarchical classification, lack of, 209–210

High/Scope Perry Preschool Project, 224

homozygous pair, 52

hooking up, 398

horizontal décalage, 277

hormonal changes, 337–338

hostile aggression, 260

hostile attribution bias, 404

human immunodeficiency virus (HIV), 82

human papillomavirus (HPV), 399

Huntington's disease, 55

Hurricane Sandy, 21–22

hygiene hypothesis, 275

hypothesis, 27

I

identity

gender, 244–245

models of, 374–375

negative, 374

positive, 374

societal investment in, 376–377

Identity Achievement, 374–375

Identity Diffusion, 374

Identity Foreclosure, 374

Identity Moratorium, 374

Identity-Role Confusion, 372–373

illnesses, middle childhood, 275–276

implicit memory, 145–146

imprinting, 20

incomplete dominance, 52–53

incremental theories, 363

independent variable (IV), 39

individualistic cultures, 170

inductive discipline, 234

Industry-Inferiority, 13, 304–305

infancy and toddlerhood

body growth in, 101–106

brain development, 106–109

cognitive development, 133–156

emotional development, 161–181

language development, 149–155

physical development, 101–127

infant-directed speech (IDS), 150

infantile amnesia, 146

infertility, 86–87

information-processing (IP) theories, 285–286

Information-Processing theories, 17

informed consent, 44

initiative and guilt, 232–233

injuries

agent factors, 206–207

early childhood, 206–207

environmental factors, 206

middle childhood, 276

sports, 343

unintentional, 276

Insecure-Avoidant (Type A) attachment, 179

Insecure-Disorganized (Type D) attachment, 180

Insecure-Resistant (Type C) attachment, 179

instrumental aggression, 260

intelligence

defined, 287

early childhood, 216

Gardner's theory of, 288–289

middle childhood, 287–289

interactive book reading, 218

interculturally mature, 415

intergenerational social mobility, 360–361

internalizing problems in adolescence, 402–405

internal working models of attachment, 178

international comparisons, 360–361

International Society for Stem Cell Research (ISSCR), 54

Internet Addiction during adolescence, 409–410

interpersonal intelligence, 288

interrelated taxonomic self, 236

intersectionality, 377–379

intersex, 241

interventions, for adolescents, 415–416

intimate partner violence in adolescence, 400–402

intrapersonal intelligence, 288

intrauterine insemination (IUI), 87

in vitro fertilization (IVF), 54, 87

iodine deficiency disorders (IDDs), 83

irreversibility, 211

I-Self, 236

J

joint attention, 143–144

K

kangaroo care, 94

Kinaaldá ceremony, 331–332

kinship care, 382

L

labor, 88–89
  dilation, 89
  expulsion, 89

lack of conservation, 210–211

lack of hierarchical classification, 209–210

language development
  early childhood, 217–221
  middle childhood, 289–290

language development in infancy and toddlerhood, 149–155
  babbling, 150
  child-directed speech, 150
  cooing, 150–151
  early literacy promotion, 154–155
  infant-directed speech (IDS), 150
  naming explosion, 152
  reading and talking, 153–155
  telegraphic speech, 152–153

Lareau, Annette, 296

late maturing, 269

latency stage of development, 12

lead, 83

learning, reading for, 292

learning theories, 13–15
  Bandura's theory, 14
  Pavlov's theory, 13–14
  Skinner's theory, 14

Letters and Word Practice, 200

LGBTQI (lesbian, gay, bisexual, transgender, questioning, intersex) community, 242, 395

lifelong patterns of development, 6–8

Lines and Patterns, 200–201

linguistic intelligence, 288

literacy in early childhood, 218–219

locomotor skills, 119

longitudinal research designs, 42–43

long-term memory, 286

Lorenz, Konrad, 20
  imprinting, 20
  theory, 20

low birth weight (LBW), 93

low depression literacy, 403

Lymphoid Growth Curve, 106

M

make-believe play, 247–249

male fertility, 86

map-making, developmental science and, 26–27

mastery goals, 312–313

masturbation, 12

maternal education, 93–94

maternal hypertension, 85

maternal postpartum blues, 96

maternal postpartum depression, 96

mathematics. *See also* numeracy
  adolescents, 359–360
  middle childhood, 294–295

Matthew Effect, 289–290

maturational timing, 338–340

measuring body growth of infants/toddlers, 102–105

medical model, 90

meditational deficiency, 357

memory in infancy and toddlerhood, 145–147
  episodic, 146
  explicit, 144–145
  implicit, 145–146
  infantile amnesia, 146
  semantic, 146

for learning in middle childhood, 292
    infancy and toddlerhood, 153–155
recasts, 218
reflective capacity, 240
reflexes, 118–119
    infancy and toddlerhood, 135–136
refugees, 414
rejected children, 317
Rejecting–Neglecting parents, 252
relational aggression, 260, 406
relational bullying, 317–318
relationships, adolescents, 391–402
    affectional orientation, 395–397
    families, 381–390
    friends/friendships, 390–392
    intimate partner violence, 400–402
    peer status, 393–394
    romantic, 396–398
    sexual activity, 398–399
representational thought, 135
research, 26–47
    bias in, 45
    correlational designs, 34–38
    data, 28–34
    developmental designs, 40–43
    ethics, 43–46
    experimental designs, 39
resource control theory, 406
respiratory distress syndrome, 93
retrieval of memory, 286
right to disconnect law, 19
risk-resilience patterns of development, 8–9

risk-taking in adolescents, 354–356
romantic relationships in adolescence, 396–398
rooting reflex, 118

S
safe sleep space creation, 112
Saidi, Samah, 293
sample of population, 29
scaffolding, 18, 234–235
Scarr–Rowe hypothesis, 62
schemes, 16
schools, 296–297
scoliosis, 84
screen time, 19
    emotional cues interpretation and, 15
secondary circular reactions (4–8 months), 136
secondary sexual characteristics, 338
second trimester of pregnancy, 75
secular trend, 202, 270
Secure (Type B) attachment, 179
self-compassion, 412–413
self-concept
    early childhood, 236–237
    middle childhood, 311–312
self-conscious emotions, 164, 233. *See also* shame vs. guilt
self-efficacy, 8
self-esteem
    early childhood, 237–238
    middle childhood, 314
self-monitoring, 282
self-recognition, 171–172
    animals, 171
    humans, 171–172
self-regulation

early childhood, 238–241
executive functions, 238
infants, 175
parent self-regulation, 240–241
self-report methods of data collection, 31–32
self-resiliency, 312–313
semantic memory, 146
sensation, 124
sensitive periods, 8
Sensorimotor stage, 135–137
    coordination of secondary circular reactions (8–12 months), 136
    mental representation (18–24 months), 137
    primary circular reactions (1–4 months), 136
    reflexes (birth to 1 month), 135–136
    secondary circular reactions (4–8 months), 136
    tertiary circular reactions (12–18 months), 137
sensory and perceptual development, 124–128
    hearing, 126–127
    perception, 124
    sensation, 124
    social smile, 124
    taste and smell, 126
    touch, 127
    vision, 124
Seok, Deborah, 149–151
separation anxiety, 164
sequential research designs, 43
seriation, 277
Sesame Workshop, 199
sex, 241
sex chromosomes, 51–52
sex-linked traits, 51–52
sexting, 407

About the Author

Kristine Anthis, PhD, is a professor of psychology at Southern Connecticut State University in New Haven. Kristine earned her BA from Saint Xavier University in Chicago and her PhD from the University of Nebraska. She also served as a fellow in the Edward Zigler Center in Child Development and Social Policy at Yale University.

She is a member of APA Division 2: Society for the Teaching of Psychology and APA Division 7: Developmental Psychology. Kristine's research interests concern emotional development throughout the life span, as well as the scholarship of teaching and learning.

Kristine has won multiple university-wide teaching awards. She has served as a reviewer for the journal *Teaching of Psychology*. She has also served as a mentor for the Society for the Teaching of Psychology and as a member of their Diversity Committee as well as their Master Teacher Committee. Kristine lives in New Haven with her wife and their son.

CPSIA information can be obtained
at www.ICGtesting.com
Printed in the USA
LVHW061147030921
696809LV00005B/51